Writing the History of Slavery

Writing History

The *Writing History* series publishes accessible overviews of particular fields in history, focusing on the practical application of theory in historical writing. Books in the series succinctly explain central concepts to demonstrate the ways in which they have informed effective historical writing. They analyse key historical texts and their producers within their institutional arrangement, and as part of a wider social discourse. The series' holistic approach means students benefit from an enhanced understanding of how to negotiate the contours of successful historical writing.

Series editors: Stefan Berger (Ruhr University Bochum, Germany), Heiko Feldner (Cardiff University, UK) and Kevin Passmore (Cardiff University, UK)

Published:
Writing Medieval History, edited by Nancy F. Partner
Writing Early Modern History, edited by Garthine Walker
Writing Contemporary History, edited by Robert Gildea and Anne Simonin
Writing Gender History (second edition), Laura Lee Downs
Writing Postcolonial History, Rochona Majumdar
Writing the Holocaust, edited by Jean-Marc Dreyfus and Daniel Langton
Writing the History of Memory, edited by Stefan Berger and Bill Niven
Writing Material Culture History, edited by Anne Gerritsen and Giorgio Riello
Writing History (third edition), edited by Stefan Berger, Heiko Feldner and Kevin Passmore
Writing Transnational History, Fiona Paisley
Writing Visual Histories, edited by Florence Grant and Ludmilla Jordanova
Writing Material Culture History (second edition), edited by Anne Gerritsen and Giorgio Riello

Forthcoming:
Writing Queer History, edited by Matt Cook
Writing Gender History (third edition), Laura Lee Downs
Writing Conceptual Histories, edited by Pasi Ihalainen and Jani Marjanen

Writing the History of Slavery

Edited by
David Stefan Doddington
Enrico Dal Lago

BLOOMSBURY ACADEMIC
LONDON • NEW YORK • OXFORD • NEW DELHI • SYDNEY

BLOOMSBURY ACADEMIC
Bloomsbury Publishing Plc
50 Bedford Square, London, WC1B 3DP, UK
1385 Broadway, New York, NY 10018, USA
29 Earlsfort Terrace, Dublin 2, Ireland

BLOOMSBURY, BLOOMSBURY ACADEMIC and the Diana logo
are trademarks of Bloomsbury Publishing Plc

First published in Great Britain 2022

Copyright © David Stefan Doddington and Enrico Dal Lago, 2022

David Stefan Doddington and Enrico Dal Lago have asserted their rights under the
Copyright, Designs and Patents Act, 1988, to be identified as Authors of this work.

Cover design: Terry Woodley
Cover image: Chained slaves mural on Door of No Return memorial, Ouidah,
Benin © Michele Burgess/Alamy; Concrete wall © Savushkin/iStock

All rights reserved. No part of this publication may be reproduced or transmitted in
any form or by any means, electronic or mechanical, including photocopying,
recording, or any information storage or retrieval system, without prior
permission in writing from the publishers.

Marisa J. Fuentes, *Dispossessed Lives: Enslaved Women, Violence, and the
Archive* (Philadelphia: University of Pennsylvania Press, 2016), pp. 1–12 and 144–8.
Reprinted with permission of the University of Pennsylvania Press.

Bloomsbury Publishing Plc does not have any control over, or responsibility for,
any third-party websites referred to or in this book. All internet addresses given
in this book were correct at the time of going to press. The author and publisher
regret any inconvenience caused if addresses have changed or sites have
ceased to exist, but can accept no responsibility for any such changes.

Every effort has been made to trace copyright holders and to obtain their permissions
for the use of copyright material. The publisher apologizes for any errors or omissions
and would be grateful if notified of any corrections that should be incorporated in future
reprints or editions of this book.

A catalogue record for this book is available from the British Library.

Library of Congress Cataloging-in-Publication Data
Names: Doddington, David Stefan, 1986- editor. | Dal Lago, Enrico, 1966- editor.
Title: Writing the history of slavery / edited by David Stefan Doddington, Enrico Dal Lago.
Description: New York, NY : Bloomsbury Academic, 2021. | Series: Writing
history | Includes bibliographical references and index.
Identifiers: LCCN 2020036014 (print) | LCCN 2020036015 (ebook) |
ISBN 9781474285582 (hardback) | ISBN 9781474285575 (paperback) |
ISBN 9781474285599 (ebook) | ISBN 9781474285605 (epub)
Subjects: LCSH: Slavery–History. | Slavery–Historiography.
Classification: LCC HT861 .W686 2021 (print) | LCC HT861 (ebook) |
DDC 306.3/6209–dc23
LC record available at https://lccn.loc.gov/2020036014
LC ebook record available at https://lccn.loc.gov/2020036015

ISBN:	HB:	978-1-4742-8558-2
	PB:	978-1-4742-8557-5
	ePDF:	978-1-4742-8559-9
	eBook:	978-1-4742-8560-5

Typeset by Integra Software Services Pvt. Ltd.
Printed and bound in Great Britain

To find out more about our authors and books visit www.bloomsbury.com
and sign up for our newsletters.

To Joe Miller

Contents

List of figures x
List of contributors xi

Introduction: Writing the History of Slavery
David Stefan Doddington and Enrico Dal Lago, Cardiff University and National University Ireland Galway 1

Part I Global approaches

1 **Defining slavery in global perspective**
David Lewis, University of Edinburgh 19

2 **Writing global histories of slavery**
Michael Zeuske, University of Cologne (Köln), University of Bonn, Universidad de la Habana 41

3 **Slavery and empire** Trevor Burnard, University of Hull 59

4 **The 'Great Divergence': Slavery, capitalism and world-economy** Dale Tomich, Binghamton University 81

5 Approaches to global antislavery
Seymour Drescher, University of Pittsburgh 113

6 Comparative and transnational histories of slavery
Enrico Dal Lago, National University of Ireland Galway 133

Part II Themes and methods

7 Political and legal histories of slavery
Sue Peabody, Washington State University 153

8 Writing national histories of slavery
Lewis Eliot, University of Oklahoma 171

9 Writing the religious history of the enslaved in the Atlantic World
Matt D. Childs, University of South Carolina 189

10 What historians of slavery write about when we write about race
Jacqueline Jones, University of Texas at Austin 227

11 Gender history and slavery
David Stefan Doddington, Cardiff University 247

12 Dispossessed lives: Enslaved women, violence, and the archive
Marisa J. Fuentes, Rutgers University, Introduced by Elizabeth Maeve Barnes, University of Reading 267

13 **Slavery, postcolonialism and the colonial archive** *Andrea Major, University of Leeds* 287

14 **Imagining slavery in Roman antiquity** *K.R. Bradley, University of Notre Dame* 307

15 **Quantitative histories of slavery** *Andrea Livesey, Liverpool John Moores University* 337

16 **Psychohistory and slavery** *Patrick H. Breen, Providence College* 361

17 **Material culture, archaeology and slavery** *Lydia Wilson Marshall, DePauw University* 377

18 **Slavery and the cultural turn** *Raquel Kennon, California State University, Northridge* 399

19 **Re-tooling memory and memory tools: America's ongoing re-memory of slavery** *Marcus Wood, University of Sussex* 417

Index 447

Figures

1. The 'Anti-Yoke' Church, Whitney Plantation 432
2. Sculptures of Slave Children in 'Anti-Yoke' Church's Chapel 434
3. *Slave Angel with Wings* in the 'Field of Angels', Whitney Plantation 435
4. The 'Wall of Honour', Whitney Plantation 438
5. The '*Allées* Gwendolyn Midlo Hall', Whitney Plantation 438
6. The Memorial to the 1811 Louisiana Slave Revolt, Whitney Plantation 442

Contributors

Elizabeth Maeve Barnes, Lecturer in Modern History, Department of History
University of Reading, UK

Keith Bradley, Eli J. and Helen Shaheen Professor Emeritus of Classics, Department of Classics
University of Notre Dame, USA

Patrick H. Breen, Associate Professor of History, History Department
Providence College, USA

Trevor Burnard, Wilberforce Professor of Slavery and Emancipation and Director, the Wilberforce Institute, at the University of Hull
University of Hull, UK

Matt D. Childs, Associate Professor of History, Department of History
University of South Carolina, USA

Enrico Dal Lago, Professor of American History, School of History and Philosophy
National University of Ireland Galway, Ireland

David Stefan Doddington, Senior Lecturer in North American History, School of History, Archaeology and Religion
Cardiff University, UK

Seymour Drescher, Distinguished Professor Emeritus of History, Department of History
University of Pittsburgh, USA

Lewis Eliot, Assistant Professor of History, Department of History
University of Oklahoma, USA

Marisa J. Fuentes, Associate Professor of Women's and Gender Studies and History; and Presidential Term Chair in African American History
Rutgers University, USA

Jacqueline Jones, Ellen C. Temple Chair in Women's History and Mastin Gentry White Professor of Southern History, Department of History; President of the American Historical Association, 2021
University of Texas at Austin, USA

Raquel Kennon, Associate Professor, Department of Africana Studies
California State University, Northridge, USA

David Lewis, Lecturer in Greek History and Culture, School of History, Classics and Archaeology
University of Edinburgh, UK

Andrea Livesey, Senior Lecturer in U.S. History, Department of History
Liverpool John Moores University, UK

Andrea Major, Professor of Colonial History, School of History
University of Leeds, UK

Lydia Wilson Marshall, Associate Professor of Anthropology, Department of Sociology and Anthropology
DePauw University, USA

Sue Peabody, Meyer Distinguished Professor of History, Department of History
Washington State University, USA

Dale Tomich, Emeritus Professor of Sociology, Department of Sociology
Binghamton University, USA

Marcus Wood, Professor of English, School of English
University of Sussex, UK

Michael Zeuske, Professor Emeritus of Latin American and Iberian History, Historical Institute, University of Cologne (Köln), Germany (1993–2018); since 2019 Senior Research Professor, Bonn Center for Dependency and Slavery Studies (BCDSS)
University of Bonn, Germany

Introduction: Writing the History of Slavery

David Stefan Doddington and
Enrico Dal Lago
Cardiff University and
National University Ireland Galway

Slavery has existed almost everywhere around the globe where humans have laid roots, and most human societies have, at one point or another, either practised forms of slavery or faced enslavement themselves.[1] While varying widely across time and place, the seemingly ubiquitous place of slavery in the human past, and the legacies, memories and the global impact of slavery and enslavement – whether personal, political, social, cultural or economic – has meant that scholars studying a wide range of regions, themes and chronologies have been drawn to the topic. Taking inspiration from these scholars and from the massive body of work they have generated in the course of over a century of studies on the history of slavery, with this volume we aim to delve into the historiographical, theoretical and methodological

---

[1] The best starting point for an understanding of the global dimension of the history of slavery, focused on its now classic definition as 'social death', remains Orlando Patterson, *Slavery and Social Death: A Comparative Study* (Cambridge, MA: Harvard University Press, 1982). For a recent reappraisal, see John Bodel and Walter Scheidel, eds, *On Human Bondage: After Slavery and Social Death* (Oxford: Wiley Blackwell, 2016).

imperatives and approaches that have driven historians in their studies of both the institution of slavery and the process of enslavement across time and space. While we do not seek to explore the history of slavery per se, nor focus on the lives of either the enslavers or the enslaved, we intend to provide a guide to how historians have used different concepts, ideas and methodologies in their efforts at reconstructing the experience of slavery by different categories of people in different times and places throughout human history. The historiography of slavery is large and immensely complicated, and, especially in the past forty years, it has expanded exponentially, often as a result of the ongoing significance of scholarly debates around particular issues. Our hope is that this volume will help academics, students and interested readers to navigate this historiography in a comprehensive and understandable way.

This volume is part of a broader academic series, *Writing History*, which was designed to provide university-level students and wider readers with accessible overviews of major historiographical, intellectual and analytical approaches that have been used by historians in their work.[2] This collection is explicitly based around a reflective consideration of the historian as practitioner, asking contributors, students and readers to engage with the disciplinary frameworks, intellectual shifts and structural forces that have shaped and continue to shape historical work on particular historical themes, such as, in this case, slavery. *Writing the History of Slavery*, thus, reveals how, why and to what effect historians have approached and explored specifically the subject of slavery, providing introductory and explanatory briefs for major themes and approaches, addressing case studies and referring to the most significant works written in the field, as well as providing suggestions for future teaching and research. The title is, of course, a misnomer: there can never be a singular history of slavery, and nor would we claim otherwise. It would be more appropriate, in fact, to talk about 'histories of slaveries', in the plural, given the enormous variety in the experience of slavery by so many different categories of people, both enslavers and enslaved, across the globe, since the start of human history.

The existence of a large degree of diversity in the types of slavery theorized and practised by different human societies in the past is, in fact, one of the

---

[2] For examples of work published in the series, see Stefan Berger, Heiko Feldner and Kevin Passmore, eds, *Writing History: Theory and Practice*, 3rd ed. (London: Bloomsbury, 2020); Stefan Berger and Eric Storm, eds, *Writing the History of Nationalism* (London: Bloomsbury, 2019); Jean-Marc Dreyfuss and Daniel Langton, eds, *Writing the Holocaust* (London: Bloomsbury, 2011); Laura Lee Downs, *Writing Gender History* (London: Bloomsbury, 2010).

main points we wish to stress, and one that comes across particularly clearly in some of the current historiography, especially the most recent multi-volume and multi-authored collective works on the history of slavery on a global scale and also the several one-volume and single-author syntheses with either a global or a New World scope.[3] Moreover, the term 'slavery' itself may be subject to scrutiny, when one thinks that it has been taken mostly to represent a static idea of an institutional system of property of human beings with little concern for the historical reality of the dynamic process of enslavement, as the pioneering work of Joseph Miller, who proposed to replace the noun 'slavery' with the active verb 'slaving', argued in a particularly compelling way.[4] These are important concerns that go beyond the correctness of the title of our book, though, and relate, instead, to central issues that are debated at several points in the chapters that follow. In this connection, it is particularly important to point out that, from the historiographical point of view, as this volume demonstrates, not only have historians approached the topic of slavery through a wide variety of methodological, intellectual and analytical frameworks, but they have also continuously debated and disagreed, sometimes fiercely, as to the positives and negatives of particular approaches and specific interpretations.

In turn, concerns over *how* historians study and represent particular elements of slavery, both theoretical and empirical, have frequently reached beyond, into wider social, political and cultural debates, and have revealed how, at the risk of a cliché, 'the past is never dead. It's not even past yet.'[5] Scholars of slavery have long acknowledged and embraced challenges to the model of an objective and singular vision of historical facts, recognizing instead the contested terrain that is represented by the remembered past. In

---

[3]For recent multi-authored works on the history of slavery, see Keith Bradley, Paul Cartledge, David Eltis and Stanley L. Engerman, eds, *The Cambridge World History of Slavery*. Vols. 1–4 (New York: Cambridge University Press, 2011–); Robert L. Paquette and Mark M. Smith, eds, *The Oxford Handbook of Slavery in the Americas* (New York: Oxford University Press, 2010); Gad Heuman and Trevor Bernard, eds, *The Routledge History of Slavery* (London: Routledge, 2011); and Enrico Dal Lago and Constantina Katsari, *Slave Systems: Ancient and Modern* (Cambridge: Cambridge University Press, 2008). For single-authored works, see especially David Brion Davis, *Inhuman Bondage: the Rise and Fall of Slavery in the Americas* (New York: Oxford University Press, 2006); Seymour Drescher, *Abolition: A History of Slavery and Antislavery* (New York: Cambridge University Press, 2009); Robin Blackburn, *The American Crucible: Slavery, Emancipation and Human Rights* (London: Verso, 2011); and Michael Zeuske, *Handbuch Geschichte der Sklaverei. Eine Globalgeschichte von den Anfängen bis heute*, 2nd ed. (Berlin: De Gruyter, 2019).
[4]Joseph C. Miller, *The Problem of Slavery as History: A Global Approach* (New Haven, CT: Yale University Press, 2012). See also Jeff Flynn and Damian Pargas, eds, *Slaving Zones: Cultural Identities, Ideologies, and Institutions in the Evolution of Global Slavery* (Leiden: Brill, 2018).
[5]William Faulkner, *Requiem for a Nun* (New York: Random House, 1951).

denying, implying or arguing for the primacy of some methods over others, or for the intellectual and socio-political imperative of one approach over another, scholars of slavery have, thus, played a critical role in revealing how history and the historian can speak both to the past and to the present. Thus, in the course of this process, scholars of slavery have created historiographical schools and traditions that have shaped in significant ways our understanding of past societies, particularly in relation to the ideologies of the dominant classes and the varieties of forms of resistance to exploitation by oppressed categories of people, whether legally enslaved or not.

Contributors to this volume were tasked with providing a reflective consideration of their own practices as historians of slavery, as well as to address some of the ways in which scholars in their field have navigated and structured their research and writing, whether on certain elements of slavery, or on experiences of enslavement or on the legacies of such practices. Our aim has been to integrate discussions of philosophical, theoretical and methodological concepts and theories with practical examples and application of such methods and approaches in studies of the history of slavery. Much outstanding existing scholarship, including the already cited collective enterprises of the *Cambridge World History of Slavery* and of the *Oxford Handbook of Slavery in the Americas*, provides readers with a systematic historical treatment with chapters on different regions where slavery was practised and within a structure that divides the latter according to either chronology or geography, or else it directly addresses, in synthetic sections, the histories of the enslaved people and the slavers, and the historical processes and phenomena that have caused enslavement, first and foremost the slave trade.[6] In doing so, these works provide much-needed syntheses of the state of the art of the field of slavery studies in relation to our historical knowledge and interpretation of past events and processes associated with the global and bi-millenarian practice of slavery, which generations of historians have painstakingly reconstructed in different parts of the world.

This volume, however, deliberately looks, instead, at the methodological toolkits and intellectual frameworks used and applied by scholars working in those areas. It asks them to reveal the process through which they have arrived at certain conclusions in their study of the history of slavery, specifically in relation to the way they have built on other scholars' work, and

---

[6]See Bradley, Cartledge, Eltis and Engerman, eds, *The Cambridge World History of Slavery*; and Paquette and Smith, eds, *The Oxford Handbook of Slavery in the Americas*.

therefore in relation to the way they either consider themselves as belonging to specific historiographical schools or not. Awareness and recognition of this is particularly important when one thinks how different historiographical schools have competed and continue to compete with each other, each by claiming to correctly interpret the incomplete surviving historical record on both enslavers and enslaved. Unlike the current superb works dealing with the history of slavery, therefore, with our volume, we do not explore the history of peoples or places connected to slavery, but rather we analyse exclusively, and by doing so we seek to illuminate the historiography of slavery, its theory and its practical applications. In other words, in revealing and deconstructing the diverse practices applied and employed by historians working in the field, the scholars who have written the chapters of this book have sought to focus on the practical application of theoretical issues and of shifting methodological demands that have affected historical research and writing, particularly in the last forty years. Ultimately, *Writing the History of Slavery* asks students and readers to recognize historians of slavery as people, researchers and writers in context, and to note how the latter has impacted upon the work they have produced. The chapters that follow this introduction examine major disciplinary and intellectual shifts inside and outside academia within the context of the development of the historiography of slavery, making use of case studies and selected examples specifically in order to connect clearly theory to practice. The contributors have addressed – each in their own different and unique way – the crucial questions of how and why historians have prioritized different methods and approaches in their research and writing, revealing, in the process, that scholars are neither removed nor immune from wider social, cultural and political currents outside the world of scholarship.

The historiography of slavery is a fruitful arena for such reflective and methodological work. Historians of slavery have been by necessity forced to address contested pasts, consider the methodological consequences of the privileging of elite voices and concomitant silencing of enslaved people, and encounter the historical afterlife of violence and exploitation. In the face of such tensions, scholars of slavery have often been at the forefront in developing new methods, championing diverse approaches to studying the past, and considering how complex and challenging histories are represented and packaged to the public. Histories of slavery have been pioneering in a number of fields: whether ensuring history is remembered 'from below', or considering intersectional issues of race, gender and class, or complicating triumphant narratives of progress and modernity. The pioneering role historians of slavery have played in shaping contemporary historiography by interrogating, complicating and re-forging anew established ideas about our past emerges clearly from all the contributions to the present volume, with many of these scholars having been at the forefront of the most significant historiographical changes of the past forty years. These changes have reshaped not only our understanding of the history of slavery but also our views of the historical interpretation of much broader themes, such as, for example, the relationship between modernity, progress, freedom and capitalism – a theme which is currently at the heart of major scholarly debate carried out in some of the most important journals in this field and in other cognate fields of historical inquiry.[7]

In their works and in their debates, scholars of slavery have continuously critically and creatively explored the mindsets and mentalities of enslavers and enslaved alike, as well as the impact of slavery on society writ large, combining the local with the global and the personal with the structural. Such diverse work has allowed for the integration and development of innumerable interdisciplinary methods and modes of research, including, but not limited to, psychoanalysis, anthropology, quantitative research and cliometrics, poststructuralism and literary studies. In turn, such work has been to the benefit of scholars across the discipline and also of all those interested in exploring the past. Continuing on the path of this established innovative and multi-disciplinary scholarship, therefore, in the present volume, contributors have explored select theoretical and methodological issues using case studies and examples from many different societies where slavery was practised around the world and at different times in history, providing, at the same time, critical summaries of the historical work

---

[7]This debate was stimulated by the publication of three major books on the history of slavery seen as strictly related to the history of modern capitalism – Walter Johnson, *River of Dark Dreams: Slavery and Empire in the Cotton South* (Cambridge, MA: Harvard University Press, 2013); Edward E. Baptist, *The Half Has Never Been Told: Slavery and the Making of American Capitalism* (New York: Basic Books, 2014); and Sven Beckert, *Empire of Cotton: A Global History* (New York: Knopf, 2015) – as well as by the pioneering studies of Dale Tomich on the 'second slavery'; see Dale Tomich, *Through the Prism of Slavery: Labor, Capital, and World Economy* (Lanham, MD: Rowan & Littlefield, 2004). For some of the most important contributions on both sides of the debate, see especially Scott R. Nelson, 'Who Put Capitalism in My Slavery?' *Journal of the Civil War Era* 5 (2015), pp. 281–304; John J. Clegg, 'Capitalis and Slavery', *Critical Historical Studies* 2 (2015), pp. 281–304; D. Rood, 'Beckert Is Liverpool, Baptist Is New Orleans: Geography Returns to the History of Capitalism', *Journal of the Early Republic* 36 (2016), pp. 151–67; Erik Mathisen, 'The Second Slavery, Capitalism, and Emancipation in Civil War America', *Journal of the Civil War Era* 8 (2018), pp. 677–99; and James L. Huston, 'Slavery, Capitalism, and the Interpretations of the Antebellum United States: The Problem of Definition', *Civil War History* 65 (2019), pp. 119–56.

done on the latter, often implementing nuances and methods coming from disciplines other than History. In chronological and geographical terms, works cited in these contributions span across the ancient Near East and the Mediterranean world, medieval Europe, the early modern and modern Atlantic world and the Americas. We are cognizant that our volume is not, and could never be, exhaustive, given the depth in the field and the range and reach of slavery on a global, world-historical, scale. However, we hope that the present edited collection has addressed the key areas in the field and that it has succeeded in representing the variety of methodological approaches, historiographical traditions, and theoretical and thematic frameworks associated to the study of the history of slavery.

The first section of the book examines how historians have attempted to explore slavery from a global perspective, revealing patterns and continuities in experiences and structures of slavery, but also differences and changes over time.[8] Although always conscious that slavery has existed almost for the entirety of human history and in almost every society of every region of the world, historians have found it incredibly challenging to write truly global histories of slavery. Partly, this was due to the widespread tendency to regionalization in the study of slavery, by which scholars tended to be experts of slavery in a particular region of the world; partly, though, the reason was also the higher degree of significance assigned to specific forms of slavery in particular areas of the world and at a particular time – specifically, the ancient Roman world and the nineteenth-century United States – as opposed to other forms of historical slavery considered of lesser importance. Only relatively recently, historians have attempted to write truly global histories of slavery, either in large collective enterprises of multi-authored volumes or in single-authored syntheses of the human experience of slavery in all places and at all times, as previously mentioned. The chapters in this first section of our book are from scholars who have engaged in either the former or the latter types of global histories of slavery and represent the state of the art of the historiography of global slavery in relation to different themes and issues.

---

[8] See David Brion Davis, 'Looking at Slavery from Broader Perspectives', *American Historical Review* 105: 2 (2000), pp. 452–66. See, also, essays by Peter Kolchin, Rebecca Scott, and Stanley Engerman in this special edition. Further work on the 'global' turn can be found in Olivier Pétré-Grenouilleau, *Les traites négrières. Essai d'histoire globale* (Paris: Gallimard, 2004); Miller, *The Problem of Slavery as History*; Zeuske, *Handbuch Geschichte der Sklaverei*; Damian Alan Pargas, 'Slavery as a Global and Globalizing Phenomenon: An Editorial Note', *Journal of Global Slavery* 1 (2016), pp. 1–4; Noel Lenski and Catherine M. Cameron, eds, *What Is a Slave Society? The Practice of Slavery in Global Perspective* (New York: Cambridge University Press, 2018).

The benefits and challenges of writing global histories of slavery emerge clearly from all the six chapters in this section. A global lens, as demonstrated in David Lewis's and Michael Zeuske's powerful chapters, can help to illuminate shifting practices and ideas over what historians have actually meant when they have spoken of 'slavery' and reveal the consequences of such definitions and terminology for scholars and activists. Mentioning different examples across time and space of persons defined as 'slaves', Lewis asks himself what actual validity has 'the single, global category of "slavery"' in relation to the enormously different historical experiences of individuals defined as 'slaves'. His conclusion is that 'the traditional ownership definition of slavery' – that is, a slave is an individual on whom the right of ownership is exercised – 'retains much utility as a tool' for comparative historical studies of global slavery.[9] Michael Zeuske, instead, details his own voyage of discovery of the global dimension of slavery, starting from his research in a specific region and historical period – nineteenth-century Cuba – and progressively expanding his horizons until he was able to write his *Handbuch der Geschichte der Sklaverei*, now in its second edition.[10] In his monumental work, Zeuske has attempted a systematization of 'phases, spaces, dimensions and processes in the global history of slaveries' – significantly a plural noun, to denote the enormous diversity in the experiences of 'slavery' in the past.[11]

Some of the most important recent debates have witnessed sharp divergences between historians over the question of how central was slavery in the making of modern global capitalism and in assessing the connections between slavery, imperialism and postcolonial politics. Trevor Burnard's chapter deals with the concept of empire in relation to the global history of slavery, and he notes how slavery and imperial expansion have been more than compatible for most of human history, from ancient to modern times, and in many areas of the world, from Europe to Africa to Asia, to the point that, until relatively recently, slavery was taken for granted specifically in relation to the history of European imperial expansion. According to Burnard, historians are now approaching a consensus, though, on the fact that 'to understand empire one needs to acknowledge the many ways in which slavery shaped imperial experiences'.[12]

---

[9] See Chapter 1 in this volume.
[10] Zeuske, *Handbuch Geschichte der Sklaverei*.
[11] See Chapter 2 in this volume.
[12] See Chapter 3 in this volume.

Dale Tomich's subsequent chapter looks specifically at the historiography, past and present, which has focused on the connections between slavery and capitalism, and he examines how historians of slavery have grappled with the economic dimensions of enslavement in the context of broad debates over capitalism, industrialization and 'modernity'. His chapter begins with a detailed analysis of Eric Williams's classic *Capitalism and Slavery*, and the responses it received.[13] It, then, continues with a critique of the 'New Economic History' approach, best represented by Robert Fogel and Stanley Engerman and of Kenneth Pomeranz's pathbreaking work in world historical studies, and finally it focuses on the important recent framework of the 'second slavery', a term which indicates the modern, global capitalist dimension of slave-based production in 'the Cuban sugar frontier, the U.S. cotton frontier, and the Brazilian coffee frontier'.[14]

Equally important in the context of the debates on modernity has been also the idea that the struggle to end slavery is a quintessential feature of our modern world. In this connection, Seymour Drescher has explored in his chapter how historical research on antislavery spoke, and continues to speak, to foundational national myths and powerful historiographical and intellectual traditions, and relates to contemporary concerns with 'modern' slavery. Drescher has noted that 'for more than a century and a half, the historiography of antislavery remained dominated by its Atlantic initiators', and that only relatively recently the historiographical focus on antislavery has expanded beyond the confines of the Atlantic paradigm; yet, 'the urge to develop comprehensive global histories of antislavery ... remains intact'.[15]

We close the opening section with Enrico Dal Lago's wide-ranging assessment of the influence of comparative and transnational historical methodologies and approaches on these global studies of slavery. In drawing together the diverse interpretive frameworks, methodologies and theoretical perspectives that have been applied by scholars working at the global level, Dal Lago provides a clear overview as to the scale of the work historians have undertaken in challenging the primacy of the nation-state through transnational and comparative assessments of slavery. He looks first at the development of historiography, from the 1940s onwards, in relation to

---

[13] Eric Williams, *Capitalism and Slavery* (Chapel Hill, NC: University of North Carolina Press, 1944).
[14] See Chapter 4 in this volume.
[15] See Chapter 5 in this volume.

historical comparisons of societies characterized by the institution of slavery across time and space, both on a global scale and on a regional basis, and then at studies focusing on the transnational practice of the slave trade at different times and in different regions of the world. Dal Lago, then, concludes with a section focusing on the new approaches represented by Joseph Miller's concept of 'slaving' as a dynamic historical process and by Michael Zeuske's global history of slaveries, which is the first step towards the full integration of comparative and transnational methodologies in the global historical study of past slave societies.[16]

The second section of the book addresses select themes and methods historians have used to examine slavery, as well as assessments as to how the types of sources that historians use, and their approach to such material, impact upon the histories written. The aim is to account for the diversity in historiographical approaches to the study of slavery across time and space through a selection of the most important issues historians have dealt with and methods they have utilized in their investigation of slave societies, slaveholders and the slaves themselves. Thus, issues related to politics, law, religion, economics, race, gender, psychology and archaeology have all influenced the historiography of slavery, leading to the creation of a large body of interdisciplinary scholarship on the subject. At the same time, methods and theories as diverse as quantitative history, postcolonial studies, history from below and the history of memory have been very influential in the different phases the historiography of slavery has gone through. This section, therefore, is designed to give students and readers an idea of the importance of these themes and methods for the past and present, and also future, historiography of slavery, by providing both summaries and case studies related to the latter and written specifically by scholars currently engaging in the study of slavery and making use of them.

The section starts with a chapter written by Sue Peabody, which looks at how the historical records found in all types of repositories of primary sources and in archives have allowed us to reconstruct political and legal histories of slavery. Peabody notes how, for most of human history, the legal records found across time and space in all societies supported the legitimacy of slavery, and only from the eighteenth century onwards, antislavery became for the first time important in legal and political terms in the Atlantic World. Peabody also notes the current historiographical focus on biographies and

---

[16] See Chapter 6 in this volume.

microhistories of the enslaved, which 'show how historians can use legal records not only to shed light on particular people in slavery and freedom, but also to ask and answer, through those records, new questions about the worlds in which the slaves lived'.[17] Lewis Eliot then explores how histories of slavery have shaped understandings and constructions of the nation-state, focusing on the contested nature of memory, race, nationalism and postcolonial struggles in the Atlantic world. After showing how historians have approached the study of slavery through national frameworks, as well as how systems of slavery have been connected to broader conceptual understandings of borders, 'insiders' and 'outsiders', Eliot asks readers to consider how 'the creation of the nation in the nineteenth century was... very much tangled with contemporary questions regarding the feasibility and acceptability of continued slaveholding'. Eliot further stresses the need for scholars to explore how 'legacies of chattel bondage continue to inform national histories' with a nuanced assessment of the pressing debates on how to confront and address the legacies of slavery.[18]

In the following chapter, Matt Childs addresses historical debates over the crucial role of religion in the lived experiences of the enslaved, using 'the era of Atlantic enslavement from the fifteenth to the nineteenth century' as a case study with a wide scope. Looking specifically at the historiography focusing on the meeting between the original African and Muslim religions of the enslaved and the Christianity of the New World's colonizers, Childs notes that the syncretistic religions born out of that meeting – such as Cuba's *Santeria*, Brazil's *Candomblé* and Haiti's *Vodun* – have been studied more by anthropologists than by historians, and that the former have mostly focused on the Creolization model of 'the history of African Christianity and African-American Christianity born out of the torturous process of slavery'.[19]

In following chapters, Jacqueline Jones, David Stefan Doddington, Marisa J. Fuentes, Elizabeth Maeve Barnes and Andrea Major show how social constructs such as race, gender and ethnicity have shaped histories of slavery, noting issues of subjectivity and considering that *who* historians focus on in their research – and how they gain access to the experiences of the enslaved – reveals structural fault lines both inside and outside of academia. Jacqueline Jones interrogates the historical category of 'race' in

---

[17]See Chapter 7 in this volume.
[18]See Chapter 8 in this volume.
[19]See Chapter 9 in this volume.

relation to the historiography of slavery, by maintaining that 'although race is a myth, the devastating consequences flowing from its multiple meanings and inhumane practices are not'. She concludes, then, that the ambiguity and contradictions associated to the word 'race' in archival documents and in other sources should alert us to the fact that the 'historians' loose and uncritical use of the term obscures more than it illuminates our study of the past'.[20] A comparable ambiguity can be observed also in the definitions of the category of 'gender', which have changed over time in relation to the different historiographical phases in the studies of slavery, as David Stefan Doddington's chapter highlights, culminating in the post-1980 scholarship, which has focused on the deconstruction of 'seemingly stable binaries of male/female to consider multiple, intersecting identities' and their impact on the experience of slavery. This historiographical shift, in turn, has generated a much welcome 'increased focus on languages of gender, the power of representations, and the relationship between masculinity/femininity', which has complicated, but also increased, our understanding of previously hidden dimensions in the lives of both the enslavers and the enslaved.[21]

In 2016, Marisa J. Fuentes published *Dispossessed Lives*, one of the most significant interventions regarding the archives of slavery since Michel Rolph-Trouillot's masterful *Silencing the Past*. Fuentes was unable to contribute to this volume but we believe readers will benefit from engaging with the vital points made in *Dispossessed Lives* as to the power dynamics embedded in 'standard' research practices, such as the use of archives and historical repositories, as well as to recognize the political and personal dimension to historical claims and historiographical debates on slavery in the Americas. We have thus provided excerpts from Fuentes's introduction and epilogue to *Dispossessed Lives*, with a guided introduction from Elizabeth Maeve Barnes, and hope that students and readers can build on the reflective and nuanced assessment of the politics in the 'production of history' to further develop their own research and writing on slavery and enslaved life.[22]

In her closely related chapter on postcolonialism and its effects on the interpretation of archival sources with regard to both the perception and the reality of slavery, Major shows that the record of slavery in British-colonized India is ambiguous and confused, because it related mostly to the

---

[20]See Chapter 10 in this volume.
[21]See Chapter 11 in this volume.
[22]See Chapter 12 in this volume.

misinterpretations of the institution by the colonizer. The deconstruction of the latter, ultimately, has resulted in the re-conceptualization of Indian slavery 'as an array of historically and regionally specific practices and statuses, each with different implications for the enslaved'.[23] Major highlights the complex methods applied by scholars to move past silences in the records and the disagreements over our capacity to do so, while also stressing the need to recognize the power of language and discourse in shaping both past and present. Alongside the specific thematic angles applied, whether race, gender or postcolonialism, then, these chapters are shaped by attention to the complexities historians face with their research in the context of historical and political debates over resistance, identities and the politics of memory and meaning.

Having examined broad thematic angles and approaches, the book moves forward with case studies where contributors have focused on the application of methods and theories to select periods and sites of slavery. Keith Bradley's chapter is an exemplary study of how to reconstruct a history of slavery from below by focusing on the case study of the Roman slave system, a task that the author acknowledges as extremely difficult because of the paucity of sources left behind by the enslaved, especially in the ancient world. Yet, by starting with the assumption that 'in everyday reality slaves responded to the conditions of servitude as individual agents capable of making decisions', Bradley is able to uncover a wide array of evidence from the most disparate sources that suggest a number of angles through which to reconstruct the experience of slavery from the point of view of the slaves; inevitably, the sheer variety of this experience, according to the different circumstances and contexts, leads Bradley to conclude that 'the Roman experience of slavery is full of contradictions and anomalies'.[24]

In the subsequent chapter, the possibilities, politics and problems of quantitative records in reconstructing the history of slavery are addressed by Andrea Livesey, with a case-study approach to Fogel and Engerman's famous/infamous cliometric study, *Time on the Cross* (1974),[25] as well as with an assessment of the methods and claims associated with the 'new' history of capitalism and slavery, best represented by scholars such as the previously cited Walter Johnson, Edward Baptist and Sven Beckert. Livesey

---

[23]See Chapter 13 in this volume.
[24]See Chapter 14 in this volume.
[25]Robert W. Fogel and Stanley L. Engerman, *Time on the Cross: The Economics of American Slavery* (New York: W. W. Norton, 1974).

challenges this scholarship by concluding that, in her own view, it is tainted by the dogmatic assumption of being able to define clearly 'the relationship of slavery and capitalism – a slippery task considering that the criteria used to define 'capitalism' varies from historian to historian', but reiterates that there are benefits to be gained when historians of slavery combine the quantitative with the qualitative.[26]

In his chapter, Patrick Breen looks at a particularly interesting approach to the study of slavery, which focuses on the attempt to understand the psychology of the enslaved. Starting by looking at sources interpreting slave psychology from the points of view of both masters and slaves, Breen, then, examines the development of modern ideas on slave psychology in the United States, from the writings of W.E.B. Du Bois to the debates following the publication of Stanley Elkins's *Slavery* (1959) and Eugene Genovese's *Roll, Jordan, Roll* (1974), and more recently in relation to Edward Baptist's *The Half Has Never Been Told* (2014).[27] He concludes with a discussion of the 'renewed interest in the psychological effects of slavery in the twenty-first-century African-American community', which has produced studies that potentially pave the way for future approaches to the psychohistory of slavery.[28] Equally novel and intriguing has been the contribution of methods of investigation and approaches coming from Archaeology in the research on past slave societies. In her chapter, Lydia Wilson Marshall expertly navigates the material turn and considers how scholars have applied both anthropological and archaeological methods to develop their understandings of slave life in different slave societies at various times and in various places across the world. Even though the practice of archaeological investigation of sites associated to slavery is only fifty years old, and still now relatively few historical studies take into account the nuances coming from the work of archaeologists, Archaeology has risen in importance in providing a better understanding of the material record of slavery in relation to evidence as diverse as the spatial organization of plantations in the Caribbean and in Africa, or the relation between either social status or ethnic identification and material culture in both Africa and the Americas. Thus, Marshall concludes her chapter with a passionate plea for much stronger

---

[26]See Chapter 15 in this volume.
[27]Stanley N. Elkins, *Slavery: A Problem in America's Institutional and Intellectual Life* (Chicago: University of Chicago Press, 1959); Eugene D. Genovese, *Roll, Jordan, Roll: The World the Slaves Made* (New York: Vintage, 1974); Baptist, *The Half Has Never Been Told*.
[28]See Chapter 16 in this volume.

interdisciplinary collaboration, and ultimately for History and Archaeology to be able 'to overcome disciplinary barriers and recognize each other as allies' in the study of past slave societies.[29]

Finally, the book concludes with two important interventions on the politics of memory, culture and representation in slavery studies. In their powerful and probing chapters, Raquel Kennon and Marcus Wood ask students and readers to consider how, and to what effect, historians, scholars and activists represent elements of slavery and attempt to speak the unspeakable. Kennon reveals how the epistemological intervention commonly known as the 'cultural turn' provided 'new methods of accounting of and for the lives and conditions of the enslaved and those who held them in slavery'. In her capacious interdisciplinary exploration of these historiographical and theoretical developments, Kennon explores how, 'by turning to "culture," a contested and mutable academic term, novelists, poets, artists, and interdisciplinary scholars from the social sciences and humanities attempt to render the ineffability of slavery's past while grappling with and against the limits of language, archival material, and cultural memory'. Kennon asks students and scholars to reflect on the power of language and discourse in their research and writing, to appreciate the power of 'naming' in the past, present and future, and provides a clarion call for scholars to work collaboratively in order to 'reimagine the critical tools and language we use to tell the stories of slavery'.[30]

Wood, in his 'short polemical introduction to slavery, memory, trauma and archives', analyses in detail the institutionalization of the memory of slavery through the case study of the Whitney Plantation, near New Orleans, and he focuses particularly on the contrast between some relatively sanitized monuments erected in remembrance of slavery, and, conversely, the brutal rendition embedded in the memorial to the 1811 German Coast slave rebellion in Louisiana. Wood, then, asks whether it is really possible to recover the truth of the slave experience in these settings with a reflective consideration as to how sites of memory are forced to balance a need to represent the brutal violence that underpinned the enslaver's power without perpetuating this language of terror. Wood concludes with an open-ended question as to whether a 'more celebratory monument at the Whitney which remembers the slaves in triumphant terms and in terms of their

---

[29]See Chapter 17 in this volume.
[30]See Chapter 18 in this volume.

revolutionary ideology' might allow for such a nuanced approach, possibly taking inspiration from the memorial of the 1811 revolt.[31]

In all the chapters of this book, therefore, the contributors reflectively consider, and ask readers to consider, how the methodological frameworks, analytical lens and presentation style that historians apply affect the histories they write. The editors and the authors of this volume do not claim comprehensiveness in all areas, but they hope that the chapters in this edited collection will provide students and readers with the opportunity to explore significant practical, theoretical and methodological concerns that have shaped the long-term scholarly investigation of the history of slavery. In focusing on the historian of slavery as practitioner, and in emphasizing the 'workings' of history, as opposed to the end product, this volume provides an attempt to make it easier for students and readers to connect often abstract ideas with real examples, by looking at general theories in conjunction with specific case studies related to the practice of slavery in the past. Most of all, it endeavours to demonstrate how both the history of slavery and historians of slavery are inevitably shaped, whether knowingly or not, by a wide diversity of contexts, cultures and theoretical and methodological frameworks, all of which have formed the bases of subsequent phases in the historiography of slavery, past and present.

---

[31] See Chapter 19 in this volume.

Part I

Global approaches

1

Defining slavery in global perspective

David Lewis

University of Edinburgh

The more we learn about slavery the more difficulty we have defining it
– David Brion Davis[1]

Let us begin with the stories of four individuals, picked more or less at random. Our first individual lived in Assyria and was named Ahat-abiša. Her father owed thirty silver shekels to a man named Zabdî; one day in 652 BC he transferred Ahat-abiša to Zabdî in restitution of that debt.[2] We know of Ahat-abiša's fate because it was recorded in cuneiform script on a clay tablet, legal evidence of her conveyance. Our second individual was named Aristarchus. Aristarchus worked as a semi-independent leather worker in Athens in the last quarter of the fifth century BC; we know of him from an inscription recording how he was confiscated and sold by the Athenian state in 414 BC because of the impious actions of his owner Adeimantus.[3] Our third individual lived two centuries ago and was named Johnson. This man was an African fluent in Mandingo and English, who learned the latter as a result of being enslaved and transported to Jamaica as a boy. Having achieved manumission, he resided in England for a number of years with

---

[1] David Brion Davis, *Slavery and Human Progress* (New York; Oxford: Oxford University Press, 1984), P. 8.
[2] *State Archives of Assyria* XIV 85.
[3] *Inscriptiones Graecae* I³ 426.14; 24–39. Discussion in David M. Lewis, *Greek Slave Systems in Their Eastern Mediterranean Context, c. 800–146 BC* (Oxford: Oxford University Press, 2018), p. 43.

his former owner before finally returning to his native country. We know of his life through the writings of the explorer Mungo Park, who hired him as an interpreter in 1795.[4] Our fourth individual is named Nadia Murad. She is an Iraqi Yazidi, and was captured by Daesh in 2014, sold several times, and subjected to severe sexual exploitation before escaping later that year. She currently works in promoting the rights of Yazidis.[5]

Scholars have labelled all of these individuals as slaves or having suffered enslavement. Why? What shared feature allows these persons' conditions at points of their lives – separated by gulfs of time and space, coming from very different cultures, undergoing many different experiences – to be grouped under a single, global category, 'slavery'? The question has attracted no small measure of controversy, and has elicited a variety of different responses. The current state of confusion is well summed up by the words of David Brion Davis, quoted in the epigraph to this chapter; for if a scholar of Davis's calibre and vision can be reduced to aporia, then the issue must be in a very sorry state indeed. The purpose of this chapter is to explore the question of defining slavery in global perspective: is it a legitimate exercise, and if so, what rules should govern the inclusion or exclusion of this or that person from the category?

I should declare an interest at the outset. The orthodox approach to defining slavery, which has persisted from antiquity to the present (but encountered critiques of various sorts, especially since the 1960s), has to do with ownership. This approach is perhaps best summed up in the League of Nations' definition of slavery of 1926 that held it to be 'the status or condition of a person over whom any or all of the powers attaching to the right of ownership are exercised'.[6] Despite various criticisms, it is this definition – or at least some close variant thereof – that seems to me to capture best what is distinctive about slavery; and I have argued at length in recent book for an ownership-focused definition.[7] That same definition has also been used

---

[4] Mungo Park, *Travels in the Interior of Africa* (London: The Folio Society, 1984 [1799]), p. 15.
[5] See 'Nadia Murad – from rape survivor in Iraq to Nobel Peace Prize' (BBC News website, 5 October 2018, [accessed 6 November 2018]).
[6] See Jean Allain, *The Slavery Conventions. The Travaux Préparatoires of the 1926 League of Nations Convention and the 1956 United Nations Convention* (Leiden; Boston: Martinus Nijhoff, 2008). My understanding of ownership as a cross-cultural category (subject of course to much local variation) draws heavily on Tony Honoré, 'Ownership' in A.G. Guest, ed., *Oxford Essays in Jurisprudence* (London; New York: Oxford University Press, 1961), pp. 107–47; further discussion in Lewis, *Greek Slave Systems* (2018), pp. 25–55; cf. Jean Allain, 'Property in Persons: Prohibiting Contemporary Slavery as Human Rights' in T. Xu and J. Allain, eds, *Property Rights and Human Rights in a Global Context* (Oxford: Hart Publishing, 2015), pp. 93–119, 107–8.
[7] Lewis, *Greek Slave Systems*.

by the co-founder of *Free the Slaves* Kevin Bales and the legal specialist Jean Allain to identify slavery in the post-abolition world of the present day, and has led to the conviction of modern enslavers.[8]

It should be noted that the ownership definition is accepted among the vast majority of slavery scholars; indeed, in large parts of the field there is no 'definitional debate' at all: it simply does not feature in recent literature on slavery in the Atlantic world; and one leading student of Roman slavery has recently declared astonishment that the traditional definition was ever questioned in the first place.[9] The debate is far more prominent among anthropologists, sociologists, specialists in modern slavery and students of African and Asian history. Naturally, it has been a serious problem for scholars with an interest in 'global' slavery studies, who must come to some manner of accommodation with their colleagues in these disciplines given the all-embracing nature of the field. This chapter, then, is not a disinterested account of the various approaches scholars have taken to defining slavery, but an overview of several key criticisms to which the orthodox view has been subjected. I aim to articulate these criticisms as clearly as possible, to use them to stress-test the orthodox view and to explore the methodological challenges that confront any attempt to define slavery as a globally valid category applicable to both historical and present-day societies. The subject is vast; within the limits of this chapter, therefore, I have had to be selective and highlight several key themes.

We begin with the question of what a definition is and what purpose it serves. The second section ('The genesis of a concept: Slavery in law and metaphor') then turns to the ancient world. My aim here is to show how the terminology of slavery – a legal relationship based on the ownership of persons – was mapped outwards onto other domains through processes of metaphorical extension. This introduced potential for confusion; it is a process still ongoing to this day, and lies at the root of some recent unorthodox approaches to the definition of slavery. The third section ('Modern studies of slavery and their expanding scope') moves from history to modern historiography, and examines how scholarship on slavery, initially focused on several familiar Western cases (Greece, Rome, the United States, the Caribbean, Brazil), expanded to explore various forms of forced labour

---

[8]Jean Allain and Kevin Bales, 'Slavery and Its Definition' in Jean Allain, ed., *The Law and Slavery: Prohibiting Human Exploitation* (Leiden; Boston: Martinus Nijhoff Publishers, 2015), pp. 502–12.
[9]Amy Richlin, *Slave Theatre in the Roman Republic* (Cambridge; New York: Cambridge University Press, 2017), p. 21.

in a much broader range of societies. It was this process that set the scene for challenges to the traditional definition to emerge during the last fifty years. I then (in the section entitled 'Finley's law') examine these challenges, especially from the sociological and anthropological traditions, and attempt to gauge whether or not they are convincing. During the nineteenth and twentieth centuries, the language of slavery was enlisted to characterize the objects of numerous humanitarian campaigns; this has led to an ever-growing indeterminacy regarding the application of the term 'slavery'. The final section ('Slavery, humanitarianism and political rhetoric') analyses the issue of modern (namely post-abolition) slavery.

As I hope to show, the confusion noted by Davis is not due to an inherent difficulty of the topic, but due to the specific historiographical trajectory of global slavery studies as it has developed over the last fifty years. It is to this historiography, I argue, that one must turn in order to understand why the current state of confusion exists.

What is a definition?

It may help to begin by asking what a definition is and what job we wish it to perform. A definition is a taxonomic tool, not an analytical tool. As Patterson has rightly noted, the point of a definition of slavery is to identify a distinct category of persons.[10] This might seem self-evident, but in fact much confusion has been caused by scholars requiring their definitions to perform other tasks of, for example, a descriptive or analytical nature.

Some scholars have treated definition as a kind of précis, a blurb meant to summarize the most historically significant aspects of slavery.[11] Such

---

[10] Orlando Patterson, *Slavery and Social Death* (Cambridge, MA: Harvard University Press, 1982), p. 21.
[11] This approach can be seen in the work of two leading scholars of ancient slavery. Lenski criticizes the property definition as an inadequate way of '*attempting to summarize* a complex phenomenon' (my emphasis), while Vlassopoulos writes that 'it is still the case that the definitions of slavery employed by historians have not yet managed to incorporate slave agency and the wider range of relationships that shape slavery'. See Noel Lenski, 'Framing the Question: What Is a Slave Society?' in Noel Lenski and Catherine M. Cameron, eds, *What Is a Slave Society? The Practice of Slavery in Global Perspective* (Cambridge: Cambridge University Press, 2018), pp. 15–57, 43; Kostas Vlassopoulos, 'Does Slavery Have a History? The Consequences of a Global Approach', *Journal of Global Slavery* 1: 1 (2016), pp. 5–27, 11. But summary/description is not the job of a definition: Lewis, *Greek Slave Systems*, pp. 26–7.

definitions tend to stray into description and prolixity.[12] A corollary of this is to see a contradiction in defining slavery in terms of property, namely that human beings are far more than just commodities, have minds of their own and have agency to affect the course of their lives.[13] This misconstrues the purpose of a definition, which is not to summarize the entire phenomenon, but to pinpoint what makes it a distinctive category. All humans have minds and agency: these factors are therefore extraneous to the task of defining a subcategory of human beings. The legal definition of slavery does not require slaves to be inert, passive pawns: rather, it simply brackets off a group of individuals who are treated as property in law or practice.[14]

Others have believed that the concept 'slavery' can only be comprehensible in association with an antonym, 'freedom'.[15] This is certainly one way in which Western societies have articulated slavery; but a concept of freedom is not necessary for a clear concept of slavery. As Jack Goody has shown, the concept 'slavery' has proven perfectly comprehensible without any antonym; and more recently Kostas Vlassopoulos has underscored that in many cultures that do have an antonym to slavery, that antonym is not freedom,

---

[12]Lenski proposes a global definition of slavery as 'the enduring, violent domination of natally alienated and inherently dishonored individuals (slaves) that are controlled by their owners (masters) who are permitted in their social context to use and enjoy, sell and exchange, and abuse and destroy them as property'. Lenski, 'Framing the question', p. 51. One could trim this down and write simply that slaves are property of their owners: the ability of the owner to enjoy, abuse, sell, natally alienate, etc. stems from this fact; these social consequences do not need to be unpacked within the definition itself. Furthermore, Lenski's definition runs into the problem that some legal systems (e.g. Shari'a law) permit slavery but forbid the owner to kill their slave. This can easily be accommodated in a cross-cultural approach to property law that admits variant restrictions on ownership. See, for example, Honoré, 'Ownership'; David Lewis, 'Orlando Patterson, Property and Ancient Slavery: The Definitional Problem Revisited' in John Bodel and Walter Scheidel, eds, *On Human Bondage: After Slavery and Social Death* (Chichester & Malden, MA: Wiley-Blackwell, 2016), pp. 31–54. However, if we follow Lenski's definition, then there were no slaves in such systems. On slavery in Shari'a law see B. Freamon, 'Definitions and Conceptions of Slave Ownership in Islamic Law' in Jean Allain, ed., *The Legal Understanding of Slavery: From the Historical to the Contemporary* (Oxford: Oxford University Press, 2012), pp. 40–60.
[13]See, for example, Julia O'Connell Davidson, *Modern Slavery: The Margins of Freedom* (New York: Palgrave Macmillan, 2015), pp. 49–51.
[14]Cf. the remarks of Moses I. Finley, *Ancient Slavery and Modern Ideology* (London: Chatto & Windus, 1980), p. 73.
[15]Most prominently, Moses I. Finley, 'Slavery' in D.L. Sills, ed., *The International Encyclopedia of the Social Sciences*, Vol. 14 (New York & London: Crowell, Collier and Macmillan, 1968), pp. 307–31, 308. More recently, Suzanne Miers, 'Slavery: A Question of Definition' in Gwyn Campbell, ed., *The Structure of Slavery in Indian Ocean Africa and Asia* (Portland, OR; London: Frank Cass, 2004), pp. 1–15, specifically, p. 2: 'No definition of slavery can be separated from the definition of its antithesis, freedom.'

but mastery or kinship.[16] Another popular approach has been to tack on various extras to the standard definition of slavery, such as Finley's claim that slaves were not just property, but were also always outsiders;[17] as Eltis and Engerman have rightly pointed out, however, 'Societies have tended to reserve enslavement for those whom they have defined as not belonging, but this has not always meant that all aliens were enslaved, or that all slaves were aliens.'[18]

On the other hand, some scholars, most prominently Joseph Miller, have objected to the very exercise of defining slavery in institutional terms; such a procedure, he argues, is 'static' and cannot capture the dynamic processes of history.[19] To deny the importance of defining slavery altogether leads to two problems. First, one cannot be precise about what one is talking about; and it remains very unclear how Miller proposes distinguishing between slaves and non-slaves. Second, as Lovejoy notes, historical societies created 'static' legal institutions for the very task of sorting individuals into the categories of slaves and non-slaves and guaranteeing their supply and control; to ignore these in favour of a 'dynamic', 'processual' history is to deny the historical significance of these institutions.[20] Above all, to reject legal categories is to engage in an unnecessary quarrel, for one need not choose either a 'static', legalistic view of history or a 'dynamic', anti-institutional view of history: historical societies are composed of fixed and moving parts, neither of which can be neglected if one aims at a rounded understanding. My point is to establish a heuristic division of labour: the task of definition is simply concerned with identifying whether or not a given person is a slave; the historian's work does not begin and end by asking this question. It is a non sequitur to claim that defining slavery in legal terms locks one into a static version of history, the agency of whose subjects simply cannot be grasped.

---

[16]Jack Goody, *The Theft of History* (Cambridge: Cambridge University Press, 2006), p. 58; Vlassopoulos, 'Does Slavery Have a History', p. 10; cf. Igor Kopytoff and Suzanne Miers, 'African Slavery as an Institution of Marginality' in Suzanne Miers and Igor Kopytoff, eds, *Slavery in Africa: Historical and Anthropological Perspectives* (Madison: The University of Wisconsin Press, 1977), pp. 3–81, 17.
[17]Finley, 'Slavery', p. 308; Finley, *Ancient Slavery and Modern Ideology*, p. 75.
[18]David Eltis and Stanley L. Engerman, 'Dependency, Servility, and Coerced Labor in Time and Space' in David Eltis and Stanley L. Engerman, eds, *The Cambridge World History of Slavery, Vol. 3: AD 1420–AD 1804* (Cambridge: Cambridge University Press, 2011), pp. 1–21, 14.
[19]Joseph Miller, *The Problem of Slavery as History: A Global Approach* (New Haven, CT: Yale University Press, 2012), pp. 1–35.
[20]Paul Lovejoy, 'Review of Miller, 2012', *American Historical Review* 118: 1 (2013), pp. 148–9.

The genesis of a concept: Slavery in law and metaphor

The legal ownership of human beings can be documented from remote periods of antiquity; slave sale contracts are known from the Old Babylonian and Old Assyrian periods, and the legal regulation of slavery is known from Sumerian documents of an even earlier date, such as the law code of Ur-Namma (2100 BC).[21] These show a fundamental similarity with slavery in the more familiar Atlantic world: the legally regulated reduction of human beings to tradeable chattel; such cases easily qualify as slavery under the 1926 League of Nations definition. A close look at the legal position of slaves in 1st millennium BC Babylonia shows that their condition satisfies all the criteria of Honoré's cross-cultural formulation of ownership.[22]

Yet antiquity also provides us with examples of one of the key complications in the definitional problem, namely the semantic extension of slave terminology; for while the reduction of human beings to the legal status of property had its own special terminology, that terminology came to be expanded in scope beyond this phenomenon proper. A look at the semantic range of some slave terms in several ancient languages may prove instructive. In Old Babylonian the slave is called a *wardum*; in Classical Hebrew, *eved*. The most common Greek term for slave is *doulos*; the most common Latin term *servus*. (Our English word 'slave', by which these words are usually translated, originates from metonymy of the term *sklavos*, 'Slav', in Byzantine Greek; Slavs were commonly enslaved in the Middle Ages.) From an early period we can observe processes of metaphorical extension by which these terms were mapped outwards from their core meaning to other domains of life.[23]

---

[21] Martha T. Roth, *Law Collections from Mesopotamia and Asia Minor* (Atlanta, GA: Scholars Press, 1995), pp. 13–22; S. Bayram & S. Çeçen, 'The Institutions of Slavery in Ancient Anatolia in the Light of New Documents', *Belleten*, 229 (1996), pp. 605–30; F. Van Koppen, 'The Geography of the Slave Trade and Northern Babylonia in the Late Old Babylonian Period' in H. Hunger & R. Pruzsinszky, eds, *Mesopotamian Dark Age Revisited* (Vienna: Verlag der Österreichischen Akademie der Wissenschaften, 2004), pp. 9–33.
[22] M.A. Dandamaev, *Slavery in Babylonia. From Nabopolassar to Alexander the Great (626–331 BC)*, trans. Victoria A. Powell, rev. ed. (DeKalb: Northern Illinois University Press, 1984), pp. 67–80; Lewis, *Greek Slave Systems*, pp. 48–52.
[23] On metaphorical extension see George Lakoff and Mark Johnson, *Metaphors We Live By* (Chicago: University of Chicago Press, 1980); April M.S. McMahon, *Understanding Language Change* (Cambridge: Cambridge University Press, 1994), pp. 174–99; George Lakoff, 'The Neural Theory of Metaphor' in R.W. Gibbs Jr., ed., *The Cambridge Handbook of Metaphor and Thought* (Cambridge: Cambridge University Press, 2008), pp. 17–38.

Thus in the ancient Near East, legal slavery served as the cultural prototype for hierarchical social relations; its terminology was enlisted to describe such asymmetrical relations even in cases where the superordinate party did not legally own the subordinate party. In the Hebrew Bible, for instance, the terms *eved* – 'male slave' (pl. *avadim*) – and *amah* – 'female slave' (pl. *amahot*) – can describe individuals held as property of an owner (Leviticus 25:44–6):

> Such male and female slaves as you may have – it is from the nations round about you that you may acquire male and female slaves. You may also buy them from among the children of aliens resident among you, or from their families that are among you, whom they begot in your land. These shall become your property: you may keep them as a possession for your children after you, for them to inherit as property.

Yet the same terminology was used to articulate asymmetrical social relations not based on legal ownership. Thus in *Genesis* when Joseph's brothers – who no longer recognize him – are accused by him of being spies, they reply (42:10):

> No, my master! Truly, your slaves have come to procure food!

Here, despite believing that they have never met him, Joseph's brothers abase themselves before a social superior by referring to him as master (*adon*) and themselves as slaves (*avadim*). This phenomenon might be compared to one in recent British history: the polite custom of signing a letter with the phrase 'your humble servant', which is strictly metaphorical and implies no true contractual relationship of service. These therefore are examples of the slave/servant metaphor being enlisted into the language of deference.

In Greece, the terminology of slavery in the Homeric epics (*c.* 700 BC) strictly applies to individuals who are the property of their owners.[24] Two key points about Greek slave terminology should be noted: first, it has an antonym, *eleutheria*, 'freedom': all members of society could be classed as either being slaves or free persons. Second is a process of metaphorical extension, operative over the centuries that followed the Homeric poems that expanded the range of subjects that the language of slavery and freedom could govern. In the sixth century BC we find the terminology of slavery used in relation to the political domination of a community by a tyrant; in the

---

[24]N.R.E. Fisher, 'Hybris, Status and Slavery' in A. Powell, ed., *The Greek World* (London: Routledge, 1995), pp. 44–84, 53–4; Edward M. Harris, 'Homer, Hesiod, and the "Origins" of Greek Slavery' *Revue des Études Anciennes* 114: 2 (2012), pp. 345–66; Lewis, *Greek Slave Systems*, pp. 60–1.

fifth century the Spartans went to war with the Athenians to 'free' the Greeks from being 'enslaved' by the Athenians – formulations that have nothing to do with legal ownership, but which recruit the terminology of the most paradigmatic asymmetrical power relationship (legal slavery) to describe other kinds of asymmetrical power relations (e.g. political domination). By the end of the fifth century BC, this terminology could be used to describe the political subjection of a city to a tyrant or a powerful neighbour, the undesirability of one citizen working as the employee of another citizen, or indeed the domination of the soul by anger, greed or lust.[25]

This highlights a central point of complication in our task: legal slavery's paradigmatic quality, embodying dynamics such as domination, subordination, but also deference and loyalty, made it a constant reference point for describing analogous phenomena; the terminology of slavery could then be mapped onto these analogous domains. The task of separating the concrete from the abstract – that is legal slavery from slave metaphors – was more easily achieved in societies where legal slavery existed. In post-abolition societies, however, the terminology of freedom is rarely, if ever, applied in its original, technical legal sense (for this is now a dead letter); as a political metaphor, however, it retains considerable value, as any observer of American political rhetoric can easily discern. 'Slavery', too, is widely appropriated in political rhetoric. As one of the most famous former slaves in history remarked,

> Now, what is this system of slavery? (…) I have found persons in this country who have identified the term slavery with that which I think it is not, and in some instances, I have feared, in so doing, have rather (unwittingly, I know) detracted much from the horror with which the term slavery is contemplated. It is common in this country to distinguish every bad thing by the name of slavery. Intemperance is slavery; to be deprived of the right to vote is slavery, says one; to have to work hard is slavery, says another (…). I am here to say that I think the term slavery is sometimes abused by identifying it with that which it is not. Slavery in the United States is the granting of that power by

---

[25]R. Brock, 'Figurative Slavery in Greek Thought' in A. Serghidou, ed., *Peur de l'esclave – Peur de l'esclavage en Méditerranée ancienne/Fear of Slaves – Fear of Enslavement in the Ancient Mediterranean (XXIXe colloque du GIREA, Rethymnon, 4–7 novembre 2004)* (Besançon: Presses universitaires de Franche-Comté, 2007), pp. 217–24; Mélina Tamiolaki, *Liberté et esclavage chez les historiens grecs classiques* (Paris: Presses de l'université Paris-Sorbonne, 2010). For a brief overview, Lewis, *Greek Slave Systems*, pp. 59–67. For the slave metaphor in Rome, see M. Lavan, *Slaves to Rome. Paradigms of Empire in Roman Culture* (Cambridge: Cambridge University Press, 2013). For a broader exploration see Mary Nyqvist, *Arbitrary Rule: Slavery, Tyranny and the Power of Life and Death* (Chicago: University of Chicago Press, 2013).

which one man exercises and enforces a right of property in the body and soul of another.[26]

As we shall see (in the section 'Finley's Law', below), this metaphorical extension of the term 'slavery' to which Frederick Douglass so objected is ongoing today, and continues to cause much confusion.

Modern studies of slavery and their expanding scope

The current global history trend has led to various ambitious studies, most recently Zeuske's *Handbuch Geschichte der Sklaverei: Eine Globalgeschichte von den Anfängen bis zur Gegenwart* (Handbook of the History of Slavery: A Global History from the Beginning to the Present) and Pétré-Grenouilleau's *Qu'est-ce que l'esclavage? Une histoire globale* (What Is Slavery? A Global History).[27] These represent the culmination of well over a century of research that – beginning from the familiar cases of, for example, Greco-Roman antiquity and the early-modern Atlantic world – expanded outwards in both space and time to incorporate every known human society. A detailed historiographical overview is impossible here, but two ambitious works ought to be singled out for special comment. First, Herman Nieboer's *Slavery as an Industrial System* (1900), which examined slavery from an ethnographical standpoint in the native societies of the Americas, the Pacific islands, central Asia, Arabia and Africa. This work is remarkable for its breadth and clarity of discussion.[28] Second, Orlando Patterson's *Slavery and Social Death: A Comparative Study* (1982). This study utilized George P. Murdock's sample of world cultures to provide the first truly global exploration of slavery; Patterson may fairly be held a founding father of today's field of global slavery studies. (Unlike Nieboer, however, Patterson

---

[26]Frederick Douglass, 'Reception speech at Finsbury Chapel, Moorfields, England, May 12th 1846'; I owe the reference to Edward Harris.
[27]Michael Zeuske, *Handbuch Geschichte der Sklaverei: Eine Globalgeschichte von den Anfängen bis zur Gegenwart* (Berlin: De Gruyter, 2013); Olivier Pétré-Grenouilleau, *Qu'est-ce que l'esclavage? Une histoire globale* (Paris: Gallimard, 2014).
[28]Nieboer's interest in slavery beyond the classical and Atlantic worlds was prefigured by much activist work during the nineteenth century that aimed at drawing the attention of colonial powers to instances of slavery and to compel intervention: see Suzanne Miers, *Slavery in the Twentieth Century. The Evolution of a Global Problem* (Walnut Creek, CA: Altamira, 2003), pp. 1–57.

rejected the ownership definition of slavery and substituted an idiosyncratic definition of his own; see further below.)

As researchers shifted their horizons outwards in space (incorporating regions such as Africa, Asia and the native societies of the Americas) and time (e.g. anthropological research using modern ethnographic studies to model the prehistory of slavery; but also sociological studies of 'modern' slavery), it is crucial to ask what criteria were (and are) utilized in judging whether or not slavery existed or exists in the cultures under investigation. If one imagines a scientist travelling into an unexplored rainforest, it seems reasonable to suppose that upon encountering an animal previously unknown to science, our scientist would attempt to categorize it according to known taxonomies, seeing (for instance) if it fits into a known genus. The same ought to be true of historians, anthropologists and sociologists who exploring a culture hitherto unknown to them can gauge whether its social structures, practices and institutions bear any resemblance to ones known to be widespread in other parts of the world. The student of slavery who newly encounters this or that form of dependant labour, therefore, is not free to co-opt these discoveries into existing categories willy-nilly, but must respect what is already known of the category; and the newly encountered phenomenon, if it does not fit into any existing categories (e.g. slavery, debt bondage, penal labour), must be treated as *sui generis*. Had such an obvious procedure been followed over the last fifty years, it would have led to a sophisticated array of categories of forced labour, some cross-culturally widespread (e.g. slavery), others less so (e.g. the Royal Navy's former practice of using press gangs to acquire naval manpower). However, one of the major problems in global studies of slavery over the past four decades has been an influential strand of research that violates this principle.

Finley's Law

In 1977 Kopytoff and Miers published a valuable collection of essays on slavery in Africa and prefaced it with a radical claim: that the traditional ownership definition was inadequate for treating African forms of slavery.[29] Their claim quickly met with criticism from M.I. Finley:

---

[29] Kopytoff and Miers, 'African Slavery', pp. 11–12; 76–8.

First, a host of, let us say, African statuses and status terms are translated as 'slaves'; second, it is observed that at essential points these so-called slaves are extremely unlike the slaves of classical antiquity or of the Americas; third, instead of reconsidering their appellation 'slaves' to their own subjects, these anthropologists angrily protest the 'ethnocentrism' of 'western' historians in order to provide a place for their own pseudo-slaves.[30]

I have called the principle implicit in Finley's criticism 'Finley's Law'; it provides a useful tool for navigating both how a global definition of slavery should be formulated, and for critiquing the various departures from this principle that have long stood unquestioned and contributed to the present state of confusion through uncritical accretion. The mistake can be seen very clearly in Kopytoff's review of the English translation of Meillassoux's *Anthropologie de l'esclavage: le ventre de fer et d'argent* (1986).[31] Meillassoux had used the traditional definition of slavery to investigate African forms of slavery; against this, Kopytoff argued that his approach was no better than investigating 'fatherhood' in Africa by insisting on examining only those cases that would qualify under a Scandinavian definition of fatherhood. In other words, Kopytoff believed in an essential, primordial phenomenon, 'slavery', of which that based on ownership was simply a 'Western' subspecies; in investigating versions of the former, he argued, one should not therefore make them conform to the narrow parameters of the latter. The criticism is something like objecting to defining a dog in terms of the attributes of a beagle, since the latter is only a subcategory of the former. But here Kopytoff made an unwarranted assumption, namely that slavery is somehow 'natural' (like fatherhood) and not a human contrivance;[32] he nowhere defined what he meant by slavery in this broader sense; and the wider sense he used seems to be composed of whatever happens to have been called 'slavery' by various persons, whether legitimately or not, with no distinction made between law and metaphor.

There is another fundamental mistake in Kopytoff's approach: a misunderstanding of the nature of property and ownership as cross-cultural

---

[30]Finley, *Ancient Slavery and Modern Ideology*, p. 69. Note how Kopytoff and Miers simply recognize as slaves anyone who has been called 'slave', without pausing to question whether or not this appellation was made legitimately. Kopytoff and Miers, 'African Slavery', pp. 3, 7 and 12.
[31]Igor Kopytoff, 'Review of Meillassoux, 1991', *American Ethnologist* 20: 2 (1993), p. 391.
[32]Even the much-maligned Roman law recognized that slavery was not natural and inevitable: Tony Honoré, 'The Nature of Slavery' in Jean Allain, ed., *The Legal Understanding of Slavery: From the Historical to the Contemporary* (Oxford: Oxford University Press, 2012), pp. 9–16, 9–10.

categories. In their introduction to the *Slavery in Africa* volume, Kopytoff and Miers argued that to say that what makes a person a slave is that he is 'property' is essentially to say: 'A slave is a person over whom certain (unspecified) rights are exercised. This does not tell us what rights are involved nor how they differ from the rights of a kin group over its ordinary members.' Because of this, 'to define "slavery" as "the legal institutionalization of persons as property" (...) is not very helpful'.[33] This was a serious error: property rights are not some vague cluster of indefinable powers; Kopytoff and Miers had effectively ignored a sophisticated debate in legal scholarship that had, by 1961, worked out those aspects of ownership that remain stable from one society to the next, and those that vary.[34]

The same error underpins the most famous challenge to the ownership definition, that of Orlando Patterson in *Slavery and Social Death*. According to Patterson, property equates to 'claims and powers vis-à-vis other persons with respect to a given thing, person, or action'.[35] However, everyone is entangled in webs of such claims and powers: 'This is what a master possesses with respect to his slave; it is also exactly what a person possesses with respect to his or her spouse, child, employee, or land.'[36] To define a slave as property fails, in Patterson's view, because everyone, 'beggar or king', is the object of some property relation, and therefore property fails to demarcate a distinct category of persons. He cites three examples of persons, clearly not slaves, apparently classed as property, by way of illustration: first, the American husband, who is apparently the property of his wife; second, sports stars traded between different clubs; third, bride-wealth in various traditional societies (payment for the bride allegedly denoting a property transaction).[37] As Paul Finkelman has rightly pointed out, however, these are not relationships based on ownership at all, but on contract; like Kopytoff and Miers before him, Patterson viewed 'property' as a vague term denoting any legal claims and powers, thus missing the distinction between ownership and contract.[38] The error is as elementary as claiming that renting a house and owning a house are essentially the same thing; the whole edifice of

---

[33]Kopytoff & Miers, 'African Slavery', p. 11.
[34]Honoré, 'Ownership'; see n. 6.
[35]Patterson, *Slavery and Social Death*, p. 22.
[36]Ibid.
[37]Ibid., pp. 21–7.
[38]Paul Finkelman, 'Review of Patterson, 1982', *The Journal of Interdisciplinary History* 15: 3 (1985), pp. 508–11, 509–11.

Patterson's critique of the ownership definition and the rationale for creating a substitute rest on this misunderstanding.[39]

An influential recent strand of anthropology contains many of the same mistakes. In his essay 'L'esclavage comme institution', Alain Testart claims that to define slavery as property freezes the institution in a narrow, Roman law framework inapplicable to other legal systems. Ownership in Roman law, he claims, was absolute, comprising the right to use (*ius utendi*), to enjoy the fruits (*ius fruendi*), and to use up or destroy (*ius abutendi*). But slaveholders in Islamic law could not kill their slaves, which does not therefore fit a property paradigm; and can we apply this framework to Africa?[40] Testart also argues that sale is not a diagnostic marker of slavery, because recruitment firms sell the labour of their workers.[41] Instead of ownership, he opts for a vague formulation of slavery as an extreme form of 'exclusion'. Like Kopytoff, Testart does not consider whether or not the labelling of certain African statuses as 'slavery' was a legitimate exercise in the first place (thus violating Finley's law); like Patterson, Testart collapses together ownership and contractual relationships (viz. treating the sale of labour and the sale of a person as the same thing); and his discussion of Roman law is misleading: despite its theoretically absolute character, *dominium* (ownership) in Roman legal practice was hemmed in by all manner of restrictions.[42] Ownership in all societies is subject to restrictions, and a property law paradigm can easily accommodate examples such as Islamic law where the killing of slaves is banned.[43] Furthermore, the ownership definition works perfectly well in many African societies (just as it applies to, e.g., early Mesopotamia),

---

[39] I make a fuller case against Patterson in Lewis, 'Orlando Patterson, Property and Ancient Slavery'; Lewis, *Greek Slave Systems*, pp. 25–55. For further debate see the essays in Allain, ed., *The Legal Understanding of Slavery* and Bodel and Scheidel, eds, *On Human Bondage*, including Patterson's response to his critics. O'Connell Davidson uncritically accepts the Patterson-Kopytoff critique of slavery as property. See O'Connell Davidson, *Modern Slavery*, pp. 45–7.
[40] Alain Testart, 'L'esclavage comme institution', *L'Homme* 38 (1998), pp. 31–69, 31–4.
[41] Testart, 'L'esclavage comme institution', p. 35.
[42] P. Birks, 'The Roman Law Concept of Dominium and the Idea of Absolute Ownership', *Acta Juridica* (1985), pp. 1–37.
[43] See Honoré, 'Ownership', which forms the methodological substratum on which Allain & Bales, 'Slavery and Its Definition', and Lewis, 'Orlando Patterson, Property and Ancient Slavery', rest. Testart writes of the property approach: 'Ces définitions eussent valu d'être examinées sérieusement si elle avaient été formulées en précisant que l'esclave se définissait *dans chaque société* par la propriété *au sens où cette société l'entend*. Peut-être une telle formulation est-elle exacte, je ne sais et nous ne pouvons le savoir tant que le recensement des diverses formes de propriétés n'a pas sérieusement été entrepris.' Yet this is exactly what Honoré's approach entails, and with which Testart does not engage; instead, he takes aim at a straw man caricature of Roman law in order to dismiss the whole idea of property. Testart, 'L'esclavage comme institution', p. 34. Pétré-Grenouilleau, *Qu'est-ce que l'esclavage?*, follows Testart on this point.

and has been utilized by leading Africanists such as the anthropologist Claude Meillassoux and the historian Paul Lovejoy.[44] The problem, then, is not that the traditional ownership definition of slavery cannot capture phenomena in pre-literate, non-state, non-Western societies or the 'small slaveries' of which Zeuske has written: it can.[45] Rather, it is a wider symptom of the tendency in twentieth-century anthropology to turn away from apparently 'Western' concepts such as property, a tendency whose legitimacy is now increasingly questioned.[46]

Slavery, humanitarianism and political rhetoric

We have seen so far that slavery can exist both in law and in metaphor; it can be found in all corners of the globe in various periods of history. We have also seen how, based on flawed understandings of legal concepts – or through other kinds of faulty method – various scholars have found the ownership definition impossible to accept, and sought to substitute their own replacements. A further layer of confusion emerges if we examine recent manifestations of the problem noted earlier, namely the broad semantic range of slave terminology in various languages. The semantic expansion of the term 'slavery' is charted in detail in Suzanne Miers's important book

---

[44] Claude Meillassoux, *The Anthropology of Slavery: The Womb of Iron and Gold* (Chicago: University of Chicago Press, 1991); Paul Lovejoy, *Transformations in Slavery. A History of Slavery in Africa*, 3rd ed. (Cambridge: Cambridge University Press, 2011).

[45] As David Brion Davis rightly notes, 'The truly striking fact, given historical changes in polity, religion, technology, modes of production, family and kinship structures, and the very meaning of "property," is the antiquity and almost universal acceptance of the *concept* of the slave as a human being who is legally owned, used, sold, or otherwise disposed of as if he or she were a domestic animal.' Davis, *Slavery and Human Progress*, p. 13. On small slaveries: Michael Zeuske, 'Historiography and Research Problems of Slavery and the Slave Trade in Global Perspective', *International Review of Social History*, 57: 1 (2012), pp. 87–111, 105–8.

[46] Useful summary of past trends and future directions in C. Hann, 'Property: Anthropological Aspects' in J. Wright, ed., *International Encyclopedia of the Social and Behavioural Sciences*, Vol. 19, 2nd ed. (Edinburgh, 2015), pp. 153–9. See also the remarks of Goody, *The Theft of History*, pp. 58–60. Kostas Vlassopoulos points out to me that in some African kin systems, individuals can be 'owned' by the kinship group; and that in some traditional societies, paternal authority can extend to selling children. I lack the specialist knowledge to comment on the former issue; and I accept his second point. A simple way out of this bind is to take the approach of Nieboer, *Slavery as an Industrial System*, p. 30, and introduce a qualification: 'Slavery is the fact that one man is the property or possession of another beyond the limits of the family proper.' Many such instances can be treated as *de facto* slavery, on which see the 'Modern Slavery' section of this chapter.

Slavery in the Twentieth Century (2003). Miers tracks this process from the early years of the abolition movement, whose constituent organizations coordinated much research into forms of forced labour across the globe during the later nineteenth century. These organizations in turn applied pressure on governments to force other nations to follow their lead in abolishing slavery, a process that, ironically, provided part of the 'civilizing' pretext for many colonial ventures that perpetrated abuses of their own, for instance the Belgian king Leopold II's acquisition of the Congo as his own private estate and the gruesome exploitation of native workers on its rubber plantations.[47]

Following the First World War, abolitionist lobbying interlocked with efforts to set up a League of Nations to forestall future wars and impose basic standards on its members; this was superseded by the United Nations, set up in the aftermath of the Second World War. It was under the aegis of these organizations that the 1926 convention on slavery and the 1956 supplementary convention established a basic taxonomy of global forms of forced labour.[48] Yet whereas the 1926 League of Nations definition of slavery aligned with the historical meaning of the term, things changed with the establishment of the UN Working Group on Slavery. At its first meeting in 1975 it was decided that the League of Nations definition was too narrow, and ought to be expanded to 'all institutions and practices which, by restricting the liberty of the individual, are susceptible of causing severe hardship and serious deprivation of liberty'.[49] It is crucial to grasp that this move lost sight of the historical, legal meaning of 'freedom' and embraced everything within its much more expansive metaphorical penumbra; by default, 'slavery' was treated in the same way. Quirk has levelled strong criticisms against the UN Working Group's method,

> where slavery has arguably come to be little more than short-hand for virtually any form of severe ill-treatment and exploitation. This situation also reflects an indefinite amalgam of literal (actual slavery) and rhetorical (a loose metaphorical association) claims. Throughout history, slavery has been regularly invoked as a rhetorical device. Familiar examples of this strategy include the concepts of 'wage slavery' and 'sex slavery' used by nineteenth century labour groups and suffragettes. When slavery was legal, the distinction between literal and rhetorical was relatively clear cut, but it

---

[47]Miers, *Slavery in the Twentieth Century*, pp. 51–3.
[48]Allain, *The Slavery Conventions*.
[49]Cited from Joel Quirk, 'Defining Slavery in All Its Forms: Historical Inquiry as Contemporary Instruction' in J. Allain, ed., *The Legal Understanding of Slavery: From the Historical to the Contemporary* (Oxford: Oxford University Press, 2012), pp. 253–77, 263.

has become increasingly ambiguous in recent times. Once slavery is held to come in any number of different forms, it is not always easy to say where slavery begins and ends.[50]

There is close on unanimous agreement among specialists that the use of the terminology of slavery to categorize phenomena as diverse as colonialism, apartheid, female genital mutilation and forced marriage is inaccurate and unwarranted;[51] and it may also prove counter-productive in the long run as a political slogan by neo-abolitionists. In order for the evocation of the term 'slavery' to pack a rhetorical punch, any phenomenon so labelled must align with the established meaning of the term. That is, if activists wish to claim that a given exploitative phenomenon *really is* slavery, it must approximate to historical cases of slavery, most vividly embodied in the Atlantic slave systems of the eighteenth and nineteenth centuries. Not everyone agrees: Snyder has recently argued that we ought to 'rethink familiar categories of analysis' such as property: 'As a human rights issue, the danger of defining slavery too narrowly is to dismiss practices that do not conform to archetypes.'[52] This approach, laudable in intent, suffers from three drawbacks. First, it treats history as if it were a palimpsest to be scraped clean and reinscribed whenever necessary. Terms such as 'property' and 'slavery' have a meaning in history that is fixed, completed and not subject to renegotiation. Put simply, it is a view that is incompatible with what happened in the past. Second, a pragmatic point: one cannot try to harness the visceral image of slavery – which is derived from history – to describe a much broader range of abuses. It is only in *alignment* with history that modern evocations have any meaning and rhetorical clout.[53] Third, Snyder's approach amounts to a kind of intellectual homeopathy, namely the belief that the more one waters

---

[50]Joel Quirk, *Unfinished Business. A Comparative Survey of Historical and Contemporary Slavery* (Paris: UNESCO, 2008), p. 32.
[51]For example, Miers, 'Slavery: A Question of Definition', pp. 12–13; Quirk, *Unfinished Business*, p. 32; Miller, *The Problem of Slavery*, p. 18; Orlando Patterson, 'Trafficking, Gender and Slavery: Past and Present' in J. Allain, ed., *The Legal Understanding of Slavery: From the Historical to the Contemporary* (Oxford: Oxford University Press, 2012), pp. 322–59; O'Connell Davidson, *Modern Slavery*, p. 6, 36; Allain and Bales, 'Slavery and Its Definition', p. 506.
[52]C. Snyder, 'Native American Slavery in Global Context' in N. Lenski and C. Cameron, eds, *What Is a Slave Society? The Practice of Slavery in Global Perspective* (Cambridge: Cambridge University Press, 2018), pp. 169–90, 190.
[53]Cf. Honoré, 'The Nature of Slavery' in J. Allain, ed., *The Legal Understanding of Slavery: From the Historical to the Contemporary* (Oxford: Oxford University Press, 2012), pp. 9–16, 16: 'Who are to be regarded as slaves in fact at the present day? This question should be answered in my view by analogy with slavery when it was a recognised institution open to criticism as contrary to nature. What was formerly accepted and is now condemned is basically the same institution.'

down a category, the more meaningful and efficacious it will become as a political slogan. That is very unlikely to work in practice.[54] As noted above, what is urgently needed is a robust taxonomic toolbox containing many precise categories of forced labour, which allows them to be understood and counteracted.

Modern slavery

A recent offshoot of the work of the abolition movement has been 'Neo-abolitionism' (as O'Connell Davidson terms it), a movement associated especially with Kevin Bales, co-founder of *Free the Slaves*.[55] The phenomenon of modern slavery poses a challenge to the question of definition explored throughout this chapter: slavery in its technical sense has long been understood as a relationship wherein one person is subjected to the legal ownership of another person (or persons, institution, state, vel sim). But in the post-abolition age (that is to say, in a global sense, since 1970), when no country in the world any longer provides a legal framework for slavery to exist, can we even speak at all of slavery, or must we root around for new terminology? Can the political potency of the term 'slavery' still be harnessed as a tool for abolitionists, without applying it to something substantively different?

Bales is well aware of the pragmatic problem of aligning modern slavery with historical slavery.[56] Yet until recently, he defined modern slavery in a fairly loose manner, identifying three criteria that qualify a person as a modern slave: (i) the use of violence over the individual; (ii) the ability to control the individual; (iii) economic exploitation of the individual.[57] This definition has rightly drawn criticism for its vagueness, inability to distinguish slavery from other forms of forced labour and poor alignment with historical slavery.[58] However, Bales has recently tightened his definition,

---

[54]Cf. Bales in his preface to Quirk, *Unfinished Business*, p. 11, and the remarks of Frederick Douglass, quoted above, on the dilution of the horror evoked by slavery if its meaning is expanded too far.
[55]O'Connell Davidson, *Modern Slavery*, p. 6.
[56]Kevin Bales, *Disposable People. New Slavery in the Global Economy* (Berkeley: University of California Press, 1999), pp. 5–6.
[57]Kevin Bales, *Understanding Global Slavery: A Reader* (Berkeley: University of California Press, 2005), p. 91.
[58]See in particular Patterson, 'Trafficking, Gender and Slavery'.

aligning it more closely with historical slavery, in collaboration with the legal specialist Jean Allain. As their argument has large implications for scholars across a range of disciplines, a review here of its main points is crucial. It involves returning to the 1926 League of Nations definition: 'The status or condition of a person over whom any or all of the powers attaching to the right of ownership are exercised.'

Let us unpack this definition following its parsing by Allain. First, it stresses the *exercise* of at least some of the powers attaching to the right of ownership over an individual.[59] However, *not all* of these need to be exercised for slavery to exist; thus a master might choose not to exercise his power to sell the slave; it is enough that he is able to do so. Second, and most significantly, slavery can either be a *status* or a *condition*. This latter point provides the key to unlocking the problem of conceptualizing slavery in a post-abolition era. In historical cases of slavery, we can understand it as a legally regulated *status*. In post-abolition societies, it must be understood as a *condition*. The difference is between slavery de jure and slavery de facto. Allain and Bales illustrate this with two parallels:

> Consider the case of a bigamist. In a majority of countries it is illegal for a married person to marry a second time. Let us say that a man gets married a second time. For that man the second marriage is illegal, the courts will not recognise it; thus he is not married de jure. However, from the courts' perspective he is married de facto; which allows for the bigamy case to proceed. A further example gets us closer to a consideration of the essence of the definition of slavery. Consider the dispute between two drug dealers over a kilogram of heroin. While neither has a de jure right of ownership of the drugs, the courts will recognise the exercise of a power attaching to such a right of ownership in a de facto sense so as to hold one or the other in violation of the laws related to possessing controlled substances. This example is instructive as it functions within a property law paradigm that is also applicable in cases of contemporary slavery. While the judge could make a determination of de facto ownership if a drug dealer was caught selling heroin, typically such cases are resolved on the simple issue of possession: did the individual have control over the heroin, did she possess it.[60]

---

[59]This point is useful for distinguishing slavery from asymmetrical familial relationships in cultures where the head of the household is able to sell his dependants into slavery. Their status is not one of slavery until sale has taken place, namely when the powers attaching to the right of ownership are actually exercised (cf. the case of Ahat-abiša, noted above). This turns enslavement from a latent possibility into a matter of fact.
[60]Allain and Bales, 'Slavery and Its Definition', pp. 505–6.

This approach to the definition of slavery has distinct advantages. First, it meaningfully aligns with the established, historical understanding of slavery as a technical status within the broader genus of forced labour, thus silencing the criticism that 'modern slavery' is an illegitimate application of the term to a much broader set of phenomena. Second, it provides a practical tool to combat modern slavery using the machinery of the law, as has occurred for example in Australia with the 2008 *Tang* case.[61] Third, it could prove useful to anthropologists, who might once more talk about 'slavery' and mean substantively the same thing as what their colleagues in history mean, rather than using it hazily to signify 'kinlessness' or 'exclusion' (although those terms may still apply as social consequences of reducing a person to the status or condition of property).[62]

Conclusion

'Slavery is arguably the most abused word in the English language.'[63] This chapter has explored several key examples of the use and abuse of the term, and their consequences for history and historiography. This brings us full circle to David Brion Davis's words in the epigraph to this chapter, true enough if read ironically. The current trend for global studies of slavery is not a field unified by method; what counts as 'slavery' has very much come to be coterminous with the subject matter of anyone who uses the term, whether or not they use the term carefully. For decades, individuals with very different definitions of slavery have been adding their work to the pile; 'Global slavery studies' is nothing more than the sum total of this work. If one assumes that everything analysed in this body of work really does count as slavery, then the result certainly will be ever-increasing perplexity in finding a workable definition. For those that use the traditional ownership definition

---

[61]Ibid.
[62]O'Connell Davidson's critique of Allain and Bales is vitiated by two errors. First, like several of the sociological and anthropological writers criticized above, she views property as a vague, amorphous bundle of rights rather than a bundle of rights and duties whose contents are to a large degree stable across cultures; she accepts the fallacious idea of absolute ownership and follows Patterson's flawed critique of property. Second, her critique of Allain and Bales focuses on Bales's earlier definition; but she does not seriously come to grips with his revised definition in collaboration with Allain, nor does she see that this is no cosmetic repackaging but a substantive shift in conceptualization. See O'Connell Davidson, *Modern Slavery*, pp. 39–46; 44–52.
[63]Miers, 'Slavery: A Question of Definition', p. 1.

of slavery, however, the outlook is not so bleak: its critics have failed to deal it a fatal blow, and it retains much utility as a tool of comparative study.

Acknowledgement

I would like to thank Edward Harris for reading and commenting on this paper in draft; responsibility for mistakes is my own.

Bibliography

Allain, J. and Bales, 'Slavery and Its Definition' in J. Allain, ed., *The Law and Slavery: Prohibiting Human Exploitation* (Leiden: Brill, 2015), pp. 502–12.

Honoré, Tony, 'Ownership' in A.G. Guest, ed., *Oxford Essays in Jurisprudence* (New York: Oxford University Press, 1961), pp. 107–47.

Kopytoff, Igor and Suzanne Miers, 'African Slavery as an Institution of Marginality' in Suzanne Miers and Igor Kopytoff, eds, *Slavery in Africa: Historical and Anthropological Perspectives* (Madison: The University of Wisconsin Press, 1977), pp. 3–81.

Lenski, Noel, 'Framing the Question: What Is a Slave Society?' in Noel Lenski and Catherine M. Cameron, eds, *What Is a Slave Society? The Practice of Slavery in Global Perspective* (New York: Cambridge University Press, 2018), pp. 15–57.

Lewis, David, 'Orlando Patterson, Property and Ancient Slavery: The Definitional Problem Revisited' in John Bodel and Walter Scheidel, eds, *On Human Bondage: After Slavery and Social Death* (Oxford: Blackwell, 2016), pp. 31–54.

Miers, Suzanne, *Slavery in the Twentieth Century. The Evolution of a Global Problem* (Walnut Creek, CA: Altamira, 2003).

Miller, Joseph, *The Problem of Slavery as History: A Global Approach* (New Haven, CT: Yale University Press, 2012).

O'Connell Davidson, Julia, *Modern Slavery: The Margins of Freedom* (New York: Palgrave Macmillan, 2015).

Patterson, Orlando, *Slavery and Social Death* (Cambridge, MA: Harvard University Press, 1982).

Testart, Alain, 'L'esclavage comme institution', *L'Homme* 38 (1998), pp. 31–69.

2

Writing global histories of slavery

Michael Zeuske

University of Cologne (Köln),

University of Bonn, Universidad

de la Habana

Slavery is ubiquitous in history, and there are many forms of it. The global history of slavery is the history of *slaving* and of the enslaved people in different types of slavery through time. It is also the social history of slavers – that is slave traders and slave owners – in all societies, in all places and throughout world history from the Neolithic era to the present.[1] It is history on a large scale, and, at the same time, microhistory.

I borrowed the important concept of *slaving* from Joseph C. Miller.[2] As I understand it, slaving describes the strategies, processes and outcomes of enslavement in a given society, and the resulting social hierarchies, for the slavers and for the enslaved. The slavers act as the agents of slaving through their capture of women, men and children, and through their use of them and their commercialization of their bodies as capital. For the slavers,

---

[1] Michael Zeuske, *Handbuch Geschichte der Sklaverei. Eine Globalgeschichte von den Anfängen bis heute,* 2nd ed. (Berlin: De Gruyter, 2019); Michael Zeuske, *Sklaverei. Eine Menschheitsgeschichte von der Steinzeit bis heute* (Stuttgart: Reclam, 2018).

[2] Joseph C. Miller, *The Problem of Slavery as History: A Global Approach* (New Haven, CT: Yale University Press, 2012), pp. 18–24.

slaving is a strategy through which they seek to improve their status rising above their marginality. 'Slaving', or, alternatively, 'the practice of slavery' – a slightly different concept also focusing on agency[3] – is a more flexible conceptual tool for an analysis of the roles played by the slavers and the enslaved in world history than the concept of 'slavery' – or 'slaveries', to reflect its many different forms – since the latter describes either customary or legal institutions, rather than dynamic historical processes.[4] Nevertheless, in this chapter, I will give a brief overview of both slaveries and slaving in global history.

When reviewing global history, it becomes apparent that there are many different stages in the development of slaveries, which include, but are by no means limited to, the four famous 'hegemonic' types of slavery (i.e. Moses Finley's 'fabulous four', in Joseph Miller's words): Roman slavery, American slavery, Caribbean slavery and Brazilian slavery.[5] To understand the proper way to do a global history of slavery, we need to presume that all societies practised slaving, had enslaved people and had slavery with their own cultural codes, laws and meanings, and they also had their own names for slavery.[6] In my view, the different stages in the development of slaveries form worldwide spatial-chronological phases in the history of slavery, which began hypothetically around 20,000–10,000/8,000 BCE (Before the Current Era). It is also important to notice that, after they began, these different phases continued until today, with the exception of the 3rd Phase (*Atlantic Slavery*), which ended with the formal abolition of slavery in the Western world, including the Americas. The present day's slaveries are types of slavery that exist without the legal ownership of human beings – according to Roman law, civil codes and traditional Anglo-American case law.

---

[3]Juliane Schiel and Stefan Hanß, 'Semantiken, Praktiken und transkulturelle Perspektiven mediterraner Sklaverei' in Juliane Schiel and Stefan Hanß, eds, *Mediterranean Slavery Revisited (500–1800). Neue Perspektiven auf mediterrane Sklaverei (500–1800)* (Zürich: Chronos Verlag, 2014), pp. 25–45; Noel Lenski and Catherine M. Cameron, eds, *What Is a Slave Society? The Practice of Slavery in Global Perspective* (New York: Cambridge University Press, 2018).
[4]Zeuske, *Handbuch der Geschichte der Sklaverei*, pp. 221–60.
[5]These are the 'slave societies' analysed by Moses Finley and Orlando Patterson. See Moses I. Finley, *Ancient Slavery and Modern Ideology* (New York: Viking Press, 1980), pp. 135–60; and Orlando Patterson, *Slavery and Social Death: A Comparative Study* (Cambridge: Harvard University Press, 1982). See also Miller, *The Problem of Slavery as History*; Kostas Vlassopoulos, 'Does Slavery Have a History? The Consequences of a Global Approach', *Journal of Global Slavery* 1: 1 (2016), pp. 5–27; Kostas Vlassopoulos, 'Finley's Slavery' in Daniel Jew, Robin Osborne, and Michael Scott, eds, *M. I. Finley: An Ancient Historian and His Impact* (New York: Cambridge University Press, 2016), pp. 76–99; and John Bodel and Walter Scheidel, eds, *On Human Bondage: After Slavery and Social Death* (Oxford: Blackwell, 2017).
[6]Zeuske, *Handbuch der Geschichte der Sklaverei*, pp. 525–63.

The *1st Phase* involved mainly enslaved women and children, or victims, and/or concrete actions of *slaving* in communities or between communities through mobility. This was a type of 'slavery without institution', which started around 20,000–8,000 BCE and still continues nowadays. More ancient than the latter was a type of slavery we might call 'sacrificial slavery', which involved the use of living humans as part of rituals requiring the death of an individual or of a group of enslaved people.

The *2nd Phase* can be identified with different types of 'house' or kin slaveries on a small scale and in relation to personal networks of kinship, affinity, clientage and association to guilds of specifically skilled people – such as hunters, warriors, ritual specialists. 'Slaving' – for lack of a better word, since there is often no name for it or no source describing it – provided mobility between groups, mostly involuntarily, but in some cases also voluntarily through clientage, or self-enslavement. In this phase, the enslaved were taken into a group or into a house, or into any habitational building, such as huts, tents, palaces or even temples.[7] This phase gave origin to a plethora of slaveries that have existed since the Bronze Age until the present day: debt slavery, collective slavery, raid slaveries, sex slavery and the slave trade. This phase also led to the most widespread and largest forms of slaveries that have existed in general in world history.[8]

The *3rd Phase* was characterized by the establishment of *Atlantic Slavery*,[9] from around 1460 to 1808/1838–1888 in the wider Western world, which included the Americas, West Africa, and also parts of East Africa and islands in the Indian Ocean. This phase includes all the 'hegemonic' slaveries mentioned earlier (aside from Roman slavery), and also other slaveries, which belonged to other phases, as well as other forms of slavery included in the 1st and 2nd Phases, specifically a variety of types of unfree labour[10]

---

[7] Alfredo González-Ruibal and Marisa Ruiz-Gálvez, 'House Societies in the Ancient Mediterranean (2000–500 BC)', *Journal of World Prehistory* 29: 4 (2016), pp. 383–437; Catherine M. Cameron, 'How People Moved among Ancient Societies: "Broadening the View"', *American Anthropologist* 115 (2013), pp. 218–31; Catherine M. Cameron, *Captives: How Stolen People Changed the World* (Lincoln: University of Nebraska Press, 2016) 19–42; Catherine M. Cameron, 'The Nature of Slavery in Small-Scale Societies' in Lenski and Cameron, eds, *What Is a Slave Society?*, pp. 151–68.

[8] Christine E. Sears, '"In Algiers, the City of Bondage": Urban Slavery in Comparative Context' in Jeff Forret and Christine E. Sears, eds, *New Directions in Slavery Studies: Commodification, Community, and Comparison* (Baton Rouge: Louisiana State University Press, 2015), pp. 201–18.

[9] Zeuske, 'Atlantic Slavery und Wirtschaftskultur in welt- und globalhistorischer Perspektive', *Geschichte in Wissenschaft und Unterricht (GWU)* 66: 5/6 (2015), pp. 280–301.

[10] Andrés Reséndez, *The Other Slavery: The Uncovered Story of Indian Enslavement in America* (Boston: Houghton Mifflin, 2016).

present in colonial territories, which became 'slaving zones'.[11] The last period in this phase was characterized by large-scale slaveries, such as the 'second slavery' and 'slavery's modernity', or 'slavery's capitalism'[12], based on 'war capitalism'[13] – first in the United States, Cuba, Brazil, Suriname and partly also in French territories – and on the capital multiplying space of the 'hidden Atlantic' (the nineteenth-century Atlantic slave trade) – first of all in relation to Cuba/Spain and Brazil/Portugal.[14] This is the only phase in the world history of slavery at whose heart lay an entire maritime commercial system of forced transportation of enslaved people, though partly also land-based: the Atlantic slave trade between the Americas and Atlantic Africa, and also parts of East Africa. Both these areas were characterized by slaving zones in their hinterland.[15] This was also the only phase that witnessed a formal end of slaveries through official government-supported emancipation laws. In a long-term global perspective, this may very well be the main reason why,

---

[11]Jeff Fynn-Paul and Damian A. Pargas, eds, *Slaving Zones. Cultural Identities, Ideologies, and Institutions in the Evolution of Global Slavery* (Leiden: Brill, 2018).
[12]Robert W. Fogel, 'American Slavery: A Flexible, Highly Developed Form of Capitalism' in J. William Harris, ed., *Society and Culture in the Slave South* (London: Routledge, 1992), pp. 77–99; Bonnie Martin, 'Slavery's Invisible Engine: Mortgaging Human Property', *Journal of Southern History* 76 (2010), pp. 817–66; Edward E. Baptist, *The Half Has Never Been Told: Slavery and the Making of American Capitalism* (New York: Basis Books, 2014); Sven Beckert and Seth Rockman, eds, *Slavery's Capitalism: A New History of American Economic Development* (Philadelphia: University of Pennsylvania Press, 2016); Dale W. Tomich, ed., *Slavery and Historical Capitalism during the Nineteenth Century* (Lanham, MD: Lexington Books, 2017). On slavery as capitalism in Cuba/Spain, see Eduardo Marrero Cruz, *Julián de Zulueta y Amondo. Promotor del capitalismo en Cuba* (La Habana: Ediciones Unión, 2006), pp. 46–79. For perspectives encompassing all, or different parts of, the Americas, see Rafael Marquese and Richard Salles, eds, *Escravidão e Capitalismo Histórico no Século XIX. Brasil, Cuba e Estados Unidos* (Rio de Janeiro: Civilização Brasileira, 2015); Mariana Muaze and Ricardo Salles, eds, *O Vale do Paraíba e o Império do Brasil nos Quadros da Segunda Escravidão* (Rio de Janeiro: 7 Letras, 2015); José Antonio Piqueras, ed., *Esclavitud y capitalismo histórico en el siglo XIX. Brasil, Cuba y Estados Unidos* (Santiago de Cuba: Casa del Caribe, 2016); Daniel Rood, *The Reinvention of Atlantic Slavery: Technology, Labor, Race, and Capitalism in the Greater Caribbean* (New York: Oxford University Press, 2017); Trevor Burnard and John D. Garrigus, *The Plantation Machine: Atlantic Capitalism in French Saint-Domingue and British Jamaica* (Philadelphia: University of Pennsylvania Press, 2016).
[13]See Sven Beckert, *Empire of Cotton: A Global History* (New York: Knopf, 2014), p. xvi.
[14]Michael Zeuske, '2018 Hidden Atlantic Atlántico oculto (Junio 2018)', available at https://www.academia.edu/36763546/2018_Hidden_Atlantic_Atlántico_oculto_Junio_2018_.doc.pdf; Michael Zeuske, 'Out of the Americas: Slave Traders and the Hidden Atlantic in the Nineteenth Century', *Atlantic Studies* 15: 1 (2018), pp. 103–35.
[15]See www.slavevoyages.org; David Eltis and David Richardson, *Atlas of the Transatlantic Slave Trade* (New Haven, CT: Yale University Press, 2010); Alex Borucki, David Eltis, and David Wheat, 'Atlantic History and the Slave Trade to Spanish America', *American Historical Review* 120: 2 (2015), pp. 433–61.

nowadays, there is no country that has legal ownership of human bodies as a basis for a type of informal slavery.[16]

The *4th Phase*, which started around 1800, is the most complex.[17] This was a period characterized, on the one hand, by the implementation of abolitionist policies and by widespread discourses linking abolition with civilization (and developing, at the same time, discourses of racism), which started first in England and France in 1808–1840, and, on the other hand, by the rise of 'new' slaveries between 1790/1840–1970.[18] It was during this phase that Western civilization became truly global, with British expansion in India, and the concurrent expansion in the Indian Ocean, the Opium Wars in China, and 'the scramble for Africa'. Under pressure from abolitionist rhetoric and as a result of the Europeans' increasing awareness of the many local names for slaveries, first of all in the Eastern hemisphere, Westerners avoided using the terms 'slavery' and 'slaves'.[19] Instead, they used traditional names to describe 'bonded labour', and they used other names for colonial forms of collective slaveries, such as 'forced labour', from the end of the nineteenth century. A similar phenomenon happened with the names used by slavers to describe forms of slavery and many other local slaveries – often part of the 1st and 2nd Phases – according to the respective cultures, in Africa, China, India, Persia, Arabia and in other Islamic countries or in countries with Islamized elites.[20] This phenomenon was concurrent, first, with large forced

---

[16]Seymour Drescher, 'The Long Goodbye: Dutch Capitalism and Antislavery in Comparative Perspective' in Gert Oostindie, ed., *Fifty Years Later. Antislavery, Capitalism and Modernity in the Dutch Orbit* (Pittsburgh, PA: University of Pittsburgh Press, 1995), pp. 25–66; Seymour Drescher, *Abolition: A History of Slavery and Antislavery* (New York: Cambridge University Press, 2009); Marcel van der Linden, ed., *Humanitarian Intervention and Changing Labor Relations. The Long-Term Consequences of the Abolition of the Slave Trade* (Leiden: Brill, 2011).
[17]Zeuske, *Sklaverei. Eine Menschheitsgeschichte von der Steinzeit bis heute*, pp. 96–126.
[18]Richard B. Allen, 'Slave Trading, Abolitionism, and New Systems of Slavery in the Nineteenth-Century Indian Ocean World' in Robert Harms, Bernard K. Freamon, and David W. Blight, eds, *Indian Ocean Slavery in the Age of Abolition* (New Haven, CT: Yale University Press, 2013), pp. 183–99; James Francis Warren, 'The Structure of Slavery in the Sulu Zone in the Late Eighteenth and Nineteenth Centuries' in Gwyn Campbell, ed., *The Structure of Slavery in Indian Ocean Africa and Asia* (London: Routledge, 2004), pp. 111–28.
[19]Andrea Major, *Slavery, Abolition and Empire in India, 1772–1843* (Liverpool: Liverpool University Press, 2012), pp. 18–38.
[20]Frederick Cooper, *Plantation Slavery on the East Coast of Africa* (Portsmouth: Heinemann, 1997); Matthew S. Hopper, *Slaves of One Master: Globalization and Slavery in Arabia in the Age of Empire* (New Haven, CT: Yale University Press, 2015); Oliver Tappe and Ulrike Lindner, 'Global Variants of Bonded Labour' in Sabine Damir-Geilsdorf et al., eds, *Bonded Labour: Global and Comparative Perspectives (18th–21st Century)* (Bielefeld: Transcript Verlag, 2016), pp. 9–34.

migrations in, and from, the Indian Ocean, China and other territories of the Eastern hemisphere,[21] as well as with the implementation of mixed forms of indentured labour, free labour and bond slaveries, based on 'war capitalism',[22] and second, with the rise of formal or informal 'second slaveries' in the Americas until 1865–1888.

It may be the case that, in this phase, there was a spread of a 'global second slavery', and that, in reality, there was 'no end after the end'.[23] In other words, the abolition of slavery resulted in the restructuring of former large-scale legal slaveries into smaller complexes of 'slaveries with no name', but with the same exploitative conditions of extremely hard work and under the same structures of production – that is plantations and other types of landed estates, also on colonial frontiers. At the same time, a similar low social status as that of slaves characterized the emancipated people after the official abolition of the type of slavery that characterized the 3rd Phase, as can be seen already in the measures taken under Toussaint Louverture in Saint-Domingue/Haiti in 1800 and in the colonial policies implemented under British pressure since around 1815. Here, as in many other cases, the so-called emancipated/liberated slaves (*recaptives*, or, in Spanish, *emancipados*) were forced to work after 'liberation/emancipation', though holding in their hands their 'freedom papers', for seven or more years under labour conditions no different from those of slavery.[24]

---

[21] Adam McKeown, 'Global Migration 1846–1940', *Journal of World History* 15: 2 (2004), pp. 155–90; Adam McKeown, 'Chinese Emigration in Global Context, 1850–1940', *Journal of Global History* 5 (2010), pp. 95–124; Richard B. Allen, 'Slave Trading, Abolitionism, and New Systems of Slavery in the Nineteenth-Century Indian Ocean World' in Damir-Geilsdorf et al., eds, *Bonded Labour*, pp. 183–99; Zeuske, 'Coolies – Asiáticos and Chinos: Global Dimensions of Second Slavery' in Damir-Geilsdorf et al., eds, *Bonded Labour*, pp. 35–57.
[22] Beckert, *Empire of Cotton*, pp. 197–229.
[23] Zeuske, *Sklaverei. Eine Menschheitsgeschichte von der Steinzeit bis heute*, pp. 212–44; see also Amalia Ribi Forclaz, *Humanitarian Imperialism: The Politics of Anti-Slavery Activism, 1880–1940* (New York: Oxford University Press, 2015).
[24] Fernando Ortiz, *Los negros esclavos* (La Habana: Ed. de Ciencias Sociales, 1976), pp. 298–305; Richard Anderson et al., 'Reports on Slavery Research: Using African Names to Identify the Origins of Captives in the Transatlantic Slave Trade: Crowd-Sourcing and the Registers of Liberated Africans, 1808–1862', *History in Africa* 40 (2013), pp. 165–91; David Eltis, 'O significado da investigação sobre os africanos escapados de navios negreiros no século XIX', *Historia: Questões & Debates*, 52 (2010), pp. 13–39; Sharla M. Fett, *Recaptured Africans. Surviving Slave Ships, Detention, and Dislocation in the Final Years of the Slave Trade* (Chapel Hill: University of North Carolina Press, 2017).

The *5th Phase* and the *6th Phase*, which I will only briefly mention in this chapter, include all the collective colonial and government-run slaveries,[25] as well as the slaveries of prisons and camps – that is the Nazi concentration camps (*KZ*); the Japanese prison camps; the Russian gulags; and the Chinese and North Korean camps – and also the so-called modern slaveries, since 1970. It is important to notice that the 3rd, 4th, 5th and 6th Phases have been also characterized by the continuous existence or by the reinvention of forms of slaveries originally implemented in the 1st and 2nd Phases.[26]

Making sense of the historiography needed for the present chapter has not been an easy task. Most of the historiographical works produced in the nineteenth and twentieth centuries have focused on Roman slavery, or on Biblical and other forms of ancient slavery, or on the large-scale 'hegemonic' slaveries I mentioned earlier, or on what we might call 'national-imperial' slaveries – despite the fact that there is nothing less 'national' or more 'transnational' than slaveries, except in the historiography and in the archival information systems. Often, the studies mentioned above have aimed at reinforcing the dominant narrative of the 'Western' discourse of abolition equalling civilization, or, as a result of the rise of Atlantic history and/or the 'new global history', they have provided an exaggerated account of a variety of 'national-imperial' slaveries, such as 'British slavery', 'French slavery' or other types of slavery in relation to other Atlantic empires – Spanish, Portuguese, Dutch, etc.[27]

Cuban historians, in fact, were the ones who began to debate and compare different slaveries around the world and to write the first 'global' histories

---

[25]Slavery in global history has two main legal dimensions: the specific relationship of 'one master vs. one slave' ('private slavery'), and the collective slavery of the *glebae adscripti* – rural populations and even entire villages bound to areas of land, which can be sold or donated, also as a privilege – as well as that of subjugated and settled people or masses of people in state-controlled camps. On collective colonial types of slaveries see Julia Seibert, 'More Continuity than Change? New Forms of Unfree Labor in the Belgian Congo, 1908-1930' in van der Linden, ed., *Humanitarian Intervention and Changing Labor Relations*, pp. 369–86; Vincent Houben and Julia Seibert, '(Un)freedom: Colonial Labour Relations in Belgian Congo and the Dutch East Indies Compared' in Ewout Frankema and Frans Buelens, eds, *Colonial Exploitation and Economic Development. The Belgian Congo and the Netherlands Indies Compared* (London: Routledge, 2013), pp. 178–92; Julia Seibert, *In die globale Wirtschaft gezwungen. Arbeit und kolonialer Kapitalismus im Kongo (1885-1960)* (Frankfurt am Main: Campus Verlag, 2016).

[26]Zeuske, Sklaverei, *Eine Menschheitsgeschichte von der Steinzeit bis heute*, pp. 41–140. See also Suzanne Miers, *Slavery in the Twentieth Century: The Evolution of a Global Problem* (Walnut Creek, CA: Altamira Press, 2003); Gwyn Campbell, Suzanne Miers, and Joseph C. Miller, eds, *Women and Slavery*, 2 Vols. (Athens: Ohio University Press, 2007–2008).

[27]Michael Zeuske, 'Historiography and Research Problems of Slavery and the Slave Trade in a Global-Historical Perspective', *International Review of Social History* 57: 1 (2012), pp. 87–111; Zeuske, *Handbuch der Geschichte der Sklaverei*, pp. 27–96.

of slavery, at a time when Cuba was at the peak of its global influence as the most dynamic example of 'second slavery' in the nineteenth century.[28] Specifically, José Antonio Saco (1797–1879), the Cuban intellectual and historian born in Bayamo, in eastern Cuba, wrote a unique 'global' history of slavery in the nineteenth century.[29] He himself owned slaves in his house. In Saco's time, the first important macro-histories of slavery focused mostly on ancient slavery, especially Greek and Roman slavery. Saco treated Roman slavery, but he focused also, much more broadly, on slavery in ancient Egypt, Babylonia, Assyria, China, India, Persia, Scythia, Carthage and other civilizations with large-scale slavery in ancient times.[30] Eduardo Torres-Cuevas, an eminent historian of slavery and the director of Cuba's National Library (*Biblioteca Nacional de Cuba*), wrote about Saco's monumental work: 'Who could possibly say that he/she knows the history of world slavery, if they have not studied one of the most important works written on the subject [Saco's *Historia de la esclavitud*], which, moreover, had a fascinating American angle, rather than a European one ?'[31]

Saco implemented a broad perspective by treating various types of large-scale slaveries and also Roman slavery. In doing so, he aimed to explain to Cuban slaveholders the reason why the contraband slave trade of the 'hidden Atlantic' ought to be abolished – also because it was controlled mainly by Spaniards and Catalans[32] – but not Cuban slavery.[33] Saco ingeniously

---

[28]Dale W. Tomich, *Through the Prism of Slavery. Labor, Capital, and World Economy* (Lanham, MD: Rowman & Littlefield, 2004); Dale Tomich & Michael Zeuske, eds, The Second Slavery: Mass Slavery, World-Economy, and Comparative Microhistories, 2 Vols., *Review: Fernand Braudel Center*, 31: 2/3 (2008).
[29]At that time, instead of 'global', the term used was 'universal' for History.
[30]José Antonio Saco, *Historia de la esclavitud desde los tiempos más remotos hasta nuestros días*, 3 Vols. [Ensayo introductorio, compilación y notas Eduardo Torres-Cuevas, Eduardo] (La Habana: Imagen Contemporanea, 2002; orig. pub. Paris: Kugelmann, 1875, and Barcelona: Impr. Jaime Jepús, 1877/78).
[31]Eduardo Torres-Cuevas, 'Ensayo introductorio. La esclavitud y su historia' in Saco, *Historia de la esclavitud*, pp. 1–25, specifically p. 2.
[32]Martín Rodrigo Y Alharilla and Lizbeth J. Chaviano, eds, *Negreros y esclavos. Barcelona y la esclavitud atlántica (siglos XVI-XIX)* (Barcelona: Icaria editorial, 2017); Rodrigo Y Alharilla and María Del Carmen Cózar Navarro, eds, *Cádiz y el tráfico de esclavos. De la legalidad a la clandestinidad* (Madrid: Silex Ediciones, 2018).
[33]Saco wrote also a history of the 'African race' (*raza Africana*) focused particularly on Hispanic America – that is the Spanish colonies in Central and South America and the Caribbean; see José Antonio Saco, *Historia de la esclavitud de la raza africana en el Nuevo Mundo y en especial en los países Americo-Hispanos*, 4 Vols. (La Habana: Imprenta de A. Álvarez, 1893). Moreover, he also wrote a history of Indian slavery in the New World; see José Antonio Saco, *Historia de la esclavitud de los indios en el nuevo mundo seguida de la historia de los repartimientos y encomiendas* [Introducción de Fernando Ortiz], 2 Vols. (La Habana: Cultural S.A., 1932). According to Eduardo Torres-Cuevas, among Saco's papers, found after his death, there were manuscripts on slavery in the French Caribbean and on slavery in the British colonies of North America and the Caribbean; see Torres-Cuevas, 'Ensayo introductorio', pp. 1–25.

explained this by referring to the disastrous developments of the western Roman Empire after the fifth century, and he argued that there had never been a place and a time in world history without slaves and slavery: 'Was there ever any people where [slavery] did not penetrate in one of its forms? Has there been, by any chance, in the annals of the world, any moment, as short as it might have been, during which it has disappeared from the earth?'[34] Saco was right in his assumptions at the time when he wrote his work, and he is still right with regard to today's world – and this despite the fact that, nowadays, nearly all the histories of slavery are written with the declared goal to condemn all its forms, including contemporary forms of slavery, as 'evil', 'un-ethical', barbaric and 'backward', and often also with the aim of supporting the end of all forms of slavery.

Besides Saco's monumental undertaking, some of the most important works written as true global histories of slavery include particularly the following. Orlando Patterson's famous *Slavery and Social Death* (1982) is a deep and wide-ranging comparative analysis focused on the historical sociology of both 'slave societies' and 'societies with slaves'[35] with the definition of the enslaved as characterized by 'social death' at its heart.[36] Suzanne Miers's *Slavery in the Twentieth Century* (2003) is a very empirical book about institutions and laws, which ends arguing about the myth of the 'abolition of slavery in the nineteenth century', and which treats the issues I related to the 4th and 6th Phases, significantly asking 'what happened after the end'?[37] Finally, Joseph C. Miller's *The Problem of Slavery as History* (2012) is a truly global study, which innovatively problematizes the concept of *slaving*, theoretically among all groups, in all societies and in all types of social formations – that is communities, networks, clans, guilds, etc. – as a strategy implemented by marginalized historical actors, the slavers, in order to improve their social status in relation to established hierarchies and so as to move from the periphery to the centre of their communities throughout world history.[38]

---

[34]Saco, *Historia de la Esclavitud*, Vol. 1, pp. 29–76, here p. 29.
[35]For the definition of 'slave societies' and 'societies with slaves', see Keith Hopkins, *Sociological Studies in Roman History*, Vol. 1: *Conquerors and Slaves* (New York: Cambridge University Press, 1978).
[36]Patterson, *Slavery and Social Death*, p. 35.
[37]Miers, *Slavery in the Twentieth Century*, pp. 47–58.
[38]Miller, *The Problem of Slavery as History*. See also Miller, 'A Theme in Variations: A Historical Scheme of Slaving in the Atlantic and Indian Ocean Regions' in Campbell, ed., *The Structure of Slavery in Indian Ocean Africa and Asia*, pp. 169–96; Joseph C. Miller, 'Slaving as Historical Process: Examples from the Ancient Mediterranean and the Modern Atlantic' in Enrico Dal Lago and Constantina Katsari, eds, *Slave Systems: Ancient and Modern* (New York: Cambridge University Press, 2008), pp. 70–102; Miller, *The Problem of Slavery as History*, pp. 18–24.

The above works inspired me as I began thinking about writing a global history of slaveries of late. In an earlier period of my life, when I lived in the GDR, I wrote my doctoral dissertation as part of an academic institution for global history called Centre for the *Allgemeine Geschichte der Neuzeit 1500-1917* (General History of the Modern Era, 1500-1917). Between 1980 and 1992, I was a member of the *Internationales Zentrum für Vergleichende Revolutionsgeschichte* (International Centre for the Comparative History of Revolutions),[39] and of the famous Research Center for the Comparative History of Bourgeois Revolutions (*Vergleichende Geschichte bürgerlicher Revolutionen*) at Leipzig, where I researched in world history (*Weltgeschichte*) by focusing, specifically, on elite Creole revolutionaries such as Simón Bolívar, Francisco de Miranda and other leaders of the *Independencia* (or *Independencias*) – the anticolonial wars for Latin American independence against Spain, from 1810 to 1830. In that scholarly context, those elites were then viewed as the 'hegemonic' group that guided the revolutionary process which separated the Spanish colonies in the continental Americas from their imperial centre in Spain, as a result of the influence of the French Revolution and the subsequent Napoleonic expansion, between 1789 and 1815.[40]

Slavery and the slaves – often called *afro-descendientes* in Spanish – are key elements to understand the movement for Latin American independence as a type of unfinished, or superficial, social revolution, which did not lead to the destruction of colonial structures, caste and racial hierarchies, and neither of slavery and slaving.[41] In fact, slaves and ex-slaves were simply incorporated into the new states, whether they were republics or empires. Jeremy Adelman has cautioned the many historians who have written books about the political and military history of the movement for Latin American independence, mostly works focusing on the history of the elites and sometimes even highly biased biographical works, that slavery and the slave trade were fundamental causes that led to the independence movements.[42]

---

[39] Michael Zeuske, 'The French Revolution in Spanish America. With Some Reflections on Manfred Kossok as Marxist Historian of "Bourgeois Revolutions"', *Review: Fernand Braudel Center* 38: 1/2 (2015), pp. 99-145.
[40] Zeuske, 'The French Revolution in Spanish America'.
[41] Michael Zeuske, 'La Independencia: Unvollendete Revolution mit Sklaverei und Bolívar' in Stefan Rinke, et al., eds, *Bicentenario: 200 Jahre Unabhängigkeit in Lateinamerika. Geschichte zwischen Erinnerung und Zukunft* (Stuttgart: Verlag Hans-Dieter Heinz. Akademischer Verlag, 2011), pp. 147-82.
[42] Jeremy Adelman, *Sovereignty and Revolution in the Iberian Atlantic* (Princeton, NJ: Princeton University Press, 2006), pp. 56-100.

In addition, I found that the enslaved people were also driving forces in the world historical processes that led to the rise of the so-called bourgeois revolutions. In this connection, when I lived in the GDR, I heard the eminent Canadian scholar of French slavery and the slave trade Clarence J. Munford, who had come to Socialist Germany to observe the process that gave birth to 'German re-unification', and who had an important influence on my views on the above issues.[43] Significantly, after German re-unification, the Research Center for the Comparative History of Bourgeois Revolutions was closed down.[44] In 1993, when the *Forschungsgemeinschaft* (German Society for the Advancement of Scientific Research, or *DFG*) provided funding to support the integration of GDR scholars into German academia, I became a historian who no longer focused on the global revolutionary elites, but on the enslaved and on the enslaved perspective on the elites, particularly in the Atlantic – the focal ocean of global history. I initially focused on the study of the enslaved in a relatively small region of Southern Cuba: the *hinterland* of Cienfuegos. The reason was that, in the later part of the period of the 'second slavery', this region was at the centre of the most advanced form of slaveholding, of a pioneering type of colonial industrialization and of world sugar production.[45]

In my first attempt at writing about slavery in southern Cuba, I wrote a very structural type of history focused on the question of whether the enslaved and the ex-slaves could be considered a class – a major issue in Marxist historiography. Subsequently, between 1993 and 2003, the experience of collaboration with Rebecca J. Scott at the University of Michigan led me to change my focus on microhistory, looking at the lives and names of slaves

---

[43]Clarence J. Munford and Michael Zeuske, 'Black Slavery, Class Struggle, Fear and Revolution in St. Domingue and Cuba, 1785–1779', *Journal of Negro History*, 73: 1-4 (1988), pp. 12–32; Clarence J. Munford, 'The "Pearl" of the Antilles Is Born: Haiti and Black Slavery – The Early Years, 1629–1715', *Jahrbuch für Geschichte von Staat, Wirtschaft und Gesellschaft Lateinamerikas (JbLA)* 28 (1991), pp. 1–19; Clarence J. Munford, *The Black Ordeal of Slavery and Slave Trading in the French West Indies, 1625–1715*, 3 Vols. [Vol. 1: *Slave Trading in Africa*; Vol. 2: *The Middle Passage and the Plantation Economy*; Vol. 3: *Culture, Terror and Resistance*] (Lampeter, UK: Edwin Mellen Press, 1991).
[44]Matthias Middell, 'Manfred Kossok – Writing World History in East Germany', *Review: Fernand Braudel Center* 38: 1/2 (2015), pp. 23–44.
[45]Michael Zeuske, '"Los negros hicimos la independencia": Aspectos de la movilización afrocubana en un hinterland cubano – Cienfuegos entre colonia y república' in Fernando Martínez Heredia, Rebecca J. Scott, and Orlando F. García Martínez, eds, *Espacios, silencios y los sentidos de la libertad: Cuba 1898–1912* (La Habana: Ediciones Unión, 2001), pp. 193–234; Michael Zeuske, 'Two Stories of Gender and Slave Emancipation in Cienfuegos and Santa Clara, Central Cuba – Microhistorical Approaches to the Atlantic World' in Pamela Scully and Diana Paton, eds, *Gender and Slave Emancipation in the Atlantic World* (Durham, NC: Duke University Press, 2005), pp. 181–98.

and investigating the well-known postcolonial theme of the 'voices of the enslaved'. At the same time, I also pursued a large-scale project on the general history of Cuba as a history of the enslaved brought there by the Atlantic slave trade, with a particular focus on their role in the formation of the Cuban nation. My engagement with the problem of identifying the names of slaves in documents and texts written after slavery[46] led me to investigate Cuba's provincial and local archives, where I researched particularly the legal records of the commercialization of human bodies of individuals who were given Christian names as slaves, and therefore were left 'without their African names'. All the legal records of slaves sold and bought included short descriptions of their bodies, whether men, women or children, and their age – which was very important for productive or reproductive values. In the records, the slaves were also described as being 'of African origin' (*bozal*), and there were further terms indicating the general cultural region of origin in Africa: *lucumí* (*yoruba*), *mandinga, gangá, mina, arará, carabalí, congo, loango, angola, macuá* or *Mozambique*.[47] Otherwise, if a slave was born in Cuba, he/she was simply called *criollo*. Further, other marks of identification that were reported in the legal records of slaves sold and bought included the presence of wounds, tattoos, scarifications, teeth's deformations[48] or diseases, and also information on whether they were prone to drink, or to revolt, or they were maroons. These legal records form effectively the main corpus of information of what we can know about the real bodies of the enslaved at the time they were undergoing the terrible experience of slavery, and as such they are different from the slave narratives, which were written by ex-slaves after they became free.[49]

---

[46]Michael Zeuske, 'Hidden Markers, Open Secrets. On Naming, Race Marking and Race Making in Cuba', *New West Indian Guide/Nieuwe West-Indische Gids* 76: 3/4 (2002), pp. 235–66; Michael Zeuske, 'The Second Slavery: Modernity, Mobility, and Identity of Captives in Nineteenth-Century Cuba and the Atlantic World' in Javier Laviña and Michael Zeuske, eds, *The Second Slavery. Mass Slaveries and Modernity in the Americas and in the Atlantic Basin* (Berlin: LIT Verlag, 2014), pp. 113–42.

[47]By looking at these cultural-ethnic markers, the buyers expected to be able to somewhat predict the 'character' of the enslaved, while the slaves used these same markers to form their religious networks and their '*naciones*' in Cuba, in Hispanic America and also in Brazil; see Jesús Guanche [Pérez], *Africanía y etnicidad en Cuba (Los componentes étnicos africanos y sus multiples denominaciones)* (La Habana: Editorial de Ciencias Sociales, 2009).

[48]Gabino La Rosa Corzo, *Tatuados. Deformaciones étnicas de los cimarrones en Cuba* (La Habana: Fundación Fernando Ortiz, 2011).

[49]Michael Zeuske, 'Die Nicht-Geschichte von Versklavten als Archiv-Geschichte von "Stimmen" und "Körpern"', *Jahrbuch für Europäische Überseegeschichte* 16 (2016), pp. 65–114. See also Vicent Sanz and Michael Zeuske, 'Microhistoria de esclavos y esclavas' in Vicent Sanz and Michael Zeuske, eds, *Millars. Espai i Història* 62: 1 (2017), pp. 9–21.

In practice, the utilization of human bodies for all types of capitalization and commodification – such as debts, loans, credits, and all other types of monetary and banking businesses – and, more generally, the treatment of human bodies as capital, so clear in the legal records of purchases and sales of slaves, were proofs of a major shift in the value systems of Europeans, who first learned how to think of human bodies as currency in their commercial transactions with West Africa, in the early days of Atlantic expansion. Thus, the investigation of legal records represented for me the first step in understanding one of the central elements in the global history of slavery: the commodification of the human body associated with enslavement. The other major elements I focused on were the names of slaves and the terms used to describe slaveries in different contexts.

In 2005, after reading and analysing around 200,000 legal records of purchase, sale and manumission of enslaved people in Cuba – out of an estimated total of 2 million – I became aware that my research was becoming increasingly focused on microhistory, and consequently less related to the type of world history that I had learned in Leipzig with Manfred Kossok, when I was a member of the Research Center for the Comparative History of Bourgeois Revolutions. Therefore, in 2006, I decided to start a new phase in my career of researcher by stepping away from my original focus on the investigation of the 'voices of the enslaved' and from issues related to postcolonial cultural history. While researching in Cuba's National Archives (the *Archivo Nacional de Cuba*), I found the papers of Ramón Ferrer, the captain of the slave ship *Amistad*, and this discovery prompted me to engage in two different projects: first, an Atlantic history of the slave trade in the era of emancipation (1808–1888) – an era I later called of the 'hidden Atlantic'[50]; second, a world history of slavery as a way to reconnect to my earlier training in History on a large scale. I began the first project with an Atlantic-wide search for Ramón Ferrer's second ship, the *Bella Antonia*, looking for its traces in the archives of London, Madrid, Seville, Lisbon, Havana and other parts of Cuba, Cataluña, Germany, Dakar, Praia/Cape Verde, São Tomé, Puerto Rico, New Orleans and other places in the United States.[51] As I did this research, I began focusing on the slave traders, on the factors in the African 'slave factories' (*factorías*), and on the 'Atlantic

---

[50]Zeuske, 'Out of the Americas', pp. 103–35; Dorothea Fischer-Hornung, 'The Hidden Atlantic: Michael Zeuske Reflects on his Recent Research', *Atlantic Studies* 15: 1 (2018), pp. 136–47.
[51]Michael Zeuske, *Amistad: A Hidden Network of Slavers and Merchants* (Princeton, NJ: Markus Wiener Publishers, 2014).

creoles' as the most important personnel in the business of slaving and in the actual relationships with the enslaved. The Atlantic slave trade effectively encapsulated the oceanic dimension of Atlantic slavery and the global and historical links between the Americas and Africa, both West Africa and East Africa. I was not able to find traces of Ramón Ferrer's ship, but I found numerous traces of the 'hidden Atlantic' – that is the Atlantic slave trade in the 'century of abolition'.[52] As a result, I published a world history of the Atlantic slave trade as part of the global history of slaveries.[53]

The other major project I pursued from 2006 was the writing of a global history of slavery. With this project, I aimed to reconnect with the world historical dimension, which had been prominent in my early training as a historian in Leipzig, by taking advantage of the boom in narratives of global history that has occurred since the end of the twentieth century. I was also influenced by the reactions to idea of the 'end of history'[54] – that is the success of liberal capitalism – and by the fact that slaves tended to be overlooked in the standard histories of capitalism.[55] I started with the relatively simple idea of looking for slaveries everywhere in time and space, maintaining two main concepts as guidelines. The first concept was the idea of human bodies as capital and consequently the idea of slavery as a form of control of human bodies, rather than a legal framework; the second concept, instead, related to the search for the identification of the different names given to slaveries all over the world by focusing on the status of the enslaved in the cultural codes, laws and customs of societies other than those of the 'hegemonic slaveries' I referred to earlier on – that is Greek and Roman slavery in the 2nd Phase, and Atlantic slavery in the 3rd Phase of my scheme.

I must point out that it is extremely difficult to write a work of global history based on archival research. Therefore, I took advantage of the micro-historical and archival skills I developed in searching through the legal records of slaves bought and sold in Cuba in order to build a bibliography of the best researched books I would need for my

---

[52] Zeuske, 'Out of the Americas', pp. 103–35.
[53] Michael Zeuske, *Sklavenhändler, Negreros und Atlantikkreolen. Eine Weltgeschichte des Sklavenhandels im atlantischen Raum* (Berlin: De Gruyter Oldenbourg, 2015).
[54] On the 'end of History', see Francis Fukuyama, *The End of History and the Last Man* (New York: Free Press, 1992).
[55] Michael Zeuske, 'Karl Marx, Sklaverei, Formationstheorie, ursprüngliche Akkumulation und Global South' in Felix Wemheuer, ed., *Marx und der globale Süden* (Köln: PapyRossa Verlag, 2016), pp. 96–144.

global-historical narrative of the history of slaveries. For my first attempt at writing a global history of slaveries I had a contract with the German publishing press *Reclam*, but this did not lead to a publishable project, because of the problems I encountered in selecting and organizing the large amount of material available on the topic. I had originally thought of organizing the material in a chronological narrative moving from 'small slaveries' – akin to Patterson's and others' 'societies with slaves' – to 'big slaveries' – akin to Patterson's and others' 'slave societies' – in all the areas of the world. However, the size of this study quickly became unmanageable, in terms of both text and footnotes.

Later, in my second attempt, around 2012, I developed a more refined model with different phases in the history of slaveries – as I explained earlier in this chapter – and I started my study with the assumptions that slaveries began as very localized phenomena driven by opportunistic reasons and that these developments occurred on a worldwide scale. In all these societies, the extreme low status, first of all, of women and children, morphed into their statuses of de-facto slaves, even though without the legal features of slavery as an actual institution. This was, effectively, what I called the 1st Phase in my scheme. An enormous help for my new conceptualization of the development of global slaveries through different historical phases came to me from the recent research on prehistoric, African and medieval slaveries in global-historical perspectives – with studies especially by Joseph C. Miller, Patrick Manning, Paul E. Lovejoy, John K. Thornton, Michael McCormick, Noel Lenski, Catherine M. Cameron, Joachim Henning, Detlef Gronenborn and Youval Rotman – and on Ottoman, Russian, Islamic and Indian Ocean slaveries – with studies especially by Ehud R. Toledano, Reuven Amitai, Stephan Conermann, Juliane Schiel, Alessandro Stanziani, Hans-Heinrich Nolte, William G. Clarence-Smith, Gwyn Campbell and Christoph Witzenrath.

Starting from the writing of the 2nd Phase of my global history of slaveries, I organized the material by keeping into account the two fundamental dimensions of time and space in viewing History on a large scale. Thus, in my view, world history referred to the chronological dimension of developments worldwide, while global history referred to the spatial dimension of global developments. Within this framework, I looked at global hemispheres – such as the Western one centred around the Atlantic Ocean, and the Eastern one centred around the Indian Ocean – at seas – such as the Black Sea, the Mediterranean, the Caribbean, the Red Sea, the Arabic Sea, the Chinese Sea and the Sulu Sea – and at large rivers and their estuaries as regions and means for the transportation and the accumulation of capital – both in written and oral forms. Concurrently, I looked at the historical presence of all types of slaveries on land – that is house slaveries, slaveries in mining areas, rural and plantation slaveries, slaveries in the building of infrastructures, state-controlled slaveries, military slaveries, etc. In this type of organization, the slave trades and the transcultural exchanges of commodities – that is slaves – which characterized them formed the very engine of accumulation of capital in global history, a capital form by human bodies, from which came the initial name I employed to describe it: '*Menschen-Kapitalismus*' (human capitalism) or '*Körper-Kapitalismus*' (body-capitalism). I accompanied the treatment of the different phases, spaces, dimensions and processes in the global history of slaveries with a chapter on statistics and with another chapter focused on the different names given to slaveries; this latter chapter allowed me to look at the local variants of slaveries around the globe within their own specific cultural dimension.[56] To be sure, though, in the first edition of my *Handbuch der Geschichte der Sklaverei* (2013), I still did not have a clear idea on how the end of Atlantic slavery in its 'second slavery' mode related to the so-called modern slaveries of today.

I, therefore, decided to write a summary of the *Handbuch der Geschichte der Sklaverei*, with the title *Sklaverei. Eine Menschheitsgeschichte* (Slavery: A Human History),[57] based on José Antonio Saco's assertion that there never was 'one second in world history without slaves and slavery'.[58] With this book, I have systematized the organization of the record on the world and global history of slaveries according to the above-mentioned phases. Furthermore, in the next edition of my *Handbuch der Geschichte der Sklaverei*, I have added a chapter on Chinese slaveries,[59] as one of the largest complex of slaveries outside the 3rd Phase, or with only some features of the 3rd Phase in relation to the Portuguese in Macao, the Spanish at Amoy, and both the Portuguese and the Spanish in Formosa/Taiwan. I have also added a chapter with the title 'No End after the End' on the link between the 'end' of Atlantic slavery in the 3rd Phase and the beginning of the subsequent phases (based on the works of Seymour Drescher).[60] Finally, I have taken into account the fast-growing bibliography on slaveries, on enslaved people

---

[56]Zeuske, *Handbuch Geschichte der Sklaverei*.
[57]Zeuske, *Sklaverei. Eine Menschheitsgeschichte von der Steinzeit bis heute*.
[58]Saco, *Historia de la Esclavitud*.
[59]Zeuske, *Sklaverei. Eine Menschheitsgeschichte von der Steinzeit bis heute*, pp. 154–71.
[60]Zeuske, *Sklaverei. Eine Menschheitsgeschichte von der Steinzeit bis heute*, pp. 212–44.

all over the world, on the relationship between slavery and capitalism, and on the history of slavery as global history. The new edition of the *Handbuch der Geschichte der Sklaverei*, in two volumes, has appeared in 2019.

Bibliography

Allen, Richard B., *European Slave Trading in the Indian Ocean, 1500–1850* (Athens: Ohio University Press, 2014).

Beckert, Sven, *Empire of Cotton: A Global History* (New York: Knopf, 2014).

Campbell, Gwyn, ed., *The Structure of Slavery in Indian Ocean Africa and Asia* (London: Routledge, 2004).

Chevaleyre, Claude, 'Acting as Master and Bondservant: Considerations on Status, Identities, and the Nature of "Bond-Servitude" in Late Ming China' in Alessandro Stanziani, ed., *Labour, Coercion, and Economic Growth in 17th–20th Centuries* (Leiden: Brill, 2013), pp. 237–72.

Dal Lago, Enrico, and Constantina Katsari, eds, *Slave Systems: Ancient and Modern* (New York: Cambridge University Press, 2008).

Forret, Jeff, and Christine E. Sears, eds, *New Directions in Slavery Studies: Commodification, Community, and Comparison* (Baton Rouge: Louisiana State University Press, 2015).

Fynn-Paul, Jeff, and Damian A. Pargas, eds, *Slaving Zones. Cultural Identities, Ideologies, and Institutions in the Evolution of Global Slavery* (Leiden: Brill, 2018).

Harms, Robert, Bernard K. Freamon, and David W. Blight, eds, *Indian Ocean Slavery in the Age of Abolition* (New Haven, CT: Yale University Press, 2013).

Lovejoy, Paul E., and Nicholas Rogers, eds, *Unfree Labour in the Development of the Atlantic World* (London: Frank Cass, 1994).

Manning, Patrick, *Slavery and African Life. Occidental, Oriental and African Slave Trades* (New York: Cambridge University Press, 1990).

Miller, Joseph C., *The Problem of Slavery as History: A Global Approach* (New Haven, CT: Yale University Press, 2012).

Witzenrath, Christoph, ed., *Eurasian Slavery, Ransom and Abolition in World History, 1200–1860* (Aldershot: Ashgate, 2015).

3

Slavery and empire

Trevor Burnard

University of Hull

Introduction

From ancient times, slavery has been associated with imperial expansion and the conquest of subject populations. All the great empires of antiquity, most of all the Roman Empire, practised slavery on a mass scale. Therefore, there is a large body of scholarship that has looked at connections between slavery and empire across time and space. This chapter will look at the development of this scholarship, with most attention paid to modern slavery, especially in the British Americas and in the United States, where the author has most knowledge, but which is also the period which resonates most with the information in the rest of this volume. What becomes clear in examining the multiple links between slavery and empire over time is that slavery and imperialism were generally compatible for most of their long histories. Thus, an examination of their interaction is less about how one institution shaped the other than about how both slavery and imperialism were mutually reinforcing. It involved one of world history's principal form of labour organization – slavery – coexisting with one of the most customary forms of political organization – empire – in our understanding of the global past.

Empires are not synonymous with slavery, but slavery is almost always an intrinsic part of most empires. That connection is not surprising given the nature of empires which might be defined as a mechanism whereby one central institution imposes its rule upon a multi-ethnic and multi-cultural set of populations in a diverse area. Empires are regularly defined as political units of large extent controlling several territories and peoples under a single sovereign authority. Of these three criteria, only sovereign authority is quantified. Size and diversity are often in the eye of the beholder. But what is central to most empires, especially modern sea-based empires ruled from Western Europe, is that the metropolis thought itself culturally superior to the subject population in colonies and forced the colonies to be under metropolitan control. In traditional empires 'it was not unusual for ethnically alien conquerors to recognize openly, and rely upon, the cultural-administrative superiority of subjugated peoples' as being in some ways superior to themselves, or at least able to provide services that the metropole could not. The reverse is true in modern empires. In short, modern empires have a 'civilizing' aspect to them, which often meant seeing enslavement 'outside' the metropolitan centre as a necessary evil for people not yet able to be considered 'civilized'.[1]

The historiography of empire and slavery

John Mackenzie, a leading historian of empire, gives us close to the agreed definition of empire in an opening statement of the Wiley-Blackwell *Encyclopaedia of Empire*, a statement thrashed out with his editorial board, so being in effect a committee-generated understanding of the phenomenon. The statement does not mention slavery, but shows that slavery was perfectly compatible with what imperialism usually is. The key part of the definition is its opening sentence, that 'an empire is an expansionist polity which seeks to form different forms of sovereignty over people or peoples of an ethnicity different from (or in some cases the same as) its own'. There is a 'ruling centre' and a 'dominated periphery' with the objectives of empire being 'the pursuit of power, wealth and security, in a self-fulfilling and supposedly self-sustaining form'. Its worldview is decidedly not democratic, being usually a view 'embracing a vision of

---

[1] Thomas T. Allsen, 'Pre-modern Empires' in Jerry Bentley, ed., *The Oxford Handbook of World History* (Oxford: Oxford University Press, 2011), pp. 362–3 (quote 363).

forms of universal government or monarchy'.[2] Slavery can easily flourish in such an institutional form. As Philip Curtin notes, while slavery has always been 'an anomalous institution in western culture', it was important in the classical Mediterranean empires of Greece and especially Rome, and after declining to insignificance in western (though not eastern) Europe as a labour system from *c.* 1000 it reappeared as 'an institution for export only' in the great maritime empires of the Americas established by Western European monarchies and states.[3] Slavery was deeply embedded in the life of the ancient Mediterranean world with no sustained opposition to slavery, despite the rise of Christianity, a religion open to both the free and the enslaved. In the greatest empire of ancient times, the Roman Empire, Roman models and practices of slavery spread throughout all the provinces of the empire, even if the role and importance of slaves in different sorts of production under the Roman Empire is unclear.[4]

Slavery remained more important as a form of labour organization outside Western Europe in the early modern period than in Western Europe itself but slavery in these areas was relatively unconnected to imperial expansion except in Russia and in the Ottoman Empire. Little work has been done on slavery and empire in Southeast Asia and even less on China[5] and while a great deal of work has been done on slavery in Africa, the nature of African societies means that it is seldom associated with the question of imperialism in Africa, though Africanists have been concerned about the impact of the Atlantic slave trade upon West African economic underdevelopment.[6] Walter Rodney famously argued that the Atlantic slave trade led to African underdevelopment.[7] Historians now dispute that claim. John Thornton has comprehensively demolished Rodney's thesis that the origins of the slave trade lay in European military and commercial superiority, that the

---

[2] John M. MacKenzie, 'The British Empire: Ramshackle or Rampaging? A Historiographical Reflection', *The Journal of Imperial and Commonwealth History* 43 (2015), pp. 99–124; John M. MacKenzie, *Encylopedia of Empire*, 4 Vols. (Oxford: Wiley-Blackwell, 2015).
[3] Philip D. Curtin, 'Slavery and Empire', *Annals of the New York Academy of Sciences* 292 (1977), pp. 3–11.
[4] Neville Morley, 'Slavery under the Principate' in Keith Bradley and Paul Cartledge, eds, *The Cambridge World History of Slavery*, Vol. 1 (Cambridge: Cambridge University Press, 2011), p. 267.
[5] But see essays by Kerry Ward on Southeast Asia, Pamela Lyle Crossley on China (two essays) in David Eltis and Stanley L. Engerman, eds, *The Cambridge World History of Slavery*, Vols. 3 and 4 (Cambridge: Cambridge University Press, 2011, 2017).
[6] Gwyn Campbell, ed., *The Structure of Slavery in the Indian Ocean, Africa and Asia* (London: Routledge, 2004); and Paul E. Lovejoy, 'Slavery in Africa' in Gad Heuman and Trevor Burnard, eds, *The Routledge History of Slavery* (London: Routledge, 2011), pp. 35–51.
[7] Walter Rodney, *How Europe Underdeveloped Africa* (Washington, DC: Blackwell, 1981).

immediate consequences of the European presence was an escalation of African warfare and that the long-term consequences of the Atlantic slave trade was the bending of the African economy to European interests. Thornton shows that the European presence in Africa before colonization begun in earnest in the mid-nineteenth century was weak, that Africans always held the upper hand in trade relations and conducted those relations for their own purposes and that outbreaks of violence occasioned by the need to acquire slaves for the Atlantic slave trade were limited and can be treated as normal parts of premodern African history.

It was Europeans, he asserts, who were in a dependent position in the Atlantic slave trade. He concludes that 'African participation in the slave trade was voluntary and under the control of African decision makers. This was not just at the surface level of daily exchange, but even at deeper levels. Europeans possessed no means either economic or military to compel African leaders to sell slaves'.[8] The commanding importance of African merchants and rulers in this imperial trade when Europeans were trading in Africa has been one of the most important findings in African scholarship on slavery and empire in the last generation. One part of the Rodney thesis, however, still stands up. Before 1800, west Africa suffered from a demographic imbalance that was not matched by inward migration. The Atlantic slave trade meant that economic, social and political development within west Africa was constrained by a loss of population.[9]

In the Ottoman Empire, slavery was more important socially and culturally than economically and enslaved people encompassed people from all walks of life, male and female, rich and poor, powerful and powerless, rural and urban, Muslim and non-Muslim. All they shared was a similar legal status as bonds-people, a status that brought with it several social impediments.[10] In the Russian Empire, the relationship of slavery to empire was complicated by the existence of serfdom. Serfdom was unknown in medieval Russia while slavery was an ancient institution. The latter was effectively abolished in the 1720s, just as Russian imperial expansion began. Serfdom had become established in the 1450s but evolved into near slavery in the eighteenth century, lasting as such for much of the first half of the nineteenth century

---

[8] John K. Thornton, *Africa and Africans in the Making of the Atlantic World, 1400–1800*, 2nd ed. (Cambridge: Cambridge University Press, 1998), p. 125 (quotation).
[9] Lovejoy, 'Slavery in Africa' in Heuman and Burnard, eds, *Routledge History of Slavery*, p. 44.
[10] Ehud R. Toledano, *As If Silent and Absent; Bonds of Enslavement in the Islamic Middle East* (New Haven: Yale University Press, 2007).

until serfdom was abolished in 1861. As in the Americas, Russia was chronically short of labour until at least the last third of the nineteenth century. Imperial expansion exacerbated this problem. For example, in 1739 Russian-style serfdom was extended to Ukraine, where peasants were forbidden by law to migrate. The abasement of the serfs continued further in 1760 when lords were permitted to banish serfs to Siberia and got military-recruit credits for such serfs. It used to be thought that Russian expansion into Central Asia ended slavery in that region but recent work by Jeff Eden suggests that such a view is incorrect. Russian efforts to foster abolition in the area, he argues, had ulterior motives as well as decidedly mixed results. Slave emancipation tended to come from slave resistance more than from imperial generosity.[11]

Critiques of empire with slavery

The main historiographical focus of slavery as part of empire concerns the Atlantic World – the New World plantation systems established by Western European empires from the sixteenth century in which, especially from the late seventeenth century, slavery was economically central and was vital to colonial politics and the relationship of the periphery towards the metropole. Increasing attention is being played to the role of slavery in the making of the Indian Ocean World but these studies, Gwyn Campbell argues, have been profoundly influenced by studies of the Atlantic slave system. They concentrate on the export of East Africans by Arabs to Zanzibar and the Persian Gulf and by Europeans to European enclaves. Campbell urges a new conceptual framework that emphasizes the peculiarity of an Indian Ocean World defined by weather (monsoons) rather than by oceans and land masses. He notes that slavery in this region needs to be understood within the context of the Indian Ocean World global economy, which was a sophisticated and durable system of long-distance exchange that linked China to Southeast and South Asia, the Middle East and Africa.[12]

---

[11]Richard Hellie, 'Migration in Early Modern Russia, 1480s–1780s' in David Eltis, ed., *Coerced and Free Migrations: Global Perspectives* (Stanford: Stanford University Press, 2002), pp. 292–323; Jeff Eden, *Slavery and Empire in Central Asia* (New York: Cambridge University Press, 2018).
[12]Gwyn Campbell, 'Slavery in the Indian Ocean World' in Heuman and Burnard, eds, *Routledge History of Slavery*, pp. 52–63. See also William Gervase Clarence-Smith, ed., *The Economics of the Indian Ocean Slave Trade in the Nineteenth Century* (London: Frank Cass, 1989).

Nevertheless, historians have been reluctant to connect slavery in the Indian Ocean World to imperialism, revelling in studying the history of migration and slavery in Southeast and South Asia without the 'stifling limitations and elitisms of imperial history'.[13] Andrea Major argues that this disinclination to see slavery in India as being relatively unconnected to empire is long lasting. She notes that the vast and rich literature on slavery and abolitionism in the British Empire has largely sidestepped India. Despite slavery in India having much in common with slavery in the Americas, Indian slavery was largely erased from British and French moral maps of the world. In the case of British India, this erasure of slavery from imperial matters reflected the intellectual and moral needs of abolitionists to construct India as the land of free labour in contrast to the West Indies as the home of slave labour. When the Liverpool merchant and Demerara slave owner Sir John Gladstone, for example, argued publicly with James Cropper, an importer of India cotton, in 1823 about the merits of slavery as a promoter of economic growth in the empire and a moral force for good for 'subordinate' peoples, Cropper assumed that slavery was purely an American rather than an Indian concern.[14]

For the Pacific, empire and slavery are more closely connected than for the Indian Ocean World, although the literature on the Pacific Ocean World is relatively sparse. No one to date has systematically treated the Pacific using methodologies drawn from the study of Atlantic history, though a recent book by David Armitage, Alison Bashford and Sujit Sivasundaram makes explicit links between the Indian, Atlantic and Pacific worlds that may lead to future scholarly investigation.[15] It is increasingly clear, however, that Atlantic and Pacific imperial histories share similar themes, notably in exploration, missionary activity, colonization and bonded labour. Bonded labour is a big theme in Pacific history before the twentieth century, with Indians moving to Fiji to work on sugar plantations and Pacific Islanders doing similar migrations to Queensland.[16] Nevertheless, the theme of slavery has not been

---

[13]Sunil Amrith, *Crossing the Bay of Bengal: The Furies of Nature and the Fortune of Migrants* (Cambridge, MA: Harvard University Press, 2015).
[14]Andrea Major, '"The Slavery of East and West": Abolitionists and "Unfree" Labour in India, 1820–1833', *Slavery and Abolition* 31 (2010), pp. 501–25; Major, *Slavery, Abolitionism and Empire in India, 1772–1843*; and Trevor Burnard and Kit Candlin, 'Sir John Gladstone and the Debate over Amelioration in the British West Indies in the 1820s', *Journal of British Studies* 57 (2018), pp. 760–82.
[15]David Armitage, Alison Bashford and Sujit Sivasundaram, eds, *Oceanic Histories* (Cambridge: Cambridge University Press, 2017), part one.
[16]Tracey Banivarua-Mar, *Violence and Colonial Dialogue: The Australian and Pacific Indentured Labour Trade* (Honolulu: University of Hawai'i Press, 2007).

conspicuous in the history of settler colonialism in the Pacific region. It is not mentioned, for example, in Alison Bashford and Stuart Macintyre's *Cambridge History of Australia*.[17] It has also not been incorporated into imperial history. For example, it is never noticed in histories of British abolitionism that in 1840, simultaneously with the abolition of slavery in the British Empire, Britain entered a treaty with Māori in New Zealand in which the British accepted the continuation of the practice of slavery within Māori society as the price of getting rangatira support.[18]

How, then, given the diversity of slave regimes in imperial settings, where slavery was less an imperial creation than a central feature of social organization that adapted itself to empire as an important kind of political organization from ancient to modern times, do we make firm conclusions about slavery and its role in creating, sustaining and disrupting empires? It is difficult to assess the historiography of slavery and empire for two different reasons. First, slavery is so central to imperial success that it is unremarkable, as in studies of slavery in the ancient world, being axiomatic to imperial expansion in ways that need no comment. In the ancient world, for example, slavery was accepted by the free as a fact of life. Imperial expansion aided the expansion of slavery, and vice versa. Moses Finley and Keith Hopkins each argued that demography and the demands of soldiers for imperial armies made it difficult to enslave Roman peasants, especially as those peasants had important political rights that discouraged their direct economic exploitation. Hopkins argued further that imperial expansion helped solve this problem by providing the Roman elite with large sums of money that allowed them to buy peasant farms, which had been undermined economically by their owners' long absences on military service abroad, sending those peasants to the city of Rome, and stocking large latifundia (landed estates) with slaves, often acquired through imperial conquest. The major effect of empire on Roman slavery, therefore, was in altering the balance of political power in the empire through depriving Italian peasants of most of their political rights.[19]

---

[17] Alison Bashford and Stuart Macintyre, *The Cambridge History of Australia*, 2 Vols. (Cambridge: Cambridge University Press, 2013).
[18] Hazel Petrie, *Outcasts of the Gods? The Struggle over Slavery in Māori New Zealand* (Auckland: Auckland University Press, 2015).
[19] Moses L. Finley, *Ancient Slavery and Modern Ideology* (Princeton: Marcus Weiner, 1990), ch. 1; Keith Hopkins, *Conquerors and Slaves* (Cambridge: Cambridge University Press, 1978), chs. 1–2; and Niall McKeown, *The Invention of Ancient Slavery?* (London: Duckworth, 2007).

Second, as in the French, British and Portuguese empires in the early modern period, slavery was so imbricated with every aspect of empire that separating out its purely imperial functions seems impossible. A famous quotation from Barbara Solow is often used to describe the centrality of slavery in American and Caribbean economic development: 'It was slavery that made the empty lands of the western hemisphere valuable producers of commodities and valuable markets for Europe and North America. What moved in the Atlantic in these centuries was predominantly slaves, the output of slaves, the inputs of slave societies, and the goods and services purchased with the earnings on slave products.'[20] John Darwin makes the same point more directly about slavery as making empires work: 'It was only by concentrating upon a few subtropical commodities raised by slave labour that agricultural colonization in the New World could be made profitable.'[21]

The result of slavery being such a pervasive presence in early modern European empires in the Americas is that accounts of slavery that are ostensibly about empire tend to be general surveys of Atlantic history. Thus, Philip Curtin's article from 1977, specifically titled 'Slavery and Empire', does not engage with the historiography of empire and how slavery might have made empire different but concentrates on slavery within empire and the institutional and social structure of slavery as it existed in the early modern period. Similarly, Christopher Bayly deals at length with slavery in his influential *Birth of the Modern World*, noting that while the slave trade and slavery came under attack in the first half of the nineteenth century, the expansion of slavery in this period, not least in the American South, Cuba and Brazil, made it probably 'the heyday of the slave system'. His interest, however, is not in slavery and empire per se but in why slavery expanded, what made it profitable in a period of free market ideology, and how the transformation of slavery in the nineteenth century had significant consequences for the representation of race.[22]

Yet the pervasiveness of slavery within imperial economies of the New World has tended to make theorists of empire underplay its importance.

---

[20]Barbara Solow, 'Slavery and Colonisation' in Barbara Solow, ed., *Slavery and the Rise of the Atlantic System* (Cambridge: Cambridge University Press, 1991), pp. 21–42.
[21]John Darwin, *After Tamerlane: The Rise and Fall of Global Empires, 1400–2000* (New York: Bloomsbury, 2008), p. 108.
[22]Curtin, 'Slavery and Empire'; C.A. Bayly, *The Birth of the Modern World, 1780–1914* (Oxford: Blackwell, 2004).

Darwin hardly mentions slavery in his award-winning history of world empires from 1400 to 2000, except to see it as vital for European economic growth. Slavery is hard to fit into his schema, with Caribbean sugar colonies being described as 'the bizarre offspring of European expansion' that had less influence on Europe than might be expected. He argues that 'until 1750 at least it might be wiser to see the Atlantic trading world as the vital prop of a commercial ancient regime rather than as a dynamic element in the industrial transformation of even the most advanced European economies'. He notes, however, that it is probably not coincidental that the promoters of slavery in the British Empire tended to be also in the vanguard of industrialization. Slavery is treated narrowly, as having large economic effects but not much social consequences, which is hardly surprising given that Darwin thinks that empire had only a 'marginal effect' on British society and culture and that ideas that Britain 'was constituted by empire' are merely to repeat a 'modish and vacuous expression'.[23]

Similarly, John Mackenzie pays little attention to slavery in his stimulating remarks on the character of empire in the British World. He disputes the contentions of major theorists of British imperialism such as Bernard Porter that 'the roots of British imperialism were material, not cultural', and acknowledges how empire caused great damage to indigenous peoples caught up in empire's 'self-sustaining dynamic'.[24] But slavery is ignored, even though his argument for the British empire being 'rampaging' rather than 'ramshackle' uses as major illustrative examples the West Indian islands of Barbados, Antigua and St. Kitts – colonies in which slavery was ever present. Mackenzie carefully notes the environmental changes that British settlers in each colony caused in their pursuit of wealth through the production of sugar, without mentioning the institution of slavery and the enslaved workers who provided the money for the settlers' 'grand plantation houses'.[25] One theme in imperial studies, he notes, has been a greater concentration on the settler colonies of the Antipodes and North America rather than on the so-called dependant empire of Africa, India and the Pacific. The emblematic book on this kind of colonization is James Belich's *Replenishing the Earth*, a wide-ranging study of a rampaging empire of explosive colonization in

---

[23]Ibid., p. 109, p. 197; John Darwin, *The Empire Project: The Rise and Fall of the British World-System, 1830–1970* (New York: Cambridge University Press, 2009), pp. 544–5.
[24]Bernard Porter, *The Lion's Share; A Short History of British Imperialism 1850–1970*, 5th ed. (Cambridge: Cambridge University Press, 2012), p. xvi.
[25]Mackenzie, 'Ramshackle or Rampaging?', p. 110.

the nineteenth century which, despite its willingness to include the United States as connected to British territories of settlement and thus part of a 'British world', virtually ignores slavery as part of its conceptual design.[26]

Slavery is downplayed in other imperial histories, notably that of the Dutch. In the first half of the seventeenth century, the Dutch Republic was the leading slave trader in the Atlantic world, with significant colonial possessions such as Brazil, Suriname and New Netherlands. The loss of Brazil in 1654 meant that slavery was less important in the Dutch world than it had been, but slave trading and slavery remained important as a major institution in Dutch colonial possessions and in its important chartered companies well into the nineteenth century. Indeed, as Marcus Vink argues, the Dutch played a pivotal role in shaping slavery in Southeast Asia, as well as the Atlantic in the seventeenth century.[27] Yet in an influential 1999 article Pieter Emmer and Wim Klooster argued strongly that if a Dutch Atlantic World existed, it did so only between roughly 1630 and 1645. They argued that the Dutch provided a model of a purely mercantile expansion that in fundamental ways 'differed from a policy designed by a central state in shaping the foundations of a maritime empire'.[28] The contemporary implication of the 1999 view is that the Dutch were not particularly implicated in the messy and morally dubious practice of colonization in the Americas in the ways that the Spanish, Portuguese, French and British were. Slavery is downplayed by Emmer and Klooster and the Dutch flair for commerce, finance and organization is highlighted. Klooster has moved back from such views, with a recent book giving a greater role to slavery than he argued in 1999. Emmer, however, has remained faithful to the ideas expressed in 1999, insisting that the Dutch were more traders than planters, with slavery playing a minimal role in shaping seventeenth- and eighteenth-century Dutch life and politics.[29]

---

[26] James Belich, *Replenishing the Earth: The Settler Revolution and the Rise of the Anglo-World, 1783–1939* (Oxford: Oxford University Press, 2009).
[27] Marcus Vink, 'The World's Oldest Trade: Dutch Slavery and the Slave Trade in the Indian Ocean in the Seventeenth Century', *Journal of World History* 14 (2003), pp. 131–77.
[28] P.C. Emmer and W.W. Klooster, 'The Dutch Atlantic 1600–1800: Expansion without Empire', *Itinerario* 23: 2 (1999), pp. 48–69.
[29] P.C. Emmer and Jos Gommans, *Rijk aan de rand van de wereld: De geschiedenis van Nederland oversee, 1600–1800* (Amsterdam: Bert Bakker, 2012); Emmer and Gommans, 'The Dutch and the Atlantic Challenge, 1600–1800' in P.C. Emmer, O. Pétre-Grenouilleau and J.V. Roitman, eds, *A deus ex machina Revisited: Atlantic Colonial Trade and European Economic Development* (Leiden: Brill, 2006), p. 164.

Slavery has recently become more central in the historiography of the French empire, especially since the declaration in 2006 by French President Jacques Chirac that every 10 May would be a day commemorating France's long involvement with slavery. Yet slavery has not been a central part of French historiography in general and discussing slavery and its links with the French empire and the major foundational event of the Haitian Revolution is often elided in scholarship both in universities and within high school curricula. In the twentieth century, the French shared what Yves Benot called a national amnesia about the history of slavery, even after a 2001 law (the *loi Taubira*) finally acknowledged the evils of France's slave holding past.[30] In 2005, however, this law was muted by another passed (and subsequently struck down in 2006) that mandated that schools had to teach the 'positive' good of French colonialism. For many French people, it is difficult to study the Haitian Revolution, as studying the Haitian Revolution in which the French under Napoleon wanted to re-enslave Haitian blacks and where they insisted on a massive sum of reparations in order for Haiti to have diplomatic recognition exposes both the hypocrisy of the French civilizing mission and the inconsistency of republican principles.[31] The tensions in the historiographic coverage of French involvement in the slave trade and in slavery came to the fore most notably in 2005, when Olivier Pétré-Grenouilleau published a provocative but historically well-justified and award-winning history of the French slave trade that took the view of parts of the French Right that denied that French colonialism was something the French needed to apologize for and who was opposed to what he termed ahistorical views of 'executioners who are solely white versus victims who are solely Black'. He was sued, unsuccessfully, by Antillais community groups for minimizing the horrors of slavery, bringing his work and views very much within the attention of mainstream French historical scholarship.[32] Yet against this must be noted an increase of work that look at slavery as an essential part of French

---

[30]Yves Benot, *La Révolution française et la fin des colonies* (Paris: La Découverte, 1987), ch. 10.
[31]Laurent Dubois, *Haiti: The Aftershocks of History* (New York: Picador, 2012), pp. 7–8, 78–84, 97–105.
[32]Olivier Pétré-Grenouilleau, *Les traits nègrières d'histoire globale* (Paris: Gallimard, 2004). The debate is summarized in Alyssa Goldstein Sepinwall, 'Atlantic Amnesia? French Historians, the Haitian Revolution, and the 2004–2006 CAPES Exam', *Proceedings of the Western Society for French History* 34 (2006), pp. 310–11. See also Cecile Vidal, 'The Reluctance of French Historians to Address Atlantic History', *Southern Quarterly* 43 (2006), pp. 153–89.

identity and French history. Works specifically on France, empire and slavery are likely to follow.[33]

Critiques of empire without slavery

To a distressing degree, analyses of slavery within empire sometimes tend to be subsumed within a fruitless argument about whether the empire was a 'good thing' or a 'bad thing'. This debate is especially strong in Britain, though echoes of it can be found in France and in the United States. Historians who want to see the British Empire as mainly a force for good tend to downplay slavery although they may stress how antislavery was a strong force in early nineteenth-century imperialism and humanitarianism. Historians who argue that imperialism was wicked tend to emphasize Britain's leading role as a slave-trading nation in the eighteenth century as an indictment of empire overall. Disputes over whether empire was a good thing or not and the role of slavery in shaping a judgement on imperialism erupt periodically within British and American universities, as at Oxford over the status of Cecil Rhodes in the university or over a five-year program into 'Ethics in Empire' at the McDonald Centre for Theology, Ethics and Public Life which critics feel is overly celebratory of imperialism, including slavery.[34]

To an extent these debates reflect the growing prominence of the public presentation of slavery as part of empire that is increasingly undertaken in museums and in landed houses.[35] In Britain, the massive public interest

---

[33]Frédéric Régent, *La France and ses Esclaves* (Paris: Grasset, 2007); François-Joseph Ruggiu, 'Une noblesse Atlantique? Le second ordre français de l'Ancien au Nouveau Monde', *Outre-Mers* 97 (2009), pp. 39–63.

[34]For bestselling polemical accounts of empire as a 'good thing' and a 'bad thing', respectively, see Niall Ferguson, *Empire: How Britain Made the Modern World* (London: Allen Lane, 2003) and Shashi Tharoor, *Inglorious Empire: What the British Did to India* (London: Hurst, 2017). For the Ethics and Empire program, see Nigel Biggar, 'Don't Feel Guilty about Our Colonial History', *The Times*, 30 November 2017. For an equally polemical but more balanced account, which indicts Britain for its involvement in slavery, see Richard Drayton, 'The Collaboration of Labour: Slavery, Empires and Globalizations in the Atlantic World, c. 1600–1850' in A.G. Hopkins, ed., *Globalization in World History* (London: Pimlico, 2002), pp. 98–114. A balanced popular account more sympathetic to empire and in which slavery is sensitively treated is Jeremy Paxman, *Empire: What Ruling the World Did to the British* (London: Viking, 2011). For the debates on slavery and leading American universities, see Alfred L. Brophy, 'Forum on Slavery and Universities: Introduction', *Slavery and Abolition* 39 (2018), pp. 229–35 and essays by Lolita Buckner Inniss, Kelley Fanto Deetz, Jody L. Allen, and Michael Sugrue, pp. 236–89.

[35]John M. MacKenzie, *Museums and Empire: Natural History, Human Cultures and Colonial Identities* (Manchester: Manchester University Press, 2009).

in 2007 in commemorations (sometimes celebrations) of the 200th anniversary of the abolition by Britain of the Atlantic slave trade brought the issue of how to talk about slavery as part of the British Empire into sharp relief for practitioners of public history. How, museum directors puzzled, was the material culture of slavery housed in museums to be displayed to a diverse range of audiences, especially as museums have moved this century from being reliquaries to being forums, places that are centres of ideas and intellectual conflict, increasingly responsive to public opinion?[36] John McAleer noted that before 2007 there was a general 'amnesia' in British museums about slavery (the same was true for French or American museums – it was only in 2012 that Nantes commemorated its slaveholding past while in 2016 French president Francoise Hollande announced a future museum devoted to slavery; the National Museum for African American Life in Washington DC opened in 2016 with a major exhibition on slavery and freedom). As recently as 1988, the idea of a Museum of Slavery was deemed unacceptable to the British public. By 2007 it was different. Nevertheless, representations of slavery in museums were tricky, as slavery, the slave trade and abolition became touchstones for views on Britain's wider imperial history. For the British government, which gave through the Heritage Lottery between £15-20 million as part of 'remembering 1807', the narrative they wanted stressed was less about expressions of 'deep sorrow and regret', as Prime Minister Tony Blair put it, 'for our nation's role in the slave trade' than for an updated Whig story of progress culminating in the abolition of the slave trade in which this event was, as Blair's successor, Gordon Brown, argued, part 'of a golden thread in British history' that recognized Britain's capacity to lead the world on issues of liberty and freedom.[37]

Thus, museums in 2007 subsequently became lightning rods for political contention over the role of slavery in British life and in British understandings of its imperial legacies. Compounding these political issues were practical ones – material objects connected to slavery were sparse and where they existed seldom reflected black resilience but rather emphasized black

---

[36]Katherine Prior, 'Commemorating Slavery 2007: A Personal View from Inside the Museums', *History Workshop Journal* 64 (2007), pp. 200–11; Douglas Hamilton, 'Representing Slavery in British Museums: The Challenges of 2007' in C. Kaplan and J.R. Oldfield, eds, *Imagining Transatlantic Slavery and Abolition* (Basingstoke: Palgrave Macmillan, 2009), pp. 127–44; and Diana Paton and J. Webster, 'Remembering Slave Trade Abolitions: Reflections on 2007 in International Perspective', *Slavery and Abolition* 30 (2009), pp. 161–7.
[37]Catherine Hall, 'Doing Reparatory History: Bringing "Race" and Slavery Home', *Race and Class* 60 (2018), pp. 3–21, 5.

suffering. As McAleer notes, 'repeated displays, however well-meaning, of objects and images traditionally used to illustrate the history of slavery can perpetuate the suffering and humiliation experienced by enslaved people and their descendants'. Museum displays also, McAleer suggests, tended to take a resolutely insular and local approach to slavery, aiming to rearticulate the meanings of slavery and abolition for British national identity rather than contextualizing the history of slavery in imperial and wider European and Atlantic history. Katherine Prior concludes that 'the 2007 events are a step in the right direction, but they also show that there is a way to go before the transatlantic slave trade becomes a standard chapter in the public's reading of British history'.[38]

It is not just in museums that more attention is beginning to be paid to slavery as central to Britain's imperial legacy. In 2007 English Heritage commissioned initial research into links with transatlantic slavery or its abolition among families who owned properties now under its care. Country houses are expressions of wealth, power and privilege and many were built in part or in whole from profits drawn from slavery. They are also vital parts today of British heritage and British tourism. Heritage professionals of all kinds have begun thinking about how slavery linkages and imperial connections might be presented to visitors. Some of these concerns are addressed in Madge Dresser and Andrew Hann's *Slavery and the British Country House* (2013) and in Sheryllynne Haggerty and Susannne Seymour's work on 'imperial careering' and the Bentinck family.[39] The results are positive, if a little mixed – slavery sells, it seems, and thus emphasizing the grisly, in the ways that medieval punishments are also highlighted at stately houses, can be a money-making exercise as much as an historical exercise.[40]

Some British historians have also tried to incorporate empire and slavery more directly into new versions of British history. Foremost among these historians is Catherine Hall, a pioneer of feminist history, who from the 1980s drew from disputes within feminism over silencing of black women an interest in the role of race in nineteenth-century British history. She noted how Britain's domestic history had been systematically demarcated from its

---

[38] John McAleer, '"That Infamous Commerce in Human Blood": Reflections on Representing Slavery and Empire in British Museums', *Museum History Journal* 6 (2013), pp. 72–86; Prior, 'Commemorating Slavery 2007', p. 201.
[39] Madge Dresser and Andrew Hann, eds, *Slavery and the British Country House* (Swindon: English Heritage, 2013).
[40] https://www.york.ac.uk/projects/harewoodslavery/about.html.

imperial history as if the two had nothing to do with each other. Her interest in making empire a more central part of British history and race more central in the historiographies of Britain and its empire led her to write an important book on the impact of colonialism on English identities in the period after the abolition of slavery, exploring the long historical links between Birmingham and Jamaica. She showed how notions of Englishness in nineteenth-century Birmingham was tied up with ideas of race and control over subordinate populations overseas who were or had once been slaves.[41]

She argues that 'the attachment to the idea of abolition as a mark of Britain's love of liberty and freedom was linked to a deep, yet disavowed, attachment in English culture to Britain's imperial power'.[42] It was similar to what Paul Gilroy, another scholar who insisted that empire and slavery were intrinsic parts of British history, called 'post imperial melancholia' where 'once the history of the Empire became a source of discomfort, shame and perplexity, its complexities and ambiguities were readily set aside'.[43] Hall turned from these thoughts on imperial melancholia to work on Zachary Macaulay, an early abolitionist with direct experience of slavery from having lived in Jamaica and a long-time resident of Sierra Leone, and his more famous son, the historian Thomas Babington Macaulay. The son, despite his father's closeness to debates over abolition, seldom wrote about history in his highly influential histories, erasing the Caribbean in his Whig version of British history as progress. Hall's aim is the exact opposite of this: she wishes to bring slavery back into discourses within British and British imperial history.[44]

She has also been involved, along with Keith McClelland, Nicholas Draper and others, on a well-funded and public-facing research project, the Legacies of British Slave-ownership (LBS) project. The aims of this project are to shift the narrative about Britain's imperial relationship with slavery from a focus on abolition, as was the case of commemorations of 2007, to one that is about the benefits associated with the business of slavery and its importance in the making of modern Britain.[45] One major work that shaped how this

---

[41]Catherine Hall, *Civilising Subjects: Metropole and Colony in the English Imagination 1830–1867* (London: Polity Press, 2002).
[42]Hall, 'Doing Reparatory History'.
[43]Paul Gilroy, *After Empire: Melancholia or Convivial Culture?* (London: Routledge, 2004).
[44]Catherine Hall, *Macaulay and Son: Architects of Imperial Britain* (New Haven: Yale University Press, 2012).
[45]Catherine Hall et al., *Legacies of British Slave-ownership: Colonial Slavery and the Formation of Victorian Britain* (Cambridge: Cambridge University Press, 2014).

project has developed is Nicholas Draper's meticulous reconstruction of the networks British slaveholders created in the early nineteenth century and how these slaveholders deployed the compensation money they were given after the abolition of slavery to invest in multiple areas of Britain's economic, social and intellectual life. Victorian Britain, Draper showed, was intimately connected with the profits and culture of Caribbean slavery.[46]

The LBS project extends this insight back in time into the eighteenth century. The works of the scholars associated with this project show multiple links in Britain between slavery and British institutions and companies. British railway and canal systems, merchant banks, insurance companies, urban developments in spa towns like Tunbridge Wells and Leamington, and a host of cultural institutions all derived legitimacy from slave-created wealth.[47] James Delbourgo has extended this theme back into the eighteenth century noting how the British Museum was founded out of the collections of Hans Sloane, who derived much of his fortune and intellectual reputation from his involvement with slavery in Jamaica.[48] The work of the LBS confirms the correctness of Eric Williams's insistence in *Capitalism and Slavery* (1944) about the contribution that slave wealth made to the development of capitalism. Hall argues that the LBS 'challenges the systemic disavowal, the knowing and not knowing of the realities of slavery that has characterized British history writing and British society'.[49]

Hall's insistence that slavery and empire went together is a new departure, as she argues, in British history but returns to much older scholarship in which empire and slavery were always linked together. The philosopher John Locke, for example, was a major theorist of liberty but an active participant in establishing slavery in South Carolina. Holly Brewer has recently contextualized Locke's ideas and actions about slavery, arguing that to understand the origins of slavery in British America, we need to pay

---

[46] Nicholas Draper, *The Price of Emancipation: Slave-ownership, Compensation and British Society at the End of Slavery* (Cambridge: Cambridge University Press, 2010).
[47] https://www.ucl.ac.uk/lbs/.
[48] James Delbourgo, *Collecting the World: Hans Sloane and the Origins of the British Museum* (Cambridge, MA: Harvard University Press, 2017).
[49] Hall, 'Doing Reparatory History'. Eric Williams's work on slavery contributions to Britain's economic progress continues to attract great historiographical attention, with the historical pendulum swinging towards seeing Williams as not just thought-provoking but persuasive. Eric Williams, *Capitalism and Slavery* (Chapel Hill: University of North Carolina Press, 1944). A key work in the rehabilitation of Williams is Joseph E. Inikori, *Africans and the Industrial Revolution in England: A Study in International Trade and Economic Development* (Cambridge: Cambridge University Press, 2002).

attention to how various laws and policies enabled slavery across the British Empire in the late seventeenth century. She notes the powerful connections between monarchy, oligarchy, lordship and slavery: all were about hereditary status, something Locke was greatly concerned about. She insists that slavery was confirmed in the Americas by force and that the power of empire was critical to each part of slavery's development.[50] Locke's commitment to slavery as a component part of empire was hardly unusual for his time, as slavery was virtually unchallenged as vital for European global expansion and domestic wealth until the Seven Years' War.

The government of Robert Walpole and his followers, for example, which ruled Britain between the 1720 and the mid-1750s, supported the interests of sugar producers almost as much as they did the interests of Britain's landed class. Around 1750, however, a few thinkers began to doubt that slavery was so vital to empire as was commonly argued in the first half of the eighteenth century. These concerns over how slavery in the British Empire undermined British moral superiority are well covered in a recent book by Jack P. Greene.[51] Benjamin Franklin, for example, argued that what Britain should be doing in its empire was fostering its growing white settler population.[52]

Adam Smith, too, saw slavery as detrimental to the long-term economic interests of the British Empire, famously advancing the virtues of the free market system over the inefficiencies of slavery.[53] His views on slavery proved highly influential, feeding into nineteenth-century criticisms of slavery as a tool of colonization by Herman Merivale, Edward Gibbon Wakefield and most famously Karl Marx. All three were concerned with aspects of classical economics and the man-land ratio in sparsely populated colonies, drawing on conventional wisdom that slavery was necessary to tropical development because of a basic disequilibrium between vast and exploitable resources and low population density. Merivale noted, in an argument closely studied by Marx, that if the basis of colonial agriculture was a staple product sold overseas, slavery was necessary to concentrate the available labour

---

[50]Holly Brewer, 'Slavery, Sovereignty, and "inheritable Blood": The Origins of American Slavery', *American Historical Review* 122 (2017), pp. 1038–78.
[51]Jack P. Greene, *Evaluating Empire and Confronting Colonialism in Eighteenth-Century Britain* (New York: Cambridge University Press, 2013), ch. 5.
[52]Benjamin Franklin, *Observations on the Increase of Mankind*, in Leonard W. Labaree et al., eds, *The Papers of Benjamin Franklin* (New Haven: Yale University Press, 1959–2018), Vol. IV, pp. 225–34.
[53]Emma Rothschild, 'Adam Smith in the British Empire' in Sankar Muthu, ed., *Empire and Modern Political Thought* (Cambridge: Cambridge University Press, 2012), pp. 184–98.

force on a comparatively small portion of available land, even though in equilibrium conditions, slave labour, as Smith insisted, was dearer than free labour. Merivale drew attention to the relationship between the core and the periphery and the role of slavery in developing the periphery which has become central to world-systems theory and also to the argument advanced by Kenneth Pomeranz that one factor that allowed Western Europe to industrialize and thus attain economic leadership from 1800 over China was what Pomeranz calls 'ghost acres' – land in the Americas that was used for agricultural production of staple commodities which allowed Europe to devote more of its land for industry.[54]

The thinking of Merivale as transmuted through Wallersteinian world-systems analysis has led to the recent manifestation of a renewed emphasis on slavery's connections with both empire and capitalism in what has been termed the 'New History of Capitalism' movement.[55] Historians associated with this movement have stressed how important slavery was to nineteenth-century economic growth and that it facilitated both American empire and British imperialism, as well. Walter Johnson, for example, looks at slavery in the nineteenth-century American South as inherently expansionist, fashioning southern claims for an American empire of slavery in Nicaragua and Cuba.[56] The most ambitious book emerging from the NHC movement is Sven Beckert's global history of cotton in which both imperialism and slavery are central. Beckert emphasizes in world-systems' style the role of the state in fostering conditions amenable for amelioration. He argues that the colonial empires of Europe had a heavy reliance on the violent expropriation of indigenous peoples and, as Solow argued, upon slavery for their economic growth. This reliance upon slavery constituted an early phase of capitalism, which Beckert identifies using the neologism 'war capitalism'. He insists that 'war capitalism' was a necessary precondition for industrial capitalism. He makes the strongest argument in present-day historiography that the Industrial Revolution originated in 'slavery, colonial domination, militarized trade and land expropriations'. Like Williams, Beckert sees the fortunes made in the slave trade and sugar planting by British entrepreneurs

---

[54]Curtin, 'Slavery and Empire', pp. 7–8; Kenneth Pomeranz, *The Great Divergence: China, Europe, and the Making of the Modern World* (Princeton: Princeton University Press, 2000).
[55]Trevor Burnard and Giorgio Riello, 'Slavery and the Industrial Revolution: State Capitalism, the Great Divergence and the Power of Consumption in the Long Eighteenth Century', *Journal of Global History* 15 (2020), 225–44.
[56]Walter Johnson, *River of Dark Dreams: Slavery and Empire in the Cotton Kingdom* (Cambridge, MA: Harvard University Press, 2013).

as a source of finance for cotton textile production and thus fundamental to British economic takeoff.[57]

Such arguments are interesting but not persuasive, as most economic history accounts of the origins of British industrialization conclude that Williams was incorrect in seeing profits from the slave trade and eighteenth-century West Indian and American plantations as more than incidental in fostering industrial economic growth.[58] Beckert draws heavily on nineteenth-century American history and assumes that cotton and slavery are inseparable. But during early industrialization, it was sugar, not cotton, that was the main crop in the Americas and sugar as a commodity played little part in the Industrial Revolution though it was vital for changing consumption habits in Britain.[59] A much more convincing account, influenced more by Karl Marx than world-systems theory, of plantation slavery being central to European imperialism and economic growth is Robin Blackburn's magisterial *The Making of New World Slavery* (1997). He provides a wealth of carefully constructed data on slavery's contribution to the European economy and concludes that 'the colonial and Atlantic regime of extended primitive accumulation allowed metropolitan accumulation to break out of its agrarian and national limits and discover an industrial and global destiny'. Slavery for Blackburn was a quintessential modern institution. He approves of Nathan Huggins's comment that 'shocking though it is, [slavery] was truly the most stark representation of what modernism and western capitalism expansion meant to traditional peoples' and starts his long book by stating that 'what has been called the "European miracle" in fact depended not only on the control of intercontinental exchanges but on the profits of slavery'. To date, Blackburn's comprehensive history of early modern slavery is the most powerful evocation of slavery being fundamental to imperialism and imperialism being, as Marx argued, how the feudal mode of production could be transformed into the capitalist mode.[60]

---

[57]Sven Beckert, *Empire of Cotton: A Global History* (New York: Knopf, 2014), p. 60 (quote).
[58]David Eltis and Stanley L. Engerman, 'The Importance of Slavery and the Slave Trade to Industrializing Britain', *Journal of Economic History* 60 (2000), pp. 123–44.
[59]Giorgio Riello, *Cotton: The Fabric That Made the Modern World* (Cambridge: Cambridge University Press, 2013), pp. 188–94.
[60]Nathan Huggins, *Black Odyssey: The African-American Ordeal in Slavery* (New York: Vintage, 1990); Robin Blackburn, *The Making of New World Slavery: From the Baroque to the Modern 1492–1800* (London: Verso, 1997), p. 6, pp. 515–16.

Conclusion

The historiography on slavery and empire is patchy. Like most history writing concerning both topics, it is distinguished by polemics – often more 'history as rhetoric' than 'history as scholarship'.[61] One strand in scholarship on empires hardly mentions slavery. Another strand makes sometimes extravagant claims for its importance. The trend in historical scholarship seems to me inescapable, however. Slavery is being brought into the historiographies of Western society in numerous and multifaceted ways. It is also being portrayed as ever more central to imperial history. At the very least, to understand empire one needs to acknowledge the many ways in which slavery shaped imperial experiences. And, vice versa, slavery cannot be studied without seeing it as usually part of larger imperial processes.

Bibliography

Blackburn, Robin, *The American Crucible: Slavery, Emancipation and Human Rights* (London: Verso, 2013).
Bradley, Keith, Paul Cartledge, David Eltis and Stanley L. Engerman, eds, *Cambridge World History of Slavery*, 4 Vols. (New York: Cambridge University Press, 2011).
Burnard, Trevor, *Jamaica in the Age of Revolution* (Philadelphia: University of Pennsylvania Press, 2020).
Craton, Michael, *Empire, Enslavement and Freedom in the Caribbean* (Princeton, NJ: Markus Wiener, 1997).
Eden, Jeff, *Slavery and Empire in Central Asia* (New York: Cambridge University Press, 2018).
Elliott, J.H., *Empires of the Atlantic World: Britain and Spain in America, 1492–1830* (New Haven, CT: Yale University Press, 2006).
Heuman, Gad, and Trevor Burnard, eds, *The Routledge History of Slavery* (London: Routledge, 2011).

---

[61] This phrase is how Eric Hilt describes Edward Baptist, *The Half That Has Never Been Told: Slavery and the Making of American Capitalism* (New York: Basic Books, 2014) which he excoriates for containing 'disastrously mishandled' economic data. Hilt, 'Economic History, Historical Analysis, and the "New History of Capitalism"', *Journal of Economic History* 77 (2017), pp. 511–36.

Morgan, Philip D., and Sean Hawkins, eds, *The Oxford History of the British Empire: Black Experience and the Empire* (New York: Oxford University Press, 2004).

Pinnen Christian, 'Slavery and Empire', *Oxford Bibliographies Online*, www.oxfordbibliographies.com

Swingen, Abigail, *Competing Visions of Empire: Labor, Slavery, and the Origins of the British Atlantic Empire* (New Haven, CT: Yale University Press, 2013).

4

The 'Great Divergence': Slavery, capitalism and world-economy

Dale Tomich

Binghamton University

Introduction

The history of *world* capitalism and *world* slavery is only beginning to be written. Until recently, slavery has predominantly been studied within the framework of particular nation-states and their colonial empires. Beginning in the 1970s historical studies of slavery bifurcated. Following the 'cultural turn', the majority of scholars turned their attention away from the social and economic history of slavery towards questions of culture, agency and meaning. On the other hand, questions of slave economy became the province of the New Economic Historians, who applied economic theory and sophisticated quantitative techniques to large bodies of data that could not be subject to analysis before the advent of computer technology. The concerns of cultural historians are far from the economics of slavery while economic history became a specialized discipline that was not readily accessible to the uninitiated. Consequently, historical studies have either turned away from macrohistorical processes and relations or treated them from a narrow and technical point of view. In recent years, however, world history, the history of capitalism, and capitalism and slavery among other problems have assumed an ever more prominent place on the current intellectual agenda.[1] Over the course of these same decades, prevailing scholarly opinion has swung from treating slavery as a backward, inefficient, precapitalist social economic relation towards regarding it as modern and capitalist. However, despite this shift in interpretation, there is no consensus and little discussion about basic questions: what do we mean by capitalism? In what way is slavery capitalist? What are the consequences of treating slavery as capitalist? And perhaps most importantly for this chapter, how do we understand capitalism and slavery as world historical relations?

How we think about each of these questions largely determines how we construct our units of analysis and organize our inquiry. The move towards concepts of world history and world capitalism requires particular caution. History, since its creation as a modern discipline during the nineteenth century, has been deeply implicated in the formation of the nation-state. Even when national history is not the object of historical inquiry, national societies, each with its own economy, polity and culture, provide, implicitly if not explicitly, the organizing theoretical framework of much historical analysis. Consequently, how we construct world history and world capitalism and slavery as objects of historical inquiry is a question of decisive theoretical significance.

This chapter will address the problem not by attempting to offer a substantive historical interpretation of the relation of slavery and capitalism, but by examining the methodological approaches and conceptual frameworks that have shaped the historiographical debates over this problem. My focus is on how concepts are used and what procedures are followed in order to construct problems, organize evidence, and make arguments and interpretations. I am particularly interested in how space and time are conceptualized in various approaches to the problem of capitalism and slavery. As Fernand Braudel argued over sixty years ago, how we understand space and time profoundly shapes

---

[1] Some representative titles include Patrick Manning, *Navigating World History: Historians Create a Global Past* (New York: Palgrave, 2003); Jürgen Osterhammel, *The Transformation of the World: A Global History of the Nineteenth Century* (Princeton, NJ: Princeton University Press, 2014); Sven Beckert, *Empire of Cotton: A Global History* (New York: Knopf, 2014); Edward Baptist, *The Half Has Never Been Told: Slavery and the Making American Capitalism* (New York: Basic Books, 2014); and Walter Johnson, *River of Dark Dreams: Slavery and Empire in the Cotton Kingdom* (Cambridge, MA: Belknap Harvard, 2013).

the way that we understand historical processes.[2] Recent debates among geographers have reiterated Braudel's emphasis on the connections between social processes and spatial relations: social relations and material process are expressed spatially and take particular geographical forms. Conversely, specific forms of spatial organization and social historical geographies are formative social relations and material processes.[3] This emphasis on the formation of spatial relations allows us to historically specify capitalism and slavery through multiple spatial scales ranging from global to local.

Building upon these insights, this chapter attempts to clarify some of the issues entailed in writing histories of slavery and world capitalism by focusing on various interpretations of the relation of slavery in the Americas and capitalist industrialization during the nineteenth century. It first examines Eric Williams's seminal *Capitalism and Slavery* (1944)[4] and subsequent criticism of his work by the New Economic Historians. In this debate, the problem of capitalism and slavery is framed as part of the colonial expansion of Europe, and more specifically as the problem of Britain and its West Indian colonies. The chapter next considers the treatment of slavery in Kenneth Pomeranz's *The Great Divergence* (2000).[5] In this work of comparative world history, New World slavery plays a decisive role in enabling Europe to industrialize and achieve far higher rates of economic growth during the nineteenth century. Finally, I will summarize my own work on what I have termed 'the second slavery'.[6] The concept of the second slavery attempts to account for the dramatic creation of new frontiers of slave commodity production – sugar in Cuba, cotton in the US South and coffee in Brazil – as part of the expansion and restructuring of the capitalist world-economy during the

---

[2] Fernand Braudel, 'History and the Social Sciences: The *Longue Durée*' [trans. Immanuel Wallerstein] in Richard Lee, ed., *The Longue Durée and World-Systems Analysis* (Albany, NY: SUNY Press, 2012), pp. 241–76.
[3] Doreen Massey, 'Politics and Space/Time', *New Left Review* 1: 196 (1992), pp. 65–84.
[4] Eric Williams, *Capitalism and Slavery* (Chapel Hill: University of North Carolina Press, 1994, orig. pub. in 1944).
[5] Kenneth Pomeranz, *The Great Divergence: China, Europe and the Making of the Modern World Economy* (Princeton, NJ: Princeton University Press, 2000).
[6] Dale Tomich, *Through the Prism of Slavery: Labor, Capital, and World Economy* (Lanham, MD: Rowman & Littlefield, 2004), pp. 56–71.

nineteenth century. This conception presents a distinct theoretical and methodological approach integrating capitalism and Atlantic slavery into nineteenth-century world history.

Historical space in the Capitalism and Slavery *debate*

The work of Trinidadian historian and statesman Eric Williams remains the starting point and fundamental reference for the historiographical debates about the relation of capitalism and slavery. Williams published his classic *Capitalism and Slavery* in 1944. The book is a work of engaged scholarship that directly challenged the prevailing historiographical canon. At the time Williams wrote, the dominant interpretation was that the abolition of the British slave trade in 1807 and British slave emancipation in 1834 were the work of the abolitionist movement in Britain and of British humanitarianism. Williams sharply emphasized economic causes and motives in opposition to the 'humanitarian school' stress on moral and political factors, and he sought to call attention to the political and economic tensions within the metropolitan-colonial relation in contrast to the humanitarians' emphasis on unilateral and disinterested British action. Within this framework, Williams systematically examined the historical relation of *capitalism* and *slavery* in order to understand the economic processes and interests that shaped the course of slavery and abolition in the British West Indies. His effort to explain the West Indian contribution to capitalist development in Britain and the consequences of capitalist development for the British West Indian colonies is a pioneering contribution to the study of what a later generation of scholars would characterize as underdevelopment. It is a significant and distinguished work of scholarship. Its conclusions may be contested, modified, accepted or rejected, but its enduring value lies in Williams's comprehensive, systematic and forceful effort to interpret industrial capitalism, colonial slavery and abolitionism within a unified historical framework. At the same time, it remains an enduring political document that was an important contribution to growing national and anti-colonial sentiment in the British West Indies and elsewhere.

Williams presents *Capitalism and Slavery* as 'strictly an economic study of the role of Negro slavery and the slave trade in providing the capital which financed the Industrial Revolution in England and of mature industrial capitalism in destroying the slave system'.[7] While it seems clear that Williams intends to treat the changing relation of capitalism and slavery as a long-term historical transformation, subsequent scholarship has broken this formulation into two separate propositions – the role of slavery in the rise of capitalism and the role of capitalism in the destruction of slavery – and treated them independently. In the remainder of this section, I will concentrate on the second proposition: the role of industrial capitalism in the destruction of West Indian slavery. This has been the most active focus of debate over Williams's work and sharply poses the various methodological approaches to interpreting slavery and capitalist development.

Williams presents a nuanced political and economic interpretation of the rise of industrial capitalism and the crisis of the slave trade and slavery in the British West Indies. He treats this process as the transformation of historically structured political, economic and social relations. He regards it as the historical transition from one form of capitalism to another. It entails the qualitative restructuring of production relations and markets in both metropolis and colony.[8] In Williams's view, West Indian slavery, the colonial system and mercantilist monopoly were inextricably linked. Their interdependence and interaction provided the organizing structure of commercial capitalism and the British colonial empire during the eighteenth century. Individually and collectively, these three interdependent elements formed a barrier to the expansion of industrial capital in Britain and

---

[7]Williams, *Capitalism and Slavery*, p. ix. In its most condensed form, Williams's argument is that 'the capitalists had encouraged West Indian slavery and then helped to destroy it. When British capitalism depended on the West Indies, they ignored or defended it. When British capitalism found the West Indian monopoly a nuisance, they destroyed West Indian slavery as the first step in the destruction of West Indian monopoly'; see Williams, *Capitalism and Slavery*, p. 169. Such emphatic formulations were characteristic of the revised text of *Capitalism and Slavery*. They have too often been seized upon by both proponents and opponents of Williams's work and condensed into an interpretation of the 'Williams' Thesis' that does not do justice to Williams's more subtle and complex argument. In this way, the question of long-term historical transformation and change through time that was of interest to Williams is removed from consideration. Instead, each proportion is treated as a separate theoretical hypothesis that can be treated independently.

[8]Williams states the general idea of a transition from commercial to industrial capitalism in several different ways with small but significant differences among the formulations. The terms of this transition are clearly stated in a letter that Williams wrote to W.T. Crouch in the course of submitting manuscript to the University of North Carolina Press: 'The book … shows how the commercial capitalism of the eighteenth century was built upon slavery and monopoly, while the Industrial capitalism of the nineteenth century destroyed slavery and monopoly'; Williams is quoted in Colin Palmer, '*Capitalism and Slavery* and the Politics of History', *Review: Fernand Braudel Center* 35: 2 (2012), p. 104.

the forces allied with the new industrial interests progressively removed them in favour of free trade.

In Williams's account, the abolition of the slave trade and slave emancipation were part of a broader political economic transformation. He delineates the tensions and conflicts between the French and British colonial empires and between the North American and West Indian colonies within the British colonial empire. The US independence deprived the British West Indian colonies of a cheap source of provisions and destroyed Britain's Old Colonial Empire creating a political and economic rival to Britain in the Atlantic.[9] A slave revolution destroyed the French colony of Saint Domingue, the world's largest sugar and coffee producer and with it the French colonial empire in the Americas.[10] The British West Indian colonies were left in a vulnerable position as the system of competing empires that had organized the Atlantic economy of the eighteenth century was dismantled. The restructuring of trade that resulted from the destruction of the mercantilist-colonial order in the Atlantic was a stimulus for the expansion and acceleration of industrial production in Britain.

Williams treats the abolition of the slave trade, slave emancipation and the abolition of the sugar duties not as a sequence of separate events, but as steps in the systematic reorganization of production and trade by industrial capital:

> The attack on the West Indians was more than an attack on slavery. It was an attack on monopoly. Their opponents were not only the humanitarians but the capitalists ... The attack falls into three phases: the attack on the slave trade, the attack on slavery, the attack on the preferential sugar duties. The slave trade was abolished in 1807, slavery in 1833, and the sugar preference in 1846. The three events are inseparable.[11]

In Williams's view, monopoly of the home market, regulated prices and limited West Indian production presented obstacles for continuous expansion of industrial capital. Abolition of the slave trade, and subsequently slavery itself, was a step in abolishing colonial monopoly and freeing capital for more productive deployment.[12]

---

[9] Williams, *Capitalism and Slavery*, pp. 108–25; Eric Williams, *The Economic Aspect of the Abolition of the West Indian Slave Trade and Slavery* [edited by Dale Tomich] (Lanham, MD: Rowman & Littlefield, 2014, orig. pub. in 1944), pp. 43–95.
[10] Williams, *Capitalism and Slavery*, pp. 146–9.
[11] Ibid., pp. 135–6.
[12] Ibid., pp. 136–52.

Williams's account is structured by his choice of Britain and its West Indian colonies as his units of analysis. This unit and its constituent elements – Britain, its colonies or the British colonial system – are taken as given. Change may occur within them but the units themselves do not change. Such a procedure creates a distinction between what is internal and what is external to each unit. The causal processes that inform Williams's analysis are taken to be internal to these units. Consequently, there can be no systematic relation between units.

Thus, Williams seeks to analyse the specific relation of capitalist development and the abolition of the slave trade and slavery *in the British West Indies*. Although he laid the groundwork for examining the problem of capitalism and the destruction of slavery, his interpretation is understandably grounded in the prevailing conception of capitalism of his day. He treats capitalism as a *national* phenomenon. He treats Britain as the classical site of capitalist development and the Industrial Revolution as well as proletarianization, the rise of an industrial middle class, and the emergence of liberal ideologies. Further, in his conception, industrial capitalism necessarily requires free trade. In contrast, Williams views the West Indian colonies as conceptually discrete and separate from British capitalism. He regards slavery as a non-capitalist relation. In contrast to the continuous expansion of industrial capital in Britain, the 'law of slave production' – soil exhaustion and the need for more slaves and livestock to secure the same level of production – retarded the expansion of production in the British slave colonies.[13] These two separate entities are linked to one another through colonialism and mercantilism to form the British colonial empire.

Constructing the problem in this way eliminates the relational character of the various terms. Williams treats the colonial slave economy as an integrated duality rather than distinctions within a unity. The unified and integral field of relations between metropolis and colonies produce the links between the two terms and make the two parts of a whole disappear from view. Instead, the terms are brought into relation with one another through complex linkages of colonial domination, mercantilist economic policy, trade, forced and unforced migration, ideology and social movements. These links are treated *as if they form the relation*. What is missing is an account of how the relation constructs the links. Consequently, the categories of

---

[13]Ibid., pp. 113–14.

capitalism and slavery, or metropolis and colony, are transformed into classificatory terms without analytical value.[14] Even as Williams proposes a broadly comprehensive *historical* interpretation, his focus on the British Empire continuously excludes the full range of causally significant relations and processes.

Since Williams construes Britain's colonial empire as an externally bounded and internally integrated conceptual and substantive unit, relations outside of this imperial unit are treated as external to the fundamental relation between Britain and its colonies. World historical relations and processes forming those units are not integrated into his causal account. Williams also recognizes the historical fact of the expansion of slavery in the US South, Cuba and Brazil during the nineteenth century. But these are treated as independent slave complexes and they do not form part of his explanatory scheme. Indeed, they enter his explanatory account only insofar as they influence British industrialization, West Indian slavery or imperial policy from the outside. Thus, his conceptual scheme implies a multiplicity of independent and parallel slave complexes, each with its own path of historical development. More central to his argument, he presents the American and Haitian Revolutions as conditions for the abolition of the slave trade and slave emancipation in the British West Indies. However, the causal mechanisms of his argument are located within the national space of Britain and its colonial dependencies. This procedure risks taking the effects of complex global-local interactions for local causes.

This analytical procedure shapes the spatial-temporal framework of Williams's causal account. While international and inter-imperial competition necessarily play a part in his formulation of the colonial-mercantile regime of commerce capitalism, it is otherwise with industrial capital. Williams emphasizes the unity of the abolition of the slave trade, slave emancipation and the abolition of preferential duties by reversing the order of events. He begins his presentation with the abolition of the Corn Laws in 1844 and moves back through slave emancipation in 1834 to the abolition of the slave trade in 1807. While this presentation unifies the sequence of events, it creates a single historical temporality, which makes it seem as if abolition and emancipation are inevitable steps in the march towards free

---

[14]Maria Sylvia de Carvalho Franco, *Homens Livres na Ordem Escravocrata* (São Paulo: Editora Ática, 1976), pp. 9–16; Francisco de Oliveira, *A Economia Brasileira: Crítica á Razão Dualista* (Petrópolis: Editora Vozes Ltda, 1981), pp. 9–13; Terence K. Hopkins, 'World-Systems Analysis: Methodological Issues' in Terence K. Hopkins and Immanuel Wallerstein, eds, *World-Systems Analysis: Theory and Methodology* (Beverly Hills: Sage Publications, 1982), pp. 151–2.

trade. In this dualistic construction, British industrial capitalism appears as if it is the dynamic source of change acting on backward, static and archaic West Indian colonies. Industrial capital is the single causal force and free trade is the necessary outcome of historical development. A unilinear process of industrialization and free trade in Britain produces a similarly unilinear sequence from abolition to emancipation in the West Indies. This formulation obscures the complexity of Williams's overall argument, which then appears reductionist and determinist. This spatial-temporal framework and the underlying conception of historical causality set the parameters for the subsequent debate over his work. By disproving his analysis of the slave trade, the whole construction falls apart.

Williams, thus, constructed the Industrial Revolution *in Britain* and its imperative for free trade as the direct and linear cause of the destruction of colonial mercantilism, abolition of the slave trade and slave emancipation. Williams's interpretation became the paradigmatic account of the incompatibility of slavery and industrial capitalism and the free market, and of the inevitability of abolition. Scholars following in his footsteps have also treated the abolition of slavery as national reiterations of the same general process. In each slave society, the emergence of capitalism led to the destruction of slavery. The result is a sequence of successive abolitions that generate a linear narrative of the incompatibility of slavery and capitalist production and exchange. World slavery is the aggregate of national slaveries.

Economic theory and history: The New Economic History

In the 1960s and 1970s, interest in *Capitalism and Slavery* was renewed and the debate over what came to be known as the 'Williams Thesis' crystallized. However, in many ways, the new debates fell along the fault lines of the initial response to the book. Williams's arguments and interpretations were supported, contested, refined and expanded in a variety of ways. Some economic historians have been generally supportive of Williams, or have challenged the arguments and data of his critics. However, most have been critical of Williams's interpretations and his evidentiary base and they are often unsympathetic to his entire project. During this period, *Capitalism and Slavery* faced rigorous challenges from a new quarter, the proponents of the New Economic History. The New Economic History provided a new approach to the analysis of historical problems grounded in the application of neoclassical economic theory and the quantification of large volumes of data. It burst onto the scene with the publication of Robert W. Fogel and Stanley L. Engerman's path-breaking *Time on the Cross* (1974).[15] Using these new quantitative techniques, Fogel and Engerman overturned the thesis of the inefficient, backward, pre-capitalist character of slavery through a powerful demonstration of the profitability and productivity of the slave economy.[16]

The New Economic Historians have put forth a new historical paradigm and presented a forceful set of analyses that has set the terms of the 'Williams debate'. Those who would align themselves with Williams in one way or another have to respond to their arguments.[17] Beyond that, the New Economic Historians have played an increasingly predominant role in defining economic history as a discipline.

The New Economic Historians have subjected *Capitalism and Slavery* to intense examination and criticism. They have constructed the debate in such a way as to attempt to prove or disprove Williams's propositions on empirical grounds. The conceptual framework of economic theory and the New Economic History necessarily transmutes Williams's concern with the historical relation of capitalism and slavery into the quite different framework of the 'economics of slavery'. The New Economic History's critique of Williams's argument that mature industrial capitalism destroyed the slave system in the British West Indian colonies is reconstructed as 'the decline thesis'.[5] Seymour Drescher, Williams's most prominent critic, summarizes the 'decline thesis' in the following terms: in the mid-eighteenth century,

---

[15] Robert W. Fogel and Stanley L. Engerman, *Time on the Cross: The Economics of American Negro Slavery* (Boston: Little, Brown and Company, 1974).

[16] The New Economic History has been subject to criticism from within and without economic history; see, for example, Paul A. David et al., *Reckoning with Slavery: Critical Essays in the Quantitative History of American Negro Slavery* (New York: Oxford University Press, 1976); and Herbert G. Gutman, *Slavery and the Numbers Game: A Critique of Time on the Cross* (Urbana: University of Illinois Press, 1976). The criticism has, by and large, focused on the findings and interpretations of the New Economic Historians.

[17] See David Eltis, *Economic Growth and the Ending of the Transatlantic Slave Trade* (New York: Oxford University Press, 1987); Seymour Drescher, *Econocide: British Slavery in the Era of Abolition* (Pittsburgh, PA: University of Pittsburgh Press, 1977); Barbara L. Solow, 'Caribbean Slavery and British Growth: The Eric Williams Hypothesis', *Journal of Development Economics* 17: 1–2 (1985), pp. 99–115; Barbara L. Solow, 'Capitalism and Slavery in the Exceedingly Long Run' in Barbara L. Solow and Stanley L. Engerman, eds, *British Capitalism & Caribbean Slavery: The Legacy of Eric Williams* (New York: Cambridge University Press, 1987), pp. 51–77; Barbara L. Solow and Stanley Engerman, eds, *British Capitalism & Caribbean Slavery: The Legacy of Eric Williams* (New York: Cambridge University Press, 1987).

the rapid rate of development of the British West Indies declined and they were unable to maintain their position as either tropical producers or customers. The inefficient anachronistic colonies became encumbrances to emergent British capitalism. The abolitionist campaigns and legislation further accelerated their decline.[18]

Drescher further breaks down the decline thesis into general propositions. First, British slavery diminished as a factor in the imperial political economy before and during abolition. Second, at the same time, the British slave colonies succumbed to competition with other slave systems in the international market. As a result, the West Indian colonies were less valuable and less vigorous in the last third of the eighteenth century than previously. Drescher notes that there is no general agreement about when the proportional decline of the West Indies began. However, the American Revolution is most often taken as the decisive event in the cycle. He continues: 'Some turning point is of course significant for any causal argument, since the decline must be shown to have preceded the major political initiatives in the dismantling process.'[19]

The New Economic Historians have devoted their energy to refuting the decline thesis through the economic analysis of large quantities of data. With few exceptions, they are quite confident that they have disproved Williams's claims on empirical grounds. Seymour Drescher contends that the British West Indies were not in decline at the time of the abolition of the slave trade in 1807. Favourable prices, increasing imports to Britain and a growing share of British trade immediately after abolition support their positive assessment of the British West Indian sugar industry after the abolition of the slave trade. Further, the acquisition of Guyana and Trinidad after 1814 brought more cultivated land into the empire than all of the cultivated land in the existing West Indian colonies. They offset slight declines in the old British West Indian colonies after 1807 and were essential to the increase of British West Indian production. In their view, the slave colonies of the British West Indies were both productive and profitable. Slave-produced sugar from the British colonies still accounted for over half of world supply in 1814.[20]

---

[18]Drescher, *Econocide*, p. 15.
[19]Ibid., pp. 15–16.
[20]Eltis, *Economic Growth and the Ending of the Transatlantic Slave Trade*, pp. 5–6; Drescher, *Econocide*, pp. 147–8.

Drescher concludes that there was no economic decline that led to abolition of the slave trade and slave emancipation in the British West Indies.[21] The only factor that prevented the British colonies from taking full advantage of the post-war boom was labour. In his well-known formulation, the abolition of the slave trade was an act of *econocide*, provoked by abolitionism in the form of a mass movement and a new liberal sensibility. It undercut the potential prosperity of the British West Indian sugar colonies and was the cause of the economic crisis, not the other way around.[22] It was the first step in an inevitable chain of events that dismantled slavery and culminated in slave emancipation. Drescher's critique of the abolition of the slave trade challenges Williams's argument at its most vulnerable point and dismantles Williams's construction of the entire sequence of events. Having refuted the economic argument for abolition, the New Economic Historians turn their attention to ideological and political explanations for abolition, the very humanitarianism that provoked Williams's intervention in the first place.

The New Economic Historians present their thesis as an objective historical account. They have produced a powerful critique of the idea that the slave formations of the Americas were backward, archaic and unproductive. However, it is inadequate to simply accept their findings as they have been presented. Any critical appropriation of their work must recognize its conceptual limitations as well as its substantive accomplishments.

The New Economic Historians replicate Williams's spatial-analytical framework and their work is subject to the same limitations. More fundamental is the question of the suitability of neoclassical theory as a tool of historical analysis and interpretation. Here, the antinomy between what Geoffrey Hodgson calls the 'barren universality' of economic theory and the contingent character of historically formed social relations and material processes generates an unproductive binary.[23] Economic theory must necessarily expel history from its domain in order to establish the conditions of its universal validity. The formalist categories of neoclassical economic theory preclude historical specification of economic development

---

[21] It should be noted that in 'A General Equilibrium Model of the Eighteenth-Century Atlantic Slave Trade: A Least-Likely Test for the Caribbean School' in Paul Unselding, ed., *Research in Economic History* 7 (1982), pp. 287–325, William A. Darity has argued that the slave-plantation complex in the Caribbean and not the slave trade is at the core of Williams's argument.

[22] Drescher, *Econocide*.

[23] Geoffrey Hodgson, *How Economics Forgot History: The Problem of Historical Specificity in Social Science* (London: Routledge, 2001), pp. 232–47.

and restrict their analysis to abstract conceptions of profitability and productivity. Social historical relations have a different status than the categories of economic analysis and are relegated to a subordinate position. The abstract universal categories of economic theory are independent of time and space; that is, they apply to all times and all spaces. Time and space themselves are not substantive relations, but rather empty categories without structure or coherence. Consequently, temporal and spatial units appear as external and secondary phenomena that can be arbitrarily aggregated and disaggregated in accordance with the problem at hand.

The establishment of the historical specificity of political economic relations is not a concern for economic theory and it has no criteria for doing so. Neither capitalism nor slavery can be specified as historical relations, nor can we speak of qualitative economic transformations or transitions such as the transition from slavery to post-slavery labour regimes. From the perspective of economic theory, the economy operates *in* social relations and history rather than *through* them. From this perspective, there is no economic distinction between capitalism and slavery. 'Slavery' is understood as an extra-economic juridical relation of property. It is 'the outcome of force and compulsion practiced by one group against others and not the outcome of voluntarily exchanged property rights'.[24] Slavery, that is, the ownership of one person by another, affects the allocation and distribution of economic resources. However, from the perspective of economic theory, it is a contingent term that falls outside the bounds of economic analysis proper.[25] It is of interest only insofar as it affects the allocation and distribution of economic resources.[26] In this approach, the term 'market' is conjoined with the term 'slavery' to characterize modern slavery. This conception facilitates the application of neoclassical economic theory to the 'slave economy' and allows profit-maximizing behaviour to achieve its clearest expression. The return on capital in the form of slaves is compared with the return on other forms of capital (i.e. those forms where free and rational choice hold) in order to determine whether a greater or lesser return on capital or greater or lesser productivity is obtained in comparison with those cases where there is free and rational allocation of resources.[27]

---

[24] Stanley L. Engerman, 'Some Consideration of Property Rights in Man', *Journal of Economic History* 33: 1 (1973), p. 44.
[25] Ibid., pp. 42–3.
[26] Ibid., p. 43.
[27] Alfred H. Conrad and John R. Meyer, *The Economics of Slavery and Other Studies in Economic History* (Chicago: Aldine, 1964), p. 45.

The implications of this theoretical approach are illustrated by Drescher's formulation of 'the decline thesis'. Williams's complex multi-layered argument, which combines national and international economic relations and domestic and imperial politics, ideology and class formation, is translated to a set of discrete, internally homogeneous and unified propositions about the 'economy' that are amenable to quantitative analysis. Relations that are not properties under observation are eliminated from consideration. By focusing on market and price competition between national units, this approach underestimates, if not ignores, the changing structure of the Atlantic economy. Foreign competitors only enter this analysis insofar as they affect conditions for British producers. Further, by treating land, labour and capital as independent factors of production, it disaggregates the historical relations through which production is organized. On the other hand, the political event of the American Revolution bears no integral relation to processes of economic development. Rather, it is a contingent event that is arbitrarily chosen to mark the beginning of the decline process. It is juxtaposed to the key event, the abolition of the slave trade in 1807, to delineate homogeneous economic segments under consideration, which are analysed though, before and after comparison. In this formulation, decline is understood as a fall in production and productivity or the falling importance of West Indian trade with Britain in the period before the abolition of the slave trade in 1807. The quantitative performance of the West Indian economy before 1807 can now be compared to that of the period after 1807. The 'decline thesis' is refuted by demonstrating that the British West Indian slave economy was profitable and productive before 1807. According to the criteria of economic theory, any subsequent decline is attributed to the abolition of the slave trade.

The New Economic Historians have been successful in challenging the interpretations of others, but have been unable to provide satisfactory interpretations of their own. In my view this is less a failure of the historians than a consequence of their approach. Here, the economy is conceptualized by a self-enclosed, internally integrated and universally applicable theory that strips it of its historical character. This theory is supplemented by a separate and contingent conception of historical social relations that are regarded as extra-economic. Further, the claims of the absolute objectivity of 'economic facts'[28] weaken the status of social historical relations. Economy

---

[28] Douglass C. North, 'Beyond the New Economic History', *The Journal of Economic History* 34: 1 (1974), pp. 1–7.

and history cannot easily be put in systematic relation to one another in such a framework. Historical relations are only brought in after the economic analysis is complete. Interpretations are ad hoc and after the fact. Thus, after rejecting the decline thesis on economic grounds, Drescher simply reverts to a version of the humanitarian argument that Williams originally criticized. Having rejected the abstractly conceived economic causes for abolition and emancipation, he turns to equally abstract political and ideological explanations and remains caught in the opposed pairing of economic versus non-economic factors. The inability of the New Economic Historians to adequately contextualize their findings leads them to reproduce the dichotomy between economic and ideological or political causes of abolition that has structured the Williams debate since its inception.

Historical space in The Great Divergence

Kenneth Pomeranz's *The Great Divergence: China, Europe and the Making of the Modern World Economy* (2000) is one of the most important and influential efforts in the new wave of scholarship that has approached the problem of capitalism and its origins in the framework of world history, rather than of European history. The book has had great influence because of the way it challenges Eurocentric accounts of economic development on the basis of empirical data and rigorous comparison. Pomeranz mobilizes a variety of methodological procedures and historical data to examine world historical processes of economic development. He develops a critical comparative approach that challenges interpretations that privilege the unique character of Europe as the source of economic modernization. Although New World slavery is not Pomeranz's main focus, he is one of the few authors to integrate slavery into a comprehensive analytical account of world history. It plays a decisive role in his account of European industrial development and the 'Great Divergence' between Europe and Asia.

In order to put European development in its world historical context, Pomeranz compares economic growth in Europe and Asia over a very long historical time. Pomeranz's account is grounded in the theoretical assumptions and methodological procedures of neoclassical economy theory and deploys them in a sophisticated comparative strategy to construct his world historical account of economic development. Economic theory's abstract and general concept of economy provides a common denominator that allows Pomeranz to make comparisons of long-term economic development, irrespective of the nature of specific economic formations. Consistent with this approach, the object of his inquiry is not capitalism as a political economic system, but rather industrialization and rapid economic growth. Thus, the decisive question for Pomeranz is the identification of disparities in the rates of growth between East and West.

Pomeranz utilizes a conception of growth that is derived from Adam Smith's *Wealth of Nations*.[29] In this framework, all economy is based on exchange. Growth is the result of productivity gains that derive from the division of labour and specialization follows from the division of labour as people try to capture the benefits of comparative advantage in the market. Producers benefit by specializing in what they are best suited to produce and exchanging with other specialized producers. The division of labour is limited only by the extent of the market. Through most of human history, factor productivity, the expansion of markets and the development of the division of labour have been limited by extra-economic constraints imposed by land and population on the ability of capital and labour to be substitutes for land in order to simultaneously expand population, raise per capita consumption, increase productivity and allow specialization in agriculture.[30]

Pomeranz constructs a conception of world history through a creative and sophisticated comparative scheme. He takes economic regions as the units of comparison. The units are fixed and independent of one another, although they may be aggregated to form larger units. Pomeranz's strategy of reciprocal comparisons simultaneously compares China (and India) to Western Europe and Western Europe to China with regard to various factors effecting economic growth. This strategy allows him to avoid the trap of explicitly or implicitly having a normative case (here Europe or Britain) against which other cases are evaluated.[31] Instead of simply comparing other regions with Europe, which allows for treating Europe as the normative case, he also compares Europe to other regions. Instead of simply asking 'Why wasn't Yangtze Britain?', Pomeranz also asks 'Why wasn't Britain Yangtze?'

---

[29] Adam Smith, *An Inquiry into the Nature and Causes of the Wealth of Nations* (London: W. Strahan and T. Cadell, 1776).
[30] Pomeranz, *The Great Divergence*, p. 211.
[31] Robert A. Nisbet, *Social Change and History: Aspects of the Western Theory of Development* (New York: Oxford University Press, 1969), pp. 189–208.

He argues Europe's market-driven development did not give it a significant economic edge over comparable regions of the world before 1800. There were no great disparities between levels of economic growth that support the idea of an internally generated European 'miracle'.[32]

However, Pomeranz emphasizes that comparison at the level of regional cases cannot explain why the acceleration of economic development happened first in Western Europe or why it happened at all.[33] In order to find an explanation for why economic development occurred first in Western Europe, Pomeranz shifts his focus from comparison between regional cases to the integrative comparative strategy that sociologist Charles Tilly terms 'encompassing comparison'. This procedure establishes (external) links between cases by locating them within an overarching macrohistorical structure or process and explains similarities of differences among them as consequences of their position within the overarching structure. This approach provides a means to discover appropriate historical cases and devise alternative explanations by fixing accounts of change to historically grounded generalizations. Cases remain self-contained and independent, but are grounded within the possibilities and constraints of the encompassing structure or process. Each case is evaluated in relation to its position within the larger structure. Tilly contends that this procedure allows us to specify causes and variations from one case to another within their time-space limits while remaining consistent with the available evidence for each case.[34]

Pomeranz finds that only in the late nineteenth century was there a significant difference in the rates of economic growth between West and East. Europe leaped ahead into sustained industrial development and created a widening gap in between West and East. In the second half of the eighteenth century, the combination of coal, steam power and mechanization enabled Western Europe and particularly Britain to greatly increase its industrial production and primary product consumption.[35] However, Pomeranz argues that this precocious industrial development could easily have been suppressed. Until 1800, ecological constraints could have forced Western Europe back on a labour-intensive path of economic development

---

[32]Pomeranz, *The Great Divergence*, pp. 206–7.
[33]Ibid., p. 25.
[34]Charles Tilly, *Big Structures, Large Processes, Huge Comparisons* (New York: Russell Sage Foundation, 1984), pp. 60, 74.
[35]Pomeranz, *The Great Divergence*, pp. 264–85.

or stopped growth altogether.[36] However, Britain was able to continue to industrial growth because it was able to construct a new kind of periphery in the New World that allowed it to overcome the ecological 'bottlenecks' existing in Europe and to exchange an ever-increasing quantity of industrial products for an ever-increasing quantity of primary products.[37]

Here Pomeranz emphasizes the pivotal role of the slave trade and New World slavery in providing an outlet for Britain's industrial output that could not be provided by the home market and that allowed British industry to break out of the environmental constraint. He argues that the importance of New World slavery resided less in the surpluses that the slave regions produced, than in the markets that they provided. Slaves were purchased from abroad and were obtained in exchange for European manufactured goods. Further, slaves produced little of their own subsistence and the level of subsistence in slave zones was much lower than that of peripheries in Eastern Europe and Asia where producers were born locally, produced for their own basic needs and had little cash to spend. Consequently, the slave colonies imported grain and timber from the British North American colonies. The income from this trade allowed the British North American colonies to also buy British manufactures. At the same time, they specialized in the production of plantation staples rather than diversifying production in order to export enough to cover the costs of buying slaves and the costs of feeding them. Thus, they were able to at once absorb the surplus production and productivity gains of the Industrial Revolution and provide an expanding supply of primary products – food and raw materials – in a way that the home market could not.[38]

Pomeranz views New World slavery as a bridge for European industrial development and the creation of a new industrial division of labour. It allowed Europe to develop industrial production and primary product consumption beyond eighteenth-century levels without disrupting European agriculture. The New World zones of slave production provided markets for European industrial goods and increased the supply of primary products required by the expansion of European proto-industry and early mechanized industries.[39] Industrial exports and primary product imports stimulated one another and established the complementarity between

---

[36]Ibid., p. 264.
[37]Ibid., p. 20.
[38]Ibid., p. 269.
[39]Ibid., pp. 263, 267.

Europe and the New World. Proto-industry 'grew up' by transferring labour to industry, which enabled industry to attract new labour and still depress wages. Consequently, European agriculture did not have to both dramatically increase its output from the same amount of land and release large numbers of workers in order to make industrialization possible. At the same time the expansion of slavery allowed overseas production to also 'grow up'. An increasing supply of primary products were acquired from abroad without requiring large amounts of European labour.[40]

The dynamics set in motion during the colonial period created the framework for a flow of resources from both slave and free areas that accelerated throughout the nineteenth century. Land-saving New World imports of primary products kept pace with European industrial production. New World imports grew and diversified after 1830. American grain, wheat, timber and other primary products fuelled European industrial growth. At the same time, the New World became an outlet for Europe's surplus population, stimulated by falling railroad and shipping costs. European migration to the New World created new consumer goods markets for European manufactures.[41] However, an unfavourable trade balance with the New World pushed European colonial expansion into Africa and Asia. By the 1880s a new industrial division of labour was established that supported European self-sustained growth and the 'Great Divergence' with Asia.[42]

Pomeranz incorporates New World slavery and the slave trade into a conception of comparative world economic history rather than confining himself to national, colonial or imperial history. However, Atlantic slavery and the colonization of the Americas are not integral to his comparative account of world economic history, and he provides no treatment of New World slavery and the slave trade that is commensurate with his analysis of Europe and Asia. Rather, he attributes the importance of New World slavery for European industrialization to a conjuncture of contingent factors.[43] They are simply mobilized at the key moment in his argument in order to account for the change in the land: labour ratio that permitted British industry to break out of the European ecological constraint. Thus, the Americas only enter Pomeranz's account when they are seen as a factor in British industrial development.

---

[40] Ibid., pp. 285–7.
[41] Ibid., p. 284.
[42] Ibid., pp. 283–7.
[43] Ibid., p. 32.

Pomeranz's argument treats Europe and the Americas as conceptually independent spaces, each with its own economy. Their interaction is the product of a fortuitous conjuncture. Each follows its own course of historical development until the American slave zones satisfy the functional needs of British industrialization. Yet even here, their histories are parallel, though complementary. This interaction creates a growing interdependence throughout the nineteenth century and results in a new, structural core-periphery relation that is part of the maturation of European industrialization and what Pomeranz terms the 'Great Divergence'.

Within the framework of his comparative approach, Pomeranz utilizes neoclassical theory to disclose the crucial role of New World slavery in British and European industrialization. However, the abstract and formal character of economic theory does not allow him to historically specify economic relations and construct an adequate account of the relation of slavery and industrialization. He posits a smooth and linear expansion of the New World slave zones and slides beyond them to the industrialization of the Americas as features of the Americas' parallel 'maturation' with Europe. His data seems to be drawn initially from the British West Indies without recognizing, despite the claims of the New Economic Historians, how limited they were, both as producers of tropical commodities and as markets for metropolitan manufactures. He fails to specify the geographic, economic, political, social and technological changes that were necessary for the creation of new, expanded spaces of slave production. This failure is linked to the limitations of economic theory, which provides no means to integrate these 'extra-economic' conditions into this account.

The contingent relation of New World slavery to European economic development in Pomeranz's analysis is constructed in accordance with the theoretical presuppositions of neoclassical theory. Geography – whether physical, social or political – is not constitutive of economy. The environmental, geographical or historical determinants of economic space are necessarily excluded from the abstractly conceived units of economic analysis. Rather, economies exist in space, but space itself is an unstructured aggregate of possible spaces infinitely divisible or expandable. The world is simply the sum of its parts. Its spaces can be added together or subdivided at will. This abstract and arbitrary conception of space underlies his failure to account for slavery and colonialism as integral aspects of European economic development.

Pomeranz compares regions with similar characteristics. The comparison of what he terms economic 'core' regions arguably forms the key to his argument. For him, 'core' is a descriptive concept rather than a relational concept. It seems to refer to any place where manufacturing, trade and, perhaps, commercial agricultural activities are concentrated – that is a particular configuration of the factors of production. That such concentrations of economic activity have existed throughout world history is not open to question. But what makes a core a core is not its morphological features, but its interrelation, interdependence and mutual formation with other zones that do not manifest the same features – that is a 'periphery'. In other words, core and periphery are formed through their relation to one another. Although they are not the primary objects of his attention, when Pomeranz incorporates the New World slave regions into his analysis, he also treats them as independent, internally integrated and self-enclosed slave economies.

To treat the core and periphery only in terms of their morphologies is of limited utility. Such a conception not only ignores the relational character of core-periphery relations, but also abstracts from the diverse and changing historical characteristics of each such zone. Each region is reduced to its lowest common denominator over long historical time. Continuity at a general level is emphasized over specific historical relations and processes forming the relations between core and periphery. Because the British 'core' and the New World slave 'periphery' are constructed as independent economies, Pomeranz conceives of the Americas as 'a new kind of *trading partner*'.[44] Thus, the links between Europe and the Americas are construed as external and contingent, for example trade or migration, but the integrity of each unit remains intact. In Pomeranz's interpretation, the expansion of the market creates more specialization in each region. In the 'core', production becomes more diverse and specialized; in the slave peripheries, greater quantities of plantation staples are produced. The 'maturation' of Europe and the Americas appears in his account as a continuous, linear market-driven process. Europe and its American trading partner 'grow up' in tandem until ever-increasing trade dependency creates a new and genuinely industrial division of labour and the world's first 'modern' core and the world's first 'modern' periphery in the 1880s. Pomeranz concludes by emphasizing

---

[44] Ibid., p. 263 (my emphasis).

the external linkages between independent entities: 'We end, then, with connections and interactions explaining what comparison alone cannot.'[45] In other words, the already given core zone is merely added to the already given peripheral zone by means of trade.

Only after Pomeranz establishes the role of New World slavery in British industrial accumulation does he go back and select historical factors that allow the Americas to play a complementary role to Europe at the time of the Industrial Revolution. These factors include the demographic collapse of the sixteenth century, mercantilism and the slave trade. However, consistent with the assumptions of economic theory, Pomeranz treats them as contingent factors that impinge on primary economic processes from the outside. They are treated not as historically formative of the relations between Europe and the New World, but as preconditions of a determined outcome. Such extra-economic factors are eclectically assembled after the purely economic analysis is completed in order to explain changes that would otherwise be incomprehensible within the terms of economic theory. Thus, distinct political, social or cultural domains are subordinated to already given 'economic facts' and any attempt to provide an integrated and comprehensive account of the historical formation of specific economic relations and processes is vitiated.

This approach emphasizes quantitative development – the material division of labour, that is, the production and exchange of things and the market. Market exchange is treated as if it was a natural outcome of production and is not historically accounted for. Instead, exchange and the market are regarded as ahistorical universals. They are the beginning and the end of historical development. Supply, demand and market price are regarded as the motors of change. Historical development reaches its culmination with universal factor mobility freed from external constraints, market exchange and self-sustained growth. This perspective emphasizes quantitative variation over qualitative change. By viewing social relations as external contingencies, it treats all forms of economic activity as commensurable and provides no criteria to adequately conceptualize specific forms of economy. Thus, the social relations of capitalism and slavery are not regarded as constitutive of historically specific forms of social production and exchange. Rather, they are construed as extra-economic factors that represent greater or lesser degrees of constraint on the mobility of the factors of production.

---

[45] Ibid., pp. 25–6.

Pomeranz has made a significant contribution to the debates over slavery and capitalism by presenting systematic quantitative analyses of the role of slavery in nineteenth-century industrialization. His work has challenged the longstanding assumption that slavery is incompatible with a modern industrial market economy. However, he has not provided a convincing historical interpretation of his findings. His explanation is a retrospective, ad hoc and arbitrary attempt to find explanations that fit the results of economic analysis. This disjuncture between economic analysis and historical interpretation is inherent in the conceptual framework of economic theory itself. While Pomeranz presents his work as an objective account of historical change, the concepts and procedures of neoclassical economic theory are fundamentally ahistorical.

The work of both the New Economic Historians and Pomeranz demonstrates the limitations of neoclassical economic theory as a tool for historical inquiry. This approach rests upon a dualistic conception of universally valid economic categories that are independent of time and space and external contingent factors that are necessarily operative in particular times and places. Its concept of economy is understood through the abstract categories of land, labour, capital and marginal utility. The assumptions of scarcity, the utility-maximizing individual, private property and market exchange that underlie the key theoretical categories are naturalized and universalized. These categories form a closed conceptual system. Conversely, nature, technology, production and exchange as substantive material-historical processes and specific forms of social relations are relegated to the status of contingent extra-economic variables. In this conceptual framework, complex historical processes and relations are subtly transformed into independent factors and stripped of their historical character. The concepts of economic and extra-economic have a different theoretical and analytical status. The result is an abstract and one-sided economic interpretation that juxtaposes economic to non-economic factors. Primacy is given to the abstract and universal categories of economic theory. The resultant dualism creates a theoretical approach that is of limited utility for the analysis of historical change.

Economic theory is intended as a guide to short- and medium-term action. By treating social relations and material processes as externalities, economic theory effectively treats them as 'given for the purpose of analysis'. In the short and medium term, it may be plausible to hold such external factors constant. However, the longer the duration of the problem at hand or the more complex the relations under consideration, the less tenable this assumption becomes. Ultimately, over the very long run, it leads to the proposition that all of history must be held constant for the purposes of economic analysis. The conceptual framework of economic theory does not treat economy as historically constituted through material-social processes. From its perspective, economy is not formative of, or formed by, historical relations. Rather, it treats economies as developing *in* history, not *through* history. Consequently, economic theory cannot specify particular forms of production and exchange, nor can it account for their historical formation. It offers no concept of historical time, nor any historical concept of space. Analysis is restricted to a given spatial-temporal framework that is determined outside of theory. Thus, economic theory removes from consideration the problems of long-term historical transformation and qualitative change through time.

In this analytical framework, capitalism and slavery are not considered as specific forms of social production. Rather, capitalism is naturalized as exchange for the market, and slavery is reduced to extra-economic coercion. Historical processes operating at the level of the world and Atlantic economies – the political processes restructuring markets, the expansion and reorganization of production, the creation of new productive spaces and of a new division of labour – are eliminated from consideration. Similarly, the ways that particular ecologies, material processes of production, technologies, and forms and scales of collective labour are combined in specific historical circumstances are not regarded as analytically significant. Despite its accomplishments, this approach excludes the very terms that are of interest for comprehending historical change. It is more important for the questions that it enables us to ask than for the answers that it provides.

The second slavery and the space-time of the world-system

In the remainder of this chapter, I present an alternative approach to the relationship between slavery and the expansion of the nineteenth-century capitalist world-economy that is based on the world-systems perspective. The emergence of new zones of slave production during the first half of the nineteenth century, what I have termed the 'second slavery', was part of the expansion and the economic and political reorganization of the capitalist world-economy.⁴⁶ The second slavery entailed the creation of extensive new geographic zones of slave commodity production, increases in the scale and intensity of production, the adoption of new technologies and the restructuring of the social relations of slavery.

The world-systems perspective allows a conceptually integrated and coherent account of the geographical and environmental conditions, material processes, and the social and political relations that transformed New World slavery and shaped its role in the restructuring of the capitalist world-economy. This perspective offers a new way of looking at these processes and interpreting them. Instead of proceeding by means of national narratives or conventional formal comparison of distinct slave societies, it allows us to frame the formation and reformation of particular regions as world-economic processes. In this way, we may trace the specific sequences of historical change that transformed slave relations in *these* new zones during *this* period and draw out their implications for our understanding of slavery and the development of the capitalist world-economy.

The New World's relation to Europe was more complex than being simply a 'new kind of trading partner'. Exchange between these two regions was not simply based on Ricardian comparative advantage. The slave plantation complexes of the New World were structurally part of the European world-economy since the sixteenth century and developed in interdependence with it. They are not comprehensible except through their interrelationship with the metropolitan core. On the reverse side of the Smithian formula, colonialism, the political appropriation of new geographical zones, the slave trade and slave labour, created new productive spaces that were the condition for, not a consequence of, the extension of the market. Relations of force and compulsion were necessary to establish historical-geographical production complexes in the New World that specialized in the production of plantation staples. These zones of slave production provided markets for European manufactures and supplied Europe with primary products, not simply at the moment of the Industrial Revolution, but in a way consistent with the historically changing levels of European development since the inception of the capitalist world-economy in the sixteenth century. Together, Europe and the New World formed an integrated division of labour that was historically made and remade. If, as Pomeranz contends, the New World slave periphery played a pivotal role in European industrialization, it arguably played an

---

⁴⁶Tomich, *Through the Prism of Slavery*.

analogous role in helping Europe reach the point at which the Industrial Revolution was possible.

The world-systems perspective, pioneered by Immanuel Wallerstein, Terence K. Hopkins and Giovanni Arrighi among others, enables us to conceptualize the second slavery. At the same time, analysis of the second slavery enables us to rework the world-systems perspective. The world-systems perspective treats capitalism as a specific historical world-economic structure. The capitalist world-economy is an evolving historical-geographical complex.[47] It is formed by an integrated world division of labour encompassing diverse forms of social labour that exchange commodities through the world market. The world division of labour and world market are politically integrated through the interstate system. The zones or regions comprising the division of labour are construed not as self-enclosed, independent and absolute spaces with external links with one another. Rather, particular zones are understood though their relative position in the organizing world-economic whole.[48]

The concept of the second slavery emphasizes the complex interrelations and tensions between global and local. The focus on global-local relations allows us to more adequately account for the historical development of particular social local formations and reconstruct the complexity of the historical processes forming and reforming the capitalist world-system. It discloses the intricate networks of social interrelations and interactions operating at all spatial scales, from the local to the global.[49] By this means we may move from an abstract conception of the capitalist world-economy to a more concrete and historical conception.

From this perspective, the local retains its particular character even as it is reproduced within the field of world-economic relations. Each particular local history is regarded as the product of the confluence of relations and processes operating across multiple spatial-temporal planes ranging from place-specific environmental conditions to the world market and interstate system. It forms a distinct historical-geographical complex that is understood not as an empirically discrete, independent and internally integrated unit with its own history, but rather as what I have elsewhere characterized as 'the local face of world process'. At the same time, the

---

[47]Vitorino Magalhães Godinho, 'Complexo Histórico-Geográfico' in J. Serrão, ed., *Dicionario de História de Portugal* (Porto: Iniciativas Editorias, 1961), pp. 130–5.
[48]Massey, 'Politics and Space/Time', pp. 80–1.
[49]Ibid., p. 80.

characteristics and significance of each local part derives from its position within the relations comprising the global whole. Each particular element or formation is *formed through* its relations with all other elements as parts of a unified and structured world-system from which they derive their meaning and function.

From this perspective, particular social formations are conceived as specific configurations of conditions, relations and processes of diverse spatial and temporal extension, which are not necessarily coterminous with the boundaries of the local unit, but rather converge to determine its individual character. Each such individual historical-geographical complex has its own history and is the product of that individual but situated history. At the same time, it is constitutive of the historical formation of the world-economic whole. Thus, the world-economy is conceived as a relation that is at once structured and structuring, the changing relation between the whole and its parts.

Formulating the problem of slave production in terms of global-local relations enables us to understand how particular slave formations are outcomes of world-systemic processes and how such formations contribute to the structuring and restructuring of the capitalist world-system. Here 'global' and 'local' are treated not as ontologically separate entities or independent 'levels' of analysis, but as opposite poles of a unified, but spatially and temporally complex and hierarchical set of relations. From this perspective, the slave formations of the Atlantic are treated not as a series of distinct and integral 'slave economies', each with its own history that is 'internal' to its boundaries, but rather as specific historical-geographic complexes that are continually made and remade through a variety of economic, political and social processes operating at diverse spatial-temporal scales, from local to global, from events to long-term developments.

The world-systems perspective inverts the logic of conventional social science or comparative history. Here, the logic of inquiry does not attempt to construct the whole by adding up the parts, nor does it look for 'lawful variations' among commensurate cases. Instead of presuming a multiplicity of independent and comparable units (societies), it presupposes a single unified world-economy in which each local part is constituted differently from the others and occupies a distinctive location within a definite spatial-temporal structure. Thus, the units under examination are neither independent of nor commensurate with one another. Rather, particular phenomena are interrelated and derive their meaning from their position in the whole.

These theoretical assumptions require distinct methodological procedures. Because global-local relations are conceived as part-whole relations, social-historical causality is necessarily tied to the complex interdependence and interaction of diverse relations. The units themselves are not taken as given. Instead, each particular unit is regarded as 'a partial outcome of complex causes and a partial cause of complex outcomes'.[50] Viewed in this way, the attributes or features of particular units are markers or points of reference for comprehending systemic processes. By analysing them within this perspective, it is possible to establish how they are formed within broader fields of relations and processes, and how they disclose world-systemic processes. While each particular complex of relations may be a unit of observation, the unit of analysis is the world-economy as a whole.

This approach radically reinterprets the question of capitalism and slavery by treating the slave formations of the Americas as integral parts of the capitalist world-economy. The US South, Cuba and Brazil are not regarded as separate slave plantation societies, each with its own economy. Rather the historical development of each of these zones is simultaneously global and local. Each zone is regarded as a distinct 'bundle of relations',[51] which is formed through broader unified world-systemic processes. In this approach, land, labour and capital are treated as substantive historical relations, rather than the abstract and universal categories of economic theory. Here, land refers to specific environmental-geographical conditions, labour is understood as human activity organized through the social relations of slavery and adapted to the material requirements of each specific crop, while capital refers to the technologies appropriate for the production of each crop. The interdependence and mutual interaction of these material, social and economic processes and relations create spatially and temporally singular zones of production. Each such space is a particular historical outcome formed through its relation to other such spaces and to the world-economy as a whole. These distinct configurations establish new commodity and financial circuits that are firmly anchored in the emergent industrial division of labour. At the same time, each zone is a part of the world-economic whole and contributes to the reconstruction of the world-economy.

---

[50]Hopkins, 'World-Systems Analysis', pp. 151–2.
[51]Eric Wolf, *Europe and the People without History* (Berkeley: University of California Press, 1982), p. 2.

This framework discloses the systemic relation of New World slavery to the processes of capitalist development and enables us to differentiate and specify particular slave formations within the historical development of the capitalist world-economy. The theoretical reconstruction of historical particulars with this framework discloses time-space differences between apparently similar phenomena – slavery, plantation, colonialism, frontiers, etc. The role, function and meaning of each are specific within the historical formation and reformation of the broader whole. Each individual historical-geographical slave complex – that is the Cuban sugar frontier, the US cotton frontier and the Brazilian coffee frontier – is a specific point of concentration of relations and processes operating on diverse spatial and temporal levels. At the same time, the world market and division of labour are remade through the historical formation of these productive zones. Thus, the concept of the second slavery does not emphasize only the distinctive character of slavery in nineteenth-century Cuba, Brazil and the US South. It also calls attention to the changing character of slavery within the expansion and reformation of the world-economy and the coexistence and interdependence of slavery, wage labour (and by implication other forms of commodity-producing labour, including combinations of coerced labour and wage labour and/or subsistence labour), and industrial production within a unified world division of labour. In this way, it contributes to our understanding of the changing character of the world-system itself.

These new zones of the second slavery were formed as parts of a distinct historical cycle of economic and geographic expansion of the capitalist world-economy that transformed the Atlantic world during the first part of the nineteenth century. The conditions for their development were world-economic processes of industrialization and urbanization, the restructuring of world markets, decolonization and the formation of nation-states in the Americas, together with the development of liberal conceptions of politics and economy. On the one hand, these zones met, through the massive redeployment and restructuring of slave labour, the growing world demand for cotton as an industrial raw material, and sugar and coffee for consumption by the working and middle classes concentrated in the urban centres of the North Atlantic. On the other hand, they were shaped by the political forces of the 'Age of Revolutions' and confronted the forces of anti-slavery and decolonization. US independence, the Haitian Revolution and Latin American independence destroyed the colonial system in the Atlantic, which had provided the structural support of the preceding slave systems, and led to the formation of independent nation-states in the Americas. At the same time, vigorous liberal and antislavery movements and ideologies appeared throughout the Atlantic world, together with multiple episodes of slave resistance, with new and diverse ideological contents, while Britain spearheaded efforts to abolish the international slave trade, the lifeblood of the second slavery. The pro-slavery politics of the second slavery were defined in relation to this politics of abolitionism and antislavery; beyond that, they were themselves frequently grounded in liberal conceptions of economy and state.[52] From this perspective, the British West Indian slave colonies entered into crisis and decline, despite the demonstrations of continued profitability and productivity by the New Economic Historians. This crisis was not a result of the slave colonies' direct relationship to industrialization in Britain. Rather, it was the consequence of the expansion and political and economic restructuring of the world-economy as a whole and the emergence of the dynamic and more productive new zones of the second slavery.

Slavery in these new agricultural frontiers was reconfigured within an unprecedented constellation of political and economic forces. Its systemic character and meaning were profoundly altered. At the core of this expansive second slavery was the redeployment of slave labour as a mass productive force, that is, the mass concentration of slave labourers devoted to monocultural staple production and the creation of new productive spaces to meet growing world market demand. Staple production in the new zones of the second slavery had to adapt to competitive and expanding postcolonial markets. Each zone was characterized by the increased geographical and economic scale of production, the expansion and intensification of slave labour, and the incorporation of new production and transportation technologies. Each led the world in the production of its particular commodity and expanded production at an unprecedented rate over the first half of the nineteenth century.

The emergence of the new zones of the second slavery restructured the overall pattern of Atlantic trade. While the US South became the leading exporter of raw cotton to Britain, the United States became the prime market for Cuban sugar and Brazilian coffee. These zones generated a demand for

---

[52]Domenico Losurdo, *Liberalism: A Counter-History* (London: Verso, 2011); Dale Tomich, ed., *The Politics of the Second Slavery* (Albany, NY: SUNY Press, 2016).

labour that brought the Atlantic slave trade, both legal and illegal, to perhaps the highest level in its history. In addition, the United States and Brazil had substantial internal slave trades. The destinations for these involuntary labourers were almost exclusively the new commodity frontiers. The zones of the second slavery were part and parcel of the formation of the liberal industrial capitalist order of the nineteenth century. They exposed the inner antagonisms and contradictions of this order.

The second slavery approach presents a substantive reinterpretation of nineteenth-century slavery, but, perhaps, more importantly, it offers a theoretical and methodological perspective that presents a new approach to understanding slavery and world capitalism. It inverts the procedures of conventional social science by taking the capitalist world-system as its unit of analysis. The capitalist world-system is understood as a historically specific formation within the more general field of world history. It provides the framework within which the relations and processes that form it may be continually specified. From this perspective, slavery is part of the complex differentiated world-economy and is constituted and reconstituted through networks of historically interdependent relations and processes operating across multiple spatial-temporal scales ranging from local to global.[53]

Slavery appears here not as an external and contingent relation but as an integral part of historical capitalism. It plays a crucial role in the expansion of industrial capital during the nineteenth century through the production of new space, the transformation of world division of labour and the expansion of the world market. The concept of the second slavery attempts to come to terms with the spatial and temporal specificity of these new frontiers of slave commodity production within the historical process reforming the world-economy as a whole during the nineteenth century. This approach implies that the relation of capitalism and slavery cannot be resolved through definitions, but rather it needs to be approached through theoretically informed empirical investigation of continually changing combinations of diverse relations – environmental, economic, social, cultural and political. Local research is constructed in a way that reveals the global. At the same time, it provides a perspective that allows us to understand broader sets of changes throughout the capitalist world-economy. The task is to comprehend the local through the global and the global through the local.

---

[53]Massey, 'Politics and Space/Time', pp. 79–81.

Bibliography

Drescher, Seymour, *Econocide: British Slavery in the Era of Abolition* (Pittsburgh, PA: University of Pittsburgh Press, 1977).

Fogel, Robert W., *Without Consent or Contract: The Rise and Fall of American Slavery* (New York: W. W. Norton & Company, 1989).

Fogel, Robert W. and Stanley L. Engerman, *Time on the Cross: The Economics of American Negro Slavery* (Boston: Little, Brown and Company, 1974).

Pomeranz, Kenneth, *The Great Divergence: China, Europe and the Making of the Modern World Economy* (Princeton, NJ: Princeton University Press, 2000).

Ryden, David Beck, *West Indian Slavery and British Abolition, 1783–1807* (New York: Cambridge University Press, 2009).

Solow, Barbara L. and Stanley Engerman, eds, *British Capitalism & Caribbean Slavery: The Legacy of Eric Williams* (New York: Cambridge University Press, 1987).

Tomich, Dale, ed., *Slavery and Historical Capitalism during the Nineteenth Century* (Lanham, MD: Lexington Books, 2017).

Tomich, Dale, *Through the Prism of Slavery: Labor, Capital, and World Economy* (Lanham, MD: Rowman & Littlefield, 2004).

Williams, Eric, *Capitalism and Slavery* (Chapel Hill: University of North Carolina Press, 2014, orig. pub. in 1944).

Williams, Eric, *The Economic Aspect of the Abolition of the West Indian Slave Trade and Slavery*, ed. Dale Tomich (Lanham, MD: Rowman & Littlefield, 2014, orig. pub. in 1944).

5

Approaches to global antislavery

Seymour Drescher

University of Pittsburgh

Antislavery, as a project directed against extreme forms of interpersonal inequality, assumed global dimensions enmeshed in other forms of inequality. It claimed adherence to a principle that the slave trade and slavery were initially fundamental transgressions against principles of religion and justice, and ultimately 'crimes against humanity'. What has been called the abolitionist revolution ultimately extended its mandate to related practices of human trafficking, bonded labour and sexual exploitation. Antislavery was also from its inception a transnational movement of state and non-state actors, coalescing over time into a civil society movement of humanitarian intervention. It became a catalyst for subsequent changes in international relations and international law.

The history of antislavery is thus associated with the development of ideas, movements and legislation, aimed primarily at the elimination of the slave trade and slavery. Challenging a ubiquitous and seemingly perennial element of human relations, antislavery first emerged within slaveholding transatlantic empires whose European metropoles had already identified themselves as zones of legal freedom.[1] The first organized abolitionist movements were cosmopolitan in ideology and intercontinental in range.

---

[1] For overviews, see Sue Peabody and Keila Grinberg, eds, Special Issue on 'Free Soil', *Slavery and Abolition* 32: 3 (2011).

Those whom they undertook to protect were non-Europeans, originally purchased beyond the boundaries of their own empires.

Relative to slavery, the historiography of antislavery deals with a much briefer period of history. In the four volumes of *The Cambridge History of World Slavery*, only the fourth, dealing with the past two centuries, offers a section devoted to abolition. It was only at the end of the eighteenth century that a number of cultural, civil and political mobilizations simultaneously coalesced to constitute what has since been designated as an international abolitionist movement.[2]

The historiography of antislavery also originated in the three original centres of its political activism. The United States, France and Britain were identified as its original sites. Not faced with the obstacles of massive revolutionary and counter-revolutionary upheavals or successive crises leading to civil war, British historians could view the processes of slave trade abolition and slave emancipation within the framework of waves of successful mass mobilizations and parliamentary victories. Their successful campaigns against the transatlantic slave trade and their Caribbean slave system allowed Britain to gain pre-eminence as the pace setter in international antislavery for more than a century after the emergence of abolitionism. Thomas Clarkson's *History of the Rise, Progress, and Accomplishment of the Abolition of the Slave Trade by British Parliament* (1808) dominated antislavery historiography.[3]

During the last third of the twentieth century, however, two earlier major challenges by Trinidadian scholars to this perspective began to command widespread attention. Eric Williams's *Capitalism and Slavery* (1944) fundamentally challenged the prevailing moral triumphalism of British historiography and its concentration on heroic abolitionist 'Saints'. Williams substituted an alternative explanation for both the rise and the fall of slavery as a continuous historical process dominated by British economic development and its ruling capitalist class. Just as British slavery's rise had fuelled the rise of its metropolitan capitalism, so its decline had directly led to the abolition of its transatlantic slave trade and its colonial slave system.

While Williams's correlation between colonial decline and British abolition was challenged by subsequent analysis of economic data, David

---

[2]David Eltis, Stanley L. Engerman, Seymour Drescher, and David Richardson, eds, *The Cambridge History of World Slavery*, Vol 4: *AD 1804–AD 2016* (New York: Cambridge University Press, 2017) [hereafter, *CHWS*], pp. 321–520. Olivier Grenouilleau, *La Revolution Abolitionniste* (Paris: Gallimard, 2017) offers a new global approach to the subject.

[3]Thomas Clarkson, *History of the Rise, Progress, and Accomplishment of the Abolition of the Slave Trade by British Parliament*, 2 Vols. (London: L. Taylor, 1808).

Brion Davis offered an alternative hypothesis, linking British abolitionism to the ideology of emergent industrial capitalism. However, as the analysis expanded beyond the British example to encompass the remainder of the Atlantic slave system, it became clear that all of the major European transatlantic slave systems first came under sustained attack when those systems were both profitable and expanding.[4]

Another Trinidadian, C.L.R. James, identified Caribbean slaves as principal agents in the history of antislavery. In *The Black Jacobins: Toussaint L'Ouverture and the San Domingo Revolution* (1938), James placed the most successful slave revolution in history at the centre of the 'Age of Revolutions'. Breaking with the Euro-American tendency to marginalize that revolution, he emphasized the Haitian slaves' embrace of the doctrines of natural rights and principle of common humanity. Their subsequent struggles offered a model of successive resistance elsewhere in local, national and transnational contexts.

Three overviews of the development of antislavery offer recent models of approaches to the evolution of antislavery over the past two centuries. In contrast to his earlier emphasis on the primacy of abolitionist arguments as the ideological counterparts of hegemonic capitalism, David Brion Davis's *Inhuman Bondage* stresses the transformation of moral perception linked to political power that enabled antislavery to become a global measure of the minimal normal standard of human achievement over the course of a century. Robin Blackburn's *American Crucible* and Seymour Drescher's *Abolition* both stress the international flow of ideas and different scenarios of power and coercion that supported, rejected and transformed antislavery over the course of two centuries.[5]

---

[4] See, inter alia, Eric Williams, *Capitalism and Slavery* (Chapel Hill: University of North Carolina Press, 1944); David Brion Davis, *The Problem of Slavery in the Age of Revolution* (Ithaca, NY: Cornell University Press, 1975); Seymour Drescher, *Econocide: British Slavery in the Era of Abolition* (Pittsburgh, PA: University of Pittsburgh Press, 1977); Laird Bergad, *The Comparative History of Slavery in Brazil, Cuba, and the United States* (New York: Cambridge University Press, 2007); and David Eltis, *Economic Growth and the Ending of the Transatlantic Slave Trade* (New York: Oxford University Press, 1987). David Beck Ryden, by restricting the time and spatial dimensions of the argument, has argued for an abbreviated version of Williams's decline thesis; see David Beck Ryden, *West Indian Slavery and British Abolition, 1783–1807* (New York: Cambridge University Press, 2009).

[5] See David Brion Davis, *Inhuman Bondage: The Rise and Fall of Slavery in the New World* (New York: Oxford University Press, 2006), and David Brion Davis, *The Problem of Slavery in the Age of Emancipation* (New York: Alfred A. Knopf, 2014); Robin Blackburn, *The American Crucible: Slavery, Emancipation and Human Rights* (London: Verso, 2011), and Seymour Drescher, *Abolition: A History of Slavery and Antislavery* (New York: Cambridge University Press, 2009). For overviews, see William Mulligan and Maurice Bric, eds, *A Global History of Anti-Slavery Politics in the Nineteenth Century* (New York: Palgrave, 2013). For recent emphasis on slave resistance see James Walvin, *Freedom: The Overthrowing of the Slave Empires* (New York: Palgrave, 2019).

Antislavery Movement

	1967–1992	1993–2018
Britain	107	297
United States	53	113
Spain	39	28
Brazil	27	29
Caribbean	26	33
France	23	54
Africa	21	65
India	4	23
Haiti	4	23
Muslim/Islamic	4	12

Antislavery

	1967–1992	1993–2018
Britain	319	805
United States	303	626
Spain	247	222
Caribbean	181	354
Africa	169	401
France	163	338
Brazil	84	221
India	36	97
Muslim/Islamic	31	106
Haiti	29	103

Source: Historical Abstracts (EBSCO), 1920–2017. I have relied on the database as a proxy for approximating the global distribution of historiographic interest during the last half-century of historical literature on the subject. The listed sites also refer to areas and populations, so that Britain includes Britons/British and orbits under their jurisdiction. I have limited the list to the top ten in each table.

In examining the pattern of emerging global perspectives on antislavery, it is important to first note some long-term patterns of change and continuity in scholarship. The tables above are drawn from the comprehensive database of Historical Abstracts (EBSCO). Their source is a database of scholarly articles on antislavery extending back to the last third of the twentieth century. I note only some of the most salient points. Historically, articles linked to British antislavery have dominated the period as a whole. I also attempted to measure the linkages between totals for combinations of two sites under British antislavery of scholarly interest identified in the database. In this regard, history appears to have repeated itself in historiography. British abolitionism long remained the world's most globalizing abolitionist project. Britain, of course, committed the most substantial fiscal, naval and diplomatic resources to the abolition of the seaborne slave trade. Its civil society demonstrated the most durable national commitment to antislavery for a century and a half. Not coincidentally, it also remained the most expansive colonializing power in the world during the long period in which abolitionist projects were transformed into instruments of global domination.

The Western Hemisphere

The above tables also indicate that scholarly interest in Haiti, the Caribbean and Africa has increased dramatically during the past two decades. Soon after the first emancipations in the Americas, in the Northern United States, Haiti became the first plantation society in the Americas to abolish slavery. Nevertheless, its achievement remained a footnote in accounts of emancipation for more than a century and a half.[6] Thereafter, generations of diplomatic isolation, endemic internal difficulties and external condescension made that nation of little interest to historians of the abolitionist process. Its legacy was often dismissed as a regressive element in a narrative framed as linked to progressive Western civilization. Only towards the end of the twentieth century did Haiti begin to be accorded a global status in the history of antislavery. With this recognition has come intensive research and diverse assessments of its impact on the developments in other areas of the Atlantic. Its impact on the imagination of the enslaved throughout the Americas and the constraints on its revolutionary potential have also been closely examined.[7]

---

[6]See the often noted comment of R.R. Palmer on Haiti in *The Age of the Democratic Revolution: A Political History of Europe and America, 1760–1800*, 2 Vols. (Princeton, NJ: Princeton University Press, 1959–1964), Vol. 1, p. 188.
[7]For assessments of the Saint Domingue revolution, see David Barry Gaspar and David Patrick Geggus, eds, *A Turbulent Time: The French Revolution and the Greater Caribbean* (Bloomington: Indiana University Press, 1997); Ada Ferrer, *Freedom's Mirror: Cuba and Haiti in the Age of Revolution* (New York: Cambridge University Press, 2014); David P. Geggus, ed., *The Impact of the Haitian Revolution in the Atlantic World* (Columbia: University of South Carolina Press, 2001), pp. 247–52;

Some historians have emphasized Haiti's strategic reluctance to offer support and large-scale aid beyond its own borders in order to ensure its survival. Many abolitionists hesitated to invoke the revolution in response to continuous anti-abolitionist invocations of violent destructiveness and the massacres attendant upon its 'servile revolution'. Historians have also stressed the relative weakness of antislavery mobilization in extended wars of independence in mainland Spanish America after 1808. Their long and increasingly brutal conflicts offered slaves alternative paths to freedom through military service rather than civil society abolitionism, while postponing general emancipation for those unable or unwilling to risk recruitment into the military. There were clearly more slaves in the Americas after half a century of wars for independence in 1825 than there had been in 1804.[8]

Historians of the United States have found that African-Americans had to weigh the benefits and risks of choosing between the British and Haitian models of opposing slavery. Even implicit public commemorations of Haiti could provoke violent retaliation. The Haitian Revolution, though, inspires assessments of its legacy as a source of anti-abolitionism as well. One approach emphasizes the revolution's 'primordial position' in the history of slavery's suppression as ipso facto evidence of its inspirational status in all subsequent episodes of resistance. Others point to its deployment as a rationale for suppressing discussion of ameliorative legislation. Anglo-American abolitionism's commitment to non-violence inspired caution

---

David Patrick Geggus and Norman Fiering, eds, *The World of the Haitian Revolution* (Bloomington: Indiana University Press, 2009). Historiographically emblematic of Haiti's position in the *Cambridge World History of Slavery* is its placement as the first chapter in its segment on abolition; see David Geggus, 'Slavery and the Haitian Revolution' in Eltis, Engerman, Drescher, and Richardson, eds, *CHWS*, Vol. 4, pp. 321–43, as well as his edited works; Laurent Dubois, *Avengers of the New World: The Story of the Haitian Revolution* (Cambridge, MA: Belknap Press, 2004); Aline Helg, *Slaves No More: Self-Liberation before Abolitionism in the Americas, 1492–1838* (Charlottesville: University of Virginia Press, 2019); David Geggus, 'Haiti and its Revolution: Four Recent Books', *Radical History Review* 115 (2013), pp. 195-202; Jeremy David Popkin, 'The Haitian Revolution comes of age: ten years of new research', *Slavery and Abolition*, 42: 2 (2021), pp. 382–401. On French antislavery's long avoidance of the revolutionary Caribbean, see Myriam Cottias, 'Le silence de la Nation: de la nation: Les « vielles colonies » comme lieu de defenitions des dogmas republicains (1848–1905)', *Outre Mers: Revue d'Histoire* 90: 1 (2003), pp. 21–45.

[8] For works emphasizing the relative weakness of Haitian-style antislavery in the Spanish American wars of independence, see Peter Blanchard, *Under the Flags of Freedom: Slave Soldiers and the Wars of Independence in Spanish South America* (Pittsburgh, PA: University of Pittsburgh Press, 2008); and Jeremy Adelman, 'The Rites of Statehood: Violence and Sovereignty in Spanish America, 1789–1821', *Hispanic American Historical Review* 90: 3 (2010), pp. 391–422.

by African-American abolitionists as well.[9] Frederick Douglass, African America's most eloquent transatlantic abolitionist speaker, refrained from invoking Haiti's revolutionary example for decades before the American Civil War.

The major manifestation of massive slave uprisings in the Caribbean has also inspired a variety of interpretations in relation to British slavery's termination. In Barbados (1816), Demerara (1823) and Jamaica (1831), thousands of slaves rose against slavery. Assessing slave resistance in the Age of Revolution often revolves around weighing the relative significance of African traditions, French Revolutionary ideology and the Haitian model of collective resistance. The three major uprisings of British slaves, however, came in direct response to metropolitan legislative initiatives to constrain the slaveholders. The insurgents addressed themselves to this situation, and eschewed the Haitian precedent. Instead, they attempted to approach the pattern of metropolitan popular contention, identifying themselves as labourers forced to work without either wages or protection against physical abuse. Captured masters signed testaments to their good treatment. All told, less than one-third of the islands' whites lost their lives in the three uprisings combined than in Nat Turner's revolt in Virginia in 1831. Not only did the metropolitan context of the uprising alter the modus operandi of the slaves, but also brutal repressions of the insurgents altered the metropolitan perceptions of the masters.[10]

Re-examinations of the last three major emancipations in the Americas have abundantly identified the role of transnational networks

---

[9]See Jeffrey R. Kerr-Ritchie, *Rites of August First: Emancipation Day in the Black Atlantic World* (Baton Rouge: Louisiana State University Press, 2007), pp. 82–3 and pp. 225–8; Mitch Kachun, *Festivals of Freedom: Memory and Meaning in African American Emancipation Celebrations, 1808–1915* (Amherst: University of Massachusetts Press, 2003); Phillipe Girard, 'The Dark Star': New Scholarship on the Repercussions of the Haitian Revolution', *Canadian Journal of Latin American and Caribbean Studies* 36: 72 (2011); and Edward Rugemer, *The Problem of Emancipation: The Caribbean Roots of the American Civil War* (Baton Rouge: Louisiana State University Press, 2008). On transnational and transracial interaction against slavery in the United States, see Manisha Sinha, *The Slave's Cause: A History of Abolition* (New Haven, CT: Yale University Press, 2016).

[10]On Anglo-American slave uprisings, see Davis, *Inhuman Bondage*, ch. 11; Seymour Drescher, 'Civilizing Insurgency: Two Variants of Slave Revolts in the Age of Revolution' in Seymour Drescher and Pieter C. Emmer, eds, *Who Abolished Slavery? Slave Revolts and Abolitionism* (New York: Berghahn Books, 2010), pp. 120–32; Michael Craton, *Testing the Chains: Resistance to Slavery in the British West Indies* (Ithaca, NY: Cornell University Press, 1982), ch. 21; and Gelien Matthews, *Caribbean Slave Revolts and the British Abolitionist Movement* (Baton Rouge: Louisiana State University Press, 2006). For a detailed examination of individual strategies, see Sue Peabody, *Madelaine's Children: Family, Freedom, Secrets, and Lies in France's Indian Ocean Colonies* (New York: Oxford University Press, 2017).

in the process. Abolitionists in the United States both black and white appealed to and celebrated the British example and offered both models of mobilization and enthusiastic support to abolitionists both black and white during the generation before the American Civil War. A second wave of civil and military mobilizations in the 1860s and 1870s accelerated the emancipation of far more slaves in the Americas than had been liberated during the preceding 'age of abolition', between 1775 and 1848. The Union's victory in 1865 revived the international movement and increased pressure on the remaining rulers of slave societies in the Americas. Both in Spain and Brazil, antislavery civil society movements emerged that were more popular and effective than any of their prior counterparts outside the Anglo-American world.[11]

Brazilian antislavery, in particular, has been increasingly identified as its society's first national social movement. As with its British and American predecessors, abolitionists adopted and extended the repertoire of prior movements: the press, a network of local associations, theatrical performances and the courts. It amplified local activities with international public opinion. The movement had the peculiar advantages of mobilizing the largest contingents of free Afro-Brazilian men and women in the Americas. Finally, when the military refused to react to massive slave flights, the legislature was compelled to legislate unconditional emancipation without compensation in 1888.[12]

---

[11]On transnational antislavery exchanges, see Lawrence C. Jennings, *French Reaction to British Slave Emancipation* (Baton Rouge: Louisiana State University Press, 1988); and Maartje Janse, 'Holland as a Little England?', *Past and Present* 229: 1 (2015), pp. 123–60. At the level of international diplomacy, see Paul Michael Kielstra, *The Politics of Slave Trade Suppression in Britain and France, 1814–1848* (New York: St. Martin's Press, 2000); and João Pedro Marques, *The Sounds of Silence: Nineteenth-Century Portugal and the Abolition of the Slave Trade* (New York: Berghahn Books, 2006). For the interaction of Atlantic civil and military mobilizations in the longer processes of Spanish abolition, see Josep M. Fradera and Christopher Schmidt-Nowara, eds, *Slavery and Antislavery in Spain's Atlantic Empire* (New York: Berghahn Books, 2013); and Christopher Schmidt-Nowara, 'The Transition from Slavery to Freedom in the Americas after 1804' in Eltis, Engerman, Drescher, and Richardson, eds, *CHWS*, Vol. 4, pp. 466–85.

[12]See Angela Alonso, *The Last Abolition: The Brazilian Antislavery Movement 1868–1888* (Cambridge: Cambridge University Press, 2021); Celso Thomas Castilho, *Slave Emancipation and Transformation in Brazilian Political Citizenship* (Pittsburgh, PA: University of Pittsburgh Press, 2016); and Jeffrey Needell, *The Sacred Cause: The Abolitionist Movement, Afro-Brazilian Mobilization, and Imperial Politics in Rio de Janeiro* (Stanford: Stanford University Press, 2020). Setting Brazilian emancipation in tri-continental perspective is Ivana Stolze Lima, Keila Grinberg, and Daniel Aarão Reis, eds, *Instituições Nefandas: O fim da escravidão e da servidão no Brasil, nos Estados Unidos e na Rússia* (Rio de Janeiro: Fundação Casa de Rui Barbosa, 2018). Brazil and the United States, the largest slaveholding societies in the Americas, also generated the hemisphere's largest interracial civil society movements. On the importance of compensated emancipation to slave-owners in the Western Hemisphere, see Frédérique Beauvois, *Between Blood and Gold: The Debate over Compensation for Slavery in the Americas* (New York: Berghann Books, 2016).

The Eastern Hemisphere

While the historiography of antislavery in the Americas is overwhelmingly interwoven with the relations between overseas colonies and European empires of slavery, its counterparts on the Eastern hemisphere are more largely intertwined with expanding empires of antislavery. Here too, Britain is far more frequently linked to the abolitionist process in Afro-Asia that any other imperial power. In Africa, British withdrawal from the slave trade in 1807 brought the issue of abolition to Africa permanently, but did not prevent the expansion of slavery in Africa for almost another century. Slavery and closely related practices of servitude remained robust in Asia as well.[13]

The Muslim World

Although British abolitionists usually represented themselves and other Europeans as operating within the framework of Christianity, their initial contacts with the Muslim world naturally stressed antislavery as equally compatible with Islamic teachings. As late as 1867, the Paris International Antislavery Conference couched its appeal to the Ottoman ruler in terms of convergent religious traditions. The Sultan replied by confidently affirming his empire's credentials as a member of the 'civilized' world, noting legislation already taken against the slave trade. Affirmations of Islam as a major obstacle to antislavery increased with the acceleration of European imperialism in Africa and the new wave of European abolitionist societies in the late 1880s. Only after Brazil emancipated its slaves in 1888 could a religious differentiation between Christian and Muslim be definitely affirmed.

---

[13]See Gareth Austin, 'Slavery in Africa, 1804–1936' in Eltis, Engerman, Drescher, and Richardson, eds, *CHWS*, Vol. 4, pp. 174–96; Michael Ferguson and Ehud R. Toledano, 'Ottoman Slavery and Abolition in the Nineteenth Century' in Eltis, Engerman, Drescher, and Richardson, eds, *CHWS*, Vol. 4, pp. 197–225; Gwyn Campbell and Alessandro Stanziani, 'Slavery and Bondage in the Indian Ocean World, Nineteenth and Twentieth Centuries' in Eltis, Engerman, Drescher, and Richardson, eds, *CHWS*, Vol. 4, p. 226; Pamela Crossley, 'Dependency and Coercion in East Asian Labor, 1800–1949' in Eltis, Engerman, Drescher, and Richardson, eds, *CHWS*, Vol. 4, pp. 540–61. For a forceful analysis of the interaction of European abolitionism and Afro-Indian Ocean bondage see Alessandro Stanziani, *Labor on the Fringes of Empire: Voice, Exit and the Law* (New York: Palgrave Macmillan, 2018). See also, Robert Harms, Bernard K. Freamon, and David W. Blight, eds, *Indian Ocean Slavery in the Age of Abolition* (New Haven: Yale University Press, 2013); Bernard K. Freamon, *Possessed by the Right Hand: The Problem of Slavery in Islamic Law and Muslim Cultures* (Leiden/Boston: Brill, 2019).

Initially, British non-governmental abolitionists who acted as advocates of emancipation before both Christian and Muslim rulers could hardly employ language that implied the superiority of their own religion or the civilizational inferiority of their interlocutors. For a short period in the mid-nineteenth century, some European abolitionists could call out Christian nations that resisted emancipation by contrasting their commitment with that of the Bey of Tunis, who decreed abolition in his own realm in the 1840s. As noted, other Muslim rulers also adopted abolition laws against the slave trade as a means of sustaining independence from both European and non-European imperial domination.[14] One must also be wary of globally identifying abolitionist pressure on Muslim rulers as 'Western'. In most of continental Europe and the Americas, non-governmental abolitionist initiatives were quite modest. Until the last third of the nineteenth century, state-sponsored international pressure remained overwhelmingly British.

In the Eastern hemisphere there is also little evidence of non-slave mobilizations or of combinations of slaves and non-slaves against their own slave systems. Slaves were often reluctant to escape their captivity unless circumstances provided post-liberation security. The lack of large-scale antislavery mobilization of the free has also been a subject of increasing attention. Compensated and free-womb liberations, a frequent strategy for many emancipations in the West, were exceptional in the Afro-Asian orbit.[15]

The Indian Ocean World

Studies of antislavery and imperialism have been consistent with the overwhelming evidence of its enhancement by European empires in the East. Historians, however, have also paid particular attention to the ways

---

[14]See, for example, Raphael Cheriau, 'L' Intervention d'Humanité or the Humanitarian Right of Intervention in International Relations: Zanzibar, France and Britain between Colonial Expansion and the Struggle against the Slave Trade from the mid-19th Century to the early 2000s', Unpublished PhD Dissertation, University of Paris and University College of Dublin, 2017; and Ismael Musah Montana, *The Abolition of Slavery in Ottoman Tunisia* (Gainesville: University Press of Florida, 2013).

[15]For an analysis of the scholarship on slave emancipation in the Muslim World, see Ehud R. Toledano, 'Abolition and Anti-Slavery in the Ottoman Empire: A Case to Answer?' in Mulligan and Bric, eds, *A Global History of Anti-Slavery Politics*, pp. 117–36; Toledano considers the divergent perspectives of William Gervase Clarence-Smith, Amal N. Ghazal, Madeline Zilfi, Larguéche Abdelhamid and Michael Salman.

in which Europeans and non-Europeans deployed strategies to delay or even counteract full emancipation from coerced labour service or sexual servitude. As with slavery in the Americas, scholars seek to integrate and compare slavery and abolition in the East. Although Africa has offered a wide field for examining Afro-Asian abolition, the Indian Ocean world has provided the principal examples for exploring contrasting patterns of antislavery and imperialism.

The Indian Ocean World had a well-established Afro-Indian slave system pre-dating that of the Atlantic and at the time of British colonial emancipation in the 1830s. Large parts of the subcontinent of India were brought under British rule even before the launching of its antislavery movement. The Subcontinent contained many times the slave population liberated by British emancipation in the 1830s. The same European power that first permanently legislated to eliminate the slaves in its transatlantic dominions also delayed similar measures in Asia for more than half a century after the emergence of nationwide British abolitionism. India remained virtually off the agenda of metropolitan abolitionists during nearly half a century of successive British mobilizations against the transatlantic slave system. With a few exceptions, British abolitionists chose to virtually ignore the existence of slavery in India as a problem until the passage of West Indian emancipation was assured in 1833.

Most historians call attention to differences between the slave system and their relation to the metropole to explain the delay. First, the contrasts with the Western variant offered rationales differentiating Indian from West Indian slavery. Morally, abolitionist propaganda made a major point of diminishing responsibility for acting against a system that long predated New World slavery. British dominion in India rested on an entirely different basis than in the plantations. The absence of major metropolitan antislavery mobilizations was matched by the absence of major servile uprisings and the absence of both contemporary public celebrations and later commemorations.[16]

Moreover, the whole premise of British abolition in India actually followed the legal model that predated the rise of abolitionism. It followed

---

[16]See Andrea Major, *Slavery, Abolitionism and Empire in India, 1772–1843* (Liverpool: Liverpool University Press, 2012), ch. 4 and ch. 7; Richard Huzzey, 'The Moral Geography of Slavery', *Transactions of the Royal Historical Society* 22 (2012), pp. 111–39; Seymour Drescher, *Pathways From Slavery* (London: Routledge, 2018), pp. 261–80; and Nancy Gardner Cassels, *Social Legislation of the East India Company: Public Justice versus Public Instruction* (London: Sage Publications, 2010), pp. 173–208.

the strategy of Lord Mansfield regarding slavery in England in 1772. The Somerset decision in 1772 ruled that, in the absence of a positive legal sanction on slavery in England, no individual could be forced by the courts or constrained by masters to obedience on the grounds that the individual was or had been a slave. Applied to the government of India, Act V, in 1843, likewise declared that its courts would no longer recognize slavery or sales of persons for debt. 'Virtual extinction' of the status would presumably follow an individual's choice to exit from all non-contractual obligations. This mode of emancipation, now historiographically tagged as 'delegalization', or a 'slow death for slavery', would persist in Afro-Asian colonies wherever judicial or official legal complicity emphasized non-interference in indigenous religious customs or voluntary servitude. Variants of this 'delegalization' became a policy model for the abolition of slavery throughout the Afro-Indian Ocean World.[17]

In some areas of Africa, as earlier in the Americas, antislavery pressure from the European metropole offered opportunities for mass exoduses from enslavement. Elsewhere individuals or families had to navigate exits from slavery through administrative complicity with masters retaining indigenous structures of sexual or hereditary bondage, only to find themselves entangled with new barriers of race or class. In both Africa and Asia, metropolitan antislavery groups came to sanction and even enthusiastically support incremental systems of emancipation. At the same time, imperial states faced the task of continuing adherence to antislavery with concurrent aims to accelerate economic development and sustain social order. Governments retained broad powers to respect local social customs while recruiting labour for major military and infrastructural needs. In turn, local imperial agents could operationally suspend or moderate imperial pressures through concern for the welfare of their subjects. Such circumstances sustained old and new forms of bondage and opportunities for new antislavery denunciations of abuse.[18]

---

[17]See Suzanne Miers, 'Slavery to Freedom in Sub-Saharan Africa: Expectations and Reality' in Howard Temperley, ed., *After Slavery: Emancipation and its Discontents* (London: Frank Cass, 2000), pp. 237-64.
[18]Paul E. Lovejoy and Jan S. Hogendorn, *Slow Death for Slavery: The Course of Abolition in Northern Nigeria 1897-1936* (New York: Cambridge University Press, 1993); Martin A. Klein, *Slavery and Colonial Rule in French West Africa* (New York: Cambridge University Press, 1998); Martin A. Klein, ed., *Breaking the Chains: Slavery, Bondage, and Emancipation in Modern Africa and Asia* (Madison: University of Wisconsin Press, 1993); and Gwyn Campbell, ed., *Abolition and Its Aftermath in Indian Ocean Africa and Asia* (London: Routledge, 2005).

The fifty years after the 1880s marked the moment of maximum convergence between antislavery and the rationale for European domination. Antislavery was legally designated by European powers as a fixed principle of international law and the clearest indicator of membership in the civilizing process. Historians have demonstrated the means by which contemporary Asian and African rulers strove to align themselves with antislavery rhetoric in order to sustain their independence, while civilians invoked Western humanitarianism as a means of liberating East Asian coolies from indentured servitude in Latin America and Africa. Abolitionist societies themselves adopted the phrase 'inferior races' to designate those brought under imperial tutelage and to justify their own mission to redeem and rescue. Any number of forms of constraint could be embedded within the explicit hierarchies of this complex project. Nor was the creation of new hierarchies limited to Europeans.[19] One enduring constant in the abolition process has involved the adoption or continuation of alternative constraints on the emancipated. Variants of this practice were evident from the earliest legislated emancipations in the United States in the 1780s to the latest in Mauritania in 1981.

Historical permutations and combinations

Studies of antislavery now entail explorations of ongoing subordination and coercion as well as of emancipation. Its origins and development within European cultural and political contexts embedded it in a fundamentally non-egalitarian international system. Euro-American abolitionists generally embraced Europe's dominant religious affiliation, its conceptions of civilization, moral progress and the beneficence of its global expansion. Moreover, given the highly competitive nature of the great powers system, it would have been impossible for European statesmen to subscribe to an international antislavery consensus if antislavery had not been a single-issue project that could make

---

[19]See, inter alia, Hideaki Suzuki, ed., *Abolitions as a Global Experience* (Singapore: NUS Press, 2016), ch. 6 and ch. 8; Daniel V. Botsman, 'Freedom without Slavery? "Coolies," Prostitutes and Outcasts in Meiji Japan's Modernization Movement', *American Historical Review* 116 (2011), pp. 1323–47; Steffen Rimner, 'Chinese Abolitionism: The Chinese Educational Mission in Connecticut, Cuba, and Peru', *Journal of Global History* 11: 3 (2016), pp. 344–64; and Howard Temperley, 'African-American Aspirations and the Settlement of Liberia' in Temperley, ed., *After Slavery*, pp. 67–92.

allowances for other forms of post-emancipation coercion. Humanitarian interventions by groups were based on this formula. If allowances had to be made for degrees of coercion, European civil or political actors were necessary to maintain surveillance and exposure of abuses within empires.[20] More rarely, action might be taken against notoriously brutal regions. In this case, it was easier to target areas of the world dominated by lesser European powers like the Portuguese and Belgians in the Congo or by indigenous rulers. The relative strength of nations in the international arena set limits on antislavery opportunities and constraints.[21]

Europe's dominant historiographical narrative of its prior millennial transformation from classical slavery to modern freedom also allowed for abolitionist tolerance of indeterminate durations of constraints beyond the legal status of slavery. The earlier expansion of European-sponsored overseas slave systems in the Americas could be portrayed as either its own deviation from a longer, more fundamental civilizational process, or a rationalization for 'intermediary' forms of coercion as disciplinary stages of the 'civilizing' process. Variants of this narrative were enshrined in successive international conventions on the slave trade and slavery from the Vienna Declaration in 1815 to the Brussels Convention in 1890 and to the League of Nations Convention on Slavery in 1926.[22]

Within these broad frameworks of imperial tutelage and native subordination, historians have now analysed patterns of action by both Europeans and non-Europeans to take advantage of opportunities imposed to ameliorate or to resist their situations.[23] Apart from the ravages of the slave trade, administrators in the chain of command mostly feared the possibility

---

[20]Frederick Cooper, 'Networks, Moral Discourse and History' in Thomas M. Callaghy, Ronald Kassimier and Robert Latham, eds, *Intervention and Transnationalism in Africa: Global-Local Networks of Power* (New York: Cambridge University Press, 2001), pp. 23–46.

[21]For a comprehensive survey, see Susan Zimmerman, 'The Long-Term Trajectory of Anti-Slavery in International Politics: From the Expansion of the European International System to Unequal International Development' in Marcel van der Linden, ed., *Humanitarian Intervention and Changing Labor Relations: The Long-Term Consequences of the Abolition of the Slave Trade* (Leiden: Brill, 2011), pp. 435–97. For one synthesis of the interplay of European metropole and empire, see Richard Huzzey, *Freedom Burning: Anti-Slavery and Empire in Victorian Britain* (Ithaca, NY: Cornell University Press, 2012).

[22]See Suzanne Miers, *Britain and the Ending of the Slave Trade* (New York: Africana Publishing Company, 1975), and Suzanne Miers, *Slavery in the Twentieth Century: The Evolution of a Global Problem* (Lanham, MD: Rowman & Littlefield, 2003).

[23]For an excellent example of how new variants of abolitionist legislation played out in the two hemispheres, emphasizing the interactions of both ex-slave and ex-masters, see Dylan C. Penningroth, 'The Claims of Slaves and Ex-Slaves to Family and Property: A Transatlantic Comparison', *American Historical Review* 112: 4 (2007), pp. 1039–69.

of large-scale economic, social and family disruption, a consideration that had prevailed in India even before the British antislavery movement first turned its attention to abolition and emancipation in the African colonies. Local representatives of the government, therefore, consciously resisted attempts to impose metropolitan values that might disrupt those of their areas of responsibility. Finally, among agents on the ground, there was little evidence of Adam Smith's dictum that free labour was more efficient than coerced labour.[24]

Diminution and diffusion: The last century of antislavery in historiography

As noted, for more than a century and a half, the historiography of antislavery remained dominated by its Atlantic initiators. Victories over slavery were encapsulated within a narrative of progressive expansion marked by successive national acts and international agreements linked to Western cultural and economic frames of reference. Major events in the twentieth century began to register a shift to new historiographical perspectives. Even before the outbreak of the Great War in 1914, antislavery's legacy had inspired analogous social movements to adapt its rhetoric and methods of agitation. While traditional frameworks of evangelical philanthropy vied with new discourses of human rights to expose abuses in the Congo, racially charged campaigns against 'Chinese slavery' in South Africa could simultaneously be deployed to ensure the return of Liberals to power in Britain.[25]

---

[24]Ehud Toledano, *As if Silent and Absent: Bonds of Enslavement in the Middle East* (New Haven, CT: Yale University Press, 2007). On the range of gender issues, see Pamela Scully and Diana Paton, eds, *Gender and Slave Emancipation in the Atlantic World* (Durham, NC: Duke University Press, 2005); and Kathryn Kish Sklar and James Brewer Stewart, eds, *Women's Rights and Transatlantic Antislavery in the Era of Emancipation* (New Haven, CT: Yale University Press, 2007). See also Suzanne Miers and Richard Roberts, eds, *The End of Slavery in Africa* (Madison: University of Wisconsin Press, 1988); Frederick Cooper, *From Slaves to Squatters: Plantation Labor and Agriculture in Zanzibar and Coastal Kenya, 1890–1925* (New Haven, CT: Yale University Press, 1980); and Andrew Zimmerman, *Alabama in Africa: Booker T. Washington, the German Empire, and the Globalization of the New South* (Princeton, NJ: Princeton University Press, 2010).
[25]See Kevin Grant, *A Civilised Savagery: Britain and the New Slaveries in Africa, 1884–1926* (London: Routledge, 2005).

Although the First World War disrupted international antislavery mobilizations that had emerged in the late 1880s, the post-war League of Nations Covenant on Slavery (1926) constituted a milestone in the legal definition of slavery and the basis for international interrogation of its ongoing impact on colonial Afro-Asia. Despite these successes, the reversals of liberalism in the following decades disempowered and demoralized all forms of humanitarian intervention. Italy's invocation of antislavery to rationalize the conquest of Ethiopia in the 1930s discredited the case of imperialist humanitarianism even before the wave of anti-colonialism following the Second World War.[26]

Slavery and forced labour also expanded exponentially in Eurasia during the Second World War. The Nuremberg tribunals enumerated slavery among the designated crimes against humanity. For the first time, agents of a state were tried and sentenced to incarceration or execution. Yet, antislavery societies appear to have played no role in publicizing or attempting to influence its proceedings. The voice of the British Anti-Slavery Society was reduced to a whisper during the Second World War and its immediate aftermath. The period clearly marked a nadir for organized antislavery. This is reflected in both contemporary and subsequent historiography as a scholarly hiatus as well.[27] Of the hundreds of articles listed under 'antislavery' in the Historical Abstracts database, only twenty-six were published between 1940 and 1955. The absence of extensive references to antislavery precedents at Nuremberg, thus, prefigured its very modest place in the global histories of slavery and antislavery.[28] Although the Universal Declaration of Human Rights (1948) designated slavery as its first violation of those rights, the newer waves of post-structural histories of antislavery have themselves focused on examples from their earlier Euro-colonial frame of reference and their examples of racial, cultural and gendered hierarchies.

---

[26]See Jean Allain, ed., *The Legal Understanding of Slavery: From the Historical to the* Contemporary (New York: Oxford University Press, 2012); Suzanne Miers, *Slavery in the Twentieth Century: The Evolution of a Global Problem* (Lanham, MD: Rowman and Littlefield, 2003); and Amalia Ribi Forclaz, *Humanitarian Imperialism: The Politics of Anti-Slavery Activism, 1880–1940* (New York: Oxford University Press, 2015). The persistence of forced labour in Western-dominated Africa during the 1930s was as significant as its surge in the Soviet Union; see Susan Pedersen, *The Guardians: The League of Nations and the Crisis of Empire* (New York: Oxford University Press, 2015), pp. 237–60.

[27]On the Nuremberg legacy, see Kim C. Priemel and Alexa Stiller, eds, *Reassessing the Nuremberg Military Tribunals: Transitional Justice, Trial Narratives and Historiography* (New York: Berghahn Books, 2012).

[28]See James Heartfield, *The British and Foreign Anti-Slavery Society, 1838–1956* (New York: Oxford University Press, 2016), pp. 417–18.

The new historiography developed in the context of a more global conception of the equality of national cultures and of an internationalism defined by human rights, rather than of Christian obligations or Western-defined processes of acculturation.[29]

As for contemporary movements against slavery, Joel Quirk observes that 'classical slavery' now occupies an altered position within a context of contemporary legal movements. The change can be documented in hundreds of currently self-designated antislavery associations. 'The Online Anti-Slavery Directory' advertises hundreds of organizations. Few include 'Anti-Slavery' in their targeted objectives. Instead they target forced, bonded and child labour; sex trafficking; forced marriage; and domestic servitude. Scholars have, thus, felt the need to approach 'contemporary' slaveries reconfigured in broader frames of reference, and themes in connected and comparative terms as movements in economy, society, culture or transgenerational microhistories of families and communities.[30]

Spatial constraints prevent a more extensive discussion of another recent development in the historiography of antislavery. A novelty of the twenty-first century has been the emergence of historical projects designed to explore the legacies of slavery as an ongoing commitment and to re-envision and repair those legacies. In 2010, *Slavery and Abolition*'s 'Annual Bibliographical Supplement' recognized the burgeoning literature on these subjects by creating a new sub-section called 'Representation and Memories'. Some of the milestones in this burgeoning field were energized by anniversary commemorations of the history of abolition. Although originating in commemorations of triumphal moments in metropolitan antislavery, they become catalysts in assessments of the legacy of slavery. A collective historiographical mobilization of descendants of slaves now contest older histories of emancipation from the perspective of the slaves, the masters and their descendants.[31] Attention has more and more circumscribed forms of coercion and targeted populations.

---

[29]Kevin Grant, 'Human Rights and Sovereign Abolitions of Slavery, c. 1885–1958' in Kevin Grant, Philippa Levine, and Frank Trentmann, eds, *Beyond Sovereignty: Britain, Empire and Transnationalism, c. 1880–1950* (New York: Palgrave, 2007), pp. 80–102.
[30]See the many transnational collective volumes cited throughout this chapter, as well as forthcoming volumes such as the already cited Lima, Grinberg and Reis, *Instituições Nefandas*; and Helg, *Slaves No More*.
[31]For major recent assessments of memorialization, see Charles Forsdick, 'Humanity's Empty Plinth: Commemorating Slavery in Contemporary France', *Atlantic Studies* 9: 3 (2012), pp. 279–97; and James Walvin, 'The Slave Trade, Abolition and Public Memory', *Transactions of the Royal Historical Society* 19 (2009), pp. 139–49.

In examining contemporary antislavery, scholars must explicitly clarify similarities and differences between 'classical' and 'contemporary' slavery, as well as variants in different areas of the world. Historians have also begun to critically investigate the global dimensions of approaches to 'contemporary slavery'. This entails close attention to the shifting definitions of slavery in a world where the traditional forms of legal slavery have been abolished by every existing national state. It is also a world in which non-governmental organizations identify themselves as antislavery human rights associations to an unprecedented extent. Historians also take account of these practices in relation to older statuses such as serfdom and indentured labour. They evoke their antislavery predecessors' dedication to the complete eradication of 'slavery in all its forms'.[32]

Equally significant, especially in the wake of the bicentennial of British slave trade abolition in 2007, academic conferences were held on every continent. Older histories of antislavery, emphasizing the rescue of the suppressed and helpless, are now joined by a historiography centred around an emphasis on slave resistance and the extent to which abolition emanates from that resistance. In parts of the world where there are fewer records of collective resistance and a continuation of post-abolition remembrance, isolation creates conditions of individual reticence to admit having descended from that still stigmatized past. Yet, the pattern and its history can quickly emerge in societies with the most persistent consciousness of slave ancestry, if a sense of collective solidarity and efficacy emerges. In such situations, the background of enslavement creates opportunities to discuss anti-enslavement from the perspective of the once enslaved.[33]

New venues for the study of slavery and abolition have also proliferated in both the Eastern and Western hemispheres in the form of university study centres, archival collections, museums, public school curricula and specialized institutes. Diaspora and local descendants of slavery demand the construction or removal of sites of memory related to the history of slavery. Projects for the remembrance and examination of non-Western legacies

---

[32] For a discussions of some of these permutations and why analysing contemporary slavery remains especially problematic in parts of the world such as India, Mauritania and Sudan, see Joel Quirk, *The Anti-Slavery Project: From the Slave Trade to Human Trafficking* (Philadelphia: University of Pennsylvania Press, 2011), esp. pp. 247–52; Allain, ed., *The Legal Understanding of Slavery*, pp. 281–374; and Annie Bunting and Joel Quirk, eds, *Contemporary Slavery: Popular Rhetoric and Political Practice* (Vancouver: University of British Columbia Press, 2017).

[33] Compare Martin A. Klein, 'Studying the History of Those Who Would Rather Forget: Oral History and the Experience of Slavery', *History of Africa* 16 (1989), pp. 209–17 with *Cahiers d'Etudes Africaines: Réparations, restitutions, réconciliations: Entre Afriques, Europe et Ameriques* 173–174 (2004).

of slavery expand.[34] The urge to develop comprehensive global histories of antislavery, noted at the beginning of this chapter, also remains intact, in seeking to integrate the long-term confluence of human interactions and attitudes that appear to have diminished the relative magnitude of slavery in all its forms.[35] Appropriately, the closing volume of the *Cambridge World History of Slavery* ends with Kevin Bales's chapter 'Coercive Labor Practices – Slavery Today' looking ahead: 'The question we face in the future is how abolition might be mobilized when cross-border intervention of the sort that Britain employed is no longer seen to be possible or acceptable.'[36]

Bibliography

Castilho, Celso Thomas, *Slave Emancipation and Transformation in Brazilian Political Citizenship* (Pittsburgh, PA: University of Pittsburgh Press, 2016).

Davis, David Brion, *The Problem of Slavery in the Age of Emancipation* (New York: Knopf, 2014).

Drescher, Seymour, *Abolition: A History of Slavery and Antislavery* (New York: Cambridge University Press, 2009).

Drescher, Seymour, *Pathways from Slavery: British and Colonial Mobilizations in Global Perspectives* (London: Routledge, 2018).

Eltis, David, Stanley L. Engerman, Seymour Drescher, David Richardson, eds, *The Cambridge World History of Slavery*, Vol. 4 *AD 1804-AD 2016* (Cambridge: Cambridge University Press, 2017).

Forclaz, Amalia Ribi, *Humanitarian Imperialism: The Politics of Anti-Slavery Activism, 1880–1940* (New York: Oxford University Press, 2015).

Fradera, Josep M. and Christopher Schmidt-Nowara, eds, *Slavery and Antislavery in Spain's Atlantic Empire* (New York: Berghahn Books, 2013).

Freamon, Bernard K., *Possessed by the Right Hand: The Problem of Slavery in Islamic Law and Muslim Cultures* (Leiden/Boston: Brill, 2019).

---

[34]For examples of this new globalizing impulse in the historiography of antislavery, see Ella Keren, 'The Transatlantic Slave Trade in Ghanaian Academic Historiography', *William and Mary Quarterly* 66: 4 (2009), pp. 975–1000.

[35]See David Eltis, 'Abolition and Identity in the Very Long Run' in Wim Klooster, ed., *Migration, Trade, and Slavery in an Expanding World: Essays in Honor of Pieter Emmer* (Leiden: Brill, 2009), pp. 227–58.

[36]Kevin Bales, 'Contemporary Coercive Labor Practices– Slavery Today' in Eltis, Engerman, Drescher, and Richardson, eds, *CHWS*, Vol. 4, pp. 573–677.

Harms, Robert, Bernard K. Freamon, and David Blight, eds, *Indian Ocean Slavery in the Age of Abolition* (New Haven; London: Yale University Press, 2013).

Klein, Martin A., ed., *Breaking the Chains: Slavery, Bondage, and Emancipation in Modern Africa and Asia* (Madison: University of Wisconsin Press, 1993).

Mulligan, William and Maurice Bric, eds, *A Global History of Anti-Slavery Politics in the Nineteenth Century* (New York: Palgrave, 2013).

Quirk, Joel, *The Anti-Slavery Project: From the Slave Trade to Human Trafficking* (Philadelphia: University of Pennsylvania Press, 2011).

Sinha, Manisha, *The Slave's Cause: A History of Abolition* (New Haven, CT: Yale University Press, 2016).

Suzuki, Hideaki, ed., *Abolitions as a Global Experience* (Singapore: NUS Press, 2016).

6

Comparative and transnational histories of slavery

Enrico Dal Lago
National University of Ireland Galway

Both comparative and transnational approaches have characterized histories of slavery carried out by professional historians in the past seventy-five years. Since the 1940s, a number of historical monographs have compared similarities and differences between aspects of slave societies in different parts of the world, while subsequent studies, from the 1980s, have investigated similarities and differences between the rise and development of different types of unfree and free labour in a number of regions and have contributed significantly to broadening our perspectives on many issues related to the historical development of slavery. In writing these studies, historians of slavery have followed distinct comparative methodologies, which, in turn, have characterized subsequent historiographical phases of comparative historical scholarship with different historiographical focuses. Conversely, even though the term 'transnational' is relatively recent, transnational studies focusing on the historical phenomena of movements of goods, people and ideas have characterized the works of many scholars of slavery at least since the 1960s. Subsequently, from the 1990s, the 'transnational turn' in world history has recast those studies as pioneering works and models for a historiographical approach focusing on the discovery of previously little-known connections between different regions of the world, as a result of the global reach of the economic, social and political ramifications of world slavery.[1]

In this chapter, in analysing the historiographical developments related to the comparative approach and to the transnational approach to histories of slavery, for the purpose of clarity, on the one hand, I treat the application of the comparative historical method in relation to *the institution of slavery* as an economic, social and political system, while, on the other hand, I look at the development of the transnational approach in relation to the study of *the historical practice of the slave trade*. My reason for this distinction is that, in general terms, comparative history analyses two or more case studies of institutions in isolation and at specific moments in time, and this has been the case also with comparative historical studies of two or more slave societies, or slave systems, or systems of unfree and free labour. Conversely, the transnational approach has always characterized those studies that focused on the historical practice of trading in slaves, because the slave trade connected, in the course of several centuries, the people of different regions and nations of the world in economic, social and political terms, thereby constituting a major transnational historical phenomenon.

With regard to comparative approaches to histories of slavery (A), we can clearly distinguish two categories of historical analysis implemented by scholars working on the institution of slavery in comparative perspective:

1. Global comparisons of slavery, focusing on similarities and differences between regional versions of the institution of slavery across the world, either synchronically (at the same point in time) or diachronically (at different times).
2. Comparisons focusing on similarities and differences between forms of slavery, or forms of unfree labour, or forms of unfree and free labour in different regions – that is in two or more specific regions – of the Atlantic world and/or the Euro-American world, or Africa, or Australasia.

---

[1] On comparative and transnational historiographical developments of world slavery, see Michael Zeuske, *Handbuch Geschichte der Sklaverei: Eine Globalgeschichte von den Anfangen bis zur Gegenwart*, 2nd ed. (Berlin: De Gruyter, 2019), pp. 27–96. With specific reference to the Euro-American World, see Enrico Dal Lago, *American Slavery, Atlantic Slavery, and Beyond: The U.S. 'Peculiar Institution' in International Perspective* (London: Routledge, 2012), pp. 1–17.

Similarly, with regard to the transnational historical practice of the slave trade (B), we can also clearly distinguish two different categories of historical analysis that have characterized scholarly studies:

1. Global and transnational studies of the historical practice of the slave trade, across times and places, throughout history and all over the world.
2. Transnational historical studies of the practice of the slave trade focusing on specific regions of the world, such as the Atlantic from the sixteenth century to the nineteenth century, or Africa or Asia from medieval times to the modern eras.

In the course of this chapter, I intend, first, to analyse the historiographical development of the two categories of analysis implemented by comparative historians with regard to the institution of slavery. Subsequently, I intend to analyse the historiographical development of the two transnational categories that have characterized the works of scholars working on the historical practice of the slave trade. Finally, I intend to briefly look at two particularly significant new approaches in relation to the development of comparative and transnational histories of world slavery, following the insights coming from the innovative work of Joseph Miller and Michael Zeuske.[2]

Comparative approaches to histories of slavery

Modern comparative approaches to the history of world slavery (A1) began with the works of David Brion Davis, who, with his crucial series on 'the problem of slavery', inaugurated a new way of looking at comparative slavery in the New World as an integrated, and very important, part of world history. In four studies published over the course of five decades – *The Problem of Slavery in Western Culture* (1966), *The Problem of Slavery in the Age of Revolutions* (1975), *Slavery and Human Progress* (1984) and *The Problem of Slavery in the Age of Emancipation* (2014) – Davis elaborated the

---

[2]Joseph C. Miller, *The Problem of Slavery as History: A Global Approach* (New Haven, CT: Yale University Press, 2012); and Zeuske, *Handbuch Geschichte der Sklaverei*. See also Peter Kolchin, 'The South and the World', *Journal of Southern History* 75: 3 (2009), pp. 565–80.

first comparative diachronic view of the ideologies related to the different types of slave systems that succeeded one another during the development of Western civilization, until slavery's eventual abolition. Beginning with Greco-Roman civilization, Davis gradually arrived, through the selection of particularly significant episodes, to treat the nineteenth century, showing clearly the degree of continuity in the ideologies that justified slavery from the ancient world to the modern world, and providing a number of comparative suggestions for further studies. Particularly important in this respect was the claim that, in contrast with the ancient, medieval and early modern societies, in which slavery went fundamentally unchallenged, in the modern world the influence of the Enlightenment and of the doctrine of natural rights, together with the spread of the classical capitalist notion of 'free' labour, led intellectuals and economists to consider slavery, for the first time in its long history, as an inhuman and backward labour system, and led to the spread of antislavery ideologies and movements.[3]

Equally influential was the most thorough single-volume comparative historical analysis of slavery to date: Orlando Patterson's *Slavery and Social Death* (1982). This complex study by a premier historical sociologist became quickly the privileged model for world histories and comparative histories of slavery shortly after it was published. By engaging in an extremely wide-ranging comparison of hundreds of slave societies in different regions of the world and at different points in history, Patterson attempted to formulate a universally valid definition of the basic constitutive elements of slavery across time and space. Eventually, Patterson encapsulated his definition in the now famous expression of 'social death', which indicated the special status of property that characterized slaves in every historical society he analysed – a status that placed them outside the social structures that regulated the life of free individuals.[4] Besides Davis and Patterson, only a handful of scholars have attempted similarly wide-ranging comparative studies of slavery across space and time. Among the few who have done so, most notable, in recent times, are Joel Quirk and Michael Zeuske. In *Unfinished Business* (2009), Joel

---

[3] David Brion Davis, *The Problem of Slavery in Western Culture* (New York: Oxford University Press, 1966); David Brion Davis, *The Problem of Slavery in the Age of Revolutions, 1770-1825* (Ithaca, NY: Cornell University Press, 1975); David Brion Davis, *Slavery and Human Progress* (New York: Oxford University Press, 1984); David Brion Davis, *The Problem of Slavery in the Age of Emancipation* (New York: Knopf, 2014).

[4] Orlando Patterson, *Slavery and Social Death: A Comparative Study* (Cambridge, MA: Harvard University Press, 1982). For a shorter, more recent, study with a similar scope and along similar lines, see Alain Testart, *L'institution de l'esclavage. Une approche mondiale* (Paris: Gallimard, 2018, orig. pub. in 2001 as *L'esclave, la dette, et le pouvoir*).

Quirk, an expert in the legal history of human bondage, has written a survey of the entirety of the historical phenomenon of slavery and its abolition at different times and in different places, both in order to arrive at some general defining features and also in order to account for the large variety of forms of slavery that have existed in the past and partly continue to exist in our present world.[5] Conversely, in his monumental *Handbuch Geschichte der Sklaverei* (Handbook of the History of Slavery, second edition 2019), Michael Zeuske has produced the most comprehensive scholarly guide to the historiography and history of slavery across time and space available in a single volume. His book is full of insights, especially with regard to the way it deals with the major historiographical issues and it attempts to systematize the scholarship and the historical evidence on slavery by dealing with broad comparable themes and features, as well as with the plethora of historical transnational links between slave societies from ancient times to the present.[6]

Most commonly, groups of experts on slavery in different times and places have taken part in wide-ranging edited collections analysing either forms of slavery or unfree labour diachronically, often by making comparisons between the ancient and modern worlds, or else by providing comprehensive world histories of slavery with chapters on the theory and practice of slavery in different historical periods and regions of the world, and thus providing implicitly ample material for broad comparisons across time and space. Among the former types of studies, most notable are *Slavery and Other Forms of Unfree Labor* (1988), edited by Leonie J. Archer; *Slave Systems: Ancient and Modern* (2008), edited by Enrico Dal Lago and Constantina Katsari; *Debt and Slavery in the Mediterranean and Atlantic Worlds* (2013), edited by Gwyn Campbell and Alessandro Stanziani; and *What Is a Slave Society?* (2018), edited by Noel Lenski and Catherine D. Cameron.[7] All the above edited collections are notable for their attempts at defining distinguishing features of slavery both through explicit and implicit comparisons of several different forms of slavery at various times and in different regions of the

---

[5]Joel Quirk, *Unfinished Business: A Comparative Survey of Historical and Contemporary Slavery* (Paris: UNESCO, 2009).
[6]Zeuske, *Handbuch Geschichte der Sklaverei*.
[7]Leonie J. Archer, ed., *Slavery and Other Forms of Unfree Labor* (London: Routledge, 1988); Enrico Dal Lago and Konstantina Katsari, eds, *Slave Systems: Ancient and Modern* (New York: Cambridge University Press, 2008); Gwyn Campbell and Alesandro Stanziani, eds, *Debt and Slavery in the Mediterranean and Atlantic Worlds* (London: Taylor and Francis, 2013); and Noel Lenski and Catherine M. Cameron, eds, *What Is a Slave Society? The Practice of Slavery in Global Perspective* (New York: Cambridge University Press, 2018).

world. Conversely, two other recent edited collection have been much more ambitious in scope by claiming to provide world histories of slavery, one in a single volume and the other in four volumes, and thus providing ample material for detailed comparative studies of slavery across time and space. The former is *The Routledge History of Slavery* (2011), edited by Gad Heuman and Trevor Burnard, while the latter is *The Cambridge World History of Slavery* (2011–), edited by Keith Bradley, Paul Cartledge, Seymour Drescher, David Eltis, Stanley Engerman and David Richardson.[8] While the Routledge volume distinguishes itself for the combination of both specific treatments of selected times and places and broad themes analysed across several different slave societies, the Cambridge four-volume work (of which three have appeared), with much more room at its disposal, represents the most comprehensive history of slavery all over the world from ancient times to the present ever published. Though both works are extremely useful for comparative historians of slavery, the *Cambridge World History of Slavery* is invaluable in terms of providing a comprehensive overview of all the forms of slavery that existed in the four historical periods (roughly the ancient, medieval, early modern and modern eras) treated in the four volumes.

Comparative approaches to slavery in specific regions of the world

The historiographical tradition of comparative slavery in specific regions (A2) is particularly rich with regard to the Atlantic and Euro-American world, where it began with the publication of Frank Tannenbaum's *Slave and Citizen* (1947). Tannenbaum sought to explain the now disproven assumption that slavery in the United States, despite its apparent similarity to slavery in Latin America, appeared much harsher than the latter in legal terms, and he found the explanation in the United States' much

---

[8]Gad Heuman and Trevor Burnard, eds, *The Routledge History of Slavery* (London: Routledge, 2011); and Keith Bradley and Paul Cartledge, *The Cambridge World History of Slavery*, Vol. 1: *The Ancient Mediterranean World* (New York: Cambridge University Press, 2011); David Eltis and Stanley L. Engerman, eds, *The Cambridge World History of Slavery*, Vol. 3: *AD1420–AD1804* (New York: Cambridge University Press, 2011); David Eltis, Stanley L. Engerman, Seymour Drescher, and David Richardson, eds, *The Cambridge World History of Slavery*, Vol. 4: *AD1804–AD2016* (New York: Cambridge University Press, 2017).

more exploitative version of capitalism, unmitigated by the Catholic Church. Although not intended as a specifically comparative work, Stanley Elkins's later work, *Slavery* (1959), did much to reinforce Tannenbaum's idea and led to the so-called Tannenbaum-Elkins hypothesis.[9] Thus, early comparative works by Herbert Klein and Carl Degler aimed at proving or disproving the 'Tannenbaum-Elkins' hypothesis. In *Slavery in the Americas* (1967), Herbert Klein focused his comparative study on Virginia and Cuba in the nineteenth century, while in *Neither Black Nor White* (1971), Carl Degler focused his comparison on the United States as a whole and Brazil, taking a broad view at the entire course of their history. It is significant that, while Klein ended up offering further support to Tannenbaum and Elkins, Degler arrived at opposite conclusions, arguing, in particular, that the slave system in Brazil was more rigid and brutal than the slave system in the United States.[10]

In the same period during which Herbert Klein and Carl Degler wrote their pioneering studies, Eugene Genovese elaborated his complex theory on the antebellum US South's slave system, and, anticipating future developments, he often added, in support of his hypotheses, important notations and discussions with comparative themes. This emerges clearly particularly in *The World the Slaveholders Made* (1969) and *Roll, Jordan, Roll* (1974), in both of which Genovese used often examples coming from his studies of other slave societies of the American continent, particularly Brazil, in order to highlight better particular aspects of his notion that the slave system of the antebellum US South was unique, because of the particular 'pre-bourgeois' features of the ideology and behaviour of southern planters, and the specific characteristics of the type of paternalism that masters exercised on their slaves in southern plantations.[11] By the 1970s, as the historiographic revolution centring upon slave agency – the broadly constituted effort to place slaves at the centre of the narrative – reached its heyday, US-originated models of interpretation of the origins and main

---

[9]Frank Tannenbaum, *Slave and Citizen* (New York: Vintage, 1946); Stanley Elkins, *Slavery: A Problem in American Institutional and Intellectual Life* (Chicago: University of Chicago Press, 1959).
[10]Herbert Klein, *Slavery in the Americas: A Comparative Study of Virginia and Cuba* (Chicago: University of Chicago Press, 1967); Carl Degler, *Neither Black Nor White: Slavery and Race Relations in the U.S. and Brazil* (Madison: University of Wisconsin Press, 1971).
[11]Eugene Genovese, *The World the Slaveholders Made: Two Essays in Interpretation* (New York: Vintage, 1968); Eugene Genovese, *Roll, Jordan, Roll: The World the Slaves Made* (New York: Vintage, 1974).

features of slavery were influencing, and were themselves influenced by, research on slave societies in the Caribbean and Latin America. This cross-fertilization led to a few explicit comparative studies, above all Gwendolyn Midlo Hall's *Social Control in Slave Plantation Societies* (1971), focused on slavery and racism as means to preserve social order in eighteenth-century St Domingue and nineteenth-century Cuba. At the same time, Genovese's *From Rebellion to Revolution* (1979) referred clearly to a comprehensive interpretation of slave revolts that went beyond the continental American horizon and looked at broader comparative points, as also an important collection edited by Genovese and Laura Foner – *Slavery in the New World* (1969) – had done at the end of the previous decade.[12]

As a result of all these developments, by the early 1980s, the comparative perspective on slavery in the Americas became an integral part of the emerging historical discipline of Atlantic History – the study of the history of the societies that created an integrated Atlantic world between the sixteenth and the nineteenth centuries. Thus, within Atlantic History, a number of studies produced from the 1980s onwards focused on either explicit or implicit comparisons between North American and Latin American varieties of slavery. This can be seen particularly in four collection of essays: *Cultivation and Culture* (1993) edited by Ira Berlin and Philip Morgan; *More than Chattel* (1996), edited by David Barry Gaspar and Darlene Clark Hine; and *Tropical Babylons* (2003), edited by Stuart Schwartz; and *The Oxford Handbook of Slavery in the Americas* (2010) edited by Robert Paquette and Mark Smith.[13] To these, we must also add five particularly important monographs: *Feitores do corpo, missionarios da mente* (2004) by Rafael Marquese; *The Comparative Histories of Slavery in Brazil, Cuba, and the United States* (2007) by Laird Bergad; *A Tale of Two Plantations* (2014) by Richard Dunn; *Planters, Merchants, and Slaves* (2015) by Trevor Burnard;

---

[12]Gwendolyn Midlo Hall, *Social Control in Slave Plantation Societies: A Comparison of Saint Domingue and Cuba* (Baton Rouge: Louisiana State University Press, 1971); Eugene Genovese, *From Rebellion to Revolution: Afro-American Slave Revolts in the Making of the Modern World* (Baton Rouge: Louisiana State University Press, 1979); Laura Foner and Eugene Genovese, eds, *Slavery in the New World: A Reader in Comparative History* (New York: Prentice Hall, 1969).
[13]Ira Berlin and Philip Morgan, eds, *Cultivation and Culture: Labor and the Shaping of Slave Life in the Americas* (Charlottesville: University of Virginia Press, 1993); David Barry Gaspar and Darlene Clark Hine, eds, *More Than Chattel: Black Women and Slavery in the Americas* (Bloomington: University of Indiana Press, 1996); Stuart Schwartz, ed., *Tropical Babylons: Sugar and the Making of the Atlantic World* (Chapel Hill: University of North Carolina Press, 2003); Robert L. Paquette and Mark M. Smith, eds, *The Oxford Handbook of Slavery in the Americas* (New York: Oxford University Press, 2010).

and *The Plantation Machine* (2016) by Trevor Burnard and John Gerrigus.[14] While the latter three monographs compared plantation life and slave management in specific regions of the Atlantic – Jamaica and Virginia in one case, St Domingue and Jamaica in another case and the British colonies in yet another case – the former two monographs, in different ways, compared explicitly and specifically the three main nineteenth-century slave societies in the Americas: the United States, Cuba and Brazil. In fact, increasingly, many scholars who have compared nineteenth-century slavery in the United States, Cuba and Brazil have found important similar features, which several historians have encapsulated in the concept of 'second slavery', following the lead, above all, of Dale Tomich's *Through the Prism of Slavery* (2004) and his edited collection *Slavery and Historical Capitalism during the Nineteenth Century* (2017).[15] In recent times, the 'second slavery' has grown increasingly in importance as a comparative approach, also as a result of its crucial link to the ever-growing scholarship on the connection between nineteenth-century slavery and the emergence of modern global capitalism – a scholarship best represented by Sven Beckert's world-ranging study *Empire of Cotton* (2014).[16]

At the same time, other comparative works have focused either on comparisons within the English-originated slave systems, or on comparisons within the non-English slave systems in the Atlantic, and have included syntheses such as *Questioning Slavery* (1996) by James Walvin, on slavery in the English-speaking parts of the Americas, and *African Slavery in Latin America and the Caribbean* (2007) by Herbert Klein and Ben Vinson – this latter the second edition of a very successful survey of slavery in the Latin American countries.[17] Also, and more importantly, from the 1990s, several major scholars have published overall comparative syntheses on Atlantic

---

[14] Rafael de Bivar Marquese, *Feitores do corpo, missionarios da mente: Senhores, letrados e o controle dos escravos nas Americas, 1660–1860* (São Paulo: Companhia das Letras, 2004); Laird Bergad, *The Comparative Histories of Slavery in Cuba, Brazil, and the United States* (New York: Cambridge University Press, 2007); Richard S. Dunn, *A Tale of Two Plantations: Slave Life and Labor in Jamaica and Virginia* (Boston, MA: Harvard University Press, 2014); Trevor Burnard, *Planters, Merchants, and Slaves: Plantation Societies in British America* (Chicago: University of Chicago Press, 2015); Trevor Burnard and John Gerrigus, *The Plantation Machine: Atlantic Capitalism in French Saint-Domingue and British Virginia* (Philadelphia: University of Pennsylvania Press, 2016).
[15] Dale Tomich, *Through the Prism of Slavery: Labor, Capital, and World Economy* (Lanham, MD: Rowan & Littlefield, 2004); Dale Tomich, ed., *Slavery and Historical Capitalism during the Nineteenth Century* (Lanham, MD: Lexington Books, 2017).
[16] Sven Beckert, *Empire of Cotton: A Global History* (New York: Vintage, 2014).
[17] James Walvin, *Questioning Slavery* (London: Routledge, 1996); and Herbert Klein and Ben Vinson, *African Slavery in Latin America and the Caribbean* (New York: Cambridge University Press, 2007).

and New World slavery, among which the most important were *The Rise and Fall of the Plantation Complex* (1990) by Philip Curtin, *The Making of New World Slavery* (1997) by Robin Blackburn, *Slavery, Emancipation, and Freedom: Comparative Perspectives* (2007) by Stanley Engerman, *From Slavery to Freedom* (1999) by Seymour Drescher, *Inhuman Bondage* (2006) by David Brion Davis, *Abolition* (2009) by Seymour Dresher and *The American Crucible* (2011) by Robin Blackburn. All of the above works have looked at the entire development of slave systems in the Americas – and thus in a very wide comparative perspective – as an essential part of world history, arguing at the same time about the crucial importance of the European background to Atlantic slavery.[18]

In this connection, since the beginning of the 1980s, a smaller group of scholars, all of them comparative historians, has argued in favour of an even wider perspective than that of Atlantic studies, pointing out the comparability between New World slavery and other types of labour – mostly 'unfree' – spread outside the Americas, and therefore extending the comparative historical approach to the entirety of the Euro-American world. By broadening the geographical scope and employing an innovative methodology, comparison through an enlarged Atlantic perspective, which includes the whole of Europe and also Africa, has proven a particularly fruitful terrain for the writing of broader types of comparative studies. These have focused particularly on slavery in the nineteenth-century American South and either unfree labour in South Africa, as in George Fredrickson's *White Supremacy* (1981); or Russian and Prussian serfdom, as in the case of Peter Kolchin's *Unfree Labor* (1987) and Shearer Davis Bowman's *Masters and Lords* (1993); or sharecropping and tenancy in southern Italy, as in Enrico Dal Lago's *Agrarian Elites* (2005). Moreover, this enlarged perspective has generated a debate on the nature of slavery and serfdom in world history, which in turn has produced comparative works even wider in scope. Particularly important among these are *Serfdom and Slavery*

---

[18]See Philip Curtin, *The Rise and Fall of the Plantation Complex: Essays in Atlantic History* (New York: Cambridge University Press, 1990); Robin Blackburn, *The Making of New World Slavery, 1492-1800: From the Baroque to the Modern* (London: Verso, 1997); Seymour Drescher, *From Slavery to Freedom: Comparative Studies in the Rise and Fall of Atlantic Slavery* (New York: Springer, 1999); David Brion Davis, *Inhuman Bondage: The Rise and Fall of Slavery in the New World* (New York: Oxford University Press, 2006); Stanley Engerman, *Slavery, Emancipation, and Freedom: Comparative Perspectives* (Baton Rouge: Louisiana State University Press, 2007); Seymour Drescher, *Abolition: A History of Slavery and Antislavery* (New York: Cambridge University Press, 2009); and Robin Blackburn, *The American Crucible: Slavery, Emancipation, and Human Rights* (London: Verso, 2011).

(1996) and *Servitude in Modern Times* (2000), one edited and the other authored by Michael Bush; *American Slavery, Atlantic Slavery, and Beyond* (2012), authored by Enrico Dal Lago; *The Second Slavery*, edited by Javier Laviña and Michael Zeuske; and *The Politics of the Second Slavery* (2016) and *New Frontiers of Slavery* (2017), both edited by Dale Tomich. All of the above have argued, in different ways, in favour of the comparability of New World slavery – whose nineteenth-century iteration, with an aggressive and exploitative capitalist ideology and practice at its core, is Tomich's 'second slavery' – with an ever wider range of case studies of unfree labour in different regions and at different times.[19]

In recent years, comparative studies have extended well beyond the Euro-American world to encompass both Asia and Africa in wide-ranging survey both of forms of slavery and also of serfdom and other varieties of unfree labour. An early and pioneering edited collection of essays, which compared the large variety of forms of bonded labour in both the Asian and African continents, institutionally, economically and socially, was *Asian and African Systems of Slavery* (1980), edited by James L. Watson; among the few more recent studies that have compared varieties of slavery across time and space in Africa and Asia, it is worth citing especially *Slavery and Resistance in Africa and Asia* (2005), edited by Edward Alpers, Gwyn Campbell and Michael Salman.[20] Specifically regarding Asia, a particularly important edited collection is *Debt and Labor in the Indian Ocean World* (2013), edited by Gwyn Campbell and Alessandro Stanziani, which gathered essays with a geographical span ranging from the Arabian Gulf to China,

---

[19]See George Fredrickson, *White Supremacy: A Comparative Study of South Africa and the U.S.* (New York: Oxford University Press, 1981); Peter Kolchin, *Unfree Labor: American Slavery and Russian Serfdom* (Cambridge, MA: Harvard University Press, 1987); Shearer Davis Bowman, *Masters and Lords: Mid-Nineteenth Century U.S. Planters and Prussian Junkers* (New York: Oxford University Press, 1993); Enrico Dal Lago, *Agrarian Elites: American Slaveholders and Southern Italian Landowners, 1815–1861* (Baton Rouge: Louisiana State University Press, 2005); Michael L. Bush, ed., *Serfdom and Slavery: Studies in Legal Bondage* (London: Longman, 1996); Michael L. Bush, *Servitude in Modern Times* (Cambridge: Polity Press, 2000); Dal Lago, *American Slavery, Atlantic Slavery, and Beyond*; Javier Laviña and Michael Zeuske, eds, *The Second Slavery: Mass Slaveries and Modernity in the Americas and the Atlantic Basin* (Berlin: Lit Verlag, 2014); Dale Tomich, ed., *The Politics of the Second Slavery* (Binghamton, NY: SUNY Press, 2016); Dale Tomich, ed., *New Frontiers of Slavery* (Binghamton, NY: SUNY Press, 2016).

[20]James L. Watson, ed., *Asian and African Systems of Slavery* (Berkeley: University of California Press, 1980); Edward A. Alpers, Gwyn Campbell, and Michael Salman, eds, *Slavery and Resistance in Africa and Asia* (London: Routledge, 2005). For an important innovative study that compares and places in transnational connection, instead, Africa and the Americas in relation to the 'second slavery', see Paul Lovejoy, *Jihad in West Africa during the Age of Revolutions* (Columbus: Ohio University Press, 2016).

and with a chronological focus on the period between the seventeenth and the nineteenth centuries.[21] Stanziani has also authored a groundbreaking work entitled *Bondage* (2014), which has pushed even further the boundaries of comparative history of slavery and serfdom by encompassing the entire Eurasia, from Russia to Central Asia and India, and analysing the institutional and social history of a wide variety of forms of bonded labour in those areas in comparative perspective.[22]

Regarding Africa, the most celebrated comparative history of the wide varieties of slave societies in the entire African continent from the sixteenth to the twentieth century remains *Transformations of Slavery* (now in its 4th edition, 2011), authored by Paul Lovejoy, which has been recently joined by *Slavery and Slaving in African History* (2014) by Sean Stillwell, who has attempted a definition of African slaveries through the comparative analysis of their various functions across time and space.[23] Important edited collections which have compared slavery and its demise in a number of regions of Africa, particularly in the nineteenth and twentieth centuries, include *Slavery in Africa* (1977) edited by Suzanne Miers and Igor Kopytoff; *Women and Slavery in Africa* (1983), edited by Claire C. Robertson and Martin A. Klein; *The End of Slavery in Africa* (1988), edited by Suzanne Miers and Richard Roberts; and *Slavery and Colonial Rule in Africa* (1999), edited by Suzanne Miers and Martin Klein. More recent studies have moved beyond Africa and attempted comparisons between slavery in Africa, Asia and the Atlantic – as in *Women and Slavery* (2007), edited by Gwyn Campbell, Suzanne Miers and Joseph Miller – and between African and American varieties of slavery and their demise – as in *The End of Slavery in Africa and the Americas* (2011), edited by Ulrike Shmieder, Katja Füllberg-Stolberg and Michael Zeuske.[24]

---

[21] Gwyn Campbell and Alessandro Stanziani, eds, *Bonded Labor and Debt in the Indian Ocean World* (London: Taylor and Francis, 2013).
[22] Alessandro Stanziani, *Bondage: Labor and Rights in Eurasia from the Sixteenth to the Early Twentieth Centuries* (New York: Berghahn, 2014).
[23] Paul Lovejoy, *Transformations of Slavery: A History of Slavery in Africa*, 4th ed. (New York: Cambridge University Press, 2011).
[24] Suzanne Miers and Igor Kopytoff, eds, *Slavery in Africa: Historical and Anthropological Perspectives* (Madison: University of Wisconsin Press, 1977); Claire C. Robertson and Martin A. Klein, eds, *Women and Slavery in Africa* (London: Heinemann, 1983); Suzanne Miers and Richard Roberts, eds, *The End of Slavery in Africa* (Madison: University of Wisconsin Press, 1988); Suzanne Miers and Martin Klein, eds, *Slavery and Colonial Rule in Africa* (London: Frank Cass, 1999); Gwyn Campbell, Suzanne Miers, and Joseph Miller, eds, *Women and Slavery*, Vol. 1: *Africa, the Indian Ocean World, and the Medieval North Atlantic*, Vol. 2: *The Modern Atlantic* (Athens: University of Georgia Press, 2007); and Ulrike Schmieder, Katja Füllberg-Stolberg, and Michael Zeuske, eds, *The End of Slavery in Africa and the Americas: A Comparative Approach* (Berlin: Lit Verlag, 2011).

Transnational approaches to histories of the slave trade

Transnational approaches to the study of world slavery are particularly evident in studies of the history of the slave trade – an activity, which was, by definition, transnational, as it put in contact different parts of the world at different times. Only a few studies, though, have looked at the history of the slave trade as a global transnational phenomenon (B1) either by focusing on the long-term connections between Africa, Europe, the Islamic world and the Atlantic, or by considering the 'Middle Passage' – the specific name of the trade in slaves from Africa to the Americas – as one of several forced migrations that have characterized modern history. Specifically, in his book *Les Traites Negrieres* (The Black Slave Trades, 2005), Olivier Pétré-Grenouilleau has looked at the slave trades from Africa to the Mediterranean and from Africa to the Atlantic in comparative perspective as constituent parts of a single 400-year-long history of impact of the African diaspora on the modern Eurasian and Atlantic worlds. Conversely, in their groundbreaking co-edited collection *Many Middle Passages* (2007), Emma Christopher, Cassandra Pybus and Marcus Rediker have situated the slave trade from Africa in the context of a global history of forced migrations of slaves, indentured servants, convicts and many other categories of individuals forcibly transported from one end to another of the Atlantic, Indian and Pacific Oceans. Together, these two works represent highly innovative global approaches to the history of the slave trade as a phenomenon tightly linked to slavery's dimensions and durability in world history.[25]

Particularly important for the transnational approach to the study of the historical practice of the slave trade in specific regions of the world (B2) has been the scholarship focusing on the Atlantic, whose initiator had been Philip Curtin. With his seminal study *The Atlantic Slave Trade* (1969), Curtin had effectively written the first comparative treatment of the Atlantic slave trade, analysing the role of the European colonizing powers, as well as looking at it also from the African and American perspectives. Curtin's main focus had been specifically on statistics and on the volume of the trade. However, his study provided a model for various types of subsequent studies, such as

---

[25]Olivier Petre-Grenouilleau, *Le traits negrieres. Essai d'histoire globale* (Paris: Gallimard, 2005); Emma Christopher, Cassandra Pybus, and Marcus Rediker, eds, *Many Middle Passages: Forced Migration and the Making of the Modern World* (Berkeley: University of California Press, 2007).

Herbert Klein's comparative monograph *The Middle Passage* (1978), which engaged in an increasingly deeper and more complex comparative analysis of both the different types of Atlantic slave trades and also the different effects that the trades had on Africa and on the Americas. Klein, then, perfected his approach in his synthetic study *The Atlantic Slave Trade* (1999).[26]

Important comparative edited collections on the transnational practice of the slave trade in the Atlantic include *Slavery and the Rise of the Atlantic System* (1993), edited by Barbara Solow; and *The Atlantic Slave Trade* (1992), edited by Joseph Inikori and Stanley Engerman.[27] As a result of the editors' and authors' strong links with the increasingly sophisticated scholarship on the Atlantic slave trade, the above collections have come to represent crucial steps in the attempts at building an overall Atlantic framework within which to fruitfully compare, by means of juxtaposition, insightful case studies originating from different slave societies in the Americas. Moreover, as Atlantic History has grown as a discipline and the Atlantic framework has become increasingly dominant among historians of slavery in the Americas, several scholars have begun to investigate thoroughly, and in comparative perspective, the African backgrounds of the slave populations of the Atlantic system. Thus, important monographs with a more or less explicit comparative dimension written since the 1990s – such as *The Black Atlantic* (1993) by Paul Gilroy; *Way of Death* (1997) by Joseph C. Miller; *Africa and Africans in the Making of the Atlantic World* (1998) by John Thornton; *Saltwater Slavery* (2007) by Stephanie Smallwood; and *Slavery and African Ethnicities in the Americas* (2007) by Gwendolyn Midlo Hall – have done much to place African culture and society at the heart of those momentous transformations that, in comparable ways all across the Americas, gave origin to an Atlantic system of slavery. While Gilroy has argued convincingly in favour of the existence of a shared Black Atlantic culture, Miller has looked at the economic interrelationships between Africa, Europe and the Americas in the Angolan slave trade, while Thornton has analysed the African societies' and elites' involvement in the early Atlantic world. Then,

---

[26] Philip Curtin, *The Atlantic Slave Trade: A Census* (Madison: University of Wisconsin Press, 1969); Herbert S. Klein, *The Middle Passage: Comparative Studies in the Atlantic Slave Trade* (Princeton, NJ: Princeton University Press, 1978); Herbert S. Klein, *The Atlantic Slave Trade*, 2nd ed. (New York: Cambridge University Press, 1999, 2010).

[27] See Barbara Solow, ed., *Slavery and the Rise of the Atlantic System* (New York: Cambridge University Press, 1993); Joseph Inikori and Stanley Engerman, eds, *The Atlantic Slave Trade: Effects on Economies, Societies, and Peoples in Africa, the Americas, and Europe* (Durham, NC: Duke University Press, 1992).

building on Thornton's pioneering work, Smallwood has written about the African perspective on the Atlantic slave trade and the latter's role in erasing and reconstituting African identities, while Midlo Hall has focused specifically on the persistence of African identities among particular ethnic groups that were brought to the New World.[28]

More recently, a number of both general and regional studies have characterized the scholarship on the Atlantic slave trade, which has continued to show the importance of the transnational approach to the study of Atlantic slavery. Among the general studies, particularly important are Marcus Rediker's *The Slave Ship* (2007), James Walvin's *Crossings* (2013), Barbara Solow's *The Economic Consequences of the Atlantic Slave Trade* (2014), David Eltis and David Richardson's *Atlas of the Transatlantic Slave Trade* (2015) and Sowande' Mustakeem's *Slavery at Sea* (2016). Either by focusing on the actual voyage across the Atlantic, or at the economic and statistical analysis of the consequences of the slave trade, or else by looking at the process of forging strong links and interdependencies between Africa, Europe and the Americas, all these studies have reiterated and emphasized the transnational dimensions of the Atlantic slave trade. The same can be said for studies focused on specific areas of the Atlantic interested by the slave trade, among which it is worth mentioning two recent studies that have dealt with the interconnections between West Central Africa and the Americas: Daniel Domingues Da Silva's *The Atlantic Slave Trade from West Central Africa* (2017); and Felipe Luiz de Alencastro, *The Trade in the Living* (2018).[29]

Important transnational studies have characterized also the scholarship on the slave trade in Africa and Asia, particularly in the Indian Ocean,

---

[28]Paul Gilroy, *The Black Atlantic: Modernity and Double Consciousness* (London: Verso, 1993); Joseph C. Miller, *Way of Death: Merchant Capitalism and the Angolan Slave Trade, 1730–1830* (Madison: University of Wisconsin Press, 1997); John Thornton, *Africa and Africans in the Making of the Atlantic World, 1440–1800* (New York: Cambridge University Press, 1998); Stephanie Smallwood, *Saltwater Slavery: A Middle Passage from Africa to American Diaspora* (Cambridge, MA: Harvard University Press, 2007); and Gwendolyn Midlo Hall, *Slavery and African Ethnicities in the Americas: Restoring the Links* (Chapel Hill: University of North Carolina Press, 2007).
[29]Marcus Rediker, *The Slave Ship: A Human History* (London: John Murray, 2007); James Walvin, *Crossings: Africa, the Americas, and the Atlantic Slave Trade* (London: Reaktion Books, 2013); Barbara L. Solow, *The Economic Consequences of the Atlantic Slave Trade* (Lanham, MD: Lexington Books, 2014); David Eltis and David Richardson, *Atlas of the Atlantic Slave Trade* (New Haven, CT: Yale University Press, 2015); Sowande' M. Mustakeem, *Slavery at Sea: Terror, Sex, and Sea in the Middle Passage* (Urbana: University of Illinois Press, 2016); Daniel B. Domingues Da Silva, *The Atlantic Slave Trade from West Central Africa, 1780–1867* (New York: Cambridge University Press, 2017); Luiz Felipe de Alencastro, *The Trade in the Living: The Formation of Brazil in the South Atlantic, Sixteenth to Seventeenth Centuries* (Binghamton, NY: SUNY Press, 2018).

which, similarly to the Atlantic, represented a focal area of coexistence and of economic and cultural exchanges between slave societies that flourished in different continents. Some of the most important scholarly works in this respect are *The Structure of Slavery in Indian Ocean Africa and Asia* (2004), edited by Gwyn Campbell; *Resisting Bondage in Indian Ocean Africa and Asia* (2007), edited by Edward Alpers, Gwyn Campbell and Michael Salman; the already cited *Debt and Labor in the Indian Ocean World* (2013), edited by Gwyn Campbell and Alessandro Stanziani; and Hideaki Suzuki's *Slave Trade Profiteers in the Western Indian Ocean* (2017).[30] Importantly, scholars have produced also important transnational studies dealing with the internal slave trades that characterized different regions within Africa and Asia – as in Patrick Manning's pioneering *Slavery and African Life* (1990), a demographic study which dealt with both Africa's internal trade and also with the Atlantic's and Indian Ocean's slave trades; and in Jeff Eden's recent work on *Slavery and Empire in Central Asia* (2018), which is the first scholarly study on the vast and neglected eighteenth- and nineteenth-century trade in Iranian and Russian slaves across the Asian continent.[31]

New approaches

Arguably, the most important new departure in terms of scholarly approaches to comparative and transnational histories of slavery is represented by Joseph Miller's implementation of the concept of 'slaving' in world history. Miller has criticized the established practice of comparing the different varieties of slavery as an institution for being static and for treating slave societies as if they were, effectively, frozen at a particular moment in time. Conversely, Miller has argued, specifically with regard to 'New World slaveries', in favour of historicizing 'slaving as a process resulting from changing strategies of people in consistent positions of marginality to the quite distinctive times and places in which they resorted to slaving to intrude on older, more

---

[30]Gwyn Campbell, ed., *The Structure of Slavery in Indian Ocean Africa and Asia* (London: Frank Cass, 2004); Edward A. Alpers, Gwyn Campbell, and Michael Salman, eds, *Resisting Bondage in Indian Ocean Africa and Asia* (London: Routledge, 2007); Campbell and Stanziani, eds, *Bonded Labor and Debt in the Indian Ocean World*; and Hideaki Suzuki, *Slave Trade Profiteers in the Western Indian Ocean: Suppression and Resistance in the Nineteenth Century* (New York: Palgrave, 2017).
[31]Patrick Manning, *Slavery and African Life: Occidental, Oriental, and African Slave Trades* (New York: Cambridge University Press, 1990); Jeff Eden, *Slavery and Empire in Central Asia* (New York: Cambridge University Press, 2018).

established interests'.[32] Thus, following Miller's suggestions, we could think of the entire world history of slavery as a succession of dynamic processes and strategies of 'slaving' occurring in different places and at different times. And therefore, Miller's intuition would bear important consequences for future comparative and transnational studies by historians of world slavery. First, the distinction between slavery and slave trade would lose its meaning, since both were parts of the historical processes and strategies of 'slaving', which, by virtue of the effects of its dynamic nature on world history, continuously created transnational links and connections between different regions of the world at different times. At the same time, one could reasonably wonder whether, instead of comparing varieties of slavery as an institution, it would be possible to compare different historical processes and strategies of slaving, either synchronically or diachronically.

Certainly, a world history of slavery written following Miller's ideas would look very different from the standard world histories of slavery that still dominate comparative and transnational historical scholarship, as Michael Zeuske's *Handbuch Geschichte der Sklaverei* clearly demonstrates. At the heart of Zeuske's work on the historiography and the history of world slavery is precisely the dynamic concept of 'slaving' as a process and a strategy, which is historicized according to the different times and places in which it occurred. At the same time, though, the preference for this approach has not prevented Zeuske from acknowledging the importance of both comparative and transnational views of the world history of slavery that have characterized older scholarly works. More than this, in an important article, published in 2008, Zeuske argued that historical comparison had grown out of its initial attempts to find static 'ideal-types' and had come to focus on comparison of historical processes, thus sharing a great deal with the dynamic nature of transnational historical approaches.[33] Therefore, Zeuske hinted at the possibility of integrating comparative and transnational approaches in the historical study of slavery, as also other scholars of slavery, among whom Peter Kolchin, have done recently in their works.[34] Arguably, by combining

---

[32]Miller, *The Problem of Slavery as History*, 14. See also Joseph C. Miller, 'Slaving as Historical Process: Examples from the Ancient Mediterranean and the Modern Atlantic' in Enrico Dal Lago and Constantina Katsari, eds, *Slave Systems: Ancient and Modern* (New York: Cambridge University Press, 2008) pp. 70–102.
[33]Zeuske, *Handbuch Geschichte der Sklaverei*; Michael Zeuske, 'Comparing or Interlinking? Economic Comparisons of Early Nineteenth-Century Slave Systems in the Americas in Historical Perspectives' in Dal Lago and Katsari, eds, *Slave Systems*, pp. 166–73.
[34]See Peter Kolchin, 'The South and the World', *Journal of Southern History* 75: 3 (2009), pp. 565–80.

together the methodologies proper of comparative and transnational approaches to the world history of slavery with the implementation of the concept of 'slaving' as a historicized process and strategy, and therefore by focusing on transnational comparisons of specific historical examples of 'slaving' across time and space, future historians will be in a better position to write an accurate historical account of the world history of human bondage from antiquity to the present.[35]

Bibliography

Beckert, Sven, *Empire of Cotton: A Global History* (New York: Vintage, 2014).
Bradley, Keith, Paul Cartledge, David Eltis, and Stanley Engerman, eds,
    The Cambridge World History of Slavery, 4 Vols. (New York: Cambridge University Press, 2011).
Campbell, Gwyn, ed., *The Structure of Slavery in Indian Ocean Africa and Asia* (London: Frank Cass, 2004).
Christopher, Emma, Cassandra Pybus, and Marcus Rediker, eds, *Many Middle Passages: Forced Migration and the Making of the Modern World* (Berkeley: University of California Press, 2007).
Dal Lago, Enrico, and Constantina Katsari, eds, *Slave Systems: Ancient and Modern* (New York: Cambridge University Press, 2008).
Heuman, Gad and Trevor Burnard, eds, *The Routledge History of Slavery* (London: Routledge, 2011).
Inikori, Joseph, and Stanley Engerman, eds, *The Atlantic Slave Trade: Effects on Economies, Societies, and Peoples in Africa, the Americas, and Europe* (Durham, NC: Duke University Press, 1992).
Miller, Joseph C., *The Problem of Slavery as History: A Global Approach* (New Haven, CT: Yale University Press, 2012).
Patterson, Orlando, *Slavery and Social Death: A Comparative Study* (Cambridge, MA: Harvard University Press, 1982).
Stanziani, Alessandro, *Bondage: Labor and Rights in Eurasia from the Sixteenth to the Early Twentieth Centuries* (New York: Berghahn, 2014).

---

[35]For an up-to-date overview of the current state of the art of comparative studies of slavery on a global scale, which takes into account both Miller's and Zeuske's works and argues for an integration of the comparative and transnational methodologies, see Matthias Van Rossum, 'Slavery and Its Transformations: Prolegomena for a Global and Comparative Research Agenda', *Comparative Studies in Society and History* 63: 3 (2021), pp. 566–98.

Part II

Themes and methods

7

Political and legal histories of slavery

Sue Peabody
Washington State University

Other than marriage, slavery may be the oldest and most widespread social institution in the world. From ancient Babylonia and Egypt to pre-Columbian societies in the Americas, to China, Africa and Europe, most societies have recognized some form of slavery and have established laws and regulations to manage it. Implicit in these legal systems is the idea that some slavery is just, legitimate and necessary – an idea that goes against virtually all modern political philosophy, from Marxism to liberal democracy. As David Brion Davis, one of the foremost historians of antislavery, noted, while the morality of slavery troubled Western philosophers from Aristotle to Locke, the sustained political campaigns to abolish slavery, beginning in the 1760s, were something wholly new in history.[1]

As widespread as slavery was in the ancient, medieval and early modern world, it also varied considerably. For example, classical Hindu authors distinguished fifteen different words to mean 'slave', depending on whether the individual had been taken captive in war, had been born to an enslaved mother, had been pawned for debt, had been given as a gift and so on.[2]

---

[1] David Brion Davis, *The Problem of Slavery in Western Culture* (Ithaca, NY: Cornell University Press, 1966), p. 13.
[2] Gyan Prakash, 'Terms of Servitude: The Colonial Discourse on Slavery and Bondage in India' in Martin A. Klein, ed., *Breaking the Chains: Slavery, Bondage, and Emancipation in Modern Africa and Asia* (Madison: University of Wisconsin Press, 1993), pp. 131–49.

Implicit in the laws regulating slavery and abolition were the political, religious and economic orders of each society: kinship and patriarchy; monarchy, democracy or military dictatorship; class, forms of sustenance, debt and exchange. As these systems varied from state to state, and because the field of history grew up with the rise of the nation-state, many of the earliest studies of slavery were focused on specific political and legal regimes.

This chapter begins with studies of particular imperial or national regimes, starting with the ancient Western world, and then moves on to the European empires that regulated slavery in the Atlantic world from the sixteenth through the nineteenth centuries. The history of slave law in the United States receives special attention, because it has had a profound influence on historiographical debates in the field. We, then, turn to several very influential works in the comparative history of slavery and abolition. Finally, we consider a recent trend in the legal history of slavery and freedom: biographical and microhistorical studies, where the lives of enslaved individuals or families become the lens through which to understand slavery and abolition within a wider frame.

The political state as a frame

The laws regulating slavery varied historically between each particular empire, nation or state, and within each state over time. Not only did the laws vary from government to government, but so did the structures of the courts, rules of evidence and precedents. Recent trends advocating comparative, global or transnational history show that, to do this well, one must first understand the particular historical institutions, legislation, social structures and cultures of one or more societies, and how these have changed over time. As a result, most historians of the past half century or so have initially focused exclusively on a single empire, nation, colony or state.

One factor that should be considered in analysing historical slave systems from the perspective of the present is that the modern concept of 'race' was not foundational to ancient or medieval slavery. The Babylonian *Code of Hammurabi* (c. 1754 BCE) of ancient Mesopotamia punished slaves more heavily than free people for the same crimes, but slaves could come from any origin (including Europe), and therefore former slaves ('freedmen') were not identifiable by colour. The Torah and Old Testament, which regulated slaveholding for Jews and early Christians, permitted the enslavement of

Hebrews, but only for a period of six years, after which 'he shall go free, for nothing' (Exodus 21:2). The association of blackness and slavery was a result of the Atlantic slave system, which did not begin to emerge until the early sixteenth century when race, as a legal construct, gradually entered some systems of law.[3]

Roman law offers the most systematic and comprehensive slave law system in the ancient world. In 1980, Moses I. Finley's *Ancient Slavery and Modern Ideology* warned modern historians not to allow ideological biases (celebration of classical culture, Marxism or racial ideology) distort their understandings of the past.[4] In the late 1980s, two historians published overviews of ancient Roman slavery. Alan Watson offered an overview of Roman slave law as *prescription*, that is, how the laws defined and regulated slavery. He included chapters on enslavement, manumission and citizenship; freedmen, patrons and the state; the slave as a thing; the slave as a man (both in non-commercial and commercial relations); the master's acquisitions through slaves; punishment of slaves; and the torture and execution of the slaves of a murdered owner.[5] The following year, Keith Bradley published a very different *descriptive* account of Roman slavery, paying, in his words, 'particular attention to what it was like – or to what I think it was like – to be a Roman slave'.[6]

The tension between these two approaches – *prescriptive* and *descriptive* – lies at the heart of the legal and political histories of slavery. Political historians consider the authorities that produced the legislation (e.g. monarchs, legislators, judges). Legal historians take the law as their essential subject, identifying the fundamental juridical principles that underlie a (supposedly internally consistent) field of jurisprudence. Social historians famously consider the history 'from the bottom up', that is from the perspective of the more oppressed members of society, and thus are less concerned with defining a coherent legal doctrine than with locating the

---

[3] The legal regulation of race is a vast topic; a good starting place on this topic is Benjamin Braude, 'The Sons of Noah and the Construction of Ethnic and Geographical Identities in the Medieval and Early Modern Periods', *William and Mary Quarterly* 54: 1 (1997), pp. 103–42.
[4] Moses I. Finley, *Ancient Slavery and Modern Ideology* (New York: Viking Press, 1980).
[5] Alan Watson, *Roman Slave Law* (Baltimore, MD: Johns Hopkins University Press, 1987). However, Watson's subsequent study, *Slave Law in the Americas* (Athens: University of Georgia Press, 1989), tends to overstate the influence of Roman law on modern slavery legislation. A clear and concise overview of Roman slave law can be found in Jane F. Gardner, 'Slavery and Roman Law' in Keith Bradley and Paul Cartledge, eds, *The Cambridge World History of Slavery*, Vol. 1: *The Ancient Mediterranean* (Cambridge: Cambridge University Press, 2011), pp. 414–37.
[6] Keith Bradley, *Slavery and Society at Rome* (Cambridge: Cambridge University Press, 1988), p. xi.

agency and resistance of those regulated by law. The best histories of slavery go beyond mere accounts of how the law prescribed behaviours for masters and slaves to consider law and reality from the perspectives of the people negotiating within them: state actors who produced the laws, the masters, the free people and the slaves themselves. In the wake of the 'linguistic turn' – a historiographical trend dating from the 1990s and shaped by methods of literary analysis – historians are increasingly sceptical of truth claims of historical documents, which were, after all, created primarily by and for the master class. It is by reading the surviving primary sources 'against the grain', that is, by asking questions that the documents themselves were not designed to answer, that historians can discover deeper truths about the past.

Prior to the arrival of Portuguese traders in the fifteenth century, forms of slavery existed in West Africa, though they are challenging to study because of the limited documentary record from this period.[7] Since household slavery was widespread in Muslim societies from Iberia and North Africa through the Middle East and South Asia to Indonesia, Islamic law (*shari'ah*) discussed slavery in many different contexts, including inheritance, marriage, and commercial and criminal law.[8] Muslim traders brought their legal practices and understandings to the lands they inhabited, and emphasized humane treatment of slaves and the manumission of female concubines who bore their master's children. It is possible that some of these principles, such as *maktuba*, or a slave's gradual manumission through self-purchase, passed into Spanish and Portuguese law as *coartacíon/coartação*.

Portuguese and Spanish monarchs issued legislation to regulate slavery within their European lands in the Middle Ages, and these laws were extended to their overseas colonies in the sixteenth and seventeenth centuries.[9] A combination of metropolitan (European) and local colonial regulations, then, evolved to address the changing demographic, economic and cultural conditions in the colonies of Latin America, Africa and Asia. The Spanish decision to ban the enslavement of indigenous Americans (*indios*) in 1542 led to the dramatic rise in the African slave trade, which, in turn, led to the

---

[7]Robin Law, *Slave Coast of West Africa, 1550–1750: The Impact of the Atlantic Slave Trade on an African Society* (New York: Oxford University Press, 1991).
[8]William Gervase Clarence-Smith, *Islam and the Abolition of Slavery* (New York: Oxford University Press, 2006), pp. 1–16; and Behnaz A. Mirzai, Ismael Musah Montana, and Paul E. Lovejoy, eds, *Slavery, Islam, and Diaspora* (Asmara: Africa World Press, 2009).
[9]Debra Blumenthal, *Enemies and Familiars: Slavery and Mastery in Fifteenth-Century Valencia* (Ithaca, NY: Cornell University Press, 2009).

codification of racial slavery, and, in turn, the imposition of racial limits to civil and political rights throughout the Americas.[10]

Slavery under French and British law was distinctive because – unlike European kingdoms with extensive contact with the Mediterranean world, such as Spain and Portugal, or the Italian city-states, which issued laws to regulate slavery in ancient and medieval times – Paris, where the French kingdom was based, and the English monarchy had no slave law when France and England began to colonize North America and the Caribbean in the seventeenth century. After developing local colonial laws in a piecemeal fashion, in 1685 the French king Louis XIV issued a comprehensive slave code (*Code Noir*) for all its Caribbean colonies (e.g. Martinique, Guadeloupe, Saint-Domingue), which was revised for the Indian Ocean colonies in 1723, and for Louisiana in 1724. Initially, France freed all slaves that travelled from its overseas colonies to the metropole – even those who escaped as stowaways on French ships – but over the eighteenth century, the planter lobby managed to eliminate this 'Free Soil Principle', and, in 1777, France banned the entry of all 'blacks, mulattoes, and other people of color' to the metropole.[11]

Likewise, each British colony (such as Jamaica, Barbados, Georgia, Virginia and Nova Scotia) gradually developed its own slave legislation, allowing for significant variation between them. Several historians have treated these variations comparatively, and there are innumerable works on each particular colony and state.[12] A good entry point for learning about slave law in the American South is Thomas D. Morris's wide-ranging synthesis, *Southern Slavery and the Law*, which systematically addresses the legal infrastructure of Southern racial slavery, slavery and property law, and how slaves were treated within the legal system, as plaintiffs, the accused and witnesses. Each US state has its own historiography of slave law.

---

[10] See Davis, *The Problem of Slavery*; and, more recently, Nancy E. van Deusen, *Global Indios: The Indigenous Struggle for Justice in Sixteenth-Century Spain* (Durham, NC: Duke University Press, 2015).
[11] Sue Peabody, '*There Are No Slaves in France*': *The Political Culture of Race and Slavery in the Ancien Régime* (New York: Oxford University Press, 1996). In southern France, the French crown actively engaged in enslaving and trading captives with Barbary pirates and rulers; see Gillian Weiss, *Captives and Corsairs: France and Slavery in the Early Modern Mediterranean* (Stanford: Stanford University Press, 2011).
[12] Elsa V. Goveia, *The West Indian Slave Laws of the 18th Century* (Barbados: Caribbean University Press, 1970); William M. Wiecek, *The Sources of Antislavery Constitutionalism in America, 1760–1848* (Ithaca, NY: Cornell University Press, 1977); A. Leon Higginbotham, Jr., *In the Matter of Color. Race and the American Legal Process: The Colonial Period* (New York: Oxford University Press, 1978).

Another key difference between the Anglo-American legal tradition and those emanating from continental Europe is the degree to which precedent-setting case law ('common law') is essential to judges' decisions. There are several key cases in Britain and the United States that have received a great deal of historical scrutiny, largely because they were significant to the abolitionist movements of these societies. The 1772 freedom suit known as 'Somerset's case', or the 'Mansfield decision', addressed the question of free soil, whether slaves who came from the overseas colonies, where slave law was well established, became free by travelling to England, which had no slave law emanating from Parliament.[13] After Britain and the United States banned the transoceanic slave trade in 1807–1808, and Britain passed its 1833 Emancipation Act, the 1839 revolt aboard the slave ship *Amistad* became a celebrated case for abolitionists, fictionalized in the 1997 Steven Spielberg film.[14] The infamous Taney decision, named after the Supreme Court justice who penned it in the 1857 case *Dred Scott v. Sandford*, excluded all black Americans, regardless of whether they were slaves or free people, from US citizenship, and was one of the crises that led to the outbreak of the American Civil War three years later.[15]

Several common themes stand out in the prescriptive study of law. For example, each government defined who could be legally enslaved and who was exempt from slavery. Generally, those deemed 'enslaveable' were outsiders, though some societies condemned their own convicts or debtors to slavery. Religion was one marker of difference: Christians prohibited Jews from owning Christian slaves and Muslims were forbidden from taking other Muslims as slaves (though conversion to the master's religion was generally insufficient to make one free). In the sixteenth century, the Spanish crown prohibited the enslavement of indigenous people (Indians), and, by 1806, the Supreme Court of Virginia ruled Indian slavery illegal.[16]

---

[13]Steven M. Wise, *Though the Heavens May Fall: The Landmark Trial That Led to the End of Human Slavery* (Boston: Da Capo, 2005) is an entry point for this well-studied case. There is a rich historiography in prior and subsequent journal articles as well.

[14]Among others, see Marcus Rediker, *The Amistad Rebellion: An Atlantic Odyssey of Slavery and Freedom* (New York: Penguin, 2013).

[15]See, for example, Kelly M. Kennington, *In the Shadow of 'Dred Scott': St. Louis Freedom Suits and the Legal Culture of Slavery in Antebellum America* (Athens, GA: University of Georgia Press, 2017); and Anne Twitty, *Before Dred Scott: Slavery and Legal Culture in the American Confluence, 1787–1857* (Cambridge: Cambridge University Press, 2016).

[16]For an early treatment of this question, see Davis, *The Problem of Slavery*, pp. 167–81. For the Virginia case, see Ariela J. Gross, *What Blood Won't Tell: A History of Race on Trial in America* (Cambridge, MA: Harvard University Press, 2008), pp. 23–5.

One of the most important features of legal systems in all slave societies was *manumission*, the process by which owners could free particular slaves, from the Latin, *manus* ('power of a master', literally 'hand') + *mittere* ('let go, release'). The methods and processes that made manumissions legitimate or forbidden by law and the condition or status of freedmen varied from state to state. For example, in some societies, masters could confer manumission by testament, and in others, slaves could initiate their freedom through self-purchase. In ancient Rome, although freedmen enjoyed citizenship rights, they were not equal to freeborn people in Roman law; they could not testify against their former masters, and the freedmen owed an obligation to support their former master, should he become impoverished.[17] In Brazil, by contrast, the manumission formula stated that freedmen were 'as if free by birth', that is with no legal impediments.[18] In the American state of Georgia, the legislature tightly controlled the masters' ability to free their slaves; in this way, the large propertied interests represented by the legislature controlled the poorer whites who might form families with their slaves (and later free them) and attempted to restrict the growth of a free non-white population.[19] In most slave societies, women and children were freed in much higher numbers than male slaves. While some of the freed women and children were the concubines, wives and children of their former masters, Rosemary Bran-Shute, among others, has shown that female slaves working in cities had greater access to a cash economy, and received partial payment in wages, which allowed them to purchase their own freedom and that of their children.[20] Conditions and regulations favouring or restricting manumission varied considerably throughout the world, and over time.

Given the extraordinarily high volume of research on the political and legal history of slavery, this chapter cites mostly articles in specific scholarly journals that often represent the vanguard of new historiographical trends. *Slavery & Abolition: A Journal of Slave and Post-Slave Studies* was founded in 1980 and is fully devoted to the history of slavery and emancipation

---

[17]Watson, *Slave Law in the Americas*, p. 34.
[18]Marc Kleijwegt, *The Faces of Freedom: The Manumission and Emancipation of Slaves in Old World and New World Slavery* (Leiden: Brill, 2006), p. 3.
[19]For an example, see 'A Master Tries to Free His Slaves in Georgia, ca. 1850–1855' in Peabody and Grinberg, *Slavery, Freedom and the Law*, pp. 88–94.
[20]Rosemary Brana-Shute, 'Sex and Gender in Surinamese Manumissions' in Rosemary Brana-Shute and Randy J. Sparks, eds, *Paths to Freedom: Manumission in the Atlantic World* (Charleston: University of South Carolina Press, 2009), pp. 175–96.

throughout the world. *Law and History Review* covers many aspects of legal history, including some of the best scholarship on the law of slavery. In addition to history journals devoted to particular times, places or topics (such as *The William and Mary Quarterly*, for colonial and early American history, the *Journal of Southern History*, the *American Journal of Legal History*, and the *Journal of Negro History*), law review journals, published by law schools, sometimes include important historical contributions, and are not usually catalogued in the standard history journal databases; a librarian can help locate the appropriate finding aid.

Slavery and the law in the United States

It is hard to overstate the effect of slavery and slave law on the history of the United States. From the origins of the Constitution to post-emancipation Reconstruction and Jim Crow to the Civil Rights movement and contemporary policing and prisons, American political and judicial institutions have been constantly influenced by slavery and its legacy.

Americans began writing the history of slave law before the American Civil War (1861–1865), which culminated in the *Thirteenth Amendment* of the United States Constitution abolishing slavery throughout the nation. Thomas R.R. Cobb, a powerful lawyer and pro-slavery advocate in Georgia, published his extensive work, *An Inquiry into the Law of Negro Slavery in the United States of America* in 1858, following the 1857 US Supreme Court's infamous Dred Scott decision. An unabashed opponent of the abolitionist movement, Cobb laced both sections of his *Inquiry* – 'An Historical Sketch of Slavery from the Earliest Periods to the Present Day' and a lengthy treatise on US slave law – with white supremacist and Christian doctrinal justifications for the enslavement of blacks.

From 1926 to 1937, Helen Tunnicliff Catterall edited a massive five-volume collection of case law, *Judicial Cases Concerning American Slavery and the Negro*. Organized by state and colony, these case summaries include local, state and federal court rulings from the United States, Canada, Great Britain and Jamaica, up to the year 1875. Each chapter includes a historical overview of a particular nation's, colony's or state's key laws and decisions, but the case summaries are not comprehensive. Unlike Cobb's *Inquiry*, Catterall's *Judicial Cases* does not present a clear bias; rather, her aim is to introduce the reader to the foundational case law through selections from the primary documents. As such, *Judicial Cases* provides a good point of entry to the historical law of slavery in the English-speaking world, with a distinctly American emphasis.

Eugene Genovese's monumental *Roll, Jordan, Roll* (1974) emphasized the master-slave relationship at the centre of American slavery. Southern law, created and practised by the most elite members of the planter class, was, in Genovese's view, hegemonic: it restricted class antagonisms 'on a terrain in which [the law's] legitimacy is not dangerously questioned'.[21] Genovese believed that the vast majority of slaves accepted the master's paternalist ideology, becoming, to a certain extent, docile and compliant participants in the system. Later historians, such as Alex Lichtenstein, challenged Genovese's interpretation, arguing that slaves had developed their own 'moral economy', or independent conceptualization of their economic and social rights, by which they justified their own actions, such as theft from the master, which the courts deemed illegal.[22] Even in considering Southern lawsuits over slaves as property (e.g. when a master sued a seller over the 'defective' qualities of a slave), historians have found evidence of autonomous slave agency.[23]

The centrality of slavery to the founding of the American nation and its subsequent development is undeniable. As Paul Finkelman has noted, 'with the exception of real estate, slaves were the most valuable form of privately held property in the United States'.[24] At the 1787 Constitutional Convention, slaveholders won virtually every debate, and slavery – despite the drafters' deliberate omission of the word – was central to many provisions in the final document. Subsequent congressional legislation, as new states joined the nation to the West, shaped the foundational legal principle of comity: the degree to which each state acknowledged the different laws of other states.[25] Slaves themselves shaped this debate, by escaping their masters and crossing state boundaries in their quest for freedom.[26]

---

[21] Eugene D. Genovese, *Roll, Jordan, Roll: The World the Slaves Made* (New York: Pantheon, 1974), p. 26.
[22] Alex Lichtenstein, 'That Disposition to Theft with Which They Have Been Branded: Moral Economy, Slave Management, and the Law', *Journal of Social History* 21: 2 (1988), p. 415.
[23] Ariela J. Gross, *Double Character: Slavery and Mastery in the Antebellum Southern Courtroom* (Princeton, NJ: Princeton University Press, 2000).
[24] Paul Finkelman, *Slavery and the Founders: Race and Liberty in the Age of Jefferson*, 3rd ed. (Armonk: Sharpe, 2014), p. x.
[25] Paul Finkelman, *An Imperfect Union: Slavery, Federalism, and Comity* (Chapel Hill: University of North Carolina Press, 1981).
[26] Richard J. Blackett, *The Captive's Quest for Freedom: Fugitive Slaves, the 1850 Fugitive Slave Law, and the Politics of Slavery* (Cambridge: Cambridge University Press, 2018).

The abolition of slavery during the American Civil War, and its enshrinement in the *Thirteenth Amendment* to the Constitution, therefore, represented a cataclysmic upheaval for the American political system. Two political historians offer contrasting interpretations of how and why that change came about. Michael Vorenberg argues the dominant view, that American politicians arrived at the constitutional resolution to the problem of slavery – as opposed to legal or regulatory reforms – only slowly and reluctantly, as a last resort. By contrast, James Oakes argues that abolishing slavery was the foremost concern of the Republican Party, with the judicial idea of 'free soil' as the cornerstone to their antislavery initiatives before and during the Civil War. According to Oakes, antislavery politicians pursued two simultaneous political strategies to abolish slavery: state abolition (with individual legislatures gradually ending slavery while compensating masters) and military emancipation (enforced by Northern troops as they conquered rebel territories, without compensation). When neither of these strategies completely ended slavery by the end of the war in 1865, northern politicians wrangled Congress to accept the *Thirteenth Amendment*.[27]

Comparative histories of slavery and abolition

The most influential and important study of slave law in the Americas, *Slave and Citizen: The Negro in the Americas*, was published by the sociologist Frank Tannenbaum, in 1947. An army stint in the US South and Tannenbaum's travels to Mexico following the revolution awakened his observations regarding race relations throughout the Americas. His post-war book, *Slave and Citizen*, argued that the Roman legal and Catholic religious traditions of Latin America – especially Brazil and Mexico – humanized the law of slavery and promoted manumission – the masters' freeing of their individual slaves. In the 'Anglo-Saxon' (i.e. British) colonies and the United States, by contrast, argued Tannenbaum, a harsher legal and religious tradition limited

---

[27]Michael Vorenberg, *Final Freedom: The Civil War, the Abolition of Slavery, and the Thirteenth Amendment* (Cambridge: Cambridge University Press, 2001) and James Oakes, *Freedom National: The Destruction of Slavery in the United States, 1861–1865* (New York: W. W. Norton, 2012).

the number of manumissions and led to harsher modern racial regimes in the English-speaking regions of the Americas.

As the US Civil Rights Movement began to effect changes in consciousness and law in the 1960s and 1970s, Tannenbaum's *Slave and Citizen* began to draw criticism from later historians. For example, while the Stanford historian Carl Degler agreed with Tannenbaum that Brazilian voters elected men of mixed ancestry more readily to high political offices than voters in the United States, he disagreed with Tannenbaum's proposed causes: the Roman legal tradition and Catholicism. Rather, Degler argued that the disproportionate number of free and enslaved men (as compared to the female population) in Brazil favoured manumission of black and mixed women and children, while the more balanced sex ratios among settlers and slaves in the United States discouraged high rates of manumission there. Moreover, the longer duration of the transatlantic slave trade in Brazil (abolished there in 1850, in contrast to the United States, effective from 1808) produced a larger African-born population well into the nineteenth century.[28] In other words, Degler argued that demographics were more important determinants than cultural traditions.

Almost a decade later, David Rankin challenged Tannenbaum from another direction, using the case history of Louisiana.[29] Louisiana offers a particularly interesting, but challenging, case study for historians of slave law because of its multiple national regimes. Settled by the French from the late seventeenth century, Louisiana received its first shipments of African slaves in 1719, and their numbers soon surpassed those of the white settlers. When France lost the Seven Years' War in 1763, Louisiana passed to Spanish control (although the majority of colonists remained French in language and culture). In 1800, Spain ceded Louisiana back to France, which sold it to the United States in 1803, after which large numbers of English-speaking Americans brought new cultural and legal traditions.[30] Rankin sided with Degler's analysis, arguing that demographic and economic conditions were

---

[28]Carl N. Degler, *Neither Black nor White: Slavery and Race Relations in Brazil and the United States* (Madison: University of Wisconsin Press, 1971).
[29]David C. Rankin, 'The Tannenbaum Thesis Reconsidered: Slavery and Race Relations in Antebellum Louisiana', *Southern Studies* 18: 1 (1979), pp. 5–31.
[30]Consequently, there is a voluminous historiography on Louisiana slave law. See especially Thomas N. Ingersoll, *Mammon and Manon in Early New Orleans: The First Slave Society in the Deep South, 1718–1819* (Knoxville: University of Tennessee Press, 1999); and Judith Kelleher Schafer, *Slavery, the Civil Law, and the Supreme Court of Louisiana* (Baton Rouge: Louisiana State University Press, 1994).

more important than cultural, religious or legal factors in determining the nature of slavery and of ensuing race relations.

Tannenbaum's argument has been revised more recently by the historians Alejandro de la Fuente and Ariela J. Gross in their collaborative work, *Becoming Free, Becoming Black*, which examines the production of white supremacy comparatively in Cuba, Virginia and Louisiana.[31] These authors agree with Tannenbaum that the relative hegemony of whites in each society at different periods rested upon the different legal regimes regulating freedom – such as the facilitation of manumission – but they also stress the social conditions and political processes that brought about the abolition of slavery and subsequently the legislation on rights for people of African descent. For example, Spanish practices facilitated manumission through self-purchase (*coartación*), which created a substantial, settled, property-owning class of free people of colour in Cuba, who asserted their political pressure and maintained social statuses similar to those of whites within the same class. By contrast, whites in Virginia and Louisiana (as it entered the United States) established a legal infrastructure based on racial discrimination and terror, with social and economic repercussions lingering into the present.

One of the most fascinating developments in global modern history is the transition from slavery to abolition, from the middle of the eighteenth century, with the abolition of the slave trade and slavery in particular regimes, to the 1926 League of Nations Slavery Convention and the 1948 Universal Declaration of Human Rights. Until the 1980s, historians' debates focused primarily on the British antislavery movement, especially whether its root causes were ideological or rooted in economic self-interest.[32] An important comparative breakthrough was Robin Blackburn's 1988 study, *The Overthrow of Colonial Slavery, 1776–1848*, which followed the abolition of slavery in Britain, the United States, France and Latin America up to the great European revolutions of 1848.[33] Blackburn's more recent book *The*

---

[31] Alejandro de la Fuente and Ariela J. Gross, *Becoming Free, Becoming Black: Race, Freedom, and Law in Cuba, Virginia, and Louisiana* (Cambridge: Cambridge University Press, 2020). For the explicit engagement with Tannenbaum, see, Alejandro de la Fuente, 'Slave Law and Claims-Making in Cuba: The Tannenbaum Debate Revisited', *Law and History Review* 22: 2 (2004), pp. 339–70; and Alejandro de la Fuente, 'From Slaves to Citizens? Tannenbaum and the Debates on Slavery, Emancipation, and Race Relations in Latin America', *International Labor and Working-Class History* 77: 1 (2010), pp. 154–73.

[32] The foundational text of this debate is Eric Williams's *Capitalism and Slavery*, first published in 1944, and reissued with a new introduction by Colin A. Palmer (Chapel Hill: University of North Carolina Press, 1994). The Williams thesis was challenged most directly by Seymour Drescher in *Econocide: British Slavery in the Era of Abolition* (Pittsburgh, PA: University of Pittsburgh Press, 1977).

[33] Robin Blackburn, *The Overthrow of Colonial Slavery, 1776–1848* (London: Verso, 1988).

American Crucible (2011) offers a wide-ranging overview of the rise and fall of Atlantic slavery. Blackburn, a Marxist, argues that Atlantic plantation slavery superseded the earlier 'traditional Mediterranean' system, where slaves occupied a variety of economic niches, from domestics to skilled artisans. Plantation slavery provided capital, markets and raw materials that advanced the Industrial Revolution. In Blackburn's view, a series of revolutions (American, French, Latin American) disrupted the power of the landowning class, so that slaves and antislavery activists seized the opportunity to dismantle the legal system of slavery in each European empire. Slavery and antislavery, according to Blackburn, produced two countervailing ideologies at the core of the modern Western world: racism and human rights. By contrast, Seymour Drescher's study, *Abolition* (2009), which preceded Blackburn's synthesis and covers much of the same historical ground, places greater emphasis on the legislative reform movements and state actions than slave resistance. Moreover, Drescher extends his analysis of slavery and abolition to show how antislavery became an effective tool in the expansion of the British Empire throughout the world, while penal slavery was at the heart of twentieth-century totalitarian states.[34]

General emancipation (as opposed to the freeing of individual slaves through manumission) posed a series of legal problems for Atlantic governments: should emancipation happen gradually, or all at once? Should masters be compensated for their loss of property? By whom? How, and at what rates? Stanley Engerman's extensive and very useful overview analyses how different governments addressed the problem of general emancipation.[35]

Immediate emancipation, whether by legislation or by lawsuit, typically did not provide compensation to masters. The independent republic of Vermont abolished adult slavery in its first constitution (1777),[36] while in 1783 the Massachusetts Supreme Court ruled that slavery was inconsistent with the state's constitutional Declaration of Rights, effectively abolishing slavery in Massachusetts.[37] The 1791 slave revolt in France's largest

---

[34] See also the historiographical survey by Lisa Ford, 'Anti-Slavery and the Reconstitution of Empire', *Australian Historical Studies* 45: 1 (2014), pp. 71–86.
[35] Stanley Engerman, 'Emancipation Schemes: Different Ways of Ending Slavery' in Enrico Dal Lago and Constantina Katsari, eds, *Slave Systems: Ancient and Modern* (New York: Cambridge University Press, 2008), pp. 265–82.
[36] Harvey Amarni Whitfield, *The Problem of Slavery in Early Vermont* (Barre: Vermont Historical Society, 2014).
[37] Higginbotham, *In the Matter of Color*, pp. 91–5.

American colony, Saint-Domingue (later Haiti), eventually led the French revolutionary government to declare general emancipation there in 1793, which was extended – at least on paper – to all French colonies by the Paris Constituent Assembly Declaration of 4 February 1794. However, due to conditions of war and planter resistance, French emancipation was only implemented in Saint-Domingue, Guadeloupe and French Guiana, before Napoleon Bonaparte overturned the 1794 decree in 1802. Only through force of arms were the former slaves in Haiti able to resist the renewal of slavery there. France would eventually abolish slavery in its remaining colonies unilaterally and with partial compensation following the Revolution of 1848.[38] Similarly, the American Civil War resulted in the immediate and uncompensated emancipation of slaves in Confederate states in 1863, and throughout the country with the *Thirteenth Amendment* of the Constitution, ratified on 31 January 1865.

The Pennsylvania legislature enacted the first gradualist model of emancipation in 1780. 'An Act for the Gradual Abolition of Slavery' freed only children born to slave mothers, and established that they were to serve a period of 'apprenticeship' to their master until the age of twenty-eight. In this way, the masters' expense of raising the children to an age of productivity was supposed to be compensated by the person's labour until the apprenticeship ended.[39] This gradualist approach meant that the entire class of slaves achieved freedom incrementally, as each new cohort achieved adulthood, as defined by law. Similar gradualist models were later implemented in Gran Columbia, Chile, and Portugal, as well as Cuba (the 1870 *Moret Law*) and Brazil (the *Rio Branco Law* of 1871), where the legislation was known as 'Free Womb' laws.[40]

The British approach to emancipation, the result of a widespread popular grass-roots antislavery campaign, was a hybrid approach. The 1833 *Slavery Abolition Act* compensated masters throughout the empire for the value of their emancipated slaves, who were designated to labour in 'apprenticeship' for a period of years. The apprenticeship system eventually broke down in 1838, but colonial legislatures passed a series of laws, including vagrancy

---

[38] Sue Peabody, 'France's Two Emancipations in Comparative Context' in Hideaki Suzuki, ed., *Abolitions as a Global Experience* (Singapore: National University Press of Singapore, 2015), pp. 25–49.
[39] Higginbotham, *In the Matter of Color*, pp. 299–310.
[40] Engerman, 'Emancipation Schemes', pp. 271–2; Camillia Cowling, *Conceiving Freedom: Women of Color, Gender, and the Abolition of Slavery in Havana and Rio de Janeiro* (Chapel Hill: University of North Carolina Press, 2013), pp. 55–60.

acts, which, in practice, compelled former slaves to continue to work on plantations, usually for the same master as before slavery. France followed this model when it abolished slavery for the second time, in 1848. Several research websites provide the names of slaveowners and the amount of compensation received, permitting analysis of the legacies of slave ownership as foundations for reparations.[41]

Legal records are a rich source to study the lives of people after emancipation. Independent Haiti developed constitutional and case law to define itself as 'Free Soil' for slaves escaping their Caribbean masters, even as it thumbed its nose at France, which in 1825 claimed millions of francs for diplomatic recognition of the fledgling nation.[42] Men and women experienced general emancipation in different ways, as recorded through legal instruments such as marriages, wills, and in unequal civil and political rights.[43]

Autobiography, biography and microhistory

One of the most important tools created by antislavery activists in the eighteenth and nineteenth centuries was the 'slave narrative': the autobiographical story of particular slaves, told in the first person, often (but not always) with the assistance of a more educated scribe who was dedicated to the abolitionist movement. While slave narratives were not strictly 'legal' in nature, they were political in their efforts to stimulate sympathy for the mistreatment of slaves and for the inhumanity of the Atlantic slave system more generally. They were also highly effective. One of the earliest, *The Interesting Narrative of the Life of Olaudah Equiano* (1789), went through nine editions and helped to generate sympathy for the campaign against the

---

[41]*Centre for the Study of the Legacies of British Slavery*, University College London, https://www.ucl.ac.uk/lbs/ and "REPAIRS: Esclavage & Indemnités: Empire colonial française du XIXe siècle" Centre International de Recherche sur les Esclavages et les Post-esclavages (CIRESC) https://esclavage-indemnites.fr/public/.

[42]Ada Ferrer, 'Haiti, Free Soil, and Antislavery in the Revolutionary Atlantic', *American Historical Review* 117: 1 (2012), pp. 40–66.

[43]Pamela Scully and Diana Paton, eds, *Gender and Slave Emancipation in the Atlantic World* (Durham: Duke University Press, 2005); Leslie Schwalm, *'A Hard Fight for We': Women's Transition from Slavery to Freedom in South Carolina* (Urbana: University of Illinois Press, 1997).

Atlantic slave trade.[44] Subsequent slave autobiographies in the United States, including *Narrative of the Life of Frederick Douglass* (1845) and *Incidents in the Life of a Slave Girl* (1861) by Harriet Jacobs, not only contributed to the abolitionist movement, but also helped define a genre in American literature.[45]

In the 1970s and 1980s, historians of medieval and early modern Europe realized that legal records were an especially rich primary source for understanding the cultures and perspectives of illiterate and low-ranking people, who otherwise left few traces in the archival documents. Historians such as Carlo Ginzburg, Emmanuel Leroy Ladurie, Natalie Zemon Davis and Arlette Farge began to write 'microhistories', that is, biographical studies of unusually well documented peasants, women and urban tradespeople who appeared in criminal or other legal records. They used legal transcripts, petitions and other judicial records to 'read against the grain', or, to pay attention to the clues these documents gave, not only about legal argument and jurisprudence, but about the lives and aspirations of common people recorded in legal settings.

In the past decade or so, there has been a virtual explosion of biographical and microhistorical studies that place enslaved individuals or families at the centre of their stories, often using evidence found in court documents. One of the first, and most important, was Annette Gordon-Reed's *The Hemingses of Monticello* (2008). Gordon-Reed reconstructed and analysed the lives of the Hemings family, who became the slaves of Thomas Jefferson through his marriage to Martha Wayles, a wealthy Virginia planter heiress. Sally Hemings eventually became the mother of several of Jefferson's illegitimate children. Gordon-Reed's Pulitzer Prize–winning book made it clear that, despite the limited quantity and types of historical sources available to historians, it is possible to carefully reimagine the lives of slaves as biographical subjects, as well as the legal principles shaping those lives.

---

[44]Olaudah Equiano, *The Interesting Narrative of the Life of Olaudah Equiano, or Gustavus Vassa, the African* (London, 1789). Vincent Caretta's biography, *Equiano, the African: Biography of a Self-made Man* (Athens, GA: University of Georgia Press, 2005), argued that the earliest chapters, describing Equiano's childhood in Africa, were fabricated. This position has been refuted by Paul E. Lovejoy, 'Olaudah Equiano or Gustavus Vassa – What's in a Name?' *Atlantic Studies* 9: 2 (2012), pp. 165–84.

[45]Frederick Douglass, *Narrative of the Life of Frederick Douglass, An American Slave, Written by Himself* (Dublin: Webb and Chapman, 1846); Linda Brent [Harriet Jacobs], *Incidents in the Life of a Slave Girl. Written by Herself* (Boston, 1861). It was Jean Fagan Yellin who revealed the true identity of the latter author in *Harriet Jacobs: A Life* (Ann Arbor, MI: Basic Civitas Books, 2004).

Another major innovation in the genre of slave microhistory and biography can be observed in James H. Sweet's recent *Domingos Álvarez*. While Gordon-Reed's book followed Thomas Jefferson, Sally and James Hemings across the Atlantic to France, Sweet's dynamic study investigated the African political and religious origins of his protagonist, Domingos Álvarez, and followed him to Brazil and then Portugal, where he faced the inquisition, leaving the most detailed records about his life. Both of these studies, along with others published more recently, including many journal articles, show how historians can use legal records not only to shed light on particular people in slavery and freedom, but also to ask and answer, through those records, new questions about the worlds in which the slaves lived.[46]

Bibliography

Blackburn, Robin, *The American Crucible: Slavery, Emancipation, and Human Rights* (London: Verso, 2011).

Catterall, Helen Tunnicliff, ed., *Judicial Cases Concerning American Slavery and the Negro* (Washington, DC: Carnegie Institution of Washington, 1926–1937).

Cobb, Thomas Read Rootes, *An Inquiry into the Law of Negro Slavery in the United States of America* [Introduction by Paul Finkelman] (Athens: University of Georgia Press, 1999. Originally published in 1858).

De la Fuente, Alejandro, and Ariela J. Gross, *Becoming Free, Becoming Black: Race, Freedom, and Law in Cuba, Virginia, and Louisiana* (Cambridge: Cambridge University Press, 2020).

Drescher, Seymour, *Abolition: A History of Slavery and Antislavery* (Cambridge: Cambridge University Press, 2009).

---

[46]Clifton Crais et Pamela Scully, *Sara Baartman and the Hottentot Venus: A Ghost Story and a Biography* (Princeton, NJ: Princeton University Press, 2009); Lea VanderVelde, *Mrs. Dred Scott: A Life on Slavery's Frontier* (New York: Oxford University Press, 2009); Randy J. Sparks, *The Two Princes of Calabar: An Eighteenth-Century Atlantic Odyssey* (Cambridge, MA: Harvard University Press, 2009); Rebecca J. Scott and Jean M. Hébrard, *Freedom Papers: An Atlantic Odyssey in the Age of Emancipation* (Cambridge, MA: Harvard University Press, 2012); Sydney Nathans, *To Free a Family: The Journey of a Mary Walker* (Cambridge, MA: Harvard University Press, 2013); Lisa A. Lindsay and John Wood Sweet, eds, *Biography and the Black Atlantic* (Philadelphia: University of Pennsylvania Press, 2014); Sue Peabody, *Madeleine's Children: Family, Freedom, Secrets, and Lies in France's Indian Ocean Colonies* (New York: Oxford University Press, 2017).

Genovese, Eugene, *Roll, Jordan, Roll: The World the Slaves Made* (New York: Pantheon, 1974).

Gordon-Reed, Annette, *The Hemingses of Monticello: An American Family* (New York: W. W. Norton & Company, 2008).

Morris, Thomas D., *Southern Slavery and the Law, 1619–1860* (Chapel Hill: University of North Carolina Press, 1999).

Peabody, Sue, and Keila Grinberg, eds, *Slavery, Freedom, and the Law in the Atlantic World* (New York: Bedford-St Martin's, 2007).

Sweet, James H., *Domingos Álvares, African Healing, and the Intellectual History of the Atlantic World* (Chapel Hill: University of North Carolina Press, 2011).

Tannenbaum, Frank, *Slave and Citizen: The Negro in the Americas* (New York: Vintage, 1947).

8

Writing national histories of slavery

Lewis Eliot

University of Oklahoma

In 1851, at the height of the British Empire's much vaunted naval anti-slave trade campaign off coastal Africa, the Wesleyan missionary and historian William Fox wrote that the abolitionism had become 'a halo of glory on our nation'. Only a few short decades after Britain's leading role in the transatlantic slave trade ended, then, antislavery had become firmly welded onto British national identity. This rapid shift significantly reorientated a British national culture that had been defined in large part by its use and defence of unfree labour for centuries.[1]

Such was the centrality of slavery to European empires since the 1500s that the institution embodied significant aspects of state identities. The total number of Africans forcibly taken to the Americas will certainly never be fully known, but the most reliable estimates place that figure at

---

[1] William Fox, *A Brief History of the Wesleyan Missions on the Western Coast of Africa* (London: Aylott & Jones, 1851), p. 88. For more on naval abolitionism, see Robert Burroughs, 'Eyes on the Prize: Journeys on Slave Ships Taken as Prizes by the Royal Navy', *Slavery & Abolition* 31: 1 (2010), pp. 99–115; Richard P. Anderson, 'The Diaspora of Sierra Leone's Liberated Africans: Enlistment, Forced Migration, and Liberation at Freetown, 1808–1863', *African Economic History* 41 (2013), pp. 103–40; John Broich, *Squadron: Ending the African Slave Trade* (New York: Abrams, 2017); Robert Burroughs and Richard Huzzey, eds, *The Suppression of the Transatlantic Slave Trade: British Politics, Practices, and Representations of Naval Coercion* (Manchester: Manchester University Press, 2018).

over 12,500,000 people. In 1807 the British Empire formerly ended its involvement in this trade and in doing so brought the question of slavery to the forefront of diplomatic discourse in Europe, Africa and the Americas. As the ending of the transcontinental consensus on the acceptability of slave labour came to an end in the early nineteenth century, visionaries, ideologues and politicians throughout the world suddenly needed to engage with the question of slavery and its place in their national cultures.[2]

This chapter examines the ways scholars of slavery have tackled the nebulous and fluid notions of nationalism and national identity. As the nursery of the modern nation state, it focuses on the Atlantic world. The Age of Revolutions birthed new states and concepts of identity, and questions of slavery and the nationality of enslaved people therefore became ever more charged. The response to these new ruminations from the architects of older imperial systems and from enslaved people themselves is equally revealing. Moving through analysis of these considerations, this chapter explains how the ostensibly conflicting institutions of slavery and the nation state reconciled, and how this influenced those of African descent both before and after widespread emancipation.

The two sages of historical nationalism, Benedict Anderson and Eric Hobsbawm, provide the most useful definitions of the nation for this exploration. This essay therefore temporally begins at the outset of the Age of Revolutions, when, per Anderson, a 'spontaneous distillation of a complex crossing of discrete historical forces' birthed the nation as a 'cultural artefact'. Hobsbawm then describes how 'ideologists of the era of triumphant bourgeois liberalism' who championed the nation then failed to engage successfully with the incompatibility of nationhood and slavery. In fact, many of the nationalist visionaries of the late eighteenth and early nineteenth centuries worked passionately to entwine liberty and unfree labour. According to Anderson, 'one key factor initially spurring the drive for independence ... was the *fear* of lower-class political mobilizations: to wit,

---

[2]This estimate is from the Trans-Atlantic Slave Trade Database, the most comprehensive quantitative analysis of the Middle Passage and concludes that the total was 12,521,337. For more see www.slavevoyages.org. For more on how British antislavery created an ideological fissure in the Atlantic world over the question of slavery, see Richard Huzzey, *Freedom Burning: Anti-Slavery and Empire in Victorian Britain* (Ithaca: Cornell University Press, 2012); Lauren Benton and Lisa Ford, *Rage for Order: The British Empire and the Origins of International Law* (Cambridge, MA: Harvard University Press, 2016). Britain was not the first state to abolish transatlantic slave trading. The newly minted French Republic did so in 1794, but Napoleon Bonaparte reversed that prohibition in 1802 and France's involvement in the Middle Passage continued until 1826.

Indian or Negro-slave uprisings'.[3] The creation of the nation in the nineteenth century was, therefore, very much tangled with contemporary questions regarding the feasibility and acceptability of continued slaveholding.

The rise of the nation state and notion of national identity matured just as the acceptability of slavery began to erode in the Atlantic world. Both established and newly formed states in Europe and the Americas then began to assess how the institution of slavery fitted into their emerging national identities and mythologies. To be sure, this was a messy progression. Examining this process explains how historians have tackled the question of slavery studies through the prism of the nation. To this end, this essay asks two questions about those investigations. Firstly, how did the reorientation of nationality as a carefully considered cultural and political marker alter the institution of slavery? And secondly, how did those states that persisted with slavery in the nineteenth century reconcile their newfound liberalism with the persistence of human bondage?

To answer these questions, this chapter is divided into two sections. The first looks to the formation of nationalist ideals in the Americas during the Age of Revolutions, beginning with the American and Haitian Revolutions and looking at the influence of their anti-colonial thought on Latin America and the British Caribbean. The second section looks to the post-Age of Revolutions era where the rapid industrializing of the Atlantic world gave both national and slaveholding ideologies a new bent, an evolution known as Second Slavery. This section looks at how this new economic order altered national approaches to both slaveholding and abolitionism in Brazil, Spanish Cuba, the United States and the British Empire. The chapter ends by looking past the end of Atlantic slavery to explain how legacies of chattel bondage continue to inform national histories.

The Age of Revolutions: Reorientating nationality

The British North American colonies were the first imperial holdings in the Atlantic world to put the modern ideals of nationalism into place in the 1770s and 1780s. Taking Anderson and Hobsbawm's definitions of the nation, the

---

[3]Benedict Anderson, *Imagined Communities: Reflections on the Origin and Spread of Nationalism* (New York: Verso Revised Edition, 1991), p. 4; Eric Hobsbawm, *Nations and Nationalism since 1780* (Cambridge: Cambridge University Press, 1990), p. 38; Anderson, *Imagined Communities*, p. 48. Italics in original.

revolutionaries of the now United States created a cultural artefact that its leadership then simultaneously espoused to their populace and projected abroad. Given the failure of these revolutionaries to reconcile their new nation with the institution of slavery, the place of human bondage within this national culture has unsurprisingly attracted considerable scholarly attention.

Though perhaps a little simplified in its highlighting of a longer tradition of slavery in the United States, the recent work of Nikole Hannah-Jones and her fellow collaborators on The 1619 Project has forced a critical public debate in American society over its national history of slavery. The 1619 Project points to the year that enslaved Africans first set foot on North American soil as the founding moment of a nation that has since identified itself primarily with the subjugation of Black people. Scholars of the United States' founding have since responded and hotly debated the veracity of these claims in popular presses. Despite their varied opinions about the relevance of the year 1619, such was the centrality of slavery to British North American life that they have nonetheless been forced to engage with the importance of the plantocracy to the birth of their nation.[4]

Insisting upon the presence of enslaved people in the origin story of the United States braids slavery and American nationalism together tightly. Analysis of, in particular, Southern states' concerns during the debates over the British North American colonial lot reveals an aristocratic class highly attuned to imperial discourses. Given the strict reliance on slavery, no economic explanation for the American Revolution makes sense without mention of enslaved people. This argument is best articulated by Woody Holton, who points to fear of enslaved uprisings (along with Native American and working-class unrest) among Virginian gentry as the impetus for leaving the British Empire and forming a new national culture. Andrew Jackson O'Shaughnessy provides a British counterpoint to Holton's work, suggesting that whatever the economic importance of the mainland American colonies to the colonists themselves, the enormous profitability of

---

[4] "The 1619 Project". *The New York Times*, 14 August 2019; Nell Irvin Painter, 'How We Think about the Term "Enslaved" Matters', *The Guardian*, 14 August 2019; Sean Wilentz, 'American Slavery and "the Relentless Unforeseen,"' *The New York Review of Books*, 14 August 2019; Allen C. Guelzo, 'Preaching a Conspiracy Theory', *City Journal*, 8 December 2019; Leslie M. Harris, 'I Helped Fact-Check the 1619 Project. The Times Ignored Me', *Politico*, 6 March 2020; and Sarah Ellison, 'How the 1619 Project Took over 2020', *The Washington Post*, 13 October 2020. For overviews of the response to the Project, including discussion of the initial letter from critiquing historians to the *New York Times* editor and initial interviews from the World Socialist Website, see, Adam Server, 'The Fight over the 1619 Project Is Not about the Facts', *The Atlantic*, 23 December 2019; 'From the Editor's Desk, "1619 and All That"', *American Historical Review* 125: 1 (2020), pp. xv–xxi.

West Indian slavery to Britain's coffers meant that the American Revolution proved a war the British Empire could afford to lose.[5]

Even those scholars who read the American Revolution as an ideological, rather than economic, event engage with the slaveholding origins of American national culture. The feudalism that Gordon Wood sees in British imperial society and from which the national architects of the United States hoped to break, certainly included slavery. Even the more progressive northern states acquiesced to the southern insistence on preserving slavery in the union. The democracy that developed in the place of colonial feudalism therefore similarly failed to satisfactorily engage in the question of slavery. In consequence, chattel bondage remained fused to the nationalism of the United States until the 1860s.[6]

The rise of this modern nationalism arrived only a few short years before the Atlantic-wide abolitionist movement evolved from a progressivist fantasy into a mainstream political crusade. This development came thanks to, in Ada Ferrer's words, the 'twin pillars of Atlantic antislavery', the passionate efforts of British abolitionist activists and, more viscerally and importantly, the Haitian Revolution of 1791. Though certainly relevant to the intersection of slavery and nationalism, the work of Britain's antislavery community took time to reverberate across the Atlantic. Their efforts, though well meaning, were nonetheless hobbled by their commitment to a peaceful emancipatory process and, aside from a few notable exceptions including Olaudah Equiano, Ottobah Cugoano and the Sons of Africa, silencing of Black voices. In contrast, the Haitian Revolution was violent, led by those of African descent, and far more suddenly dragged the question of slavery to the forefront of revolutionary minds in the early national period.[7]

---

[5] Woody Holton, *Forced Founders: Indians, Debtors, Slaves, and the Making of the American Revolution in Virginia* (Chapel Hill: University of North Carolina Press, 1999); Andrew Jackson O'Shaughnessy, *An Empire Divided: The American Revolution and the British Caribbean* (Philadelphia: University of Pennsylvania Press, 2000). For a broader temporal look at a similar issue, see Alan Taylor, *The Internal Enemy: Slavery and War in Virginia, 1772–1832* (New York: W. W. Norton, 2013). On how the regional economic issues Holton explores informed a national revolution, see T.H. Breen, *The Marketplace of Revolution: How Consumer Politics Shaped American Independence* (Oxford: Oxford University Press, 2005). This line of United States national history has since been synthesized in Alan Taylor, *American Revolutions: A Continental History, 1750–1804* (New York: W. W. Norton, 2016). Some have taken the importance of slavery to the revolutionary story even further, in particular Alfred Blumrosen, Ruth G. Blumrosen, and Steven Blumrosen, *Slave Nation: How Slavery United the Colonies and Sparked the American Revolution* (Naperville, IL: Sourcebooks, 2005).

[6] The seminal work in this regard is Bernard Bailyn, *The Ideological Origins of the American Revolution* (Cambridge, MA: The Belknap Press, 1967). This mode of argument has since been taken up by Gordon S. Wood, in particular in Wood, *The Radicalism of the American Revolution* (New York: Vintage, 1991) and Wood, *The Creation of the American Republic, 1776–1787* (Chapel Hill: University of North Carolina Press, 1998).

[7] Ada Ferrer, 'Cuban Slavery and Atlantic Antislavery', *Review* 31: 3 (2008), pp. 267–95, 267. Though those of African descent were heavily involved in the British abolitionist movement, their contributions were often silenced by 'pragmatic' voices who hoped to sterilize the abolitionist cause and so gain more ground. See, Gretchen Gerzina, *Black England: Life before Emancipation* (London: John Murray, 1995); Gretchen Gerzina, ed., *Britain's Black Past* (Liverpool: Liverpool University Press, 2020); Ryan Hanley, *Beyond Slavery and Abolition: Black British Writing, c. 1770–1830* (Cambridge: Cambridge University Press, 2018).

The seminal analysis of the Haitian Revolution and its role in advancing nationalism throughout the Atlantic world is the work of C.L.R. James. James points to the vital leadership of Toussaint Louverture to explain how Haitian rebels violently asserted their rights to self-determination in the face of a French state which professed revolutionary ideals but could not comprehend the intersection of Blackness and nationalism. Scholarship since James's pioneering study has examined how the actions of Haitians of African descent rang throughout the Atlantic world. The destruction of French rule in Saint Domingue inspired enslaved Africans beyond Hispaniola to even more urgently reject their bondage and in ways that recalled the nationalism of Haitian rebels. Haiti's declaring of independence in 1804 similarly forced the leaders of the nascent national movements of the early nineteenth century to engage with a Black Republic that represented the ideals they espoused without the ideologically limiting coffle of slavery.[8]

The last twenty years have witnessed a renewed interest in the Haitian Revolution. The works of in particular David Geggus and Laurent Dubois have looked to integrate the creation of Haitian nationalism as a cultural artefact into the narrative of the enslaved uprising and its aftermath. Jeremy Popkin then tackled the complex and nuanced relationship between the end of French rule in Saint Domingue and the abolition of Haitian slavery and in doing so explained how antislavery became an integral aspect of nationality.[9]

Inspired by these analyses, scholars of other regions in the Americas then developed a fascination with the ways the ideological tenets of the Haitian

---

[8]C.L.R. James, *The Black Jacobins: Toussaint L'Ouverture and the San Domingo Revolution* (London: Secker & Warburg, 1938); Laurent Dubois, *A Colony of Citizens: Revolution and Slave Emancipation in the French Caribbean, 1787-1804* (Chapel Hill: University of North Carolina Press, 2004); Matthew D. Childs, *The 1812 Aponte Rebellion in Cuba and the Struggle against Atlantic Slavery* (Chapel Hill: University of North Carolina Press, 2006); Lauren Dubois, 'An Enslaved Enlightenment: Rethinking the Intellectual History of the French Enlightenment', *Social History* 31: 1 (2006), pp. 1-14; João Pedro Marques, 'Slave Revolts and the Abolition of Slavery: An Overinterpretation', in Seymour Drescher and Pieter C. Emmer, eds, *Who Abolished Slavery? Slave Revolts and Abolitionism* (New York: Berghahn Books, 2010), pp. 3-77. For the importance of this text, see Rachel Douglas, *Making the Black Jacobins: C.L.R. James and the Drama of History* (Durham, NC: Duke University Press, 2019). For contextual information about the colony of Saint Domingue, see John D. Garrigus, *Before Haiti: Race and Citizenship in French Saint-Domingue* (New York: Palgrave Macmillan, 2006).
[9]David P. Geggus, *Haitian Revolutionary Studies* (Bloomington: Indiana University Press, 2002); Laurent Dubois, *Avengers of the New World: The Story of the Haitian Revolution* (Cambridge, MA: The Belknap Press, 2004); Jeremy D. Popkin, *You Are All Free: The Haitian Revolution and the Abolition of Slavery* (Cambridge: Cambridge University Press, 2010). The approaches of Geggus and Dubois were influenced heavily by the seminal work of Carolyn E. Fick, *The Making of Haiti: The Saint Domingue Revolution from Below* (Knoxville: University of Tennessee Press, 1990).

Revolution permeated throughout the western hemisphere. The work of the Haitian rebels was particularly attractive to enslaved people in the Americas. Not only did they gain their freedom, but they also overthrew their colonial masters and achieved independence. The promise of self-determination without racial or imperial subjugation was a particularly enticing prospect to enslaved people and the independent Haiti had admirers throughout the western hemisphere. As a result, the leaders of national movements in Latin America needed to be highly attuned to the thoughts and ideologies of those of African descent when crafting their new nations. David Brion Davis and Robin Blackburn have explored how Haitian ideologies spread throughout the region, while Matt Childs, Matthew Smith and Marixa Lasso have highlighted instances of the direct influence of Haitian rebels on enslaved rebellions elsewhere in the Americas.[10]

Thanks to the centrality of slavery over the course of the Haitian Revolution and its enormous influence throughout the region, nationalizing states in Latin America approached the question of slavery rather differently than the United States had done a generation earlier. This has, though, only recently received historiographical engagement. The long-accepted thesis on the causes and progress of independence movements in South America is best surmised by John Lynch, who eschewed analysing the political ideals of independence and instead focused on its social and economic practicalities. He similarly looked to rebellion leadership as the ideological fulcrums of independence. Though certainly an important aspect of the discourse of liberty, Lynch avoided engaging with the reception of their approaches among rank-and-file revolutionaries. This meant that his exploration of independence narratives remained incomplete. And most enduringly, Lynch championed an analytical approach to Latin American nationalism that focused on the resulting multitude of states, a lens of analysis that occluded

---

[10]David Brion Davis, 'Impact of the Haitian Revolution', in David P. Geggus, ed., *The Impact of the Haitian Revolution in the Atlantic World* (Columbia: University of South Carolina Press, 2002), pp. 3–9; Robin Blackburn, 'The Force of Example', in Geggus, ed., *The Impact of the Haitian Revolution*, pp. 15–22; Juan R. González Mendoza, 'Puerto Rico's Creole Patriots and the Slave Trade after the Haitian Revolution', in Geggus, ed., *The Impact of the Haitian Revolution*, pp. 58–71; Matt D. Childs, '"A Black French General Arrived to Conquer the Island": Images of the Haitian Revolution in Cuba's 1812 Aponte Rebellion', in Geggus, ed., *The Impact of the Haitian Revolution*, pp. 135–56; Marixa Lasso, 'Haiti as an Image of Popular Republicanism in Caribbean Colombia: Cartagena Province (1811–1828), in Geggus, ed., *The Impact of the Haitian Revolution*, pp. 176–92; Matthew J. Smith, *Liberty, Fraternity, Exile: Haiti and Jamaica after Emancipation* (Chapel Hill: University of North Carolina Press, 2014); Laurent Dubois and Richard Lee Turits, *Freedom Roots: Histories from the Caribbean* (Chapel Hill: University of North Carolina Press, 2019).

the commonalities between the myriad revolutionary groups at work in early nineteenth-century Latin America.[11]

Though an impressive archival analysis of the social roots of nationalist thought in South America, Lynch paid only cursory attention to the role of non-white people in the successes of independence. Recent responses to this oversight have forcefully re-entered the question of race and slavery in the Latin American nationalism of the Age of Revolutions. Marixa Lasso is perhaps most effusive in her rejection of Lynch's findings. Her examination of the Colombian independence movement reveals the vital role that enslaved people played in both designing and securing national liberty. Lasso argues that Colombians of African descent forced revolutionary leaders to support emancipation and the revolution there was only successful because of the support of free people of colour.[12]

Others have taken Lasso's assertions even further. Ernesto Bassi argues that not only were enslaved and free people of African descent vital actors in Colombian independence movements but that they also had the ability to move across borders, thereby undermining the white-centric ideals of

---

[11]John Lynch, *The Spanish American Revolutions, 1808–1826* (London: Weidenfeld and Nicolson, 1973). For more recent examples of this approach, albeit with more attention to the ideological aspects of Latin American nationalism, see James E. Sanders, *The Vanguard of the Atlantic World: Creating Modernity, Nation, and Democracy in Nineteenth-Century Latin America* (Durham: Duke University Press, 2014); Anthony McFarlane, *War and Independence in Spanish America* (Abingdon: Routledge, 2008). Lynch's assertions about social upheaval contributing to independence movements suggests a watershed of liberalism, though recent reconsiderations of Iberian Atlantic society suggest a longer history of unrest and conflict over sovereignty. For more, see Jaime E. Rodriguez O., *The Independence of Spanish America* (Cambridge: Cambridge University Press, 2009); Jeremy Adelman, *Sovereignty and Revolution in the Iberian Atlantic* (Princeton: Princeton University Press, 2009).

[12]As a chapter specifically about the intersection of nationalism and African slavery, there is no space to engage in the similarly vital role that native Americans played in the independence stories of Latin America. For this side of the historiography, see, among many others, Florencia A. Mallon, *Peasant and Nation: The Making of Postcolonial Mexico and Peru* (Berkley: University of California Press, 1995); Ariel de la Fuente, *Children of Facundo: Caudillo and Gaucho Insurgency during the Argentine State-Formation Process (La Rioja, 1853–1870)* (Durham, NC: Duke University Press, 2000); Brooke Larson, *Trials of Nation Making: Liberalism, Race, and Ethnicity in the Andes, 1810–1910* (Cambridge: Cambridge University Press, 2004); Marcela Echeverri, *Indian and Slave Royalists in the Age of Revolution: Reform, Revolution, and Royalism in the Northern Andes, 1780–1825* (Cambridge: Cambridge University Press, 2016); Ben Vinson III, *Before Mestizaje: The Frontiers of Race and Caste in Colonial Mexico* (Cambridge: Cambridge University Press, 2018); Marixa Lasso, *Myths of Harmony: Race and Republicanism during the Age of Revolution, Colombia, 1795–1831* (Pittsburgh: University of Pittsburgh Press, 2007). Similarly important in ensuring the story of slavery was included in national stories in Latin Americas are Aline Helg, *Liberty and Equality in Caribbean Colombia, 1770–1835* (Chapel Hill: University of North Carolina Press, 2004). For how a similar process played out for Indian communities, see Sinclair Thompson, *We Alone Will Rule: Native Andean Politics in the Age of Insurgency* (Madison: University of Wisconsin Press, 2003); Rebecca A. Earle, *The Return of the Native: Indians and Myth-Making in Spanish America, 1810–1930* (Durham, NC: Duke University Press, 2007).

nationalist leadership. The white architects of the early national period in Latin America did not account for a subaltern community connected by race that ignored newly drawn state borders. Aline Helg further underlines the power that those of African descent held, charting the process of manumissions across the western hemisphere to reveal both the role that free people of colour played in independence movements but also their formative role in the ideological foundations of post-Age of Revolutions notions of liberty.[13]

The importance of those of African descent in the end of imperial rule and, in the case of much of Latin America, slavery itself, did not lead to racial equality. The ruling classes of many of these new nations worked hard to preserve a system of racialized labour exploitation without the now seemingly provincialized structures of unfreedom. Beyond Haiti, therefore, the political impetus for liberal nationalism was not as a critique of the 'malignant tendency' to preserve 'the revival of large-scale slavery' in the Atlantic. Rather, it was an unrelated yearning for cultural belonging whose architects hoped to preserve a system of chattel bondage that proved increasingly at odds with post-independence liberalism. Though slavery no longer existed in parts of the post-Age of Revolutions Americas, certain states continued to rely upon it. As a result, their national identities became still more firmly tied to slavery.[14]

Second Slavery: Reconciling liberty and unfreedom

The liberal political underpinnings of the Age of Revolutions created a juxtaposition with plantocratic slave labour systems as the predominant mode of wealth creation in the Americas. Given the extent to which plantations were engrained in national psyches, a clean economic break from slave labour in the Americas remained impossible. This gave rise to the era of the Second Slavery. This term refers to the period after the abolition of

---

[13]Ernesto Bassi, *An Aqueous Territory: Sailor Geographies and New Grenada's Transimperial Greater Caribbean World* (Durham, NC: Duke University Press, 2017); Aline Helg, *Slave No More: Slave No More: Self-Liberation before Abolitionism in the Americas* trans. Lara Vergnaud (Chapel Hill: University of North Carolina Press, 2019).
[14]Anderson, *Imagined Communities*, p. 60.

British transatlantic slave trading in 1807 when the centuries-old consensus on the acceptability of African enslavement in the Americas came to an end. For the purposes of this chapter, it also signifies the increasingly evident incompatibility of liberal national culture and enslavement as it existed in the colonial Americas.[15]

Because of this ideological conflict, the rise of Second Slavery effectively denotes the changed relationship between slaveholding and capitalism that developed in response to the industrializing of the Atlantic world in the nineteenth century. New zones of slave-built commodity production emerged in Brazil, Cuba and the United States South that dramatically tightened the rhetorical proximity between enslaved workers and a perpetually growing class of consumers both locally and beyond the ocean. This evolved form of chattel ended concerns that, as a system of labour, slavery was incompatible with industrialization and relied upon mercantile monopolies to be financially stable. The resulting shrinkage of Atlantic economic space triggered new debates over the place of African enslavement in a global marketplace once it became clear that slavery was in fact well-suited to industrialization and thrived in competitive markets.[16] This economic justification for industrialized slaveholding overruled any consequences from slavery being out of place politically in the post-Age of Revolutions era.

The newly independent Brazil, formed in 1822, experienced numerous enslaved rebellions while in its infancy. The state nevertheless perpetuated its plantocracy until well into the 1880s. The sheer number of imported Africans, far more than anywhere else in the Americas during the Age of Slavery, meant that even in independence, Brazilian national culture remained

---

[15] Anthony E. Kaye, 'The Second Slavery: Modernity in the Nineteenth-Century South and the Atlantic World', *Journal of Southern History* 75: 3 (2009), pp. 627–50; Dale W. Tomich, 'Civilizing America's Shore: British World-Economic Hegemony and the Abolition of the International Slave Trade (1814–1867), in Dale W. Tomich, ed., *The Politics of the Second Slavery* (Albany: State University of New York Press, 2016), pp. 1–24; Rafael Marquese and Tâmis Parron, 'International Proslavery: The Politics of the Second Slavery', in Tomich, ed., *The Politics of the Second Slavery*, pp. 25–56; Daniel B. Rood, *The Reinvention of Atlantic Slavery: Technology, Labor, Race, and Capitalism in the Greater Caribbean* (Oxford: Oxford University Press, 2017).

[16] Christopher Schmidt-Nowara, 'Spain and the Politics of the Second Slavery, 1808–1868', in Tomich, ed., *The Politics of the Second Slavery*, pp. 57–82; Luis Miguel Garciá Mora, 'The Paths of Freedom: Autonomism and Abolitionism in Cuba, 1878–1886', in Tomich, ed., *The Politics of the Second Slavery*, pp. 113–44; Ricardo Salles, 'Passive Revolution and the Politics of the Second Slavery in the Brazilian Empire', in Tomich, ed., *The Politics of the Second Slavery*, pp. 145–72; Dale W. Tomich, 'The Second Slavery and World Capitalism: A Perspective for Historical Inquiry', *International Review of Social History* 63: 3 (2018), pp. 477–501.

tightly associated with the institution of slavery. The racial exclusion that typified Brazilian national society mirrored its colonial experience as the state's racial minority looked to the past to maintain white supremacy. Those of African descent worked hard to undermine these efforts and, as they had done in the colonial era, made use of the court system to assert their place in the nation state. Their continued subjugation proved possible only because of a European desire for Brazilian-grown produce, in particular sugar and coffee, that undermined any moral campaign against unfree labour.[17]

The economic success of Brazilian goods abroad did not stop increased pressure from those of African descent to end slavery domestically. Beyond the courts, enslaved people and free people of colour worked hard to gain a foothold in Brazilian national culture. Debates over abolition increased political engagement among those of African descent and created a state that ideologically included people of colour for the first time. Though the abolition of slavery in 1888 was not a watershed moment for the rights of Black people, the end of Brazilian Second Slavery underscores the tight connection between enslavement and the national identity of Brazil.[18]

Though still a colony, Spanish Cuba nonetheless experienced the combined effects of Second Slavery and the rise of nationalism in the western hemisphere. During the mid-nineteenth century, Cuba experienced dozens of enslaved uprisings, most famously the mutiny aboard *La Amistad* in 1839 and the Conspiracy of *La Escalera* of 1841–4. Even as increased industrialization entrenched existing labour systems in the face of national ideologies, the events of the 1790s in Saint Domingue continued to shape slavery in Cuba. Some scholars have examined the extent to which British agents nurtured these moments of resistance. According to Robert Paquette,

---

[17] The most famous of these was the Malê Revolt that occurred in 1835 in the city of Salvador, Bahia. For an exhaustive treatment, see João José Reis, *Slave Rebellion in Brazil: The Muslim Uprising of 1835 in Bahia*, trans. Arthur Brakel (Baltimore: Johns Hopkins University Press, 1993). The deep roots of Brazilian slave culture are well explained in Stuart B. Schwartz, *Sugar Plantations in the Formation of Brazilian Society: Bahia, 1550–1835* (Cambridge: Cambridge University Press, 1985); Stuart B. Schwartz, *Slaves, Peasants, and Rebels: Reconsidering Brazilian Slavery* (Urbana-Champaign: University of Illinois Press, 1992); Roquinaldo Ferreira, *Cross-Cultural Exchange in the Atlantic World: Angola and Brazil during the Era of the Slave Trade* (Cambridge: Cambridge University Press, 2012). It was ultimately that moral pressure that caused Brazilian emancipation, though this only occurred in 1888. For more see Bronwen Everill, *Not Made by Slaves: Ethical Capitalism in the Age of Abolition* (Cambridge, MA: Harvard University Press, 2020).

[18] Dale T. Graden, *From Slavery to Freedom in Brazil: Bahia, 1835–1900* (Albuquerque: University of New Mexico Press, 2006); Celso Thomas Castilho, *Slave Emancipation and Transformations in Brazilian Political Citizenship* (Pittsburgh: University of Pittsburgh Press, 2016); Walter Fraga *Crossroads of Freedom: Slaves and Freed People in Bahia, Brazil, 1870–1910*, trans. Mary Ann Mahony (Durham, NC: Duke University Press, 2016).

abolitionists from Britain attempted to undermine the Second Slavery of Spanish Cuba, while Aisha Finch explains that Black people were more instrumental in upsetting the plantocracy on the island. Others, including Joseph Miller, James Sweet and Manuel Barcia have noted the pan-African commonalities between those of African descent in the Americas that underline the need to understand the existence of a pervading African identity that rebutted European imperial or American national distinctions.[19]

Despite the highlighting of a pan-African identity beyond the comprehension of white masters, there were connections between Black resistance to slavery and budding Cuban independence movements during the nineteenth century. The Haitian Revolution created an economic vacuum in the transatlantic sugar market that Cuban planters rushed to fill and in doing so worked to industrialize Cuban sugar production. This remade slavery in Cuba and the institution developed a hue that was both unique to the island and reflected a proto-nationalist relationship between creole planters and their enslaved laborers.[20]

---

[19] For a detailed analysis of the mutiny on *La Amistad*, see Michael Zeuske, *Amistad: A Hidden Network of Slavers and Merchants* trans. Steven Rendell (Princeton: Markus Wiener, 2015). On the Conspiracy of *La Escalera* see Michele Reid-Vasquez, *The Year of the Lash: Free People of Color in Cuba and the Nineteenth Century Atlantic World* (Athens: University of Georgia Press, 2011); Aisha K. Finch, *Rethinking Slave Rebellion in Cuba: La Escalera and the Insurgencies of 1841–1844* (Chapel Hill: University of North Carolina Press, 2015). See also Robert L. Paquette, *Sugar Is Made with Blood: The Conspiracy of La Escalera and the Conflict between Empires over Slavery in Cuba* (Middletown: Wesleyan University Press, 1988); Dale T. Graden, *Disease, Resistance, and Lies: The Demise of the Transatlantic Slave Trade to Brazil and Cuba* (Baton Rouge: Louisiana State University Press, 2014); Joseph C. Miller, 'Retention, Reinvention, and Remembering: Restoring Identities through Enslavement in Africa and under Slavery in Brazil', in José C. Curto and Paul E. Lovejoy, eds, *Enslaving Connections: Changing Cultures of Africa and Brazil during the Era of Slavery* (New York: Humanity Books, 2004), pp. 81–124; James H. Sweet, '"Not a Thing for White Men to See": Central African Divination in Seventeenth-Century Brazil', in Curto and Lovejoy, eds, *Enslaving Connections*, pp. 139–48; Manuel Barcia, *The Great African Slave Revolt of 1825: Cuba and the Fight for Freedom in Matanzas* (Baton Rouge: Louisiana State University Press, 2012); Manuel Barcia, *West African Warfare in Bahia and Cuba: Soldier Slaves in the Atlantic World, 1807–1844* (Oxford: Oxford University Press, 2014).

[20] Ada Ferrer, *Freedom's Mirror: Cuba and Haiti in the Age of Revolution* (Cambridge: Cambridge University Press, 2014); Christopher Schmidt-Nowara, *Slavery, Freedom, and Abolition in Latin America and the Atlantic World* (Albuquerque: University of New Mexico Press, 2016). For the challenges combining Black and national identities, see Pieter C. Emmer, 'The Price of Freedom: The Constraints of Change in Postemancipation America', in Frank McGlynn and Seymour Drescher, eds, *The Meaning of Freedom: Economics, Politics, and Culture after Slavery* (Pittsburgh: University of Pittsburgh Press, 1992), pp. 23–48; Michel-Rolph Trouillot, 'The Inconvenience of Freedom: Free People of Color and the Political Aftermath of Slavery in Dominica and Saint-Domingue/Haiti', in McGlynn and Drescher, eds, *The Meaning of Freedom*, pp. 147–82; David Kazanjian, *The Colonizing Trick: National Culture and Imperial Citizenship in Early America* (Minneapolis: University of Minnesota Press, 2003).

The relationship between enslaved people and planters developed a more urgent tone as the Cuban wars for independence began in 1868. Both Rebecca Scott and Ada Ferrer are adamant that Cuba's Black majority was instrumental in securing the separation of the island from Spain. The participation in Cuban nationalism from those of African descent not only racialized the wars and thereby further mixed slavery and national culture on the island, but also meant that enslaved people were equally responsible for ending Cuban slavery and Spanish colonization.[21]

The legacy of Black Cubans' contributions to the national cause during the nineteenth century has prompted further questions about the place of Blackness in national mythologies. These questions have driven comparative histories that analyse the place of those of African descent in post-colonial nations in the Americas. Looking beyond the nation comparatively unveils Black political, if not economic, involvement in the creation of national mythologies in Brazil and Cuba that did not occur in the post-emancipation United States or the British West Indies.[22]

To scholars of unfree labour systems, Second Slavery had perhaps the most interesting influence on the nationalism of the United States. Competing narratives emerged that further coloured an already intense regionalism

---

[21] Rebecca J. Scott, *Slave Emancipation in Cuba: The Transition to Free Labor, 1860–1899* (Princeton: Princeton University Press, 1985); Ada Ferrer, *Insurgent Cuba: Race, Nation, and Revolution, 1868–1898* (Chapel Hill: University of North Carolina Press, 1999). Others have engaged in similar narratives from elsewhere in the Spanish Caribbean. This historiography is particularly rich in the field of Dominican independence. See Anne Eller, *We Dream Together: Dominican Independence, Haiti, and the Fight for Caribbean Freedom* (Durham, NC: Duke University Press, 2016); Milagros Ricourt, *The Dominican Racial Imagery: Surveying the Landscape of Race and Nation in Hispaniola* (New Brunswick: Rutgers University Press, 2016); Dixa Ramírez, *Colonial Phantoms: Belonging and Refusal in the Dominican Americas, from the Nineteenth Century to the Present* (New York: New York University Press, 2018). This literature was heavily influenced by Julius Scott's long-unpublished 1986 PhD thesis, since released as Julius S. Scott, *The Common Wind: Afro-American Currents in the Age of the Haitian Revolution* (New York: Verso, 2018).

[22] For comparative analyses, see Rebecca J. Scott, *Degrees of Freedom: Louisiana and Cuba after Slavery* (Cambridge, MA: The Belknap Press, 2008); Alejandro de la Fuente and Ariela J. Gross, *Becoming Free, Becoming Black: Race, Freedom, and Law in Cuba, Virginia, and Louisiana* (Cambridge: Cambridge University Press, 2020). For work specifically on Brazil see Barbara Weinstein, *The Color of Modernity: São Paulo and the Making of Race and Nation in Brazil* (Durham, NC: Duke University Press, 2015); Yuko Miki, *Frontiers of Citizenship: A Black and Indigenous History of Postcolonial Brazil* (Cambridge: Cambridge University Press, 2019). For analysis of the British Empire see Thomas C. Holt, *The Problem of Freedom: Race, Labor, and Politics in Jamaica and Britain, 1823–1938* (Baltimore: Johns Hopkins University Press, 1991); Alexander X. Byrd, *Captives and Voyagers: Black Migrants across the Eighteenth-Century British Atlantic World* (Baton Rouge: Louisiana State University Press, 2008); Rosanne Marion Adderley, *'New Negroes from Africa': Slave Trade Abolition and Free African Settlement in the Nineteenth-Century Caribbean* (Bloomington: University of Indiana Press, 2006); Natasha Lightfoot, *Troubling Freedom: Antigua and the Aftermath of British Emancipation* (Durham, NC: Duke University Press, 2015).

between northern free states and slaveholding southern plantocracies. Both sides claimed to represent the true national identity of the country, a debate that eventually laid out the battle lines for the American Civil War of the 1860s. The industrial revolutions of the nineteenth century created such a demand for slave-grown cotton that, economically, the southern states took on the mantle for the whole national culture.[23]

The economic importance of chattel slavery to the American South meant that despite the decentralization of slavery in the United States, unfree labour remained an essential element of the national culture. This global demand for enslaved-grown crops fuelled the expansionary attitudes of pro-slavery southerners and led to their imposing their parochial economic structures elsewhere in the union through entrenchment of federal power. The temporality of this imposition has been analysed as well. While some, including Walter Johnson and Sven Beckert, believe that the economic importance of slavery to the national culture of the United States grew out of pre-independence systems, others, in particular Don Fehrenbacher and Joshua Lynn see a change in the nature of slavery that informed the early republic and antebellum eras.[24]

Though there certainly was an abundance of internal factors that contributed to the marriage of slavery and American nationalism, there also existed external forces that worked to solidify slavery in the national culture of the United States. Despite the industrializing of many of the Atlantic economic zones of commodity production, the integral role of slavery to that global marketplace meant that southern planters developed a distinct regional culture at odds with national norms. This meant that by the antebellum era, the southern planter minority had perhaps more in

---

[23] On the regionalist origins of the American Civil War, see, among many others, James McPherson, *Battle Cry of Freedom: The Civil War Era* (Oxford: Oxford University Press, 2003); Bruce Levine, *The Fall of the House of Dixie: The Civil War and the Social Revolution that Transformed the South* (New York: Random House, 2014); Don H. Doyle, *The Cause of All Nations: An International History of the American Civil War* (New York: Basic Books, 2014); Jonathan Daniel Wells, *A House Divided: The Civil War and Nineteenth-Century America* (Abingdon: Routledge, 2017).

[24] Walter Johnson, 'The Pedestal and the Veil: Rethinking the Capitalism/Slavery Question', *Journal of the Early Republic* 24: 2 (2004), pp. 299–308; Walter Johnson, *River of Dark Dreams: Slavery and Empire in the Cotton Kingdom* (Cambridge, MA: The Belknap Press, 2013); Sven Beckert, *Empire of Cotton: A Global History* (New York: Vintage, 2015); Edward E. Baptist, *The Half Has Never Been Told: Slavery and the Making of American Capitalism* (New York: Basic Books, 2016). On the role of southerners in the federal government, see Don E. Fehrenbacher, *The Dred Scott Case: Its Significance in American Law and Politics* (Oxford: Oxford University Press, 2001); Don E. Fehrenbacher, *The Slaveholding Republic: An Account of the United States Government's Relations to Slavery* ed. Ward M. McAfee (Oxford: Oxford University Press, 2001); Joshua A. Lynn, *Preserving the White Man's Republic: Jacksonian Democracy, Race, and the Transformation of American Conservatism* (Charlottesville: University of Virginia Press, 2019).

common with the rural slaveowners of Brazil and the Spanish Caribbean than with United States northerners of similar social standing. The roots of these elite divisions stretched back to before independence and mean that it is conceivable that the persistence of slavery in the American South thwarted any chance for a truly free national mythology to form in the United States.[25]

There existed a similar disconnect in the British Empire to do with the place of antislavery in its national culture. Since Eric Williams prompted fresh explorations of British abolitionism in the 1940s, antislavery has remained a topic of fascination for historians. Williams's work, pointing to the economically prudent ending of the British legal involvement in transatlantic slavery, inspired a reconsidering of the nature of antislavery in the British Empire. The Williams Thesis sparked huge backlash against the notion that white guilt did not factor into the ending of British slaving. Whether a factor in antislavery or not, the shift away from slavery in the Empire dramatically altered a national culture that had until then been heavily informed by engagement with an Atlantic slaveholding economy. There has still been no satisfactory conclusion to the questioning of the Williams Thesis, given the extent to which slavery was ingrained into British imperial culture until 1834.[26]

---

[25]Edward B. Rugemer, *The Problem of Emancipation: The Caribbean Roots of the American Civil War* (Baton Rouge: Louisiana State University Press, 2008); Matthew Pratt Guterl, *American Mediterranean: Southern Slaveholders in the Age of Emancipation* (Cambridge, MA: Harvard University Press, 2013); Edward B. Rugemer, *Slave Law and the Politics of Resistance in the Early Atlantic World* (Cambridge, MA: Harvard University Press, 2018).

[26]For a synthesis of the historiography of abolitionism, see Seymour Drescher, *Abolition: A History of Slavery and Anti-Slavery* (New York: Cambridge University Press, 2009); Manisha Sinha, *The Slave's Cause: A History of Abolition* (New Haven: Yale University Press, 2017). For Williams's work, see Eric Williams, *Capitalism and Slavery* (Chapel Hill: University of North Carolina Press, 1944). For Williams's enduring legacy, see Colin Palmer, *The Legacy of Eric Williams: Caribbean Scholar and Statesman* (Mona: University of the West Indies Press, 2015). *Capitalism and Slavery* evolved from Williams's D.Phil thesis from the University of Oxford, awarded in 1938. This has since been posthumously published as Eric Williams, *The Economic Aspect of the Abolition of the West Indian Slave Trade and Slavery* ed. Dale W. Tomich (Lanham, MD: Rowman & Littlefield, 2014). See also David Brion Davis, *The Problem of Slavery in Western Culture* (Ithaca: Cornell University Press, 1966); Howard Temperley, *British Antislavery 1833-1870* (Columbia: University of South Carolina Press, 1972); David Brion Davis, *The Problem of Slavery in the Age of Revolution, 1770-1823* (Ithaca: Cornell University Press, 1975); Seymour Drescher, *Econocide: British Slavery in the Era of Abolition* (Pittsburgh: University of Pittsburgh Press, 1977); Howard Temperley, 'Abolition and the National Interest', in Jack Hayward, ed., *Out of Slavery: Abolition and After* (London: Frank Cass, 1985), pp. 86–109; David Eltis, *Economic Growth and the Ending of the Transatlantic Slave Trade* (Oxford: Oxford University Press, 1987); Seymour Drescher, *Capitalism and Antislavery: British Mobilization in Comparative Perspective* (Oxford: Oxford University Press, 1987); Robin Blackburn, *The Overthrow of Colonial Slavery, 1776-1848* (New York: Verso, 1988); Selwyn H.H. Carrington, *The Sugar Industry and the Abolition of the Slave Trade, 1775-1810* (Gainesville: The University Press of Florida, 2002); Seymour Drescher, *The Mighty Experiment: Free Labor versus Slavery in British Emancipation* (Oxford: Oxford University Press, 2004); Claudius K. Fergus, *Revolutionary Emancipation: Slavery and Abolitionism in the British West Indies* (Baton Rouge: Louisiana State University Press, 2013).

Even so, after the emancipation of Britain's West Indian enslaved people, antislavery became a vital characteristic of Britishness. Recent work from David Lambert, Christopher Brown and Richard Huzzey has examined the role of abolitionism in Britain's national ideology, in particular its role in domestic and foreign politics. Their analyses explain how abolitionism provided oftentimes opposing groups a common foreign enemy who countered much of what was lauded as civil in British national culture. Studies of British abolitionism have also included discussions over the nature of the freedom presented to those of African descent in the Empire, in particular the relationship between Black slavery and white-class struggle. This only further engrained the question of slavery, albeit as a blight on the Atlantic world, as part of British culture.[27]

Second Slavery solved the incompatibility of slavery and nationalism that characterized race relations during the Age of Revolutions in the Americas. This new, industrialized, slavery allowed planters to continue profiting from unfree labour despite the advent of liberal nationalism in Brazil and the United States and allowed colonists in Cuba to reject calls for independence until late in the nineteenth century. In contrast, antislavery became a national marker in Britain, where a culture of abolitionism developed in opposition to the slaveholding economies that emerged after the birth of the modern nation state.

---

[27]David Lambert, *White Creole Culture, Politics, and Identity during the Age of Abolition* (Cambridge: Cambridge University Press, 2005); Christopher Leslie Brown, *Moral Capital: Foundations of British Abolitionism* (Chapel Hill: University of North Carolina Press, 2006); Huzzey, *Freedom Burning*. See also Adam Hochschild, *Bury the Chains: Prophets and Rebels in the Fight to Free an Empire's Slaves* (New York: Houghton Mifflin Harcourt, 2005); David Brion Davis, 'Slavery, Emancipation, and Progress', in Donald A. Yerxa, ed., *British Abolitionism and the Question of Moral Progress in History* (Columbia: University of South Carolina Press, 2012), pp. 13–36; Lamin Sanneh, 'Slavery, Antislavery, and Moral Progress: A Comparative Historical Perspective', in Yerxa, ed., *British Abolitionism*, pp. 81–98; David Brion Davis, *The Problem of Slavery in the Age of Emancipation* (New York: Alfred A. Knopf, 2014). On the role of anti-slave trade activity on British imperialism, see Seymour Drescher, 'Emperors of the World: British Abolitionism and Imperialism', in Derek R. Peterson, ed., *Abolitionism and Imperialism in Britain, Africa, and the Atlantic* (Athens: Ohio University Press, 2010), pp. 129–49; Michael Craton, 'Proto-Peasant Revolts? The Late Slave Rebellions in the British West Indies, 1816–1832', *Past & Present* 85 (1979), pp. 99–125; David Beck Ryden, *West Indian Slavery and British Abolition* (Cambridge: Cambridge University Press, 2009); Robin Blackburn, *American Crucible: Slavery, Emancipation, and Human Rights* (New York: Verso, 2011); Benton and Ford, *Rage for Order*; David Kazanjian, *The Brink of Freedom: Improvising Life in the Nineteenth-Century Atlantic World* (Durham, NC: Duke University Press, 2016).

Conclusion

Despite British politicians' engagement with antislavery as an aspect of nationalism, white supremacy endured. As other Atlantic states, including Cuba, Brazil, and the United States, began to replace slavery with antislavery as national cultural artefacts in the later nineteenth and early twentieth centuries, the presence of sizeable free minorities of African descent concerned white national ideologues throughout the Atlantic world. This, combined with a renewed appetite for aggressive imperial expansion in Africa among European states meant that even with abolition, slavery remained a topic of frequent discourse in the development of national ideologies.[28]

As an enslaved person could not be of a nation that espoused the tenets of liberty, nationalist ideologues excluded those enslaved people from membership to the state during the Age of Revolutions. After emancipation, nation states throughout the Atlantic world reconciled their new-fangled identities without the institution of slavery. The legacy of exclusion of those of African descent based on slavery continued after emancipation, grounded in racial divisions. The scholars of slavery who have interrogated this dichotomy reveal that the predominance of the slavery question during the creation of national identities means that, in essence, national histories are histories of slavery.

---

[28]Paul Gilroy, *There Ain't No Black in the Union Jack* (Chicago: University of Chicago Press, 1987) is the best articulation of this argument for the exclusionary origins of British national culture but looking at slavery in the Atlantic world demonstrates that this was not unique to Britain. For the response of those of African descent, see Paul Gilroy, *The Black Atlantic: Modernity and Double-Consciousness* (Cambridge, MA: Harvard University Press, 1993). For more on African colonization, see G.N. Nzoigwe, 'Reflections on the Berlin West Africa Conference, 1884–1885', *Journal of the Historical Society of Nigeria* 12: 3–4 (1984), pp. 9–22; Stig Forster et al. (eds.), *Bismark, Europe, and Africa: The Berlin Conference, 1884–1885 and the Onset of Partition* (London: Oxford University Press for the German Historical Institute, 1988); Robin Law, 'Abolition and Imperialism: International Law and the British Suppression of the Atlantic Slave Trade', in Peterson, ed., *Abolitionism and Imperialism*, pp. 150–74; Bronwen Everill, *Abolition and Empire in Sierra Leone and Liberia* (Cambridge: Palgrave Macmillan, 2012); Matthew Craven, 'Between Law and History: The Berlin Conference of 1884–1885 and the Logic of Free Trade', *London Review of International Law* 3: 1 (2015), pp. 31–59; Padraic X. Scanlan, 'Blood, Money, and Endless Paper: Slavery and Capital in British Imperial History', *History Compass* 14: 5 (2016), pp. 218–30

Bibliography

'The 1619 Project'. *The New York Times*, 14 August 2019.

Brown, Christopher Leslie, *Moral Capital: Foundations of British Abolitionism* (Chapel Hill: University of North Carolina Press, 2006).

Castilho, Thomas Celso, *Slave Emancipation and Transformations in Brazilian Political Citizenship* (Pittsburgh: University of Pittsburgh Press, 2016).

Dubois, Laurent, *A Colony of Citizens: Revolution and Slave Emancipation in the French Caribbean, 1787–1804* (Chapel Hill: University of North Carolina Press, 2004).

Ferrer, Ada, *Freedom's Mirror: Cuba and Haiti in the Age of Revolution* (Cambridge: Cambridge University Press, 2014).

Gilroy, Paul, *There Ain't No Black in the Union Jack* (Chicago: University of Chicago Press, 1987).

Holton, Woody, *Forced Founders: Indians, Debtors, Slaves, and the Making of the American Revolution in Virginia* (Chapel Hill: University of North Carolina Press, 1999).

Huzzey, Richard, *Freedom Burning: Anti-Slavery and Empire in Victorian Britain* (Ithaca: Cornell University Press, 2012).

Johnson, Walter, *River of Dark Dreams: Slavery and Empire in the Cotton Kingdom* (Cambridge, MA: The Belknap Press, 2013).

Lasso, Marixa, *Myths of Harmony: Race and Republicanism during the Age of Revolution, Colombia, 1795–1831* (Pittsburgh: University of Pittsburgh Press, 2007).

9
Writing the religious history of the enslaved in the Atlantic World

Matt D. Childs

University of South Carolina

The enterprise of human enslavement has coercively and intimately bonded with religion for much of recorded history. Masters have utilized religion as one of the primary tools in converting people into property in their designs of human domination. Slaves have ingeniously asserted their humanity through invoking religion to counter their enslavement through strategies of resistance. Given the central role religion has played in defining the institution of slavery for masters and slaves alike, it is not surprising that there is a voluminous scholarship on the topic from institutional, intellectual, political, social and cultural perspectives. Indeed, the relationship between slavery and religion is so central to our understanding of the history of slavery, it's hard to find scholarship that does not address the topic in one form or another, either directly or indirectly, centrally or obliquely.

This chapter analyses how historians have framed and studied the relationship between slavery and religion. In examining this very broad and even lengthier body of scholarship, I focus on literature dealing with the topic that covers primarily the era of Atlantic enslavement from the fifteenth to the nineteenth centuries to give the analysis some coherence, and more humbly reflect my own limited area of expertise. Within that temporal and geographic framework, I draw from African, Caribbean and Latin American studies of slavery and religion, and survey the scholarship on the United States from the perspective of 30,000 feet, with occasional dive bombs to leave a few droppings on its dense and sophisticated, albeit often parochial historiography. After a very cursory overview of slavery and the monotheistic faiths of Judaism, Islam and Christianity, followed by a brief examination of the relationship between slavery, the Roman Empire and Christianity, I then turn to Atlantic slavery. Given the Christian Church as an institution has been a prolific generator of primary sources, I analyse how the empirical documentation of ecclesiastical sources has been used by scholars of slavery in various ways to write the history of Atlantic enslavement. Finally, I turn to a thematic treatment of how historians have employed religion as a category of analysis to tell the history of slavery from comparative, intellectual, social, cultural and gendered perspectives. This chapter tips more to telling the history of the enslaved than the enslavers, and focuses mainly on the population of African descent, even though I recognize there is a large literature on indigenous enslavement in its pre-Columbian and post-Columbian variants, as well as other forms of bonded labour relations such as indentured servants. In surveying the historiography of the topic spread across time, place, empires and nations in the Atlantic World, it becomes readily apparent that historians are far more interested in writing about Christianity among the enslaved, than the religious histories of the population of African descent and their diverse belief systems.

Monotheistic perspectives, imperial models and ecclesiastical sources

All three of the dominant monotheistic faiths of the Judeo-Christian-Islamic tradition recognized slavery in their key religious texts, which subsequently has cast a long shadow over both pro- and antislavery positions. The Hebrew Bible, commonly called the Old Testament in Christian writings, has many references to slaves and slavery, most notably in *Exodus*, *Deuteronomy* and *Leviticus*. These references and their subsequent incorporation into the Christian Bible as the Old Testament provided a sacred text from which slavery could be justified, and also challenged. Whether dramatically fleeing slavery through the liberating story in *Exodus*, or recognizing the authority of masters and commentary on the treatment of slaves in *Deuteronomy* and *Leviticus*, among other passages, the Hebrew Bible and the Old Testament prominently featured slavery in their most important passages. Consequently, the Bible is probably the most exegeted work on the topic of slavery. Historian David Brion Davis's intellectual treatment of these contradictions addressed by Church Fathers and Theologians has shown that the Christian Church came to accept slavery as a natural law adapted and modified for sinful humans, even while it upheld the ideal of a spiritual utopia in which all of humanity could be free. When slavery went from being an accepted to an unacceptable institution and challenged at a systemic level from political, intellectual and cultural perspectives (rather than at the individual level) in the eighteenth and nineteenth centuries, pro-slavery and antislavery forces appropriated these Biblical passages for their intense debates.[1]

Although not as important as the Bible in eliciting debates and justifying political and moral positions on the question of abolition in the Americas, Islam and in particular Islamic law shaped the experiences and expectations of the enslaved subsequently brought to the Americas. The Quran contains numerous references to slaves, the treatment of slaves by masters and the process of manumission for slaves. In the ninth and tenth centuries jurists elaborated on these passages to develop a series of laws to govern slavery. As Islam spread from the Arabian Peninsula across the Sahara and into West Africa, many slaves brought to the Americas carried with them an understanding of Islamic slave laws. Historian Paul Lovejoy has examined Islamic slave practices such as self-purchase, hiring out slaves to other masters, or working on their own and turning over their wages to their masters. In the Sokoto Caliphate for example, one of the largest slave societies in West Africa and a source for slaves brought into the Americas, the concept known as *murgu* involved a payment made by slaves to their master for the right to work on their own account.

---

[1] See, for example, David Brion Davis, *The Problem of Slavery in Western Culture* (Ithaca, NY: Cornell University Press, 1966); *The Problem of Slavery in the Age of Revolution, 1770–1823* (Ithaca, NY: Cornell University Press, 1975); and *In the Image of God: Religion, Moral Values, and our Heritage of Slavery* (New Haven, CT: Yale University Press, 2001). For a selection of excerpts from the Bible dealing with slavery, see Stanley Engerman, Seymour Drescher, and Robert Paquette, eds, *Slavery* (Oxford: Oxford University Press, 2001), pp. 7–8, 60–1, and 93–6.

Through the payment of *murgu*, slaves could purchase their own freedom, marry, maintain separate households and acquire some legal and social separation from master's dominion. African familiarity with this practice likely aided some slaves in the Americas. In Brazil and Cuba, for example, slaves used their knowledge of *murgu* and applied the concept to their New World environment as they strategized about freedom through the Iberian practice of *coartación* and *cortacāo*, whereby slaves had a legal right to purchase their freedom. Consequently, although very few masters were Muslims in the New World, the slaves understanding of Islamic law influenced their experiences and expectations of enslavement on the other side of the Atlantic from a religious perspective even when they were engaged in what a Christian colony would have largely regarded as a secular economic transaction.[2]

The Roman Empire and in particular its laws and imperial methods for organizing conquered territories and extracting labour through slavery served as a model for the development of Atlantic Slavery. The New World slave empires of the Portuguese, Spanish, British, French and Dutch had studied the Roman Empire and drew inspiration and justification for how Rome extended its civilization through Europe and the Mediterranean. Although the conversion of enslaved populations conquered through warfare and evangelization in acquired territories was not as pronounced for the Roman Empire as it would be for the Spanish and Portuguese, that connection served as an important historic example in braiding together empire, religion and slavery. Historian Jeffrey Fynn-Paul found that as the relationship between empire, monotheism and slavery became solidified in the first millennium, it resulted in areas on the borders of Roman Empire being defined as 'slaving zones' for a source of labourers. Similarly, on the East Roman frontier zone, the process of conversion and focusing on captive women became a conscious strategy of extending Roman civilization and

---

[2]See Paul E. Lovejoy, 'Murgu: The Wages of Slavery in the Sokoto Caliphate', *Slavery & Abolition: A Journal of Slave and Post-Slave Studies* 14: 1 (1993), pp. 168–85; Paul E. Lovejoy, 'Muslim Freedmen in the Atlantic World: Images of Manumission and Self-Redemption' in Paul E. Lovejoy, ed., *Slavery on the Frontiers of Islam* (Princeton, NJ: Markus Wiener Publishers, 2004), pp. 233–58, esp. 243–4. For a selection of excerpts from the Quran dealing with slavery, see Engerman, Drescher, and Paquette, eds, *Slavery*, pp. 99–100. Also see Daniel B. Domingues da Silva, David Eltis, Nafees Khan, Philip Misevich, and Olatunji Ojo, 'The Transatlantic Muslim Diaspora to Latin America in the Nineteenth Century', *Colonial Latin American Review* 26: 4 (2017), pp. 528–45; Manuel Barcia, 'West African Islam in Colonial Cuba', *Slavery & Abolition* 35: 2 (2014), pp. 292–305.

religious institutions into conquered territories. As Spain solidified its control in mainland Latin America and brought indigenous civilizations under its rule, and the Catholic Church expanded through the hemisphere along with the state, references and comparison to the Roman emperor Constantine and his embrace of Christianity became more common as a historic model to emulate.[3]

Rome not only served as an example for how to link religion, empire and slavery, but its legal culture shaped the record keeping of many New World slave systems through its notarial conventions reflected in secular and non-secular sources. For the sake of clarity and brevity, ecclesiastical sources can be broken down into three types that have influenced how historians have written the history of slavery and religion: social, cultural and intellectual.

Social historians of slavery have long utilized church-generated sources to write what has become known as 'history from below'. Utilizing baptismal records historians have reconstructed family relations and fictive and extended kin networks. Analysing these sources historians have shown how elements of family structure became reassembled, and the central role of women in maintaining and building slave communities through serving as godmothers, often to multiple godchildren. Similarly, last wills and testaments of masters, slaves and free people of colour have allowed scholars to analyse the social experience of slaves listed as inventoried property, but also as authors of their own wills as well. Burial certificates of slaves have been analysed to assess life span and the impact of slavery on the health of the enslaved. As these serial sources record gender, race, ethnicity and legal status, historians have employed them for demographic analysis to differentiate the many experiences of enslavement spread across space and time. Recognizing the utility of these ecclesiastical sources for writing the history of slavery, several digitization efforts have been completed and are currently in process to make them more widely available such as the Slave Societies Digital Archive (formerly Ecclesiastical and Secular Sources for Slave Societies), directed by Jane Landers and hosted at Vanderbilt

---

[3]Jeffrey Fynn-Paul, 'Empire, Monotheism and Slavery in the Greater Mediterranean Region from Antiquity to the Early Modern Era', *Past & Present* 205 (November 2009), pp. 3–40; Andrea Sterk, 'Mission from Below: Captive Women and Conversion on the East Roman Frontiers', *Church History* 79: 1 (March 2010), pp. 1–39; Anthony Pagden, *Lords of all the World: Ideologies of Empire in Spain, Britain and France, c. 1500–c. 1800* (New Haven, CT: Yale University Press, 1995), p. 32.

University, which preserves endangered ecclesiastical documents related to Africans and African-descended peoples in New World slave societies.[4]

Ecclesiastical sources have also provided rich ethnographic and cultural insights into the lives and thoughts of the enslaved. The Spanish and Portuguese Inquisitions operated in Latin America during the colonial period and had investigative bodies in Mexico, Peru, Colombia and Brazil. Similar to the methods religious historians of medieval and early modern Europe developed to look into peasant, popular and plebeian belief systems through such techniques as microhistory, the Catholic church's investigations into what it deemed unorthodox religious practices produced rich documentary records of the enslaved. Historians have used these sources to examine beliefs and rituals that expressed ideas and worldviews that can be traced back to Africa. Similarly, the investigations by the inquisition also show how colonial masters' own religious practices and customs were being transformed by the cosmologies of the enslaved. Beyond inquisitional sources, church investigations and documents generated through canon law have been used by historians of slavery to examine such issues as slaves appealing to the church to intervene in legal matters and the church investigating abuses of slaves. The British and American slave societies did not generate a similar body of documentation from an ecclesiastical perspective. However, when certain religious practices such as obeah were outlawed in the nineteenth century, secular judicial bodies began investigating them that produced similarly rich records for the practices and customs of the population of African descent. As many of the legal documents dealing with religious practices record the transcribed spoken words of the slaves, and sometimes in African languages, albeit

---

[4]For more than fifty years historians have been writing the social history of the enslaved through ecclesiastical sources; for examples see Frederick P. Bowser, *The African Slave in Colonial Peru, 1524–1650* (Stanford: Stanford University Press, 1974); Stuart B. Schwartz, *Sugar Plantations in the Formation of Brazilian Society, Bahia 1550–1835* (Cambridge: Cambridge University Press, 1985); Gwendolyn Midlo Hall, *Africans in Colonial Louisiana: The Development of Afro-Creole Culture in the Eighteenth Century* (Baton Rouge: Louisiana State University Press, 1992); Jane G. Landers, *Black Society in Spanish Florida* (Urbana: University of Illinois Press, 1999); Herman L. Bennett, *Africans in Colonial Mexico: Absolutism, Christianity, and Afro-Creole Consciousness, 1570–1640* (Bloomington: Indiana University Press, 2003); and Sherwin K. Bryant, *Rivers of Gold, Lives of Bondage: Governing through Slavery in Colonial Quito* (Chapel Hill: University of North Carolina Press, 2014). For digitization of ecclesiastical sources see examples such as 'Slave Societies Digital Archive': https://www.slavesocieties.org_British Endangered Archives Programme of 'Diaspora Collections at the Major Archives of the Province of Matanzas Cuba (EAP060)': https://eap.bl.uk/project/EAP060.

mediated through the coercive techniques of the investigating body, they have been a rich source for writing the cultural history of the enslaved.[5]

In contrast to the Latin American slave societies that generated extensive ecclesiastical notarial and judicial sources, the Protestant slave societies through the genres of autobiographical narrative of conversion and spiritual diary recording produced a large corpus of texts for historians to examine the cultural and intellectual dimensions of slavery and religion. Beginning in the eighteenth century and continuing through the nineteenth century, hundreds of slave narratives were published that provided details on the individual experiences of slaves often through a religious framework of conversion, such as in the autobiography of Oladauh Equiano. These accounts testified to how earthly masters prevented slaves from having an individual relationship with a spiritual master. As the abolitionist movement developed at the end of the eighteenth century, the writing, publishing and dissemination of these texts became testimonials in the service of denouncing slavery. Historians have paired these texts with the American WPA slave interviews conducted in the 1930s to work from a large body of consciously self-reflective texts with extensive interior insights (*ego*) into religious and spiritual matters. Ever since the publication of these autobiographical accounts, historians have utilized these narratives to analyse the religious, intellectual and cultural history of the enslaved and their relationship to masters.[6]

---

[5]See, for example, Gonzalo Aguirre Beltrán, *La población negra de México: Estudio etnohistórico* (Mexico City: Fondo de Cultura Económica, 1946); Laura de Mello E Souza, *O diabo e terra de Santa Cruz: feitiçaria e religiosidade popular no Brasil colonial* (São Paulo: Companhia das letras, 1986); Laura A. Lewis, *Hall of Mirrors: Power, Witchcraft, and Caste in Colonial Mexico* (Durham, NC: Duke University Press, 2003); James H. Sweet, *Recreating Africa: Culture, Kinship, and Religion in the African-Portuguese World, 1441–1770* (Chapel Hill: University of North Carolina Press, 2003); Joan Cameron Bristol, *Christians, Blasphemers, and Witches: Afro-Mexican Ritual Practice in the Seventeenth Century* (Albuquerque: University of New Mexico Press, 2007); Diana Paton, *The Cultural Politics of Obeah: Religion, Colonialism and Modernity in the Caribbean World* (Cambridge: Cambridge University Press, 2015); the special issue of *Atlantic Studies*, 12. 2 (2015) titled 'Obeah: Knowledge, Power, and Writing in the Early Atlantic World'; and Pablo F. Gomez, *The Experiential Caribbean: Creating Knowledge and Healing in the Early Modern Atlantic* (Chapel Hill: University of North Carolina Press, 2017).

[6]Among the many scholars that use these texts see John W. Blassingame, *The Slave Community* (Oxford: Oxford University Press, 1972); Eugene D. Genovese, *Roll, Jordan, Roll: The World the Slaves Made* (New York: Random House, 1974); Charles Joyner, *Down by the Riverside: A South Carolina Slave Community* (Urbana: University of Illinois Press, 1984); William L. Andrews, *To Tell a Free Story: The First Century of Afro-American Autobiography, 1760–1865* (Urbana: University of Illinois Press, 1986); Vincent Carretta, *Equiano, the African: Biography of a Self-Made Man* (Athens: University of Georgia Press, 2005); James Sidbury, *Becoming African in America: Race and Nation in the Early Black Atlantic* (Oxford: Oxford University Press, 2007); Ras Michael Brown, *African-Atlantic Cultures and the South Carolina Lowcountry* (Cambridge: Cambridge

The contrast in the generation of ecclesiastical sources between Catholic and Protestant slave societies influenced historian Frank Tannenbaum's formulation on the comparative differences between Iberian and British slavery in his now classic *Slave & Citizen* (1946). Tannenbaum argued that the institutions of the law and the church in Iberian slave societies served as a mediating force in limiting masters' authority and provided a political and cultural space for former slaves to become citizens. By contrast, in British America legal and religious institutions did not serve the same buffering role for the enslaved, and the limited rights accorded to former slaves in post-emancipation societies could be explained by the absence of such institutions. Subsequently known as the 'Tannenbaum Thesis', it remains one of the longest ongoing debates in the historical literature on New World slavery.[7]

The 'Tannenbaum Thesis' has shown a remarkable resilience for staying relevant as each new generation 'rediscovers' the book's insights. At the time of the fiftieth anniversary of the publication of his essay in 1996, the book had sold over 100,000 copies. The ongoing importance of the 'Tannenbaum Thesis' for shaping slave studies has resulted in several historiographical assessments of his argument over the last twenty years. Scholars today are not interested in the facile positions of what slave society was the 'worse' or 'better', or proving that Tannenbaum was right about this colony/nation, but wrong about that one, which animated earlier assessments in the 1960s and 1970s. Over the last twenty years scholars have found that Tannenbaum was onto something in recognizing the role of the Catholic Church as an important institution in shaping the experience of slaves (in addition to the law). However, unlike the argument in *Slave & Citizen* that is more of an essay rather than a monograph supported by detailed research, historians now stress the initiative and actions of slaves themselves. The 'Neo-Tannenbaum' approach emphasizes how slaves utilized, flexed and employed the church to mediate their experiences, rather than seeing the church itself as an independent and benevolent arbitrator of the relationship between master and slaves. For these scholars, it is often the voluminous ecclesiastical sources documenting the actions of the slaves that are ushered in support of

---

University Press, 2012); Tera W. Hunter, *Bound in Wedlock: Slave and Free Black Marriage in the Nineteenth Century* (Cambridge, MA: Belknap Press, 2017). For methodological treatment of these sources, see Sharon Ann Musher, "'Contesting the Way the Almighty Wants It:" Crafting Memories of Ex-Slaves in the Slave Narrative Collection', *American Quarterly* 53: 1 (2001), pp. 1–31.
[7]Frank Tannenbaum, *Slave & Citizen: The Negro in the Americas* (New York: Alfred A. Knopf, 1946).

their position of the relevance of the church in shaping the slave experience. In other words, the Tannenbaum 'thesis' is often 'proofed' by the voluminous documentation generated by the church in Latin America (as well as legal records), and the absence of such materials for British America.[8]

In summary, the Christian Church, whether Catholic or Protestant, and its generation of ecclesiastical sources have provided much of the foundation for the empirical documentation historians have employed in their studies. These sources have decisively influenced how the history of religion and slavery has been written. But even more broadly, without religious sources much of the history of Atlantic slavery would not be written at its current level of depth and detail.

Conceptualizing transformations in the religions of the enslaved from the discipline of history

In surveying the historiography of slavery and religion as it relates to Atlantic Slavery, the single overarching topic that has framed most studies is how African cosmologies became transformed into New World belief systems. This mirrors the overall thrust of slave studies writ large that examine how a human became transformed into a commodity, a person transformed into property, a people transformed into a racial-juridical category. Methodologically and conceptually studying these processes has proved challenging for the historical profession due to its prioritizing Western history over non-Western history. Historians have long abandoned and denounced the enlightened idea that Europe had a 'history' that could be recovered through professional and scientific research methods, whereas Africa, Latin America and Asia had stories and customs that are better suited for the expertise of anthropologists, archaeologists and folklorists. Put succinctly, Europe's history was sophisticated enough to merit empirical historical analysis, whereas Africa, Asia and Latin America's history was

---

[8]For various assessments of the 'Tannenbaum Thesis' and a bibliography of the numerous works influenced by his study, see the special issue of *Law and History Review*, 22: 2 (Summer 2004); and Alejandro de la Fuente, 'From Slaves to Citizens?: Tannenbaum and the Debates on Slavery, Emancipation, and Race Relations in Latin America', *International Labor and Working-Class History* 77 (Spring 2010), pp. 154–73.

more myth than fact. Despite the profession's correction and disavowal of Eurocentric history since the 1960s, earlier legacies can still be discerned. For example, regardless of all the innovations in capturing the experiences of the indigenous population in Latin American history through reading indigenous language texts and employing multi-disciplinary perspectives, Pre-Columbian history still remains largely the work of anthropologists and archaeologists while 'colonial' and 'modern' Latin American history remains the work of historians. To cite just one example, the *Oxford Handbook of Latin American History* (2010) provides detailed information on the history of indigenous populations spread over several chapters, yet all of them focus on the post-Columbian period. Latin America enters the historical profession as a historical topic fully once the Europeans arrive on the scene at the end of the fifteenth century; everything prior ends up being a pre-history.[9]

For histories of Africa the same problem presents itself, but in a different form. The periodization of African history is usually divided into pre-colonial, colonial and postcolonial. Consequently, African history is defined by the presence or absence of Europeans. Unlike European history that has developed a periodization and chronological breaks particular to its own internal history dynamics (medieval, early modern, modern), African history periodization is defined most prominently by the external history dynamics of Europeans. Historian James Sweet has pointed out the multiple ramifications of this problem from methodological, conceptual, epistemological and ontological angles. In response, Africanists have developed innovative methodologies for dealing with a primary source base that often is not tied to a written text and does not fetishize the archive. For example, oral histories and the study of historical memory have been a staple of African history for decades, but only now are regarded as *au currant* for the historical profession as a whole. Scholars outside of African studies have been hesitant to recognize these methods and approaches despite the

---

[9] For the historical profession and the division between the West having a 'history' while the non-West being a people 'without a history', see the summary in Georg G. Iggers, *Historiography in the Twentieth Century: From Scientific Objectivity to the Postmodern Challenge*, with a new epilogue (Middletown, CO: Wesleyan University Press, 2005). *The Oxford Handbook of Latin American History*, ed. Jose Moya (Oxford: Oxford University Press, 2010) is not unique in demonstrating how periodization often follows disciplinary specialization as a survey of Latin American history journals such as the *Hispanic American Historical Review* and *The Americas* shows even while they have focused on indigenous history topics. For a critique of this 'pre-history' approach, see Juliana Barr, 'There's No Such Thing as "Prehistory": What the Long Durée of Caddo and Pueblo History Tell Us about Colonial America', *The William and Mary Quarterly* 74: 2 (April 2017), pp. 203–40.

humanities embrace and celebration of multi-disciplinary perspectives. The disciplinary 'borders' between history and non-history, or the even more permeable multi-disciplinary 'frontiers' that shapeshift depending on scholarly perspective, have produced an unequal primary source base and secondary literature on the topic of African religions compared with the history of the enslaved in the Americas. The discrepancy between primary documentation and secondary literature that handicaps our understanding of Africa's past, yet prioritizes its history of enslavement as subjects of history rather than agents of their own history, has resulted in *Silencing the [African] Past* to invoke Michel-Rolph Trouillot's formulation.[10]

These issues are more than just academic and philosophical musings, and cannot be so easily dismissed as a defensive rant in support of non-Western history from a partisan perspective. Rather, for the purpose of this chapter in assessing the writing of history of slavery and religion, my point is that it's actually easier for historians to study how cosmologies in Africa became religions in the Americas because of the basic ideas that structure history as a discipline. The tradition of historical writing with a thematic focus on religion has a long history of examining how various heterogeneous religious systems became incorporated into Catholic and Protestant orthodoxy as a process of centralization and modernization whether through the Roman Empire, medieval kingdoms, absolutist monarchs or republican democracies in step with the liberal march of history. From the particular to the universal. By contrast, African religions that display parallel belief systems, eclectic incorporation of multiple cosmologies, religious authority not tied to a text, secret and undocumented initiation ceremonies, and a stubborn disregard for time as a linear process have made it difficult to analyse these customs, traditions and belief systems through a Western historical framework.

If history as a discipline prioritizes change over time as the benchmark of scholarly analysis and narrative presentation, what does the scholar do when confronted with a topic from the past with an imperfect documentary base that does not lend itself easily to historical analysis? For some scholars, these phenomena whether religious, social or cultural are just too ahistorical, empirically impoverished, and do not display enough change over time to be

---

[10]James H. Sweet, 'Reimagining the African-Atlantic Archive: Method, Concept, Epistemology, Ontology', The *Journal of African History* 55: 2 (July 2014), pp. 147–59; also see the similar comments by Joseph C. Miller, 'History in Africa/Africa and History', *American Historical Review*, 104: 1 (February 1999), pp. 1–32; Joseph C. Miller, *The Problem of Slavery as History* (New Haven, CT: Yale University Press, 2012), esp. ch. 4; and Michel-Rolph Trouillot, *Silencing the Past: Power and the Production of History* (Boston, MA: Beacon Press, 1995), esp. 70–107.

studied from a social scientific or humanistic perspective. Fortunately, these discrepancies in method and the particular analytical and investigatory perspectives of historical sub-disciplines whether they are African, American or European are now recognized as an opportunity not to have one method colonize another, or coercively impose one disciplinary standard on another, but more beneficially learn the different ways to write the history of slavery and religion in the Atlantic World.[11]

Pre-colonial African history and the religious perspectives of the enslaved

Over the last thirty years, one of the great innovations in writing the religious history of the enslaved has been the development of pre-colonial African historiography. Previously, scholars studying the religious beliefs of the enslaved in the Americas often used contemporary descriptions of folk customs and telescoped backwards to explain historical religious practices. With the publications by scholars such as Joseph Miller, Robin Law, Linda Heywood, Paul Lovejoy, Sandra Greene, Patrick Manning, Edna Bay and John Thornton, a corpus of secondary texts provided detailed historical analysis of pre-colonial Africa. This new historiography paired with English becoming the *lingua franca* of academic scholarship, which has now made it far more easier for monoglot American historians in particular to read secondary literature outside of their own fields. If these texts were not written in English, they would have been largely ignored by scholars outside of African studies. Just as important, this historical scholarship was written in a framework that enriched our understanding of pre-colonial African history, but also spoke directly to central issues animating the scholarship

---

[11]Operating from a normative assumption to find dramatic changes without specifying what would be a threshold or a barometer of such change to make it noteworthy of study, Philip Morgan concludes: 'My basic argument is that although Africa's integration into the Atlantic world over three and a half centuries was impressive, it was still quite limited. Even by 1820, Atlantic influences were unequally diffused throughout Africa; much of the continent had hardly been penetrated by them.' See Philip D. Morgan, 'Africa and the Atlantic, c. 1450 to c. 1820' in Jack P. Greene and Philip D. Morgan, eds, *Atlantic History: A Critical Appraisal* (Oxford: Oxford University Press, 2009), pp. 223–48, p. 224.

on slavery in the Americas. No longer could an Americanist, Europeanist or Latin Americanist slavishly claim that we simply do not have enough knowledge about pre-colonial African history to answer these questions with confidence. To elaborate on one notable example of this trend, John Thornton's influential *Africa and Africans in the Making of the Atlantic World* (1992, 2nd ed. 1998) provided scholars of Atlantic slavery a clear and concise presentation of African belief systems and cultural frameworks drawing upon his detailed knowledge of West African history and his gift of synthesis. Thornton's expertise in the Kingdom of Kongo and the Portuguese colony of Angola resulted in him seeing far more similarities in belief systems and stressing religious changes and conversion to Christianity began in Africa, and not the Americas. As a result, transformations in belief systems from African to Christianity could be traced in both places and not a New World development alone. Thornton's work became widely assigned in undergraduate courses and graduate seminars and when demographic data on the importance of West Central Africans as the largest region for the origins of slaves brought to the Americas was firmly established through the Trans-Atlantic Slave Trade Database, it made his insights all the more relevant for understanding the religious practices of the enslaved in the Americas.[12]

---

[12] Joseph Miller, *Way of Death: Merchant Capitalism and the Angolan Slave Trade, 1730–1830* (Madison: University of Wisconsin Press, 1988); Patrick Manning, *Slavery and African Life: Occidental, Oriental, and African Slave Trades* (Cambridge: Cambridge University Press, 1990); Robin Law, *The Slave Coast of West Africa, 1550–1750: The Impact of the Atlantic Slave Trade on an African Society* (Oxford: Clarendon Press, 1991); Sandra E. Greene, *Gender, Ethnicity, and Social Change on the Upper Slave Coast: A History of Anlo-Ewe* (Portsmouth, NH: Heinemann, 1996); Edna G. Bay, *Wives of the Leopard: Gender, Politics, and Culture in the Kingdom of Dahomey* (Charlottesville: University of Virginia Press, 1998); Paul Lovejoy, *Transformations in Slavery: A History of Slavery in Africa*, 2nd ed. (Cambridge: Cambridge University Press, 2000); Robin Law, *Ouidah: The Social History of a West African Slaving 'Port', 1727–1892* (Athens: Ohio University Press, 2004); John Thornton, *Africa and Africans in the Making of the Atlantic World, 1400–1800*, 2nd ed. (Cambridge: Cambridge University Press, 1998). My experience of having Thornton's text assigned in classes taken for my BA, MA, and PhD at three different institutions in the 1990s was not unique as an example of its widespread use. For further development of Thornton's approach on the convergence of African religions, see 'The Kingdom of Kongo and Palo Mayombe: Reflections on an African-American Religion', *Slavery & Abolition* 37: 1 (2016), pp. 1–22. David Eltis, David Richardson, Stephen D. Behrendt, and Herbert S. Klein, eds, *The Trans-Atlantic Slave Trade: A Database on CD-ROM* (Cambridge: Cambridge University Press, 1999). For a selection of publications based upon interpreting the data, see David Eltis and David Richardson, eds, *Routes to Slavery: Direction, Ethnicity and Mortality in the Transatlantic Slave Trade* (London: Frank Cass, 1997); and David Eltis and David Richardson, eds, *Extending the Frontiers: Essays on the New Transatlantic Slave Trade Database* (New Haven, CT: Yale University Press, 2008). The 1999 slave trade database has been updated and augmented by new data and is now available on an open-access website at http://www.slavevoyages.org.

Thornton's text quickly became a representative model of how to link African and American belief systems by stressing similarities and convergences rather than cosmological differences and divergences. For some scholars, however, Thornton had overstated the degree of conversion among the general population. In addition, some readers were not perceptive enough to distinguish the exceptional Catholic presence in the Kingdom of Kongo and Angola with other locations in West Africa. For some, Thornton's model of religious change could apply to all of Atlantic Africa. Historian James Sweet utilized some of the same sources Thornton employed, but in particular scoured through Portuguese Inquisition records to perform an exegetical analysis of Kongo and Angolan traditions that could trace many non-Catholic beliefs and practices back to Africa. Sweet emphasized that African belief systems could be practised in parallel with Catholic beliefs, and one did not necessarily supplant the other despite the best hopes of Christian missionaries and their optimistic reports confidently documenting large-scale conversions. Putting sources generated in Brazil in dialogue with sources from West Central Africa, Sweet chronicled the ongoing practice of divinations, ordeals, ritual burials, revelations, dietary restrictions, cures and culturally constructed gendered identities as evidence of the ongoing centrality of Angolan, Kongo and Mbundu religion for the enslaved in Africa and the Diaspora.

In Thornton's interpretive framework, African and Christian belief systems converged, whereas Sweet stressed Africans practised parallel belief systems – one did not supplant or necessarily contradict the other regardless of how Christian religious scholars at the time and since have classified parallel beliefs as heresy. The temptation to create an argument that explains conversion whether in the service of denouncing colonial rule as an ideological enterprise, or showing the creativity of the enslaved in injecting African beliefs into Christianity as a form of resistance has resulted in historians overlooking the obvious. For many who lived under empires, kingdoms, polities and stateless societies in pre-colonial Africa, practising multiple religions was neither an exceptional expression of hybridity nor indicative of the cosmopolitan cultural literacy of Atlantic Creoles, but simply the norm.[13]

---

[13] James H. Sweet, *Recreating Africa: Culture, Kinship, and Religion in the African-Portuguese World, 1441–1770* (Chapel Hill: University of North Carolina Press, 2003).

An indication of how African culture became reshaped by Atlantic slavery can be discerned by looking at cosmological beliefs and the terms the enslaved used to describe their experience of being converted into a human commodity. Among the Africans exported from the Kongo-Angolan region by the Portuguese, they often referred to each other as 'malungo', which was a Kimbundu-derived religious word that could mean either brother, relative, comrade and, in Brazil, shipmate. But 'malungo' was more than just a religious tie of solidarity born out of enslavement in Africa and the traumatic experience of the transatlantic slave trade. It also referred to a Central African deity that had the authority to re-establish broken kin relations and create new hierarchies of lineage. Consequently, the slave trade and the process of enslavement made some African deities more powerful and potent, not weaker or failed gods eclipsed by Christianity and its saints.

Among the enslaved Africans exported from the Bight of Benin, several deities associated with cholera and smallpox became more prominent as the slave trade intensified. In the Kingdom of Dahomey, Sakpata, the god of smallpox climbed the deity pantheon as the slave trade penetrated into the interior of West Africa spreading death and disease in its destructive wake. As enslaved Africans called upon the supernatural to seek out assistance and guidance in dealing with their enslaved illness, these transformations in belief systems through the elevation of deities serve as a cultural index at the level of religious consciousness of being converted from Africans to Atlantic slaves. Sakpata priests became increasingly powerful as adherents sought out their healing powers resulting from the intensification of the slave trade. Consequently, Dahomean King Agaja singled out the Sakpata priests and their followers for enslavement and exported them to the Americas to remove the local supernatural threat. This turned a religious problem of imperial rule in Dahomey into an Atlantic cosmological phenomenon. The act of enslaving, banishing and exiling the Sakpata priests via the transatlantic slave trade served to funnel this religious knowledge and healing practices throughout the Americas.[14]

---

[14]Robert W. Slenes, "'Malungu, ngamos vem!'": África coberta e descoberta do Brasil', *Revista da Universidade de São Paulo* 12 (1991–1992), 48–67; Law, *Ouidah*, 90, 93; Luis Nicolau Pares, *A formação do camndomblé: História e ritual da nação jeje na Bahia* (Campinas: Editora da Unicamp, 2006); James H. Sweet, *Domingos Álavres, African Healing, and the Intellectual History of the Atlantic World* (Chapel Hill: University of North Carolina Press, 2011).

Competing paradigms for studying the religious beliefs of the enslaved

When it comes to understanding the transformation in religious practices of enslaved Africans once they began the process of rebuilding their lives in the Americas, scholars have debated for nearly a century over interpretive frameworks that have produced considerable heat and some light on the matter. The pioneers in the field of slave religious and cultural studies were anthropologist Melville Herskovits, who created a typology of cultures identifying those that were more or less African depending on cultural practices; Brazilian sociologist Nina Rodrigues, who studied enslaved Muslims; and Cuban anthropologist Fernando Ortiz, who coined the term 'transculturation' to convey the new culture that emerged between Spanish and African interactions. All three scholars charted important empirical and conceptual territory, but they tended to read current religious practices observed through fieldwork among people of African descent in the twentieth century back onto the past. For example, one common feature in their analyses was a tendency to regard African cultures as being 'transplanted' in their entirety, and thus being a clear 'continuation' and 'survivals' of African beliefs and practices.[15]

By contrast, in a widely influential essay from 1976 and subsequently revised and updated, historical anthropologists Sidney Mintz and Richard Price argued that as result of what they concluded was the random nature of the slave trade, Africans imported into the Americas 'did not compose at the outset, groups' that could be identified with a single specific and unifying religious belief system traced to an Old World homeland. Rather, they argued that African slaves brought to the New World represented 'crowds' of disparate groups and cultures 'and very heterogeneous crowds at that'. Mintz and Price did not ignore the religious and cultural traditions Africans brought with them, and even analysed some of their practices, but they forcefully suggested that scholarship should examine the creation of Creole

---

[15] An excellent intellectual account of their work and others who shaped the early field of studying African religious practices (and culture more broadly) in the Americas can be found in Kevin A. Yelvington, 'The Invention of Africa in Latin America and the Caribbean: Political Discourse and Anthropological Praxis, 1920–1940' in Kevin A. Yelvington, ed., *Afro-Atlantic Dialogues: Anthropology in Diaspora* (Santa Fe, NM: School of American Research, 2006); Melville J. Herskovits, *The Myth of the Negro Past* (New York: Harper, 1941); Nina Rodrigues, *Os Africanos no Brazil* (São Paulo: Companhia Editora Nacional, 1935); and Fernando Ortiz, *Contrapunteo cubano del tabaco y el azúcar* (Havana: J. Montero, 1940).

cultures and innovations in the New World in response to 'what they [slaves] undeniably shared at the outset was their enslavement'. Mintz and Price cautioned scholars against looking for similarities between Old World and New World African religious practices and beliefs. One scholar's confirmation of the continuation of a belief system from Africa to the Americas as a verifiable African 'survival' or 'retention', for another scholar could easily be classified as a false positive where similarity in cultural outcome becomes causality in historical arguments about resistance to enslavement. Instead, Mintz and Price focused on how diverse African cultures came together and began to form and invent new bonds of association and religious practices born out of slavery through the process of creolization.[16]

Since the 1970s, the literature on slavery in the Americas, especially on United States slavery, has generally followed the Mintz and Price Creolization model with its emphasis on New World innovations in the formation of African-American religious belief systems. Ira Berlin, for example, built upon the 'creolization model' by connecting the paradigm to early African-European interactions when he developed the term 'Atlantic Creole'. According to Berlin, 'Atlantic Creoles' emerged during the encounter between Africans and Europeans in West Africa during the sixteenth century. These transatlantic cultural brokers served as cultural and religious intermediaries between nascent slave communities and European settler communities, were often fluent in multiple languages and were able to deftly bridge cultural divides. Twenty years after Berlin first coined the term 'Atlantic Creole', it has now become a regular title in books and articles on slave culture and religion in the Americas with special attention drawn to the remarkable skills and fascinating lives of these individuals.[17]

At the same time Berlin was developing the concept of the 'Atlantic Creole', African Diasporic studies began to challenge the Mintz and Price Creolization model. Scholars such as John Thornton and Paul Gilroy argued that the African Diaspora was a process shaped by events and experiences

---

[16] Sidney W. Mintz and Richard Price, *The Birth of African-American Culture: An Anthropological Perspective* (Boston, MA: Beacon Press, 1992), 18–19.
[17] Ira Berlin, *Many Thousand Gone: The First Two Centuries of Slavery in North America* (Cambridge: Harvard University Press, 1998), pp. 17–46, see esp. p. 42 for the link between expression of Christian belief and Atlantic-Creole identity. For authors who build upon and employ Berlin's model, see Randy J. Sparks, *The Two Princes of Calabar: An Eighteenth-Century Atlantic Odyssey* (Cambridge: Harvard University Press, 2004); Linda M. Heywood and John K. Thornton, *Central Africans, Atlantic Creoles and the Foundation of the Americas, 1585–1660* (Cambridge: Cambridge University Press, 2007); and Jane G. Landers, *Atlantic Creoles in the Age of Revolutions* (Cambridge: Harvard University Press, 2010).

on both sides of the Atlantic. As previously mentioned, historians of pre-colonial Africa dating back to the 1970s, but even more importantly a new generation of African historians trained in the 1990s and 2000s from an Atlantic perspective, took an increasing interest in studying slavery in Africa and the Americas. Their work, which collectively can be referred to as the 'African Atlantic' approach, often directly engaged with and challenged Mintz and Price's creolization paradigm.[18]

The development of pre-colonial African historiography went hand in hand with a revolution in studying the transatlantic slave trade by collaborative scholarly efforts, computer assistance and the construction of long-term data sets spanning centuries. As a result, it has become easier for scholars to eschew the generic non-descriptive terms 'Africa' and 'African', and identify more precisely the cultural origins of slaves, their likely religious beliefs and their New World destinations. The statistical databases on the transatlantic slave trade assembled by an international team of researchers headed by David Eltis and work on transatlantic cultural links between Africa and the Americas by the scholars brought together by Paul Lovejoy's Nigerian Hinterland Slave Trade Project at York University gathered a massive amount of demographic and biographic source material on the lives and experiences of slaves in the Diaspora. The quantitative and qualitative data in these works fundamentally challenges the conclusions made by Mintz and Price about the random nature of the slave trade that supposedly resulted in a 'crowd' of different cultures and a heterogeneous mix of religious beliefs. The original database from 1999 is constantly being updated and

---

[18]Thornton, *Africa and Africans in the Making of the Atlantic World*; Paul Gilroy, *The Black Atlantic: Modernity and Double Consciousness* (Cambridge, MA: Harvard University Press, 1993). For the budding scholarship on pre-colonial African history from an Atlantic Perspective, see for example Miller, *Way of Death*; Lovejoy, *Transformations in Slavery*; Gomez, *Exchanging Our Country Marks: The Transformation of African Identities in the Colonial and Antebellum South* (Chapel Hill: University of North Carolina Press, 1998); Sweet, *Recreating Africa*; Linda M. Heywood, ed., *Central Africans and Cultural Transformation in the American Diaspora* (Cambridge: Cambridge University Press, 2002); Kristin Mann, *Slavery and the Birth of an African City, Lagos, 1760–1900* (Bloomington: Indiana University Press, 2007); Rebecca Shumway, *The Fante and the Transatlantic Slave Trade* (Rochester, NY: University of Rochester Press, 2011); G. Ugo Nwokeji, *The Slave Trade and Culture in the Bight of Biafra: An African Society in the Atlantic World* (Cambridge: Cambridge University Press, 2010); Walter Hawthorne, *From Africa to Brazil: Culture, Identity, and an Atlantic Slave Trade, 1600–1830* (Cambridge: Cambridge University Press, 2010); Toby Green, *The Rise of the Trans-Atlantic Slave Trade in Western Africa, 1300–1589* (Cambridge: Cambridge University Press, 2012); Roquinaldo Ferreira, *Cross-Cultural Exchange in the Atlantic World: Angola and Brazil during the Era of the Slave Tarde* (Cambridge: Cambridge University Press, 2012); and Mariana P. Candido, *An African Slaving Port in the Atlantic World: Benguela and Its Hinterland* (Cambridge: Cambridge University Press, 2013).

now contains detailed information on 36,000 slaving voyages. As a result, of all the voluntary and involuntary migratory streams that brought people to the Americas from 1500 to 1850, the most detailed information we have is for enslaved Africans. Historians have begun to identify specific migrations patterns from statistical and cultural sources that link slave-exporting regions in Africa with specific destinations in the Americas. Increasingly scholars are focusing on a single exporting region in Africa and a single destination in the Americas to trace out in detail how religious beliefs were transferred and transformed through the slave trade.[19]

These interpretative paradigms for writing the religious history of the enslaved in the Atlantic World have strengths and weaknesses. The 'creolization' model gets at the heart of the creative adaptive process all slaves had to go through but does not distinguish this process very clearly from the creative adaptations to new environments that all migrants, slave or free, had to go through. The 'African Atlantic' approach, in the words of Paul Lovejoy, 'is important because it places the "middle passage" in the middle' of the slaves' experiences. Nevertheless, this approach underplays how African cultural forms and religious beliefs were developed within and during New World enslavement. The 'Atlantic Creole' model conceptually bridges the 'creolization' model and the 'African Atlantic' approach, but here some problems are readily apparent. Most of the literature on 'Atlantic Creoles' focuses on those Africans who were conversant and accepted into European worlds, and these scholars use certain markers of Western civilization such as fluency in European languages and the mastery of writing. And most importantly for the purposes of this chapter, they most frequently practised a European religion. In addition, there were many generations of Atlantic Creoles in the Americas, not just an initial generation. For Berlin, Atlantic Creoles are a generational phenomenon produced through initial African-

---

[19]David Eltis, David Richardson, Stephen D. Behrendt, and Herbert S. Klein, eds, *The Trans-Atlantic Slave Trade: A Database on CD-ROM* (Cambridge: Cambridge University Press, 1999). For the activities and publications of Paul Lovejoy's Nigerian Hinterland Slave Trade Project, see http://www.yorku.ca/nhp/areas/nhp.htm. For the history and ongoing updates to the *Trans-Atlantic Slave Trade Database*, see https://slavevoyages.org. See for example the chapters in Kristin Mann and Edna Bay, eds, *Rethinking the African Diaspora: The Making of the Black Atlantic World in the Bight of Benin and Brazil* (London: Frank Cass Publishers, 2001); Linda Heywood, ed., *Central Africans and Cultural Transformations in the American Diaspora* (Cambridge: Cambridge University Press, 2002); Toyin Falola and Matt D. Childs, eds, *The Yoruba Diaspora in the Atlantic World* (Bloomington: Indiana University Press, 2005); José C. Curto and Paul E. Lovejoy, eds, *Enslaving Connections: Changing Cultures of Africa and Brazil during the Era of Slavery* (Amherst, NY: Humanity Books, 2004); Gwendolyn Midlo Hall, *Slavery and African Ethnicities in the Americas: Restoring the Links* (Chapel Hill: University of North Carolina Press, 2005).

European interactions. Yet, every time European traders created new zones and entrepots for the transatlantic slave trade to thrive, a new group of 'Atlantic Creoles' came into existence.

Richard Price offered a sophisticated, albeit playful defence of the creolization model in an essay artfully titled 'On the Miracle of Creolization'. Price affirmed its interpretive framework, but conceded that it was hard to prove from a social scientific perspective as it implies a specific culture in Africa can be identified with empirical documentation and then methodically charted how it changed in the Americas. Leaving aside the point that even the Vatican has a minimum threshold of two documented examples to recognize a miracle as a religious phenomenon, Price's 'Miracle of Creolization' article did not resolve the matter or move the debate forward with new evidence or a case study to prove his point. Instead, he argued that creolization as linked to identity was more of a discursive phenomenon than a social phenomenon. Indeed, as a discursive device to explain culture change from various beliefs to a new one, creolization as an interpretive paradigm resonates most eerily with American historians and the US official motto of *E plurubus unum*, which is worth remembering the founding fathers created to mask over social divisions and imagine a unified nation. And given this chapter is about slavery, I would be remiss if I did not mention the obvious: the American Founding Fathers were slave owners. The problem of how to study the religious beliefs and more specifically the changes in those beliefs is a Gordian Knot. Historians unable to find an easy solution come up with loopholes and write around the problem. Regardless of their imperfection, these ongoing debates over conceptual models powerfully underscore there is no single way to write the history of religion for the enslaved, but many that require multiple perspectives to understand the various religions spread across space and time in the New World.[20]

---

[20]Paul E. Lovejoy, 'Identifying Enslaved Africans in the African Diaspora' in Paul E. Lovejoy, ed., *Identity in the Shadow of Slavery* (London: Continuum, 2000), p. 2; Richard Price, 'The Miracle of Creolization: A Retrospective', *NWIG-New West Indian Guide/Nieuwe West Indische Gids* 75: 1–2 (2001), pp. 35–64; Richard Price, 'On the Miracle of Creolization' in Kevin A. Yelvington, ed., *Afro-Atlantic Dialogues: Anthropology in Diaspora* (Santa Fe, NM: School of American Research, 2006), pp. 115–47. For further commentary on the various approaches to studying the religion and culture of the enslaved in the Americas, see the chapters 'Religion and Slavery' by Douglas Ambrose and 'Slave Culture' by Kevin Dawson both in Robert L. Paquette and Mark M. Smith, eds, *The Oxford Handbook of Slavery in the Americas* (Oxford: Oxford University Press, 2010), pp. 378–98 and 465–88; Matt D. Childs, 'Slave Culture' in Gad Heuman and Trevor Burnard, eds, *The Routledge History of Slavery* (Abingdon, VA: Routledge, 2010); and Paul Christopher Johnson and Stephan Palmié, 'Afro-Latin American Religions' in Alejandro de la Fuente and George Reid Andrews, eds, *Afro-Latin American Studies: An Introduction* (Cambridge: Cambridge University Press, 2018), pp. 438–85.

Syncretic or African religions?

From the very beginning of Atlantic enslavement in the fifteenth century, syncretic religions emerged in the slave societies of Africa and the Americas that recreated an African spiritual realm. As indigenous African religions were not tied exclusively to a specific text or scripture, they regularly evolved by incorporating other deities and beliefs. This tendency towards syncretism, coupled with the familiarity Africans already had with Islam and Christianity prior to arrival in the Americas, culturally prepared Africans to adapt their religions to Christianity and practise them in parallel and overlapping ways. Africans from Yorubaland, for example, channelled deities called *orisas* into Roman Catholic saints. This syncreticism between Yoruba *orisas* and Roman Catholic saints gave birth to some of the central religious beliefs and practices of Candomble in Brazil, Santeria in Cuba and Vodun in Haiti. For example, in Brazil, Ogun, the orisha of iron and war, is matched with St George who carries a sword, whereas in Cuba, Ogun is commonly linked with Saint Peter who holds an iron key. In Haiti, iconography depicting Saint Jerome in battle carrying a metal sword linked him to Ogun as the deity of blacksmiths. Changó, the orisha god of thunder and lightening, is linked to Santa Bárbara because her father was struck dead by lightning as a punishment for killing her when she refused to give up her Christian faith. The millions of enslaved Africans carried to Cuba, Brazil and Saint Domingue from the seventeenth to the nineteenth centuries resulted in a constant influx of belief systems, which created the demographic conditions for syncretic religions to thrive. It should be stressed, however, that religious continuities required a transformation of African religious imagery and symbols in the New World. For some scholars these are clear examples of the 'creolization' of Yoruba orishas into Catholic saints and the incorporation of Christianity, whereas for others it exemplifies the transference of an African cosmology that is only recorded as Christianity by the historical archive reluctant to recognize African belief systems.[21]

---

[21] For an ethnographically rich, historically documented and theoretically complex analysis of this process and the debates over how to study these religious phenomenon, see the works J. Lorand Matory, *Black Atlantic Religion: Tradition, Transnationalism, and Matriarchy in the Afro-Brazilian Candomble* (Princeton, NJ: Princeton University Press, 2005); Luis Nicolau Parés, *The Formation of Candomblé: Vodun History and Ritual in Brazil*, trans. Richard Vernon (Chapel Hill: University of North Carolina Press, 2013); and in particular the debate between the two of them in *The Americas*, 72: 4 (October 2015), pp. 607–42.

However one classifies such representations as either Creole or African, scholars tend to agree that the Catholic empires of the New World showed far greater toleration for African religious practices despite their much bemoaned inquisition of Black Legend lore. By contrast, these cultural and religious forms are far less numerous in Protestant British, Dutch and later the United States. Spain and Portugal organized enslaved and free Africans into religious brotherhoods in the New World by grouping them together by place of origin. Mariza de Carvalho Soares's detailed examination of religious brotherhoods in Rio de Janeiro documents how Africans who shared a similar ethnicity often formed their own sodalities. These brotherhoods provided an institutional framework for an ethnic/cultural identity through the Catholic Church. The same phenomenon occurred throughout the Spanish empire whereby religious brotherhoods made up of Africans could be found from the northern borderlands of Saint Augustine to the far southern extreme of Buenos Aires.[22]

On the Spanish Caribbean island of Cuba, for example, the presence of Catholic brotherhoods that included the population of African ancestry can be traced to the sixteenth century. In 1573 the Havana Town Council reported that Africans took part in the procession of Corpus Christi, and several wills indicate they regularly made donations to sodalities. Jane Landers found that many African ethnic groups proliferated in Havana and organized important brotherhoods. Most of the brotherhoods selected a patron saint that they honoured on his or her feast day with elaborate festivals and ceremonies. As an eighteenth-century Havana Bishop lamented, these brotherhoods often disregarded their religious duties and sacraments and created 'scandalous and grave disorders ... when they congregate on festival days'. These societies thrived in port cities throughout Latin America, and were largely an urban phenomenon. By carving out an institutional space for themselves within the Catholic Church, Africans refashioned their New

---

[22]Mariza de Carvalho Soares, *Devotos da cor: Identidade étnica, religiosidade e escravidão no Rio de Janeiro, século XVIII* (Rio de Janeiro: Civilização Brasileira, 2000); Bowser, *The African Slave in Colonial Peru, 1524-1650*, 249-50, 339; Nicole von Germeten, *Black Blood Brothers: Confraternities and Social Mobility for Afro-Mexicans* (Gainesville: University of Florida Press, 2006); Landers, *Black Society in Spanish Florida*, ch. 5; George Reid Andrews, *The Afro-Argentines of Buenos Aires, 1800-1900* (Madison: University of Wisconsin Press, 1980), 142-51.

World institutions to speak, in part, to their places of origin and religious beliefs from the other side of the Atlantic.[23]

The origins of the New World African lay brotherhoods can be traced to Catholic brotherhoods of Spanish origin, but analogous societies were common to West and Central Africa. At the port of Old Calabar and surrounding regions in the Bight of Biafra, an all-male secret society known as Ekpe formed as early as the second half of the seventeenth century. According to Paul Lovejoy and David Richardson, Ekpe society created a series of associations through religious and patron-client relations that regulated the behaviour of its members. The secret organization crossed the Atlantic and resurfaced in nineteenth-century Cuba through an altered form in the Abakuá society. In the Yoruba Kingdom of Oyo a semi-secret organization known as the Ogboni society advised the King on religious and political matters. When Yorubaland funnelled thousands of Africans to Cuba and Brazil in the nineteenth century, detailed knowledge of the organization crossed the Atlantic and influenced the Catholic brotherhoods. Latin American colonial administrators and Catholic priests regarded African participation in religious brotherhoods as an extension of European sodalities and evidence of their successful evangelization and conversion efforts. The organizations for Africans, however, did not represent something entirely of Iberian origin, but an Old World African religious institution modified to a New World setting.[24]

Protestant slave societies of the Americas also produced their own variants of African-influenced Christianity. From the seventeenth to the nineteenth centuries, masters and missionaries in the British Caribbean and United States went from showing very little interest in the spiritual well-being of

---

[23]Landers, *Black Society in Spanish Florida*, ch. 5; David Wheat, *Atlantic Africa and the Spanish Caribbean, 1570-1640* (Chapel Hill: University of North Carolina Press, 2016); Quote from document reprinted in Levi Marrero, *Cuba: Economía y sociedad, del monopolio hacia la libertad comercial (1701-1763)* (Madrid: Editorial Playor, 1980), VIII: 159; Philip A. Howard, *Changing History: Afro-Cuban Cabildos and Societies of Color in the Nineteenth Century* (Baton Rouge: Louisiana State University Press, 1998); and Matt D. Childs, '"The Defects of Being a Black Creole": The Degrees of African Ethnicity in the Cuban Cabildos de Nación' in Jane A. Landers and Barry Robinson, eds, *Slaves and Subjects: Blacks in Colonial Latin America* (Albuquerque: University of New Mexico Press, 2006), pp. 209-45.
[24]Paul E. Lovejoy and David Richardson, 'Trust, Pawnship, and Atlantic History: The Institutional Foundations of the Old Calabar Slave Trade' *American Historical Review* 104 (1999), 347-9; Ivor L. Miller, *Voice of the Leopard: African Secret Societies and Cuba* (Jackson: University Press of Mississippi, 2009); Robin Law, *The Oyo Empire, c. 1600-c. 1836: West African Imperialism in the Era of the Atlantic Slave Trade* (Oxford: Oxford University Press, 1977), 61.

slaves to demonstrating a religious zeal that helped produce a distinct Afro-American Christianity. The emergence of evangelical Christianity with its emphasis on a personal relationship with god, rather than access to God through exclusive instruction by theologically trained scholars, braided with slave populations born and raised in North America during the eighteenth and nineteenth centuries. In particular, Baptists and Methodists took an active evangelizing role. Some groups even spoke out against slavery and allowed slaves and free people of colour to form their own independent churches, such as First African Baptist Church in Augusta, Georgia and the African Methodist Episcopal Church, formed by Richard Allen. Employing biblical scripture, slaves created a distinct Afro-American Christianity that linked their religious experiences to stories of the biblical exodus of the Jews from Egypt. Slaves in the United States and the British Caribbean refashioned their religious worldview to claim that they were God's chosen people who would be redeemed from slavery and racial oppression through conversion. Slaves forged the beliefs of Evangelical Christianity that swept through the Anglo-Protestant world into a weapon to attack master dominion. By comparison, there are few equivalents from the Catholic French, Spanish or Portuguese slave societies of the Americas where Biblical inspiration from the Old Testament and mastery of the written word of the Bible served as powerful tools in shaping the slaves' religious experience.[25]

Religion and slave revolts

Since the 1960s the theme of resistance has figured as one of the central topics in the historiography of New World slavery. Space constraints do not allow a full examination of how slaves bonded together religion and resistance to challenge their master's authority on a daily basis to assert their humanity by demanding religious holidays, creating a spiritual sense of a self outside of the temporal world where they had been reduced to property, countering a hegemonic Christian worldview that justified slavery with a counter-hegemonic religious response, or by simply engaging in fellowship

---

[25]See, for example, Genovese, *Roll, Jordan, Roll*; Sylvia R. Frey and Betty Wood, *Come Shouting to Zion: African American Protestantism in the American South and British Caribbean to 1830* (Chapel Hill: University of North Carolina Press, 1998); Erskine Clarke, *Dwelling Place: A Plantation Epic* (New Haven, CT: Yale University Press, 2005), esp. pp. 152–66; James Sidbury, *Becoming African in America: Race and Nation in the Early Black Atlantic* (Oxford: Oxford University Press, 2007).

with other humans to construct a community. Instead, I am going to focus on how religion has been incorporated into accounts of slave revolts throughout the hemisphere.[26]

Undoubtedly, the Haitian Revolution stands alone as the most important slave revolt during the history of Atlantic Slavery. The Haitian Revolution began with a massive uprising in August 1791 that would culminate in 1804 with the only independent black republic in the Western Hemisphere. Haiti's historical starting point represents a singular event of human accomplishment. The African background of the slaves, their culture and their religion proved essential in determining the course of events in Haiti. Among the slaves drawn from various locations within Africa, some from the Kingdoms of Kongo and Dahomey looked back to their place of origin as they legitimated and organized their struggle in Haiti. A few slaves claimed loyalty to the King of the Kongo, and believed he would send troops to aid their cause. Likewise, they also blended African and European political traditions by drawing inspiration from the *Declarations of the Rights of Man and Citizen* and carrying African amulets for protection in battle. Many of the leaders of the Haitian Revolution had their own conjurers that provided supernatural powers for themselves and their armies before they went into battle. Culturally, in terms of the ideas that informed slaves and free people of colour to rise in rebellion, emancipation rumours, monarchical degrees, royalist ideology and, in particular, vodun beliefs from the beginning to the end served as a constant well to draw legitimacy from in their struggle for freedom.[27]

In 1800, reports rocked Richmond, Virginia, that slaves planned to revolt and take the capital city. Virginia officials quickly arrested the suspected

---

[26] For accounts of slavery and resistance the literature is vast; overviews can be found in Douglas R. Egerton, 'Slave Resistance' in Robert L. Paquette and Mark M. Smith, eds, *The Oxford Handbook of Slavery in the Americas* (Oxford: Oxford University Press, 2010); James Sidbury, 'Resistance to Slavery', and Gad Heuman 'Slave Rebellions', both in Gad Heuman and Trevor Burnard, eds, *The Routledge History of Slavery* (Abingdon, VA: Routledge, 2010).

[27] My account of the Haitian Revolution is drawn from C.L.R James, *The Black Jacobins: Toussaint L'Overture and the San Domingo Revolution*, 2nd ed. (New York: Vintage, 1963); Carolyn E. Fick, *The Making of Haiti: The Saint Domingue Revolution from Below* (Knoxville: University of Tennessee Press, 1990); Laurent Dubois, *Avengers of the New World: The Story of the Haitian Revolution* (Cambridge: Harvard University Press, 2004); Trouillot, *Silencing the Past*; David Patrick Geggus, *Haitian Revolutionary Studies* (Bloomington: Indiana University Press, 2002); John K. Thornton, 'African Soldiers in the Haitian Revolution', *Journal of Caribbean History* 25: 1–2 (1991), pp. 58–80; John K. Thornton, '"I Am the Subject of the King of Congo": African Political Ideology and the Haitian Revolution', *Journal of World History* 4: 2 (1993), pp. 181–214; Terry Rey, *The Priest and the Prophetess: Abbé Ouviere, Romaine Riviere, and the Revolutionary Atlantic World* (Oxford: Oxford University Press, 2017).

rebels, had them questioned and then punished them for what would subsequently become known as Gabriel's Conspiracy, named after the slave leader owned by Thomas Prosser. How the slave rebels made sense of what freedom meant and legitimated their cause point to important differences in the religious, cultural and social dynamics of slave societies in the Atlantic World in the eighteenth and nineteenth centuries. At a religious level, Gabriel and his followers forged the beliefs of Evangelical Christianity that swept through the Anglo-Protestant world into a weapon to attack master dominion. By comparison, there are few equivalents from the Iberian slave societies of the Americas where Biblical inspiration from the Old Testament served such a powerful role in building violent antislavery movements. In organizing the revolt, literacy and mastery of the written word often acquired through studying and preaching from the Bible served as a divine weapon not only for providing logistics and planning, such as forged passes, but court testimony makes clear that writing held special emancipatory powers, and often served as criteria for leadership roles.[28]

The British Caribbean experienced a cycle of slave insurrections after 1800 that hammered the final nails into slavery's coffin. After twenty years of debate, the British Parliament abolished the transatlantic slave trade in 1807. As news and stories of parliamentary debates and the formation of abolitionist societies crisscrossed the Atlantic often carried by Baptist missionaries, slaves in the British Caribbean learned that they had a few allies in London. Two of the biggest rebellions occurred in the colonies of Demerara in 1823 and Jamaica in 1831. As a concession to British abolitionists, masters allowed missionaries to minister to the slaves. Demeraran slaves appropriated the missionaries' Evangelical language and symbols and turned Sunday church services, which brought enslaved labourers together from various plantations, into organizational opportunities for the rebellion. When the rebellion broke out in August 1823, in a matter of weeks, the slave army numbered as large as 12,000 and controlled nearly sixty plantations. When the colonial governor met with the slaves and asked why they revolted in an attempt to end the rebellion through negotiation, they boldly demanded

---

[28] For Gabriel's Conspiracy, see James Sidbury, *Ploughshares into Swords: Race, Rebellion, and Identity in Gabriel's Virginia, 1730–1810* (Cambridge: Cambridge University Press, 1997); James Sidbury, 'Saint Domingue in Virginia: Ideology, Local Meanings, and Resistance to Slavery, 1790–1800', *Journal of Southern History* 63: 33 (August 1997), pp. 531–52; Douglas R. Egerton, *Gabriel's Rebellion: The Virginia Slave Conspiracies of 1800 and 1802* (Chapel Hill: University of North Carolina Press, 1993); Gerald W. Mullin, *Flight and Rebellion: Slave Resistance in Eighteenth-Century Virginia* (Oxford: Oxford University Press, 1972), pp. 140–63.

"'Our rights'". The governor recognized how the slaves had wed the radical beliefs of Christianity emphasizing equality of all men before God with abolition rumours. The slaves told the Governor that 'God had made them of the same flesh and blood as the whites; they were tired of being slaves; their good King has sent orders that they should be free, and they would not work any more'. After the slaves made it clear that they would not return to slavery, the British colonial state brought to bear its full military force and violently subdued the insurgents.[29]

The Demerara Rebellion served as a prelude to the largest slave revolt in the British Caribbean eight years later. Erupting in Jamaica on Christmas Day in 1831, the slave revolt included 20,000 to 30,000 slaves, who blanketed the western end of the island leaving torched canefields and smouldering plantations in their path. The rebellion subsequently became known as the 'Baptist War' in an act of historical revisionism to put the blame on Baptist missionaries who actively evangelized in the region, rather than recognizing the slaves' strike for freedom. As part of their missionary strategy to have the converted do the converting, the Baptists encouraged free people of colour and slaves to run their own church services. Inside the security of church services, Jamaican slaves began to plot their rebellion as early as April 1831. The leader of the rebellion, deacon Samuel 'Daddy' Sharpe, used his religious position to move from plantation to plantation ministering to his flock and spreading plans of insurrection. Several slaves testified that Sharpe told them that the King had declared them free, but their masters and colonial officials would not recognize the order. The Jamaican slave rebels used the disruption in the plantation labour regime during the holidays leading up to Christmas to spread the news that they had been declared free. They made a pact and vowed not to work as slaves after 25 December; just as Christ was born to save the world, they would be reborn to make their freedom. Only after several months of bitter fighting did Jamaican authorities subdue the insurrection. The Jamaican Baptist War sent masters, the Jamaican Assembly, and the British Parliament a powerful message of the huge costs required for maintaining slavery as a system of human domination. In the aftermath of

---

[29]For an analysis of the Demerara Rebellion see Emília Viotti da Costa, *Crowns of Glory Tears of Blood: The Demerara Slave Rebellion of 1823* (New York: Oxford University Press, 1994), quote p. 216; Robin Blackburn, *The Overthrow of Colonial Slavery, 1776–1848* (London: Verso Press, 1988), pp. 428–31; Michael Mullin, *Africa in America: Slave Acculturation and Resistance in the American South and British Caribbean, 1763–1831* (Urbana: University of Illinois Press, 1992), pp. 249–53; Michael Craton, *Testing the Chains: Resistance to Slavery in the British West Indies* (Ithaca, NY: Cornell University Press, 1982), passim and esp. pp. 335–39.

the rebellion, the need to reform slavery and place it on the 'peaceful' road to gradual abolition with compensation for masters, as opposed to immediate emancipation by the slaves' own hands, now seemed more urgent than ever. In 1838, slavery, under the guise of a four-year apprenticeship system, came to an end in the British Caribbean.[30]

Similar to the British Caribbean, Bahia, Brazil, witnessed an elevated commitment by Africans to end slavery by violent insurrection during the first decades of the nineteenth century. From 1807 to 1835, more than twenty revolts, plantation uprisings, maroon rebellions and foiled conspiracies occurred in Bahia and the surrounding plantation hinterland called the Recôncavo. The largest insurrection, the Malê Rebellion, occurred in 1835 and reflected the migratory and religious patterns carried by the transatlantic slave trade. As a result of reviving and expanding sugar plantation agriculture in Northeastern Brazil in the wake of the Haitian Revolutions, combined with the rapid decline of the Oyo Empire in West Africa due to incessant warfare, ethnic Yorubans, known in Brazil as Nagôs, arrived in Bahia by the thousands. Historian João Reis's brilliant work on the revolt has shown that many of the rebels shared a Diasporic Muslim culture, and they continued practising their Islamic faith in Brazil. The start of the rebellion coincided with the religious fete of Our Lady of Guidance (quite appropriately), which allowed for greater freedom of movement in the city and countryside. Islam, however, represents the single most distinguishing religious feature of the Malê Rebellion. When Africans went into battle to end their enslavement, they wore white robes, and carried amulets that contained folded Koranic verses written in Arabic containing fiery and revolutionary messages. Moreover, Muslims figured prominently among the rebel's leadership. Similar to Gabriel's Conspiracy, mastery of reading and studying religious texts and the power of literacy served to structure the movement.[31]

---

[30] Craton, *Testing the Chains*, pp. 291–321; Blackburn, *Overthrow of Colonial Slavery*, pp. 432–68; Mullin, *Africa in America*, pp. 253–60.

[31] My analysis of the 1835 Malê Rebellion is drawn from João Jose Reis, *Rebelião escrava no Brasil: A história do levante dos malês em 1835*, rev. ed. (São Paulo: Companhia das Letras, 2003); Reis, *Slave Rebellion in Brazil: The Muslim Uprising of 1835 in Bahia*, trans. Arthur Brakel (Baltimore, MD: Johns Hopkins University Press, 1993); Paul E. Lovejoy, 'Background to Rebellion: The Origins of Muslim Slaves in Bahia', *Slavery & Abolition* 15: 22 (1994), pp. 151–80; Jack Goody, 'Writing, Religion, and Revolt in Bahia', *Visible Language* 20 (1986), pp. 318–43; and Manuel Barcia, *West African Warfare in Bahia and Cuba: Soldier Slaves in the Atlantic World* (Oxford: Oxford University Press, 2014).

The centrality of religion in strategies and plans of action by the enslaved to challenge slavery as an institution of human domination remains the great thematic bind in analysing resistance whether expressed in African, syncretic, Christian or Islamic forms. As historian Douglas Egerton concluded in surveying various revolts, 'whether the creed was Baptist or Catholic, Muslim or a pre-Islamic West African derivation, a devout sense of faith inspired numerous leaders from Southampton to Bahia to believe the heavens were on the side of the oppressed'. Numerous other conspiracies, revolts and rebellions could be listed as further testament to this phenomenon whether Palmares in Brazil, the Stono Revolt in Colonial South Carolina, the Aponte Rebellion in Cuba, the Nat Turner revolt in Virginia or the Jamaican Maroons to just list a few that would document the cultural connection between religion and slave resistance.[32]

Gendered perspectives on writing the religious history of the enslaved

Continuing with the theme of resistance and religion, incorporating gender as a category of analysis has produced notable insights, and even new interpretations of how to frame the writing of the history of the enslaved. In Cuban historiography, one of the most debated historical events of the nineteenth century is the *La Escalera* Rebellion, or *La Escalera* Conspiracy. Named after the Spanish word for 'ladder', which slaves and free people of colour were tied to when horrifically whipped and brutally punished, historians have debated over whether there even was a conspiracy; was it the product of white fear and paranoia; did British abolitionists catalyse the revolt; did judicial and political authorities make the mixed-race free mulatto poet Placido the leader of the conspiracy to silence alliances between free people of colour and slaves; and even whether the revolts that broke out on various plantations over several months were coordinated as part of a collective plan of insurrection, or localized sporadic rebellions. Historian Aisha Finch's methodologically sophisticated and creative analysis centred on gender to show what so many historians may have forgot and just ignored. Her chapter five title quotes a repeated refrain from the judicial

---

[32]Douglas R. Egerton, 'Nat Turner in a Hemispheric Context' in Kenneth S. Greenberg, ed., *Nat Turner: A Slave Rebellion in History and Memory* (Oxford: Oxford University Press, 2003), p. 137.

testimony of the investigation: 'And the Women also Knew.' Finch's careful reading of sources shows how the slave 'rebel' was constructed through the judicial process as a 'male' figure with 'masculine' characteristics of heroism, bravery, strength and militancy, which subsequent historians have largely followed. Men were threatening to the colonial order built on enslaved plantation labour, whereas from the perspectives of male masters and the colonial state that created a notably gendered archive of repression, women were passive and manageable. However, in organizing the rebellion, connecting plantation to plantation, spreading news of the conspiracy from rural to urban areas, women were far more important in bringing the rebellion to fruition than men, and assumed important leadership roles such as that of Carlota Lucumí. Some women leaders and participants built solidarities through their central role in harnessing Afro-Cuban sacred traditions whether of Kongo or Yoruba derivation. Recognizing the important role of women in these endeavours, Finch concludes that scholars should 'reexamine the complicated position of women at the nexus of a number of different insurrectionary and spiritual labors' that placed them in an elevated position in carrying out plans for rebellion. A re-reading of the archive and historical events linking religion, resistance and gender results in not just 'finding' women as more active historical participants that add depth and detail to our historical knowledge, but actually a new interpretive thesis on long-standing historiographical topics.[33]

Pairing gender and slavery can lead scholars to rethink how to write the religious history of the enslaved. As previously mentioned, the Iberian enslavers allowed slaves and free people of colour to form religious brotherhoods, which often congregated a specific African cultural group or ethnicity. Looking at these Catholic religious associations beyond an institutional framework to narrow in on the internal gender dynamics of these organizations reveals how women actively participated in the *brother*hoods, and often outnumbered men. These sodalities elected both a

---

[33]Aisha K. Finch, *Rethinking Slave Rebellion in Cuba: La Escalera and the Insurgencies of 1841–1844* (Chapel Hill: University of North Carolina Press, 2015), quote p. 220. For accounts of *La Escalera*, see José Luciano Franco, *La gesta heroica del Triunvirato* (Havana: Editorial de Ciencias Sociales, 1978); Robert L. Paquette, *Sugar Is Made with Blood: The Conspiracy of La Escalera and the Conflict between Empires over Slavery in Cuba* (Middletown, CO: Wesleyan University Press, 1988); Gloria García, *Conspiraciones y revueltas: la actividad política de los negros en Cuba (1790–1845)* (Santiago: Editorial Oriente, 2003); Manuel Barcia, *Seeds of Insurrection: Domination and Resistance on Western Cuban Plantations, 1808–1848* (Baton Rouge: Louisiana State University Press, 2008); Michel Reid-Vasquez, *The Year of the Lash: Free People of Color and the Nineteenth-Century Atlantic World* (Athens: University of Georgia Press, 2011).

'King' and a 'Queen' to govern them and spelled out the electoral processes in their charter constitutions. Brazilian historian Mariza de Carvalho Soares studied one such group that when the king died, the queen sought to rule over the entire brotherhood, including its male members. While males served as the leaders of the societies, women shaped who ran the organizations since they often outnumbered men. Females flexed their numerical superiority through voting for leaders and deciding the financial affairs, often to the consternation of the male members. Although Catholic confraternities could be found in Europe that catered to the spiritual well-being of women, the degree to which women and men jointly participated in New World brotherhoods made up of the population of African descent stands in marked contrasts with how the Church often segregated men and women by gender in Europe. As brotherhoods were above all urban institutions in the slave societies of the Americas, females had a demographic advantage over men when it came to membership and authority within the organizations. The enslaved plantation economies of the New World produced a geographically gendered division of labour for the population of African descent. While men and women lived and laboured in both rural and urban areas, women and especially free women of colour could be found most prominently in cities. In urban port cities bordering the Atlantic, women dominated the markets as vendors of goods and actively participated in the cash economy. Consequently, not only did they often outnumber men in the brotherhoods, but they also disproportionately influenced the wealth of these organizations by contributing membership dues and making donations. When historians look at the internal dynamics and organizational structure of these brotherhoods, many appear as a hidden form of African matriarchy institutionalized through Catholicism.[34]

Similarly, braiding together gender, religion and slavery can also reshape our understanding of Protestant African-American Christianity. To illustrate this trend in historical writing, two biographies of enslaved women who became free show how gendering the history of religion and slavery results in moving women from the margins to the centre of scholarly analysis. Jon Sensbach's transatlantic biography of a mixed-race woman named Rebecca

---

[34] Mariza de Carvalho Soares, 'Can Women Guide and Govern Men?: Gendering Politics among African Catholics in Colonial Brazil' in Gwyn Campbell, Suzanne Miers, and Joseph C. Miller, eds, *Women and Slavery: The Modern Atlantic*, Vol. 2 (Athens: Ohio University Press, 2008), pp. 79–99; Matt D. Childs, 'Gendering the African Diaspora in the Iberian Atlantic: Religious Brotherhoods and the Cabildos de Nación' in Sarah E. Owens and Jane E. Mangan, eds, *Women of the Iberian Atlantic* (Baton Rouge: Louisiana State University Press, 2012), pp. 230–62.

traces her personal transformation from enslaved to free through her life in Antigua, Saint Thomas, Europe and then the Gold Coast of West Africa where she died in 1780. As a slave on the Danish island of St Thomas, she became free and played an instrumental role working with Moravian missionaries in building a Black congregation. After living in Central Europe for three years, she then settled on the Gold Coast in the service of mission work. Sensbach shows how Rebecca was part of a small but vibrant community of early Protestant activists of African ancestry who through a spiritual framework began to challenge the 'paradox' to convert Africans and treat them as religious equals, even while Protestantism and its many denominations supported slavery. Related, but from a different perspective of turning the unknown historical figure Rebecca into a lens to examine Protestantism and slavery, is Vincent Carretta's biography of Phillis Wheatley that turns a well-known religious literary figure respected for her artful 'manipulator of words' into a 'manipulator of people'. Wheatley became a celebrity in her own life though the publication of her poems, which eventually resulted in her manumission, and entering correspondence circles with the likes of George Washington and Benjamin Franklin. Carretta's careful reading of her published texts paired against contextual primary and secondary sources enabled him to see how her middle passage experience and time in London during the Somerset Decision (1772), which held slavery was not supported by common law in England and Wales, shaped her authorial skills in using Christianity to challenge slavery. Taken together, these two biographies show how braiding together religion, slavery and gender provides an early glimpse into what will be the central themes and challenges of the Protestant abolitionist movements of the nineteenth century.[35]

Conclusion

In the broader historiography of slavery, few topics have figured so prominently in scholarly writings as religion from conceptual, methodological, empirical and historiographical perspectives. Slavery as a concept for societal organization was embedded into monotheistic faiths,

---

[35] Jon F. Sensbach, *Rebecca's Revival: Creating Black Christianity in the Atlantic World* (Cambridge, MA: Harvard University Press, 2005); and Vincent Carretta, *Phillis Wheatley: Biography of a Genius in Bondage* (Athens: University of Georgia Press, 2011), quote p. 137.

indigenous religions in Africa and the Americas, and served as a model in empire-building from antiquity to the New World. From the perspective of the methodological models to interpret slavery, some of the longest and ongoing debates in the historical profession whether it is the 'Tannenbaum Thesis' counterpointing Iberian Catholic slavery versus Protestant British slavery, or 'creolization' versus 'African-Atlantic' approaches, religion has functioned as the rudder that holds the keel in line to keep arguments afloat. From the perspective of analysing the empirical documentation that historians have employed, writing the history of the enslaved in the Americas simply could not be done at its current level of sophistication and nuance without ecclesiastical sources. From a historiographical perspective, religion has been paired most notably with social, cultural and gendered perspectives, almost all of which have been written through the interpretive prism of resistance in some form whether that is individual resistance, everyday resistance, cultural resistance or collective violent acts of armed resistance.[36]

History as a discipline has been far more focused and far more comfortable with analysing how the population of African descent injected their own beliefs systems into Christianity. Much of the literature on the religion of the enslaved in the Atlantic World is really the history of African Christianity and African-American Christianity born out of the torturous process of slavery. From this interpretive angle, Christianity becomes creolized by the slaves themselves and creates a shared and common belief system with their enslavers, even while it provides spiritual, cultural and intellectual tools to limit master dominion and critique their exploitation. The theme of a shared but separate past in the fight for inclusion into national history runs deep through the intellectual odyssey of race and slavery in the Atlantic World – whether it's manifested through DuBois concept of 'Double Consciousness', José Martí's position of 'With All and For All' or José Vasconcelos formulation of the 'Cosmic Race'. The interpretive inflection in analysing how African beliefs became transformed to New World Christianity echoes the political history of accounting for how racialized populations transformed their colonial status into fighting for citizenship rights and inclusion in the nation-

---

[36]This point is based upon my impression from surveying the field as a whole (qualitative) rather than a statistical analysis of articles and books (quantitative) on the subject. However, just looking at the winners and finalists of the Fredrick Douglass Book Prize given out annually since 1999 'for the most outstanding non-fiction book in English on the subject of slavery, resistance, and/or abolition' would confirm such a characterization of the field, see https://glc.yale.edu/frederick-douglass-book-prize/past-winners.

state. The resonation of religious history with political history has produced a vibrant, dynamic and voluminous historiography like two tuning forks that play off each other in synchronicity to produce a louder sonic impact.[37]

The Creolization approach, however, has muted out far too many historical topics in writing the religious history of the enslaved. African religions and 'neo-African' religions in the Americas such as Santeria, Candomblé and Vodun continue to be the work largely of anthropologists, whereas historians are more comfortable working with the change over time model and narrative structure of Christian creolization. The dialogue between past and present continues to plough deep disciplinary divides in determining what religions are suitable for historical analysis and which ones are more applicable for anthropological approaches. Given that the only exceptional feature of American slavery may be the fact that its historians have exercised an exceptional impact in dictating the research agenda of slavery and religion in the Atlantic World, it may be time to look to scholars based in other countries for inspiration. Read from the vantage point of today, perhaps Michael A. Gomez was a little too harsh when he concluded a 1999 historiographical essay with: 'Scholars of North American slavery need to either reconsider the African antecedent as playing a major role in the histories and cultures of the people of African descent and thereby retool, or they need to consider changing to a field of inquiry in which they can more accurately demonstrate their expertise.' Since then, there have been some notable improvements in the sophistication of American scholars writing about Africans as historical subjects in their own right through Atlantic World and Diasporic frameworks, rather than only slaves as historical topics.[38]

---

[37]See, for example, David Luis-Brown, *Waves of Decolonization: Discourse of Race and Hemispheric Citizenship in Cuba, Mexico, and the United States* (Durham, NC: Duke University Press, 2008); Juliet Hooker, *Theorizing Race in the Americas: Douglass, Sarmiento, Du Bois and Vasconcelos* (New York: Oxford University Press, 2017); and Paulina L. Alberto and Jesse Hoffnung-Garskof, '"Racial Democracy" and Racial Inclusion: Hemispheric Histories' in Alejandro de la Fuente and George Reid Andrews, eds, *Afro-Latin American Studies: An Introduction* (Cambridge: Cambridge University Press, 2018), pp. 264–316.

[38]Michael A. Gomez, 'African Identity and Slavery in the Americas', *Radical History Review* 75 (1999), pp. 111–20. Responses to Gomez's critique include Stephanie Smallwood, *Saltwater Slavery: A Middle Passage from Africa to American Diaspora* (Cambridge, MA: Harvard University Press, 2007); Jason R. Young, *Rituals of Resistance: African Atlantic Religion in Kongo and the Lowcountry South* (Baton Rouge: Louisiana State University Press, 2007); Vincent Brown, *The Reaper's Garden: Death and Power in the World of Atlantic Slavery* (Cambridge, MA: Harvard University Press, 2008); Ras Michael Brown, *African-Atlantic Cultures and the South Carolina Lowcountry* (Cambridge: Cambridge University Press, 2012); Kevin Dawson, *Undercurrents of Power: Aquatic Culture in the African Diaspora* (Philadelphia: University of Pennsylvania Press, 2018).

Given Brazil has the longest history of New World Slavery and imported ten times as many Africans as the United States, we should turn here for new methodological and interpretive models to enrich our studies. To end on a positive note with an example to follow, historian João Reis, the doyen of Brazilian slavery studies, has published a fascinating biography that explores the contradictory world of an African religious leader. His study *Domingos Sodré, um sacredote africano: Escrvadão, liberade e candomblé na Bahia do século XIX* (2008) is a highly textured social, cultural and religious biography of a one-time slave turned freed African in Bahia, Brazil. Reis brings the contradictory Domingo Sodré to life to flesh out the religious history of nineteenth-century urban slavery. Through a socio-cultural biography of a man who was born in Africa, toiled as a slave in Brazil, earned his freedom, became an influential candomblé priest, headed a group that purchased the freedom of slaves through a manumission junta, was a slave owner himself, and practised Catholic rituals and customs, his book ranges widely across topics. While well aware of scholarly debates emanating out of North American scholarship, the book does not fall into the historiographical traps of charting all change over time as examples of creolization, or reading every religious practice as indication of African survivals. In the epilogue, Reis points out the shortcomings of both creolization and African approaches. Sodré's life was amazing, but not because he operated in what to the modern reader was contradictory religious worlds. That contradiction was not so contradictory to his contemporaries. Sodré was considered a *ladino* – born in Africa but conversant in the languages and customs of his homeland, other parts of Africa that he learned in the Diaspora, and from Brazil. Far more cosmopolitan than the colonial powers that considered him primitive and in need of their enlightened Christianity to bring him to modernity. Not quite African; and not quite Brazilian. Not a bozal; and not a creole. Working both sides of cultural inputs from the Atlantic was a process of *ladinização* (ladinoization) rather than creolization that posits arrival at a future cultural destination. Reis's work deserves to be read widely and he is undoubtedly the most well-known and translated Brazilian scholar of slavery in the United States. But, is it even realistic to hope that the Portuguese language terms *ladino* and *ladinização* developed out of Brazilian historiography will become the new interpretive paradigm for studying the religion and culture of the enslaved in the Atlantic World? If Richard Price can describe creolization as a 'miracle', I can certainly hope for my own *milagreiro* (miracle worker) to conjure a new historiographical vision for the future.[39]

Acknowledgements

The author wishes to thank Pat Sullivan and the History Center at the University of South Carolina for giving him the opportunity to workshop this chapter. Special thanks to the Atlantic History Writing Group (Lewis Eliot, Melissa DeVelvis, Pat O'Brien, Caleb Wittum; Zoie Horency; Nathalia Cocenza; DJ Polite, Rebekah Turnmire, Neal Polhemus and Helen Marodin) for their critique of an earlier version.

Bibliography

Brown, Ras Michael, *African-Atlantic Cultures and the South Carolina Lowcountry* (New York: Cambridge University Press, 2012).
Falola, Toyin and Matt D. Childs, eds, *The Yoruba Diaspora in the Atlantic World* (Bloomington: Indiana University Press, 2005).
Finch, Aisha K., *Rethinking Slave Rebellion in Cuba: La Escalera and the Insurgencies of 1841–1844* (Chapel Hill: University of North Carolina Press, 2015).
Mintz, Sidney W. and Richard Price, *The Birth of African-American Culture: An Anthropological Perspective* (Boston, MA: Beacon Press, 1992).
Parés, Luis Nicolau, *The Formation of Candomblé: Vodun History and Ritual in Brazil*, trans. Richard Vernon (Chapel Hill: University of North Carolina Press, 2013).
Paton, Diana, *The Cultural Politics of Obeah: Religion, Colonialism and Modernity in the Caribbean World* (New York: Cambridge University Press, 2015).

---

[39] João José Reis, *Domingos Sodré, um sacredote africano: Escrvadão, liberade e candomble na Bahia do século XIX* (São Paulo: Companhia das Letras, 2008); João José Reis, *Diving Slavery and Freedom: The Story of Domingos Sodré, an African Priest in Nineteenth-Century Brazil*, trans. H. Sabrina Glendhill (Cambridge: Cambridge University Press, 2015). For further comments by Reis on *ladino* and *landinização* see his chapter 'African Nations in Nineteenth-Century Salvador, Bahia' in Jorge Cañizares-Esguerra, Matt D. Childs, and James Sidbury, eds, *The Black Urban Atlantic in the Age of the Slave Trade* (Philadelphia, PA: University of Philadelphia Press, 2013), pp. 63–82, esp. 81–2.

Reis, João Jose, *Rebelião escrava no Brasil: A história do levante dos malês em 1835*, rev. ed. (São Paulo: Companhia das Letras, 2003).

Sensbach, Jon F., *Rebecca's Revival: Creating Black Christianity in the Atlantic World* (Cambridge, MA: Harvard University Press, 2005).

Soares, Mariza de Carvalho, *Devotos da cor: Identidade étnica, religiosidade e escravidão no Rio de Janeiro, século XVIII* (Rio de Janeiro: Civilização Brasileira, 2000).

Sweet, James H., *Domingos Álavres, African Healing, and the Intellectual History of the Atlantic World* (Chapel Hill: University of North Carolina Press, 2011).

10

What historians of slavery write about when we write about race

Jacqueline Jones
University of Texas at Austin

For such a short and seemingly innocuous word, 'race' has been the source of untold misery for many hundreds of millions of people over the centuries. Race is not real, for it presupposes that all of humankind can be categorized into a small number of distinct groups ('races'), and that these groups exist on a hierarchy according to their members' biologically determined intelligence and culture. And so, because the word 'race' is ubiquitous today, any discussion of its use must begin with a reminder that the idea is as false as it is insidious.[1] Although race is a myth, the devastating consequences flowing from its multiple meanings and inhumane practices are not. Indeed,

---

[1] See for example Ashley Montagu, *Man's Most Dangerous Myth: The Fallacy of Race*, 6th ed. (Walnut Creek, CA: AltaMira Press, 1997); Barbara J. Fields, 'Ideology and Race in American History' in J. Morgan Kousser and James M. McPherson, eds, *Region, Race, and Reconstruction: Essays in Honor of C. Vann Woodward* (New York: Oxford University Press, 1982), pp. 143–77; Nina G. Jablonski, 'The Evolution of Human Kin and Skin Color', *Annual Review of Anthropology* 33 (January 2004), pp. 585–623. This is not to deny the prevalence of certain diseases among specific populations, that is, epidemiological regionalisms. See David Reich, 'How Genetics Is Changing Our Understanding of "Race"', *New York Times*, 23 March 2018. Obviously the literature on the history of slavery is immense, and many historians could be cited for each point made in the text. However, because of space limitations, I have kept documentation to a minimum. The reader should keep in mind that the beginning of each footnote should begin with 'For example, see ….'

the very idea depends upon mechanisms of legal and physical coercion to enforce it. At the same time, it is noteworthy that in some instances members of a group victimized by the idea have appropriated the word and used it as a weapon of resistance: the politics of 'racial solidarity' unites people who share a common history, not a 'race'.

This chapter explores some of the ways that historians have used, explored and challenged the notion of 'race' (and its rendering in the English language) as it informs their studies of slavery in the Western Hemisphere. The temporal and regional parameters of this chapter allow us to focus on the Americas during the age of empire-building, followed by the age of independent nation-building. Indeed, the idea of race emerged consonant with Europeans' efforts to conquer and exploit vast reserves of labour in the 'New World' – Indigenous peoples as well as forced migrants from Africa – and to wrest riches (some real, some illusory) from their colonies. Certain new countries in the Americas – most notably the United States – framed their national project in 'racial' terms in order to integrate the institution of slavery into their collective narrative of rebellion against and ultimate triumph over a colonial power. 'Race', then, has been central not only to the economic development of the Western Hemisphere but also to the varieties of myth-making that shaped the lives of all people living there.

Most scholars acknowledge that they must reckon with race because over time, in concert with the development of global capitalism, it constituted the ultimate rationale for the commodification of vulnerable human bodies. Yet a survey of various uses of the word 'race' suggests the challenges it poses to historians. Some use the word as *shorthand* for other terms and concepts. The idea of race takes the form of *pseudo-scientific theory* that informed the policies and tactics of empire-builders in their determination to subordinate specific peoples. The effort to deploy race as the underpinning of whole societies was a *violent process that unfolded over many generations*. Scholars recognize that race reinforces, complements and defines *other critical variables* in shaping social identities. In essence, race was a *political strategy*, an argument used to justify the unjustifiable and excuse the inexcusable. Race has always been a *malleable idea* with inconsistent and contradictory meanings, although scholars have found it a useful *point of comparison* between colonial societies of British, Spanish and Portuguese origins. During the era of slavery, some people of colour opposed the idea of race, and treated it not as fact but as a *contested notion*, while others appropriated the term for their own use and turned it into a *rallying cry of the oppressed*. In short, historians of slavery are obligated to approach race as a term that calls for scrutiny and scepticism, since it lacks precision as a category of social analysis. These multiple meanings of the word 'race' form the central premise of this chapter, and each meaning deserves at least brief explication here.

Systems of human bondage in the Americas included not just chattel slavery practised by peoples of European descent who enslaved peoples of Indigenous and African descent, but also various forms of slavery practised by Indigenous groups that enslaved each other as well as peoples from other groups, including at times Hispanic and Anglo intruders.[2] In cases where Indians enslaved captives of war, European traders and explorers, and members of other kin groups, slavery conformed to customary practices and not necessarily the imperatives of 'racial difference'.[3] In contrast, misguided notions of profound, immutable 'racial' differences were relevant – and, in the case of the United States, central – to the development of chattel slavery as practised by Europeans and their descendants in the Americas.

Some historians of slavery put the word 'race' in quotation marks as a reminder to the reader that the assumptions behind it are false, while others try to avoid it directly, or use the term 'racial ideologies' instead.[4] Nevertheless, despite the limitations of the word, it is not unusual for scholars to use it and its variants as *shorthand* for 'black', 'of African descent', or some other vague signifiers.[5] Thus an historian might note that, under the US South's 'peculiar institution', one 'race' subordinated another, producing 'racism', a kind of prejudice that tainted all 'race relations'.[6] These uses of the term are misleading and only serve to reify it. To state the obvious, from the beginning of slavery in the New World, bondwomen of African descent gave birth to children with white fathers; to label those children 'black' conforms to (US) cultural conventions but obscures historical reality. Slavery was not a 'racial' institution; it was a legal institution, with the status of the mother determining the status of the child regardless of that child's skin colour, father or ancestral

---

[2] Andrés Reséndez, *The Other Slavery: The Uncovered Story of Indian Enslavement in America* (New York: Mariner Books, 2017).
[3] James F. Brooks, *Captives and Cousins: Slavery, Kinship, and Community in the Southwest Borderlands* (Chapel Hill: University of North Carolina Press, 2002).
[4] For the 2009 edition of my 1985 book *Labor of Love, Labor of Sorrow: Black Women, Work, and the Family from Slavery to the Present* (New York: Basic Books, 2009) I made this disclaimer in the Introduction: 'I avoid use of the words "race" or "racism," preferring instead to focus on racial ideologies and the way they were deployed.' (p. xiv).
[5] R. Douglas Cope, *The Limits of Racial Domination: Plebeian Society in Colonial Mexico City, 1660–1720* (Madison: University of Wisconsin Press, 1994), pp. 83–4.
[6] Eugene D. Genovese, *Roll Jordan Roll: The World the Slaves Made* (New York: Vintage, 1976), p. 3, p. 21, p. 31.

line. In that sense the distinctiveness of slavery as a labour system derived not from a particular division of labour – in the antebellum South poor white people picked cotton too – but from the central fact that it depended upon the enslaved woman's reproductive labour.[7] The term 'racial slavery' elides this central fact, and implies (wrongly) that, for example, any enslaved person in the United States possessed a lineage that could be traced back exclusively to Africa, unbroken by progenitors belonging to other groups.

Those scholars who use the term 'race' would probably claim that it is a familiar way to refer to the enslavement of people of African descent – but its widespread and too often uncritical, unthinking use only serves to reinforce the myth of race. Still, it is not unusual for historians to use the term 'racial slavery' to differentiate a system characterized by enslaved people of African descent with systems characterized by slavery based on other factors – whether the slave was a war captive or part of an enemy's kin network, for example.

The ubiquitous phrase 'race relations' presupposes an essential kind of interaction between people contingent only on their 'racial' identification without any attention to the contextual relationship between them – as employer/employee, landlord/tenant, co-workers, co-religionists and so forth.[8] For example, the punishment of an enslaved field worker by a white overseer, or the decision by an enslaved cook to burn the biscuits for her mistress's dinner party, is not an example of 'race relations', but forms of interaction contingent on the unequal power between master and slave. (Unfortunately, the Library of Congress designates 'race relations' as an official category of literature, nonfiction or otherwise, giving the misleading impression that the term is a valid concept that scholars can use with precision.) Like 'racial slavery', the term 'race relations' obscures critical historical facts essential to our understanding of the institution of bondage and how it worked during different periods in different places. In a related vein we might also note the problematic term 'mixed race', which suggests that, for example, one parent is 'white' and the other 'black', when in fact the 'black' parent is probably descended from people of multiple 'racial' heritages, and not just African.

Some scholars argue that 'race' is shorthand – or the 'front man' – for a hierarchical system that is more accurately termed *caste*. In this view, race

---

[7]Wendy Warren, *New England Bound: Slavery and Colonization in Early America* (New York: Liveright, 2017), p. 156.
[8]Michael West, *The Education of Booker T. Washington: American Democracy and the Idea of Race Relations* (New York: Columbia University Press, 2006).

is both a visible manifestation of inequality and a distraction that keeps us from acknowledging the larger structures that undergird that inequality. Caste is a system based on and enforced *via* laws, political institutions, labour exploitation, cultural practices, iconography, and psychological manipulation. Slavery laid bare the caste system embedded in US society, but the end of slavery did not signify the end of caste. In order to understand the destructive and all-encompassing nature of caste relationships, one must look to other nations – to India, and the means by which the 'Untouchables', the *Dalits*, the lowest caste, are subordinated, and to Nazi Germany, with its horrific program to destroy the Jews, a program modeled after the US system of Jim Crow segregation and state-sponsored terror. According to theorists of caste, then, the institution of bondage rendered obvious the caste system which, post-emancipation, has remained intact, rigid, though less obvious.[9]

In some studies, 'race' is deployed not as shorthand for a whole constellation of human relationships, but as a specific body of thought. In these instances, historians of slavery reckon with the significance of race as a *pseudo-scientific theory* that gave licence to what we today would call crimes against humanity. The age of empire-building in the early seventeenth century coincided with an Enlightenment impulse to classify and categorize – at first minerals, plants, and animals, and then human beings. The Spanish term for race, *raza*, originally referred to purebred horses, and only later to various ethnic groups.[10] Not coincidentally, then, the development of human bondage in the Americas proceeded lockstep with the development of 'scientific' thought on differences among various groups of people, based on their geographical origins, history, language and culture. Indeed, it is difficult to determine which was cause or effect – the theory of race or the institution of bondage. In 1677, William Petty, a British economist associated with the English Royal Society, propounded a hierarchy of humanity based on intelligence and 'manners', with the 'Guinea negroes' (i.e. enslaved people) at the lowest rungs.[11] In an era of revolutionary nation-building and robust English slave-trafficking, David Hume in his 1753–4 essay 'Of National Characters' argued, 'I am apt to suspect the negroes and in general

---

[9]Isabel Wilkerson, *Caste: The Origins of Our Discontents* (New York: Random House, 2020), p. 18.
[10]See these two essays in the volume edited by Margaret R. Greer, Walter D. Mignolo and Maureen Quilligan, eds, *Rereading the Black Legend: The Discourses of Religious and Racial Difference in the Renaissance Empires* (Chicago, IL: University of Chicago Press, 2007); Kathryn Burns, 'Unfixing Race', pp. 188–201; and Walter D. Mignolo, 'What Does the Black Legend Have to do with Race?', pp. 312–24.
[11]Ibram X. Kendi, *Stamped from the Beginning: The Definitive History of Racist Ideas in America* (New York: Nation Books, 2016), p. 55.

all other species of men (for there are four or five different kinds) to be naturally inferior to the whites. There never was a civilized nation of any other complexion than white, nor even any individual eminent either in action or speculation.' This sentiment was echoed by white opinion-makers including President Thomas Jefferson and Princeton University President Samuel Stanhope Smith, lending political heft and intellectual credence to the idea of race.[12]

By the 1830s, elites were arguing that race was a fact and not just a scientific theory. Whites in Virginia recoiled at the slave rebellion led by Nat Turner, and studied his remains for clues about him and his presumed genetic proclivity for murder and mayhem.[13] Samuel George Morton's *Crania America, Or, a Comparative View of the Skulls of Various Aboriginal Nations of North and South America, To Which Is Prefixed an Essay on the Varieties of the Human Species* appeared in 1839, around the time of the forced removal of the southeastern Indians from their homelands into Indian Territory (present-day Oklahoma), and also the time that formal agitation against slavery ceased among whites in the South.[14] In attempting to secure recognition of the British for the Confederate States of America by justifying the preservation of slavery, emissaries of the would-be new nation cited studies such as Arthur Gobineau's 'Essay on the Inequality of the Human Races' (1853) and those of the Mobile, Alabama, physician Josiah Nott, who advanced the theory of polygenesis, which held that blacks belonged to a species of being wholly different from whites.[15]

The duration of US slavery from the early seventeenth century until 1865 – and the fact that it was so deeply embedded in the nation's northern and southern economies – presumably proved that the institution was 'natural', that is, based on 'scientific principles' not unlike those of gravity or the rotation of the Earth around the Sun. The presumed continuity between the degraded status of the enslaved tobacco worker of 1650 and that of the enslaved cotton picker of 1860 gave credence to the idea of the immutability of racial differences through time. According to this logic, the rigours of fieldwork, over the generations unaltered by labour-saving technologies,

---

[12]Kendi, *Stamped*, p. 132; Patrick Rael, *Eighty-Eight Years: The Long Death of Slavery in the United States, 1777–1865* (Athens: University of Georgia Press, 2015), p. 39.
[13]Daina Ramey Berry, *The Price for their Pound of Flesh: The Value of the Enslaved, from Womb to Grave, in the Building of a Nation* (Boston, MA: Beacon Press, 2016), pp. 101–2.
[14]Claudio Saunt, *Black, White, and Indian: Race and the Unmaking of an American Family* (New York: Oxford University Press, 2006), p. 58.
[15]Don H. Doyle, *The Cause of All Nations: An International History of the Civil War* (New York: Basic Books, 2017), p. 36, p. 144, p. 191.

demonstrated a biological determinism revealed in the unchanging racial division of labour. Pro-slavery ideologues purporting to be scientists could promote and embellish these prejudices by suggesting that blacks were 'naturally' obedient and cheerful, content with their lot.[16] These views were not exclusive to southern whites; in 1865 a Union officer described the former slaves in racial terms: 'They are a race of peculiarly keen feelings and domestic tendencies, and they have fewer means of withdrawing from their griefs than we [i.e., whites] have.'[17] Historians of slavery, then, of necessity have probed the symbiotic relation between ideologies of racial difference on the one hand and the imperatives of forced labour on the other.[18]

Yet race existed as more than a set of pernicious pseudo-scientific ideas concocted at a specific point in time. In fact, 'Racializing' humans was a *violent, centuries-long process* that eventually collapsed thousands of ethnic groups into three 'races' – White, Red and Black (with an occasional nod to the unhelpful designation 'mixed race'). In Europe, on the continent of Africa, and in what is now North and South America, native ethnic groups distinguished themselves from each other by their different languages, cultures, governmental structures and religion; and, in many instances, they fought prolonged, bloody wars over these differences. (Of course, ethnicity, like 'race', is a malleable concept, never fixed.[19]) Gradually those particular ethnic distinctions receded, to be replaced by a tri-partite 'racial' classification, one that reflected the exigencies of particular times and places, but in all instances relied on mechanisms of brute power.[20]

Some scholars argue that the process of race-making began onboard the slave ship, when all European crew members regardless of ethnicity or rank became 'white', and all captives regardless of ethnicity became 'black'.[21] In general, though, most historians would agree that the process unfolded

---

[16] John Blassingame, *The Slave Community: Plantation Life in the Antebellum South*, rev ed. (New York: Oxford University Press, 1979), p. 227.

[17] Qu. in Herbert Gutman, *The Black Family in Slavery and Freedom, 1750–1925* (New York: Vintage Books, 1977), p. 22.

[18] The process of racializing groups culminated in the late nineteenth century, when scholars in the new fields of anthropology and sociology conflated European ethnicity with race, producing treatises on 'the Jewish race' and 'the Italian race'. See for example David R. Roediger, *Working Toward Whiteness: How America's Immigrants Became White: The Strange Journey from Ellis Island to the Suburbs* (New York: Basic Books, 2006).

[19] Alan Gallay, *The Indian Slave Trade: The Rise of the English Empire in the American South, 1670–1717* (New Haven, CT: Yale University Press, 2003), p. 9.

[20] James Sidbury and Jorge Cañizares-Esguerra, 'Mapping Ethnogenesis in the Early Modern Atlantic', [plus forum] *William and Mary Quarterly* 68 (April 2011), pp. 181–246; Edward Baptist, *The Half Has Never Been Told: Slavery and the Making of American Capitalism* (New York: Basic Books, 2016).

[21] Marcus Rediker, *The Slave Ship: A Human History* (New York: Penguin Books, 2008).

unevenly and over many generations. Some argue that during the earliest years of colonization, the idea of race as a driving force in everyday human relations did not exist.[22] For example, seventeenth-century Chesapeake planters tended to lump subordinate labourers into a single category of promiscuous people resistant to labour discipline – whether they were Indian hirelings, English indentured servants or newly imported enslaved Africans. All these groups were presumed dangerous, a continual threat to their landed masters and mistresses. Within an Atlantic world of colliding European and Indian empires, it was difficult if not impossible to attach temperamental or other personal qualities to a phenotype.[23]

Early eighteenth-century South Carolina low country planters expressed strong preferences for certain ethnic groups as they surveyed the human cargoes of slave ships docked at Charles Town. Presumably different groups were readily identifiable to potential buyers by their geographical origins, native language and distinctive patterns of ritual scarification, and particularly prized by their willingness and capacity to work hard. Over time, however, the descendants of these enslaved peoples shed these identifying characteristics and became African-American, or 'black'.[24] In the revolutionary Atlantic World, cosmopolitan creoles of African descent derived status and legal protection from their roles as soldiers and members of the Catholic Church, and from their legal rights as citizens of the Spanish empire. Some creole elites of colour enjoyed a degree of geographical and economic mobility, and some were able to secure at least a modest amount of schooling for themselves and their children. In contrast, enslaved people of African descent toiling on large sugar plantations in Cuba lacked any protection and faced brutal discrimination, reduced to an undifferentiated category based on their 'race'. This fate awaited virtually all enslaved people in the antebellum United States.[25]

---

[22] Alex Borucki, *From Shipmates to Soldiers: Emerging Black Identities in the Rio de la Plata* (Albuquerque: University of New Mexico Press, 2015).
[23] Jacqueline Jones, *A Dreadful Deceit: The Myth of Race from the Colonial Period to Obama's America* (New York: Basic Books, 2013), pp. 1–46.
[24] Michael A. Gomez, *Exchanging Our Country Marks: The Transformation of African Identities in the Colonial and Antebellum South* (Chapel Hill: University of North Carolina Press, 1998).
[25] Jane Landers, *Atlantic Creoles in the Age of Revolutions* (Cambridge, MA: Harvard University Press, 2011); Rashauna Johnson, *Slavery's Metropolis: Unfree Labor in New Orleans during the Age of Revolutions* (Cambridge: Cambridge University Press, 2018); Aisha K. Finch, *Rethinking Slave Rebellion: La Escalera and the Insurgencies of 1841–1844* (Chapel Hill: University of North Carolina Press, 2015); Jack D. Forbes, *Africans and Native Americans: The Language of Race and the Evolution of Red-Black Peoples*, 2nd ed. (Champaign: University of Illinois Press, 1993).

It is also possible to chart how this levelling process eroding ethnicity and culminating in 'race' in the United States gradually spread west from eastern seaboard plantation economies, where blacks were considered a 'race' by the 1700s, to the Texas-Mexico borderlands, where fluid forms of Spanish categorization based on indigeneity, gender, kinship and nationality prevailed until the following century. Emboldened by their growing numbers within these borderlands, Anglos exercised the military might needed to reduce all people of colour to non-white races. In cases such as this, demography, not biology, was destiny.[26]

An argument can be made for the idea that, at least in the United States, the history of slavery is the history of race-making. The first colonists in the Chesapeake region justified enslaving Africans who were neither Christian nor English-speaking, but discarded those considerations once the descendants of these workers became English-speaking Christians. At that point slaves were defined not by their language or religion, but by their 'race'.[27] The Catholic priests in California missions gave thanks to God when they believed they had converted Indians to Christianity, but conversion did not negate a racial hierarchy established before conversion, when all Indians were 'heathens'.[28]

This process of defining and enforcing race was fundamentally different in New England. There, after the Revolution, whites claimed that the hardships endured by newly emancipated slaves – especially their poverty and their menial labour – were emblematic of the shortcomings of their 'race', giving lawmakers and employers a reason to continue to discriminate against them. In this and other areas, making race went hand in hand with making class and, indeed, the two were often mutually reinforcing, with the black 'race' associated in the minds of whites with intergenerational poverty.[29]

However powerful the notion of race, it was not all-powerful in shaping human relationships. No individuals defined themselves solely by the 'race' assigned to them; they embraced or were forced to accept multiple social signifiers. Race is then *one of many variables* that forged individual identity

---

[26]Juliana Barr, *Peace Came in the Form of a Woman: Indians and Spaniards in the Texas Borderlands* (Chapel Hill: University of North Carolina Press, 2007), pp. 288–91.
[27]Ira Berlin, *Many Thousands Gone: The First Two Centuries of Slavery in North America* (Cambridge, MA: Belknap Press, 2000); Anthony S. Parent, *Foul Means: The Formation of a Slave Society in Virginia, 1660–1740* (Chapel Hill: University of North Carolina Press, 2003).
[28]Benjamin Madley, *An American Genocide: The United States and the California Indian Catastrophe, 1846–1873* (New Haven, CT: Yale University Press, 2017).
[29]Joanne Pope Melish, *Disowning Slavery: Emancipation and 'Race' in New England, 1780–1860* (Ithaca, NY: Cornell University Press, 2000); Jones, *Dreadful Deceit*, pp. 97–144.

and the configuration of specific societies. Historians of slavery seek to account for and describe the relative effects of other hierarchical systems of social classification that shape communities and nations and coexist along with ideologies of race. These additional systems, all of which are marked by power differentials, include gender, kinship, age, wealth, religion, political rights, ethnicity and military supremacy, to name just a few. In other words, the hegemonic nature of race should not blind us to other kinds of authority based on notions of superiority and inferiority.[30] At the same time, it seems reasonable to suggest that racial ideologies were not just one other factor affecting an enslaved person's life, but rather that all other factors were often if not always somehow subsumed under, twisted by, these ideologies.[31] In any case, generalizations by definition fuel stereotypes about the inherent intelligence and dignity of whole groups of people. Thus, in the antebellum United States, whites described all members of the 'African race' as childlike, emotional and simpleminded, not unlike the stereotypes about all women at the time.

Closely related to the meaning of race as a process, evolving over time and following plantation economies, is race as a cynical ploy, a *political strategy* – in other words, a means of rationalizing the enslavement of subordinate groups in pursuit of specific goals, profits and political power foremost. Dividing subordinate groups from one another by anointing them members of separate races was a key element of this strategy. Here the vulnerability of certain mass populations is a major theme, though, paradoxically, one that is at once self-evident but also often overlooked. The forced migration of millions of men, women and children from Africa was possible because they came from home societies that lacked powerful, seafaring nation-states that could rescue and redeem these captives on the high seas. In contrast, at the beginning of colonization, Indians far outnumbered European colonists, and so proved more difficult to enslave.

It is worth noting that distinctions based on the idea of race proved of little value to the earliest European colonists who dealt with Africans and Indians. Africans *qua* slave traders and Indians *qua* members of powerful political confederations achieved whites' respect because of their numbers and control of resources. In the African interior, native traders orchestrated

---

[30] Tiya Miles, *The House on Diamond Hill: A Cherokee Plantation Story* (Chapel Hill: University of North Carolina Press, 2012).
[31] Brenda E. Stevenson, *Life in Black and White: Family and Community in the Slave South* (New York: Oxford University Press, 1997), p. xi.

the commerce in war captives, and in the European New World colonies, large, hostile Indigenous populations represented an existential threat to empire-building in those areas. In other words, in their roles as traders or warriors operating in their home territory, Africans and Indians insisted upon and often received the respect due them. Europeans conducted negotiations with the leaders of these groups as befit diplomatic or economic relations between equal partners representing nations or other sovereign groups. When and where these groups lost their power and became vulnerable to enslavement, planters and ideologues used the concept of 'race' to rationalize their subordination.

Race, then, had its uses: It provided the intellectual scaffolding for a system of labour exploitation and oppression. Perhaps the most telling example of this cynical ploy was the desperate speculation about racial difference in the works of Thomas Jefferson, author of the Declaration of Independence and later third president of the United States. Jefferson generalized about all black people in his *Notes on the State of Virginia* (written between 1781 and 1783) to justify their enslavement. He also sought to defend the Founding Fathers who excluded them from a polity founded on the proposition that 'all men are created equal'.[32]

Race was useful in other contexts as well. Some historians have suggested that the southeastern Cherokee consciously adopted the idea of race at a time and in a place – during the post-removal period, when they had been forced out of their native grounds and into Indian Territory (present-day Oklahoma). By embracing the idea of race, the Cherokee could accomplish several goals simultaneously: they could appropriate the labour of a group stripped of all rights under US law to abet their own nation's transition from subsistence hunting and gathering to staple crop agriculture; they could act 'white', as a 'civilized people' in Anglo terms; and they could claim superiority over black people in general. The Cherokee and other native groups paid a high price for this calculated move. Kin groups consisting of 'mixed race' members were shattered and a shared history among Indians and Africans was denied, leaving the Cherokee nation fractured and divided.[33] Ultimately whites turned the idea of race back on all Indian groups and either promoted state-sponsored genocide or confined them to reservations in a calculated move to dispossess them of their land.

---

[32]Edmund S. Morgan, *American Slavery, American Freedom* (New York: W. W. Norton, 1975).
[33]Fay A. Yarbrough, *Race and the Cherokee Nation: Sovereignty in the Nineteenth Century South* (Philadelphia: University of Pennsylvania Press, 2007).

Whether or not other Indian groups adopted this strategy of accepting and promoting the idea of race, a strategy that led to 'racial slavery', or simply enslaved the most vulnerable group in the United States at the time, is a matter of debate among scholars.[34] In any case, it is difficult to generalize from group to group (to compare, for example, the Cherokee to the Creek), kin network to kin network, and even person to person when it comes to studying how various indigenous leaders used the idea of race in pursuit of their own self-aggrandizement.[35] In considering race as a rationale, it is nearly impossible to discern when people truly believed the idea, or when they invoked it as a convenient way to mask their own power-grab. Or perhaps this presumed distinction between the ideological and the material is irrelevant in any case.[36] And, not surprisingly, rigid laws enforcing racial discrimination at times masked more fluid practices on the ground.[37] Still, the growing significance of race in slave-holding Indian cultures did not erase other competing factors that shaped identity – lineage, kinship, gender and culture, for example.[38]

If race was a political strategy deployed by a certain group and tailored to circumstances, then it is not surprising to find that the idea was ever *malleable*, used in contradictory and inconsistent ways. At times elites made exceptions to the rigid rules of race – for example, when their own kin were involved (the enslaved children of their masters). Southern whites equated the 'black race' with slavery, but at the same time accommodated themselves to the fact that not only were some people of colour free, a few were even slave owners.[39] In other instances whites contradicted themselves, using divergent meanings of the word simultaneously. Some used the word to mean their

---

[34]Theda Perdue, *Slavery and the Evolution of Cherokee Society, 1540-1866* (Knoxville: University of Tennessee Press, 1987); Barbara Krauthamer, Tiya Miles, Cecilia E. Naylor, and Circe Sturm, 'Rethinking Race and Culture in the Early South', *Ethnohistory* 53 (Spring 2006), pp. 399–405; Katherine Osburn, *Choctaw Resurgence in Mississippi: Race, Class, and Nation Building in the Jim Crow South, 1830-1977* (Lincoln: University of Nebraska Press, 2014); Kathryn E. Holland Braund, 'The Creek Indians, Blacks, and Slavery', *Journal of Southern History* 57 (1991), pp. 601–36.
[35]Christina Snyder, 'Conquered Enemies, Adopted Kin, and Owned People: The Creek Indians and their Captives', *Journal of Southern History* 73 (2007), pp. 255–8.
[36]Daniel Littlefield, *Africans and Creeks: From the Colonial Period to the Civil War* (New York: Praeger, 1979).
[37]Gary Zellar, *African Creeks: Estelvste and the Creek Nation* (Norman: University of Oklahoma Press, 2007).
[38]Circe Sturm, 'Blood Politics, Racial Classification, and Cherokee National Identity: The Trials and Tribulations of the Cherokee Freedmen', *American Indian Quarterly* 22 (Winter–Spring 1998), pp. 230–58.
[39]Michael P. Johnson and James L. Roark, *Black Masters: A Free Family of Color in the Old South* (New York: W. W. Norton, 1986).

own (white) family, and others considered it a synonym for (white) lineage or property ownership, making translating the language of race a perpetual challenge for historians.[40]

In the early nineteenth-century US South, Cuba and Brazil, planters could oversee vast 'tropical' workforces – enslaved people defined as a 'race' – and at the same time depend on the industrial skills of some of those workers to install technologies (sugar and flour mills, railroads, for example) that would make crop production and processing more efficient and profitable. In other words, the mechanical know-how of a few enslaved men helped to shape the labour of the many supposedly racially inferior 'tropical' field hands.[41] Meanwhile, in New England, whites disparaged the newly freed slaves as simultaneously 'naturally' impoverished, lazy dependents on the one hand and job-seeking predators on the other. In the United States, many people conflated the 'black race' with 'slavery', despite the facts that the majority of whites did not own slaves;[42] 'race pride' could rest on fragile foundations, but it could also provoke a Civil War.

During that conflict, the planters who claimed that their enslaved work forces were docile, grateful creatures quickly switched their assessment in order to account for what they feared were the bloodthirsty 'traitors' within their midst – black men and women who served as spies and non-military combatants in the service of the Union army.[43] In the antebellum US South, textile mill owners claimed that enslaved men, women and children were docile and obedient, perfectly suited for mill-operative work. Later in the century, mill owners, intent on reserving these jobs for whites, argued that blacks were unsuited for and unable to work in factories because as a race they 'lacked mechanical sense'.[44] In any case, notions of black inferiority were never sufficient to control a large and restless population; those notions were meaningful only to the extent that whites could enforce them with the

---

[40]Tessie P. Liu, 'Race and Gender in the Politics of Group Formation: A Comment on Notions of Multiculturalism', *Frontiers* 12 (1991), pp. 155–65; Cheryl I. Harris, 'Whiteness as Property', *Harvard Law Review* 106 (June 1993), pp. 1707–91.
[41]Daniel P. Rood, *The Reinvention of Atlantic Slavery: Technology, Labor, Race, and Capitalism in the Greater Caribbean* (New York: Oxford University Press, 2017).
[42]Walter Johnson, *River of Dark Dreams: Slavery and Empire in the Cotton Kingdom* (Cambridge, MA: Harvard University Press, 2017), p. 64, p. 72.
[43]Stephanie McCurry, *Confederate Reckoning: Power and Politics in the Civil War South* (Cambridge, MA: Harvard University Press, 2012); Jacqueline Jones, *Saving Savannah: The City and the Civil War* (New York: Knopf, 2008), p. 158.
[44]Jacqueline Jones, *American Work: Four Centuries of Black and White Labor* (New York: W. W. Norton, 1998), pp. 222–32.

whip and the pistol, and control the built and natural landscape in which both groups lived.[45]

Modern-day historians at times use race as an analytical category, an *illuminating pressure-point of comparison* between the United States and other parts of the Western Hemisphere.[46] In this sense race serves as a lens through which to explore larger themes related to national development. Complicating matters is the fact that the Spanish word for race, *raza*, differs in meaning from its English counterpart. Thus, the use of the word 'race' in a Latin American context is problematic, as are other terms commonly used by historians of the United States, including 'Negro' and 'colored'. Nevertheless, no labels related to race, skin colour or ethnicity could ever adequately capture the lived experience of any group or individual.[47]

Latin American societies, both colonial and independent, tended to take a more nuanced view of 'race', and situated individuals in the legal realm according to several criteria, including class, cultural heritage and a wide spectrum of skin colours. Where the United States at times distinguished 'black' people from 'mulattoes' (a person of white and African heritage), Hispanic cultures used the terms *mestizo* (Spanish or white and indigenous descent), *pardo* (brown), *indio* (Indian), *Moreno* (black), *zambo* (African and indigenous descent), *quinteronone* (one-fifth African descent) and *-cuarterón* (one-quarter African descent). This terminology did not negate the significance of race however, but rather offered a dizzying array of permutations that ultimately solidified it. Perhaps a fitting substitute for race in the Spanish context is 'socio-racial status', with all the contingent factors that this vague term implies.[48]

The presence of large numbers of Indians and the prevalence of intermarriage among members of these groups and people of European and African descent remained defining characteristics of Latin societies in contrast to the colonies that eventually became the United States. In colonial Peru, for example, indigenous Andeans and people of African descent were

---

[45]Ryan A. Quintana, 'Planners, Plantations, and Slaves: Producing the State in Early National South Carolina', *Journal of Southern History* 81 (February 2015), pp. 79–116; Stephanie M.H. Camp, *Closer to Freedom: Enslaved Women and Everyday Resistance in the Plantation South* (Chapel Hill: University of North Carolina Press, 2004).

[46]Alan Taylor, *American Revolutions: A Continental History, 1750–1804* (New York: W. W. Norton, 2016), p. 15, p. 22, p. 266, p. 272.

[47]Matthew Restall, *The Black Middle: Africans, Mayas, and Spaniards in Colonial Yucatan* (Stanford, CA: Stanford University Press, 2013).

[48]Ann Twinam, *Purchasing Whiteness: Pardos, Mulattos, and the Quest for Social Mobility in the Spanish Indies* (Stanford, CA: Stanford University Press, 2015), p. 10, p. 43.

situated within a *casta* classification, considered inferior to Europeans. Still, the label 'Indian' conferred more legal rights than did 'black'.[49] And *casta* was too an elastic term to be used with much precision from one place or time period to another. In these and other ways societies created by Spanish and Portuguese colonizers eschewed the hard, fast and ultimately arbitrary black-white binary favoured by Anglos in British North America and then the United States.[50]

As noted above, powerful colonial institutions, including the state, the church and the military at times, served as buffers between people of colour and the harsh definition of race that evolved in British North America. Furthermore, prosperous persons of mixed African/white descent in Spanish America could purchase (between the 1760s and the 1810s) the rights and privileges associated with whiteness by means of *gracias al sacar*, 'whitening petitions'.[51] American colonies and later states failed to develop such a means of upward mobility for non-white persons. In the United States, local courts went to great lengths to establish the 'race' of someone whose origins were indeterminate, often insisting a person was 'black' because of any rumoured or real African heritage, regardless of skin colour.[52]

Indeed, some might argue that the various terms to signify skin colour and class in colonial Latin America amounted to a 'pigmentocracy', where differences in physical appearance and lineage constituted a hierarchy – one more complicated than the word 'race' would allow, but one where certain statuses (and hence individuals) were considered superior to and more worthy of rights and privileges than others.[53] Most historians of Latin America now however argue that in these societies, sources of identification remained fluid, depending on the particular social context as well as the individual's reputation. In other words, one's clothing, occupation, comportment and personal displays of wealth generally might prove crucial to one's position in society.[54] In contrast, in the United States by the late antebellum period, even the few well-to-do free people of colour people laboured under strictures similar to those imposed upon their enslaved kin toiling in the fields; and

---

[49]Rachel Sarah O'Toole, *Bound Lives: Africans, Indians, and the Making of Race in Colonial Peru* (Pittsburgh, PA: University of Pittsburgh Press, 2012), pp. 161–5.
[50]Restall, *Black Middle*, p. 31.
[51]Twinam, *Purchasing Whiteness*.
[52]Ariela J. Gross, *What Blood Won't Tell: A History of Race on Trial in America* (Cambridge, MA: Harvard University Press, 2010).
[53]Magnus Morner, *Race Mixture in the History of Latin America* (Boston, MA: Little Brown, 1967).
[54]Cope, *Limits*; Twinam, *Purchasing Whiteness*, p. 63.

these liabilities would continue after emancipation, when the rigidity of racial classifications superseded the achievements of any one person. Thus, a dignified college-educated black man who dressed in the Victorian style could not escape the daily humiliation of public segregation and the daily dangers that deprived him not only of his right to vote but also protection from random physical attacks. In the United States, the notion of a 'black race' was all encompassing and unforgiving.

The United States gained its independence as a nation committed to slavery, and thus had a vested interest in the rationale of a binary system of race – one is either 'black' or 'white' – as a way to provide a rough political equality for all white men regardless of class.[55] Some historians have argued that the new nation was built upon a superstructure of 'whiteness' that posited a monumental conflict between the founders and their followers on the one hand and the supposedly monolithic forces of Indian and black allies of the British on the other.[56] In New England, patriotism came to be associated with service during the Revolutionary War, supposedly eliminating black men from the nexus of citizenship and whiteness that defined the new nation (and ignoring the fact that black men did serve in the Continental Army where they were allowed to do so).

Profits derived from the labour of enslaved workers in the South fuelled the northern industrial and market revolutions of the first half of the nineteenth century, demonstrating (to elites) that national progress, the expansion of cotton cultivation and the production of cotton cloth were one and the same.[57] The apogee of US nationalism, westward expansion in the age of slavery, was contingent upon racializing Mexicans, Indians and people of African descent.[58] In contrast, many emerging countries in Latin America embraced nation-building and the abolition of slavery at the same time, though those twin goals did not necessarily end discrimination and social prejudice based on status differentials that marginalized people of colour.[59]

---

[55] Anthony W. Marx, *Making Race and Nation: A Comparison of South Africa, the United States, and Brazil* (Cambridge: Cambridge University Press, 1998).
[56] Robert G. Parkinson, *The Common Cause: Creating Race and Nation in the American Revolution* (Chapel Hill: University of North Carolina Press, 2016).
[57] Sven Beckert, *Empire of Cotton: A Global History* (New York: Vintage, 2015).
[58] Reginald Horsman, *Race and Manifest Destiny: The Origins of American Racial Anglo-Saxonism* (Cambridge, MA: Harvard University Press, 1981).
[59] Greg Grandin, *The Empire of Necessity: Slavery, Freedom, and Deception in the New World* (New York: Picador, 2015).

Historians also acknowledge that race had its vocal dissenters; the idea was a flash point, a *contested notion* among slave-era contemporaries, especially black revolutionaries, intellectuals, preachers and activists. The rebels on the French colony of the island of St Domingue defended their right to their freedom by invoking Enlightenment ideas of natural rights. They proclaimed, 'all being children of the same father created in the same image ... We are your equal, then, by natural right.'[60] Likewise, Boston's David Walker, in his provocative 'Appeal, in Four Articles: Together with a Preamble to the Coloured Citizens of the World' of 1829, argued for a Christian view that posited the equality of all humankind. A free man of colour, Walker charged that whites' belief in race amounted to a 'dreadful deceit' that they visited upon themselves, a tissue of lies meant to mask the exploitation of black labour in the North as well as the South.[61] Throughout the Western Hemisphere, black Freemasons laid claim to the dignity that should be accorded all men regardless of their religion, 'race' or national origin.[62]

In the antebellum United States, black abolitionists and preachers disputed contemporary notions of race, especially the theory of polygenesis. The college-educated John Brown Russworm suggested that differences in climate were responsible for producing difference in superficial physical attributes such as skin colour. William Whipper argued that black people might change their behaviour by seeking education and living a respectable life, and thus put to rest the notion of race as a form of biological determinism. However, by the time Whipper had begun to expose the fiction of race (and its corollary, skin 'colourism'), that fiction was so firmly a part of national discourse that even sympathetic whites and blacks considered his views outside the realm of practical politics.[63]

If some antebellum black people disputed the idea of race, others embraced the word but not its traditional meaning, using it as a *rallying cry of the oppressed*. In keeping with its malleability, race could serve as a

---

[60] Qu. in Landers, *Atlantic Creoles*, p. 73.
[61] Peter P. Hinks, *To Awaken My Afflicted Brethren: David Walker and the Problem of Antebellum Slave Resistance* (University Park: Pennsylvania State University Press, 1996).
[62] Stephen Kantrowitz, '"Intended for the Better Government of Man": The Political History of African American Freemasonry in the Era of Emancipation', *Journal of American History* 96 (2010), pp. 1001–26.
[63] Manisha Sinha, *The Slave's Cause: A History of Abolition* (New Haven, CT: Yale University Press, 2016), pp. 63–4, pp. 201–4; Joan E. Bryant, *Reluctant Race Men: Black Opposition to the Practice of Race in Nineteenth-Century America* (New York: Oxford University Press, 2018); Mia Bay, *The White Image in the Black Mind: African-American Ideas about White People, 1830–1925* (New York: Oxford University Press, 2000).

means of resistance among those defined in racial terms by their oppressors. In this sense 'racial solidarity' – at times expressed through the adjective 'African' applied to the names of churches and benevolent societies – bound together people constrained by arbitrary laws and customs. Enslaved people in the eighteenth-century British North American colonies could forge a transnational identity – and with it specific forms of political activism – based on their shared suffering as exiles from their homeland, slaves or former slaves, and Christians. This collective identity bound together New England seamen to South Carolina field hands and immigrants to Nova Scotia and Sierra Leone. Historians disagree on the origins of this phenomenon – for example, whether 'racial solidarity' captures a universal pan-African black experience, or whether it is a class-based phenomenon very much rooted in time and place.[64]

Certainly the term 'racial solidarity' implies that all other forms of identity are subsumed under this one overarching category, a problematic assumption considering the power of gender, class and place to distinguish people of colour from each other.[65] In any case the term should not obscure the divergent interests and even in some instances violent clashes between and among men and women in bondage. Those conflicts challenge the notion of an essentialist slave community based on bonds of blood or 'race'.[66]

Finally, we must recognize that the devastating consequences of the idea of race – material legacies in the form of impoverished and disadvantaged populations – have functioned as an *impetus* for modern scholars who recognize that the history of slavery continues to resonate today. In fact, a case can be made for the idea that the rich historiography related to slavery is a product of what some scholars euphemistically term ongoing 'racial issues in the Americas'. It is true that the word 'race' is a fact of life in modern scholarship, in the news media, in and outside the academy. Of course, even people who would dispute the fundamental meaning of race – as a means of classifying individuals and cultures within a 'racial' hierarchy – still use the term routinely. At the same time, scholars are studying a relatively new

---

[64]James Sidbury, *Becoming African in America: Race and Nation in the Early Black Atlantic* (New York: Oxford University Press, 2007); James Sidbury, *Ploughshares into Swords: Race, Rebellion, and Identity in Gabriel's Virginia, 1730–1810* (Cambridge: Cambridge University Press, 1997), pp. 4–5; Ben Schiller, 'U. S. Slavery's Diaspora: Black Atlantic History at the Crossroads of "Race," Enslavement, and Colonisation', *Slavery and Abolition* 32 (July 2011), pp. 199–212.
[65]Evelyn Brooks Higginbotham, 'African-American Women's History and the Metalanguage of Race', *Signs* (Winter 1992), pp. 251–4.
[66]Jeff Forret, *Slave against Slave: Plantation Violence in the Old South* (Baton Rouge: Louisiana State University Press, 2015).

aspect of 'race' – the trend towards turning away from racial and ethnic classifications, at least for official, governmental purposes. Nevertheless, the US Census Bureau persists in asking a 'race question' and offers specific categories that are supposedly exclusive of one another – White, Black or African-American, American-Indian or Alaska Native, Asian, Native Hawaiian or Other Pacific Islander. These categories are a muddle, signifying long-discredited pseudo-scientific racist designations (White), self-identifiers regardless of heritage or appearance (black or African American), Indigeneity by place of residence (Alaska or Hawaii) or origins in a particular region of the world (Asian).[67]

It is unlikely that historians of slavery (or historians of any subject for that matter) will relinquish use of the word 'race' anytime soon. Obviously, when confronted with the word in primary or archival sources, scholars must reckon with it and its often contradictory and confusing contemporaneous meanings. However, ongoing scholarship will no doubt continue to reveal that historians' loose and uncritical use of the term obscures more than it illuminates our study of the past.

Acknowledgements

The author would like to acknowledge the help of Ann Twinam, especially for the sections on Latin America.

Bibliography

Bryant, Joan E., *Reluctant Race Men: Black Opposition to the Practice of Race in Nineteenth-Century America* (New York: Oxford University Press, 2018).

Fields, Barbara J., 'Ideology and Race in American History' in J. Morgan Kousser and James M. McPherson, eds, *Region, Race, and Reconstruction: Essays in Honor of C. Vann Woodward* (New York: Oxford University Press, 1982).

Gomez, Michael A., *Exchanging Our Country Marks: The Transformation of African Identities in the Colonial and Antebellum South* (Chapel Hill: University of North Carolina Press, 1998).

---

[67] https://www.census.gov/topics/population/race/about.html.

Higginbotham, Evelyn Brooks, 'African-American Women's History and the Metalanguage of Race', *Signs* 17: 2 (1992), pp. 251–4.

Jones, Jacqueline, *A Dreadful Deceit: The Myth of Race from the Colonial Era to Obama's America* (New York: Basic Books, 2017).

Kendi, Ibram X., *Stamped from the Beginning: The Definitive History of Racist Ideas in America* (New York: Nation Books, 2016).

Melish, Joanne Pope, *Disowning Slavery: Emancipation and 'Race' in New England, 1780–1860* (Ithaca, NY: Cornell University Press, 2000).

Osburn, Katherine, *Choctaw Resurgence in Mississippi: Race, Class, and Nation Building in the Jim Crow South, 1830–1977* (Lincoln: University of Nebraska Press, 2014).

Parkinson, Robert G., *The Common Cause: Creating Race and Nation in the American Revolution* (Chapel Hill: University of North Carolina Press, 2016).

Restall, Matthew, *The Black Middle: Africans, Mayas, and Spaniards in Colonial Yucatan* (Stanford, CA: Stanford University Press, 2013).

Saunt, Claudio, *Black, White, and Indian: Race and the Unmaking of an American Family* (New York: Oxford University Press, 2006).

Sidbury, James, *Becoming African in America: Race and Nation in the Early Black Atlantic* (New York: Oxford University Press, 2007).

Sturm, Circe, 'Blood Politics, Racial Classification, and Cherokee National Identity: The Trials and Tribulations of the Cherokee Freedmen', *American Indian Quarterly* 22 (1998), pp. 230–58.

Twinam, Ann, *Purchasing Whiteness: Pardos, Mulattos, and the Quest for Social Mobility in the Spanish Indies* (Stanford, CA: Stanford University Press, 2015).

Wilkerson, Isabel, *Caste: The Origins of Our Discontents* (New York: Random House, 2020).

11

Gender history and slavery

David Stefan Doddington
Cardiff University

When the American ex-slave Harriet Jacobs wrote in her 1861 autobiography that 'slavery is terrible for men; but it is far more terrible for women', she emphasized how the sexual violence of white enslavers added another layer of oppression onto enslaved women.[1] Distinctions based on gender and sex appear regularly in the dynamics of slavery and the experiences of enslavement across time and space, notwithstanding regional specificities and sensitivity to chronological concerns. Writing about slavery in eleventh-century England, Wulfstan, Bishop of Worcester, noted the different fates of women and men based on the expectation, and the stark realities, of reproductive exploitation: 'For [the English] would buy men from all over England and sell them off in Ireland in the hope of profit, even putting on sale girls whom previously they had sexually abused and who were now pregnant.'[2] While both women and men suffered in slavery, Wulfstan and Jacobs – some 800 years apart – highlighted how the consequences of that suffering could manifest differently.

---

[1] Harriet Jacobs, *Incidents in the Life of a Slave Girl. Written by Herself* (Boston, MA: Published for the Author, 1861), p. 119.
[2] *Vita Wulfstani of William of Malmesbury*, ed. R.R. Darlington (London: Offices of the Society, 1928), p. 43; 'Life of Bishop Wulfstan of Worcester' in *Three Lives of the Last Englishmen*, trans. Michael James Swanton (New York: Garland Press, 1984), p. 126; Cited in Sally McKee, 'Slavery' in Judith Bennett and Ruth Karras, eds, *The Oxford Handbook of Women and Gender in Medieval Europe* (Oxford: Oxford University Press, 2013), pp. 281–92, p. 288. Both women and men faced the threat of sexual abuse, but reproductive exploitation is flagged as unique to women.

Rather than focus on gendered experiences in slavery or examine how gender shaped practices of enslavement, however, this chapter seeks to explore how social, cultural and political questions and concerns relating to gender and sex have influenced historians and historical work on slavery. I outline some of the approaches, methods and theories that have shaped academic histories of slavery and gender, making use of examples addressing the anglophone Americas, but also histories of slavery in antiquity and medieval Europe.[3] In doing so, I consider the transnational elements of such work and stress the significance of gender to our understandings of slavery at the local and global level.

Histories of gender and slavery cannot be purely predicated on biological or reproductive distinctions between women and men. Nor can we assume that to speak of gender is to speak only of women. However, pioneering work on the topic which emerged in the latter half of the twentieth century spoke to political, intellectual and methodological changes both inside and outside of the academy and connected to wider international networks of feminist political activism. Scholars strove to recover the voices and experiences of women in the past, as well as to address historical and contemporary concerns relating to gendered power relations. Much of the early material that could be categorized as 'gender history' in slave studies had a social or experiential angle, but scholars advancing this work also forced a critical rethinking of the analytical frameworks applied to their period of study. If women, and not men, were the focal point of study, could we truly speak of a 'demise' of slavery in medieval Europe; was resistance in the US South only the act of 'exceptional men'?

Disciplinary shifts associated with the cultural turn from the late 1980s generated diverse studies that examined men and masculinities, deconstructed seemingly stable binaries of male/female to consider multiple,

---

[3]While not covered in this chapter, select work on gender and slavery in Africa, Asia and the wider Americas includes Claire C. Robertson and Martin A. Klein, eds, *Women and Slavery in Africa* (Madison: University of Wisconsin Press, 1983); Maria Jaschock and Suzanne Miers, eds, *Women and Chinese Patriarchy: Submission, Servitude, and Escape* (Hong Kong: Hong Kong University Press, 1994); Bernard Moitt, *Women and Slavery in the French Antilles* (Bloomington: University of Indiana Press, 2001); Sandra Lauderdale Graham, *Caetana Says No: Women's Stories from a Brazilian Slave Society* (New York: Cambridge University Press, 2002); Eric Alan Jones, *Wives, Slaves, and Concubines: A History of the Female Underclass in Dutch Asia* (DeKalb: Northern Illinois University Press, 2010); Madeline C. Zilfi, *Women and Slavery in the Late Ottoman Empire: The Design of Difference* (New York: Cambridge University Press, 2010); Camilla Cowling, *Conceiving Freedom: Women of Color, Gender, and the Abolition of Slavery in Havana and Rio de Janeiro* (Chapel Hill: University of North Carolina Press, 2013); Matthew S. Gordon and Kathryn A. Hain, eds, *Concubines and Courtesans: Women and Slavery in Islamic History* (New York: Oxford University Press, 2017).

intersecting identities, and addressed the significance of the gendered discourse that shaped power relations in slave systems. How, for example, did contested ideas on femininity or masculinity – on what it meant to be a woman or a man – shape ideas and manifestations of power and powerlessness? Building on these challenges, historical work on gender and slavery is now marked by a theoretical eclecticism, with both a continued interest in experiences and identities, and an appreciation of the significance of gender to society, culture and power relations.

Women's history

Although enslaved individuals such as Jacobs were all-too aware of how gender had shaped their worlds, academic work on slavery from the first half of the twentieth century rarely considered the different experiences of women and men. 'Professional' history was mostly written by white men and about white men; some historians barely acknowledged women as historical actors. The most prominent historian of the US South prior to the Second World War, Ulrich B. Phillips, opened his racist defence of American slavery with the statement 'for a man to be property may seem barbaric and outrageous', before conflating a passive acceptance of the logic of racial slavery with the alimony payments twentieth-century men were 'legally required' to pay their ex-wives.[4] When later scholars such as Kenneth Stampp addressed slave resistance, this was made synonymous with masculinity: 'Though the history of southern bondage reveals that men can be enslaved under certain conditions, it also demonstrates that their love of freedom is hard to crush.'[5]

Similar gendered trends could be found in other work on slavery. In Gwyn William's *The Vikings* (1968), he noted 'the slave *him*self was the foundation of Viking life at home', while in P.H. Sawyer's *Kings and Vikings* (1982), he declared: 'that there were slaves, freed*men* and different ranks of free*men* need not be doubted.'[6] In relation to wider themes in the field, important work from the 1950s to the 1970s had addressed large-scale economic

---

[4]Ulrich B. Phillips, *Life and Labor in the Old South* (Boston, MA: Little, Brown, and Company, 1929), p. 160.
[5]Kenneth Stampp, *The Peculiar Institution: Slavery in the Antebellum South* (New York: Knopf, 1956).
[6]Gwyn Jones, *A History of the Vikings* (New York; London: Oxford University Press, 1968); P.H. Sawyer, *Kings and Vikings* (New York: Methuen, 1982). Italics mine.

shifts in medieval Europe, focusing on an apparent transition from slavery to feudalism and the consequent 'demise' of slavery. Major quantitative projects in the same period acknowledged, but rarely explored, that from the late twelfth century women were forming 'a growing majority among the slaves traded by Christians in European and non-European markets'.[7] An emphasis for many historians remained on a transition *away* from slavery as the dominant mode of production within Europe. In a historiographical survey of the field published in 1995, Susan Mosher Stuard argued this was because scholars assumed that the important figure in ascertaining the significance of slavery was that of the man: 'a good half-century of research presents the demise argument in terms of men gaining rights or freedom in the rural countryside.' And yet, Stuard explained, 'shifting the lens from the male slave to the female … changes the picture', altering our understanding of social, economic and gendered structures in medieval Europe.[8]

Much work addressing gender and slavery from the 1970s through to the 1990s had an openly revisionist angle. Scholars who were inspired by and engaged in transnational feminist activism and thought looked to correct the omission of women from histories of slavery. An outburst of social history from the 1960s had seen many historians explore how marginalized groups responded to oppression and put these struggles at the centre of their histories.[9] Feminist historians were critical, however, of the continued emphasis within this scholarship on men as the universal figure and stressed the need to consider intersectional issues surrounding race, gender and class. Erlene Stetson, writing about US slavery, recalled how black female scholars from this era 'felt betrayed by historians whose liberal views allowed them to envision the reality of male slaves (to a degree) but not that of female

---

[7]This point is emphasized in McKee, 'Slavery', p. 285. For the wider literature, see Marc Bloch, 'Mediaeval Inventions' in *Land and Work in Mediaeval Europe*, trans. J.E. Anderson (London: Routledge, 1967), p. 178; Marc Bloch, *Slavery and Serfdom in the Middle Ages: Selected Essays*, trans. William R. Beer (Berkeley: University of California Press, 1975); Pierre Dockès, *Medieval Slavery and Liberation*, trans. Arthur Goldhammer (Chicago, IL: University of Chicago Press, 1982); Charles Verlinden, *L'esclavage dans l'Europe médiévale*, 2 Vols. (Bruges: De Tempel, 1955-1977). A significant outlier here was Iris Origo, 'The Domestic Enemy: The Eastern Slaves in Tuscany in the Fourteenth and Fifteenth Centuries', *Speculum* 30: 3 (1955), pp. 321–66.
[8]Susan Mosher Stuard, 'Ancillary Evidence for the decline of medieval slavery', *Past & Present* 149 (1995), pp. 3–28, p. 3. Stuard's argument has been addressed in Alice Rio, *Slavery After Rome, 500-1100* (Oxford: Oxford University Press, 2017), pp. 160-74.
[9]John Blassingame, *The Slave Community: Plantation Life in the Antebellum South* (New York; Oxford: Oxford University Press, 1972); Michael Craton, *Searching for the Invisible Man: Slaves and Plantation Life in Jamaica* (Cambridge, MA: Harvard University Press, 1978); Susan Treggiari, *Roman Freedmen During the Late Republic* (Oxford: Clarendon Press, 1969).

slaves. We had a sense of fighting the world'.[10] Angela Davis explained how research on enslaved women in the Americas could challenge contemporary myths about black women, as well as destabilize normative assumptions that feminism was synonymous with white, middle-class women: 'It is not for the sake of historical accuracy alone that such a study should be conducted, for lessons can be gleaned from the slave era which will shed light upon Black women's and all women's current battle for emancipation.'[11] The political as well as intellectual imperatives to examine the lives of women were likewise central to pioneering work in ancient history. Sarah B. Pomeroy's 1975 book, *Goddesses, Whores, Wives, and Slaves*, 'was conceived when I asked myself what women were doing while men were active in all areas traditionally emphasized by classical scholars'. The sense of a scholarly recovery of women in the past was clear. So, too, was that this reflected contemporary concerns: 'the story of women in antiquity should be told now, not only because it is a legitimate aspect of social history, but because the past illuminates contemporary problems in relationships between men and women.'[12]

Historians of slavery influenced by social history and intersectional feminism hoped to address the experiences and diverse roles of women, whether enslaved, part of a non-slaveholding (under)class, or even enslavers.[13] They insisted that sexual dynamics were fundamental to understanding slavery almost everywhere it had existed. To explore demographics or economics, or the political and legal structures of slavery, was inevitably to talk of interactions between women and men. The Roman law *partus sequitur ventrem*, for example, meant that children

---

[10]Erlene Stetson, 'Studying Slavery – Some Literary and Pedagogical Considerations on the Black Female Slave' in Gloria T. Hull, Patricia Bell Scott, and Barbara Smith, eds, *All the Women Are White, All the Blacks Are Men, but Some of Us Are Brave: Black Women's Studies* (Westbury: The Feminist Press, 1982), p. 62.
[11]Angela Davis, *Women, Race, and Class* (New York: Random House, 1982), p. 4; bell hooks, *Ain't I a Woman: Black Women and Feminism* (Boston, MA: South End Press, 1981).
[12]Sarah B. Pomeroy, *Goddesses, Whores, Wives, and Slaves: Women in Classical Antiquity* (New York: Shocken Books, 1975), pp. x–xii.
[13]Important work on women as enslavers/non-slaveholders includes Catherine Clinton, *The Plantation Mistress: Woman's World in the Old South* (New York: Pantheon, 1982); Elizabeth-Fox Genovese, *Within the Plantation Household: Black and White Women of the Old South* (Chapel Hill: University of North Carolina Press, 1988); Cecily Jones, *Engendering Whiteness: White Women and Colonialism in Barbados and North Carolina* (Manchester: Manchester University Press, 2002); Thavolia Glymph, *Out of the House of Bondage: The Transformation of the Plantation Household* (New York; Cambridge: Cambridge University Press, 2008); Margaret Sommerville, *Sex and Subjection: Attitudes to Women in Early-Modern Society* (London: Arnold, 1995); William Foster, *Gender, Mastery, and Slavery: From European to Atlantic World Frontiers* (London: Palgrave Macmillan, 2010).

born to enslaved women were born into slavery. Slave systems in antiquity and medieval Europe were sustained through conquest, but also through productive and reproductive exploitation.[14] Continuity in the sexual elements of enslavement were evident in European colonists' assumption or adaptation of this law in the Americas, with the transnational significance accorded to reproductive exploitation evident in legislation passed across the Atlantic world. The Virginia act of 1662 that decreed 'all children borne in this country shall be held bond or free only according to the condition of their mother' was only one of many across the Atlantic world that confirmed sexual relations as fundamental to entrenching hierarchies and power.[15] As historian Catherine Clinton argued: 'slavery was not simply a system of labour extraction but a means of sexual and social control as well.'[16] While some early (male) critics of women's history questioned the validity of work on the topic, these pioneering scholars proved that to study gender relations was to study power.[17]

The 'invisible (wo)man' – Experience and identity

Historians were attuned to the methodological problems they faced in trying to uncover the experiences or roles of women in slave systems. Alienation and powerlessness marked both the everyday lives and the

---

[14]Jane Gardner, *Women in Roman Society & Law* (London: Routledge, 1990), pp. 206–9; Ruth Mazo Karras, *Slavery and Society in Medieval Scandinavia* (New Haven, CT: Yale University Press, 1988), pp. 50–6; Keith Bradley, *Slavery and Society at Rome* (Cambridge: Cambridge University Press, 1994), pp. 33–5; Walter Schediel, 'Quantifying the Sources of Slaves in the Roman Empire', *Journal of Roman Studies*, 87 (1997), pp. 156–69. Legal changes relating to slavery's heritable status are discussed in Sally McKee, 'Inherited Status and Slavery in Renaissance Italy and Venetian Crete', *Past & Present*, 182 (2004), pp. 31–54.

[15]Jacqueline Jones, *Labor of Love, Labor of Sorrow: Black Women, Work and the Family from Slavery to the Present* (New York: Basic Books, 1985), p. 43. An excellent summary of the transnational significance of gendered legislation can be found in Sasha Turner, 'The Invisible Threads of Gender, Race, and Slavery', *Black Perspectives* (2017).

[16]Catherine Clinton, '"Southern Dishonour": Flesh, Blood, Race and Bondage' in Carol Bleser, ed., *In Joy and Sorrow: Women, Family, and Marriage in the Victorian South, 1830–1990* (New York; Oxford: Oxford University Press, 1990), pp. 52–69, p. 52.

[17]On hostility scholars faced, see Deborah Gray White, '"Matter Out of Place": Ar'n't I a Woman? Black Female Scholars and the Academy', *Journal of African American History* 92: 1 (2007), pp. 5–12; hooks, *Ain't I a Woman*, p. x.

historical afterlife of all enslaved people, and this was worsened by gendered asymmetries of power.[18] In *Ar'n't I a Woman* (1985), the first full-length monograph on enslaved women in the United States, Deborah Gray White stressed how the 'double burden' of racism and patriarchy which enslaved women faced also affected historical research: 'Whites wrote most of antebellum America's records and African-American males wrote just about all of the antebellum records left by blacks. To both groups the female slave's world was peripheral.'[19] Susan Mosher Stuard described the problems and scepticism she (and others) faced in the 1950s while seeking to research medieval women: 'anyone seeking information on women in medieval archives was told firmly that none existed.'[20] Pomeroy emphasized how problems inherent to all social histories of antiquity were harder still when looking for the voices of women: 'In a period when the history of men is obscure, it naturally follows that the documentation for women's lives is even more fragmented.'[21] This invisibility was yet more pronounced in relation to enslaved women.

Scholars argued, however, that a creative and interdisciplinary approach could provide access to the world of enslaved women, reveal how slavery mattered to contemporaries, and shift existing historiographical narratives and trends. White, for example, mined traditional archival records but also addressed testimony from enslaved people 'in light of what anthropologists know about women who do similar things in analogous settings.'[22] In their studies on enslaved women in the British Caribbean, Hilary Beckles and Barbara Bush stressed the need to combine traditional modes of research with 'historical imagination ... a certain degree of intuition and empathy', and 'informed speculation' to address silences and gaps in the official repositories.[23] In a more recent discussion on the historiography of gender

---

[18]Michel-Rolph Trouillot, *Silencing the Past: Power and the Production of History* (Boston, MA: Beacon Press, 1995); Marisa J. Fuentes, *Dispossessed Lives: Enslaved Women, Violence, and the Archive* (Philadelphia: University of Pennsylvania Press, 2016).
[19]Deborah Gray White, *Ar'n't I A Woman? Female Slaves in the Plantation South* (New York; London: W. W. Norton, 1999; reprint, 1985 edition), pp. 23–4.
[20]Susan Mosher Stuard, 'The Chase after Theory: Considering Medieval Women', *Gender & History* 4 (1992), pp. 135–46, p. 138.
[21]Pomeroy, *Goddesses, Whores, Wives, and Slaves*, p. xviii.
[22]White, *Ar'n' t I A Woman*, pp. 23–4.
[23]Hilary Beckles, *Natural Rebels: A Social History of Enslaved Black Women in Barbados* (London: Zed Books, 1989), pp. 176–7; Barbara Bush, *Slave Women in Caribbean Society, 1650–1838* (London: Currey, 1990), p. 90, p. 121, p. 148, p. 167. See also Lucille Mathurin Mair, *The Rebel Woman in the British West Indies during Slavery* (Kingston: Institute of Jamaica, 1975).

and slavery in medieval Britain and Ireland, David Wyatt (2009) explained how work on the topic had been furthered by 'enter[ing] the realm of speculation' and reading between the lines of legal codes, chronicles, religious texts and epic literature.[24] In addressing the roles and experiences of women in slavery, scholars emphasized the need to widen the scope of what was considered acceptable as historical evidence, to read against the grain of sources to showcase how gender relations underpinned slave systems, and to think creatively and critically about the full range of actors and interactions in a given society.

Many early scholars stressed how women's experiences in slave systems differed to those of men. A significant component of this scholarship examined sexual violence, with the seemingly timeless and transnational element of this dimension of enslaved women's lives revealed by scholars of antiquity, medieval Europe and the Americas.[25] In her studies on Viking society, Ruth Mazo Karras addressed the continuities here: 'as in *all* slaveholding societies male slaveholders had sexual access to their slaves, and they often purchased women for that purpose alone.'[26] Outside of exploitation and resistance, however, other questions were asked: how might experiences or understandings of pregnancy, childbirth and childcare impact upon women's lives? How did patterns of work differ according to actual and imagined differences between women and men? What type of kinship structures could enslaved people build and what significance did the family have for them? Did women and men resist slavery or assert mastery in the same way?

Alongside a critical re-assessment of source material created by enslavers, historians of slavery in the United States were able to make use of published slave narratives, albeit authored predominantly by men, to profitably answer

---

[24]David Wyatt, *Slaves and Warriors in Medieval Britain and Ireland, 800-1200* (Leiden; Boston: Leiden University Press, 2009), pp. 52-3.
[25]Origo, 'The Domestic Enemy'; Ruth Mazo Karras, 'Concubinage and Slavery in the Viking Age', *Scandinavian Studies* 62 (1990), pp. 141-62; Gardner, *Women in Roman Society*; Moses Finley, *Ancient Slavery and Modern Ideology* (Princeton, NJ: Markus Wiener Publishers, 1998), p. 46, 163-4; Darlene Clark Hine, 'Rape and the Inner Lives of Black Women in the Middle West: Preliminary Thoughts on the Culture of Dissemblance', *Signs* 4: 4 (1989), pp. 912-21; Thelma Jennings, '"Us Colored Women Had to Go through a Plenty": Sexual Exploitation of African American Slave Women', *Journal of Women's History* 1: 3 (1990), pp. 45-74; Brenda Stevenson, *Life in Black and White: Family and Community in the Slave South* (New York; Oxford: Oxford University Press, 1996).
[26]Karras, 'Concubinage and Slavery', 141. Italics mine.

some of these questions.²⁷ Narratives of enslaved women were highlighted and, as in the case of Jean Fagan Yellin's work on Harriet Jacobs's *Incidents in the Life of a Slave Girl,* corroborated in the face of both contemporary and academic scepticism as to their veracity. Yellin explicitly noted how her work with *Incidents* came while making 'an effort to make amends for ignoring women in my earlier writing'.²⁸ Scholars who stressed the usefulness of the more evenly gendered body of interviews conducted with elderly ex-slaves as part of the Works Progress Administration project in the 1930s also interrogated and deconstructed the scepticism other scholars held towards these records, speaking to wider methodological debates over how best to access the social world of enslaved people.²⁹ A significant outpouring of research on women and gender in the United States developed in the 1990s based upon these types of records, with a number of key monographs, edited collections and articles stressing the importance of studying women, gender and slavery.³⁰

Testimony from enslaved people in the ancient and medieval period proved more elusive for scholars of slavery.³¹ Male enslavers or elite beneficiaries of slavery were both the authors and subjects of most historical material available on slave systems, and these writers typically either took for granted the ubiquity of slavery in their societies or explicitly ignored and belittled enslaved people. Yet, as scholars have revealed, information on the lives of women and on the significance of gender relations was embedded in much contemporaneous writing, as well as popular and material culture. By reading against the grain of family and epic sagas or poems, archaeological and material traces, legal codes, chronicles and religious texts, historians of medieval or ancient slavery exposed how gender shaped elements of

---

²⁷John Blassingame, 'Using the Testimony of Ex-slaves: Approaches and Problems', *Journal of Southern History* 41: 4 (1975), pp. 473–92, p. 480; Frances Smith Foster, '"In Respect to Females …": Differences in the Portrayals of Women by Male and Female Narrators', *Black American Literature Forum*, 15: 2 (1981), pp. 66–70.
²⁸Harriet Jacobs, *Incidents in the Life of a Slave Girl. Written by Herself*, ed., Jean Fagan Yellin (Cambridge, MA: Harvard University Press, 1987), pp. vii–xxv.
²⁹White, *Ar'n't I A Woman*, pp. 23–4; –, 'Black Female Scholars and the Academy', pp. 9–10; Saidiya Hartman, *Scenes of Subjection: Terror, Slavery, and Self-Making in Nineteenth-Century America* (New York; Oxford: Oxford University Press, 1997), pp. 10–12.
³⁰Select collections include Bleser, ed., *In Joy and Sorrow*; Catherine Clinton and Nina Silber, eds, *Divided Houses: Gender and the Civil War* (New York; Oxford: Oxford University Press, 1992); David Barry Gaspar and Darlene Clark Hine, eds, *More Than Chattel: Black Women in Historical Perspective* (Bloomington: Indiana University Press, 1996); Catherine Clinton and Michele Gillespie, eds, *The Devil's Lane: Sex and Race in the Early South* (New York: Oxford University Press, 1997).
³¹Pomeroy, *Goddesses, Whores, Wives, Slaves*, p. 190; Bradley, *Slavery and Society*, p. 178.

slavery. Expectations of sexual access to enslaved women are clear in much of the documentary evidence, but so, too, are quotidian dimensions of slave life. The 'comedic' use of names such as 'Slattern, Serving-Maid, Cinder Wench' for enslaved women in the Old Norse *Rígsþula* poem, for example, indicated the type of work enslaved women were expected to do in these societies, and symbolized their overall subaltern position.[32] Epic poems and tragedies of antiquity, including Homer's *Odyssey* and *Iliad*, or Euripides's *Trojan Women*, likewise offered insights into both the gendered violence associated with enslavement and more mundane elements of slavery, such as distinctions in labour between women and men.[33]

Comedies and dialogues, while likewise shaped by elite views or exaggerated for effect, were used by scholars to examine how gender underpinned social relations and shaped the lives of classical contemporaries.[34] For example, Xenophon's *Oikonomikos*, a dialogue on household management in ancient Greece, explained how male and female 'qualities' influenced work roles: 'the god, from the very beginning', had 'designed the nature of woman for the indoor work and concerns and the nature of man for the outdoor work'. These ideas extended to the work arrangements of enslaved people in this elite household. Men worked in the fields, including planting, ploughing and holding supervisor roles; women performed domestic duties and were presumed to be sexually available to their enslavers.[35] Gendered ideals captured in such documents shaped wider social and political relations in antiquity. In her study on women and Roman law, for example, Jane Gardner

---

[32] Karras, *Slavery and Society*, pp. 51–60; Ruth Mazo Karras, 'Servitude and Sexuality in in Medieval Iceland' in Gisli Pallson, ed., *From Sagas to Society: Comparative Approaches to Early Iceland* (Enfield Lock: Hisarlik Press, 1992), pp. 289–304; Judith Jesch, *Women in the Viking Age* (Woodbridge: Boydell & Brewer, 1991), pp. 185–202; Kirsten A. Seaver, 'Thralls and Queens: Female Slavery in the Medieval Norse Atlantic' in Gwynn Campbell, Suzanne Miers, Joseph Miller, eds, *Women and Slavery: Africa, the Indian Ocean World, and the Medieval North Atlantic* (Athens: Ohio University Press, 2007), pp. 147–69, p. 150; Wyatt, *Slaves and Warriors*, pp. 141–3. The men also have pejorative names. The fact one son was named *Kefser* (bedmate) could indicate that enslaved men were presumed sexually accessible.

[33] *Odyssey* 9.39–42, 22. 422–3; Euripides, *The Trojan Women*, 252–75, 500–1; Moses Finley, *The World of Odysseus* (London: Chatto & Windus, 1956), p. 61. For source critiques of epic literature, see Elaine Fantham, Helene Peet Foley, Natalie Boymel Kampen, Sarah B. Pomery, and H. Alan Shapiro, eds, *Women in the Classical World: Image and Text* (New York; Oxford: Oxford University Press, 1993), pp. 10–53; Christiana Franco, 'Women in Homer' in Sharon L. James and Sheila Dillon, eds, *A Companion to Women in the Ancient World* (Malden, MA: Wiley-Blackwell, 2012), pp. 54–66; Emily Wilson, 'Slaves and Sex in the *Odyssey*' in Deborah Kamen, C. W. Marshall, eds, *Slavery and Sexuality in Classical Antiquity* (Madison: University of Wisconsin Press, 2021), pp. 15–40.

[34] Pomeroy, *Goddesses, Whores, Wives, Slaves*, p. x; Rob Tordoff, 'Slaves and Slavery in Ancient Greek Comedy' in Ben Akrigg and Rob Tordoff, eds, *Slaves and Slavery in Ancient Greek Comic Drama* (New York: Cambridge University Press, 2013), pp. 1–63.

[35] Xenophon, *Oeconomicus*, ed. and trans. Sarah Pomeroy (Oxford: Oxford University Press, 1994), p. 7, pp. 20–5, pp. 35–9, pp. 314–17.

addressed patterns of manumission based on a small sample of surviving documents. Enslaved women appear to have been more regularly 'freed' by a sexual partner, likely with an expectation of marriage. This was inextricable from the coercive sexual practices of slavery and wider patriarchal structures. Enslaved men (in smaller numbers) more frequently freed themselves using a *peculium*, which they had greater opportunities to build up because of the wider variety of jobs available to men, *as* men.[36] The everyday life of enslaved people was rarely the central point of such source material. However, by reading against the grain and cross-referencing different sources, scholars revealed how gender shaped both slavery and freedom.

Some of the most rewarding work shaped by these methodological and intellectual innovations came in relation to slave resistance in the Americas. Many contemporaries had conflated resistance with both masculinity and militancy, with ex-slave Josiah Henson, for example, claiming it was 'a woman's instinct' to instead cling 'to hearth and home'.[37] Early historians took their cue from such sources. Feminist scholars challenged these historical claims, which had also been used to denigrate black women in the present, paint them as passive, even accommodationist, in nature, or infer that their suffering was lesser to that of men.[38] Revisionist scholars stressed, therefore, that women's opportunities for resistance were not shaped by 'instinct' or biological essentialism. Instead, they were restricted by gendered *ideas* that associated caring responsibilities with femininity or which prevented them from gaining mobile or skilled work roles that might facilitate flight. If famed rebels like Frederick Douglass used resistance to demonstrate 'how a slave was made a man', enslaved women like Harriet Jacobs were instead told: 'nobody respects a mother who forsakes her children.'[39] Expectations that women would be carers, community pressure to remain with children

---

[36]Gardner, *Women in Roman Society*, pp. 225–6; Nick R. E. Fisher, *Slavery in Classical Greece* (London: Bristol Classical Press, 1993), p. 68; Matthew J. Perry, *Gender, Manumission, and the Roman Freedwoman* (New York; Cambridge: Cambridge University Press, 2014), pp. 44–9; Allison Glazebrook, 'Gender and Slavery' in Stephen Hodkinson, Marc Kleijwegt, and Kostas Vlassopoulos, eds, *The Oxford Handbook of Greek and Roman Slaveries* (Oxford: Oxford University Press, 2017), p. 9. Distinctions in work roles had similar impact in the Americas. See White, *Ar'n't I a Woman*, pp. 76, 128–30; Marietta Morrissey, *Slave Women in the New World: Gender Stratification in the Caribbean* (Lawrence: University Press of Kansas, 1989), pp. 65–8, pp. 161–3.
[37]Josiah Henson, *Autobiography of the Rev. Josiah Henson* (London; Ontario: Schuyler, Smith, 1881), p. 79.
[38]Michelle Wallace, *Black Macho and the Myth of Superwoman* (New York: Dial Press, 1978), p. 16.
[39]Frederick Douglass, *Narrative of the Life of Frederick Douglass, an American Slave; Written by Himself* (Boston, MA: Anti-Slavery Office, 1845), pp. 65–6; Jacobs, *Incidents in the Life of a Slave Girl*, p. 139.

(alongside desire) and restrictions on the mobility of women based on gendered assumptions, not biology, led to fewer women taking permanent flight than men.[40]

Scholars insisted, however, that enslaved women were not passive. Barbara Bush, Brenda Stevenson, Darlene Clark Hine and David Barry Gaspar, among others, revealed how women across the Americas were involved in a constant, day-to-day struggle against slavery that undermined the system and ensured enslaved people maintained a sense of personal dignity and communal support.[41] Others proved that, while sexual exploitation was a fundamental part of the brutality of slavery, enslaved women demonstrated agency through reproductive resistance, whether in the form of violence, contraceptive methods shared in a female slave network, or even suicide and infanticide.[42] Such work also helped deconstruct essentialist views that equated femininity solely with motherhood. Historians thus emphasized the need to rethink the boundaries drawn between violent and passive resistance. Scholars such as Beckles revealed how enslaved women's 'aggressive survivalist consciousness' underpinned the creation of families and communities that made possible all other forms of resistance.[43] Building on these methodological and conceptual advances, historians have proven, time and time again, that enslaved women in the Americas responded to slavery in ways that defied their dehumanization, and prioritized community, solidarity and survival.[44]

---

[40]This was argued in a comprehensive study on runaways in the American South, suggesting how far the argument has been accepted: John Hope Franklin and Loren Schweninger, *Runaway Slaves: Rebels on the Plantation* (New York; Oxford: Oxford University Press, 1999), p. 212.

[41]Bush, *Slave Women*, pp. 51–82; Gaspar and Hine, eds, *More Than Chattel*; Verene Shepherd, Bridget Brereton, and Barbara Bailey, eds, *Engendering History: Caribbean Women in Historical Perspective* (New York: St Martin's Press, 1995).

[42]Darlene Clark Hine and Kate Wittenstein, 'Female Slave Resistance: The Economics of Sex' in Filomina Chioma, ed., *The Black Woman Cross-Culturally* (Cambridge: Schenkman, 1981), pp. 289–99; Jennings, 'Us Colored Women'; Liese M. Perrin, 'Resisting Reproduction: Reconsidering Slave Contraception in the Old South', *Journal of American Studies* 35: 2 (2001), pp. 255–74; Bush, *Slave Women*, pp. 143–8, 165–6; Nikki. M. Taylor, *Driven Toward Madness: The Fugitive Slave Margaret Garner and Tragedy on the Ohio* (Athens: Ohio University Press, 2016).

[43]Beckles, *Natural Rebels*, ix, 153.

[44]Outstanding work on slave resistance and community building on this legacy includes Stephanie Camp, *Closer to Freedom: Enslaved Women and Everyday Resistance in the Plantation South* (Chapel Hill: University of North Carolina Press, 2004); Steeve O. Buckridge, *The Language of Dress: Resistance and Accommodation in Jamaica, 1750–1890* (Kingston: University of the West Indies Press, 2004); Emily West, *Chains of Love: Slave Couples in Antebellum South Carolina* (Urbana: University of Illinois Press, 2004); Daina Ramey Berry, *Swing the Sickle for the Harvest Is Ripe: Gender and Slavery in Antebellum Georgia* (Urbana: University of Illinois Press, 2007).

Gender, power and representation

Much work on gender and slavery focused on the experiences of enslaved women, but developments in the discipline associated with the cultural turn in the late 1980s also saw a shift in focus for some. Building on the theoretical work on gender by Joan Scott, Judith Butler and Evelyn Brooks Higginbotham, to name only a few, scholars of slavery increasingly addressed the significance of gender as a linguistic, psychoanalytical and cultural construction, as well as a means of signifying power between and within groups and in society.[45] They showed how gendered ideas had been mobilized by contemporaries to support or attack slavery, to strengthen associations and identities, and establish the limits of inclusion/exclusion. These shifts also led scholars to examine how men navigated a gendered world, and to reveal how binary oppositions between man and slave, as well as man and woman, were used to signify social hierarchies and shape the platforms of resistance, mastery and identity formation in slave systems.[46] Academic histories of slavery thus increasingly moved beyond the social world of enslaved people to examine how gender was culturally constructed, as well as to stress the significance of gendered discourses in shaping worldviews relating to slavery in transnational and comparative contexts. As Jennifer L. Morgan noted in her influential work *Laboring Women* (2004): 'Gender functioned as a set of power relationships through which early slaveowning settlers and those they enslaved defined, understood, and adjusted the confines of racial slavery.'[47]

---

[45]Joan Scott, 'Gender: A Useful Category of Historical Analysis', *American Historical Review* 91: 5 (1986), pp. 1053–75; Evelyn Brooks Higginbotham, 'Beyond the Sound of Silence: Afro-American Women in History', *Gender & History* 1: 1 (1989), pp. 50–67, – 'African-American Women's History and the Metalanguage of Race', *Signs* 12: 2 (1992), pp. 251–74.
[46]Darlene Clark Hine and Earnestine Jenkins, eds, *A Question of Manhood: A Reader in U.S. Black Men's History and Masculinity* (Bloomington: Indiana University Press, 1999–c. 2001); Edward Baptist, '"The Absent Subject": African American Masculinity and Forced Migration to the Antebellum Plantation Frontier' in Craig Thompson Friend and Lorri Glover, eds, *Southern Manhood: Perspectives on Masculinity in the Old South* (Athens: University of Georgia Press, 2004), pp. 136–74; Craig Williams, *Roman Homosexuality: Ideologies of Masculinity in Classical Antiquity* (Oxford: Oxford University Press, 1999); Trevor Burnard, *Mastery, Tyranny & Desire: Thomas Thistlewood and His Slaves in the Anglo-Jamaican World* (Chapel Hill: University of North Carolina Press, 2004).
[47]Jennifer L. Morgan, *Laboring Women: Reproduction and Gender in New World Slavery* (Philadelphia: University of Pennsylvania Press, 2004), p. 7. On p. 4, Morgan specifically notes the transnational significance of reproduction as an organizational and analytical principle as much as crops or plantation/regional demographics.

A hallmark of the cultural turn was the concept that language shapes worlds, and this was evident in studies by Kathleen Brown and the aforementioned Morgan, who revealed how gendered values were used by Europeans to rationalize the exploitation of Africans and Amerindians.[48] In her study on colonial Virginia, Brown considered how ideas on gender were transmitted, resisted and refashioned by contemporaries. Rather than take for granted categories like gender, race or class, Brown emphasized the need to engage with discourses of gender, defined 'as the use of language delineating a community and its interests', as well as to consider change over time. Brown examined how linguistic structures and cultural constructs served as a means of expressing and signifying power and giving meaning to the world colonial Americans, Native peoples and Africans lived in: 'by providing the medium through which people defined and communicated acceptable boundaries for behavior, and indeed, perceived that behavior, languages of race and gender had a role in constituting practice.'[49]

Morgan, explicitly building on Brown's work, noted further the significance of cultural representations in legitimizing slavery. Travel accounts, images and writings from white Europeans served to *create* the image of Africans as 'others' who were eligible for enslavement. An emphasis on cultural production in relation to power was evident throughout. To Morgan, Europeans acquired the psychological distance necessary to enslave an 'other' 'in part through manipulating symbolic representations of African women's sexuality'. Constant references to outlandish sexual organs, the conflation of Africans with animals, and lurid descriptions of easy childbirth and loose family relationships appeared to offer 'proof' of 'an immutable difference between Africans and Europeans, a difference ultimately codified as race'. These representations had very real effects:

> By the time the English made their way to the West Indies, decades of ideas and information about brown and black women predated the actual encounter. In many ways, the encounter had already taken place in parlors and reading rooms on English soil, assuring that colonists would arrive with a battery of assumptions and predispositions about race, femininity, sexuality, and civilization.[50]

---

[48] Kathleen M. Brown, *Good Wives, Nasty Wenches, & Anxious Patriarchs: Gender, Race, and Power in Colonial Virginia* (Chapel Hill: University of North Carolina Press, 1996); Morgan, *Laboring Women*. See also Hartman, *Scenes of Subjection*, pp. 86, 103–12.
[49] Brown, *Good Wives, Nasty Wenches*, pp. 3–5, p. 368.
[50] Morgan, *Laboring Women*, p. 8, p. 49.

In the same period, scholars of ancient slavery also addressed representation as a means of moving beyond the silences that had frustrated earlier classicists. In *Women and Slaves in Greco-Roman Culture* (1998), Sandra Joshel and Sheila Murnaghan analysed how linguistic and cultural constructions distinguished women and slaves 'from free men by their social subordination and their imagined otherness'. They emphasized the significance of social, cultural and linguistic binaries in constructing and articulating social realities and hierarchies. The cultural constructs of gender and slavery were used to symbolize and speak to power and powerlessness in a patriarchal slave society: 'the ancient Greeks and Romans relied on the polarities of male/female and free/slave in order to understand themselves and to organize their societies.'[51] In *Slaves and Other Objects* (2003), Page DuBois revealed the near-constant binary oppositions between slave and free in material and popular culture, noting how these served as a means of articulating identity and providing meaning in the classical world, for enslavers and enslaved alike. DuBois also stressed the importance of engaging with slavery and the sexual abuse of women as part of a gendered political discourse as well as lived experience. Representations of women enslaved in tragedies were deployed by contemporaries 'as a metaphor to invoke possibilities of domination and submission of one city-state in its relations with another'.[52] Ideas on power and powerlessness were constituted through a gendered worldview, often with specific reference to slavery.

The emphasis on gender as a means of signifying power was taken up in David Wyatt's work on slavery in medieval Britain and Ireland (2009). Building on the ideas of Karras, Wyatt stressed the socio-cultural significance of slavery rather than the economic dimensions, as well as how practices of enslaving/enslavement served to mark out social and gendered hierarchies.[53] Wyatt noted, for example, how the condition of slavery was 'conceived and characterised in terms of sexual submission'. Sexual violence against *all* enslaved people served as a means of

---

[51]Sandra R. Joshel and Sheila Murnaghan, eds, *Women and Slaves in Greco-Roman Culture: Differential Equations* (London: Routledge, 1998), p. 3, pp. 12–13. See also Paul Cartledge, *The Greeks: A Portrait of Self and Others* (Oxford: Oxford University Press, 1993), pp. 133–65.
[52]Page DuBois, *Slaves and Other Objects* (Chicago, IL: University of Chicago Press, 2003), p. 4. See also Jennifer Glancy, *Slavery in Early Christianity* (New York; Oxford: Oxford University Press, 2002), pp. 9, 117–53.
[53]Ruth Mazo Karras, *Sexuality in Medieval Europe: Doing Unto Others* (New York: Routledge, 2005).

constructing masculine identity for male enslavers: 'the act of enslavement was equated with a symbolic act of rape and sexual possession irrespective of biological gender.' The metaphor enabled the act: enslaved men who 'were characterised and associated with normative feminine qualities' were both perceived as being prone to sexual assault, but also real victims of sexual violence.[54] A gendered approach to slavery thus illuminated wider understandings of power and belonging in the medieval world. As Wyatt revealed, the 'conceptual and social world' of contemporaries was constructed through gendered binaries of 'power and weakness; honour and shame; between belonging and not belonging; between "being" and "not being"; *between freedom and slavery.*'[55]

Historians therefore combined an interest in the social world of enslaved people and enslavers with concerns over the wider cultural resonance of ideas on gender – on what it meant to be a woman or a man, and how these were inextricably linked – in slave systems. Stephanie McCurry's work on politics and society in the antebellum South, for example, revealed how ideas of masculinity were used to unite enslavers and non-slaveholding whites, as 'masters' of their 'small worlds', while Craig Williams considered how sexual activities between enslaver and enslaved in Roman society, and the gendered binary of penetrator/penetrated, worked to establish status and selfhood. Henrice Altink examined how abolitionists in Britain made the abuse against women and the violation of gendered norms emblematic of the horrors of slavery, and used this to marshal antislavery sentiment among women, while Trevor Burnard addressed how the sexual violence of enslavers like Thomas Thistlewood in Jamaica worked to foster both the personal and the political mastery expected in slave societies.[56] This interplay between experience and ideas, between the cultural and the social, continues to mark studies on gender and slavery.

---

[54]See also Thomas Foster, 'The Sexual Abuse of Black Men under American Slavery', *Journal of the History of Sexuality* 20: 3 (2011), pp. 445–64.

[55]Wyatt, *Slaves and Warriors*, pp. 211–13, p. 241. Broad discussions on masculinity, medieval Europe, and the Icelandic sagas can be found in Gareth Lloyd Evans, *Men and Masculinities in the Sagas of Icelanders* (Oxford: Oxford University Press, 2019). More information on sexual power relations can be found in Ruth Mazo Karras, *Unmarriages: Women, Men, and Sexual Unions in the Middle Ages* (Philadelphia: University of Pennsylvania Press, 2012).

[56]Stephanie McCurry, *Masters of Small Worlds: Yeoman Households, Gender Relations, and the Political Culture of the Antebellum South Carolina Low Country* (New York: Oxford University Press, 1995); Williams, *Roman Homosexuality*; Henrice Altink, *Representations of Slave Women in Discourses on Slavery and Abolition, 1780-1838* (London: Routledge, 2007); Burnard, *Mastery, Tyranny & Desire*. See also Pamela Scully and Diana Paton, eds, *Gender and Slave Emancipation in the Atlantic World* (Durham, NC: Duke University Press, 2005).

Gender and slavery

Historians have opened new avenues into examining the gendered lives of women and men, enslaver and enslaved alike, as well as revealed how slave systems operated under a battery of assumptions and beliefs over gender and sex. Some of the most significant theoretical and empirical insights into slavery over the past few decades have come through a gendered analysis. In Marisa J. Fuentes's *Dispossessed Lives* (2016), Sowande' Mustakeem's *Slavery at Sea* (2017) and Deirdre Cooper Owens's *Medical Bondage* (2018), we see complex meditations on the intractability of archival silences, but also fresh insights into the diverse experiences and the multiplicity of identities that can be buried within the categories 'women' or 'men'.[57] Mustakeem, for example, notes how distinctions of age affected gendered experiences of the slave trade, while Owens considers how enslaved and Irish immigrant women faced similar, and yet different, manifestations of reproductive violence, and reveals the intersections of race, sex and gender in shaping 'modern' medicine. In her compelling book, Fuentes reiterates the necessity of reading against the 'violence in and of the archive', noting how problems encountered by pioneers in the field remain a concern: 'nothing prepared me for the encounter with the paucity of material about enslaved women, the complete absence of material by enslaved women, and the intensity of archival and physical violence on enslaved women that I would struggle with over the next decade.'[58] Notwithstanding this candid reflection, Fuentes provides a powerful example of how to blend theoretical insights relating to identities, space and power with empirical research, demonstrating how a study of gender speaks to the most vital themes in the histories of slavery.

Methodological concerns relating to gender and slavery likewise remain a significant point of debate elsewhere. Madeline Henry wrote in 2011 that classicists 'who write about slavery usually render the experience

---

[57] Fuentes, *Dispossessed Lives*, p. 5; Sowande' Mustakeem, *Slavery at Sea: Terror, Sex, and Sickness in the Middle Passage* (Urbana: University of Illinois Press, 2017); Deirdre Cooper Owens, *Medical Bondage: Race, Gender, and the Origins of American Gynaecology* (Athens: University of Georgia Press, 2017). See also Sasha Turner, *Contested Bodies: Pregnancy, Childrearing, and Slavery in Jamaica* (Philadelphia: University of Pennsylvania Press, 2017); Stephanie Jones-Rogers, *They Were Her Property: White Women as Slave Owners in the American South* (New Haven: Yale University Press, 2019). On masculinity: Sergio Lussana, *My Brother Slaves: Friendship, Masculinity, and Resistance* (Lexington: Kentucky University Press, 2016); Randy Browne, *Surviving Slavery in the British Caribbean* (Philadelphia: University of Pennsylvania Press, 2017); David Stefan Doddington, *Contesting Slave Masculinity in the American South* (New York; Cambridge: Cambridge University Press, 2018).
[58] Fuentes, *Dispossessed Lives*, p. 144.

of men normative' while Deborah Kamen and C. W. Marshall recently noted that 'the sexual life of enslaved people has continued to be relatively understudied.'[59] And yet, exciting work seeks to correct this. Jennifer Glancy, Kyle Harper and Matthew Perry have addressed how gendered assumptions shaped both attitudes to slavery and the lives of enslaved people in the Roman world and stressed the need to examine cultural representations of the body and gendered ideologies to move beyond silences in the records. Harper, for example, argued that 'the sexual exploitation of slaves was built into the social mechanics of sexuality in the Roman empire', and the 'exploitation of slaves was ingrained into the whole fabric of late antique sexuality'.[60] Slaves may not have been spoken about directly, but their assumed presence (and presumed sexual access to them) shaped the politics of sexual respectability, family dynamics and the identities of women and men, both enslaver and enslaved. Historians such as Kathy Gaca, Allison Glazebrook and Debra Blumenthal have interrogated the diverse experiences of enslaved women and men, examined the cultures of honour and shame that shaped understandings of masculinity and mastery in the ancient and medieval world, and addressed both the lived realities of sexual violence and the gendered connotations of such exploitation.[61] Indeed, Deborah Kamen and C. W. Marshall have argued that scholars must continue to explore the sexual and gendered dynamics of slavery. They insist as to the value of comparative approaches to slave systems and, building on Saidiya Hartman's notion of 'critical fabulation', stress the need for boldness in applying 'a degree of speculation', alongside a critical reading of the scattered evidence left to

---

[59] Madeleine Henry, 'The Traffic in Women: From Homer to Hipponax, from War to Commerce' in Allison Glazebrook and Madeleine Henry, eds, *Greek Prostitutes in the Ancient Mediterranean, 800 BCE–200 CE* (Madison: University of Wisconsin Press, 2011), pp. 14–34, p. 14; Deborah Kamen and C.W. Marshall, 'Introduction: Mere Sex Objects?', in Kamen and Marshall, eds, *Slavery and Sexuality*, pp. 3–15, p. 6.

[60] Kyle Harper, *Slavery in the Late Roman World, AD275–425* (Cambridge: Cambridge University Press, 2011), pp. 283–5; Perry, *Gender, Manumission*; Glancy, *Slavery in Early Christianity*.

[61] Kathy Gaca, 'Ancient Warfare and the Ravaging Martial Rape of Girls and Women: Evidence from Homeric Epic and Greek Drama' in Mark Masterson and Nancy Sorkin, eds, *Sex in Antiquity: Exploring Gender and Sexuality in the Ancient World* (London: Routledge, 2015), pp. 278–98; Allison Glazebrook, 'A Hierarchy of Violence? Sex Slaves, *Parthenoi*, and Rape in Menander's *Epitrepontes*', *Helios* 42: 1 (2015), pp. 81–101; Debra Blumenthal, *Enemies and Familiars: Slavery and Mastery in Fifteenth-Century Valencia* (Ithaca, NY: Cornell University Press, 2009); Jennifer Glancy, 'Early Christianity, Slavery, and Women's Bodies' in Bernadette Brooten, eds, *Beyond Slavery: Overcoming Its Religious and Sexual Legacies* (Basingstoke: Palgrave-Macmillan, 2010); Rebecca Winer, 'The Enslaved Wet Nurse as Nanny: The Transition from Free to Slave Labor in Childcare in Barcelona after the Black Death (1348)', *Slavery & Abolition* 38 (2017), pp. 303–19.

us, to explore gender, sexuality, and slavery. As they put it: 'speculation of this sort is worthwhile if it gives us a better sense for the experience of marginalized individuals in antiquity.' These themes, methods and concerns are vital in any understanding of slavery and slave systems. A gendered lens has proven indispensable in addressing the experiences of enslavers and enslaved alike and illuminating the structures and dynamics of slavery both local and global.[62]

Conclusion

This chapter has provided an overview of some key themes, approaches and methods relating to the study of gender and slavery. This is by no means comprehensive, but patterns, continuities and challenges can be taken up by students interested in the subject. If much pioneering work focused on the experiences of women and challenged the assumption that the male experience was normative, developments associated with the cultural turn saw an increased focus on languages of gender, the power of representations and the relationship between masculinity and femininity. Gender relates to both personal identities and political, social and cultural structures, speaking to ideas and expressions of power and powerlessness, of insider/outsider. As an all-encompassing discourse that shapes multiple facets of life, gender has proved to be a vital category of analysis for historians of slavery and slave systems.

Acknowledgements

I would like to thank David Wyatt and Alex McAuley for their advice relating to studies on antiquity and medieval slavery. Tracey Loughran, Mark Williams and Keir Waddington generously provided comments. All errors are my own.

Because of space limitations, I have kept documentation to a minimum. The reader should keep in mind that the beginning of each footnote should begin with 'For example, see ….'

---

[62]Kamen and Marshall, 'Mere Sex Objects?', in Kamen and Marshall, eds, *Slavery and Sexuality*, p. 6. On critical fabulation see, Saidiya Hartman, 'Venus in Two Acts,' *Small Axe* 26, 12: 2 (June 2008), pp. 1–14. See also Raquel Kennon's chapter in this volume.

Bibliography

Brown, Kathleen M., *Good Wives, Nasty Wenches, & Anxious Patriarchs: Gender, Race, and Power in Colonial Virginia* (Chapel Hill: University of North Carolina Press, 1996).

Bush, Barbara, *Slave Women in Caribbean Society, 1650-1838* (London: Currey, 1990).

Fuentes, Marisa J., *Dispossessed Lives: Enslaved Women, Violence, and the Archive* (Philadelphia: University of Pennsylvania Press, 2016).

Glancy, Jennifer, *Slavery in Early Christianity* (Oxford: Oxford University Press, 2002).

Joshel, Sandra R. and Sheila Murnaghan, eds, *Women and Slaves in Greco-Roman Culture: Differential Equations* (London: Routledge, 1998).

Morgan, Jennifer L., *Laboring Women: Reproduction and Gender in New World Slavery* (Philadelphia: University of Pennsylvania Press, 2004).

Perry, Matthew, *Gender, Manumission, and the Roman Freedwoman* (New York; Cambridge: Cambridge University Press, 2014).

Pomeroy, Sarah B., *Goddesses, Whores, Wives, and Slaves: Women in Classical Antiquity* (New York: Shocken Books, 1975).

White, Deborah Gray, *Ar'n't I A Woman? Female Slaves in the Plantation South* (New York; London: W. W. Norton & Company, 1999, reprint, 1985 edition).

Wyatt, David, *Slaves and Warriors in Medieval Britain and Ireland, 800-1200* (Leiden; Boston: Leiden University Press, 2009).

12

Dispossessed lives: Enslaved women, violence, and the archive

Marisa J. Fuentes
Rutgers University
Introduced by Elizabeth Maeve Barnes
University of Reading

In 2016, Marisa J. Fuentes published *Dispossessed Lives*, one of the most significant interventions regarding the archives of slavery since Michel Rolph-Trouillot's *Silencing the Past*. Given the importance of Fuentes's intervention, the editors asked me to provide an introduction to her work for this volume. Fuentes insists in *Dispossessed Lives* that we must grapple with the limits to documentary knowledge on the enslaved produced by their enslavers, and she emphasizes how historical knowledge of slavery is shaped by power dynamics in and outside of academia. It is a searingly reflective piece of work, with nuanced assessments of the politics and power struggles embedded in research practices, historical claims and historiographical debates, as well as a sobering reminder of the traumas inherent for scholars immersed in a history full of horrors. Fuentes nonetheless shows how historians can apply a range of methods and practices to critically and creatively explore the lives of enslaved people, as well as the dynamics of slavery itself.

Archives – collections of records and documents – are challenging for all historians of marginalized people. The documents that a society produces, and those it chooses to preserve, reflect and sustain the power dynamics and inequalities embedded in that society. The types of evidence available to historians are therefore determined by two key factors: source creation and document preservation. Prior to the twentieth century, source creation was heavily limited by relatively low literacy rates. Without either the ability, access or the need to put pen to paper, illiterate people appear in documents only as subjects referred to by other authors. Their thoughts and feelings go unremarked upon, and their interior lives unrecorded. Even when marginalized people did have the ability to make their mark – through writing, artistic expression, crafts – archives have always prioritized preserving what is immediately useful alongside subjective assessments of what is deemed of historic 'value'. Financial records, legal files, government proceedings and other similar documents were kept because people needed to refer to them. It is only with recent advances in archiving practices, driven by the emergence of social history, that archives dedicated to preserving records of daily life have emerged.

The archive of slavery, therefore, is both vast and desolate. Slavery in the Americas was a massive global economic system and as such produced a wealth of records. Ships logs, plantation accounts, taxation records and censuses all offer a range of information about the number of enslaved people in certain areas, their sale value, their movements and the products of their labour. The diaries and correspondence of white enslavers are filled with details about the interactions between enslaver and enslaved, including social ties and the realities of plantation life. Newspapers document enslaved people's criminal behaviour – including flight, theft and violence – as well as the barbaric punishments meted out by the authorities. The nature of what was recorded and survives in the archive is testament to the realities of the institution, however. Historians can access very little of enslaved people's own words – especially outside of the United States – and as a result have only minimal direct access to the thoughts, feelings and experiences of enslaved people themselves. Generally denied literacy, refused the right to testify in legal spaces and side-lined in processes that shaped their lives, enslaved people had little opportunity to mould the documentation produced about them. What they did produce was largely ephemeral, denied the significance that would demand preservation.

Like all historians of slavery in the Caribbean, Marisa Fuentes's geographical focus limits her to an archive that is almost entirely lacking in sources produced by enslaved people themselves. Indeed, in *Dispossessed Lives*, Fuentes makes use exclusively of documents created by free individuals. Absent the voices of the enslaved, Fuentes applies unconventional methods to the traditional archive – the records of enslavers, documents produced by the colonial administration, personal files of white men and women – to illuminate both the realities of enslavement for women in Barbados and the nature of the archive itself. In spotlighting the ways archival records shape the meanings of race, gender and bondage, both at the time they were produced and in historical practice, Fuentes demands that we reflect on our work as historians as well as on the past itself.

Faced with an archive that offers only fragments of Black experiences, and with sources that foreground the violence and violations inflicted on enslaved women, Marisa Fuentes crafts an approach grounded in the historiography of women and slavery, colonial studies and the theories of Black feminist scholars. Fuentes's primary method is 'reading along the bias grain', a phrase informed by a tailoring technique in which material is cut at a certain angle to produce elasticity. By 'reading along the bias grain', Fuentes can stretch the archival material beyond its apparent limitations, highlighting silences and reflecting on what is left unsaid. Through using contextual information, Fuentes is able to flesh out fragments into rich descriptions of enslaved people's lives. In shifting the perspective of a source from its white author to an enslaved subject, Fuentes highlights contradictions, distortions and fabrications. Critically, through foregrounding known prejudices in the archive, Fuentes reflects on power imbalances in the documents themselves. In drawing on methods from scholars across disciplines, and shaping her own innovative approach, Marisa Fuentes pushes the discipline of history beyond the ostensible limits of the traditional archive. The difficulties Fuentes explores, and the strategies she employs to navigate the limitations of historical documentation, can speak to scholars of slavery across time and space. It is hoped this edited chapter can help showcase the complex power dynamics present in the 'production of history'.

N.B. In-text references to chapter material in Dispossessed Lives *remain but readers should note these are signposts to work outside of this present volume. Ellipses mark where material has been abridged but the content is unchanged, including US spelling/punctuation.*

Marisa J. Fuentes, *Dispossessed Lives: Enslaved women, violence, and the archive* (Philadelphia: University of Pennsylvania Press, 2016).

Introduction (pp. 1-12)

Dispossessed Lives constructs historical accounts of urban Caribbean slavery from the positions and perspectives of enslaved women within the traditional archive.[1] It does so by engaging archival sources with black feminist epistemologies, critical studies of archival power and form, and historiographical debates in slavery studies on agency and resistance. To trace the distortions of enslaved women's lives inherent in the archive, this book raises questions about the nature of history and the difficulties in narrating ephemeral archival presences by dwelling on the fragmentary, disfigured bodies of enslaved women. How do we narrate the fleeting glimpses of enslaved subjects in the archives and meet the disciplinary demands of history that requires us to construct unbiased accounts from these very documents? How do we construct a coherent historical accounting out of that which defies coherence and representability? How do we critically confront or reproduce these accounts to open up possibilities for historicizing, mourning, remembering, and listening to the condition of enslaved women?

This study probes the constructions of race, gender, and sexuality, the machinations of archival power, and the complexities of 'agency' in the lives of enslaved and free(d) women in colonial Bridgetown, Barbados. A microhistory of urban Caribbean slavery, it explores the significance of an urban slave society that was numerically dominated by women, white and black. By the turn of the eighteenth century, Barbados sustained an enslaved female majority whose reproduction rates contributed to a natural increase in the slave population by 1800.[2] Similarly, white women made up a slight majority of the island's white population and owned predominantly female slaves who, in turn, allowed white women a measure of economic independence.[3] This unusual demography and the underexplored, intra-gendered relationships between different groups of women mark an important shift from the extant scholarly focus on white men's domination of black and brown women in slave societies.

EDITORS' NOTES: Footnote numbers do not correspond directly with *Dispossessed Lives* due to the abridged nature of this chapter. Notes for further reading have been edited for brevity. For full citations see: Fuentes, *Dispossessed Lives*.

[1] The traditional archive refers to the majority of documents produced during the era of slavery in the British Caribbean by colonial administrators, planters, white men and women, and governing bodies in the metropole.
[2] Hilary Beckles, *Natural Rebels: A Social History of Enslaved Women in Barbados* (Kingston: Ian Randle, 1989), p. 7.
[3] Hilary Beckles, *Centering Woman: Gender Discourses in Caribbean Slave Society* (Kingston: Ian Randle, 1999), p. 63.

Despite its small size in relation to other Caribbean islands, an examination of Barbados, and in particular Bridgetown, enhances our understanding of how race, gender, and sexuality were formed in British Atlantic slave societies and how these constructions of identity directed and influenced the life experiences of urban enslaved women. Unlike similar works on enslaved women of the antebellum U.S. South that draw on the limited voices of the enslaved, this book does not feature sources written by enslaved people themselves.[4] On the contrary, the very nature of slavery in the eighteenth-century Caribbean made enslaved life fleeting and rendered access to literacy nearly impossible. Yet the women who appear in the archival fragments on which this book draws offer a crucial glimpse into lives lived under the domination of slavery—lives that were just as important as those of more visible and literate people in this period, who most consistently left an abundance of documentary material. Throughout this work I interrogate the quotidian lives of enslaved women in Bridgetown and account for the conditions in which they emerge from the archives. This is done to bring attention to the challenges enslaved women faced and the continued effects of white colonial power that constrain and control what can be known about these women in the archive. Instead of a social history of enslaved life in Bridgetown and Barbados, I examine archival fragments in order to understand how these documents shape the meaning produced about them in their own time and our current historical practices. In other words, this is a methodological and ethical project that seeks to examine the archive and historical production on multiple levels to destabilize the British colonial discourse invested in enslaved women as property. The impetus to 'recover' knowledge about how enslaved women made meaning from their lives is an important aspect of the historiography of Caribbean slavery. A significant amount of historical scholarship now exists showing how these women enacted their personhood despite their experiences of dehumanization and commodification.[5] This

---

[4]Here I am not arguing that antebellum slavery histories have a wealth of sources to draw on from the enslaved perspective. Instead, I want to point out that the records of colonial Caribbean slavery are even sparser and there are strikingly few narratives left by enslaved women. For more information on the Caribbean slave narratives that do exist, see Nicole N. Aljoe, 'Caribbean Slave Narratives', in John Ernest, ed., *The Oxford Handbook of African American Slave Narratives* (New York: Oxford University Press, 2014), pp. 362–70.

[5]For scholarship on enslaved women in the U.S. and Caribbean, see Adele Logan Alexander, *Ambiguous Lives: Free Women of Color in Rural Georgia, 1789–1879* (Fayetteville: University of Arkansas Press, 1991); Henrice Altink, *Representations of Slave Women in Discourses on Slavery and Abolition, 1780–1838* (New York: Routledge, 2007); Edward Baptist, '"Cuffy," "Fancy Maids," and "One-Eyed Men": Rape, Commodification, and the Domestic Slave Trade in the United States', *American Historical Review* 106 (December 2001), pp. 1619–50; Edward Baptist and Stephanie M.H. Camp, eds, *New Studies in American Slavery* (Athens: University of Georgia Press, 2006); Beckles, *Centering Woman and Natural Rebels*; Daina Berry, *Swing the Sickle for the Harvest Is Ripe:*

book builds on that scholarship; indeed, it has allowed me to ask a different set of questions concerning the body of the archive, the enslaved body in the archive, and the materiality of the enslaved body. This work seeks to understand the production of 'personhood' in the context of Bridgetown and this British Caribbean archive, while troubling the political project of agency.[6] It articulates the forces of power that bore down on enslaved women, who sometimes survived in ways not typically heroic, and who sometimes succumbed to the violence inflicted on them. Each chapter examines one woman in the context of eighteenth-century Bridgetown as she came into archival view. The chapters are titled after the women who are named in the fragments I explore when possible, in order to contest their fragmentation and to challenge the impetus of colonial authorities to objectify enslaved people in the records by generic namings such as 'Negro' or 'slave.'

From p. 4-8 of the introduction Fuentes sets out some of the key limitations to the archives of slavery and asks her readers to critically reflect upon the methodologies and approaches scholars can apply to explore the lives of enslaved people, in general, and enslaved women, in particular.

[...] Over two decades of scholarship on the social histories of gender and slavery and theoretical work on the politics of the archive serve as the foundation for this book's emphasis on historical production and the archives of enslaved women in Caribbean slavery. These social histories of

---

Gender and Slavery in Antebellum Georgia (Urbana: University of Illinois Press, 2007) ... [.] For innovative historical scholarship on women who did not leave an archive, see Camilla Townsend, *Malintzin's Choices: An Indian Woman in the Conquest of Mexico* (Albuquerque: University of New Mexico Press, 2006) and Natalie Zemon Davis, *Women on the Margins: Three Seventeenth-Century Lives* (Cambridge, Mass: Harvard University Press, 1997). For a range of theoretical work on the archive, see Antoinette Burton, *Archive Stories: Facts, Fictions, and the Writing of History* (Durham, N.C: Duke University Press, 2005); Dipesh Chakrabarty, *Provincializing Europe: Postcolonial Thought and Historical Difference* (Princeton, NJ: Princeton University Press, 2000); Natalie Zemon Davis, *Fiction in the Archives: Pardon Tales and Their Tellers in Sixteenth-Century France* (Stanford, Calif: Stanford University Press, 1987); Jacques Derrida and Eric Prenowitz, *Archive Fever: A Freudian Impression* (Chicago: University of Chicago Press, 1996); Gayatri Chakravorty Spivak, 'Can the Subaltern Speak?' in Lawrence Grossberg and Carl Nelson eds, *Marxism and the Interpretation of Culture* (Urbana: University of Illinois Press, 1988), pp. 271–315; Carolyn Steedman, *Dust: The Archive and Cultural History* (New Brunswick, N.J: Rutgers University Press, 2002) ... [.]
[6]For a critique of narratives of resistance in slavery studies, see the work of literary scholar Jenny Sharpe in *The Ghosts of Slavery: A Literary Archaeology of Black Women's Lives* (Minneapolis: University of Minnesota Press, 2003), pp. xiv-vi. Sharpe draws on a range of scholars interested in complicating notions of agency including Michel-Rolph Trouillot, who states, 'Everything can become resistance to the point that we are not sure whether or not the word stands for an empirical generalization, an analytical category, or a vague yet fashionable label for unrelated situations'. Trouillot, 'In the Shadow of the West: Power, Resistance and Creolization in the Making of the Caribbean Region', in Wim Hoogbergen, ed., *Born Out of Resistance: On Caribbean Cultural Creativity* (Utrecht: ISOR, 1995), p. 9.

enslaved women's everyday lives allow me to focus specific attention on the questions of archival fragmentation and historicity without reproducing their labors on the historical, social, and economic circumstances of slavery in the Atlantic world.[7] Driven by questions of historical production in the context of archives that are partial, incomplete, and structured by privileges of class, race, and gender, my work follows the path- breaking scholarship of Deborah Gray White, Jennifer Morgan, Camilla Townsend, and Natalie Zemon Davis, who found ingenious ways to use known biases within particular archives to ask seemingly impossible questions of subjects whose presence, when noted, is systematically distorted. Scholars in the fields of colonial slavery and women's history more broadly understand and contend with scant sources from the enslaved perspective, and this is particularly true in the colonial British Caribbean.

This study also draws attention to the nature of the archives that inform historical works on slavery by employing a methodology that purposely subverts the overdetermining power of colonial discourses. By changing the perspective of a document's author to that of an enslaved subject, questioning the archives' veracity and filling out miniscule fragmentary mentions or the absence of evidence with spatial and historical context our historical interpretation shifts to the enslaved viewpoint in important ways. As previous scholarship has generated substantial knowledge about how enslaved women made meaning in their lives despite commodification and domination, my book does not simply seek to recover enslaved female subjects from historical obscurity. Instead, it makes plain the manner in which the violent systems and structures of white supremacy produced devastating images of enslaved female personhood, and how these pervade the archive and govern what can be known about them. Rather than leaving enslaved women 'vulnerable to the readings and misreadings of whoever chooses to make assumptions about them,'[8] my book probes the

---

[7] Recent or forthcoming scholarship continues a scholarly interest in the plantation societies of the Caribbean with a focus on Barbados. Trevor Burnard's forthcoming book, *Planters, Merchants, and Slaves: Plantation Societies in British America, 1650–1870* (Chicago: University of Chicago Press, 2015) renews attention to the strivings and aspirations of British colonists in their attempts to profit from developing plantation systems. Justin Roberts, *Slavery and the Enlightenment in the British Atlantic, 1750–1807* (New York: Cambridge University Press, 2013) conducts a study of plantation regimes in early modern Virginia, Barbados, and Jamaica, and Simon Newman, *A New World of Labor: The Development of Plantation Slavery in the British Atlantic* (Philadelphia: University of Pennsylvania Press, 2013) returns to seventeenth-century Barbados to examine the system of indentured servitude and its foundational impact on the development of racial slavery.
[8] Townsend, *Malintzin's Choices*, p. 7.

construction of enslaved women in the archival records, using methods that at once subvert and illuminate biases in these accounts in order to map a range of life conditions that profoundly challenge assumptions about the 'slave experience' in Caribbean systems of domination.

What would a narrative of slavery look like when taking into account 'power in the production of history?' That is, how do slaveholders' interests affect how they document their world, and in turn, how do these very documents result in persistent historical silences?[9] What would it mean to be critical of how our historical methodologies dependent on such sources often reproduce these silences? There is not a paucity of sources about slavery in the Caribbean from the words and perspectives of white authorities and slave owners. In fact, there are vital archival materials that describe the contours of enslaved women's work and reproduction in the Caribbean. Using sources such as probate records, inventories of property, and descriptions of punishment and profit, scholars have mined the words and worlds of colonial authorities for clues to how the enslaved lived, worked, reproduced, and perished. Indeed, there are few if any new sources in this field; and *Dispossessed Lives* uses some of these same records but draws different conclusions by productively mining archival silences and pausing at the corruptive nature of this material.[10] The objectification of the enslaved allowed authorities to reduce them to valued objects to be bought and sold, used to produce profit and to retain and bequeath wealth. It also made the enslaved disposable when they could no longer labor for profit. This same objectification led to the violence in and of the archive. Enslaved women appear as historical subjects through the form and content of archival documents in the manner in which they lived: spectacularly violated, objectified, disposable, hypersexualized, and silenced. The violence is transferred from the enslaved bodies to the documents that count, condemn, assess, and evoke them, and we receive them in this condition. Epistemic violence originates from the knowledge produced about enslaved women by white men and women in this society, and that knowledge is what survives in archival form. With sole reliance on the empirical matter of the eighteenth-century Caribbean, we can only create historical narratives that reproduce these violent colonial discourses. The work of this book is to make plain how and why this knowledge was created

---

[9] For a discussion of 'power and historical production', see Trouillot, *Silencing the Past*.
[10] I am indebted to the generosity of Barbadian historians including Dr. Pedro Welch and Dr. Karl Watson, who shared their vast knowledge and personal archival research with me over the last decade. Many of the sources they shared are used in this book. I have reinterpreted these sources using analyses interrogating archival power.

and reproduced, and to employ new methodologies that disrupt this process in order to illuminate subjugated, 'marginalized and fugitive knowledge [and perspectives] from,' enslaved women.[11]

In each chapter I contend with the historical paradox and methodological challenges produced by the near erasure of enslaved women's own perspectives, in spite and because of the superabundance of words white Europeans wrote about them. By applying theoretical approaches to power, the production of text, and constructions of race and gender to the written archive, I question historical methods that search for archival veracity, statistical substantiation, and empiricism in sources wherein enslaved women are voiceless and objectified. The subjects in this study, the laborers, the enslaved women, men, and children, lived their 'historical' lives as numbers on an estate inventory or a ship's ledger and their afterlives often shaped by additional commodification. The very call to 'find more sources' about people who left few if any of their own reproduces the same erasures and silences they experienced in the eighteenth-century Caribbean world by demanding the impossible. Paying attention to these archival imbalances illuminates systems of power and deconstructs the influences of colonial constructions of race, gender, and sexuality on the sources that inform our work. This enables a nuanced engagement with the layers of domination under which enslaved women and men endured, resisted, and died. This is a methodological project concerned with the ethical implications of historical practice and representations of enslaved life and death produced through different types of violence.

Violence pervades the histories of slavery and this book. The violence committed on enslaved bodies permeates the archive, and the methods of history heretofore have not adequately offered the vocabulary to reconstitute 'the depth, density, and intricacies of the dialectic of subjection and subjectivity' in enslaved lives.[12] A legible and linear narrative cannot sufficiently account for the palimpsest of material and meaning embedded in the lives of people shaped by the intimacies and ubiquity of violence. Therefore, this book dwells on violence in its many configurations: physical, archival, and epistemic. The most obvious instances are physical— the ways violence inflicted on enslaved bodies turned them into objects in slave societies. Chapter 5 features and reproduces the inordinate accounts of

---

[11] Avery F. Gordon, *Ghostly Matters: Haunting and the Sociological Imagination* (Minneapolis: University of Minnesota Press, 2008), p. xviii. For an important discussion of the relationship between 'evidence and history', see Burton, *Archive Stories*, p. 1.
[12] Gordon, *Ghostly Matters*, p. 8.

enslaved women's beatings in the records of the slave trade abolition debates. This reproduction brings to the fore how the excessive nature of such images works to silence these violent experiences beneath the titillated gazes of white men, abolitionist sensationalism, and historiographical skepticism, as well as our unavoidable complicity in replicating these accounts in order to historicize them.

Violence, then, is the historical material that animates this book in its subtle and excessive modes—on the body of the archive, the body in the archive and the material body.[13] Focusing on the 'mutilated historicity' of enslaved women (the violent condition in which enslaved women appear in the archive disfigured and violated), this book shows how 'the violence of slavery made actual bodies disappear.'[14] For example, Chapter 4 assesses execution records of enslaved women and men to challenge our understanding of colonial laws. In a system that forbade the enslaved a legal voice, the arbitrary and capricious nature of enslaved 'crime' and punishment comes to the fore and challenges our readings of enslaved resistance. It also explicates the reach of these laws, which in 1768 demanded that the bodies of executed slaves be weighted down and thrown into the sea to prevent the enslaved community from rituals of mourning. Colonial power subsequently made the archive complicit in obscuring the offenses committed against the enslaved through the language of criminality. My work resists the authority of the traditional archive that legitimates structures built on racial and gendered subjugation and spectacles of terror. This violence of slavery concealed enslaved bodies and voices from others in their own time and we lose them in the archive due to those systems of power and violence. Each chapter contends with these circumstances and uses different methods to draw out the link between violence, archival disappearance, and historical representation in the fragmentary records in which enslaved women materialize. The nature of this archive demands this effort.

Dispossessed Lives uses archival sources at times 'for contrary purposes.'[15] I stretch archival fragments by reading *along the bias grain* to eke out extinguished and invisible but no less historically important lives.[16] In Chapter 3, for example, I use the court case of sexual entanglement between

---

[13] Many thanks to Melanie J. Newton for helping me with this formulation. Personal Communication, October 2014.
[14] Newton, Personal Communication.
[15] Hartman, *Scenes of Subjection*, p. 11.
[16] This method is explained more fully in Chapter 2. It is the way I describe a methodology by which the archival record is stretched to accentuate the figures of enslaved women whose presence influences ontological conditions of others but who are not mentioned in particular archives.

two white men and a married white woman to discuss the ways the presence and expectations of enslaved women in Bridgetown gave white women particular forms of power. Beliefs about enslaved women also enabled a young enslaved boy, owned by one of the men in the case, to dress as a woman in order to access public spaces without being perceived as a threat. Here the absence of explicit representations of enslaved women does not mean they have no bearing on the subjectivities and possibilities for other people in this society. I purposely fill out their absence as one way to address the above methodological questions. *Dispossessed Lives* demonstrates what other knowledge can be produced from archival sources if we apply the theoretical concerns of both cultural studies and critical historiography to documents and sources. It is an argument that history can still be made, and we can gain an understanding of the past even as we consciously resist efforts to reproduce the lived inequities of our subjects and the discourses that served to distort them.

From p. 9-12 of the introduction Fuentes deconstructs common labels and terminology applied by historians of slavery, such as 'agency' and 'resistance,' and considers the personal and political dimensions to scholarly efforts to conceptualise and understand enslaved peoples' actions, choices, and the limitations placed upon them.

[...] Since the late 1990s, scholars from a range of fields, including history, have challenged and refined the concept of agency as it applies to enslaved people. In her now definitive book, Saidiya Hartman argues that agency connotes the idea of 'will' and 'intent,' both of which were foreclosed by the legal condition of chattel slavery.[17] Walter Johnson contends that agency as a trope originated from noble origins in the Civil Rights era but should be carefully interrogated for the conflation of its meaning with resistance and humanity in slavery scholarship.[18] These scholars argue that the issue of 'redress' is inescapable in writing histories of black life as the legacies of racism, racialized sexism, and poverty continue to haunt our present. In this effort, Hartman's concerns shed light on the contradictions, exclusions, and demands of black people in post- emancipation liberal humanist discourses

---

This analysis is achieved without destroying the integrity (historical veracity) of the original archival documents. It is a different approach to colonial records than in Ann Laura Stoler's important work, *Along the Archival Grain*, where she skillfully reveals the weaknesses in colonial power through an affective reading of nineteenth-century Dutch colonial documents. In my approach I am specifically interested in what can be gleaned from the imbalances in which enslaved women are either invisible or distorted in their representations in the traditional archive.

[17]Hartman, *Scenes of Subjection*, esp. pp. 52–6.
[18]Walter Johnson, 'On Agency', *Journal of Social History* 37 (2003), p. 120.

of rights and duties.[19] She asks us to consider to what extent our work on the past is in service of redress and therefore what is the historian's relationship to her subjects? To what end do we write these narratives?[20]

At stake here are the ways in which scholars, working within the paradigm of traditional African American historiography, insist that agency—akin to resistance—is still the most appropriate lens through which to examine slave life.[21] Stephanie Camp contends that 'slave resistance in its many forms is a necessary point of historical inquiry, and it continues to demand research.'[22] Camp recognizes that studies of resistance have changed but, she argues, we 'need not [abandon] the category altogether.'[23] The present study troubles similar tropes of agency in Chapters 2 and 3 by examining the lives of white and free(d) women of color whose social and economic power relied on patriarchy and slave ownership.[24] In Chapter 2 I address this issue in relationship to Rachael Pringle Polgreen, a mixed-race slave-owning woman in Barbados.[25] Using the scholarship of Michel-Rolph Trouillot and Saba Mahmood, I question the application of sexual agency to enslaved and free(d) women's sexual relations with white men in the context of this slave society where many enslaved and free women were subjected to unequal power relations and violence. Focusing specifically on women also deconstructs 'resistance' as armed, militaristic, physical, and triumphant—a vision of resistance particularly resonant in the Caribbean with its histories of large-scale uprisings.

---

[19]Hartman, *Scenes of Subjection*, p. 6. Johnson has recently reprised this conversation in *Slavery's Ghost: The Problem of Freedom in the Age of Emancipation* (Baltimore: Johns Hopkins University Press, 2011), p. 8–30. This book revisits the limits of freedom for African Americans in the post-emancipation era as Hartman discussed in *Scenes of Subjection*.
[20]Hartman, 'Venus in Two Acts', *Small Axe* 12: 2 (2008), p. 10.
[21]Justin Roberts lodges a similar and important critique against the paradigm of agency as resistance in histories of slavery in *Slavery and the Enlightenment in the British Atlantic, 1750-1807*, see esp. 'Introduction', pp. 1–25. Roberts points to the traditional and classic texts in British Atlantic history over the last several years to argue that the power dynamics and violence of early modern plantations were more complex than the historiography and framework of agency reveals. However, this critique originates much farther back in the scholarship on 'subaltern' histories, and we have benefited from critical interdisciplinary engagement from a wide variety of scholars in anthropology and feminist, African diaspora and cultural studies, many of whose publications date to the early 1990s. Moreover, a gendered reading of resistance/agency narratives further complicates this paradigm, challenging the notion of agency as a gender neutral phenomenon. At stake then, is how agency is deployed in the scholarship on slavery and how enslaved women are represented in this narrative as 'sexual agents'.
[22]Camp, *Closer to Freedom*, p. 2.
[23]Ibid.
[24]For a longer discussion of how agency is gendered in feminist scholarship, see Saba Mahmood, *Politics of Piety: The Islamic Revival and the Feminist Subject* (Princeton, NJ: Princeton University Press, 2005).
[25]See also Marisa J. Fuentes, 'Power and Historical Figuring: Rachael Pringle Polgreen's Troubled Archive', *Gender and History* 22 (November 2010), p. 3.

In counterpoint to definitions of agency, the concept of 'social death' addresses how the enslaved were constrained by law, commodification, and subjection. In recent years, scholars have expanded on Orlando Patterson's pivotal text *Slavery and Social Death* (1982), detailing the process by which Africans were made into property and how the condition of slavery in the past adversely affects how they can be accounted for historically. Still, prominent scholars reassert the imperative of resistance studies. In Vincent Brown's important analysis of social death, he urges us away 'from seeing slavery as a condition to viewing enslavement as a predicament, in which enslaved Africans and their descendants never ceased to pursue a politics of belonging, mourning, accounting, and regeneration.'[26] Chapter 4, however, reminds us of the extent of power wielded by authorities and how the enslaved were subjected to arbitrary executions at the caprice of their owners and colonial officials, therefore limiting their strategies of mourning and shaping the perceptions of enslaved humanity and resistance.

Arguably, as many have noted, concepts of agency, resistance, and social death, perhaps even more than in other historical fields, continue to influence the ways we write and think about the enslaved and about systems of slavery and domination. *Dispossessed Lives* maintains that these historiographical debates are as important as illuminating the actions of the enslaved, because they have implications for what we have come to know and the limits of what we can know about the history of slavery. While the majority of studies of slavery have focused on the antebellum U.S. South, the British Caribbean offers a different tale, one in which slavery depended on a factory of violence in sugar production unsurpassed in North America. Life spans for most of the enslaved were brief and the physical distance from imperial control allowed particular types of atrocities on their bodies. On an island like Barbados, where sustained or permanent flight was nearly impossible, 'rival geographies'—spaces created by the enslaved in defiance of the restrictions of plantation life—were threatened by surveillance, dangerous waterways, and deplorable material conditions.[27] This study does not suppress the historical

---

[26]Vincent Brown, 'Social Death and Political Life in the Study of Slavery', *American Historical Review* 114: 5 (December 2009), p. 1248; my emphasis.
[27]Stephanie Camp deploys this term in *Closer to Freedom*, xxix. Its original incantation is credited to Edward Said, who used it to describe 'resistance to colonial domination' (18). Camp applied the term to the antebellum South. She was aware that alternate spaces were never autonomous from slave holders' power or trespass, but she explains that 'rival geography did, however, provide space for private and public creative expression, rest and recreation, alternative communication, and importantly, resistance to planters' domination of slaves' every move' (19).

efforts of enslaved people to resist their circumstances. Rather, it presents the agonizing decisions they made in the face of violent retribution from colonial authorities. Dwelling on these uncomfortable junctures in history highlights the messy and contradictory behaviors of enslaved people. This book's theoretical underpinnings at once read along the bias grain of the archive[28] and against the politics of the historiography to gain nuanced understandings of what Avery Gordon calls 'complex personhood' and the minute details of fragmentary lives that are challenging for historians to access.[29]

The fields of women's and gender studies and black feminist theory give significant attention to knowledge production and the intersectional experiences of women; and these fields frame the questions with which I approach this history and these enslaved female subjects. This study argues that there was something particular about being enslaved and female in slave societies even as it resists more traditional concepts of gender; it dwells purposely on feminist epistemological questions concerning how (historical) knowledge is produced about enslaved female subjects through the archive. I draw on a range of interdisciplinary black feminist scholars, including historians, cultural studies scholars, and novelists who interrogate how black women have been represented historically and contemporarily; their sexual violations; and their hypersexualized images.[30] Moreover, these scholars use analyses of race and gender to destabilize the power of dominant knowledge and representations of women of the African

---

[28]Taking the phrase from tailoring, in which fabric is cut at an angle to produce elasticity: reading along the bias grain stretches the archive to accentuate the presence of enslaved women when not explicitly mentioned in certain documents. See Chapter 3 for the application of this method.
[29]Gordon, *Ghostly Matters*, pp. 4–5.
[30]There is a vast and substantial canon of Black feminist scholarship on issues of representation and epistemology. The texts that influenced and are cited in this study include Jean Besson, 'Reputation and Respectability Reconsidered: A New Perspective on Afro-Caribbean Peasant Women', in Janet Momsen, ed., *Women and Change in the Caribbean: A PanCaribbean Perspective* (London: James Currey, 1993), p. 15; Jennifer DeVere Brody, *Impossible Purities: Blackness, Femininity, and Victorian Culture* (Durham, NC: Duke University Press, 1998); Sabine Broeck, 'Enslavement as Regime of Western Modernity: Re-Reading Gender Studies Epistemology Through Black Feminist Critique', *Gender Forum: An Internet Journal of Gender Studies* 22 (2008); Elsa Barkley Brown, '"What Has Happened Here": The Politics of Difference in Women's History and Feminist Politics', *Feminist Studies* 18: 2 (1992), pp. 295–312; Katherine E. Browne, *Creole Economics: Caribbean Cunning Under the French Flag* (Austin: University of Texas Press, 2004); Hazel V. Carby, 'Policing the Black Woman's Body in an Urban Context', in Kwame Appiah and Henry Louis Gates Jr, eds, *Identities* (Chicago: University of Chicago Press, 1995), pp. 735–55 ... [.] For a more comprehensive list organized by field, see Sherri L. Barnes, *Black American Feminisms: A Multidisciplinary Bibliography*, University of California, Santa Barbara Libraries, http://blackfeminism.library.ucsb.edu/ (accessed 7 June 2015).

diaspora. My focus on the centrality of enslaved women to the project of slavery follows in the wake of such work and elucidates the manner in which their specific sexualized identities and social constructions placed them in particular roles and positions in Caribbean and Barbadian slave societies. It also demonstrates how gender and sexuality were shaped and produced in a society where white and Afro- Barbadian women outnumbered men. Building on Jennifer Morgan's scholarship, which illustrates how reproduction signified a central experience for enslaved women, I consider the ways in which sexuality was inhabited, performed and consequential for urban female slaves.

Finally, this book examines our own desires as historical scholars to recover what might never be recoverable and to allow for uncertainty, unresolvable narratives, and contradictions. It begins from the premise that history is a production as much as an accounting of the past, and that our ability to recount has much to do with the conditions under which our subjects lived. This is a project concerned with an ethics of history and the consequences of reproducing indifference to violence against and the silencing of black lives. Our responsibility to these vulnerable historical subjects is to acknowledge and actively resist the perpetuation of their subjugation and commodification in our own discourse and historical practices. It is a gesture toward redress.

Epilogue (pp. 144-48)

[…] I want to return to the beginning, to the roots of my methodological and ethical concerns and underscore what it means to reckon with the tragic permanency of historical silence and erasure. There will always be unanswerable questions from an archive that cannot fully redress the loss of historical perspectives and insights from the enslaved. I went to Barbados searching for something I would never find. Emerging empty-handed from these archives, the silence deafening, I was confronted head on with the questions this book has attempted to answer. I had intended to write about the ways enslaved women labored, built communities, and experienced the confinements of urban life. I had talked extensively with historians who had done archival work in the region and gathered their tips and advice on organizing my time as I went to search for my subjects in the historical records. Yet nothing prepared me for the encounter with the paucity of material about enslaved women, the complete absence of material by enslaved women, and the intensity of archival and physical violence on enslaved women that I would struggle with over the next decade.

There were none of the voices I sought to document; no whole figures emerged that I could trace beyond a momentary mention. The women I did find were battered, beaten, executed, and overtly sexualized. They were listed on estate inventories only as Phoebe, Mimba, or 'Broken Back Betty,' and sometimes only as 'negroe'—stripped bare of all that was meaningful in their lives. Bequeathed in wills and deeds, or counted and dying on slave ships, they could not tell me about these conditions or what they thought, how they loved, or from where they came. The permanent loss of this knowledge was harrowing. Looking back now, I understand how both naïve and hopeful I was going into this project. I believed I would find 'that one source' no one else had yet discovered. I would be able to tell a story from the standpoints and thoughts of the women about whom I wished to write. I would discover a document that revealed the inner everyday lives of the enslaved in plain language that I could simply translate. I encountered images of Rachael Pringle Polgreen across the island made into dolls, posters, and postcards—her caricature (re)commodified for twenty-first-century tourists. I scoured a century of execution compensation records and read about Molly and numbers of other women who had been executed, and I found the conditions of their lives buried with them. There was nothing about age, family life, or the circumstances leading to their convictions. I could not prove, at the time, what I felt to be true: the system of slavery assumed enslaved people were criminals when they were instead victims of an impossible legal structure. I discovered a court case where an enslaved boy dressed in women's clothes with a hidden dagger walked across town at night, dragged into the affairs of white Barbadians, yet silenced within the frame of law. Not even his name was mentioned. The few surviving newspapers contained brief advertisements of runaway slaves; one of them was Jane, conjured by the variety of scars on her body. Her owner mentioned no relatives or considered the life she left behind when she was captured and brought across the Atlantic.

I was drawn to each of these people by the loss of their histories and my unfulfillable desire to recuperate something about them. I found only their archival mention, fragment, or image, and knew something must be said. At the time of their discovery I did not yet know what they embodied, only that they represented a range of theoretical concerns I began to ponder because of their incomplete and violated nature. My questions shaped the way I would seek to bring these women into history, as well as a way to bring the discipline of history into a more transparent and reflexive frame. It was the context and the manner in which enslaved women were silenced that provoked my focus on addressing this process of erasure and the violence of their physical, historical, and archival condition.

After twenty-two months of archival research in Barbados, England, and South Carolina, I returned to the United States with a determination to address the issue and causes of archival silence. Through the life of this project I worked within a historical disciplinary structure that required more sources to make the project 'viable' and within the logic of historical methodology, which purported that a history of silence could not be written when there was not enough material to fill an article, let alone a book. I resolutely thought about and challenged the process from which these disciplining rules and (desires) emanated. The women in the book—Jane, Agatha, Rachael, Joanna, Molly, and the many more whose names did not survive—required more than the limits a single discipline allowed, and I spent the next several years developing methodological pathways into their lives. These included explorations about their historical or historiographical representations, thinking through the theoretical significance of colonial power in the realm of law and punishment, and changing the archival language and gaze to reflect the gaze and perspective of the women in the fragments.

History is produced from what the archive offers. It is the historian's job to substantiate all the pieces with more archival evidence, context, and historiography and put them together into a coherent narrative form. The challenge this book has confronted is to write a history about what an archive does not offer. My theoretical questions guided me to move toward particular methodologies that would assist me in explicating the limits and possibilities of enslaved women's historical subjectivities. Molly, for example, symbolizes both the violence of slavery on bodies and the violence of the laws that prevent the enslaved from claims of humanity and innocence. Rachael Pringle Polgreen's metanarrative demonstrates the troubling and silencing nature of historical production—it shows the way her rehearsed narrative obscures her perpetuation of slavery's violence. Jane and the unnamed women in the final chapter illuminate the manner in which mutilation—physical and symbolic—conditioned their historicity leading to questions about the impossibility of recovery. The nature of the archive from which they emerge requires this effort. We cannot redeem or rescue them, but we can reconsider their pain.

This project has not been without risk for me, and perhaps for my readers as well. It has not hewn to those historical practices that require a vast empirical base from which to generalize. There is political risk in presenting seemingly 'defeated' and disfigured subjects and of presenting 'too much death' and violence. And, there is risk in the archival encounter. Confronting sources that show only terror and violence are a danger to the researcher who sees her own ancestors in these accounts. To sit with these sources requires the capacity to hold and inhabit deep wells of pain and horror. One must persist for years in this 'mortuary' of records to bring otherwise invisible lives to historical representation in a way that challenges the reproduction of invisibility and commodification. This process of historicization demands strategies to manage the emotional response one has to such brutality in order to persist with these subjects—to be willing to take up and sit with this aspect of human degradation and to find meaning. When writing Chapter 5 I spent weeks reading hundreds of accounts of dismembered, burned, and whipped enslaved women and men. There were many times I had to put the documents down and walk away. But I knew I had to gather myself and return to them. I have by now spent years absorbing the brutalizations inflicted on people of African descent and witnessing the process by which—'humans [cease] to be.'[31] To spend time in this temporal and geographical space is to risk emotional strength. It obliterates the possibility of objectivity. It is an exercise in endurance.

When I teach courses in early modern Caribbean history and slavery, I assign my students a final paper requiring them to analyze a primary source from the era and region we have covered over the semester. Several class days are spent practicing with different documents, some of which I used for this book. We read wills left by women of color, compare the Code Noir to the Barbados Slave Acts, and read the Haitian and American declarations of independence together to analyze language and the meanings of freedom. The students' enthusiasm turns into agony and anxiety when they have to choose their own source to analyze for their final assignment. They have many questions about where to look, what constitutes an appropriate source, and what is the required number of secondary sources they will need to contextualize their document. What is most striking however, is the repeated question that sometimes rises into complaint: how do I find a source written by an enslaved person or from their perspective? Aside from

---

[31] M. Nourbese Philips, *Zong!* (Middletown, Conn: Wesleyan University Press, 2008), p. 196.

the few surviving slave narratives there are some students who wish to write about the gendered violence particular to the experience of enslaved women, or routine and everyday life of slavery but find the records at best empty of this concern; at worst there are documents in which slave owners blame the women for their 'insatiable desires' or reduce enslaved people to their price or physical debility. At the heart of my students' question is the realization of how difficult it is to narrate from a place of silence. It then dawns on them that their assignment is as much about working with what is there as with what is not. This is the same concern I had struggled with when I began this project over a decade ago.

Dispossessed Lives insists that historical studies of the black Atlantic inform the ways in which race, gender, and sexuality continue to shape the lives of African-descended people worldwide. It is a history of how people of African descent became disposable, when black lives were objectified and thus vulnerable to the caprice, lusts, and economic desires of colonial authorities. It documents the strategies and structures that made black Atlantic lives subject to violence of thought and action. It offers material to reflect on the stakes of resistance in such systems and the reproduction of raced and gendered configurations of vulnerability. It begins to mark the way that the archive and history have erased black bodies and how the legacies of slavery—the racialized sexism and the legal, socioeconomic, and physical violence against people of African descent—manifest in the violence we continue to confront. It is a gesture toward a reckoning of our own time. It is a history of our present.

13

Slavery, postcolonialism and the colonial archive

Andrea Major
University of Leeds

'There is no slavery in the dominions of the East India Company', abolitionist lawyer James Stephen boldly, but erroneously, declared in 1807, 'unless the condition of a few domestic life servants may deserve the name; and even these are so treated that their bondage can scarcely be distinguished from freedom'.[1] The absence of an overt slave plantation economy on the West Indian model led to the assumption among late-eighteenth- and early-nineteenth-century abolitionists that chattel slavery barely existed in Britain's Eastern possessions, and what little was found there was deeply embedded in indigenous institutions and bore little resemblance to its West Indian counterpart. As a result, various forms of coerced labour in South and South East Asia were relegated to the peripheries of nineteenth-century antislavery debate. They subsequently remained marginal concerns in mainstream historiographies of slavery and abolition that tended to focus overwhelmingly on North America and the Caribbean.[2] From the 1980s onwards, however, scholars began to challenge the dominance of the Atlantic experience for understanding slavery, and to uncover more complicated histories of 'unfree' labour

---

[1] James Stephen, *The Dangers of the Country* (London: Samuel F. Bradford, 1807), p. 115.
[2] David Brion Davis, for example, dismisses Indian slavery in a single footnote in *The Problem of Slavery in the Age of Revolution, 1770–1823* (New York: Oxford University Press, 1999), p. 155.

around the world. Studies focusing on local slaveries and slave trades in South America, Africa, the Middle East and the Indian Ocean presented alternative experiences of coerced labour and different typologies of bondage.[3] While still under-researched compared to the numerous and detailed studies that map out the Atlantic slave trade, scholars increasingly found ways to overcome some of the practical and methodological problems posed by an unevenly represented, politically fractured, and socially and culturally heterogeneous Indian Ocean world, integrating sources from various archives to piece together the diverse experiences, and complex commercial networks through which African and Indian slaves, convicts and indentured servants moved around the region.[4]

Writing histories of slavery in the context of European colonies in South and South East Asia has raised a number of theoretical and methodological issues, relating both to the often fluid, multifaceted, and ambivalent nature of 'unfree' labour in these regions, and to the difficulties involved in reading both vernacular and colonial archives. As Tanika Sarkar points out, in colonial India, Western conceptions of chattel slavery were not necessarily helpful in defining what constituted enslavement, or delineating this from other forms of servitude and obligation, because almost all forms of labour were influenced by extra-economic compulsions and few were ever entirely 'free'.[5] Developments in postcolonial theory since the late 1970s have, however, offered new methodological tools for reading the complex socio-economic formations that underpinned slavery in India as they were refracted through often problematic colonial archives, as well as for deconstructing influential Western discourses about the nature and meanings of enslavement itself. Important studies by Indrani Chatterjee and Gyan Prakash, among others, have explored the ways in which complex relationships between caste, class, kinship, indenture, debt bondage and slavery within India can be used to challenge accepted nineteenth-century discourses of 'slavery' and 'freedom', and provide more nuanced interpretation of Indian social, economic

---

[3]See, for example, W.G. Clarence-Smith, *The Economics of the Indian Ocean Slave Trade in the Nineteenth Century* (London: Frank Cass, 1989); Richard B. Allen, *Slaves, Freedmen, and Indentured Laborers in Colonial Mauritius* (New York: Cambridge University Press, 1999); Gwyn Campbell, ed., *The Structure of Slavery in Indian Ocean Africa and Asia* (London: Frank Cass, 2004); Gwyn Campbell, ed., *Abolition and Its Aftermath in Indian Ocean Africa and Asia* (London: Routledge, 2005).
[4]For an excellent recent overview of this, see Richard B. Allen, *European Slave Trading in the Indian Ocean, 1500–1850* (Columbus: Ohio University Press, 2015).
[5]Tanika Sarkar, 'Bondage in the Colonial Context' in Utsa Patnaik and Manjari Dingwaney, eds, *Chains of Servitude: Bondage and Slavery in India* (Madras; Hyderabad: Sangam, 1985), p. 97.

and labour relations.[6] In doing so they have revealed a diverse history of slavery and unfree labour in South Asia that long predates the emergence of the colonial and capitalist networks that underpinned the imperial project, but which were fundamentally impacted and altered by them. Postcolonial approaches to writing the history of slavery in India thus raise two sets of inter-related questions: what do Western attempts to apply their own constructions of slavery and freedom to other contexts tell us about subjectivities and assumptions of the colonial observer, and how do we strip these away to recover the diverse lived experiences and local meanings of enslavement in colonized societies?

The Slavery Convention signed at Geneva in 1926 defines slavery as 'the status or condition of a person over whom any or all of the powers attaching to the right of ownership are exercised'. All-encompassing in its vagueness, this generic definition masks the myriad statuses, processes and experiences that characterized enslavement in different parts of the world. As Gyan Prakash argues, absolute and binary constructions of 'slavery' and 'freedom' are themselves the product of post-Enlightenment ideas of individualism and capitalist economy. As a result, they are often inapplicable to pre-colonial societies where various issues of status and obligation interacted to form relationships of dependence that went beyond systems of monetary exchange.[7] While historians continue to use terms such as 'slavery' and 'free labour' to describe Indian conditions, Ravi Ahuja argues that this does not necessarily mean that free wage labour is accepted as the norm, but rather reflects a pragmatic deployment of well-known definitions because 'incisive alternative theoretical concepts are still not at hand'.[8] In South and South East Asia, relationships of extreme dependence could take many forms, and did not always neatly map onto typologies of slavery constructed in relation to the Atlantic world. Orlando Patterson's definition of slavery as extreme power imbalance, maintained by violence and resulting in the 'social death' of the enslaved, for example, is not necessarily applicable to the South Asian

---

[6]See Indrani Chatterjee, *Gender, Slavery and Law in Colonial India* (New Delhi: Oxford University Press, 1999); Indrani Chatterjee and Richard Maxwell Eaton, eds, *Slavery & South Asian History* (Bloomington: Indiana University Press, 2006); Gyan Prakash, 'Terms of Servitude: The Colonial Discourse on Bondage and Servitude in India' in Martin A. Klein, ed., *Breaking the Chains: Slavery, Bondage, and Emancipation in Modern Africa and Asia* (Madison: University of Wisconsin Press, 1993); Gyan Prakash, *Bonded Histories: Genealogies of Labor Servitude in Colonial India* (Cambridge: Cambridge University Press, 1990).
[7]Prakash, *Bonded Histories*, pp. 1–11.
[8]Ravi Ahuja, 'Labour Relations in an Early Colonial Context: Madras, c. 1750–1800', *Modern Asian Studies* 36: 4 (2002), pp. 793–826, p. 795.

context, in which slaves could take on a number of different social and cultural roles and identities, sometimes simultaneously, or in quick succession.[9] Some were held as chattels, with the 're-isolation, institutionalized coercion and systemic exploitation, outsider status or essential kinlessness' that implies, but for others the boundary between slavery and relationships of dependence was more porous and upward mobility was possible.[10] As a result, definitions of slavery in South Asia are difficult to pin down. Tanika Sarkar suggests it is best understood as a labour relationship categorized by 'the master's absolute, unconditional control over the person, labour and children of the slave', while Richard Eaton sees it as 'the condition of uprooted outsiders, impoverished insiders – or the descendants of either – serving persons or institutions on which they are wholly dependent'.[11] Either definition encompasses a range of different labour relationships, involving varying patterns of servitude and ownership, with generally accepted aspects of the slave experience such as natal alienation, persons as property, chattel status, violence, coercion, race, kinlessness, dishonour or 'social death' intersecting with other features such as caste, kinship, debt and reciprocity.[12]

The difficulty applying well-worn definitions of slavery to the South Asian context and the lack of a 'master narrative' of Indian slavery may play a part in explaining its omission from both late-eighteenth- and nineteenth-century antislavery discourse, and from more recent historiographies of slavery and abolition.[13] Writing in 1999, David Brion Davis blamed the 'blindness of antislavery leaders to East Indian slavery' on 'scanty and unreliable information, and the peculiar nature of Indian slavery itself'.[14] These assumptions are problematic if we are to understand colonial attitudes to Indian slavery, and the social formations and labour relations which constituted it, because they both underestimate the size of the nineteenth-century colonial archive on Indian slavery, and take its contents at face value. Taking Davis's statement as a starting point, this chapter will explore some of the problems inherent in using the colonial archive to uncover, locate and write histories of slavery

---

[9] Orlando Patterson, *Slavery and Social Death: A Comparative Study* (Cambridge, MA: Harvard University Press, 1982).
[10] Markus Vink, '"The World's Oldest Trade": Dutch Slavery and Slave Trade in the Indian Ocean in the Seventeenth Century', *Journal of World History* 14: 2 (2003), pp. 131–77, p. 136.
[11] Sarkar, 'Bondage in the Colonial Context', p. 97; Richard Maxwell Eaton, 'Introduction' in Chatterjee and Eaton, eds, *Slavery & South Asian History*, p. 2.
[12] Eaton, 'Introduction', p. 1.
[13] Eaton, 'Introduction', p. 1.
[14] David Brion Davis, *The Problem of Slavery in the Age of Revolution, 1770–1823* (Ithaca, NY: Cornell University Press, 1975), p. 155.

in South Asia. Using the 1828 *Parliamentary Papers* on 'Slavery in India', and particularly their coverage of agricultural slavery in early nineteenth-century South India, as a case study, it will discuss the influence of various imperial imperatives and orientalist assumptions on the representation of Indian forms of bondage in colonial discourse, before concluding with a discussion of some recent postcolonial historiography that seeks to provide a more complex and nuanced picture of unfree labour in India.

Indian slavery and the colonial archive

Although dwarfed by the vast body of material produced on slavery in the Americas and Caribbean, several accounts of slavery in South Asia were produced by colonial officials, missionaries and other travellers in the early nineteenth century. The East India Company itself produced extensive collections of correspondence on the subject dating back to 1772. These were published in volumes of *Parliamentary Papers* in 1828, 1834, 1837, 1841 and 1843, providing perhaps the largest single repository of English-language sources on slavery in early colonial India available to historians.[15] So extensive was the 1828 volume that during a discussion of the subject in Parliament in 1833, Sir Robert Inglis lamented that no abridged synthesis had been made available, as not every Member could spare time to wade through nearly a thousand folio pages.[16] The publication of the first volume of *Parliamentary Papers* in 1828 was publicized in the specialist press: the *Asiatic Journal*, for example, carried a detailed commentary on them over several articles. They also formed the basis for the chapter on slavery in Rev James Peggs's *India's Cries to British Humanity* (1830).[17] The inclusion of slavery as an issue in this famous missionary tract suggests that the British evangelical public had access to information about Indian labour conditions, yet unlike Peggs's other topics – sati, infanticide and idolatry – major missionary society publications rarely reported on the issue. While they offer a rich resource

---

[15]*Parliamentary Papers* on 'Slavery in India'/'East Indian Slavery', 1828 (125), 1834 (128), 1837–8 (697), 1839 (138), 1841 (262), (54), (238), 1842 (507), 1843 (525) (hereafter *PP* 1828, *PP* 1837–8, etc.).
[16]Robert Inglis, *HC Deb*, 26 July 1833, Vol. 20, pp. 14–50; p. 17–18.
[17]J. Peggs, *India's Cries to British Humanity: Relative to the Suttee, Infanticide, British Connexion with Idolatry, Ghaut Murders, and Slavery in India*, 2nd ed. (London: Seely and Son, 1830).

for historians, their arrangement in chains of official correspondence limited their accessibility to and impact on contemporary readers. Rev Thomas Price, writing in 1837, reported that his colleague Mr Pringle had 'waded through' the *Parliamentary Papers*, 'but could not make out anything from it', and that even Peggs's summary of the contents did not 'exhibit the actual state of slavery in India so as to attract the attention of the public to it'.[18] Nor did they elicit much response from the abolitionist press. The *Anti-Slavery Monthly Reporter* briefly noted their publication but claimed their contents did not alter their view of East Indian slavery.[19] As I have argued elsewhere, the muted and ambivalent response of British abolitionists to the question of Indian slavery goes beyond simple ignorance of the Indian context, and reflects the discursive problems that exploitative Indian labour conditions posed for an antislavery discourse that was already invested in the idea of India as a potential free labour alternatives to the West Indies.[20] Ironically, it was West Indian apologists, keen to undermine the argument that East Indian trade offered an ethical alternative to slave produce, who paid most attention to the apparent revelations about Indian labour conditions. Drawing their information from sources such as Francis Buchanan's *A Journey from Madras through the Countries of Mysore, Canara and Malabar* (1807) and a selective reading of the *Parliamentary Papers*, George Saintsbury and Joseph Marryat, among others, publicly challenged abolitionist assumptions about the moral superiority of 'free-grown' East India sugar by emphasizing the existence of both slavery and extreme poverty on the subcontinent.[21]

As with all colonial texts, nineteenth-century publications dealing with slavery in India cannot be taken at face value and often tell the reader more about the subjectivities of their author/s than they do about the socio-economic realities of Indian labour conditions. As such, they must be read critically and against the grain if they are to yield useful insights into the functioning of Indian labour relationships. As Edward Said so influentially argued in *Orientalism* (published in 1978), complex power hierarchies and imperatives of domination and control informed all Western attempts to 'know' the so-called East.[22] As a result, all expressions

---

[18]Rev Thomas Price, *Slavery in America: With Notices of the Present State of Slavery and the Slave Trade throughout the World* (London: G. Wightman, 1837), p. 79.
[19]*Anti-Slavery Monthly Reporter* 2: 41 (October 1828).
[20]For more, see Andrea Major, *Slavery, Abolitionism, and Empire in India, 1772–1843* (Liverpool: Liverpool University Press, 2012).
[21]See, for example, George Saintsbury, *East India Slavery* (London: C. Tilt, 1829).
[22]Edward Said, *Orientalism* (New York: Pantheon, 1978).

of Western 'understanding' of the East are political and are shaped by consciously or subconsciously imbibed preconceptions and assumptions. The pursuit of knowledge in the colonial context was never disinterested, because the knowledge that was created was repeatedly put at the service of the colonial administration.[23] In the context of the study of slavery, the body of colonial knowledge that was produced on the subject represents a series of constructions informed by the assumptions, ideologies and imperatives of the imperial project. Colonial (mis)interpretations of Indian socio-religious customs such as caste impacted on their understanding of Indian slavery, while wider imperatives of stability, revenue collection and control also shaped their assessment of it. The codification of racial/cultural characteristics, and the assignation of immutable 'essences' to Indian society simplified the process of understanding by creating an unchanging frame of reference for events and phenomena that contrasted unfavourably with the European observers' own self-identity. The depiction of Indians as passive, apathetic and weak, for example, led some colonial officials to assert that they were naturally fitted for foreign domination and bondage, while ideas about the immutability of caste identity led colonial officials to designate some groups as born slaves.

Although some academics have dismissed Said's reworking of the relationship between knowledge and colonial power – Ernest Gellner, for example, claimed that *Orientalism* was 'entertaining, but intellectually insignificant' – for most Said's ideas have become crucial to any reinterpretation of the processes of Western understanding and representation of 'oriental' societies and cultures.[24] Many, including Gayatri Spivak and Homi Bhabha, view it as the foundation stone of postcolonial theory. This is not to suggest, of course, that *Orientalism* does not contain ideological and theoretical flaws, inconsistencies and paradoxes that have been the subject of sustained critique and analysis in postcolonial studies. The portrayal of a unified colonial discourse marginalizes counter-hegemonic trends and dissenting voices, while insufficient attention to multi-directional flows of information, influence and ideas oversimplifies the processes by which colonial power was discursively maintained. Thus, Lisa Lowe suggests that European orientalism should be viewed not as a single

---

[23]See Bart Moore-Gilbert, *Post-Colonial Theory: Contexts, Practices, Politics* (London: Verso, 1997), p. 38.
[24]Cited in John MacKenzie, *Orientalism: History, Theory and the Arts* (Manchester: Manchester University Press, 1995), p. 10.

overarching discourse, but as multiple, heterogeneous and contradictory, consisting of an uneven matrix of situations across different cultural and historical sites. She stresses the fluidity both of discourse, which she views as a 'complex and uneven terrain composed of heterogeneous textual, social and cultural practices', and of hegemony, which she views as a process of negotiation, consent and compromise between dominant and subaltern groups.[25] Any study of Indian slavery undertaken using colonial archives and English-language sources must be sensitive to these complexities, not only because discussion of slavery in India took place in numerous different forums and contexts – from British pro- and antislavery publications, to East India Company Board of Revenue consultations – but also because colonial observers themselves had multiple identities, as colonizers, administrators, evangelicals, abolitionists, scholars, entrepreneurs, and, in the early years of colonial expansion, slaveholders and traders.

If the *Parliamentary Papers* provide a wealth of correspondence on Indian slavery, any information they provide is refracted through the prism of a colonial discourse shaped by the political and ideological imperatives of the East India Company state. As one contemporary observer noted, 'This big book treats the subject much in the same manner as the planter magistrates and senators of Jamaica might be expected to report on Negro slavery, if the House of Commons called on them to exhibit its nature.'[26] In a similar vein, Indrani Chatterjee suggests that they are less a repository of 'facts' about Indian labour conditions, than a record of a 'triangulated conversation' between East India Company officials, the Presidency and Supreme Governments and the home authorities, around issues of colonial governance, slavery and abolition.[27] Some colonial officials did provide extensive reports on slavery and other labour conditions in their localities, but even these are problematic sources for reconstructing the nature, functioning and lived experience of Indian slavery, as I'll discuss in the next section. What they do offer are important insights into how East India Company officials interpreted Indian society and their own relationship to it, as rulers, administrators and occasionally reformers. These interpretations as they were produced on the ground were not always consistent, of course,

---

[25]Lisa Lowe, *Critical Terrains: French and British Orientalisms* (Ithaca, NY: Cornell University Press, 1992), p. 11.
[26]Price, *Slavery in America*, 79.
[27]Indrani Chatterjee, 'Renewed and Reconnected Histories' in Chatterjee and Eaton, eds, *Slavery & South Asian History*, p. 31.

varying between officials based on their personality, ideological position, position within the East India Company hierarchy and the immediate local imperatives of governance. Moreover, the sometimes conflicting accounts of colonial officials in the field were often synthesized, simplified and sanitized as they progressed up through the EIC hierarchy. Unwelcome revelations, difficult contradictions and regional and local complexities were ironed out as information passed from local officials to the Presidency Governments, the Court of Directors and eventually to Parliament and sections of the British public sphere. As such, these records themselves, and the publications that were based on them, offer a window onto multi-dimensional global interactions and processes of colonial control that linked changing East India Company ideas and policies to metropolitan debates, the formation of imperial and humanitarian ideologies, and wider social, political and economic discourses about slavery, trade and empire, the nature of EIC rule in India, and Britain's imperial identity.

Colonial constructions of Indian slavery

David Brion Davis's second suggestion – that the 'peculiar' nature of Indian slavery itself accounts for its failure to impact British abolitionist debates – also raises some important questions. Contemporary observers and more recent historians have both assumed fundamental differences between East and West Indian slavery, based on the different ways in which it functioned in the two locations. Indian forms of bondage did not involve some key defining features that were thought to characterize slavery in early nineteenth-century philanthropic discourse; the 'certain spaces (the ship, the plantation) and practices (especially the use of the whip and the treadmill) … [and] … the juxtaposition of particular racialised bodies (white enslavers/black enslaved)' that Lambert and Lester discuss as representing 'easily identifiable and denouncable metonyms for slavery'.[28] As a result, the very application of the term 'slavery' to certain labour conditions in India could be contested. Yet an over-emphasis on the difference between East

---

[28]David Lambert and Alan Lester, 'Geographies of Colonial Philanthropy', *Progress in Human Geography* 28: 3 (2004), pp. 320–41, p. 337.

and West Indian forms of slavery obscures some of the useful insights that can be drawn when they are placed in the same analytical frame. Colonial officials saw sufficient similarities to deploy the terminology of slavery – albeit unevenly and problematically – to the coercive labour relationships they encountered in India. The issue is not whether the various forms of bondage in India fit precisely with modern typologies of slavery, but what the differential designation of certain practices as slave or 'slave-like' in colonial and evangelical discourse can tell us about the processes of colonial knowledge formation.

Attempts to project the New World plantation model onto South Asian forms of slavery are clearly problematic, yet nor can we simply assume that because Indian slavery was not exactly like Atlantic plantation slavery, it was entirely unique, or dismiss it as an atypical 'Oriental exception to some ideal type'.[29] It has been argued that surplus landless labour in India created a different context for slavery compared to that in the New World, where the adoption of a highly coercive slave system was predicated on a critical shortage of free labour to work the available land.[30] In contrast, slavery in India has been characterized as connected to status, 'unproductive' domestic labour and agricultural subsistence, rather than to capitalist production on an industrial scale. This, together with the apparent absence of a racial element to slave oppression, led some colonial observers to argue that Indian slavery was relatively benign. Governor-General Lord William Bentinck, for example, believed that it was 'divested ... of all the cruel features which characterised the African trade'.[31] Though obviously denied certain rights and freedoms, Indian slaves were considered to enjoy more existential security than free labourers, and their position was often compared favourably both to West Indian slaves and to the average poverty-stricken Indian peasant. Such assumptions about the relatively benign nature of Indian slavery have been influential, but it is important to contextualize them with reference to the discursive imperatives of the colonial state. Slavery was a difficult and potentially destabilizing social issue for a colonial government that was caught between rising abolitionist sentiment at home and its reliance on coercive labour strategies and the acquiescence of the Indian slaveholding elites for the maintenance of its power in India.

---

[29]Eaton, 'Introduction', p. 3.
[30]Howard Temperley, 'The Delegalization of Slavery in British India', *Slavery & Abolition* 21: 2 (2000), pp. 169–87, p. 173.
[31]*PP* 1837–1838, 56.

The colonial archive on slavery in India contained within the *Parliamentary Papers* contains debates about three main overlapping areas – European slave trafficking in and from India; the internal traffic in women and children (and their subsequent enslavement within the home, or in dancing troops, brothels and mendicant religious orders); and agricultural and caste-based slavery and debt bondage, mostly discussed in the context of South Indian agrarian relations. Such groupings are themselves problematic, of course. As Chatterjee notes, the experience of African slavery in the New World led British observers arbitrarily to 'divide the world made by the slave holders into neat little spheres – one where adult men laboured outdoors, and another where women and children laboured at tasks which could never be measured, and therefore remained undervalued as domestic labour'.[32] Moreover, as Dharma Kumar demonstrates, the term 'slavery' did not adequately describe the many forms of bondage existing within 'traditional' agrarian relations, which ranged from 'chattel slavery to debt peonage' and also incorporated various caste-based obligations.[33] There was considerable debate about whether specific local conditions amounted to actual slavery, or whether other terms – 'allodial slave of the soil', 'agricultural serf', 'villein', '*adscriptus glebae*' or 'conditional servant for life' – were more appropriate. 'Faced with these groups, which were clearly in some degree or other of servitude', Kumar notes, colonial officials fell back on 'a palimpsest of definitions, none of which fitted South Indian conditions'.[34]

Colonial officials were divided as to the moral and material implications of allowing various systems of 'unfree' labour to continue. In working through this issue, colonial officials were influenced by a range of ideas and pressures that shaped their interpretation of the systems that they observed. Their responses clearly indicate the practical imperatives of a colonial government wary of any measures that might undermine the stability and profitability of its control, even as they also indicate moral distaste for the institution of slavery itself. During the 1810s and 1820s, when the issue of ameliorating Indian agricultural slavery was first mooted, the East India Company was still in the process of establishing its rule. Maximizing and stabilizing tax revenues was vital to finance military activity on the external and internal frontiers of the colonial state, so any innovations that might

---

[32] Indrani Chatterjee, 'Abolition by Denial' in Campbell, ed., *Abolition and Its Aftermath in the Indian Ocean Africa and Asia*, p. 151.
[33] Chatterjee, *Gender, Slavery and Law*, 5.
[34] Dharma Kumar, 'Caste and Landlessness in South India', *Comparative Studies in Society and History* 4: 3 (1962), pp. 337–63, 342.

potentially jeopardize this were treated with caution. At the same time, many colonial officials articulated their own opposition to slavery in a way that equated 'Britishness' with freedom, setting themselves apart from both the Indian elite and West Indian planters. C.M. Lushington, the Collector at Trichinopoly, for example, began his defence of the South Indian slave system by emphasizing that the very idea of slavery was 'revolting and abhorrent to an Englishman'.[35] Such competing imperatives underpinned a discursive reconstruction of Indian agricultural slavery as qualitatively different to its West Indian counterpart.[36] 'There cannot … be a doubt that the slavery prevalent among the lower classes of the Hindus is of a very different and opposite nature from that so strongly and justly reprobated in England', the Board of Revenue reported in 1819.[37] Because slavery in South India did not involve natal alienation, the middle passage or violent enslavement in a foreign land, colonial officials maintained that it could not be compared to the transatlantic trade – no matter how miserable the actual condition in which Indian slaves were found. Thus, although several colonial officials reported on the squalid conditions, harsh treatment and evident malnutrition of Indian agricultural slaves – and some, including Francis Buchanan and Catholic Missionary the Abbe Dubois, even considered their state of to be worse than that of enslaved Africans in the West Indies – the generally accepted view was that agrarian slavery in South India was a relatively mild form of bondage that actually offered greater existential security than free labour.[38] In the context of growing colonial need to acquire and control labour for its agricultural enterprises, 'slavery' in South India was thus configured as being primarily caste-based, mild, static and hereditary, characteristics that not only provided a rationale for non-interference, but also allowed it later to be usefully juxtaposed against 'indenture', which, despite its many coercive features and increasingly draconian legislation, was deemed mobile and based on free contract.[39]

Contradictions within colonial accounts of South Indian labour condition reflect the wide regional variation in agricultural practice in the area under study. They also prompt us to question dominant colonial paradigms and the reliability of the evidence on which they were based. Very few of the colonial officials who offered opinions on Indian slavery

---

[35] *PP* 1828, p. 839.
[36] *PP* 1828, p. 921.
[37] *PP* 1828, pp. 816–17.
[38] For more on this see Major, *Slavery, Abolitionism and Empire in India*, p. 201.
[39] See Major, *Slavery, Abolitionism and Empire in India*, p. 222.

had direct access to information from the slaves themselves – as the Board of Revenue put it, 'with this description of person, the government officers have seldom had any direct communication'.[40] Rather they relied on their native officers, or local landholders, for information, many of whom were slave owners themselves.[41] Yet even taking this into account, colonial interpretations of Indian slavery are inconsistent with the evidence, as their Indian informants themselves acknowledged that slaves might be bound, flogged, locked up, put in the stocks, have noses slit or amputated and be 'punished in such manner as it would please [his master], provided it does not deprive him of life'.[42] While such punishments must be understood in the context of both the penal power sanctioned in existing labour law and the quotidian violence of the East India Company state's agrarian relations, colonial officials' willingness to overlook evidence of brutality raises question about the wider agenda underlying their investment in the image of the well-treated Indian slave.

If colonial interpretations of Indian slavery were distorted by the practical imperatives of the colonial state, they were also shaped by orientalist attitudes to India that allowed certain social and labour relationships to be dismissed as inextricably entwined with the Hindu 'tradition' of caste. With its hereditary occupations, obligations, rules of conduct, and penalties of ostracism and social death, colonial officials frequently likened the caste system to a form of enslavement. As J. Vaughan, then Collector for Malabar, put it, 'What is Hindoo jurisprudence, in some points of view, but a state of slavery to customs, any deviation from which is punished by being out-casted, and driven from every privilege they religiously value?'[43] The extreme functioning of caste disabilities in parts of South India in particular led many British colonial officials to conceptualize so-called 'Untouchables' as at best existing in 'slave-like' relationships of dependence with the higher castes, and at worst comprising actual 'slave-castes'.[44] Considered polluting, even at a distance, they were denied admission to markets, temples, public roads and wells, while simultaneously being

---

[40]Benedicte Hjejle, 'Slavery and Agricultural Bondage in South India in the Nineteenth Century', *Scandinavian Economic History Review* 15: 1–2 (1967), pp. 71–126, p. 77.
[41]Hjejle, *Slavery and Agricultural Bondage*, p. 94.
[42]One report noted of an errant slave that 'formerly he would be flogged, put in the stocks, and his nose cut off; but at present the latter mode of punishing is never resorted to', implying that the other two still occurred; see *PP* 1828, p. 847 *et seq.*
[43]*PP* 1828, p. 846.
[44]Chatterjee, *Gender, Slavery and Law,* p. 6. 'Untouchable' is, of course, a highly pejorative colonial term for groups who would now identify as *dalits* (meaning 'oppressed').

subject to a range of labour and other obligations and expectations that replicated slavery. In this way, as Kooiman points out, their 'social degradation received a ritual sanction, although their labour power provided the major foundation on which local society rested'.[45] Unlike enslaved Africans, who had been 'brought within the memory of man from a distant country', however, India's agricultural slaves were thought to have existed in that state since time immemorial, having been born into immutable, socially sanctioned slavery.[46] As C. Hyde, the collector for Southern Arcot, put it, 'the Sudra tribe are naturally born in a state of servitude; and although some of the superior of the subdivisions of that tribe in modern days have emancipated themselves from this degrading thraldom, yet the lower castes are always looked upon as natural slaves'.[47]

Of course, contemporary historians now question the extent to which the caste system described by evangelical observers and colonial officials ever really existed. Although British commentators saw it as an ancient, universal and rigid hierarchy that left no room for social mobility or individuality, in pre-colonial India caste identity was neither as all-encompassing, nor as fixed as colonial accounts implied. Indeed, Susan Bayly argues that far from being a longstanding 'traditional' formulation, the basic structure of caste society only emerged in the century before the advent of colonial rule and reflected the political expediencies of influential new groups, rather than timeless religious ideals.[48] It was British colonial ethnographers, as well as subsequent anthropologists and sociologists, who looked at India's multi-layered, complex and often fluid social systems and attempted to reduce them into a static social hierarchy of 'castes' based on birth and ritual divisions between purity and pollution. This is not to suggest that the colonial state 'invented' caste, but rather that through their attempts to understand, codify, categorize and count the people of India, previously dynamic and negotiable social systems became increasingly fixed and were invested with a sense of immutability and permanence that they had not always possessed.[49] In pre-colonial India the distinction between 'free-born'

---

[45]Dick Kooiman, 'Conversion from Slavery to Plantation Labour: Christian Mission in South India (19th Century)', *Social Scientist* 19: 8/9 (1991), p. 59.
[46]See, for example, Robert Inglis, *HC Deb*, 17 July 1833, Vol. 19, pp. 797–807.
[47]*PP* 1828, pp. 871.
[48]See Susan Bayly, *Caste, Society and Politics in India from the Eighteen Century to the Modern Age* (Cambridge: Cambridge University Press, 1999).
[49]For more, see Nicholas B. Dirks, *Castes of Mind: Colonialism and the Making of Modern India* (Delhi: Permanent Black, 2004).

and so-called slave-castes would not have been as clear-cut nor as absolute as colonial accounts suggest. While the existence of a ritual dimension to labour exploitation did blur the boundaries between economic enslavement and caste obligation, too close an association between low-caste status and slavery would be misleading. Not all slaves came from this social background, for while a higher caste individual could not become the slave of a lower one, they could become enslaved to their caste equals, or superiors, through debt bondage, or loss of caste. Conversely, not all lower castes and *dalits* were slaves, and those who were occupied a range of statuses and experienced different limitations on their freedom and obligations to their caste superiors. Although slave groups tended to occupy the very bottom of the caste hierarchy, there were further divisions within them, and each sub-group appeared to have firmly articulated rights and disabilities that differed according to status and region.[50]

The tendency of colonial officials to understand relationships of agricultural dependence, obligation and oppression through the lens of caste is not surprising, given their wider understanding of that system's role in structuring all Indian social interactions. The emphasis on the relationship between caste and unfree forms of labour has also influenced more recent historiography of slavery and abolition, however, which has broadly assumed that this relationship made Indian forms of bondage unique and exceptional. Thus, Howard Temperley argues that slavery in India was primarily distinguished from other forms by 'its intimate relationship with the Indian caste system. From top to bottom it was characterized by strongly-held notions of hierarchy and deference, one result of which was that there was no ready way of distinguishing where obligations associated with slavery ended and other types of obligation began'.[51] The difficulty with such interpretations, as Indrani Chatterjee so convincingly argues, is that our conception of the caste system has itself been shaped by colonial officials and scholars, many of whom were influenced by plantocratic ideals and slave systems in other parts of the world. Influential orientalist scholar Henry Colebrooke, for example, was himself an aspiring planter, and Chatterjee believes that this influenced the way in which he conflated the manual labour performed by low-caste groups with a loss of citizenship and origins in slavery.[52] Thus Chatterjee

---

[50] See *PP* 1828, pp. 548–52; Buchanan, *A Journey from Madras*, p. 370.
[51] Temperley, 'The Delegalization of Slavery in British India', pp. 169–70.
[52] Chatterjee, *Gender, Slavery and Law*, p. 6.

notes that the idea of 'social disabilities inherited in the blood', which were a prominent feature of colonial conceptions of caste, bore many similarities to the legal and social frameworks of North American slavery.[53] From this perspective, colonial officials who discussed Indian slavery in terms of caste status were not simply faithfully describing an immutable system but contributing to the colonial construction of caste itself.

Conclusion: Uncovering experiences of slavery

If postcolonial approaches have helped to elucidate and deconstruct some of the assumptions, ideologies and agendas underpinning the colonial (mis)representations of slavery in India, they have also fed into more complex and nuanced interpretations of the lived experience of bondage on the subcontinent and suggested new ways of thinking about slave-status. Rather than a simple teleology of enslavement, resistance and emancipation, Indian slavery has been reconceptualized as an array of historically and regionally specific practices and statuses, each with different implications for the enslaved.[54] These have sought to move beyond categories imposed by colonial discourses of slavery drawn from the Atlantic experience, and problematize attempts to compartmentalize different regional and historical manifestations according to existing norms. Thus, Tanika Sarkar's separation of Indian forms of slavery into skilled but unproductive domestic labour in the households of the indigenous elite and productive agrestic slavery that produced a surplus in the form of agricultural crops has been criticized by Indrani Chatterjee for reproducing colonial categories and simplifying the wide range of service and labour obligations that existed in pre-colonial and colonial India.[55]

Rather than accept traditional dichotomies such as of 'slave' or 'free', 'domestic' or 'agricultural', 'capitalist' or 'traditional', recent studies of unfree labour in South Asia have tended instead to embrace the blurred boundaries and contradictions inherent in diverse and varied relationships of exploitation and dependence. Domestic slaves might perform limited

---

[53]Chatterjee, *Gender, Slavery and Law*, p. 7.
[54]Eaton, 'Introduction', p. 1.
[55]Chatterjee, *Gender, Slavery and Law*, p. 3.

agricultural labour, while the women of agrestic slave castes might be subject to sexual exploitation. Household slavery might sometimes have been structured by ideas of kinship and reciprocity, but it was not necessarily 'benign', while agricultural or caste-based slavery might bleed into and out of debt bondage and other forms of servitude and obligation. Loans or advances of money marked the bonding labourers to their masters in a relationship that was neither exactly slave nor entirely free.[56] Powerful local elites, or moneylenders, might hold the right to the person and labour of their debtor indefinitely, without that debtor specifically being denoted a slave. In other areas 'debt bondage' was thought to characterize agrarian relationships between individuals and even whole castes. In theory, debtor relationships were terminable on the paying off of the loan, but in practice clearing even relatively small debts often proved impossible and those held in debt bondage often slipped into a condition of permanent and inheritable dependency and thus slavery.[57] Gyan Prakash argues that although the British re-imagined these relationships as 'debt bondage' after 1843, in fact the relationships of dependence between *Kamia* labourers and their masters in Bihar were based on status rather than monetary exchange.[58]

In colonial and pre-colonial India, nearly all members of society were embedded in wider social hierarchies and networks, demarcated by obligations and responsibilities that complicate any discussion of 'freedom' and 'unfreedom' in the Western sense. Nor did enslaved individuals always remain permanently in that state. Slavery could be a transitional condition, through which some people in South Asia moved, with various personal and collective outcomes.[59] Domestic slaves could be integrated into both the affective and political networks of the kin/clan group, although they could also equally be excluded again, while Indian labouring classes simultaneously experienced both high levels of social mobility and appalling levels of existential insecurity.[60] As a result, individuals could assume various social roles, as petty commodity producers, 'free wage labourers', debt servants or slaves, almost concurrently, or within a relatively short time span.[61] Slaves could also develop complex and nuanced relationships

---

[56] See Prakash, *Bonded Histories*; Jan Breman, *Labour Bondage in West India: From Past to Present* (New Delhi: Oxford University Press, 2007).
[57] Eaton, 'Introduction', p. 6.
[58] See Prakash, 'Terms of Servitude', p. 131 *et seq.*
[59] Eaton, 'Introduction', p. 8.
[60] Ahuja, 'Labour Relations', p. 825.
[61] Ahuja, 'Labour Relations', p. 825.

of kinship and reciprocity with their owners. As Ramya Sreenivasan demonstrates for the Rajput states, the boundaries between lineage, clan and *jati* were not absolute, but rather were intertwined with histories of slavery and evolved through the management of slave labour as much as they did through the more well-known networks of marriage alliances between elite households.[62] Thus although Orlando Patterson has emphasized kinlessness or 'social death' as crucial to the condition of slavery, Indrani Chatterjee and Sumit Guha argue that kinship and kinlessness were not simply biological states in pre-colonial India, but were socially constructed and negotiated conditions that could be fluid and complex.[63] Feeding and clothing could transform unconnected strangers into kin as nurturing and commensality could constitute bonds of kinship and authority, while the incorporation of waifs, captives or slaves into the household increased its social capital.[64] Thus rather than conforming to absolute distinctions of slavery and family drawn from Western conceptions of both the Atlantic model of slavery and the discrete and biological boundaries of the nuclear family, Chatterjee and Guha argue that we should view slavery and kinship in pre-colonial India as existing within a continuum.[65]

Authentic 'slave voices' in India, as elsewhere, are notoriously difficult to uncover. Slaves, by virtue of their status, rarely left records or accounts of their experiences, and often had limited opportunities for self-expression. Indirect slave testimonies can be found in a diverse range of sources, however, ranging from court cases, police records, and newspaper reports, to family chronicles and personal papers. Indrani Chatterjee describes the 'hide and seek nature of slavery in … vernacular records', as slave voices are refracted through elite accounts of various sorts.[66] These records, as Eaton notes, are often 'fragmentary, opaque and tainted with the politics of the day'.[67] Indian chroniclers often wrote slaves out of their histories, while the records of the British colonial state contain equally significant erasures, misrepresentations and rationalizations.[68] Slave voices and experiences are further obscured by the ambivalent terminology used to denote slave status in both vernacular

---

[62] Ramya Sreenivasan, 'Drudges, Dancing Girls, Concubines: Female Slaves in Rajput Polity, 1500–1850' in Indrani Chatterjee and Richard M. Eaton, eds, *Slavery & South Asian History* (Bloomington and Indianapolis IN: Indiana University Press, 2006), pp. 7, 136–62.
[63] Indrani Chatterjee and Sumit Guha, 'Slave-Queen, Waif-Prince: Slavery and Social Capital in Eighteenth-Century India', *Indian Economic & Social History Review*, 36: 2 (1999), p. 167.
[64] Chatterjee and Guha, 'Slave-Queen, Waif-Prince', p. 170.
[65] Chatterjee, *Gender, Slavery and Law*, p. 171.
[66] Chatterjee, 'Renewed and Connected Histories', p. 32.
[67] Eaton, 'Introduction', p. 9.
[68] Eaton, 'Introduction', p. 9.

and colonial accounts, with terms like concubine, bondsman and vassal being employed by colonial observers to indirectly denote possible enslavement.[69] Uneven record-keeping practices in some Indian courts were compounded by norms of respectability that proscribed the discussion of women in public.[70] Meanwhile, colonial policies exacerbated the reluctance to explicitly name slaves as such, as their emphasis on legitimate biological ancestry and purity of descent lead to the dispossession of older slave-born lineage members, and encouraged reticence about slave origins among family record keepers.[71] Both postcolonialism and subaltern studies have offered tools to approach these challenges, with increased emphasis on 'the fragment' as a valuable historical artefact, as well as analytical and discursive tools to dismantle colonial prose.[72] In the process, postcolonial scholars have sought new ways of conceptualizing slavery that are appropriate to the South Asian context and do not rely on Western definitions and assumptions about its functioning. Thus Chatterjee argues that slavery in India is best understood as 'a dialectic of captivity and transfers along a socially integrated continuum, as a dialectic between alienation and intimacy, not as a static problem of "unfreedom", coerced labour, "commodity" or "property"'.[73] Thus, rather than define slavery in absolute terms of 'free' versus 'slave', we should foreground locally specific usages and relationships, and be aware that these changed both regionally and over time.[74] Moreover, while it is possible to catch glimpses of the intimate social functioning of Indian slavery through the colonial archive, the images of Indian slavery that it contains are not empirical realities, but rather the product of various overlapping, and sometimes conflicting, colonial discourses.

Bibliography

Allen, Richard B., *European Slave Trading in the Indian Ocean, 1500–1850* (Columbus: Ohio University Press, 2015).

---

[69] Chatterjee, *Gender, Slavery and Law*, p. 1; Chatterjee, 'Renewed and Connected Histories', p. 26.
[70] Sreenivasan, 'Drudges, Dancing Girls, Concubines', pp. 136–8.
[71] Eaton, 'Introduction', p. 9.
[72] For example, see Ranajit Guha, 'The Prose of Counter-Insurgency' in Ranajit Guha, ed., *Subaltern Studies II* (New Delhi: Oxford University Press, 1983).
[73] Chatterjee, 'Renewed and Connected Histories', p. 19.
[74] Chatterjee, 'Renewed and Connected Histories', p. 19; Chatterjee, *Gender, Slavery and Law*, p. 4.

Baak, Paul E., 'About Enslaved Ex-Slaves, Uncaptured Contract Coolies and Unfreed Freedmen: Some Notes about and Labour in the Context of Plantation Development in Southwest India, Early Sixteenth Century-Mid 1990s', *Modern Asian Studies* 33: 1 (1999), pp. 121–57.

Campbell, Gwynn, ed., *The Structure of Slavery in Indian Ocean Africa and Asia* (London: Frank Cass, 2004); and Campbell, Gwynn, ed., *Abolition and Its Aftermath in Indian Ocean Africa and Asia* (London: Routledge, 2005).

Chatterjee, Indrani, *Gender, Slavery and Law in Colonial India* (New Delhi: Oxford University Press, 1999).

Chatterjee, Indrani and Richard Maxwell Eaton, eds, *Slavery & South Asian History* (Bloomington: Indiana University Press, 2006).

Hjejle, Benedicte, 'Slavery and Agricultural Bondage in South India in the Nineteenth Century', *Scandinavian Economic History Review* 15: 1–2 (1967), pp. 71–126.

Kumar, Dharma, *Land and Caste in South India* (Cambridge: Cambridge University Press, 1965).

Major, Andrea, *Slavery, Abolitionism, and Empire in India, 1772–1843* (Liverpool: Liverpool University Press, 2012).

Prakash, Gyan, *Bonded Histories: Genealogies of Labor Servitude in Colonial India* (Cambridge: Cambridge University Press, 1990).

Prakash, Gyan, 'Terms of Servitude: The Colonial Discourse on Bondage and Servitude in India' in Martin A. Klein, ed., *Breaking the Chains: Slavery, Bondage, and Emancipation in Modern Africa and Asia* (Madison: University of Wisconsin Press, 1993).

Sarkar, Tanika, 'Bondage in the Colonial Context' in Utsa Patnaik and Manjari Dingwaney, eds, *Chains of Servitude: Bondage and Slavery in India* (Madras; Hyderabad: Sangam, 1985).

Viswanath, Rupa, *The Pariah Problem: Caste, Religion, and the Social in Modern India* (New York: Columbia University Press, 2014).

14

Imagining slavery in Roman antiquity

K.R. Bradley

University of Notre Dame

The whole commerce between master and slave is a perpetual exercise of the most boisterous passions, the most unremitting despotism on the one part, and degrading submissions on the other.
— Thomas Jefferson, *Notes on the State of Virginia*

Introduction: The issue

A.E. Housman once expressed the opinion 'that civilization without slavery is impossible'. Slavery, as Housman saw it, was in the case of Roman civilization its 'chief institution', and it was indeed an institution that was never widely contested. A memory of a remote Golden Age of social equality and justice was recalled every December in the annual celebration of the Saturnalia, but the brief days of liberation that slaves then enjoyed never gave rise to a movement for the permanent restoration of social harmony through slavery's removal; nor did the eschatological prospect of a communitarian era offered by the Sibylline oracular tradition produce any ameliorative effect.[1] In late antiquity, the Cappadocian Gregory of Nyssa developed

---

[1] Housman in Archie Burnett, ed., *The Letters of A.E. Housman*, Vols. 1–2 (Oxford: Clarendon Press, 2007), Vol. 1, p. 556 (3 January 1924); A. E. Housman, *The Confines of Criticism: The Cambridge Inaugural 1911* (Cambridge: Cambridge University Press, 1969), p. 34. Never widely contested:

theological arguments to persuade Christians of the equality of all human beings in the sight of God, and to prove the injustice of slave ownership, urging his followers to free their slaves in anticipation in the sinful present of the equality of all in the heavenly eternity to come. Practical fulfilment of his ideas was possible in the ascetic mode of life to which he and his family were committed, and similar effects, though surely minimal, may have been felt in comparable Christian communities. Yet theological argument, devoid of political support, did not become the basis of a realizable social programme for systemic change, and Salvian duly found the behaviour of Christian slave owners in his day as disgraceful as ever. Throughout Rome's history, a slaveless world was, with few exceptions, no more than mythically imaginable. Every slave consequently will have considered preposterous the particular claim of Philo (*Leg.* 13) that Rome witnessed a golden age in the reign of Tiberius.[2]

My remit in this chapter is to examine the Roman slavery system from below, from the perspective of those who knew enslavement first-hand.[3] The task is formidable, if not impossible, because there is little evidence from slaves themselves from which their perceptions might be recovered. The 'despotism' of their owners is easily accessible, but the 'degrading

---

Peter Garnsey, *Ideas of Slavery from Aristotle to Augustine* (Cambridge: Cambridge University Press, 1996). Saturnalia: Arthur O. Lovejoy, and George Boas, *Primitivism and Related Ideas in Antiquity* (New York: Octagon Books, 1965), pp. 23–102 (add for celebration from Vindolanda *TV* II Tablet: 301). Tradition: *Orac. Sib.* 2.319–24; 8.110–11; 14.351–5 with J.J. Collins, 'Sibylline Oracles (Second Century B.C. – Seventh Century A.D.): A New Translation and Introduction' in James H. Charlesworth, ed., *The Old Testament Pseudepigrapha* (Garden City, NY: Doubleday, 1983), pp. 459–60; J.L. Lightfoot, *The Sibylline Oracles, With Introduction, Translation, and Commentary on the First and Second Books* (Oxford: Oxford University Press, 2007), pp. 529–30.
[2]Gregory: Ilaria Ramelli, *Social Justice and The Legitimacy of Slavery: The Role of Philosophical Asceticism from Ancient Judaism to Late Antiquity* (Oxford: Oxford University Press, 2016), pp. 172–89 (cf. Kyle Harper, *Slavery in the Late Roman World, AD 275–425* [Cambridge: Cambridge University Press, 2011], p. 346), 190–211; cf. Lactantius, *Div. Inst.* 5.14.15–17. Salvian: Keith R. Bradley, 'Roman Slavery: Retrospect and Prospect', *Canadian Journal of History* 43 (2008), pp. 497–8. Slaveless: see D. Konstan, 'A World without Slaves: Crates' Thêria' in C.W. Marshall and George Kovacs, eds, *No Laughing Matter: Studies in Athenian Comedy* (London: Bristol Classical Press, 2012), pp. 13–18.
[3]The project is a supplement to Keith R. Bradley, *Slavery and Society at Rome* (Cambridge: Cambridge University Press, 1994), and synthesizes items of evidence either new or insufficiently discussed, together with developments in scholarship from the interim. I continue to find inspiration in the studies of M.I. Finley, especially Moses I. Finley, 'Slavery' in D.L. Sills, ed., *International Encyclopedia of the Social Sciences*. Vol. 14 (New York: Macmillan, 1968), pp. 307–14, the trenchant critique of Vlassopoulos – in Kostas Vlassopoulos, 'Finley's Slavery' in Daniel Jew, Robin Osborne, and Michael Scott, eds, *M.I. Finley: An Ancient Historian and His Impact* (Cambridge: Cambridge University Press, 2016), pp. 76–99 – notwithstanding, and I draw unapologetically on various contributions of my own written since 1994.

submissions' as slaves truly experienced them, as too what Housman disparagingly termed 'the mental habits of the slave', less so.[4] How then to proceed? In what follows I illustrate from select items of evidence – literary, legal, documentary, material – something of the broad conditions that governed the lives of slaves, and draw what I think are reasonable inferences on the servile response to them. The evidence inherently privileges the views of slave owners and their representatives, but there is no alternative but to confront and work with it.[5] In doing so, I assume that in everyday reality slaves responded to the conditions of servitude as individual agents capable of making decisions dependent upon the emotions their owners understood them to experience – their resentment of injustices, their hopes, fears, joys, and sorrows – the determining force of which in history is assured; and in view of the vagaries of human nature and the heterogeneity of Rome's slave population, I assume also an array of responses to be discernible, servile inertia or passivity apart.[6]

First, however, a proviso. Rome's history extended across a millennium. At its height Roman power stretched from Portugal and Morocco to Iran and Syria, and from Scotland to Libya and Egypt. The process of imperial expansion (and retrenchment) was dynamic and constantly changing, with a huge variety of peoples, all culturally distinctive, falling subject to Roman rule. Apuleius's remarks (*De deo Socr.* 148–9) on the religious variety of the Mediterranean world in his day are enough to register the point. What it means, therefore, to call Rome, at once a city and an empire, a 'slave society' – a common and legitimate practice – is problematical since allowance has to be made for factors of time and place.[7] Slave population ratios cannot

---

[4]Housman, *The Confines of Criticism*, p. 42.
[5]Nothing is gained by dismissing the written record as rhetoric: Katherine Shaner, *Enslaved Leadership in Early Christianity* (New York: Oxford University Press, 2018).
[6]Emotions: Cato, ORF³ fr.58; Cicero, *Ad fam.* 11.28.3; cf. Philo, *Quod omnis probus* 100. Assured: Ramsay MacMullen, *Feelings in History, Ancient and Modern* (Claremont, CA: Regina Books, 2003).
[7]Keith R. Bradley, 'Freedom and Slavery' in Walter Scheidel and Alessandro Barchiesi, eds, *The Oxford Handbook of Roman Studies* (Oxford: Oxford University Press, 2010), pp. 625–6; cf. John Bodel, 'Death and Social Death in Ancient Rome' in John Bodel and Walter Scheidel, eds, *On Human Bondage: After Slavery and Social Death* (Malden, MA and Oxford: Wiley Blackwell, 2017), pp. 81–108; Noel Lenski, 'Framing the Question: What Is a Slave Society?' in Noel Lenski and Catherine M. Cameron, eds, *What Is a Slave Society? The Practice of Slavery in Global Perspective* (Cambridge: Cambridge University Press, 2018), pp. 15–57; Noel Lenski, 'Ancient Slaveries and Modern Ideology' in Lenski and Cameron, eds, *What Is a Slave Society?*, pp. 106–47; Kyle Harper and Walter Scheidel, 'Roman Society and the Idea of "Slave Society"' in Lenski and Cameron, eds, *What Is a Slave Society?*, pp. 86–105.

help as a basis of definition because accurate numerical information on the Roman population at large, in any era or location, is non-existent, while any notion that an emergent capitalist market economy should be an all-important definitional criterion overlooks the fact that slave-owning by Greeks, Jews, Egyptians, Carthaginians and others long preceded Roman territorial expansion. In any case 'slave society' and 'slave economy' are not synonyms. The creation and development of a body of law throughout the millennium regulating relations between slave and free evident at Rome, in both senses, may be of greater relevance, with the principle that 'all men are either free men or slaves' of fundamental significance.[8] If indeed anything beyond bland generalizations about slavery in 'ancient Rome' or 'among the Romans' is to be achieved, a construct is required that allows Satto, a house-born slave in the household of the Celtic merchant Blussus, who traded with the Roman army on the Rhine, to be collocated with the seven slaves, some purchased, others house-born, in the Egyptian household of the soldier Julius Acutianus and his *de facto* spouse Cornelia, with the slave potters of Italy whose handiwork could be highly prized, and with the hundreds of domestic slaves individually owned by Roman grandees in the city.[9] I prefer therefore to understand Rome's slave society, macroscopically and diachronically, as a slave *culture*, in which ownership of human property was always regarded as normative, and the slave, a rightless and kinless outsider associated principally with capture in warfare, as the social antithesis of the free Roman citizen whenever and wherever situated. Slavery was a state equivalent to death, as proved by the preference for suicide over enslavement from prisoners of war, and a consequence of a culturally distinct aspect of Roman mentality, the 'desire to dominate', which can be easily overlooked

---

[8] Law: Jane Gardner, 'Slavery and Roman Law' in Keith Bradley and Paul Cartledge, eds, *The Cambridge World History of Slavery*, Vol. 1: *The Ancient Mediterranean World* (Cambridge: Cambridge University Press, 2011), pp. 414–37. Principle: *Dig.* 1.5.3.

[9] W. Selzer, *Römische Steindenkmäler: Mainz in Römischer Zeit, Katalog zur Sammlung in der Steinhall* (Mainz: Verlag Phillip von Zabern, 1988): no. 10 (pp. 95–8); P. Cattaoui VI 1–23 with J.A. Straus, 'L'Idiologue a raison', *Chronique d'Égypte* 78 (2003), pp. 217–20; William L. Westermann, *The Slave Systems of Greek and Roman Antiquity* (Philadelphia, PA: The American Philosophical Society, 1955), pp. 91–4; Bradley, *Slavery and Society at Rome*, p. 11. See especially Leonard A. Curchin, 'Social Relations in Central Spain: Patrons, Freedmen and Slaves in the Life of a Roman Provincial Hinterland', *Ancient Society* 18 (1987), pp. 75–88; Leonard A. Curchin, 'Slaves in Lusitania: identity, demography and social relations', *Conimbriga* 56 (2017) pp. 75–108; and Jonathan Edmondson, 'Family Life within Slave Households at Augusta Emerita: The Epitaph of the Cordii', *Anas* 15/16 (2002–2003), pp. 201–38, on developments in Roman Spain.

in global comparisons. (Subjection to empire, or even to love, was a natural metaphorical shift.) Distortion of its historical character, and its enormities, is inevitable if treated sceptically or dispassionately.[10]

Regulation

For slave owners, slavery was a source of labour, services and social prestige. How were these benefits secured? The Roman agronomists followed Greek predecessors on household regulation in recommending a combination of incentives, rewards, threats and punishments as stimulants for good performance that resemble practices in later slavery history.[11] The emergence from a mediaeval Arabic translation of a text probably from the age of Nero, the *Oikonomikos* of the Greek author Bryson, underscores the extent of the practices implicit in their recommendations. The text's chief assumption is that slaves, conceptualized as socio-economic necessities and alienable commodities, must be carefully managed in order to elicit obedience from them. The slave owner is encouraged to display sympathy and to show kindness to his slaves, yet it is axiomatic that they are to be punished when they cause offence: a first mistake can be ignored, but for subsequent infractions increasingly severe verbal correction is stipulated and finally physical punishment. Periods of rest are recommended for maximal productivity, but all opportunity for excessive independence of action or thought is disallowed. The model to be followed, suitably modified for human property, is the regime for controlling animals, the ideal being not to rule by terror but to induce compliance by making slaves respect their owners. Optimal performance is to be expected from the young, because they are considered willing to obey and to accept responsibilities promptly, while disaffection is to be

---

[10]Death: Philo, *Quod omnis probus* 118–19, 134; Seneca, *Ep.* 77.18; Appian, *BC* 4.76–80. Aspect: Sallust, *Cat.* 2.2; Tacitus, *Ann.* 1.10; Augustine, *De civ. D.* 1 praef. Shift: M. Lavan, *Slaves to Rome: Paradigms of Empire in Roman Culture* (Cambridge: Cambridge University Press, 2013); Roam Lyne, 'Servitium Amoris', *Classical Quarterly* 29 (1979), pp. 117–30. Distortion: Niall McKeown, *The Invention of Ancient Slavery?* (London: Duckworth, 2007); Westermann, *The Slave Systems of Greek and Roman Antiquity*, p. x.

[11]Keith R. Bradley, 'The Bitter Chain of Slavery', *Dialogues d'histoire ancienne* 41 (2015), pp. 155–63; Enrico Dal Lago and Constantina Katsari, 'Ideal Models of Slave Management in the Roman World and in the Ante-Bellum South' in Enrico Dal Lago and Constantina Katsari, eds, *Slave Systems: Ancient and Modern* (Cambridge: Cambridge University Press, 2008), pp. 187–213.

pre-empted by purchasing slaves ethnically distinct from the owner. The owner in turn is to provide adequate material support and not to make unreasonable or illegal demands. There is no compromise, however, on the expectation of total compliance. Bryson's final prescription, a typical divide-and-conquer strategy, is to establish a hierarchy of servile statuses within the household governed by the degree of favour in which the master holds his slaves, his aim being to secure obedience through fostering rivalry in winning and rising in the master's regard. In effect, slaves are to collude in their own victimization by being conditioned to internalize the propriety of their subject status.[12] All of this is consistent with piecemeal indications of a constant consciousness among slave owners of the attentions ownership of human property required. Philodemus (*De oec.* 9.26–44) advocated rewarding industrious slaves with extra supplies of food and rations of wine, and Plutarch (*Mor.* 459B-D) thought that more could be accomplished by restraint and a kindly disposition than by instruments of violence used in anger. The regulations reflected at the private level what Roman law expressed publicly, rendering questionable a definition of slavery in which slaves appear as objects distinct from their human masters.[13] Judged from the servile point of view, the template of prescriptions commonly found in the tradition of household regulation presented the victims of enslavement with a set of behavioural choices by which their personal interests might best be served. This is the leading idea which guides the present discussion.

Contingency

A partially preserved census inscription from Cycladic Thera suggests one type of outcome. The manner in which it records the names and, in many cases, the ages of 152 rural slaves who belonged to an unnamed slave owner suggests patterns of rural slave management and experience that may have applied more broadly in the Roman Mediterranean. A more or less equal ratio of adult males and females seemingly allowed slaves to form quasi-marital

---

[12]Simon Swain, *Economy, Family, and Society from Rome to Islam: A Critical Edition, English Translation, and Study of Bryson's Management of the Estate* (Cambridge: Cambridge University Press, 2013), pp. 55–72. Corsicans, notably, had a particular reputation for intractability: Strabo 5.2.7.
[13]Lenski, 'Framing the Question', p. 51.

unions, and through reproduction to live in nuclear-styled families, as with the couple Eutychos, aged 40, and Theodoula, aged 25, who had two children, Lampadion and the four-year-old Eutychos. The predominance of slave mothers in the inscription is a sign that manumission of slave fathers around the age of thirty was predictable, especially for men in positions of responsibility, women being less likely to be manumitted while still capable of producing new slave offspring. Equally, however, the considerable number of named older males indicates that manumission was by no means universal.[14] In sum, the document points to practical implementation on a slave owner's part of the agronomists' prescriptions to permit opportunities for familial relationships and eventual manumission as means of fostering servile compliance and productivity. It is of late Imperial date, however, and from a remote location in the southern Aegean. Exactly how representative therefore of practices it is elsewhere is a genuine issue, not least because of the perennial question of whether absentee slave owners commonly had personal knowledge of their rural slave complements. Items of legal and material evidence raise less benign possibilities for servile living conditions and consequent responses.

The Roman law on remedies available to slave owners for damage and injury to their slaves is a convenient example. It extended from the era of the Twelve Tables to that of Justinian, a huge interval during which the principle remained firm regardless that the slave owner was entitled to compensation for diminution of the value of his slave property caused by a third party. If Roman lawyers sometimes defined slavery as contrary to nature,[15] it can hardly at any time have seemed so to the vast majority of Rome's population, slaves included. In the conservative Roman legal mind property and privilege took pride of place. Two elements stand out as plausible representations of social experience.

First, the frequency of references to the wounding, killing and abduction of slaves can give no indication of the incidence of such eventualities, but the situational details described suggest the hazards that might affect slaves at any time: a doctor's negligence, starvation, ambush, traffic accidents, war, an unfortunately tossed javelin on the training ground, the hand of a barber struck by a misthrown exercise ball – these are just a few of the causes of slaves' deaths intriguingly introduced. (The physical spoliation of the face and other parts of the body, painful and shaming, caused by

---

[14]Kyle Harper, 'The Greek Census Inscriptions of Late Antiquity', *Journal of Roman Studies* 98 (2008), pp. 106–16; Harper, *Slavery in the Late Roman World*, pp. 74–6.
[15]*Dig*.1.5.4.1.

branding and tattooing might be compared.[16]) Violent associations between damage and injury are of course inevitable; but brutality emerges from the law as a fundamental condition of servile life. The praetor was generous in forbidding a man to beat another man's slave 'contrary to sound morals', but the law did not object to beating the slave when its corrective value was in play. Jurists likewise could distinguish 'mere interrogation' and 'mild intimidation' from 'torture' when discussing the taking of evidence from slaves, or raise the concept of 'extreme cruelty'; yet the axiom that the slave's body was subject to physical constraint was never questioned, which meant that slaves, as sensate human beings, always had before them the prospect of the whip, the lash or the fist.[17] At times 'humanity' or 'compassion' could prompt someone to release the chained slave from his shackles, or allow him to run away or harbour him after escape; but such signs of sympathy are notable by their rarity. More prominent is the law's Catonian preoccupation with protecting the financial well-being of the slave owner, as a result of which, especially in the rules established to calculate loss due to damage or injury, sympathy for the slave is to be dismissed. The severing of a prize slave painter's thumb is of interest only as an item affecting his economic worth.[18]

Secondly, the heterogeneity of the slave population is striking, as in the discretion permitted to the praetor in granting an action for injury, where the position as well as the character of the slave concerned made a difference: the 'common slave' or 'drudge' did not belong to the same category as the 'steward', while 'a troupe of actors or musicians' may have fallen in between.[19] It follows that common cause was unlikely to have resulted from simple juridical status. Indeed, it was expected that one slave might collaborate in causing damage and injury to another, or that one might abduct another in order to replace him as the price of his manumission.

---

[16]*Dig.* 9.2.7.8; 9.2.9.2; 9.2.9.3; 9.2.52.2; 19.2.13.pr.; *Paul. Sent.* 2.4.3; *Dig.* 9.2.9.4; 9.2.7.11.pr. See in full J.D. Harke, *Corpus der römischen Rechtsquellen zur antiken Sklaverei.* Teil III. *Die Rechtspositionen am Sklaven.* 2: *Ansprüche aus Delikten am Sklaven* (Stuttgart: Franz Steiner Verlag, 2013). Spoliation: D. Kamen, 'A Corpus of Inscriptions: Representing Slave Marks in Antiquity', *Memoirs of the American Academy in Rome* 55 (2010), pp. 95–110.

[17]*Dig.* 47.10.15.34; 47.10.15.38; *Cod.* 6.2.20. *Dig.* 47.10.15.41; 24.3.24.5. *Dig.* 47.10.15.35; 9.2.27.17. The shaming effect of the *furca* was known to Plutarch (*Mor.* 280E).

[18]*Dig.* 4.3.7.7; 11.3.5.pr.; Justinian, *Inst.* 4.3.16. Alan E. Astin, *Cato the Censor* (Oxford: Oxford University Press, 1978), pp. 261–6. Gaius, *Inst.* 3.217; *Dig.* 9.2.27.17; *Coll.* 2.4.1; *Dig.* 9.2.33.pr. *Dig.* 9.2.23.3.

[19]*Dig.* 47.10.15.44; 9.2.22.1.

It was also expected that despite his natural inferiority the slave was persuasible and morally corruptible: the good slave could be made bad and the bad slave worse, with a host of harsh consequences: physical harm, theft, flight, incitement of other men's slaves, mishandling of the *peculium*, implication in love affairs and evil arts, truancy, time-wasting at public entertainments, sedition, fraud.[20] Judgement of corruption was expressed, as in all matters, in terms laid down by the slave-owning establishment, with no awareness of the irony involved in the assumption that items of property devoid of legal personality were capable of many forms of human, and often subversively human, action.

As for material evidence, the 'creolized' culture of African slaves in the New World has led to a search for something similar in Roman antiquity, one result being the attractive proposition that locally enslaved slaves and their descendants in Roman Britain built living quarters in the pre-Roman form of the Celtic roundhouse that excavation has revealed at Vindolanda in northern England and among the high Imperial villa complexes of the south. This both pays attention to regional particularism and posits an answer to the notoriously difficult problem of identifying servile living areas.[21] Examination, moreover, of the architecture, decorations and physical settings of the remains of the Campanian cities and villas destroyed by the eruption of Mt Vesuvius has produced bold theories about the everyday lives of slaves: the House of the Menander at Pompeii contained areas in which domestic slaves are thought to have been capable of lingering and disappearing from sight, actively frustrating their owners' wishes as they moved through the house to perform their duties, while the zebra stripes with which some of the walls of a villa at Oplontis were decorated are said to have functioned as signs for slaves to follow when moving from one area to another, efficiently but unobtrusively. Further, the late architectural development of the remarkable villa at Settefinestre seems to show a preoccupation with surveillance of rural slaves consistent with

---

[20]*Dig.* 41.3.4.16–17; 41.4.10. *Dig.* 11.3.5.1; 11.3.1.4; 11.3.1.5.
[21]Jane Webster, 'Archaeologies of Slavery and Servitude', *Journal of Roman Archaeology* 18 (2005), pp. 161–79; Jane Webster, 'Less Beloved: Roman Archaeology, Slavery and the Failure to Compare', *Archaeological Dialogues* 15: 2 (2008), pp. 103–23. Problem: Keith R. Bradley, 'Slavery and Archaeology', *Journal of Roman Archaeology* 16 (2003), p. 573, on Fredrick Hugh Thompson, *The Archaeology of Greek and Roman Slavery* (London: Duckworth, 2003), pp. 67–130.

directives on slave management found in the agronomists' record.[22] The important presumption in such views is that slaves actively responded to their subject status, as the law earlier cited intimates. Domestic architecture itself, however, cannot prove but only suggest slave experience.[23]

So too with the remains of buildings thought to have been used as sites of slave-trading. Mass enslavements of enemies defeated in warfare were common during Rome's Republican wars of empire-building and sometimes in the Imperial age as well. Merchants distributed the victims from points of captivity to regions where their labour and services were required, and transportation over vast distances could be involved.[24] (This was true even in less fractious times. In the mid-third century AD the nine-year-old boy Zoilus was sold by one owner to another in Alexandria after having been imported a year earlier by sea from Macedonia.)[25] Remnants of buildings thought to have been centres of exchange in the distributive process have been found at a cluster of sites – Delos, Ephesus, Pompeii, Herculaneum, Ostia, Lepcis Magna, Rome itself – and archaeologists have interpreted elements within them as indications of the means by which potentially dangerous new slaves were controlled, fed and otherwise accommodated – platforms for inspection prior to sale included. No building, however, has to my knowledge been incontestably identified as a purpose-built slave market, and the true significance of the architectural remnants concerned remains controversial. Literary evidence is required to confirm that the prospect of enslavement was a nightmare.[26]

---

[22] Sandra Joshel and Lauren Hackworth Petersen, *The Material Life of Roman Slaves* (New York: Cambridge University Press, 2014).
[23] Michele George, 'Domestic Architecture and Household Relations: Pompeii and Roman Ephesos', *Journal for the Study of the New Testament* 27: 1 (2004), pp. 13–14, 21. For a different type of material (osteological) investigation, see Ulrike Roth, 'Food, Status, and the *Peculium* of Agricultural Slaves', *Journal of Roman Archaeology* 18 (2005), pp. 278–92: slaves in rural Italy of the late Republic perhaps had dietary access to meat more commonly than typically supposed.
[24] Merchants: John Bodel, 'Towards a Study of Roman Slave-Traders', *Journal of Roman Archaeology* 18 (2005), pp. 181–95; see D.C. Braund and G.R. Tsetskhadze, 'The Export of Slaves from Colchis', *Classical Quarterly* 39 (1989), p. 117 on raiding. Distances: J.A. Straus, *L'Achat et la vente des esclaves dans l'Égypte romaine: Contribution papyrologique à l'étude de l'esclavage dans une province orientale de l'empire romain* (Munich: K.G. Saur, 2004).
[25] PSI XII 1254.
[26] Controversial: Filippo Coarelli 'L'"Agora des Italiens": Lo *statarion* di Delo?', *Journal of Roman Archaeology* 18 (2005), pp. 196–212; Paolo Braconi, 'Il "Calcidico" di Leptis Magna era un mercato di schiavi?', *Journal of Roman Archaeology* 18 (2005), pp. 213–19; Elizabeth Fentress, 'On the Block: *catastae, chalcidica* and *cryptae* in Early Imperial Italy', *Journal of Roman Archaeology* 18 (2005), pp. 220–34; Monika Trümper, *Graeco-Roman Slave Markets: Fact or Fiction?* (Oxford: Oxbow Books, 2009). Nightmare: Ausonius, *Ephem.* 8.18.

During transportation, as in other situations found in the law above, slaves were subjected to shackling, and the archaeological record is rich in examples of chains, fetters, manacles and other barbaric restraints. They cannot all be associated with enslavement; free convicted criminals might also be held in chains. But like the images of bound captives commonly found in Roman sculpture, especially triumphal monuments, they vivify the incidental references of literary texts.[27] A group of sixteen small figurines of high Imperial date from military sites in Britain and along the Rhine-Danube frontier showing prisoners chained at the neck, wrists and ankles is particularly graphic. They seem to represent the initial enslavement of prisoners intended for markets in the Roman heartland, with the captives' heavily leonine heads again implying connections in the Roman mind between slaves and wild animals.[28] The physical and psychological effects were presumably severe, comparable to the master's objectification of the slave body that underlay the collaring of recaptured runaways. At a relatively early date Lucilius (917–8W) associated a collared fugitive with a dog.[29]

Fathoming the meaning to contemporaries of such objects and of the multiplicity of representations of slaves in paintings, mosaics and statuary is a daunting enterprise. The slave child-minders from elite households visible in biographical sarcophagi raise complex questions about emotional bonds between slave and free while simultaneously displaying the status of commemorators and servile functionality. Black slaves shown as decorative elements of everyday objects – perfume-holders, a body-scraper, bronze counterweights, furniture appurtenances, an inkwell, nail-heads – express exoticism and apotropaic power. Other household utensils fashioned as slaves draw on themes of authority, subordination and deference, and representations of Cupid as a punished child offer signs of physical restraint, torture, sexual exploitation and resistance that reflect and reinforce the

---

[27] Restraints: Fredrick Hugh Thompson, 'Iron Age and Roman Slave-shackles', *Archaeological Journal* 150 (1993), pp. 57–168. Images: Keith R. Bradley, 'On Captives under the Principate', *Phoenix* 58 (2004), pp. 298–318.

[28] Figurines: R. Jackson, 'Bronze Bound Captives: Symbols of Slavery' in N. Crummy, ed., *Image, Craft and the Classical World: Essays in Honour of Donald Bailey and Catherine Johns* (Montagnac: Instrumentum Monog. 29, 2005), pp. 143–56. Animals: Keith R. Bradley, 'Resisting Slavery at Rome' in Bradley and Cartledge, eds, *The Cambridge World History of Slavery*, Vol. 1, pp. 59–78. Prisoners: Quintilian, *Inst.* 8.3.67–9; Hermogenes, *Progym.* 48 (Rabe), Oppian, *Hal.* 2.313–8, 5.553–61.

[29] Collaring: Jennifer Trimble, 'The Zoninus Collar and the Archaeology of Roman Slavery', *American Journal of Archaeology* 120 (2016), pp. 447–72.

immanence of slavery in Roman culture. So a series of acute studies finds.[30] An investigation of a late Imperial set of mosaics illustrating the schooling of an upper-class boy attended by his slave pedagogue is truly perplexing. One scene shows the man beating the bare-bottomed child, another a threat of further punishment. A parent could evidently permit the subordinate servile figure to discipline his child, and display the act in a lavish artistic medium for all to see, in a manner inverting the 'normal' exercise of authority over the slave by the free slave owner.[31] How this apparent paradox was resolved in real life is one of the difficulties of social interaction produced by a slave society. Given that variations within status groups were enormous, it is too simplistic to believe that the social status of the viewer alone determined which associations were most strongly understood in artistic representations.[32] The chief value of the evidence lies in the conditional complexities of slave life portrayed. Slaves themselves, however, of every description, saw themselves constantly depicted as inferior beings.

Voices

The items considered so far point to some of the circumstances by which the lives of slaves were constrained, with incidental notice emerging of the ways in which the mechanisms of management provoked servile responses. As indicated at the outset, however, direct testimony from slaves themselves is minimal. To Philo (*Quod omnis probus* 48), slavery was in the nature of things a state of voicelessness: a non-person by definition had nothing to say. But in reality of course speech was essential for communication, and trusted slaves trained to perform important functions could easily correspond with

---

[30]Michele George, 'Family and *familia* in Roman Biographical Sarcophagi', *Mitteilungen des Deutschen Archäologischen Instituts, Römische Abteilung* 107 (2000), pp. 191–207; Michele George, 'Images of Black Slaves in the Roman Empire', *Syllecta Classica* 14 (2003), pp. 161–85; Michele George, 'Slavery and Roman Material Culture' in Keith Bradley and Paul Cartledge, eds, *The Cambridge World History of Slavery*, Vol. 1, pp. 385–413; Michele George, 'Cupid Punished: Reflections on a Roman Genre Scene' in Michele George, ed., *Roman Slavery and Roman Material Culture* (Toronto: University of Toronto Press, 2014), pp. 158–79.
[31]Constantin A. Marinescu, Sarah E. Cox, and Rudolf Wachter, 'Paideia's Children: Childhood Education on a Group of Late Antique Mosaics' in Ada Cohen and Jeremy B. Rutter, eds, *Constructions of Childhood in Ancient Greece and Rome* (Princeton, NJ: American School of Classical Studies at Athens, 2007), pp. 101–14.
[32]John R. Clarke, *Art in the Lives of Ordinary Roman: Visual Representation and Non-Elite Viewers in Italy, 100B.C.-A.D. 315* (Berkeley: University of California Press, 2003).

their owners: Cicero's Tiro is the supreme example.[33] Questions of literacy aside, however, how safe it was to commit to writing anything that might be construed as controversial was doubtless a concern, and how common for slaves to communicate in writing among themselves is beyond knowledge. Freedom of speech was impossible without freedom, and caution was always necessary to limit provocation.[34] Declamatory exercises could be assigned to elite young pupils in which they spoke as slaves appealing against harsh sentences – a pedagogue facing crucifixion for apparently murdering his dissolute charge, a slave about to be unjustly punished at the whim of his mistress, a *meretrix*, with whom he was in love – but if the 'voices' consequently heard were sympathetic they are hardly authentic.[35] A rare document from Egypt of the high Imperial age shows a young slave barber who had recently completed his apprenticeship deferentially writing to his former master with news of employment in a new household, and in a poet's imagination a slave could make a request from his owner for burial at life's end.[36] Desperation seems to underlie a letter from classical Athens sent to his mother by an apparent slave apprentice working in a foundry: 'I have been handed over to a man thoroughly wicked; I am perishing from being whipped; I am treated like dirt – more and more!'[37]

A case has been made from a contextual examination of the comedies of Plautus that the voices of slaves were deliberately excluded from the historical record, both by representatives of the slave-owning classes who created the Roman literary tradition as it now exists, and by slaves themselves who adopted silence as a strategy of coping with the pressures slavery imposed upon them. On this view, Plautus's *Mercator* obscures the violence inherent in slavery by the sentimentality of its plot, *Persa* illustrates the strategic silence of the objectified slave to which all slaves had recourse for the sake of frustrating their owners' wishes and *Captivi* reveals the limits of servile speech and the range of responses that followed: accommodation to the master's authority under the threat of physical punishment, defiant

---

[33]Susan M. Treggiari, *Freedmen in the Roman Republic* (Oxford: Oxford University Press, 1969), pp. 261–2.
[34]Seneca, *De ira* 3.24.2; cf. Philo, *Quod omnis probus* 99; 148.
[35]Calpurnius Flaccus, *Decl.* 17, 33.
[36]P.Oxy. 3809; *Anth. Pal.* 7.162.
[37]D.R. Jordan, 'A Personal Letter Found in the Athenian Agora', *Hesperia* 69 (2000), pp. 91–103; Edward M. Harris, 'Notes on a Lead Letter from the Athenian Agora', *Harvard Studies in Classical Philology* 102 (2004), pp. 157–70; F.D. Harvey, '"Help! I'm Dying Here": A Letter from a Slave', *Zeitschrift für Papyrologie und Epigraphik* 163 (2007), pp. 49–50.

self-assertion and forms of tricksterism that allowed a human identity to emerge within the confines of servitude.[38] A conspiratorial expunging of the historical record, however, is an inherently questionable proposition, and I prefer to regard Plautus's comedies as documents opening up access to a range of active servile responses to slavery that both playwright and audience understood. Indeed, a compelling analysis attentive to the pivotal moment of Roman military engagement to which the plays belong foregrounds the horrors incessant warfare inflicted on Plautus's contemporaries – familial disruption, social and geographical dislocation, constant vulnerability to enslavement, the plight of those who became the fodder of the slave trade – and reveals how the plays represent the residue of live dramatic performances by actors themselves often slaves before audiences sensitive to the disruptions of warfare in their midst in which many slaves were present.[39] In vivid comedic mode, they critique the unavoidable products of enslavement – kidnapping, brutal chastisement, sexual exploitation – yet simultaneously give voice to slaves' hopes of recovering familial ties, repatriation, freedom and a full humanity. The 'degrading submission' involved in the sale of female flesh in *Persa*, its humorously ruseful plot aside, is one example on this view of the resistant spirit that infuses Plautine theatre.[40] Ultimately, I imagine, Roman comedy offers an ironic running commentary on the definition of freedom as the body's security from physical coercion: even the gentle Terence did not balk from specifying the differing types of instrument with which slaves were customarily beaten.[41]

A particular type of servile expression can be seen in the innumerable memorials slaves and ex-slaves erected to the dead, the manumitted far more than the enslaved. From the plaques that accompanied the cinerary urns deposited in the *columbaria* of Rome, Ostia and Puteoli, a certain autonomy has been perceived in the choice of expressions used to commemorate the deceased, and an egalitarian community spirit posited in the households

---

[38]Roberta Stewart, *Plautus and Roman Slavery* (Malden, MA and Oxford: Wiley-Blackwell, 2012), pp. 27, 46, 50–5, 79, 191.
[39]Amy Richlin, *Slave Theater in the Roman Republic: Plautus and Popular Comedy* (Cambridge: Cambridge University Press, 2018).
[40]Richlin, *Slave Theater in the Roman Republic*, pp. 256–64.
[41]Definition: Philo, *Quod omnis probus* 17. Terence: Saara Lilja, *Terms of Abuse in Roman Comedy* (Helsinki: Suomalainen Tiedeakatemia, 1965), p. 55. See Keith R. Bradley, 'Moments in the History of Roman Slavery: A Review Article', *Latomus* 75 (2016), pp. 348–9, with Cicero, *Rosc.* 46–7, and M. Leigh, *Comedy and the Rise of Rome* (Oxford: Oxford University Press, 2004), pp. 6–8.

concerned. Similarly, funerary inscriptions from the German provinces have been taken to show slaves' individuality.[42] The epitaphs and reliefs of the so-called freedmen monuments common in the Latinate West certainly attest the familial and other bonds that could be established in the servile population at large, including bonds between slaves or former slaves and their masters and patrons. The record on a stele from Ferrara of the slave child Festius who died accidentally and was remembered by a father stricken that his son did not live long enough to be set free is both touching and disturbing, and the elaborate gravestone from Mainz a patron set up to his freedman Iucundus, a *pecuarius* murdered by an anonymous slave who subsequently committed suicide, is a striking example from an outlying region of a slave owner's concern for a man who had once been his property.[43] On the other hand, many inscriptions are formulaic in content, and the commemorative moment was not a time for unconventional ideas. Funerary epigraphy moreover often reveals both the restrictions on personal liberty that remained after slaves were set free and the obligations decedent slave owners imposed on the manumitted – to maintain their burial monuments, for instance, and to conduct future religious rituals in their honour. Nor must the simple fact be forgotten that slave owners had the capacity to ban the interment of individual slaves in family tombs, just as they had the testamentary right to forbid manumission: the concept of *callida humanitas* was often in play.[44] Slaves who found the means to set up dedications, fulfil vows and convey gifts are identifiable, and their human character and capacity are well in evidence. (Their origins, however, are seldom recorded.[45]) They appear nevertheless to have exercised initiative only in conventional ways, and no signs emerge of a distinctively servile medium of self-expression or of a distinctive slave culture of the kind observable elsewhere in the global history of slavery. This is especially true of slaves' religious activities. Activity there was, and certain preferences in religious practices may have existed;

---

[42]Dorian Borbonus, *Columbarium Tombs and Collective Identity in Augustan Rome* (New York: Cambridge University Press, 2014); Bassir Amiri, *Esclaves et affranchis des Germanies: Mémoire en fragments. Étude des inscriptions monumentales* (Stuttgart: Franz Steiner Verlag, 2016), pp. 43, 45.
[43]*CIL* V 2417; XIII 7070.
[44]*CIL* VI 8857, 13732; Egidio Incelli, 'Le Rapport maître-esclave et les modalités de manumission dans l'empire romain' in Monique Dondin-Payre and Nicolas Tran, eds, *Esclaves et maîtres dans le monde romain: Expressions épigraphiques de leurs relations* (Rome: École Française de Rome, 2017), p. 38.
[45]H. Solin, 'Zur Herkunft der römischen Sklaven (Zugleich eine Ergänzung von M. Bang, *Die Herkunft der römischen Sklaven* 1910)' in Heinz Heinen and Johannes Deissler, eds, *Menschenraub, Menschenhandel und Sklaverei in antiker und moderner Perspektive* (Stuttgart: Franz Steiner Verlag, 2008), pp. 99–130.

but there is nothing that can be called exclusively servile.[46] As with other aspects of their history, this must be attributed to slaves' internalization of the cultural norms prevalent in Roman society at large, the ultimate proof of which lies in the regularity with which former slaves themselves became slave owners as their circumstances improved over time.[47]

Funerary evidence illustrates above all therefore the manner in which those slaves and ex-slaves implicated in acts of commemoration chose to adopt the norms of established society and to accommodate themselves to the *status quo*, often with proud reference to the crafts and trades by which they had achieved assimilationist success, or in the case of women in gender-specific terms.[48] Not that those who were set free should be thought typical of the Roman slave population as a whole. Since funerary inscriptions show that countless numbers of slaves were manumitted over time, Roman slavery can sometimes be conceptualized as a process in which a gradual transition from enslavement to freedom and full citizenship was virtually guaranteed.[49] I am disinclined to accept this idea, and wonder what the followers of Eunus, Athenion, Spartacus and other leaders of revolt might have thought of it. Manumission records show how some slaves worked within the boundaries of servitude for the sake of personal advantage or were rewarded for the dutiful performance of their functions. It is impossible, however, to assess in comparable detail cases where manumission never occurred, which means that there is no justification for designating Roman slavery an 'open' system in contrast to other 'closed' systems in the universal history of slavery. Account has also to be taken of the category of Junian Latins, a surely significant constituency.[50]

---

[46]John A. North, 'The Ritual Activity of Roman Slaves' in Stephen Hodkinson and Dick Geary, eds, *Slaves and Religions in Graeco-Roman Antiquity and Modern Brazil* (Newcastle: Cambridge Scholars Publishing, 2012), pp. 67–91.
[47]R. Duthoy, 'La Fonctionalité sociale de l'Augustalité', *Epigraphica* 36 (1974), pp. 134–54.
[48]Michele George, 'Social Identity and the Dignity of Work in Freedmen's Reliefs' in Eve D'Ambra and Guy P.R. Métraux, eds, *The Art of Citizens, Soldiers and Freedmen in the Roman World* (Oxford: Archaeopress, 2006), pp. 19–29; Leslie Shumka, 'Inscribing Agency: The *Mundus Muliebris* Commemorations of Roman Italy', *Phoenix* 70 (2016), pp. 77–103.
[49]John Bodel, 'Death and Social Death in Ancient Rome' in Bodel and Scheidel, eds, *On Human Bondage*, pp. 81–108; cf. Joseph C. Miller, *The Problem of Slavery as History: A Global Approach* (New Haven, CT: Yale University Press, 2012).
[50]Paul Weaver, 'Where Have All the Junian Latins Gone? Nomenclature and Status in the Early Empire', *Chiron* 20 (1990), pp. 275–304; Paul Weaver, 'Children of Junian Latins' in Beryl Rawson and Paul Weaver, eds, *The Roman Family in Italy: Status, Sentiment, Space* (Canberra and Oxford: Oxford University Press, 1997), pp. 55–72.

The writings of two men who were once slaves themselves are of special interest. First Publilius Syrus, a composer in the age of Cicero of the popular theatrical entertainments called mimes. Some 700 lines remain from his work, self-standing maxims that were extracted from his plays and that became a repository of proverbial wisdom suitable for instructing pupils in Roman schools due to their moralistic import. The maxims embody a conventional Roman moral code that a figure who began his life as an enslaved Syrian, a total outsider, fully absorbed as he grew to maturity and became in time an insider who accepted the values of the society into which he had been forcibly translated, with the premium placed on freedom taken as fundamental and the cleavage between freedom and slavery strongly felt. The platitude (*Sent.* 413) that to live under another person's control is the depth of misery no doubt expressed a sentiment with which many slaves identified, and possibly it had a special resonance for Publilius himself.[51] But it was not a call to arms, and overall his maxims exhibit no deeply personal signs of a slave's experience of slavery. Publilius takes slave-owning for granted, acknowledges the master's implicit greater human worth and the absence of fear the slave should ideally display to his owner, and assumes the master's expectation of complete servile loyalty (*Sent.* 363, 534). The *Sententiae* authenticate therefore that genuine process of servile assimilation to which I have earlier alluded. For those born into slavery or enslaved as children, the process began as soon as they learned to perform simple tasks and interacted with free members of their households, absorbing the habits of enslavement just as their free counterparts absorbed the habits of mastery.[52]

Secondly, the *Discourses* of the Stoic philosopher Epictetus. Born a slave in Phrygian Hierapolis, Epictetus at some point fell into the possession of the imperial freedman Epaphroditus but was allowed under the Flavians to study at Rome with the philosopher Musonius Rufus and was eventually set free. He subsequently established a school at Nicopolis in Epirus where he

---

[51] Orlando Patterson, *Slavery and Social Death: A Comparative Study* (Cambridge, MA: Harvard University Press, 1982), p. 77. On the leaders of slave revolts, see Keith Bradley, *Slavery and Rebellion in the Roman World, 140 BC–70 BC* (Bloomington, IN: Indiana University Press, 1989)

[52] Christian Laes, 'Child Slaves at Work in Roman Antiquity', *Ancient Society* 38 (2008), pp. 235–83; E. Herrmann-Otto, 'Kindsein im römischen Reich' in H. Heinen, ed., *Kindersklaven-Sklavenkinder: Schicksale zwischen Zuneigung und Ausbeutung in der Antike und im interkulturellen Vergleich* (Stuttgart: Franz Steiner Verlag, 2012), pp. 171–201; cf. Keith R. Bradley, *Apuleius and Antonine Rome: Historical Essays* (Toronto: University of Toronto Press, 2012), pp. 181–204.

taught eminent pupils.[53] The period of his enslavement cannot be precisely determined but is likely to have covered at least the formative years of his childhood and early adulthood. The subject of freedom and slavery dominates his work.[54] Incidental details vividly illustrate the ordinary buying and selling of slave merchandise, the subjection of slaves to physical coercion, the temporary release offered by the Saturnalia, the formalities of manumission before a Roman magistrate.[55] More interestingly, however, insight is sometimes detectable into slave psychology as the details are introduced. Every slave wishes to be free, Epictetus says, but the material demands of independence once manumission has taken place sometimes lead to regret for the forfeited security of the slave household, in which food and shelter had been provided as a matter of course (4.1.33–37). Through deliberate disobedience slaves might annoy their masters, but wilfulness runs the risk of punishment, and a beating is a sharp reminder of errors of judgement (2.20.29–31). Slaves may decide to abscond, a seemingly commonplace activity, but if so they have to draw on reserves of opportunistic self-reliance for survival, unable ever to be confident of not suddenly being recognized and re-enslaved (1.9.7–8; 1.29.59–63; 3.26.1–2). A certain sympathy emerges from the way Epictetus reflects on slaves' capacity to act independently and on the consequences of their actions, attributable perhaps to personal knowledge and his own experience: it was believed that the lameness from which he came to suffer was due to maltreatment while still in slavery. Such sympathy, however, is very limited. His interest in freedom and slavery has far less to do with the real-life conditions of the world around him than with the inner world of the individual and the individual's attainment of spiritual contentment.[56] The burdens of slavery therefore are of no concern to him. He adopted the familiar Stoic position that in principle all human beings are of equal worth (1.13), but his insistence on the achievement of personal contentment and the irrelevance to this end of external circumstances prevented application of the idea to any practical ameliorative purpose. If anything, Epictetus's counsel to slaves was a counsel of accommodation: strength of character is the means by which to endure victimization, and

---

[53] A.A. Long, *Epictetus: A Stoic and Socratic Guide to Life* (Oxford: Oxford University Press, 2002), pp. 10–11; Fergus Millar, 'Epictetus and the Imperial Court' in Fergus Millar, eds, *Rome, The Greek World, and the East, Vol. 2: Government, Society, and Culture in the Roman Empire* (Chapel Hill: The University of North Carolina Press, 2004), pp. 105–19.
[54] Jackson P. Herschbell, 'Epictetus: A Freedman on Slavery', *Ancient Society* 26 (1995), pp. 185–204.
[55] 1.19.19–21; 2.12.17–25; 2.21.11; 3.25.9–10; 1.25.8; 4.1.58; 2.1.25–26.
[56] Long, *Epictetus*, p. 1.

physical injury is not harmful if nobly borne (4.1.127).[57] Slaves, moreover, are far less useful than citizens and magistrates, so that deviation from their place in the chain of utility is discountenanced (2.23–24). Epictetus appreciated that direct action, by escape or suicide, was an instinctual response to any form of captivity (4.1.24–27). But human enslavement was due to providence and providence was to be accepted as no more than a state of mind without demur (4.104–106).[58]

Whatever Epictetus had endured in slavery does not become, then, a subject for an elaborately intimate history or a record of what the transition from slavery to freedom meant to the manumitted slave. His career typifies the reality that the Roman slave could sometimes acquire an education, prosper and come to have widespread influence, but his words are not the work of a radical activist. They betray at times indeed a sense of social myopia, as in the proposition that senatorial status brought with it a special form of slavery (4.1.40).[59]

The degree to which the Stoic gospel of providential compliance affected the Roman slave population as a whole cannot be measured. Presumably, however, it was not the preserve of an intellectual elite alone.[60] Trimalchio's much garbled enunciation of the doctrine of the brotherhood of mankind is sufficient indication that a man of his station could be expected to have picked up a smattering of Stoicism, and an analogy is offered by the Platonist Celsus's later evidence on the widespread familiarity of Christian stories and teachings, in refuting which he notably referred to the cause of Epictetus's lameness.[61] Consequently, the effect among slaves of learning that their condition was of no significance in the pursuit of individual contentment, and that all that mattered was submission to the status to which the divine will had assigned them, was to discourage all prospect of concerted agitation against the slavery system, and even of individual opposition to the slave owner's power. Stoicism was by definition a barrier to social change, and ironically it is in this that the value of Epictetus's 'voice' lies. What his teaching meant in everyday life for the men and women compelled to suffer the consequences of irrational outbursts of anger from their owners – as the

---

[57] P.A. Brunt, *Studies in Stoicism* (Oxford: Oxford University Press, 2013), p. 336.
[58] Herschbell, 'Epictetus', p. 201, with reference to *Ench.* 14.
[59] G.E.M. de Ste Croix, *The Class Struggle in the Ancient Greek World from the Archaic Age to the Arab Conquests* (London: Duckworth, 1981), p. 423.
[60] *Contra*: Brunt, *Studies in Stoicism*, p. 336.
[61] Petronius, *Sat.* 71.1; Origen, *C.Cels.* 3.55; 3.59; 7.53 (Epictetus); cf. Bradley, *Apuleius and Antonine Rome*, pp. 216–17.

Epicurean Philodemus (*De ira* 5) had listed them, beating, kicking, blinding, even murder – it is difficult to say. Many might be imagined to have followed its dictates with a certain resignation. Congruent with the directives of Bryson and his predecessors, Stoic doctrine encouraged its adherents to uphold, not to challenge, the established social order.[62]

Complexity compounded

Documents of early Imperial date from Puteoli, Pompeii and Herculaneum show slaves and ex-slaves in family businesses engaged in commercial activities of many kinds that required education and training in finance, and, as far as their owners and patrons were concerned, reliability and trustworthiness. The opportunities servile functionaries were permitted for independent financial decision-making and the display of initiative were considerable; and in carrying out their responsibilities a freedom of movement was enjoyed in high contrast to the rigid prescriptions of control embodied in the management tradition.[63] Ex-slaves may in fact have dominated family businesses, but slaves can also be seen closely involved in making and recovering loans, arranging securities, writing leases and witnessing commercial exchanges, transactions that were founded on the quintessential Roman virtue of mutual trustworthiness (*fides*) that bound unequals together.[64] Simultaneously, however, slaves other than family agents notably appear as loan securities, seemingly without distress to the agents themselves, and ex-slaves, manumitted I imagine by their former owners in return for loyal service, in turn become slave owners in their own right.[65] Likewise, servile agents were aware as they carried out their

---

[62] de Ste Croix, *The Class Struggle in the Ancient Greek World*, p. 142; cf. C.E. Manning, 'Stoicism and Slavery in the Roman Empire', *Aufstieg und Niedergang der römischen Welt* II 36.3: 1518–43.

[63] In the Augustan era the slave Lysas, owned by P. Annius Plocamus of Puteoli, is attested in Egypt's eastern desert on the road to Berenice: David Meredith, 'Annius Plocamus: Two Inscriptions from the Berenice Road', *Journal of Roman Studies* 43 (1953), pp. 38–40.

[64] Ex-slaves: Henrik Mouritsen, *The Freedman in the Roman World* (Cambridge: Cambridge University Press, 2011), pp. 206–47. Slaves: for example, TP Sulp. 45, 46, 78, 79. *Fides*: Arnaldo D. Momigliano, *On Pagans, Jews, and Christians* (Middletown, CT: Wesleyan University Press, 1987), p. 78 (see Publilius, *Sent.* 596: 'The skilled slave holds part of his master's power').

[65] TP Sulp. 49; 85–7. TP Sulp. 48 Jean Andreau, *Les Affaires de Monsieur Jucundus* (Rome: École Française de Rome, 1974), p. 206.

assignments that sales of slaves by auction on the open market, sometimes due to loan forfeitures in agreements they themselves had arranged, were routine matters of everyday business, the altogether mundane aspect of which is perceptible in wax writing-tablets from the Agro Murecine recording the activities of the Sulpicii, a group of early Imperial bankers at Puteoli, and comparable material from the archive at Pompeii of the banker L. Caecilius Iucundus.[66] Sale was so common and so risk-laden that it produced a handbook from the medical writer Rufus of Ephesus to guide the purchaser through the transaction: avoid a hasty decision, beware of fraudulent dealers, inspect the merchandise thoroughly, investigate its history. Every part of the slave's body was to be checked for integrity before the exchange was completed.[67]

In anomalous circumstances such as these, to penetrate servile mentality becomes hopelessly frustrating. Awareness of personal subjection, identification with the profit-seeking interests of the family firm through assimilative education and training, appreciation through association with manumitted co-workers of prospects of personal advancement and upward mobility in both status and wealth, constant awareness of the commodified nature of slave property on the auction block – such jarring and confusing features illustrate the many facets of social relations to which Roman slavery could give rise, and in which many disparate and incongruous features were understood as entirely compatible with one another. At Ephesus, publicly owned slaves are attested as purchasers of slave infants.[68] Altogether, however, the benefits servile financial agents enjoyed in their lives might well be thought to have encouraged the accommodationist attitude towards the social *status quo* observable in other contexts: there was little incentive to challenge a system in which personal rewards and eventual freedom could be realistically anticipated. The lives of these slaves were vastly different from those of their rural counterparts who were kept in chain gangs and housed

---

[66] TP Sulp. 42–4, 77, 85–7, 90–3 with D.F. Jones, *The Bankers of Puteoli: Finance, Trade and Industry in the Roman World* (Stroud, Gloucs: Tempus, 2006), pp. 137–8; Andreau, *Les Affaires de Monsieur Jucundus*, p. 104 (nos. 20, 45, 49, 62, 74); Gregory Rowe, 'Trimalchio's World', *Scripta Classica Israelica* 20 (2001), pp. 225–45. See additionally Jean-Jacques Aubert, *Business Managers in Ancient Rome: A Social and Economic Study of Institores, 200 B.C.–A.D. 250* (Leiden: Brill, 1994); Richard Gamauf, 'Slaves Doing Business: The Role of Roman Law in the Economy of a Roman Household', *European Review of History* 16 (2009), pp. 331–46.
[67] Swain, *Economy, Family, and Society from Rome to Islam*, pp. 270–9; cf. Ammianus Marcellinus 29.4.4 (*merces*); Symmachus, *Ep.* 2.78.2 (*sanitas*); Plut. *Mor.* 209C (soft white bodies a disadvantage on the block).
[68] Shaner, *Enslaved Leadership in Early Christianity*, pp. 13–14, 37.

in *ergastula*, in no way comparable to the 'barbaric' German captives whose blonde hair provided a steady supply of fancy wigs for fashionable Roman matrons.[69]

A sharp contrast, however, emerges from other documents preserved on papyrus from Roman Egypt – private letters, records of local court proceedings, wills and receipts for the exchange of goods – that like the Italian commercial documents expose the lived reality of antiquity directly. The servile element of the population of Roman Egypt was relatively small, and most slaves were engaged in domestic occupations rather than agriculture. Proximity to slave owners for the majority is an obvious inference. Among this population, however, acts of intransigence are well attested: slaves ran away, stole from their owners, assaulted them verbally and physically, caused damage to property, and refused to carry out their obligations.[70] The frequency and incidence of such events are (again) immeasurable, but the record is voluminous enough to render comprehensible the urgency of the prescriptions, in any context or location, of slave owners such as Bryson. None of the intransigent acts is unique to the slave population; free persons committed crimes as well. Motivations will have differed, however, given that slaves were liable at all times to forms of treatment – confinement, beating, burning, torture, sexual abuse – considered inappropriate for persons of free status.[71] Many slaves in the mostly small Egyptian households lived in quasi-familial settings with their owners and may have felt themselves integrated to some degree into domestic communities. But the record of criminous behaviour cannot be underestimated, and the 'crimes' of slaves are best understood as acts of slave resistance. Naturally enough, the documentary papyri obscure this connection. But the types of act they attest are precisely those, as I have insisted in the past, that the agronomists and others, with much complaint, identified as the forms of servile recalcitrance against which slave owners had constantly to guard.[72]

---

[69]Ovid, *Amores* 1.14.45–50. *Ergastula*: J. Molina Vidal, J.I. Grau Mira, F. Llidó, J.F. Álvarez Tortosa, 'Housing Slaves on Estates: A Proposed *ergastulum* at the Villa of Rufio (Giano dell'Umbria)', *Journal of Roman Archaeology* 30 (2017), pp. 402–6.

[70]J.-A. Straus, 'Esclaves malfaiteurs dans l'Égypte romaine' in Gaelle Tallet and Christiane Zivie-Coche, eds, *Le Myrte et la rose: Mélanges offerts à Françoise Dunand par ses élèves, collègues et amis* (Montpellier: Cahiers de l'ENiM, 2014), pp. 23–31.

[71]J.-A. Straus, 'Esclaves maltraités ou punis dans l'Égypte romaine', *Chronique d'Égypte* 90 (2015), pp. 134–46.

[72]Bradley, 'Resisting Slavery at Rome', with earlier references.

Here I stress the apparently endemic problem of flight, which emerges, again in legal evidence, as an item of special concern in the aedilician edict regulating the sale of slaves. The law required the vendor to declare at the time of sale whether the slave being sold had a history of absconding. If he stated that the slave was not a fugitive and was later shown to have made a false statement, the sale could be rescinded and the purchaser appropriately compensated.[73] In the jurists' discussions of the circumstances in which flight might occur, the key feature for present purposes is the emphasis placed on servile intent. In the first instance, the jurists defined absconding as a defect of the mind, not a physical defect, recognizing the slave's human capacity to act purposively to conceal himself from his master. It made no difference if a slave changed his mind after escaping and returned to the household; what mattered was acting with intent, and remorse – a human emotion – was of no consequence.[74] In some circumstances, running away was justifiable: self-preservation from dangers posed by an enemy, a brigand, a fire, the collapse of a building, an abusive instructor or temporary manager, or from cruel treatment: as long as the slave returned afterwards, he was not considered a fugitive. It was not flight itself but the motive that was all-important. Consequently a slave who hid in the household awaiting an opportunity to escape, but who had not actually run away, was to be considered a fugitive unless he were waiting for an angry master's temper to subside. Likewise with a slave who ran away to seek the intervention of a friend when his master was about to beat him, or who intended to commit suicide or was simply absent overnight, or who ran away to seek his mother's help in importuning his master against some apparent misdeed, or who as a *vicarius* accompanied a fleeing slave: was he aware of what was happening and did he actually intend to escape? A farm slave who ran away but was apprehended before he had fully left the estate was deemed a fugitive because he had meant to escape; yet a slave who ran away to seek asylum before a statue of the emperor but who did not intend to escape was not.[75] The jurists evidently understood the real-life circumstances that controlled slave behaviour – incidents of slaves committing suicide by drowning in the Tiber cannot be figments – and in their scrupulous attention to detail they made every effort to enter the thought processes of the slaves affected by those

---

[73] *Dig.* 21.1.1.
[74] *Dig.* 21.1.4.3; 21.1.17.pr. *Dig.* 21.1.17.1–2.
[75] *Dig.* 21.1.17.3. *Dig.* 21.1.17.4; 21.1.17.5; 21.1.17.7. *Dig.* 21.1.17.8; 21.1.17.12; cf. 21.1.43.1–3.

circumstances.[76] Their insistence on ascertaining the motives that actuated servile behaviour is crucial for historical purposes: to have some indication of what was in slaves' minds when they took action as they did is to approach an understanding of slavery 'from below'.

The historical record at large has an obsessive interest in fugitive slaves and commonly presents them in jaundiced terms. Every incident of flight, however, must be seen in the light of the legal evidence as due to a deliberate decision made by a slave in response to the conditions of subjection by which the slave was bound; and from the jurists' statement that to have run away was to have acquired a form of freedom,[77] the desire to become free must in many cases be acknowledged as an especially powerful motivating force. It was an advantage that slaves were not always easily distinguishable from free persons – although fugitives might be purchased *in absentia* by a new owner determined to track them down – and it is no surprise that enormous resources were deployed for their recovery.[78] In turn, all the forms of misbehaviour with which slaves are associated have to be regarded as similar responses. Thefts, destruction of property by arson, murderous revolt against the owner and his family – these are all listed to sobering effect by Philodemus (*De ira* 5) as the consequences of the slave owner's resort to brutality and abuse when unable to control his anger. (Little wonder that Philodemus thought the runaway slave fortunate.) Wilful acts of defiance, ranging from major revolt through petty sabotage of property and deliberate dissembling to sexual manipulation, were permanent features of the Roman slavery system; and

---

[76]*Dig.* 21.1.17.6. *Dig.* 21.1.17.4–7; cf. Philo, *De fuga* 3: fear as a motive for flight. See in full Yann Rivière, 'Recherche et identification des esclaves fugitifs dans l'Empire romain' in Jean Andreau and Catherine Virlouvet, eds, *L'Information et la mer dans le monde antique* (Rome: École Française de Rome, 2002), pp. 115–96; Georg Klingenberg, *Corpus der römischen Rechtsquellen zur antiken Sklaverei.* Teil X. *Juristisch speziell definierte Sklavengruppen*, 6: *Servus Fugitivus* (Stuttgart: Franz Steiner Verlag, 2015).

[77]*Dig.* 21.1.17.10.

[78]Distinguishable: *CIL* IX 2438 with Mirelle Corbier, '*Fiscus* and *Patrimonium*: the Saepinum Inscription and Transhumance in the Abruzzi', *Journal of Roman Studies* 73 (1983), pp. 126–31; Michele George, 'Slave Disguise in Ancient Rome', *Slavery and Abolition* 23 (2002), pp. 41–54; Serena Connolly, '*Quasi libera quasi ancilla*: Diogenia and the Everyday Experience of Slaves', *American Journal of Ancient History* 3–4 (2004–2005), pp. 171–88. Determined: P.Oxy. 5166. Resources: Christopher J. Fuhrmann, *Policing the Roman Empire: Soldiers, Administration, and Public Order* (New York: Oxford University Press, 2012), pp. 34–5; cf. Stephen Llewelyn, 'P. Harris I 62 and the Pursuit of Fugitive Slaves', *Zeitschrift für Papyrologie und Epigraphik* 118 (1997), pp. 245–50.

this remained true in the late Imperial age despite the oppressive message of resignation to their plight, fully consistent with earlier Stoic doctrine, delivered to slaves by Christian clerics such as John Chrysostom.[79]

Confirmation of this perspective 'from below' comes from a sequence of dreams recorded and explained by the dream-interpreter Artemidorus. In one example (1.45; 5.91), a slave dreamed that he had three sets of genitals. The outcome was that the slave was set free and acquired three names in place of the single name by which he had previously been known; the first two names were those of the man who had manumitted him. The dream self-evidently refers to a slave who was manumitted according to Roman conventions, the man adding the *praenomen* and *nomen* of his former master to the original slave name that he retained as a *cognomen*. Artemidorus does not say when or where the manumission took place, but he reports the dream with assurance. In a second example (4.24), a slave with the common slave name of Syrus dreamed that his feet had no soles. He was subsequently burned alive. This was a dream Artemidorus found in his reading, but as with the first example it presumes that a slave had once made his experience known and it evidently achieved some notoriety. In another example (2.15), a slave dreamed that he struck some frogs with his fist, the outcome being that he became his master's steward: the frogs signified the ordinary household slaves and the striking of the fist stood for the issuing of orders from an overseer. In an exceptionally sensationalistic case (4.61), a slave dreamed that his master prostituted his wife to him: no ill-will arose between the men, as would have happened had the dream involved the slave's seduction of the woman and her consequent commission of adultery; instead the master placed all his property in the slave's trust and made him his steward in charge of his entire household. Equally striking is a dream (1.78) in which a slave masturbated his master, to a favourable result: the slave became the pedagogue and caretaker of his owner's children, symbolized in the dream by the man's genitalia which the slave held in his hands. In contrast, a slave so treated in a dream

---

[79]Bradley, 'Resisting Slavery at Rome'; cf. Joao J. Reis, 'Slavery in Nineteenth-Century Brazil' in David Eltis, Stanley L. Engerman, Seymour Drescher, and David Richardson, eds, *The Cambridge World History of Slavery*, Vol. 4: *AD 1804–AD 2016* (Cambridge: Cambridge University Press, 2017), pp. 146–53; Robert L. Paquette, 'Slave Resistance' in Eltis, Engerman, Drescher, and Richardson, eds, *The Cambridge World History of Slavery*, Vol. 4, pp. 272–95. Chrysostom: Chris L. de Wet, *Preaching Bondage: John Chrysostom and the Discourse of Slavery in Early Christianity* (Berkeley: University of California Press, 2015). On Philodemus see Voula Tsouna, *The Ethics of Philodemus* (Oxford: Oxford University Press, 2007), pp. 214–15.

by his owner was subsequently punished with a flogging. A further instance (4.64) concerns a slave who dreamed that he was murdered by his master, and a second slave who dreamed that a fellow-slave murdered him. The first slave was manumitted, but not the second. The logic of the dream was that death signified freedom, and that the master had the power of life and death over a slave that the fellow-slave did not. One was set free therefore but not the other. What dreams of being murdered might reveal about the dreamers' states of mind I do not know – a reasonable guess is that slaves often lived in a climate of fear, and fear, indeed, despite Publilius, was said to be the mark of the slave[80] – but the underlying assumption of the slave owner's absolute authority is obvious. In another case (4.69), a slave dreamed that he was playing a game of ball with Zeus. It meant in view of the game's competitive nature that the slave was treating his master, symbolized by the god, on an equal and therefore inappropriate footing: he was too outspoken. The result was that the slave quarrelled with his master and incurred his displeasure, the game involving a contentious breach of the deference the master expected from his slave. Another example (4.81) tells of another Syrus to show that dreams of serving funerary meals were inauspicious – Syrus's owner died after being given such a meal – and a final record (5.85) tells of a slave who dreamed that he was given a boiled egg by his mistress, which he ate after throwing away its shell. The result was that the mistress, who was pregnant, died after giving birth. On orders from her husband the slave then took charge of the infant and reared the child. The rationale was that the worthless shell, the wife's body, was discarded while the inner egg, the child, provided the slave with a means of sustenance.

This catalogue may be taken to indicate the concerns of slaves in their everyday relationships with their owners and the kinds of questions they might at times put to oracles. Would they be set free? Would they come to terms with their owners? Should they fear being sold?[81] The dreams all appear to be genuine, and the meanings given to them are not hypothetical. Artemidorus knew what had happened to the slaves concerned and his record permits something of authentic servile experience to be communicated. As always his evidence is indirect. But his interpretations come from a manual composed for and about a world in which a certain proportion of the population was bound together by its collective unfreedom, and because his interpretative logic was conditioned by the socio-cultural realities of

---

[80] Diogenes Laertius 6.75; Lactantius, *Div. Inst.* 4.4.2.
[81] *Sortes Astrampyschi* 3, 46, 74.

that world, his evidence must be taken as plausible. It is hardly in doubt that his book was comprehensible to contemporary readers. Artemidorus's interpretations were dictated by the contingencies of slavery as an institution and the responses slaves made to them. The anxieties they embody suggest as characteristic of servile mentality at large an inordinate degree of desperation.[82]

Resolution

To the extent that it can be recovered and understood at all, the Roman experience of slavery is full of contradictions and anomalies, and Housman's phrase, 'the mental habits of the slave', is far too reductionist to cover every aspect of the experiences that emerge from the evidence available, its many prejudices and shortcomings notwithstanding. Conformity to and compliance with the norms of established society were expected from slaves *tout court*, and in innumerable instances, especially when opportunities for education and advancement were in prospect, manumission, enrichment and sometimes even political power were the rewards of what must be regarded as often a servile strategy of acquiescence to authority. On the other hand, the power exercised by slave owners could exceed levels of acceptability and arouse reactions clandestine, dangerous and violent. Mutual fears and suspicions could never have been far absent.[83] The unpredictability of the slave owner's authority might induce distress in the domestic steward awaiting from his master a reckoning of his accounts; but the slave owner could never discount the possibility that a Diogenes would not simply lie down on the auction block and ridicule the auctioneer, that a resentful Politoria would not solicit from a practitioner of magic a harmful *defixio*, or that the rebel leader Athenion would not appear again.[84] The parameters of power were variable and fluid, the relationship between master and slave a matter of constant negotiation. What seems incontrovertible is that despite

---

[82]Keith R. Bradley, 'Artemidorus and the Dreams of Slaves', *Classica et Mediaevalia* 66 (2015), pp. 191–219.
[83]Anastasia Serghidou, ed., *Fear of Slaves – Fear of Enslavement in the Ancient Mediterranean* (Besançon: Presses Universitaires de Franche-Comté, 2007).
[84]Galen, *De praecog.* 6.11–13. Plutarch, *Mor.* 466E; cf. Diogenes Laertius 6.29. Anton Alvar Nuño, 'Le Malheur de Politoria: Sur la malédiction d'une esclave contre sa matrone' in Dondin-Payre and Tran, eds, *Esclaves et maîtres dans le monde romain*, pp. 113–27. Appian, *Mithr.* 59.

the absence of significantly direct testimony from slaves, Roman slave owners were fully conscious of the human nature of their human property and of the need to accommodate, by one means or another, the property's human emotions if their own privileged positions were to be successfully maintained and their desires adequately met. Equally, whatever individual or sometimes sporadically collective acts of opposition to slavery manifested themselves, even the most intellectually accomplished slaves, as the example of Epictetus above all illustrates, did not attempt to promulgate a reformist agenda in opposition to traditional social norms. The philosophical notion that slavery was contrary to nature never came to carry sufficient weight to produce radical social change, one explanation for which might lie in the fact that the master-slave relationship was only one, if the most extreme, in a series of unchangingly patriarchal and hierarchical relationships by which Roman society was organized, in all of which power and authority were disproportionately structured. No ideological movement strong enough to shake the foundations of society can be seen to have arisen. From the vantage point of the slave, held above all in the violent, shameful, subject condition of what the Sibylline tradition called 'the yoke of slavery', the chief preoccupation, I imagine, was often if not always that of how to survive in a society which set no store in the worth of the individual human being, and in which human equality existed only in mythical memory and aspirational fantasy.[85] The great variability of the decisions slaves had to make is perhaps best proven by the contrasting acts of loyalty and disloyalty, with factors of revenge strongly perceptible, in the civil wars of the Late Republic.[86]

Whatever rationalizations of this sort might be advanced, however, stumbling blocks obtrude. I find it difficult to understand the sentiments of slaves like the Urbanus from Aquileia and the Barnaeus and Salama from Capua, as they carried out their duties in the service of owners who collected the Roman tax on manumission.[87] Could cordiality ever have prevailed in the circumstances their labour involved? Slavery remains in my view the most problematical aspect of Roman social history about which to generalize, in view of the huge variety of circumstances contained in the historical record – including the strange phenomenon of voluntary slavery[88]

---

[85]Yoke: *Orac. Sib.* 3.508–10; 3.537; 3.567; 4.102–4; 8.123–5.
[86]Valerius Maximus 6.8; Appian, *BC* 1.73; 4.22, 29, 39, 49, 51.
[87]*CIL* V 36; X 3875.
[88]Richard Duncan-Jones, *Power and Privilege in Roman Society* (Cambridge: Cambridge University Press, 2016), pp. 142–53.

– that reflect the limitless vagaries and complexities of human behaviour that a slave society produces. Almost anything was possible. Lenaeus, a freedman of the great Cn. Pompeius, was said by Suetonius (*Gramm.* 15.3) to have cast off his chains and escaped to his homeland while a boy still in slavery, and after receiving an education to have returned with the price of his freedom, but to have been manumitted *gratis* because of his learning. The incident has been dismissed as romantic fiction.[89] But how can the truth be known? Even more bizarre is an incident reported by Tertullian (*Nat.* 1.16.14–19). A boy of elite Roman status kidnapped and sold into slavery was later purchased by his unwitting father and, as a slave, sexually exploited by both parents, who only came to know their son's true identity through the nurse and pedagogue who had once cared for him. They subsequently killed themselves. The boy, as a sentient being, can hardly have failed when on the auction block, like every slave in the same predicament, to comprehend his reduction to a state of complete objectification; and Tertullian, always indignant, can in this instance for once be forgiven for his raillery against Roman conventionality. In the last analysis, slavery casts an indelible shadow over the long duration of Rome's history and its peoples' achievements. It unsettles and disturbs. Aeneas, I observe, did not encounter slave owners in Tartarus. To understand the experiences of the millions of its victims from within strains the capacity of the historian almost to breaking point – and it is the imagination of a poet that is of final avail:

> A bondsman and a slave, a stranger to pleasure,
> bent at the same trade for forty years
> over his bench, he lines up the new
> coins that the people of Nicaea issue.
> He'll hold up one, another he'll measure;
> and attentively, his eyes fogged by old age,
> he examines them to make sure the inscription is true.
> If he makes another mistake, they said, he'll be tortured,
> and his hands are trembling.
> 'With Severus as king the world enjoys good fortune.'[90]

---

[89]Robert A. Kaster, *C. Suetonius Tranquillus:* De Grammaticis et Rhetoribus [Edited with a Text, Translation, and Commentary] (Oxford: Oxford University Press, 1995), pp. 181–2.
[90]C.P. Cavafy, '[Bondsman and Slave]' in C.P. Cavafy, *Collected Poems* [Translated with Introduction and Commentary by D. Mendelsohn] (New York: Knopf, 2009), p. 112.

Bibliography

Bradley, Keith R., *Slavery and Society at Rome* (Cambridge: Cambridge University Press, 1994).

Bradley, Keith R. and Paul A.C. Cartledge, eds, *The Cambridge World History of Slavery*, Vol. 1: *The Ancient Mediterranean World* (Cambridge: Cambridge University Press, 2011).

Finley, Moses I., *Ancient Slavery and Modern Ideology* [expanded edition, ed. Brent D. Shaw] (Princeton, NJ: Markus Wiener Publishers, 1998, orig. pub. in 1968).

Fitzgerald, William, *Slavery and the Roman Literary Imagination* (Cambridge: Cambridge University Press, 2000).

Garnsey, Peter, *Ideas of Slavery from Aristotle to Augustine* (Cambridge: Cambridge University Press, 1996).

Harper, Kyle, *Slavery in the Late Roman World, AD 275–425* (Cambridge: Cambridge University Press, 2011).

Hopkins, Keith, *Conquerors and Slaves, Sociological Studies in Roman History*, Vol. 1 (Cambridge: Cambridge University Press, 1978).

Joshel, Sandra and Lauren Hackworth Petersen, *The Material Life of Roman Slaves* (New York: Cambridge University Press, 2014).

Mouritsen, Henrik, *The Freedman in the Roman World* (New York: Cambridge University Press, 2011).

Schiavone, Aldo, *Spartacus* (Cambridge, MA: Harvard University Press, 2013).

15

Quantitative histories of slavery

Andrea Livesey
Liverpool John Moores University

In the preface to the *Evidence and Methods* volume to *Without Consent or Contract*, Historian Robert William Fogel wrote that by revealing his methodology, he hoped to 'expose the limits' of his own study.[1] Bizarre as such an opening admission might seem, this statement was unmistakably shaped by criticisms received after the 1974 publication of the most controversial quantitative study of slavery, *Time on the Cross*. Fogel's statement, however, heeds an important warning for any historian, quantitative or other: every study is shaped by its limits, and the ability to recognize the limits of our evidence, methodology and conclusions is a crucial skill within the historian's toolkit. This is especially important for historians of slavery, for whom our subject matter constantly urges us to reconsider the limits of our own evidence and methodology.[2]

Quantitative methodologies originated in the social sciences, yet over the last seventy years they have been incorporated into more traditional histories to various extents. Quantitative methods range from simple descriptive statistics (e.g. counting, finding averages) to methods known

---

[1] R.W. Fogel, *Without Consent or Contract: Evidence and Methods* (New York: W. W. Norton, 1989), p. xiii.
[2] R.W. Fogel and S. Engerman, *Time on the Cross: The Economics of American Negro Slavery* (New York: Little Brown and Company, 1974), hereafter *TOTC*.

as 'inferential statistics' (more advanced statistical techniques such as significance testing, probability, distributions and confidence intervals). Most students of history, and indeed most historians, will only draw on the first of these two categories, after all, and as this chapter will demonstrate, one can learn much from simply counting (when coupled with sound qualitative knowledge). However, knowing what statistics mean and when to use them (and importantly, when *not* to use them) is vital.[3]

While methods have varied, practitioners of quantitative history have had one simple goal in incorporating quantitative methods into their analysis: to challenge the reliability of literary evidence. Pat Thane, in her work on ageing, has argued that the turn to methodologies adopted from the social sciences has coincided with an 'increasing awareness of the multiple forms of social diversity within all societies, and, in consequence, the need for greater complexity of analysis'. Similarly, according to Robert Darcy and Richard Rohrs, this challenge to the reliability of literary sources 'coincided with greater interest in groups, which, because of their numbers and diversity, defied traditional research methods'.[4] When we consider this in the context of the methodological development of slavery studies in the United States, there is a clear correlation with the greater availability (or attention) to sources previously overlooked, particularly the large body of interviews with formerly enslaved people collected by the Federal Writers' Project in the 1930s, and published by George P. Rawick in the 1970s.[5]

Sources written by enslaved people, even in the United States where first-hand accounts of slavery are most numerous, are dwarfed by the extensive body of evidence left behind by their enslavers. The elusive nature of sources written by enslaved people, in addition to the constant moulding and remoulding of approaches and language (often shaped by contemporary socio-political landscapes), has led to a constant questioning of all source material. In dealing with histories of slavery, however, no methodology has

---

[3]Manuals and extensive guides on how to put together samples, account for biases, test results and statistical methods can be found in the 'evidence and methods' supplements to past quantitative work on slavery – for example, Fogel, *Without Consent or Contract*; Fogel and Engerman, *Time on the Cross: Evidence and Methods* (New York: Little, Brown and Company, 1974). Additional material can be found in R. Darcy and R.C. Rohrs, *A Guide to Quantitative History* (Westport, CT: Praeger, 1995).
[4]P. Thane, 'Social Histories of Old Age and Aging', *Journal of Social History* 37: 1 (2003), p. 93; Darcy and Rohrs, *A Guide to Quantitative History*, p. 2.
[5]G.P. Rawick, ed., *The American Slave: A Composite Autobiography, Series One and Two*, Vols. 1–19 (Westport: Greenwood Press, 1972); *Supplement Series One*, Vols 1–12 (Westport: Greenwood Press, 1979); *Supplement Series Two*, Vols. 1–10 (Westport: Greenwood Press, 1979).

received such energetic criticism as quantitative history. If historians have supposed to identify a 'historical truth' (whatever that might mean), it is quantitative historians (sometimes known as new economic historians and cliometricians) who have come closest to claiming access to this. For example, Fogel and Engerman stated the following in the introduction to *Time on the Cross*: 'This will be a disturbing book to read. It requires forbearance on the part of the reader and a recognition that what is set forth represents the honest efforts of scholars whose central aim has been the discovery of *what really happened* [italics mine].'[6] As this chapter will reveal, however, a truth set out by the numbers is just as ambiguous and fleeting as any other theory or interpretation that rests upon a body of source material shaped by subjugated people and their oppressors. But, despite quantification as a methodology falling out of favour among a great number of historians of slavery in recent years, it is no *less* valid an approach, and it has formed an important part of the iterative methodological development of the study of slavery.

Historians and counting

Historical debates on how best to study the experiences and lives of enslaved people started relatively late in history departments and would also have been deemed relatively unimportant by scholars whose work was shaped by, or actively shaped, white supremacy. When Ulrich B. Philips wrote *American Negro Slavery* in 1918, few white scholars would have questioned the sample of white sources used to form his argument that slavery was based on a system of intimate benevolent paternalism.[7] In the wake of the Civil Rights Movement, however, the field moved on. As a new generation of black and white scholars entered the academy to study the history of enslaved people, historians were increasingly held to account for their conclusions, and questioned as to how they arrived at them. Sources from the formerly enslaved, including the large body of Works Progress Administration (WPA) interviews, were more widely used and became the cornerstone of most

---

[6]Fogel and Engerman, *TOTC*, p. 8.
[7]U.B. Philips, *American Negro Slavery: A Survey of the Supply, Employment and Control of Negro Labor as Determined by the Plantation Regime* (New York: D. Appleton and Company, 1918).

histories of slavery. This switch reflects, better than any, the politicization of historical methodology when related to the study of slavery. With the near abundance of material subsequently available to historians of slavery in the United States, historians were presented with a new challenge: how to best organize material that reflected so many divergent experiences into a study that reflected a 'common enslaved experience', and that could be translated into workable conclusions.

Historians had used quantitative methodologies in earlier studies on slavery. The path-breaking work of scholar and politician Eric Williams, for example, examined the economic structures and materialist dynamics related to abolitionism and emancipation in the British Atlantic. However, the self-termed 'new economic historians' were more forthright in assessing the benefits of a quantitative approach to all areas of slavery and slave life.[8] Fogel and Engerman, as part of this cohort, were the first to apply this methodology in an attempt to understand the realities of day-to-day interpersonal relationships under slavery, which of course has wide-ranging implications for the understanding of black experiences throughout the African diaspora in slavery and in freedom. Moving through the literature produced by US Historians since the 1970s, this chapter will explore debates over the group of historical methodologies that can be defined as quantitative and reflect critically upon the influence of select key quantitative history[ies] to our understanding of slavery. The chapter will be arranged into three sections that reflect three dominant approaches to the quantitative study of slavery: the first section is an analysis of the 'New Economic History' approach to quantitative history, which will centre on a case study of the treatment of sexual violence and family life in *Time on the Cross*. Next, the section on 'Post-1980 Quantitative Studies' will explore approaches to similar material and alternative sampling methods by Michael Tadman, Emily West and others who challenged Fogel and Engerman's conclusions and contributed important statistics on the domestic slave trade, demographics and cross-plantation marriages. Finally, the focus will turn to works produced by scholars working on the 'New History of Capitalism', whose members

---

[8] E. Williams, *Capitalism and Slavery* (Chapel Hill: University of North Carolina Press, 1944). Williams's work revealed the impact of African slavery on British economic development and claimed that profits from slavery helped to fertilize the British Industrial Revolution. See also Kenneth Morgan's re-evaluation of the Williams thesis in K. Morgan, *Slavery, Atlantic Trade and the British Economy, 1660–1800* (London: Cambridge University Press, 2000).

include Walter Johnson, Edward Baptist and Daina Ramey Berry. These works put the financial behaviour of slaveholders at the centre of combined quantitative and social history-style analysis in order to reflect on the real effect that capitalism under slavery had on the lives of enslaved people.

New Economic History and Slavery (1974–)

When *Time on the Cross* was first published in 1974, Fogel and Engerman claimed to have discovered 'unbelievable' things about the slave system.[9] Yet, the work became one of the most notable scholarly controversies in the historiography of American slavery. In the years following its publication, the work came under scrutiny from a range of scholars and formed the focal point of conference panels, retaliatory monographs and edited collections, even spilling out into the public sphere in a way that is quite unusual for academic work.[10] In fact, it still attracts attention in both the field and the classroom. In the end, it was the extent that their conclusions – and their self-congratulatory tone – diverged from those that were produced through the newly emerging social history approaches of the Civil Rights Era that meant their methods were scrutinized with an irate precision by their contemporaries. Fogel and Engerman put together a set of ten 'principle characteristics' of the slave economy that included an assertion that 'slavery was rational and profitable', and perhaps more controversially, that 'the belief that slave breeding, sexual exploitation and promiscuity destroyed the black family was a myth'.[11] This latter assertion will be the focus of a case study for this section.

---

[9]Fogel and Engerman, *TOTC*, p. 8.
[10]See H.G. Gutman, *Slavery and the Numbers Game* (Urbana: University of Illinois Press, 1975); P.A. David, H.G. Gutman, R. Sutch, P. Temin, G. Wright, and K. Stampp, eds, *Reckoning with Slavery: Critical Essays in the Quantitative History of American Negro Slavery* (New York: Oxford University Press, 1976); G.M. Walton, ed., 'A Symposium on Time on the Cross', *Explorations in Economic History* 12: 4 (1975). Symposia were held at the University of Rochester in October 1974 and the University of Mississippi in October 1975. The criticisms of the participants were published in the aforementioned volumes.
[11]Fogel and Engerman, *TOTC*, p. 5.

The scale of the critical attention received and the extent that its more controversial conclusions are used in the classroom has helped to form historians' own collective memory of both the book and a particular historiographical moment. In the context of the 1970s post-Civil Rights Era, and a coordinated scholarly backlash to the Moynihan report, minority scholars and their allies saw a threat in the work as it challenged beliefs and threatened agendas.[12] Despite many historical fields now paying close attention to quantitative techniques, scholars of slavery have been sceptical, often linked back to the reception and problematic interpretations contained in *Time on the Cross*.

According to Fogel and Engerman, 'the interpretation of facts always involved a leap beyond those facts'.[13] This 'leap', admitted by Fogel and Engerman, exposed the gulf between the numbers and how they relate to an argument: in short, numbers never speak for themselves. The sense that conclusions painted as scientific, objective and based on quantitative methodologies were founded on flawed data and involved interpretative leaps was highlighted more by their critics than by Fogel and Engerman themselves, and the separation of the first volume from the evidence and methods volume was a significant point of controversy. Peter Kolchin, in a review of *Time on the Cross*, highlighted both of these problems:

> There is a danger that because *some* of Fogel and Engerman's conclusions are based on quantitative analysis, readers will assume that *all* of their conclusions are based on such analysis. The danger is all the greater because the evidence is confined to a volume that most readers will not see.[14]

Kolchin highlighted the inherent danger in the reader being expected to accept conclusions based on good faith, given that most would not have access to the second volume.

---

[12] What became known as 'The Moynihan Report' was published in 1965 as *The Negro Family: The Case for National Action* by the US Department of Labor by Daniel Patrick Moynihan, Assistant Secretary of Labor. Moynihan claimed that the increasing welfare dependency of black American families was a result of a 'steady disintegration' of the black family structure since emancipation (p. 14), https://web.stanford.edu/~mrosenfe/Moynihan's%20The%20Negro%20Family.pdf (accessed 11 June 2019).
[13] Fogel and Engerman, *TOTC: Evidence and Methods*, p. 26.
[14] P. Kolchin, 'Review: Toward a Reinterpretation of Slavery', *Journal of Social History* 9: 1 (1975), p. 107.

Case study: Forced reproduction in Time on the Cross

One of the most controversial conclusions that Fogel and Engerman came to was on 'forced reproduction'. This contributed to their position on the stability of enslaved families. According to Fogel and Engerman: 'The family was the basic unit of social organisation under slavery ... [i]t was to the economic interest of planters to encourage the stability of slave families and most of them did so.' In order to arrive at this conclusion, Fogel and Engerman attempted to access the psyche of enslavers through applying quantitative methodologies to the reproductive patterns of enslaved people. They claimed to have calculated the average age of enslaved mothers at the birth of their first child from probate records. However, in assessing their workings, one can see that the evidence they referred to was, in fact, 'the distribution of the ages of mothers at the birth of their first *surviving* child [emphasis mine]'. Of course, in the nineteenth century, and especially under such horrific conditions as enslavement, there was often a gulf between the age of a woman at the birth of her *first* child and first *surviving* child. Fogel and Engerman's data told them (and their readers) that the average age at 'first' birth was 22.5 (and a median of 20.8). This, they wrote, contradicted the common belief that young teenage girls were often made mothers at age twelve, thirteen or fourteen.[15] Herbert Gutman wrote an extended critique of *Time on the Cross* in his monograph *Slavery and the Numbers Game*, published shortly after Fogel and Engerman's work.[16] Gutman's critique included general questions on Fogel and Engerman's methodology, but, as above, he also argued that the way that data was collected from probate records was problematic. Gutman countered that when we look at the source base used, Fogel and Engerman's argument about 'prudish' sexual more collapses. He wrote that 'put simply, a probate record (like a census enumeration) offers the historians no clue whether the oldest child in a household (or family) was the first-born'.[17]

---

[15]Fogel and Engerman, *TOTC*, p. 137.
[16]H.G. Gutman, *Slavery and the Numbers Game: A Critique of Time on the Cross* (Urbana: University of Illinois Press, 1975), pp. 142–53.
[17]Ibid., 151.

This limited data was used by Fogel and Engerman to make a leap in analysis that led to problematic and potentially harmful conclusions. In a non-contraceptive society, the late average age at first birth indicated to the cliometricians that there were other factors at play in limiting the birth rate, and this is where the 'leap' between the 'facts' and their interpretation came in, that 'slave parents closely guarded their daughters from sexual contact with men' and that 'in a well-fed, non-contraceptive population in which women are quite fecund after marriage, only abstinence would explain the relative shortage of births in the late-teen ages'. This, to Fogel and Engerman, meant that enslaved people were 'prudish' rather than promiscuous, putting in place two simple polemic definitions of sexual behaviour and attitude.[18]

Once this figure for the age at 'first' birth had been gleaned (which, in addition to the problems listed above would have depended on accurate accounting for age in record groups, in addition to accurate calculations of age of menarche [first period] for enslaved adolescents), it would then be used to make conclusions on three areas of study:

1. the profitability of 'slave breeding',
2. the causes of the high rate of natural increase among US enslaved populations when compared to those in the West Indies and
3. the sexual mores of enslaved people.

As Fogel and Engerman insisted that 'slave labourers' were highly efficient and productive labourers – and as such implied that enslaved people were reactors to the stimuli of enslavers – enslaved familial behaviour 's no more than a reaction to rational planter (or enslaver) economic uli. Fogel and Engerman removed the agency of enslaved people to ide that the economic needs and calculations of planters coincided gthen and sustain 'stable slave families'. 'That morality and good practice should collide', wrote Fogel and Engerman, 'created neither ir consternation among most planters'.[19] However, as a number vere soon to demonstrate, Fogel and Engerman's evidence of ts related to child-bearing did not speak to benevolent otected enslaved families. Attitudes and beliefs about black

---

'C, pp. 137–8.
sonance with recent studies of capitalism and slavery where planters nic beings. The turn in the new histories of slavery and capitalism is s thought to have on the moral character of the enslaver.

sexuality among white enslavers were not taken into account as these did not fit into a simple quantitative analysis.

Harriet Jacobs described such white male attitudes when she wrote of the age of fifteen as a 'sad epoch in the life of a slave girl' an age at which she became aware of, and a victim of, the sexual transgressions of male enslavers.[20] Fogel and Engerman's statistics found a median age of first live birth as 20.8 years, which for them meant a leap in analysis to conclude that those in Southern society were in favour of refraining from sexual activity until a later age. This did not take into account the emotive first-hand testimony of formerly enslaved people, such as Harriet Jacobs. Testimony from the 1930s would also counteract their claims. Lulu Wilson reported to the Texas Writers' Project that both she and her mother were singled out for forced reproduction at different ages. She told her interviewer:

> My maw says she took with my paw and I was born but some time passed and didn't no more younguns come and so they said my paw was too old and wore out for breedin' and they wanted her to take with this here other buck. So the Hodges set the [***] hounds on my paw and run him away from the place and maw said he went to the free state. So she took with my step paw and they must of pleased the white folks that wanted [enslaved people] to breed like livestock 'cause she birthed nineteen children.

Her enslaver sold the majority of her siblings into the domestic slave trade, and it was up to her stepfather 'who was a fool for his young ones' at the end of the war to 'tramp half way 'round the country gatherin' up the young 'uns they done sold 'way'. Lulu herself was just thirteen or fourteen when her 'mistress' made her marry and subsequently brought a doctor to the plantation to tell her, 'less'n I had a baby, old as I was and married, I'd start in on spasms. So it twan't long 'til I had a baby'.[21]

The fact that even a few young enslaved girls would give birth at age thirteen, fourteen or fifteen holds a significance that stands aside from a quantitative majority. This testimony deserved more attention, despite forming part of a smaller sub-sample, as it hints at a truth that is not accounted for within a quantitative study: to the individual who had been forced to 'breed' at an early age, the statistical significance of her experience would have been wholly irrelevant. This very point goes back to the difficulty

---

[20] H. Jacobs, *Incidents in the Life of a Slave Girl*, originally published Boston (1861), https://docsouth.unc.edu/fpn/jacobs/jacobs.html (accessed 1 December 2018).
[21] Rawick., *American Slave, Supp. Ser. 2, Vol. 5, Pt. 4,* 1571.

of using statistics to identify trends in large groups, which could lose sight of the individual. Peter Kolchin addressed this in his review of *Time on the Cross* when he noted that 'it is unlikely that most slaves calculated that only 13 percent of interregional slave sales broke up families, or that such information would have been especially reassuring to them'.[22]

Aside from the leaps in analysis and faulty interpretation of the records, there were also problems with the sampling that Fogel and Engerman used. 'Sampling' is the process of identifying a small number of cases for analysis, rather than spending much time preparing data on an extensive source base. Fogel and Engerman used just thirty plantation manuscripts to come to their conclusions, which Gutman used to argue that 'not a shred of quantitative evidence in either volume of T/C' shows that 'most' planters 'encouraged the stability of slave families'.[23] Neither their sample size nor 'leap' of analysis held up this conclusion.

Fogel and Engerman, however, are not the only historians to have used data for quantitative analysis that was unlikely to be accurate. In fact, in their challenge to Fogel and Engerman's claims that enslaved women *did not* bear children until they were physically able, James Trussel and Richard Steckel used height-by-age data in order to estimate the mean age of slaves at menarche (the date of their first period). Their analysis lay on empirically derived biomedical generalizations that relate to the age at which girls experience the peak of their adolescent growth spurt (the largest annual increase). Menarche happens, on average, one year later. This data required critical reading as to its validity as it is highly likely that the enslaved person's age was estimated by height from the official that measured her. Therefore, their data was probably predicated on guesses from enslavers and traders in enslaved people.[24] Despite grand claims of a scientific method that could revolutionize the discipline, cliometricians were unable to check the authenticity of each of their data points from which their generalizations were derived.

While this is just one example of the controversies that *Time on the Cross* engendered, it demonstrates the harm caused by detachment from the academic and socio-political context of one's research. Social science research methods generally work on a cumulative basis, and Fogel and

---

[22]Kolchin, 'Toward a Reinterpretation of Slavery', p. 107.
[23]Gutman, *Slavery and the Numbers Game,* 94. For original argument, see Fogel and Engerman, *TOTC*, pp. 83–4, 119–25.
[24]J. Trussell and R. Steckel, 'The Age of Slaves at Menarche and Their First Birth', *Journal of Interdisciplinary History* 8: 3 (1978), pp. 477–505.

Engerman are likely to have prescribed to this belief of iterative development of scholarship (likely expecting that others would build on and fill in the gaps in their research), without the necessary emotional awareness of the impact of their tentative conclusions. They underestimated sexual violence, forced reproduction and punishment, but all of these problems come down to the fact that the conclusions exceeded the capacity of the data.

Post-1980s quantitative studies

A somewhat less controversial area of study has been the quantitative calculations made on the interregional slave trade in the United States. In the nineteenth century, abolitionists had claimed that slavery had only survived in the 'net-exporting' states (Upper South states that exported more enslaved people through the domestic slave trade than they imported), due to a high incidence of 'slave-breeding' farms (farms that were set up specifically with the purpose of 'breeding' enslaved people). In states of the Upper South the 'rearing' of slaves was described in some abolitionist pamphlets as the 'chief source' of income. They hinted at 'stud farms', and pointed to the destruction of the slave family and highlighted not only the sexual abuse of enslaved women and children but also the moral corruption of whites of 'all classes, all professions, both sexes, and all ages', all of whom were involved in the 'rearing' and sale of slaves.[25]

The first sophisticated analysis of the domestic slave trade was conducted by Fogel and Engerman who systematically demonstrated the profitability of slavery both in newly colonized lands and in older net-exporting states, which went against the traditional abolitionist accusations of 'slave-breeding' enterprises in the Upper South. While correct in this part of their analysis, Fogel and Engerman fell down with their demographic analysis of the enslaved people moved as part of the domestic slave trade. They concluded that the domestic slave trade separated few families, relying on data which came from the branch of the trade from the Chesapeake to New Orleans.[26]

---

[25] The Executive Committee of the American Anti-Slavery Society, *Slavery and the internal slave trade in the United States of North America; being replies to questions transmitted by the committee of the British and Foreign Anti-Slavery Society for the abolition of slavery and the slave trade throughout the world* (London, 1841), p. 22, http://archive.org/stream/slaveryinternals00ameruoft/slaveryinternals00ameruoft_djvu.txt (accessed 10 April 2015).
[26] Fogel and Engerman, *TOTC*, pp. 78–86.

In this data set, there seemed to be very few children sold without a parent, a trend which seemingly confirmed Fogel and Engerman's statements on the stability of the slave family and was used to further claim that enslavers rarely separated enslaved families. In 1988, Michael Tadman published *Speculators and Slaves*, which led to a fundamental rethinking of the scope and significance of the internal slave trade. Tadman noted the methodological problems in Fogel and Engerman's work. Fogel and Engerman based their conclusions on an extensive database of New Orleans bills of sale to take account of marriage separations and children sold without either parent. Yet, these bills of sale only show forcible separations *at the point of sale*, rather than at the point of leaving their original plantation (likely to have been in the Upper South). Tadman's work showed, however, that the New Orleans trade was a statistical anomaly and had a preponderance of young field-age males, men who were desired by enslavers in the sugar parishes around New Orleans. This demographic breakdown was not replicated in slave trading elsewhere in the United States. Through their sampling error, therefore, Fogel and Engerman allowed space for a more benevolent impression of southern slaveholders. Tadman noted that 'use of mother-and-offspring lots does not reveal, for any market, the full extent of the forcible separation of spouses. Many women sold without husbands and (for reason of infidelity, child mortality, or child sale) without children might also have been parted from their husbands by the trade'.[27]

In addition, Tadman was able to present quantitative evidence against Fogel and Engerman's assertion that the majority of inter-regional movements of enslaved people were due to planter migrations rather than the inter-regional slave trade. Through calculations of age structures (supported by calculations based on shipping records and a detailed study of slave traders in South Carolina) Tadman was able to demonstrate that fully 60–70 per cent of inter-regional movements of enslaved people were through the slave trade rather than planter migrations.[28] By using statistics of slave sales to calculate the lifetime probability that an enslaved person might be separated from a spouse, Tadman separated the data into age cohorts and multiplied the cohort-specific sales rate by the proportion married in the general population. By aggregating these figures, Tadman found that 'about one in five of the first marriages of Upper South slaves

---

[27]M. Tadman, *Speculators and Slaves: Masters Traders and Slaves in the Old South* (Madison: University of Wisconsin Press, 1989), p. 134.
[28]Ibid., p. 31.

would have been broken by the trade'.[29] Most importantly, for the purpose of this chapter, Tadman's work often demonstrates the value of simple counting over complex statistical techniques. In doing so he is able to incorporate this data into a viable historical narrative that diverges little from, but offers incredible weight to, narratives of loss and harm told by formerly enslaved people.[30] Such labour-intensive work is likely to be embarked upon by neither students nor historians working under the expectation of frequent publication. Nevertheless, this method can be replicated in other less obvious areas of enslaved life.

From the 1970s, when George P. Rawick began the huge task of locating and publishing the thousands of WPA interviews, growing numbers of historians have made use of these sources. Almost all of these historians, though, have mined the interviews for quotations and have taken a qualitative approach to this source base.[31] The publication in the 1970s of George P. Rawick's collections of WPA interviews with the formerly enslaved in the 1930s revolutionized the study of enslaved lives, and has been a constant feature of histories of slavery since that time. Economic historians and cliometricians have, however, rarely used this material for the purpose of quantification, seeing it as too subjective for quantitative analysis.[32] However, some slavery specialists have used a methodology of simple quantification (again demonstrating that statistical techniques need not be complicated), based on a large body of source material and contextualized with a strong background knowledge of the slave system.

Paul Escott's *Slavery Remembered*, a study of interviews with the formerly enslaved, is essentially a qualitative study, but to support arguments on select issues Escott took a quantitative approach. Escott's comparisons of the information given in interviews conducted by white and black interviewers revealed, if it wasn't already clear, that the racial context of the 1930s made

---

[29]Ibid., pp. 169, 285. See also J.B. Pritchett, 'Quantitative Estimates of the United States Interregional Slave Trade, 1820–1860', *Journal of Economic History* 61: 2 (2001), pp. 467–75.

[30]See, for example, the testimony recorded in O.V. Rogers-Albert, *The House of Bondage, or, Charlotte Brooks and Other Slaves*, https://docsouth.unc.edu/neh/albert/albert.html (accessed 10 June 2019). On the traumas of seeking to find lost family after emancipation, see H. A. Williams, *Help Me to Find My People: The African American Search for Family Lost in Slavery* (Chapel Hill: University of North Carolina Press, 2012).

[31]E. Genovese, *Roll, Jordan, Roll: The World the Slaves Made* (New York: Pantheon Books, 1974); F. Yarborough, 'Power, Perception, and Interracial Sex: Former Slaves Recall a Multiracial South', *Journal of Southern History* 71 (2005), pp. 559–89.

[32]See, for example, J. Hirsch, 'Reading and Counting', *Reviews in American History* 8: 3 (1980), pp. 312–17.

a significant impact on the interviews. Such information offers a guideline for historians in working qualitatively with these same sources.[33] The most serious quantitative examination of these sources came from Stephen Crawford in his important, though unpublished, PhD, 'Quantified Memory' (1980).[34] Crawford's work remains the only essentially quantitative study of the interviews. For this dissertation he used the first set of the interviews that were published by Rawick (sixteen volumes of WPA interviews together with a further volume carried out by Fisk University students). He used these sources to quantify aspects of slave life ranging from workload and diet to family life and sexual exploitation.

Again, Crawford carefully considered factors such as the differences in the responses of the interviewees when there was a black and a white interviewer. For example, Crawford found that in the overall sample, 50 per cent of the ex-slaves interviewed by blacks characterized their masters as 'good' or 'very good', compared to 71 per cent of those interviewed by whites.[35] This also applied to questions over parentage. Crawford found that formerly enslaved people were often reluctant to claim white parentage when talking to white interviewers and were especially reluctant to report that their 'master' was their father.[36] Depending on whether the formerly enslaved person was interviewed by a white or black interviewer (with the black interviewers gaining the higher results), Crawford's statistics tell us that 6 to 10 per cent of the formerly enslaved interviewees reported having white fathers.[37] In his analysis of single-parented, mother-headed households, 15 per cent of these were due to the formerly enslaved person having a white father. He calculated that enslaved women who had their first child by their 'master' then went on to have fewer children than those women who had their first child by a black man. Therefore, Crawford reasoned, the enslaver could suffer economically by having a sexual relationship with his enslaved people (which follows the model of Fogel and Engerman in *Time on the Cross*).[38] The methodology employed by Crawford, and Escott, demonstrates that it is possible, and also relatively simple, for quantitative historians to

---

[33] P.D. Escott, *Slavery Remembered: A Record of Twentieth Century Slave Narratives* (Chapel Hill: University of North Carolina Press, 1979), pp. 10–11.
[34] Escott, *Slavery Remembered*; S. Crawford, 'Quantified Memory: A Study of the WPA and Fisk University Slave Narrative Collections', unpublished PhD, University of Chicago (1980).
[35] Ibid., p. 40.
[36] Ibid., p. 41.
[37] Ibid., p. 162.
[38] Ibid., p. 159.

establish a range of error that qualitative historians can use for a guideline. Both historians calculate the likely upper and lower boundary of reports of sensitive issues (such as sexual violence) when interviewed by a white or black interviewer, though the conclusions do not always necessarily have a close engagement with contradictory evidence from qualitative material.

In *Chains of Love* (2004), historian Emily West used WPA slave testimonies, records of enslavers, and quantitative methods to uncover the relationships of enslaved couples, their family dynamics, and patterns of individual and collective resistance. West combined a quantitative and a textual approach in order to calculate a *minimum estimate* of the extent of interracial sexual encounters in antebellum South Carolina by totalling all those who had either a direct or an indirect knowledge of sexual violence by whites in the WPA testimony. Rather than sampling the full WPA interview collection (a technique used by Paul D. Escott), West studied the full body of South Carolina WPA interviews.[39] The manner in which West interprets the numbers is significant. West noted the gender of those who discussed interracial sex (majority male) and put this into the context of 1930s social and racial etiquette to conclude that men were more willing to discuss sexual issues (whether first- or second-hand) with interviewers.[40] This common-sense approach to interpretation of the data meant that the conclusions are not over-stated, and that the methodology was clear and astute.

While this chapter, thus far, has discussed just a small illustrative sample of quantitative histories of slavery, some clear principles of good practice can be established for future research, as well as highlighting some pitfalls that others have fallen into in the past. The overriding problem encountered when combining quantitative analysis and slavery has been the inability of some practitioners to separate social science methodology and history. Historical sources are different to those encountered in other disciplines. When historians work with samples of material it is intrinsically different in character than the body of material that is collected during investigations in the social sciences. Historical source sets are rarely randomly sampled from a more complete data set, nor deliberately collected with the purpose of lending themselves to statistical analysis – we do not get to choose what remains out of the fragments of the past. For example, the WPA interviews

---

[39]While West does use all available interviews, the WPA interviews were conducted with a limited number of formerly enslaved people who were still alive in the 1930s; therefore, the interviews used already a limited sample of people emancipated after the Civil War.
[40]E. West, *Chains of Love: Slave Couples in Antebellum South Carolina* (Urbana: University of Illinois Press, 2004).

were never meant to be a random sample of the total slave population. In fact, records show that they were collected according to the local knowledge, will and friendships of the interviewer.[41] There is rarely a scientific principle underlying the collection or compilation of historical source sets, and archives and other sites of historical memory are marked by gaps, losses, omissions, anachronism and even 'violence'.[42] Outside of the issues of source material, historians also need to balance the significance of individuals and groups in favour of larger trends that may miss certain cultural nuances.

Indeed, criticisms of quantitative history often focus on a distinction between the traditional narrative and a drier quantitative analysis.[43] Fogel and Engerman calculated the rate of whippings on southern plantations and came up with the figure of 0.7 whippings per enslaved person per year. This figure does not represent the fear of whipping, nor the trauma that one enslaved person might have experienced through watching their mother, father, child, sibling or spouse being whipped.[44] Walter Johnson wrote that 'we are accustomed to thinking of sounds as fleeting, as impressions that end when our eardrums cease to vibrate – but these memories tell of sounds that were as lasting as the scars on the former slaves' bodies'.[45] A balance between quantitative and qualitative research methods, therefore, can be revealing, not just of wider patterns in a society, but of certain exceptions. This balance thoroughly exploits sources in order to encourage a more nuanced understanding of the past.

Economic vitality studies of the twenty-first century

Quantitative methodology remains a touchstone of economic-historical study of American slavery, and in an attempt to formulate new arguments

---

[41] Based on forthcoming research of author on Louisiana Writers' Project.
[42] On the production of knowledge of slavery and the archive see M. Fuentes, *Dispossessed Lives: Enslaved Women, Violence, and the Archive* (Philadelphia: University of Pennsylvania Press, 2016); M.R. Trouillot, *Silencing the Past: Power and the Production of History* (Boston, MA: Beacon Press, 1995).
[43] Darcy and Rohrs, *A Guide to Quantitative History*, pp. 1–6.
[44] Fogel and Engerman, *TOTC*, p. 145.
[45] W. Johnson, *River of Dark Dreams: Slavery and Empire in the Cotton Kingdom* (Cambridge, MA: Harvard University Press, 2013).

linking nineteenth-century slavery (in particular) to the development of modern capitalism, historians of slavery in the 2010s have sparked debate on a scale little seen in our field since the publication of *Time on the Cross*.[46] Key proponents of this 'new' theory include Walter Johnson, Edward Baptist and Sven Beckert, who combine narrative sources with statistical methods in an attempt to incorporate human experience into questions relating to slavery's profitability, enslaver/enslaved relations, and the reasons for slavery's demise. Baptist was the most candid in setting out the reformist nature of this approach in *The Half Has Never Been Told,* where he wrote that the first 'major assumption' of historians is that 'as an economic system – a way of producing and trading commodities – American slavery was fundamentally different from the rest of the modern economy and separate from it'.[47] Yet, since the days of Eugene Genovese and Elizabeth Fox-Genovese who, following Gramsci's cultural hegemony model, argued that slaveholders were 'in, but not of', the capitalist world economy', no major work in US history has argued that slavery was not a rational economic system, acutely connected to wider Atlantic financial interests.[48]

---

[46]This task becomes even more complicated considering that the criteria used to define 'capitalism' vary from historian to historian (not taking into account definitions used in other disciplines). Marx's theory of capital differs to the classic Anglo-American interpretation of capitalism as a desire to make money, which is part of human nature that involved rational human actors who maximize their advantages – an ideology first penned during the Scottish Enlightenment, but appeared with increasing frequency from the time of the Cold War. For further discussion see P. Coclanis, 'The Economics of Slavery' in R.L. Paquette and M.M. Smith, eds, *The Oxford Handbook of Slavery in the Americas* (Oxford; New York: Oxford University Press, 2010), pp. 489–512; Scott Reynolds Nelson, 'Who Put Their Capitalism in My Slavery', *Journal of the Civil War Era* 5: 2 (2015), pp. 289–310.

[47]E. Baptist, *The Half Has Never Been Told: Slavery and the Making of American Capitalism* (New York: Basic Books, 2014), p. xviii.

[48]E. Fox-Genovese and E.D. Genovese, *Fruits of Merchant Capital: Slavery and Bourgeois Property in the Rise and Expansion of Capitalism* (New York: Oxford University Press, 1983), pp. 3–61. See also E.D. Genovese, ed., *Introduction to Historical and Theoretical Perspectives*, vol. 1 of *The Slave Economies* (New York: Wiley, 1973), pp. 1–3; and Genovese, *Introduction to Slavery in the International Economy*, vol. 2 of *The Slave Economies* (New York: Wiley, 1973), pp. 1–3. See also D.R. Egerton, 'Markets without a Market Revolution: Southern Planters and Capitalism', Journal of the Early Republic 16 (1996), pp. 207–21.While beyond the US-specific focus of this chapter, there has also been a wave of scholarship that has sought to move past spatial and temporal boundaries to explore Atlantic slavery from the colonial era onwards, and integrate studies of capitalism, modernity and slavery on a hemispheric, even global perspective. This approach, commonly labelled 'Second Slavery', encourages scholars to think about concepts such as capitalism and modernity in relation to local-global relations. See Dale Tomich, *Through the Prism of Slavery: Labor, Capital, and World Economy* (Lanham, MD: Rowman & Littlefield, 2004), pp. 56–71; Tomich, ed., *The Politics of the Second Slavery* (Albany, NY: SUNY Press, 2016); R. Blackburn, 'Why the Second Slavery?' in D. Tomich, ed., *Slavery and Historical Capitalism in the Nineteenth Century* (New York: Lexington Books 2017).

Not all of the recent 'history of capitalism' school employ quantitative methods; Walter Johnson, for example, puts in place a world-systems model of capitalism that relies on mainly qualitative material – the relationship of the *forces of production* to the *relations of production*, to put it in Marx's terms. Johnson explored the dispossession of native people, deadly steamboat explosions, environmental degradation, financial crises, and the daily coercion and violence of plantation work, plus sexual violence inflicted on enslaved women. This, according to Gavin Wright, gave valuable insight for economic historians who 'can easily become preoccupied with analytical abstractions and conventional quantitative measures'.[49] Yet, Wright, a leading economic historian himself, noted how such positives were countered by the limited, even faulty, quantitative analysis based on a lack of understanding of economic theory. For example, Johnson states that planters' money was tied up in land and slaves, overlooking the fact that sales of land and slaves were mere transfers that 'did not absorb resources in the aggregate'. Also, in a similar way to Edward Baptist (explored below), Johnson notes that cotton productivity increased six-fold between 1820 and 1860, but, unlike Baptist, does not make any attempt to explain the quantitative reasoning or factors that led to this growth.[50]

One of the primary criticisms of Johnson et al. is that of 'historical presentism'. Johnson's 'carceral landscape', with 'starving' enslaved people, invited his readers to envisage a straightforward trajectory from nineteenth-century slavery through to mass incarceration and the struggling underclass of global capitalist enterprise.[51] Philip Morgan questioned Johnson's use of sources, noting that the narrative style 'does not raise questions of typicality, representativeness, or balance', a charge which Edward Baptist takes on in *The Half Has Never Been Told*.[52] Baptist calculated that slavery was profitable with a competitive cotton market and productivity gains that were passed onto consumers in the form of lower prices. But it was the way this productivity was calculated that historians well-versed in quantitative methodology took issue with: The so-called 'pushing system' of labour, as described

---

[49] G. Wright, 'Book Review: River of Dark Dreams: Slavery and Empire in the Cotton Kingdom', *Journal of Economic Literature* 52: 3 (2014), pp. 877–9. See also G. Winant, 'Book Review, River of Dark Dreams: Slavery and Empire in the Cotton Kingdom', https://nplusonemag.com/issue-17/reviews/slave-capitalism/ (accessed 8 July 2019).
[50] Johnson, *River of Dark Dreams*, p. 244.
[51] Ibid., pp. 227, 180.
[52] P. Morgan, 'Book Review, River of Dark Dreams: Slavery and Empire in the Cotton Kingdom', *American Historical Review* 119: 2 (2014), p. 463.

by Baptist, meant that the rate of cotton productivity and efficiency rose startlingly over time – slave owners, through the calculated and systematic use of 'torture' (whipping, etc.), increased productivity on southern cotton plantations by 400 per cent between 1800 and 1860. The charges levelled at Baptist were numerous, but most fell into the categories of (1) misreporting and miscalculating data, (2) ignoring sampling techniques and lack of understanding of quantitative methodology and (3) using conclusions drawn from faulty quantitative methods to write 'evocative' history.[53]

To begin with (1) Misreporting of data, we turn to Trevor Burnard's review essay of *The Half Has Never Been Told*. From Table 4.3 we learn from Burnard that there are some serious inaccuracies and misleading statistics reported:

> Baptist wants to show that infant mortality rates in the antebellum South were extraordinarily high and the same as in West Africa and the Caribbean. So he cites Jack E. Eblen for infant mortality in the antebellum South, but without adding Eblen's warning that his figures may be too high. Then he chooses the lowest figures on infant mortality for any West Indian slave population that Higman has found, without telling the reader that Higman warns us that his figures for Jamaica are surprisingly low and that he prefers the much higher figures for other West Indian slave societies.

Burnard accused Baptist of using figures that best suited his argument when a 'more nuanced and accurate reporting of data would complicate what he wants us to believe'.[54] Baptist's detailed response to Burnard admitted the errors in transcription, but stuck to the conclusion that 'the rate of infant mortality on the South's cotton frontier seems to have approached the rate in Caribbean slave societies'.[55] It is interesting to note that while Baptist references other works by Michael Tadman, he left out Tadman's quantitative calculations on rates of natural increase/decrease in US sugar plantations in the parishes of Louisiana, compared to the sugar plantation of the Caribbean. These calculations demonstrate the demographic consequences of sugar slavery when compared to US cotton plantations, and add nuance both to Baptist's argument and to Burnard's affront.

---

[53] For summary review, see J. Murray, A. Olmstead, T. Logan, J. Pritchett and P. Rousseau, 'The Half Has Never Been Told: Slavery and the Making of American Capitalism', *Journal of Economic History* 75: 3 (2015), pp. 919–31.
[54] T. Burnard. 'The Righteous Will Shine Like the Sun: Writing an Evocative History of Antebellum American Slavery', *Slavery and Abolition* 36: 1 (2015), p. 182. Original table in Baptist, *The Half Has Never Been Told*, p. 123.
[55] E. Baptist, 'The Response', *Slavery and Abolition* 36: 1 (2015), p. 191.

Tadman argued that natural increase in North America was 'the product of circumstances equivalent in important ways to those associated with modern "Third World" populations that is, populations where very high death rates are compensated for by even higher birth rates. North American natural increase came about *despite an experience of bitter exploitation and suffering*'. Baptist, however, did not account for this knowledge that came from looking at the crop differences between the Caribbean and the United States. Tadman calculated the weighting of factors involved in the lack of children present on sugar plantations compared to cotton plantations. He calculated that the scarcity of potential childbearing women in the sugar parishes would have been responsible for 40 per cent of the child shortage, so the combination of low fertility and high child mortality would have accounted for the remaining 60 per cent.[56] Simply put, there are other factors associated with the rates of mortality that run adjacent to the will of the master. The presence of an internal slave trade, environmental conditions, the disease environment, crop-specific demands of labour would all affect rates of natural increase and infant mortality entirely outside of the control of the profit-making calculations of the master. Baptist, therefore, could be correct that the mortality rates of the United States and the British Caribbean *may* have approached similar rates, but *the numbers do not speak for themselves* – there is a wider context that would lead the informed reader away from concluding that the mortality rates were a product of more than just the rapacious, torturing, capitalist enslaver, as Baptist would have his reader believe.

The next charge brought against Baptist was that of ignoring sampling techniques and a lack of understanding of quantitative methodology. To explore this, we return to Baptist's charge that the 'whipping machine' technology employed by enslavers increased productivity by 400 per cent from 1800 to 1860. In fact, Fogel and Engerman in 1974 made a similar claim that 'Slave Agriculture was not inefficient compared with free agriculture'. According to Fogel and Engerman, slave farms had a significant productivity advantage due to both 'positive' and 'negative' incentive (positive being rewards, negative being punishment). This claim led to criticism that resulted in the aforementioned response to *Time on the Cross, Reckoning with Slavery* (1976), which again resulted in the 'positive' incentive element of the analysis being completely retracted from Fogel's follow-up work,

---

[56] M. Tadman, 'The Demographic Cost of Sugar: Debates on Slave Society and Rates of Natural Increase in the Americas', *The American Historical Review* 105: 5 (December 2000), pp. 1534–75.

Without Consent or Contract, where he argues that 'slaves on intermediate or large plantations worked about 76 per cent more intensely per hour than did free southern farmers or slaves on *small plantations* [emphasis mine]'.[57] If, then, we take Baptist's analysis that the increase in productivity on large plantations was due to the 'whipping machine', then Baptist does not explain why this technology was not put in place on the smaller farms.[58]

In a review of Baptist's work, Stanley Engerman pointed out that 'Baptist accepts that the productivity of slaves in producing cotton increased over time, but rather than attribute some of this either to the movement to better lands, or to improved managerial techniques, or to improvements in seeds, or possibly to an increase in slave heights and strength ... his preferred explanation is attribution to increasing use of "torture"'.[59] What Baptist does not do, that Fogel and Engerman actually did very well in *Time on the Cross*, is use 'Total Factor Productivity' to make their calculations. 'Total Factor Productivity' takes into account not just the simple increase in outputs but calculates the output per unit of all inputs into the production system, which includes the land, labour and capital. So, like with the case of the calculations on the infant mortality rates in the United States compared with the Caribbean, Baptist does not take into account all of the factors that might skew his argument – the expansion of slavery into the south-western frontier is one particularly important omission.

The interpretative problems encountered by Baptist and others need not discourage quantitative methods. The source material is available, and it is increasingly available online to an incredible scale.[60] If plantation managers, and others involved in the slave economy, were using quantitative management and accounting practices then it makes sense that historians can follow this paper trail.[61] Scholars are increasingly attuned to the intersection between capitalist impulse and human relationships, the 'boisterous passions', described by Thomas Jefferson, that controlled the behaviour of

---

[57] Fogel, *Without Consent or Contract*, pp. 78–9.
[58] For a more extended version of this argument see the excellent critical blogpost on 'Baptism by Blood Cotton' on pseudoerasmus.com (accessed 1 April 2019).
[59] S. Engerman, 'Review of the Business of Slavery and the Rise of American Capitalism, 1815–1860 by Calvin Schermerhorn and The Half Has Never Been Told: Slavery and the Making of American Capitalism by Edward E. Baptist', *Journal of Economic Literature* 55: 2 (2017), pp. 637–43.
[60] See, for example, *Voyages: The Trans-Atlantic Slave Trade Database*, https://www.slavevoyages.org/voyage/; *The Berry Slave Value Database*, https://www.openicpsr.org/openicpsr/project/101113/version/V1/view.
[61] Seen most recently in C. Rosenthal, *Accounting for Slavery: Masters and Management* (Cambridge, MA: Harvard University Press, 2018).

enslavers. Yet enslavers did not always act in predictable ways, and it is this microhistory that quantitative analysis alone does not allow for. The most recent quantitative studies would also benefit from incorporating more fully the contributions of women to the development of the capitalist system in the nineteenth century. Gendered lines of inquiry are almost completely absent from the New History of Capitalism school. In these works, women rarely appear except as raped and commodified. Both Baptist and Johnson use evocative, yet sloppy, language and analogies, to describe sexual violence against enslaved women. Baptist reduces the rapacious power of slaveholders to market 'fetishism', while Johnson describes slaveholder's rape as 'converting semen into capital'. Both writers fall into the trap of, while trying to represent the worst of mastery, relegating enslaved women to helpless victims or secondary actors in the process of reproduction. Recently published works by Stephanie E. Jones-Rogers and Marie Molloy, while not quantitative in their methodology, add much needed scholarship on the economic behaviours of slaveholding women.[62]

Combining quantitative analysis and ideas from the 'New History of Capitalism' school, Daina Ramey Berry's *The Price for Their Pound of Flesh* (2017) merges economic patterns of appraisals of slave value with testimony from the formerly enslaved, switching between values on enslaved bodies set out by enslavers and 'soul values', an internal judgement of value by the enslaved that escaped commodification. Berry used the data from probate records collected by Fogel and Engerman, and combined it with plantation records, diaries, trading company records, bills of sale, receipts, auction reports, insurance companies, titles, deeds, gifts, court records, medical records and virtually any written document she could find that included name, age, sex, monetary value and year data. Berry's database contains values of nearly 90,000 people from the Upper and Lower South from birth to death.[63] She juxtaposed the market value of enslaved people

---

[62]Marie Molloy, *Single, White, Slaveholding Women in the Nineteenth-Century American South* (Columbia: University of South Carolina Press, 2018); Stephanie E. Jones-Rogers, *They Were Her Property: White Women as Slave Owners in the American South* (New Haven, CT: Yale University Press, 2019). For a more general discussion on the exclusion of women's history from recent histories of capitalism, see also, A.D. Stanley, 'Histories of Capitalism and Sex Difference', *Journal of the Early Republic* 36 (2016), pp. 344–50; E. Hartigan-O'Connor, 'Gender's Value in the History of Capitalism', *Journal of the Early Republic* 36 (2016), pp. 614–35.

[63]D.R. Berry, *The Price for Their Pound of Flesh: The Value of the Enslaved from Womb to Grave, in the Building of a Nation* (Boston, MA: Beacon Press, 2017), p. 208.

(the price at which they were sold) with the appraisal value (assessed by owners, banks and insurers), and in doing this, she reimagined the life cycles of enslaved people. With the value of elderly enslaved people paralleling that of children ten and under, enslaved people started and ended their lives not having to compete against the 'price tag put upon their bodies'.[64] Berry was able to challenge economic historians by matching their big data and combining it with a sophisticated social and cultural analytical framework. Berry's work is unique in her constant referral to the 'soul value' of enslaved people – the self-worth of enslaved people is privileged in a manner that is unusual for economic studies.

Conclusion

Each section of this chapter has demonstrated that good quantitative history is not just 'quantitative'. Numbers are not neutral, and the methodological challenge of quantitative history is being able to constantly balance historical sense and statistics. A knowledge of the circumstances of the data, and an awareness of how such data might be used for good in the present, without overstating, and in line with qualitative sources produced (primarily) by the formerly enslaved. This type of work takes both mental agility, and the ability and stamina that long detailed quantitative study requires. The fact is that many of the large-scale quantitative projects within other disciplines are conducted by groups of researchers and can take years to put together. Yet, there is still scope for quantitative work to be done effectively within the confines of a time-limited project, thesis or dissertation. Given a certain degree of background knowledge a lot can be learned by simply counting. But in the same manner, the assessment of usefulness, or representativeness of a set of data, is an art that depends on judgement, knowledge and experience. Mathematical equations rarely lend themselves well to human behaviour alone, so the usefulness of any calculation will depend as much on the judgement of the historian as the input of data and the calculation done on a calculator or computer program. Historians of slavery, therefore, cannot just leave the counting to the people who 'do numbers'.

---

[64]Ibid., p. 132.

Bibliography

Baptist, E., *The Half Has Never Been Told: Slavery and the Making of American Capitalism* (New York: Basic Books, 2014).

Berry, D.R., *The Price for Their Pound of Flesh: The Value of the Enslaved from Womb to Grave, in the Building of a Nation* (Boston, MA: Beacon Press, 2017).

David, P.A., H.G. Gutman, R. Sutch, P. Temin, G. Wright and K. Stampp, eds, *Reckoning with Slavery: Critical Essays in the Quantitative History of American Negro Slavery* (New York: Oxford University Press, 1976).

Escott, P.D., *Slavery Remembered: A Record of Twentieth Century Slave Narratives* (Chapel Hill: University of North Carolina Press, 1979).

Fogel, R.W. and S. Engerman, *Time on the Cross: The Economics of American Negro Slavery* (New York: Little Brown and Company, 1974).

Johnson, W., *River of Dark Dreams: Slavery and Empire in the Cotton Kingdom* (Cambridge, MA: Harvard University Press, 2013).

Tadman, M., *Speculators and Slaves: Masters Traders and Slaves in the Old South* (Madison: University of Wisconsin Press, 1989).

West, E., *Chains of Love: Slave Couples in Antebellum South Carolina* (Urbana: University of Illinois Press, 2004).

Williams, E., *Capitalism and Slavery* (Chapel Hill: University of North Carolina Press, 1944).

16

Psychohistory and slavery

Patrick H. Breen

Providence College

Antebellum psychology of slavery

In the March 1844 issue of the *Southern Literary Messenger*, C.B. Hayden launched a new front in the debate over slavery. He published a survey 'On the Distribution of Insanity in the U. States'. The short article congratulated Americans on their great good fortune of not having insanity rates as high as those in Europe, but he asked if America's 'free institutions in which we glory' might actually 'promote' insanity. The question became only more provocative as he drilled into the 1840 census data on insanity. He noted that the insanity among blacks was markedly higher in the northern states, highest in Maine where one in fourteen black residents was insane. In contrast, the rate of insanity among blacks in the south was much lower: the slave state with the highest rate of insanity, Missouri, had about a third the rate of black insanity of any free state. Louisiana, with less than one case per forty-three hundred black residents, had 1 per cent the rate of black insanity reported in Massachusetts. Even regional reports, Hayden argued, supported his thesis. Eastern Virginia, which had many more slaves than in what would become West Virginia, had a significantly lower rate of insanity. 'The negro of the South … cares not for the morrow, well knowing, that another will provide what he shall eat, what he shall drink, and wherewithal he shall be clothed.'[1] Hayden's article garnered an immediate response. James McCune Smith, an African-American medical doctor who had graduated from the University of Glasgow, attacked Hayden's contention that one in fourteen blacks in Maine was insane. Examining the census data, Smith found that six Maine towns had more insane blacks than black residents. As a result, Smith rejected Hayden's conclusions. In fact, he asserted that Hayden's reading of the psychological effects of slavery was backwards. To Smith, slavery was debilitating. 'Freedom', on the other hand, 'has not made us mad; it has strengthened our minds by throwing us on our own resources'.[2]

Hayden's insanity thesis was not the only controversial interpretation of slave psychology made in the antebellum period. In September 1851, Samuel Cartwright, a New Orleans doctor physician writing in the southern periodical *DeBow's Review*, developed a different argument about the psychology of slavery. He coined the term 'Drapetomania'. Coming from the words for 'mad or crazy' and 'runaway slave', Cartwright intended to trace the psychological roots of the tendency slaves had to flee their owners. He also coined terms for other diseases, including Dysæsthesia Æthiopica. Slaves suffering from this infirmity tended to 'break, waste and destroy everything that they handle ... tear, burn or rend their own clothing, and paying no attention to the rights of property, steal others to replace what they have destroyed'. According to Cartwright, this disease 'is easily curable': the afflicted slaves should be put 'to some hard kind of work in the open air and sunshine, that will compel him to expand his lungs, as chopping wood, splitting rails, or sawing with cross-cut or whip saw'.[3] While Cartwright insisted that his new terminology was based upon 'sound psychological principles', the opponents of slavery mocked his racist psychology. Frederick Law Olmsted, for instance, observed that in colonial times the runaways were '*generally white men*, convicts sold for

---

[1]C.B. Hayden, 'On the Distribution of Insanity in the U. States', *The Southern Literary Messenger* 10: 3 (March 1844), pp. 178–81, p. 180. This was not the first discussion of the psychological effects of slavery. Fifty years earlier, Thomas Jefferson observed that the children of slaveholders, 'nursed educated, and daily exercised in tyranny, cannot but be stamped with its odious peculiarities'. Thomas Jefferson, *Notes on the State of Virginia* (Philadelphia, 1788), p. 172, at https://docsouth.unc.edu/southlit/jefferson/jefferson.html
[2]James M'Cune Smith, 'Freedom and Slavery for African-Americans', 29 January 1844, in Carter G. Woodson, ed., *The Mind of the Negro as Reflected in Letters During the Crisis 1800–1860* (Mineola, NY: Dover, 2013), p. 276.
[3]Samuel Cartwright, 'Diseases and Peculiarities of the Negro Race', *De Bow's Review* 11: 3 (September 1851), pp. 331–8.

their crimes .... Owing, probably to the neglect of sufficient quarantine precautions, *Dysæsthesia Ethiopica* ... was not confined to the Ethiopian stock, but, perhaps, from their then more close association in the labors of the plantation, it too frequently, also, attacked the white slaves'.[4]

While Olmsted lampooned Cartwright's outlandish theories, the psychological effects of slavery were no laughing matter for former slaves. In *The Narrative of the Life of Frederick Douglass*, 1845, Douglass described 'the soul-killing effects of slavery', which he tried to portray when he recounted the sexually charged sadistic torture of his Aunt Hester or even Douglass's own suicidal impulses. During the year that Douglass was sent to live with a slave breaker, he recalled that he 'was broken in body, soul, and spirit. My natural elasticity was crushed ... the cheerful spark that lingered about my eye died; the dark night of slavery closed in upon me; and behold a man transformed into a brute!' Sixteen years later, Harriet Jacobs vividly described for her readers the psychological anguish she faced as female slave, both in dealing with the lecherous entreaties of her slave master and also the constant anxiety for the fate of her own children. In *Incidents in the Life of a Slave Girl*, she also recalled how her own grandmother, Molly Horniblow, 'broke down under the weight of anxiety and toil'.[5] During the years leading up to the Civil War, the psychological effects of the institution of slavery was a vital question.

W.E.B. Du Bois and the psychology of slavery

After the Civil War, the debate over the psychological effects of slavery flagged. In part this was because many decided that the racial problems were no longer the most pressing issues facing the nation. Following the Civil War, slavery was dead. And many people – both white and black – had no intention of revisiting some of the most painful parts of this

---

[4]Frederick Law Olmsted, *A Journey in the Seaboard Slave States with Remarks on Their Economy* (New York: 1856), p. 226.
[5]Frederick Douglass, *The Narrative of the Life of Frederick Douglass: An American Slave Written by Himself* (1845), 'soul-killing', p. 14; 'brute', p. 63; on Hester, pp. 5–8; on suicidal impulses, p. 41; https://docsouth.unc.edu/neh/douglass/douglass.html; Harriet Jacobs, *Incidents in the Life of a Slave Girl, Written by Herself*, ed. and Intro. by Jean Fagan Yellin (Cambridge: Harvard University Press, 1987), p. 123.

chapter in American history. The movement away from close readings of the psychological effects of slavery was also tied to developments in the field of history. In the late nineteenth century, a new model for doing academic history was imported to America from Germany, where scholars had championed archival research and close analysis of primary sources. Students including many new doctoral students would go to the archives to find out in Leopold von Ranke's phrase 'wie es eigentlich gewesen' or 'what actually happened'. Because of the nature of the archival collection, however, what they found in the archives tended to be what powerful people and institutions had left records of, something that made it easy to study politics and diplomacy and harder to study slavery, let alone the 'Peculiar Institution's' psychological effects.[6]

The rise of academic history also made it less likely that formally trained historians would be interested in the topic. The schooling requirements of the new research universities created a new barrier for less privileged students. Although some blacks were able to earn doctorates, that credential did not open the doors to employment at the best universities in the United States, which meant that the founding generations of academic historians were trained by people who were focused on technique and largely uninterested in developing a new interpretation of slavery. In fact, to this new generation of historians of the South – many trained by Columbia University Professor William Archibald Dunning and known colloquially as the Dunning School – the central racial problem in American history was not the legacy of slavery, but the problems of Reconstruction, which Dunning had unsympathetically described as 'the disasters of negro political supremacy'.[7] Even so, not all of Dunning's students studied Reconstruction. The most important student of slavery of this era was Georgia-born Ulrich Bonnell

---

[6] Frederick Douglass alludes to this problem at the start of his fictional *The Heroic Slave*, when he notes that Madison Washington 'a man who loved liberty as well as did Patrick Henry – who deserved it as much as Thomas Jefferson, – and who fought for it with a valor as high, an arm as strong, and against odds as great, as he who led all the armies of the American colonies through the great war for freedom and independence, lives now only in the chattel records of his native State'. See Douglass, *The Heroic Slave* (Cleveland, 1853), p. 175, at http://utc.iath.virginia.edu/africam/affifda1t.html. W.E.B. Du Bois also makes a similar point about a later period in African-American history, when he observed, 'The chief witness in Reconstruction, the emancipated slave himself, has been almost barred from court. His written Reconstruction record has largely been destroyed and nearly always neglected.' See *Black Reconstruction, 1860–1880* (New York: Atheneum 1992), p. 721.
[7] William Archibald Dunning, *Reconstruction, Political and Economic, 1865–1877* (New York: Harper and Brothers, 1907), p. 114. While Dunning was the most important of his era's scholars on the South, he was hardly alone. For Du Bois's survey of the field, see his 'The Propaganda of History' in *Black Reconstruction in America*, pp. 711–29.

Phillips. Phillips taught at the University of Michigan and Yale and in 1918 published *American Negro Slavery*. Phillips's stoutest defender, Eugene D. Genovese, lauds Phillips's mastery of the archival sources on slavery in the South. Yet even Genovese had to accept Stanley Elkins's critique that Phillips 'did not take the Negroes seriously as men and women', hardly a propitious foundation for a psychological history of slavery.[8]

As a result, the most psychologically astute work on the psychology of slavery, *The Souls of Black Folks,* was out of step with the profession. While Du Bois's training was completely ordinary and his first history was methodologically orthodox, he grew disenchanted with the modern historical project. In one of his autobiographies, Du Bois recalled a moment when the problem of the new dispassionate historical scholarship became perfectly clear. In April of 1899, Du Bois heard the news that Sam Hose, a black man in central Georgia, had killed his landlord's wife. Realizing the danger of the moment, Du Bois composed 'a carefully and reasoned statement' that he intended to deliver to the Atlanta *Constitution*, but he learned that Hose had been lynched before he could reach Joel Chandler Harris's offices. According to his autobiography, Du Bois was shaken by this lynching and upon reflection concluded two things: 'first, one could not be a calm, cool, and detached scientist while Negroes were lynched, murdered and starved; and secondly, there was no such definite demand for scientific work of the sort that I was doing.'[9]

Du Bois's growing awareness of the shortcomings of problems with the field did not turn him entirely from history – he continued to write historical works even after he left the academy in 1910 – but Du Bois became less

---

[8] Eugene D. Genovese, 'Ulrich Bonnell Phillips & His Critics', foreword to Ulrich Bonnell Phillips, *American Negro Slavery: A Survey of the Supply, Employment and Control of Negro Labor as Determined by the Plantation Regime* (Baton Rouge: Louisiana State University Press, 1966), p. xix. Stanley Elkins makes much the same assertion phrased slightly differently in his introduction to *Slavery: A Problem in American Institutional and Intellectual Life*, 3rd ed., revised (Chicago: University of Chicago Press, 1959, 1976), p. 10.

[9] W.E.B Du Bois, *The Suppression of the African Slave-Trade to the United States of America, 1638–1870* in Nathan Huggins, ed., W.E.B. Du Bois: *Writings*, The *Suppressions of the African Slave-Trade*, *The Souls of Black Folks, Dusk of Dawn, Essays* (New York: Library of America, 1986), quote on p. 3; W.E.B. Du Bois, *The Autobiography of W. E. B. Du Bois: A Soliloquy on Viewing My Life from the Last Decade of Its First Century* (New York: Dover, 1964), p. 222. Du Bois's story of a sudden realization with the problem of academic history seems simplistic as he already had written a sociological analysis of blacks in Philadelphia, which freed him from writing solely about the past, and even more so because the *Atlantic Monthly* had published his most methodologically innovate piece of historical writing in 1897, two years before the lynching. See W.E.B Du Bois, 'Strivings of the Negro People', *The Atlantic Monthly* (August 1897), at https://www.theatlantic.com/magazine/archive/1897/08/strivings-of-the-negro-people/305446/.

willing to restrict his writing to the new rules of the discipline. For example, *The Souls of Black Folks* abandoned the fiction of an impartial author. Writing in the first-person, Du Bois developed the idea that the racism and oppression created what he termed 'double-consciousness'. According to Du Bois, the self of black Americans was essentially conflicted: 'an American, a Negro; two souls, two thoughts, two unreconciled strivings; two warring ideals in one dark body.' Du Bois then put this psychological division at the centre of African-American History: 'The history of the American Negro', he contended, 'is the history of this strife,—this longing to attain self-conscious manhood, to merge his double self into a better truer self.' In his later years, Du Bois would become more explicitly Freudian, but his early training as a student of William James at Harvard had opened the door for Du Bois to explore the complex interactions of racism and the psyche in ways that most of his contemporaries did not.[10]

Psychoanalysis and the psychohistory of slavery

Du Bois's sensitive writings on the psychological effects of slavery and racism stood as exceptional. Most academic historians writing about America were not concerned about the subject, and, even if they had been, as a group they were methodologically unprepared to handle the topic.[11] But changes in the world of psychology in time gave academic historians

---

[10]W.E.B Du Bois, *The Souls of Blacks Folk*, in *W. E. B. Du Bois: Writings*, pp. 364–5. For a great review of the history of the term 'double consciousness', see John P. Pittman, 'Double Consciousness' in Edward N. Zalta, ed., *The Stanford Encyclopedia of Philosophy* (Summer 2016), at https://plato.stanford.edu/archives/sum2016/entries/double-consciousness/ Following the publication of *The Souls of Black Folks*, Du Bois avoided the phrase 'double consciousness' – it never appeared again in his writing – and he eventually adopted a Freudian theory of self, which he found helpful in contesting a 'liberal' or unified theory of self, which Du Bois found unsatisfying and ultimately incapable of explaining the intransigence of white racism. For Du Bois's Freudian turn, see his 1940 *Dusk of Dawn*, in *W. E. B. Du Bois: Writings*, p. 770. See also Shannon Sullivan, 'Remembering the Gift: W. E. B. Du Bois on the Unconscious and the Economic Operations of Racism', *Transactions of the Charles S. Pierce Society* 39: 2 (Spring 2003), pp. 205–25. In the 1990s, writers used the language of 'double consciousness' at an unprecedented rate. See https://books.google.com/ngrams

[11]Henry Adams, the other great figure who produced a psychologically rich autobiography, *The Education of Henry Adams*, had, like Du Bois, been trained in the German methods and also, like Du Bois, left academic history.

new tools to begin writing works in the sub-discipline of psychobiography. And no figure is more important in this development than Sigmund Freud. For Freud, the conscious was just one part of the mind. People had unconscious feelings, thoughts and urges that also shaped their identities in essential ways. Neuroses, such as anxiety and depression, could be traced to a conflict between the unconscious urges (which Freud labelled the 'id') and the demands of the rational self (the 'ego') and the internalized rules of society (the 'superego'). At first, Freud developed his theory as a way to work 'towards the explanation of psychoses', but as he developed ways of exploring the unconscious, he believed that psychoanalysis offered the potential to treat mental health problems.

Freud also saw the potential of psychoanalysis for explaining the actions of prominent historical figures. In 1910, Freud published the first modern psychobiography, a portrait of Leonardo da Vinci. Other psychoanalysts followed Freud's lead. Within a few decades, psychoanalysts and their followers had produced scores of psychobiographies.[12] Despite the popularity of these psychobiographies, academic historians were slow to adopt the techniques of psychoanalysis to their own work. In part this could be understood as a reticence to master a second discipline (especially one as fragmented as psychology, which quickly split into many different schools that each had its own approach to the mind), but it also reflected a scepticism of the inferences supported mainly by psychoanalytic theory.

---

[12]Sigmund Freud, *Leonardo da Vinci: A Psychosexual Study of Infantile Reminiscence*, trans. A.A Brill (New York: Moffat, 1916), at https://www.bartleby.com/277/1.html; Meyer Schapiro, 'Leonardo and Freud: An Art-Historical Study', *Journal of the History of Ideas* 17: 2 (1956), pp. 147–78; Donna Arzt, 'Psychohistory and Its Discontents', *Biography* 1: 3 (Summer 1978), pp. 1–36. See Walter Isaacson, *Leonardo da Vinci* (New York: Simon and Schuster, 2017). Freud based his reading of Leonardo on a mistranslation, but that setback did not prevent Freud from attempting two more psychobiographies, one of Fyodor Dostoevsky and another, posthumously published by his co-author William C. Bullitt, of Woodrow Wilson. Some psychohistorians insisted that Bullitt corrupted the biography of Wilson, but recent work makes it clear that Freud was in fact a co-author of *Thomas Woodrow Wilson: A Psychological Study* (1967). See Ben Yagoda, 'What Drove Sigmund Freud to Write a Scandalous Biography of Woodrow Wilson?' *The Smithsonian* (September 2018), at https://www.smithsonianmag.com/history/what-drove-sigmund-freud-write-scandalous-biography-woodrow-wilson-180970042/. For listings of early psychobiographies, including Fritz Wittels, *Sigmund Freud, His Personality, His Teachings and His School* (London, 1924), see Terry H. Anderson, 'Becoming Sane with Psychohistory', *The Historian* 41: 1 (November 1978), pp. 1–20. See William Todd Schultz's 'Introducing Psychobiography' in *Handbook of Psychobiography* (New York: Oxford University Press, 2005), pp. 3–18 for an account of the resistance to psychobiography from the academic discipline of psychology.

Eventually the discomfort of some historians with the methods of psychoanalysis declined, especially after the publication of Alexander L. George and Juliette L. George's 1956 *Woodrow Wilson and Colonel House: A Personality Study*, and Erik Erikson's 1958 *Young Man Luther: A Study in Psychoanalysis and History*. In December 1957, William L. Langer delivered a presidential address to the American Historical Association titled 'The Next Assignment', in which he tasked the profession to enrich 'our historical understanding through the exploitation of the concepts and findings of ... psychoanalysis'. By the 1980s, many historians and other social scientists had produced psychoanalytically informed biographies of figures such as Andrew Jackson, Thomas Jefferson and Abraham Lincoln.[13]

Among the most prominent and controversial of these psychobiographies was Fawn M. Brodie's *Thomas Jefferson: An Intimate History*, a book that self-consciously adopted psychoanalysis to 'explore the hitherto hidden mysteries of' her subject. In this biography, Brodie argued that Jefferson fathered Sally Hemings's children. To make this argument, she tapped typical sources, including newspaper accounts and the recollections of Sally Hemings's son, Madison. But these sources had always been seen as problematic by Jefferson scholars, so Brodie argued that evidence that 'Sally Hemings had become for Jefferson a special preoccupation may be seen' in Jefferson's daily journal. For example, Brodie observed that soon after the young Sally Hemings arrived in France, Jefferson used the word 'mulatto' eight times in describing the landscape, something Brodie reads as revealing Jefferson's new preoccupations.

---

[13]John W. Blassingame, *The Slave Community: Plantation Life in the Antebellum* South, *Revised and Enlarged Edition* (New York: Oxford University Press, 1972, 1979), quote on p. 284; Alexander L. George and Juliette L. George, *Woodrow Wilson and Colonel House: A Personality Study* (New York: International Publishers, 1968); Erik Erikson, *Young Man Luther: A Study in Psychoanalysis and History* (New York: W. W. Norton, 1958); Erik Erikson, *Dimensions of a New Identity* (New York: W. W. Norton, 1974); Charles B. Strozier, *Lincoln's Quest for Union: Public and Private Meanings* (New York: Basic Books, 1982); Dwight G. Anderson, *Abraham Lincoln: The Quest for Immortality* (New York: Knoft, 1982). See also Winthrop D. Jordan, *White over Black: Attitudes toward the Negro, 1550–1812* (Chapel Hill: University of North Carolina Press, 1968). For related collections, see Robert J. Brugger, *Our Selves, Our Past: Psychological Approaches to American History* (Baltimore, MD: Johns Hopkins University Press, 1984), and Peter N. Stearns and Jan Lewis, *An Emotional History of the United States* (New York: New York University Press, 1998). For examples of scholars opposed to the claims of psychobiography, see Jacques Barzun, *Clio and the Doctors: Psycho-History, Quanto-History and History* (Chicago: University of Chicago Press, 1974); Gerald Izenberg, 'Psychohistory and Intellectual History', *History and Theory* 14: 2 (May 1975), pp. 139–55; and David E. Stannard, *Shrinking History: On Freud and the Failure of Psychohistory* (New York: Oxford University Press, 1980).

Brodie's book was incredibly popular – it was selected as the main selection of the Book-of-the-Month Club – but the psychoanalytic apparatus became an object of ridicule for academic historians, especially those who rejected Brodie's central contention of the long-standing sexual relationship between Hemings and Jefferson. Even those who think that Brodie was right about Jefferson and Hemings criticized her reliance on psychoanalysis. Annette Gordon-Reed, who had argued strongly for the relationship even before DNA evidence suggested that Brodie was right about Jefferson's relationship to Sally Hemings's children, noted that Brodie 'handed her detractors a club with which to beat her about the head and shoulders by employing Freudian symbolism to support her claims'.[14] Gordon-Reed's wariness exemplifies a larger disillusionment with the place of psychobiography in academic historiography. By the end of the twentieth century, Freud no longer enjoyed the standing he once did among professionals or within the reading public. Both professional historians and popular audiences have been affected by the increased use of psychotropics, and other forms of psychotherapy, to treat psychological problems, something that has decreased the saliency of Freudian psychoanalysis within the larger culture.

At the same time, academic history has changed its focus in a way that made historians less interested in biographies in general, let alone psychobiographies. As the profession has emphasized writing 'history from below', historians have become more interested in the stories of the least privileged people in society. In terms of slavery, this requires turning away from an exclusive concern with the slaveholders and writing the stories of slaves. But slaves rarely produced (and society rarely preserved) the type of records that a psychobiographer needs. Among slaves and former slaves, Frederick Douglass stands out as an exceptional former slave who produced voluminous records of the type that a psychobiographer could mine, but even his new standard biography, David Blight's *Frederick Douglass*, uses

---

[14]Annette Gordon-Reed, *Thomas Jefferson and Sally Hemings: An American Controversy* (Charlottesville: University of Virginia Press, 1997), p. 4. For examples of the negative responses to Brodie's *Thomas Jefferson*, see Newell G. Bringhurst, 'Fawn Brodie's *Thomas Jefferson*: The Making of a Popular *and* Controversial Biography', *Pacific Historical Review* 62: 4 (November 1993), pp. 433–54, especially pp. 452–4. See also Newell G. Bringhurst, *Fawn McKay Brodie: A Biographer's Life* (Norman: University of Oklahoma Press, 1999). Recently, Lois W. Banner has a more favourable view of Brodie's work, noting that Brodie used 'Freud and Erikson to inform her narrative without overwhelming it'. See Lois W. Banner, 'AHR Roundtable: Biography as History', *The American Historical Review* 114: 3 (2009), p. 580.

none of the tools of the psychoanalyst, focusing instead on Douglass's prophetic character.[15] Given the way that psychobiography has fallen out of favour, it is not surprising then that the use of the term has declined dramatically since peaking in the late 1980s.[16]

Stanley M. Elkins and Eugene D. Genovese on the slave personality

In 1959, Stanley M. Elkins's *Slavery: A Problem in American Institutional and Intellectual Life* proposed a different approach to the minds of slaves. Rather than trying to do a version of psychoanalysis on specific historical figures, Elkins suggested that the personalities of people who had been enslaved could be conceived as a group. Drawing heavily on the work of Bruno Bettelheim, who had written on the psychological effects of the German concentration camps on the camps' victims, Elkins drew an analogy between the concentration camps and American slave plantations. Just as the victims of the concentration camps were psychologically scarred by their experiences, the people who lived their lives as slaves had their personalities shaped by the institution of slavery. According to Elkins, the most common result was for the enslaved to adopt the role of 'Sambo', a

---

[15] See David W. Blight, *Frederick Douglass: Prophet of Freedom* (New York: Simon and Schuster, 2018). During the bicentennial of Frederick Douglass birth, one book, Danjuma G. Gibson's *Frederick Douglass, a Psychobiography*, adopts the language of psychobiography. But Gibson's book is not a traditional psychobiography, in that Gibson, a theologian, eschews 'the psychosocial objectives generally put forth by traditional psychoanalytic theory, objectives such as oedipal resolution, conflict-free spaces, object seeking, relational seeking, and so on'. Danjuma G. Gibson's *Frederick Douglass, a Psychobiography: Rethinking Subjectivity in the Western Experiment of Democracy* (Cham, Switzerland: Palgrave Macmillan, 2018), p. 11. Perhaps the most successful psychobiography of Frederick Douglass is Peter Walker's essay on Douglass in *Moral Choices*. Walker's approach draws more heavily from William James than Freud. See Peter Walker, *Moral Choices* (Baton Rouge: Louisiana State University Press, 1978).

[16] According to Google's Ngram viewer, 'psychobiography' has declined more than 75 per cent between a peak in 1988 and 2008, the most recent year Google had released. In contrast, the word 'biography' has also declined, but less than 30 per cent from a peak in 1987. See https://books.google.com/ngrams. Lewis Perry's scepticism of the future of psychohistory – evident in the change of the title for a review essay on psychohistory from 'Psychohistory Comes of Age' to 'Has Psychohistory Come of Age?' – reflected his 'disappointment, both in its achievements and in its reception by the historical profession'. See Lewis Perry, 'Has Psychohistory Come of Age?' *The History Teacher* 19: 2 (February 1986), p. 280.

person who evinced the characteristics of 'the perpetual child'. Not all slaves were Sambos, Elkins admitted, but he contended that 'Sambo was by far the most pervasive' role adopted by American slaves.[17]

Elkins's argument that American slavery warped the psychological development of the majority of American slaves set off a tremendous debate about the slaves' personalities. Many rejected Elkins's thesis flatly, following instead Herbert Aptheker, who had concluded his seminal 1941 *American Negro Slave Revolts* with the assertion that 'discontent and rebelliousness were not only exceedingly common, but, indeed, characteristic of American Negro slaves'.[18] Others accepted that there were slaves who acted like Sambos, but they rejected that these actions were authentic expressions of the slaves' personalities. To the extent that the Sambo character existed under American slavery, the characteristic childish behaviours were self-consciously adopted by slaves as a way of ameliorating the tribulations of slavery. Mary Agnes Lewis, for instance, observed that 'the possibility that conformity and compliance might be extorted without significant personality distortion' was not a possibility that Elkins considered.[19]

Others rejected Elkins's thesis on the grounds that the analogy was poorly constructed. The concentration camps were terrible institutions that totally redefined their prisoners' lives. Slavery – albeit it an undeniably horrible institution – left the oppressed, in the words of Earl E. Thorpe, 'more "elbow room"' than the prison camps for slaves to develop their own personalities.

---

[17]Stanley Elkins, *Slavery: A Problem in American Institutional and Intellectual Life*, 3rd ed., revised (Chicago: University of Chicago Press, 1959), p. 130, p. 131.
[18]Herbert Aptheker, *American Negro Slave Revolts: Nat Turner, Denmark Vesey, Gabriel, and Others* (New York: New World Paperbacks, 1943), p. 374. See also Gerald W. Mullin, *Flight and Rebellion: Slave Resistance in Eighteenth-Century Virginia* (New York: Oxford University Press, 1972); Peter H. Wood, *Black Majority: Negroes in Colonial South Carolina from 1670 through the Stono Rebellion* (New York: W. W. Norton, 1974); Douglas R. Egerton, *Gabriel's Rebellion: The Virginia Slave Conspiracies of 1800 and 1802* (Chapel Hill: University of North Carolina Press, 1993); Douglas R. Egerton, *He Shall Go Out Free: The Lives of Denmark Vesey* (Madison, WI: Madison House, 1999); Stephanie M.H. Camp, *Closer to Freedom: Enslaved Women and Everyday Resistance in the Plantation South* (Chapel Hill: University of North Carolina Press, 2004); and Walter C. Rucker, *The River Flows On: Black Resistance, Culture, and Identity Formation in Early America* (Baton Rouge: Louisiana State University Press, 2006).
[19]Mary Agnes Lewis, 'Slavery and Personality' in Ann Lane, ed., *The Debate over Slavery: Stanley Elkins and His Critics* (Urbana: University of Illinois Press, 1971), p. 81. See also Orlando Patterson, 'Quashee' in Lane, ed., *The Debate over Slavery*, pp. 210–19; Earl E. Thorpe, 'Chattel Slavery and Concentration Camps' in Lane, ed., *The Debate over Slavery*, pp. 23–42; and Bertram Wyatt-Brown, 'The Mask of Obedience: Male Slave Psychology in the Old South', *American Historical Review* 93: 5 (December 1988), pp. 1228–52.

Elkins's argument forced historians who rejected it to look for ways that slaves created their own worlds, something that led to an unprecedented outpouring of scholarship on slave family life, culture and religion. In various ways, these scholars all rejected Elkins's thesis that childishness was the most common characteristic of American slaves.[20]

Following this burst of scholarship, most historians of slavery rejected Elkins's work, but the most important work on slavery to emerge in the 1970s, Eugene D. Genovese's *Roll, Jordan, Roll*, built a new interpretation of slavery on the foundation that Elkins had created. In his review of Elkins's *Slavery*, Genovese outlined two main critiques of Elkins's work: first, Elkins presented the Sambo figure as specifically American, while Genovese saw the Sambo figure as a universal product of slavery. Second, he rejected the way that Elkins contrasted Sambo to Nat Turner. To Genovese, 'Sambo, in short, was Sambo only up to the moment that the psychological balance was jarred from within or without; he might then well have become Nat Turner, for every element antithetical to his being a Sambo resided in his nature'. Genovese drew explicitly on the ideas of Hegel, Marx and Gramsci, but elsewhere he noted that the ideas of slave personality in *Roll, Jordan, Roll*, 'draws heavily on Freudian theory, although I saw no need to present an explicit model'. Genovese never fully flushed out the psychological underpinnings of his magnum opus, but in a 1975 essay for *Review of Radical Economics*,

---

[20]Earl E. Thorpe, 'Chattel Slavery and Concentration Camps' in Lane, ed., *The Debate over Slavery*, p. 39; John W. Blassingame, *The Slave Community: Plantation Life in the Antebellum South, Revised and Enlarged Edition* (New York: Oxford University Press, 1972, 1979); George P. Rawick, *From Sundown to Sunup: The Making of the Black Community* (Westport, CN: Greenwood Press, 1972); Leslie Howard Owens, *This Species of Property: Slave Life and Culture in the Old South* (New York: Oxford University Press, 1976); Herbert G. Gutman's *The Black Family in Slavery and Freedom, 1750–1925* (New York: Vintage, 1976); Albert J. Raboteau, *Slave Religion: The 'Invisible Institution' in the Antebellum South* (New York: Oxford University Press, 1978, 1980); Thomas L. Webber, *Deep Like the Rivers: Education in the Slave Community, 1831–1865* (Urbana: University of Illinois Press, 1978); Lawrence W. Levine, *Black Culture and Black Consciousness: Afro-American Folk Thought from Slavery to Freedom* (New York: Oxford University Press, 1977); Charles Joyner, *Down by the Riverside: A South Carolina Slave Community* (Urbana: University of Illinois Press, 1984); Sterling Stuckey, *Slave Culture: Nationalist Theory and the Foundations of Black America* (New York: Oxford University Press, 1987); and Michael A. Gomez, *Exchanging Our Country Marks: The Transformation of African Identities in the Colonial and Antebellum South* (Chapel Hill: University of North Carolina Press, 1998). While this vein of scholarship moved away from Elkins's thesis, some of these scholars' rejection of Elkins's work was not always absolute. For example, Sterling Stuckey rejects Elkins even as he accepts that 'slavery caused not a few bondmen to question their worth as human beings – this much, I believe we can posit with certitude'. Even Blassingame's otherwise path-breaking work on slave community adopts the same personality theory that Elkins introduced. See Sterling Stuckey, 'Through the Prism of Folklore: The Black Ethos in Slavery' in Lane, ed., *The Debate over Slavery*, p. 246; and John W. Blassingame, *The Slave Community*, esp. pp. 284–322.

his wife and frequent collaborator, Elizabeth Fox-Genovese, outlined one way of using a version of Freudian ego psychology to understand the idea of paternalism within a slave society that was central to both Genovese and Fox-Genovese's work.[21]

The psychohistory of slavery in the twenty-first century

Despite the importance of *Roll, Jordan, Roll* – historian Walter Johnson described it as 'the *locus classicus* for some of the most powerful and important ideas that have shaped the discussion of slavery for the last quarter century' – the opaque psychological foundations of the book did little to promote interest in the psychology of slavery and recent historians have deemphasized the psychological effects of slavery. Just as biographers have moved away from psychobiographies, historians of slavery have described slavery in ways that focused on the way that slaveholders restrained and traded black bodies, on the ways that slavery fit in within a growing capitalist world. Edward Baptist, for example, organized his award-winning *The Half Has Never Been Told: Slavery and the Making of American Capitalism* with chapter titles that focus on body parts of slaves. In the chapter titled 'Heads', Baptist alludes not to the psychological effects of slavery, but to 'the severed heads of rebels' who died after the German Coast Uprising of 1811. Within mainstream historiography, Herbert Aptheker's view of resistance has become a default position and the primary explanation for why there were not more examples of outright resistance was not psychological but political and military power. As Walter Johnson put it, 'it seems hard to argue that

---

[21]Eugene D. Genovese, 'Rebelliousness and Docility in the Negro Slave: A Critique of the Elkins Thesis', in Lane, ed., *The Debate over Slavery*, pp. 43–74, p. 71; Eugene D. Genovese, 'Toward a Psychology of Slavery: An Assessment of the Contribution of *The Slave Community*' in Al-Tony Gilmore, ed., *Revisiting Blassingame's The Slave Community: The Scholars Respond* (Westport, CN: Greenwood Press, 1978), p. 41, n. 1; Elizabeth Fox-Genovese, 'Poor Richard at Work in the Cotton Fields: A Critique of the Psychological and Ideological Presuppositions of *Time on the Cross*', *Review of Radical Political Economics* 7: 3 (October 1975), pp. 67–83. For the historical reception of Elkins's thesis, Peter Kolchin finds that 'historians have been virtually unanimous in finding that Elkins erred' in his depiction of the world of slavery. Peter Kolchin, *American Slavery, 1619–1877* (New York: Hill and Wang, 1993), p. 138.

Southern slaveholders ever transformed rule into consent – that they ever, in the final instance, succeeded in ruling by anything other than force.'[22]

To the extent that the current consensus that slaves were essentially rational agents who have been overwhelmed by the power of the slaveholders is to be challenged, the challenge appears to come from historians working on revising the benign portrait of the slave community that appeared in response to Elkins's work. As early as 1983, Peter Kolchin observed that 'the revisionist portrait of the slave community seems distorted if not implausible'. Kolchin's suspicions of more dissension within the slave quarters than the previous generation of scholars suggested has been borne out by the research of a new generation of historians including Brenda Stevenson, Dylan C. Penningroth, Emily West, Anthony Kaye and Jeff Forret.[23]

While most traditional academic historians have approached psychohistory warily, other scholars and healthcare providers have a renewed interest in the psychological effects of slavery in the twenty-first-century African-American community. In a guide 'Best Practice Highlights: African Americans/Blacks' posted on the website of the American Psychiatric Association, Rahn K. Bailey observes that 'historical adversity', of which slavery is the first example, has contributed 'to socioeconomic disparities experienced by Blacks in America today'. Likewise, Joy DeGruy, whose doctorate is in social work, has coined the phrase 'Post Traumatic Slave Syndrome' to describe the problematic psychological inheritance of the descendants of slaves. Some scholars have found the language of trauma especially resonant during the era of the Black Lives Matter movement. While the language of trauma is easily employed by historians of slavery, there are problems involved in trying to adopt the framework of trauma

---

[22]Walter Johnson, 'A Nettlesome Classic Turns Twenty-Five', *Commonplace* 1: 4 (July 2001), http://www.common-place-archives.org/vol-01/no-04/reviews/johnson.shtml; Edward E. Baptist, *The Half of the Story Has Never Been Told: Slavery and the Making of American Capitalism* (New York: Basic Books, 2014), p. 73. In contrast, Nell Irvin Painter, whose curiosity about psychohistory continued even into the twenty-first century, observed dryly that her ongoing 'interest in psychology and other social sciences inspires a certain wariness among my colleagues'. Nell Irvin Painter, *Southern History Across the Color Line* (Chapel Hill: University of North Carolina Press, 2002), p. 5.

[23]Peter Kolchin, 'Reevaluating the Antebellum Slave Community: A Comparative Perspective', *Journal of American History* 71: 3 (December 1983), pp. 579–601, p. 582; Peter Kolchin, *American Slavery*; Brenda Stevenson, *Life in Black and White: Family and Community in the Slave South* (New York: Oxford University Press, 1996); Dylan C. Penningroth, *The Claims of Kinfolk: African-American Property and Community in Nineteenth-Century South* (Chapel Hill: University of North Carolina Press, 2003); Emily West, *Chains of Love: Slave Couples in Antebellum South Carolina* (Urbana: University of Illinois Press, 2004); Anthony E. Kaye, *Joining Places: Slave Neighborhoods in the Old South* (Chapel Hill: University of North Carolina Press, 2007); and Jeff Forret, *Slave against Slave: Plantation Violence in the Old South* (Baton Rouge: Louisiana State University Press, 2015).

studies to the study of slave psychology. In 'Trauma and Other Historians: An Introduction', Yoav Di-Capua asks, 'The psychoanalytic model of trauma is structured on the ideas of a well-defined modern subject or self, but does it apply to societies at large? Do collectives exhibit the same symptoms as traumatized individuals, such as intrusion, dissociation, and repetition?' Ron Eyerman, a sociologist, has done the most to answer this question with respect to the African-American community, but in discussing slavery, Eyerman has turned the question from the trauma of slavery, as traditionally understood by historians, to a 'collective memory' which he finds primarily in the African-American community in the generations following slavery. In doing so, his work is within mainstream trauma theory, which distinguishes the 'psychological process independent from the specific traumatic event', but provides a less helpful roadmap for historians who want to focus upon the experiences of slavery rather than the ways that later generations remembered the traumatic history of slavery.[24]

Bibliography

Barzun, Jacques, *Clio and the Doctors: Psycho-History, Quanto-History and History* (Chicago: University of Chicago Press, 1974).

Blassingame, John W., *The Slave Community: Plantation Life in the Antebellum South* (New York: Oxford University Press, 1972).

---

[24] Rahn K. Bailey, 'Best Practice Highlights: African Americans/Blacks', *American Psychiatric Association*, https://www.psychiatry.org/psychiatrists/cultural-competency/education/best-practice-highlights/best-practice-highlights-for-working-with-african-american-patients (accessed 16 June 2019); Joy DeGruy, *Post Traumatic Slave Syndrome: America's Legacy of Enduring Injury and Healing* (Oakland, CA: Uptone Press, 2005). For an example of the language of trauma being adopted by the Black Lives Matter movement, see Samuel R. Aymer, '"I Can't Breathe": A Case Study—Helping Black Men Cope with Race-Related Trauma Stemming from Police Killing and Brutality', *Journal of Human Behavior in the Social Environment* 26: 3–4 (2016), pp. 367–76; Yoav Di-Capua, 'Trauma and Other Historians: An Introduction', *Historical Reflections* 41: 3 (Winter 2015), pp. 1–13; Ron Eyerman, *Cultural Trauma: Slavery and the Formation of African-American Identity* (New York: Cambridge University Press, 2001), p. 5. For the overview of mainstream trauma theory, see Nathaniel Vincent Mohatt, Azure B. Thompson, Nghi D. Thai, Jacob Kraemer Tebes, 'Historical Trauma as Public Narrative: A Conceptual Review of How History Impacts Present-Day Health', *Social Science and Medicine* 106 (April 2014), pp. 128–36. For examples of scholars working on the memory of slavery, see Soyica Diggs Colbert, Robert J. Patterson, and Aida Levy-Hussen, eds, *The Psychic Hold of Slavery: Legacies in American Expressive Culture* (New Brunswick, NJ: Rutgers University Press, 2016); Alan Rice and Johanna C. Kardux, 'Confronting The Ghostly Legacies of Slavery: The Politics of Black Bodies, Embodied Memories and Memorial Landscapes', *Atlantic Studies* 9: 3 (2012), pp. 245–72.

Colbert, Soyica Diggs, Robert J. Patterson, and Aida Levy-Hussen, eds, *The Psychic Hold of Slavery: Legacies in American Expressive Culture* (New Brunswick, NJ: Rutgers University Press, 2016).

Du Bois, W.E.B., *Writings, The Suppressions of the African Slave-Trade, The Souls of Black Folks, Dusk of Dawn, Essays*, ed. Nathan Huggins (New York: Library of America, 1986).

Elkins, Stanley M., *Slavery: A Problem in American Institutional and Intellectual Life* (Chicago: University of Chicago Press, 1959).

Eyerman, Ron, *Cultural Trauma: Slavery and the Formation of African-American Identity* (New York: Cambridge University Press, 2001).

Fox-Genovese, Elizabeth, 'Poor Richard at Work in the Cotton Fields: A Critique of the Psychological and Ideological Presuppositions of *Time on the Cross*', *Review of Radical Political Economics*, 7: 3 (1975), pp. 67–83.

Kovel, Joel, *White Racism: A Psychohistory* (New York: Columbia University Press, 1970).

Lane, Ann, ed., *The Debate over Slavery: Stanley Elkins and His Critics* (Urbana: University of Illinois Press, 1971).

Rice, Alan and Johanna C. Kardux, 'Confronting the Ghostly Legacies of Slavery: The Politics of Black Bodies, Embodied Memories and Memorial Landscapes', *Atlantic Studies*, 9: 3 (2012), pp. 245–72. DOI: 10.1080/14788810.2012.702524

17

Material culture, archaeology and slavery

Lydia Wilson Marshall

DePauw University

In 1968, African-American archaeology began with Charles Fairbanks's excavation of 'slave cabins' at Kingsley Plantation, Florida.[1] Fellow archaeologists quickly followed Fairbanks's lead in excavating other slave-related sites. Before long, African-American archaeology developed into a robust and vibrant field in the United States, the Caribbean and broader Latin America. Yet, some fifty years after that first pioneering excavation at Kingsley, archaeological studies remained essentially absent from the historical literature about slavery in the Americas. At the turn of the twenty-first century, few such historical studies cited archaeological research; even fewer integrated material data into their interpretations.[2] Even today, thoroughly interdisciplinary studies of American slavery remain rare. Archaeology also has made little contribution to historians' understanding of enslaved people in ancient Rome; classical historians tend to underestimate slavery's material imprint and the power of artefacts to expand our

---

[1] Charles H. Fairbanks, 'The Kingsley Slave Cabins in Duval County, Florida, 1968', *The Conference on Historic Site Archaeology Papers* 7 (1972), pp. 62–93.
[2] Daniel L. Fountain, 'Historians and Historical Archaeology: Slave Sites', *Journal of Interdisciplinary History* 26: 1 (1995), pp. 67–77.

understanding of the institution.[3] Likewise, in Africa, historians of slavery but rarely call upon archaeological data in constructing their arguments.[4]

The call for collaboration between historians and archaeologists of slavery is not new. The pioneering archaeologist of slavery Charles Fairbanks himself argued that 'only full cooperation [between historians and archaeologists] will yield significant results. We must guard against the idea that either discipline has the magic key to complete understanding'.[5] While interdisciplinary research about slavery has increased over the past two decades, impediments to a productive partnership persist. For example, even with their field's recent 'material turn', few historians have been formally trained in the analysis of material culture.[6] In addition, archaeologists do not often publish in historical journals or present their data in ways that are accessible and useful to historians.[7] The schism between archaeology and history is also rooted in each field's disciplinary goals, conventions and sources.

Archaeology and history

Archaeology in the United States and increasingly in Europe is associated with the broader field of anthropology. Thus, much archaeological writing remains rooted in a comparative and generalizing social science tradition. That is, archaeologists tend to push past the particularities of their case studies towards the analysis of more universal patterns of human behaviour. While many historians seek to build the most particularistic, detailed and locally specific understandings of past life possible, archaeologists maintain more of a comparative eye and seek patterns that extend cross-regionally

---

[3]Nico Roymans and Marenne Zandstra, 'Indications for Rural Slavery in the Northern Provinces' in Nico Roymans and Ton Derks, eds, *Villa Landscapes in the Roman North: Economy, Culture and Lifestyles* (Amsterdam: Amsterdam University Press, 2011), pp. 161–77. Jane Webster, 'Archaeologies of Slavery and Servitude: Bringing "New World" Perspectives to Roman Britain', *Journal of Roman Archaeology* 18 (2005), pp. 161–79.
[4]Paul J. Lane and Kevin C. MacDonald, 'Introduction: Slavery, Social Revolutions and Enduring Memories' in Paul J. Lane and Kevin C. MacDonald, eds, *Slavery in Africa: Archaeology and Memory* (Oxford: Oxford University Press, 2011), pp. 1–21.
[5]Fairbanks, 'The Kingsley Slave Cabins in Duval County, Florida, 1968', p. 1.
[6]Anne Gerritsen and Giorgio Riello, 'Introduction: Writing Material Culture History' in Anne Gerritsen and Giorgio Riello, eds, *Writing Material Culture History* (London: Bloomsbury, 2015), pp. 1–13.
[7]John Bedell, 'Archaeology and Probate Inventories in the Study of Eighteenth-Century Life', *Journal of Interdisciplinary History* 31: 2 (2000), pp. 223–45.

or cross-culturally.⁸ This difference in disciplinary goals complicates the integration of historical and material data, as these data were collected towards different ends.

Historians' long-standing reluctance to engage archaeological data is also motivated by an outdated perception of archaeology as an alien 'scientific' discipline.⁹ In the 1960s, the theoretical movement 'New Archaeology' (now mostly known as processual archaeology) promoted the field as hypothesis-driven, objective and scientific. Yet, many archaeologists now recognize their field as essentially interpretive. With the cross-disciplinary ascendancy of postmodernism in the 1980s, postprocessualist theory developed in archaeology. Characterizing archaeological inquiry as subjective and interpretive, postprocessualism undermined archaeology's designation as a science. This interpretive turn in archaeology is important to remember as we consider the most serious challenge to the interdisciplinary study of slavery: varying sources.¹⁰

In 1995, historian Jan Vansina wryly observed, 'most historians feel hopelessly lost when reading debates about the fine print of the seriation of pottery styles or the different interpretations of C14 dates, which so often provide the intellectual excitement at archeaological get-togethers.'¹¹ Vansina identified the primary impediment to collaboration between the fields as a difference in sources. Historical and material data sets, he argued, were fundamentally incompatible: while historians study written and oral messages, archaeologists analyse 'mute' artefacts.¹² Yet, in a postprocessual framework, objects are far from mute. That is, as historians themselves increasingly recognize, 'objects themselves are not simply props of history, but tools through which people shape their lives'.¹³ This more active view of material culture reminds researchers to pay attention to how objects are used in cultural reproduction and the negotiation of social relationships.¹⁴

---

⁸Jan Vansina, 'Historians, Are Archeologists Your Siblings?' *History in Africa* 22 (1995), pp. 369–408.
⁹Peter Robertshaw, 'Sibling Rivalry? The Intersection of Archeology and History', *History in Africa* 27 (2000), pp. 261–86.
¹⁰Mary C. Beaudry, Lauren J. Cook, and Stephen A. Mrozowski, 'Artifacts and Active Voices: Material Culture as Social Discourse' in R. McGuire and R. Paynter, eds, *The Archaeology of Inequality* (Oxford: Basil Blackwell, 1991), pp. 150–91.
¹¹Vansina, 'Historians, Are Archaeologists Your Siblings?', pp. 369–70.
¹²Ibid., p. 370.
¹³Gerritsen and Riello, 'Introduction: Writing Material Culture History', p. 2.
¹⁴Stephen T. Driscoll, 'The Relationship Between History and Archaeology: Artefacts, Documents, and Power' in Stephen T. Driscoll and Margaret R. Nieke, eds, *Power and Politics in Early Medieval Britain and Ireland* (Edinburgh: Edinburgh University Press, 1988), pp. 162–87.

Indeed, with scrutiny, the epistemological rationale for dividing the fields of history and archaeology appears little more than arbitrary. After all, documents themselves are also material culture. The division of the categories 'object' and 'document' is a modern cultural creation that reflects literate bias.[15] Questioning existing disciplinary divisions and moving towards greater cooperation between archaeologists and historians are especially important for the study of slavery. Both historians and archaeologists of slavery face a partial record. Historians piece together the lives of the enslaved from documents that were typically written by slave owners. Such documents may elide those aspects of enslaved people's lives that were not considered worthy of recording or were hidden from slave owners. In addition, 'much of the writing about slavery, as of any submerged group, was designed to reinforce the established system'.[16] Anthropologist Claude Lévi-Strauss even argued that, for most of human history, *the* foremost function of written language was to facilitate slavery.[17] The archaeological record of slavery is likewise incomplete. Only some of the daily activities of enslaved people have material residues, and only some of these residues will preserve and be discovered by archaeologists. Moreover, if decontextualized, any object by itself can say very little about slavery. Historical and archaeological sources are usefully considered in tandem not to simply check one record against the other but to critically consider their convergences and divergences in telling a more complex and complete story.

Material culture, space and the study of slavery

History experienced a broad material turn in the early twenty-first century. The call to move 'beyond words'[18] pushed historians of slavery to more critically assess the materiality of the practice. Such materially focused historical analyses did not always rely on archaeological data. However, they often pursued interpretive themes also taken up by archaeologists of slavery. This chapter section reviews the intersection of archaeological and historical

---

[15]Driscoll, 'The Relationship between History and Archaeology', pp. 165–6.
[16]Fairbanks, 'The Kingsley Slave Cabins in Duval County, Florida, 1968', p. 1.
[17]Claude Lévi-Strauss, *Tristes Tropiques* (London: Picador, 1973), p. 393.
[18]Leora Auslander, 'Beyond Words', *American Historical Review* 110: 4 (2006), pp. 1015–44.

efforts to analyse material culture and the use of space; in particular, it considers how objects and space were deployed in slave owners' strategies of coercion and control.

Plantations' spatial organization and built environments have long occupied archaeologists' attention. The ways in which plantation buildings were positioned and plantation space allocated has helped archaeologists better understand planters' efforts to supervise enslaved workers, reinforce these workers' subjugation and enhance their economic productivity.[19] In Cuba, for example, archaeologist Theresa A. Singleton has analysed how slave owners manipulated plantation space to control enslaved people: there, plantation owners built tall walls around slave villages to restrict the movement of residents and used high bell towers as a kind of panopticon.[20] Following Michel Foucault, a panopticon is a viewpoint that facilitates total surveillance without allowing those being observed to know whether or not they are being watched at any particular moment.[21] Because of this uncertainty, enslaved people working in view of a panopticon will begin to monitor themselves, as if they are always being watched, thus participating in their own subjugation. James Delle identified similar patterns of surveillance in Jamaica using what archaeologists call viewshed analysis. Viewshed analysis uses spatial modelling to establish what is visible from any single standpoint on a landscape. At Jamaica's Clydesdale Plantation, Delle established that the overseer's house maintained two distinct vantage points: from the entrance of his house, the overseer could monitor the 'slave village', and from his veranda, he could observe enslaved labourers as they processed harvested coffee. Following Singleton, Delle argued that the ultimate purpose of this spatial arrangement was to establish a panopticon, thus promoting a sense of total surveillance: even in moments when enslaved workers were in reality unobserved by the overseer, the spatial placement of his house ensured that these slaves would monitor themselves as if they were being watched.[22]

---

[19]Theresa A. Singleton, 'Archaeology and Slavery' in Mark M. Smith and Robert L. Paquette, eds, *The Oxford Handbook of Slavery in the Americas* (New York: Oxford University Press, 2010), pp. 702–24.
[20]Theresa A. Singleton, 'Slavery and Spatial Dialectics on Cuban Coffee Plantations', *World Archaeology* 33: 1 (2001), pp. 98–114.
[21]Michel Foucault, *Discipline and Punish: The Birth of a Prison* (New York: Random House, 1975).
[22]James A. Delle, 'The Habitus of Jamaican Plantation Landscapes' in James A. Delle, Mark W. Hauser, and Douglas V. Armstrong, eds, *Out of Many, One People: The Historical Archaeology of Colonial Jamaica* (Tuscaloosa, AL: The University of Alabama Press, 2011), pp. 122–43.

Architectural historians have been less likely than archaeologists to rely explicitly on the notion of a panopticon. However, they have also long studied how plantations' landscape and spatial organization may both support and reflect power relationships between residents. Indeed, some influential architectural and landscape studies of plantations predate history's broader turn towards the analysis of material culture in the early twenty-first century. For example, in the early 1990s, American studies scholar John Vlach argued that 'slave quarters were only incidentally meant as residences; they were, foremost, the planters' instruments of social control'.[23] In his analysis of plantation landscapes, Vlach paid attention to visibility in a way that presaged archaeologists' later widespread adoption of viewshed analysis. He argued that enslaved villages established some distance away from the planter's residence and screened from view by trees would be able to create a more autonomous sense of community than those located where surveillance was more total.[24] Sometimes, however, plantation organization less reflected planters' efforts to establish dominance over slaves and more their efforts to advertise this dominance and the concomitant 'orderliness' of the plantation space to other slave owners. For example, historian Dell Upton argued that the careful row-like arrangements of slave houses visible from a plantation's great house reflected a 'white landscape' meant for consumption by a planter's neighbours and other white visitors.[25]

Spatial data demonstrate that efforts to subordinate enslaved workers were often closely entwined with planters' efforts to advertise that subordination to others. Mgoli was a nineteenth-century clove plantation on Pemba Island, now part of Tanzania. At Mgoli, archaeological excavations by Sarah Croucher uncovered a hard packed outdoor clove-drying floor made with stones and rubble just adjacent to the house of the plantation owners who were Omani colonists. Next to the clove-drying floor was a *baraza*, a long stone bench running along the front of the planter's house. Baraza were typical architectural features of elite coastal Eastern African houses and well established by the nineteenth century. They provided a location of hospitality and socializing for elite men. The baraza at Mgoli provided a means of supervising enslaved workers at a critical time in clove processing; incorrect

---

[23]John Michael Vlach, *Back of the Big House: The Architecture of Plantation Slavery* (Chapel Hill: University of North Carolina Press, 1993), p. 165.
[24]Ibid., p. 235.
[25]Dell Upton, 'White and Black Landscapes in Eighteenth-Century Virginia', *Places* 2: 2 (1984), pp. 59–72.

drying methods posed consider financial risk because of the possibility of crop loss. Yet, at the same time, the baraza would have provided a space for socializing between Mgoli's owner and other elite men. The proximity of the baraza to the clove-drying floor served not just economic but also social functions: the presence of enslaved labourers at work would have demonstrated and reinforced these men's high status by comparison.[26]

Efforts to monitor and confine enslaved people are reflected in slave-related architecture from a wide variety of temporal and geographic contexts. Stone-built towers were ubiquitous in rural ancient Greece and several remain standing today. Classical scholars first interpreted these towers as possible military defensive forts. However, they were often located a considerable distance from large settlements and away from extant political borders. Instead, written accounts strongly imply these towers were used for the temporary imprisonment of slaves, for example enslaved women at night. Their height also would have allowed many such structures to act as points of surveillance to monitor slaves at work during the day. These towers' association with slavery is further reflected by their consistent geographical coincidence with Greek landscapes of agriculture and mining where the enslaved laboured.[27] Slavery in ancient Greece and colonial America differed in fundamental ways. Most significantly, no specific ethnicity was associated with enslaved status in Greece while, in the Americas, the African origin of bondspeople ultimately marked them as enslaveable. Nonetheless, slave-related architecture in both settings reflects slave owners' overarching concern with controlling their slaves by controlling their use of space.

Historian Stephanie Camp has argued that 'at the heart of the process of enslavement was a geographical impulse to locate bondspeople in plantation space'.[28] To prove her point, Camp first analysed the widespread use of the pass system in the United States to restrict slave movement outside of plantations. She additionally noted out that, even within the plantation, American slave owners also sought to control enslaved people's movements. For example, some sent their overseers to check on slaves while they were sleeping and promised punishment to anyone found out of place.[29] Spatial

---

[26]Sarah K. Croucher, *Capitalism and Cloves: An Archaeology of Plantation Life on Nineteenth-Century Zanzibar* (New York: Springer, 2015), p. 130.
[27]Sarah P. Morris and John K. Papadopoulos, 'Greek Towers and Slaves: An Archaeology of Exploitation', *American Journal of Archaeology* 109: 2 (2005), pp. 155–225.
[28]Stephanie M.H. Camp, 'The Pleasures of Resistance: Enslaved Women and Body Politics in the Plantation South, 1830–1861', *Journal of Southern History* 68: 3 (2002), pp. 533–72, p. 534.
[29]Camp, 'The Pleasures of Resistance', p. 546.

dynamics as revealed by both historical and archaeological data reveal how central the use and control of space was to broader strategies to control and subordinate slaves. Material culture can help us trace these strategies across time and space. The architectural similarities that archaeologists have identified between stone-built towers in ancient Greece and high bell towers in colonial Cuba are not coincidental: They reflect a shared preoccupation with the surveillance of enslaved workers. By analysing built landscapes of slavery and unpacking how their spatial organization was used as a means of control, we can begin to extrapolate continuities in how slavery was practised. That is, we can better understand how enslaved people's subordination was achieved in a variety of temporal and geographic settings.

Slaveholders reinforced enslaved people's subordinate status not just through control of space but also by limiting their access to material goods. In West Africa, captives were often stripped before boarding ships bound for the Americas; many remained naked for the entirety of the Middle Passage.[30] In the Americas, archaeologists have found clues to the material rupture associated with passage over the Atlantic. For example, despite their ubiquity in West Africa, very few cowrie shells have been recovered at archaeological sites associated with enslaved people in the Americas. This near absence points to the difficulty the enslaved would have faced trying to carry ornaments or other objects from their homelands.[31]

Following this rupture, enslaved people's access to material culture continued to be mediated and controlled by slave owners. In the Caribbean, for example, enslaved artisans, drivers and watchmen maintained a comparatively 'elite' status as compared to field labourers, at least from white slave owners' perspective. Historian Justin Roberts has argued that the status of this 'better sort' of slave was materially reflected in their greater access to food, clothing and even superior building materials for their homes. While no slaves could legally own property, the material goods these workers amassed improved their quality of life and helped buttress their authority over the enslaved people whom they supervised. Indeed, ultimately, such was the purpose of these goods.[32] By providing varying material provisions,

---

[30]Jerome S. Handler, 'The Middle Passage and the Material Culture of Captive Africans', *Slavery & Abolition* 30: 1 (2009), pp. 1–26.
[31]Ibid., pp. 5–6.
[32]Justin Roberts, 'The "Better Sort" and the "Poorer Sort": Wealth Inequalities, Family Formation and the Economy of Energy on British Caribbean Sugar Plantations, 1750–1800', *Slavery & Abolition* 35: 3 (2014), pp. 458–73.

plantation owners sought to establish a hierarchical system within the enslaved population that would contribute to the greater efficiency and profitability of the plantation while also inspiring loyalty among slaves positioned on top of this hierarchy. In this way, the better provisioning of some enslaved workers contributed to the continuing subordination of all.

However, greater access to high-status goods did not invariably signal a higher social status for enslaved people. On Eastern Africa's Swahili Coast, enslaved captives – for example, women marketed as concubines – might be lavishly dressed for the slave market and would be again redressed after their purchase. Historian Jeremy Prestholdt has convincingly argued that this redressing, along with the renaming of captives, represented slave owners' domination; these acts worked together to negate the identities and experiences of enslaved people prior to their capture. Indeed, even when concubines were adorned by their owners with expensive ornaments and lavish clothing, Prestholdt maintains that such apparel was far from representing any power on the part of these enslaved women themselves. Rather, it 'exemplified the divestment of the enslaved's abilities to define themselves physically'.[33]

The inadequacy of simply equating social status and material culture is also revealed by archaeologist John Otto's pioneering work at Canon's Point Plantation, St Simons Island, Georgia, in the 1970s and 1980s. Otto demonstrated several similarities between the material consumption patterns of black enslaved labourers and white overseers at Canon's Point. While there were some material distinctions identified between these groups (for instance, overseers' houses were generally better built than the structures that slaves inhabited), the similarities were more striking. For example, both overseers and slaves consumed little refined blue transfer-printed pearlware and whiteware ceramics as compared to the plantation's owners. Trash deposits from both overseer and slave residences also point to a common dependence on hunting wild animals to supplement rations provided by the plantation owner. Faunal evidence – that is animal bone – additionally suggests both overseers and enslaved people favoured cooked stews that would provide the maximum nourishment from any meat they obtained.[34] However, we should be cautious to read too much into

---

[33]Jeremy Prestholdt, *Domesticating the World: African Consumerism and the Genealogies of Globalization* (Berkeley: University of California Press, 2008), p. 123.
[34]John Solomon Otto, 'Race and Class on Antebellum Plantations' in Robert L. Schuyler, ed., *Archaeological Perspectives on Ethnicity in America: Afro-American and Asian American Culture History* (Farmingdale, NY: Baywood Publishing Company, 1980), pp. 3–13.

these material similarities. Certainly, the archaeological record reveals the economic exploitation of both overseer and enslaved groups. Yet, of course, in no way was the social status of these two groups equivalent. As Otto argued, even poorer whites like overseers 'received immeasurable symbolic rewards from having skin colour identical to the planters'.[35]

A broader limitation of the studies overviewed in this section is their predominant focus on slaveholders' perspectives. For example, while the comparatively greater access to food and clothing afforded to enslaved drivers, artisans and watchmen indicates their greater social status from white slave owners' perspective, it says little about their position as perceived by other enslaved people. As archaeologist Charles E. Orser, Jr., has argued, 'for slaves, those people who could heal the sick, preach, teach, entertain, and fool the master – in short, who could tend to the needs of the slave community – were accorded the highest social positions in slave society'.[36] Since the mid-twentieth century, social history or 'history from below' has been committed to studying the lives of subordinated people. By casting a wide net over many different kinds of sources, historians have become increasingly successful in circumventing the exclusively white perspective that permeates much written documentation in colonial and antebellum America. For one, to better understand the 'world that slaves made',[37] scholars have pursued a broader understanding of their relationship with material culture. Importantly, material culture can help us better understand not only slaveholders' strategies of coercion but also experiences of enslaved people that sat far outside the attention or control of their owners.

In the mid-1930s, the Federal Writers' Project of the Work Projects Administration (WPA) collected over 2,000 accounts from formerly enslaved people in the United States. While historians have used these oral histories to better understand the contours of slavery for well over fifty years, the analysis of slaves' use of material culture in these accounts has only been taken up in earnest in the twenty-first century. In their study of slave foodways, Herbert Covey and Dwight Eisnach used WPA accounts to demonstrate the ingenuity and resourcefulness of enslaved cooks facing

---

[35]John Solomon Otto, 'Black Folks and Poor Buckras: Archeological Evidence of Slave and Overseer Living Conditions on an Antebellum Plantation', *Journal of Black Studies* 14: 2 (1983), pp. 185–200, p. 197.
[36]Charles E. Orser, Jr., 'The Archaeological Analysis of Plantation Society: Replacing Status and Caste with Economics and Power', *American Antiquity* 53: 4 (1988), pp. 735–51, p. 740.
[37]Eugene D. Genovese, *Roll, Jordan, Roll: The World The Slaves Made* (New York: Pantheon Books, 1974).

material shortages: interviewees recalled cooks using glass bottles as rolling pins, baking small 'hoecakes' on old tobacco hoes and using mussel shells as spoons or ladles.[38] The WPA archive additionally provides insight into the materiality of healing practices. For example, the formerly enslaved Emmaline Heard reported the preparation of 'conjuring bags' filled in part with dried and powdered insect parts and maintaining obvious ritual significance.[39] Oral histories collected by the WPA offer more direct access to the perspectives of enslaved people and helpfully bypass the biases and blind spots of written accounts created by and in the interest of slave owners. Yet, in relying on WPA accounts, historians are limited by choices made by interviewers in the 1930s – for example, what questions to ask and what level of detail to record. Archaeological data are thus well positioned to broaden and deepen our historical understanding of the material culture of enslaved people.

Material culture, space and the enslaved

In the twenty-first century, there has been increasing interpretive emphasis in both history and archaeology on enslaved people as social actors. In 1982, historical sociologist Orlando Patterson's seminal *Slavery and Social Death* relied on comparisons between ancient and historical slavery to highlight slave owners' systematic efforts to strip enslaved people of their humanity and objectify them.[40] It is hard to overstate the influence of Patterson's work on scholars of slavery across the disciplines – sociology, history, anthropology, archaeology and so on. The concept of social death, in particular, provided a new means by which to analyse the social status of slaves and the process of enslavement. While Patterson's comparative vision and synthesis of wide-ranging data remain widely admired, his book's fundamental assumption has come under recent fire. Patterson

---

[38]Herbert C. Covey and Dwight Eisnach, *What the Slaves Ate: Recollections of African American Foods and Foodways from the Slave Narratives* (Santa Barbara, CA: Greenwood Press, 2009), pp. 60–5.
[39]Sharla M. Fett, *Working Cures: Healing, Health, and Power on Southern State Plantations* (Chapel Hill: University of North Carolina Press, 2002).
[40]Orlando Patterson, *Slavery and Social Death: A Comparative Study* (Cambridge, MA: Harvard University Press, 1982), pp. 35–76.

posited that enslaved captives suffered a social death in which they lost the social positions they had held in their natal societies and became kinless non-persons. Such alienation was certainly the intention of slave owners. However, researchers increasingly recognize that slaves retained some measure of agency and created social structures independent from their owners.

In other words, enslaved people were not socially dead: people did not in actuality become things under slavery, regardless of whether they were treated as such by slave owners.[41] Historian Vincent Brown argued particularly forcefully against the theory of social death, suggesting that – whatever disorientation and hardships they faced – African women aboard slave ships bound for the Americas were not 'the living dead; [rather] they were the mothers of gasping new societies'.[42] Recognizing the enslaved as people rather than objects is a necessary foundation from which to analyse their use of material culture. Considering slaves' use of material culture propels our analysis beyond slave owners' strategies of coercion and control; it allows us to better understand how bondspeople negotiated their oppression and created social worlds apart from their enslavers.

This chapter section pays particular attention to the use of material culture by enslaved people in the United States, where archaeologists and historians have studied slavery in great depth. I focus on slave material culture in the United States because of its broader comparative relevance: the patterns of cultural creation and persistence identified here can give us insight into enslaved people's use of material culture in times and places with less robust archaeological and historical records. The hope is to begin to identify a language of material engagement that crosses geographic and cultural boundaries. Enslaved captives arrived to the Americas with disparate cultural orientations and a wide variety of geographic origins in Africa. Out of this diversity came the beginnings of more unified African-American cultures. African-American cultural creation remains a strong interpretive focus for archaeologists in the United States. In this section, I first review major theoretical strands influencing the archaeology of slavery in the United States; I then show how recent theoretical shifts have deepened our understanding of enslaved people's use of material culture and space.

---

[41] Nicholas T. Rinehart, 'The Man That Was a Thing: Reconsidering Human Commodification in Slavery', *Journal of Social History* 50: 1 (2016), pp. 1–23.
[42] Vincent Brown, 'Social Death and Political Life in the Study of Slavery', *American Historical Review* 114: 5 (2009), pp. 1231–49, p. 1241.

African-American archaeology has been deeply influenced by debates and ideas originating in the wider field of anthropology. Melville Herskovits's conception of 'Africanisms' and James C. Scott's analysis of resistance have been of particular use to archaeologists. In the 1940s, Melville Herskovits and the sociologist E. Franklin Frazier commenced a debate that would dominate scholarship about African-Americans for a generation. In particular, they disagreed over how much African culture enslaved captives retained once in the New World. Given the extreme trauma of the Middle Passage, Frazier argued that African cultural traditions could not survive the journey over the Atlantic. Instead, captives and their descendants created new practices and norms fashioned after European American cultural and social organization.[43] Herskovits disagreed, arguing that African culture survived its passage to the New World. He worked to identify what he called 'Africanisms' – cultural traits retained from the continent by people of African descent.[44]

Early practitioners of African-American archaeology typically took up Herskovits's side: he inspired decades of archaeological attention to the role of African heritage in African-American cultural creation, including in religion, house style and diet. In the twenty-first century, the field has shifted towards a more middling position on the debate, recognizing both cultural disruption and continuity. Archaeologists have also been more cognizant of the potential harm in over-focusing on Africanisms in that researchers start to 'search for Africa, not for an understanding of African America'.[45] Archaeologists today tend to focus on the many strands that contributed to the creation of African-American culture, including multiple distinct African traditions. Rather than arguing over whether African-American culture is built on an African or European-American foundation, archaeologists are more apt to trace the effects of multiple cultural currents, including indigenous American cultures.

A second major influence on the field of African-American archaeology is James C. Scott's 1985 classic ethnography *Weapons of the Weak*.[46]

---

[43]Edward Franklin Frazier, *The Negro in the United States* (New York: Macmillan, 1949).
[44]Melville J. Herskovits, *The Myth of the Negro Past* (New York: Harper and Brothers, 1941).
[45]Theresa A. Singleton and Mark Bograd, 'Breaking Typological Barriers: Looking for the Colono in Colonoware' in James A. Delle, Stephen A. Mrozowski, and R. Paynter, eds, *Lines that Divide: Historical Archaeologies of Race, Class, and Gender* (Knoxville, TN: University of Tennessee Press, 2000), pp. 3–21, p. 8.
[46]James C. Scott, *Weapons of the Weak: Everyday Forms of Peasant Resistance* (New Haven, CT: Yale University Press, 1985).

Scott's analysis focused on Malaysian peasants' everyday resistance to their oppressors, providing a useful and more universal framework for understanding those acts of resistance that fell well short of armed rebellion or revolution. Archaeologists widely embraced Scott's theoretical tack. His approach gave scholars in African-American archaeology a vocabulary to analyse how smaller acts (like breaking tools, feigning illness or lack of understanding, working slowly, or absconding from work for short periods) were nonetheless acts of resistance against the slaveocracy.

Archaeological attention to enslaved people's resistance was a necessary corrective to persistent master narratives emphasizing slaves' docility or laziness. In the twenty-first century, however, archaeologists have also increasingly recognized the limitations of such an interpretive approach. As applied in archaeology, the at-one-time-revolutionary domination-and-resistance model became a catchall framework in which an expanding array of acts was deemed resistance. That is, archaeologists were so eager to see resistance that the concept's over-application diluted its explanatory power. To put the problem succinctly, domination and resistance models sometimes provided a *pre-determined* explanation for behaviour (i.e. resistance to domination) that was applied regardless of variation in the archaeological data.[47] Also problematically, in these models, enslaved people were only recognized as exercising agency in *reaction* to slave owners' domination. Today, archaeologists increasingly recognize that enslaved people's social worlds extended to corners inaccessible to slave owners. By moving beyond an exclusionary focus on resistance, archaeologists are able to better recognize and analyse enslaved African-Americans' relationships and interactions with each other and with others, such as Native Americans.

These recent shifts – away from 'Africanisms' and away from the constraints of domination-and-resistance models – have deepened archaeologists' understanding of enslaved people's interaction with and use of material culture. Colonoware is a type of pottery that is ubiquitous on many plantation sites in the southeastern United States as well as other contexts of enslavement, including small farms and urban households. Colonoware is low-fired, meaning that it is fired on an open flame rather than in a contained kiln. It is hand-built by coiling long pieces of clay rather

---

[47]Charles E. Orser and Pedro Paulo A. Funari, 'Archaeology and Slave Resistance and Rebellion', *World Archaeology* 33: 1 (2001), pp. 61–72, p. 63.

than turned on a potter's wheel. It is also typically unglazed. This pottery was originally dubbed 'Colono-Indian Ware' by archaeologist Ivor Noël Hume in the early 1960s. Hume had encountered this pottery in his excavations at Colonial Williamsburg; the name he gave the pottery ware reflected both the time period he associated with it and whom he assumed were its producers, Native Americans. When later encountered on plantations in slave contexts, colonoware was at first interpreted following Hume's logic. Very early studies assumed that Native American potters had made and sold the ware even when found in African-American contexts. However, as early as the late 1970s, some archaeologists argued that colonoware was in fact produced by enslaved people of African descent and represented an 'Africanism' or cultural continuity to West African pottery traditions.[48]

More recently, archaeologists have begun to approach colonoware as a type of object that transcends ethnic identification, instead occupying what has been called an 'intercultural' space. That is, scholars have begun to explore how colonoware's form and patterns of use reflect the combination of many cultural currents, including African, Native American and European-American traditions. In the lowcountry of South Carolina, colonoware recovered at slave-related sites consisted primarily of open bowls and globular pots; some scholars have argued these vessel shapes reflect the persistence of a soup-based culinary tradition with roots in West Africa.[49] On the other hand, in the Virginian Chesapeake, colonoware on plantations encompasses a much wider variety of vessel shapes, many of which align with specific and formal English forms, such as porringers and handled cups. These distinctions demonstrate geographically based variance in the relative dominance of African and European-American influence on colonoware pot form. Some archaeologists have suggested these differences in vessel shape may reflect the distinct work regimes and dominant crops in each region. Gang labour in Virginia on tobacco plantations required the continued close supervision of enslaved people by their owners and hired white overseers. Rice cultivation in South Carolina, by contrast, often isolated enslaved labourers from close observation by and interaction with white people since rice fields were geographically dispersed. Thus, the forms of colonoware pottery in Virginia may reflect the greater European influence that enslaved

---

[48]Leland G. Ferguson, 'Looking for the "Afro" in Colono-Indian Pottery', *The Conference on Historic Site Archaeology Papers* 12 (1977), pp. 68–86.
[49]Leland G. Ferguson, *Uncommon Ground: Archaeology and Early African America, 1650–1800* (Washington, DC: Smithsonian, 1992), p. 106.

people there experienced.[50] Attention to the coexistence of multiple cultural currents pushes archaeological analysis past its once exclusionary focus on Africanisms and towards a more nuanced understanding of African-American cultural creation.

Subfloor pits have been another central focus of African-American archaeology. These holes, dug into earthen house floors, are commonly identified on plantations in the southeastern United States. Indeed, these pits' prevalence has led archaeologists to sometimes rely on them as markers of enslaved people's houses even when other construction materials are absent. For example, subfloor pits are often the only lasting indication of houses in fields that were later ploughed, other material indicators having been displaced or disintegrated. Early interpretations of these pits often emphasized their potential role as 'hidey holes' in which to conceal goods pilfered by enslaved people from their owners.[51] However, with their field's movement away from restrictive domination-and-resistance models, archaeologists have started to consider many more potential functions. For one, these pits sometimes served as root cellars, to protect crops from frost over the winter months. Such a practical function is mentioned in some accounts of life from formerly enslaved people. The use of pits as root cellars is also reflected archaeologically in their frequent placement in front of hearths; archaeologists have additionally recovered pollen from sweet potato and corn in soil collected from the bottoms of some pits.[52] However, other pits are located away from hearths and are also dug too shallow to have been practically useful as root cellars.

Additional uses identified by archaeologists for subfloor pits include personal or family storage spaces and, most extraordinarily, religious ancestral shrines. Most such pits are simply filled in with trash at the time of house collapse; thus, the materials that archaeologists recover in pits may not reflect what they held during their period of use. Nonetheless, there are subfloor pits whose excavated contents indicate more deliberate placement of materials rather than a haphazard trash deposit. For example, archaeologist Patricia Samford compared Igbo religious shrines in West

---

[50]James Deetz, 'Archaeology at Flowerdew Hundred' in Theresa A. Singleton, ed., *'I, Too, Am America': Archaeological Studies of African American Life* (Charlottesville: University of Virginia Press, 1999), pp. 39–46, p. 43.
[51]William M. Kelso, *Kingsmill Plantations, 1619-1800: Archaeology of Country Life in Colonial Virginia* (Orlando, FL: Academic Press, 1984), p. 201.
[52]Patricia M. Samford, *Subfloor Pits and the Archaeology of Slavery in Colonial Virginia* (Tuscaloosa: University of Alabama Press, 2007), pp. 123–37.

Africa to four subfloor pits in three different structures at the Utopia Quarter of Virginia's Kingsmill Plantation. These pits yielded complete and unbroken metal artefacts like iron hoes and scythes as well as copper alloy pot handles. The metal objects were accompanied by tobacco pipes, animal bones, broken and complete wine bottles, and grape pollen residue. Pointing out several similarities to West African Igbo ancestral shrines, Samford argued these pits held offerings to ancestors, including not only food but also poured wine libations.[53] By moving away from an exclusionary focus on enslaved people's resistance, archaeologists have begun to study and understand those aspects of life that stretched beyond the gaze and power of slave owners.

Of course, the colonial and antebellum United States is far from representing the wide diversity of times and places in which slavery has occurred in human history. Colonoware and subfloor pits won't help anyone better understanding slavery in ancient Rome, for instance. Yet, there is a broader lesson that emerges from the above analyses: the need to move the analysis of slavery beyond the master-slave relationship. For example, much like the ancestor shrines described above, ancient Roman graffiti written and drawn by enslaved people reveals a vibrant interior world beyond their owners' control or notice.[54] How, then, can historians integrate the kinds of material data emphasized in this chapter section into their own analyses? Archaeological data provides a foothold into the analysis of the physical material world that enslaved people inhabited; it may also help historians better understand corners of that physical world that lay beyond the attention, supervision and understanding of slave owners.

Expanding the analytical lens: Slavery as a time-deep process

One persistent problem facing archaeologists who study slavery is the difficulty of defining a material signature of the practice. Indeed, even in places and time periods when written documents indicate that slavery was a robust and well-established institution, material evidence of domination or restraint is

---

[53]Samford, *Subfloor Pits and the Archaeology of Slavery in Colonial Virginia*, pp. 149–73.
[54]Jane Webster, 'Less Beloved: Roman Archaeology, Slavery and the Failure to Compare', *Archaeological Dialogues* 15: 2 (2008), pp. 103–23.

but rarely unearthed. For example, only a few dozen gang chains and shackles have been identified by archaeologists from Roman-era Europe.[55] The scarcity of such objects has led some scholars to posit that slavery is archaeologically invisible.[56] Others have come out against this supposition, arguing, for example, that violent iconography depicting the subjugation of captives reflects real-life violence and subjugation. Beyond iconography, enslaved people's bodies themselves can be used to identify the practice. Archaeologists have used slaves' skeletal remains to illustrate their recurrent violent abuse, longstanding malnutrition and physical overwork. Captives' natal origins have also been studied via human remains. Entering the body through food, strontium chemical isotopic signatures in bones and teeth reflect local geology; thus, since adult teeth form in childhood and do not remodel like bone, dental strontium isotopic levels can be used to identify captives or slaves raised in an area geologically distinct from where they died.[57]

Another way some archaeologists have begun to move beyond the conundrum of identification is to focus on slavery as a process as opposed to a thing[58] – that is to shift attention away from material markers of slave status or domination and towards markers of the large-scale processes that slavery engendered. Regional-level analyses in Africa have demonstrated how increases in slave raiding prompted greater use of defensive architecture and settlement placement; for example, hilltop lookouts in Tsavo, Kenya,[59] and subterranean structures called *souterrains* in Dahomey (Benin)[60] both offered defensive benefits that surpassed any practical challenges of their habitation, such as difficulties in the procurement of food. As another example, maroons or runaway slaves residing in the Great Dismal Swamp in the southeastern United States were economically isolated from the external world; imported items are almost absent among the artefacts

---

[55]Timothy Taylor, 'Believing the Ancients: Quantitative and Qualitative Dimensions of Slavery and the Slave Trade in Later Prehistoric Eurasia', *World Archaeology* 33 (2001), pp. 27–43.
[56]J. Alexander, 'Islam, Archaeology and Slavery in Africa', *World Archaeology* 33: 1 (2001), pp. 44–60.
[57]Lydia Wilson Marshall, 'Introduction: The Comparative Archaeology of Slavery' in Lydia Wilson Marshall, ed., *The Archaeology of Slavery: A Comparative Approach to Captivity and Coercion* (Carbondale: Southern Illinois University Press, 2015), pp. 1–23.
[58]Ann B. Stahl, 'The Slave Trade as Practice and Memory: What Are the Issues for Archaeologists?' in Catherine M. Cameron, ed., *Invisible Citizens: Captives and Their Consequences* (Salt Lake City: University of Utah Press, 2008), pp. 25–56.
[59]Chapurukha Kusimba, 'Archaeology of Slavery in East Africa', *African Archaeological Review* 21 (2004), pp. 59–88.
[60]J. Cameron Monroe, 'Cities, Slavery, and Rural Ambivalence in Precolonial Dahomey' in Marshall, ed., *The Archaeology of Slavery*, pp. 192–214.

recovered through excavations in the swamp.[61] While material scarcity is not invariably a function of slave or former slave status, here it reflects the need for self-emancipated people to detach from broader colonial society: while not marking slavery in every occurrence, here, with historical context intact, it is clear the scarcity of imported goods is a consequence of swamp residents' former enslavement.

In advocating for a process-oriented approach to slavery, some scholars have questioned the need to 'prove' that slavery existed at all. Given the ubiquity of slavery in modern, historic and ancient societies, archaeologist Timothy Taylor posited that we can practically 'assume access to coerced labor as *a priori*, in the same way as access to drinking water is assumed'.[62] In a similar vein, archaeologist Catherine Cameron has used anthropological and historical data to make a case for the global ubiquity of captives in ancient small-scale societies. She argued not only that captives were numerous in such societies but also that they shaped these societies in profound ways, as bearers of culture and as intermediaries and interpreters between different cultural groups.[63] While she has implored archaeologists to develop more methods for the material identification of slavery, Cameron is equally forceful when arguing for archaeologists to move beyond a fixation on material markers of slave status to the interpretive hard work of understanding slavery's effects and consequences.

In some ways, these analytical moves – into time periods pre-dating historical records and away from an emphasis on material identification – may make emerging research on the archaeology of slavery seem potentially less useful to historians. However, what this new research allows is a re-conceptualization of the material world as being shaped by slavery in ways that cut far deeper than the use of tools of restraint. A house, a cup, a needle, a marble – all these may be as much objects of slavery as shackles or chains because their production, consumption and use was shaped by slave systems. This emphasis on slavery as a practice also moves archaeology

---

[61]Daniel O. Sayers, A *Desolate Place for a Defiant People: The Archaeology of Maroons, Indigenous Americans, and Enslaved Laborers in the Great Dismal* Swamp (Gainesville: University Press of Florida, 2014).

[62]Timothy Taylor, 'Ambushed by a Grotesque: Archaeology, Slavery, and the Third Paradigm' in Michael Parker Pearson and I.J.N. Thorpe, eds, *Warfare, Violence and Slavery in Prehistory* (Oxford: Archaeopress, 2005), pp. 225–33.

[63]Catherine M. Cameron, *Captives: How Stolen People Changed the World* (Lincoln: University of Nebraska, 2016).

out of a position in which it identifies slavery to one in which it analyses and interprets the institution. It thus strengthens archaeologists' potential to partner with historians in a way that does more than 'add flavour'[64] to historical analyses.

Conclusion: The strength of an interdisciplinary approach to slavery

In a description that still bristles many archaeologists today, Ivor Noël Hume – himself an archaeologist – described his field as the 'handmaiden to history' in 1964.[65] This position was one Hume held onto for the span of his career. In 2011, he remarked, 'you know, I called archaeology the "handmaiden of history." I think I coined that phrase. And it is. In most cases it expands history and it dots i's and crosses t's you know'.[66] Archaeologists have overwhelmingly rejected Hume's characterization because of the implicit subservient position in which it places their field as a helping hand to historians. However, there is another more generous and radical way to understand Hume's position. In his 2011 interview, Hume went on to state that 'I became an historian, a social historian who uses the artefacts to illuminate and expand what we think we know'.[67] In claiming the discipline of history as his own, Hume challenged the epistemological distinction between the fields. It's not so much that archaeology should serve history, in this view of Hume, but rather that interpretations of slavery's past should not be siloed into discrete analyses of artefacts, textual records and oral accounts that stymy and impede fuller understanding. Given the incomplete records that both historians and archaeologists of slavery face, the depth and nuance of our interpretations depends on our ability to overcome disciplinary barriers and recognize each other as allies.

---

[64]Driscoll, 'The Relationship between History and Archaeology', p. 136.
[65]Ivor Noël Hume, 'Archaeology: Handmaiden to History', *North Carolina Historical Review* 41: 2 (1964), pp. 215–25.
[66]Ivor Noël Hume and H.M. Miller, 'Ivor Noël Hume: Historical Archaeologist', *The Public Historian* 33: 1 (2011), pp. 9–32, pp. 23–4.
[67]Hume and Miller, 'Ivor Noël Hume: Historical Archaeologist', p. 24.

Bibliography

Cameron, Catherine M., ed., *Invisible Citizens: Captives and Their Consequence* (Salt Lake City: University of Utah Press, 2008).

Croucher, Sarah K., *Capitalism and Cloves: An Archaeology of Plantation Life on Nineteenth-Century Zanzibar* (New York: Springer, 2015).

Fairbanks, Charles H., 'The Kingsley Slave Cabins in Duval County, Florida, 1968', *The Conference on Historic Site Archaeology Papers* 7 (1972), pp. 62–93.

Fennell, Christopher C., *Crossroads and Cosmologies: Diasporas and Ethnogenesis in the New World* (Gainesville: University Press of Florida, 2007).

Ferguson, Leland G., *Uncommon Ground: Archaeology and Early African America, 1650–1800* (Washington, DC: Smithsonian, 2011).

Lane, P.J. and K.C. MacDonald, eds, *Slavery in Africa: Archaeology and Memory* (Oxford: Oxford University Press, 2011).

Marshall, Lydia Wilson, ed., *The Archaeology of Slavery: A Comparative Approach to Captivity and Coercion* (Carbondale: Southern Illinois University Press, 2015).

Orser, Charles E., Jr. and Pedro Paulo A. Funari, 'Archaeology and Slave Resistance and Rebellion', *World Archaeology*, 33: 1 (2001), pp. 61–72.

Singleton, Theresa A., ed., *"I, Too, Am America": Archaeological Studies of African American Life* (Charlottesville: University of Virginia Press, 1999).

18

Slavery and the cultural turn

Raquel Kennon
California State University, Northridge

'Sixty Million and more', the provocative four-word dedication of Toni Morrison's Pulitzer Prize–winning novel *Beloved* (1987), famously alludes to the incalculable number of African people captured and lives lost over the course of the transatlantic slave trade, the estimated sum total of people forcibly transported and enslaved in the Americas for more than three and a half centuries.[1] Invoking the death tolls of war and searing tabulations of genocide, with 'Sixty Million and more' Morrison raises the difficult issue of quantifying those souls deemed 'human cargo', Black flesh turned commodity in a transgenerational, geopolitical economic system rooted in racial capitalism that forcibly extracted labour to make the modern world.[2] Although the consensus among historians is a far lower

---

[1] Toni Morrison, dedication in *Beloved* (New York: Knopf, 1987), [i].David Brion Davis, 'Foreword', in David Eltis and David Richardson, eds, *Atlas of the Transatlantic Slave Trade* (New Haven: Yale University Press, 2010), p. xvii; Colin A. Palmer, *The First Passage: Blacks in the Americas, 1502–1617* (Oxford: Oxford University Press, 1995), p. 23. For an overview of twentieth-century historians' attempts to determine the volume of the slave trade, see Herbert S. Klein, *The Atlantic Slave Trade* (Cambridge: Cambridge University Press, 1999), pp. xx–xxi.

[2] For a reading of connotations of the word 'soul' and its relation to notions of Christian salvation in antislavery movement and slave narratives, see Walter Johnson, *Soul by Soul: Life Inside the Antebellum Slave Market* (Cambridge, Mass: Harvard University Press, 1999), pp. 9–10. For a discussion of the distinction between 'body' and 'flesh' as cultural text, see Hortense J. Spillers, 'Mama's Baby, Papa's Maybe: An American Grammar Book', in *Black, White, and in Color: Essays on American Literature and Culture* (Chicago: The University of Chicago Press, 2003), pp. 206–9. See also Baby Suggs' sermon on loving one's 'flesh that weeps, laughs', Morrison, *Beloved*, pp. 88–9.

figure of approximately twelve and a half million Africans enslaved in the New World, the true and accurate size of the slave trade and the terrors the enslaved endured remain 'unknown' and 'unknowable', to borrow Valerie Smith's language.[3] Morrison's astonishing narrative envisioning of the interior life of her protagonist, Seethe, the enslaved mother who makes agonizing choices to sustain her children, in fact, reveals the extent to which slavery's unknowable horrors defy representation in number or language.

The inability to calculate what Eli Faber calls slavery's 'grim and cruel enormity' attests to the irreducibility of this global tragedy to a definitive number of lives lost or single narrative account.[4] It is precisely this quantitative and discursive resistance to a singular, authoritative scientific accounting that has propelled what scholars designate as the 'cultural turn'.[5] *Beloved* embodies these animating tensions at the core of the turn towards culture in slavery studies, the generative contradictions that emerge from the 'interrelated but distinct bodies of archival material' that Stephanie Smallwood observes are 'one, quantitative, and the other largely textual'.[6] By turning to 'culture', a contested and mutable academic term, novelists, poets, artists and interdisciplinary scholars from the social sciences and humanities

---

On capitalism, race, and slavery, see Cedric J. Robinson, *On Racial Capitalism, Black Internationalism, and Cultures of Resistance*, ed. H.L.T. Quan (Pluto Books, 2019); Edward E. Baptist, *The Half Has Never Been Told* (New York: Basic Books, 2014); Eric Williams, *Capitalism & Slavery* (Chapel Hill: University of North Carolina Press, 1994). For scholarly criticism on comparative atrocities, public reaction to the echoes of the 'six million' of the Holocaust and the implication of 'six times ten', and other resonances of Morrison's dedication, see, for example, Naomi Mandel, '"I Made the Ink": Identity, Complicity, 60 Million, And More', *Modern Fiction Studies* 48: 3 (Fall 2002), pp. 581–613; Caroline Rody, 'Toni Morrison's Beloved: History, "Rememory," and a "Clamor for a Kiss"', *American Literary History* 7: 1 (Spring, 1995), pp. 92–119; Juda Bennett, *Toni Morrison and the Queer Pleasure of Ghosts* (Albany: State University of New York Press, 2014); Walter Clemons, 'The Ghosts of "Sixty Million and More"', in Barbara H. Solomon, ed., *Critical Essays on Toni Morrison's Beloved* (New York: Prentice Hall, 1998), p. 46; Nellie McKay and William L. Andrews, eds, *Toni Morrison's Beloved: A Casebook* (New York: Oxford University Press, 1999).

[3] Valerie Smith, '"Circling the Subject": History and Narrative in Beloved', in Henry Louis Gates Jr. and Anthony Appiah, eds, *Toni Morrison: Critical Perspectives Past and Present* (New York: Amistad, 1993), p. 354.

[4] Eli Faber, *Jews, Slaves, and the Slave Trade: Setting the Record Straight* (New York: New York University Press, 1998), pp. 1–2.

[5] For a discussion of the shift to viewing science as 'part of culture, not above it', see Victoria E. Bonnell and Lynn Hunt, eds, *Beyond the Cultural Turn: New Directions in the Study of Society and Culture* (Berkeley and Los Angeles, California: University of California Press, 1999), p. 14.

[6] Stephanie E. Smallwood, *Saltwater Slavery: A Middle Passage from Africa to American Diaspora* (Cambridge, Mass: Harvard University Press, 2007), p. 4.

attempt to render the ineffability of slavery's past while grappling with and against the limits of language, archival material and cultural memory. The magnitude of the African lives summoned in Morrison's dedication, then, exposes the incalculability of this global atrocity which exceeds the empirical tools of scientific method. The novel powerfully sheds light on slavery's racial intimacies and arrangements of power and domination that Christina Sharpe terms 'monstruous' in the sense of 'a set of known and unknown performances and inhabited horrors, desires and positions produced reproduced, circulated, and transmitted, that are breathed in like air and often unacknowledged to be monstrous'.[7]

Morrison's inclusion of 'and more' further signals the impossibility of (re)solving the violence fuelling this racial calculus, of knowing the exact aggregate number of enslaved Africans who survived in mind and body, of numbering those who perished from the brutalities of the slave system, or by death at their own hands, or their mother's hands, like the fictional Sethe and her historical inspiration, Margaret Garner, attempting to save her children from the terrors of enslavement. Morrison recalls in *The Origin of Others* 'deliberately' choosing 'not to investigate' the 'facts', had they been available, of Margaret Garner's infanticide, 'I wanted to rely fully on my own imagination. My principal interest was in trying to fathom the mother-in-law's inability to condemn her daughter-in-law for murder'.[8] 'The murdered child', Morrison elaborates, is at 'the novel's center and spread'; 'Imagining her was for me the soul of art and its bones'.[9] The amplifying conjunction in the dedication, 'and more', emphasizes the unfathomable and monstrous calculations of slavery, of those who never survived the barracoon, or the horrors of the Middle Passage, those who, fettered, jumped overboard into the Atlantic Ocean before reaching those distant shores, or persevered toiling under the lash in the New World, or those who miraculously managed to steal themselves away into the mountains or free territory, outside the law that sanctioned their bondage. The turn towards culture attends to those names and stories often left unrecorded by early to mid-twentieth-century prevailing modes of researching and theorizing modern slavery.

---

[7]Christina Sharpe, *Monstrous Intimacies: Making Post-Slavery Subjects* (Durham: Duke University Press, 2010), p. 3.
[8]Toni Morrison, *The Origin of Others* (Cambridge, Mass: Harvard University Press, 2017), p. 82.
[9]Ibid., p. 91.

This chapter explores how the 'cultural turn' as epistemological intervention broadens the parameters of slavery scholarship beyond traditional historiographies, conventional sociological analytic frameworks and literary criticism produced in isolation. It extends across disciplinary boundaries to provide new methods of accounting of and for the lives and conditions of the enslaved and those who held them in slavery. The cultural turn promotes far-reaching, eclectic, polemical, refreshingly innovative and cross-disciplinary slavery research which seeks to represent the lives of the enslaved when imagination is the only tool accessible to address the disturbing silences in the archive. 'Critical fabulation', as Saidiya Hartman terms it, is a 'writing practice' which involves 'laboring to paint as full a picture of the lives of the captives as possible'.[10] This theoretical approach, Hartman argues, is a 'double gesture' that 'can be described as straining against the limits of the archive to write a cultural history of the captive, and, at the same time, enacting the impossibility of representing the lives of the captives precisely through the process of narration'.[11] The 'cultural turn' elevates methodologies such as critical fabulation as serious modes of analysis. This reorientation towards culture coincides with recent scholarly interrogations of slavery's archive which urge reformulations of the research questions asked of the archive, and prompt new ways of reading and interpreting archival materials even as it recognizes the impossibility of precise narrative representation.

In what follows, I offer a brief overview of the 'cultural turn' and several of its various analytic threads of signification within a broader academic context. I then focus on the turn to cultural analysis as it has developed specifically within comparative slavery studies in the last decades by examining several ground-breaking texts which have ushered in new critical approaches to the field and shifted theoretical frameworks related to notions of representation, identity and authenticity. In the subsequent section, I take up questions of slavery's archive and digital databases, with an emphasis on the recent scholarly debates and interventions in critical terminology and naming. I conclude by revisiting the conceptualization of 'rememory' in Morrison's *Beloved*, an enduring theme and critical term that has emerged from the cultural turn, which returns us to the issue of quantification in the classic novel's dedication.

---

[10]Saidiya Hartman, 'Venus in Two Acts', *Small Axe* 26:12: 2 (June 2008), pp. 1–14, p. 11.
[11]Ibid., p. 11.

Historicizing the 'Cultural Turn'

The 'cultural turn' is characterized by myriad significations across the academic disciplines. In its simplest gloss, it signifies, beginning with its rise in the late 1970s in the wake of the linguistic turn, a move away from the presumed objectivity and rigor of positivist, natural science applications in scholarly research, and instead valorizes wide-ranging cultural analysis in social science fields as distinct as cultural anthropology, economics, psychology and geography.[12] Although transdisciplinary scholars have developed multiple complex, shifting, at times competing, conceptualizations of 'culture', which variously have come to encompass manifold elements including, but not limited to, value systems, beliefs, customs, rites, rituals, art, habits, language, worldviews, translations, symbols and traditions, theorists have yet to arrive at an authoritative definition that holds across the social sciences, humanities and cultural studies.[13] Doris Bachmann-Medick, who distinguishes between the German language *Kulturwissenschaften* and the related Anglophone cultural studies, in fact, challenges the notion of a single comprehensive cultural turn.[14] Rather, she argues that this shift in scholarly attention is composed of a 'chain' or 'constellation' of different 'cultural turns' such as the interpretive turn, the reflexive turn and the post-colonial turn, each with subcategories including the 'affective turn' and the 'technological turn' that, taken together, might be organized around the larger rubric of the 'cultural turn'.[15] As Gabriel Rockhill and Alfredo Gomez-Muller similarly argue, the concept and question of 'culture' has spurred '*intensive* and

---

[12] Bonnell and Hunt, eds, *Beyond the Cultural Turn*, p. 4, pp. 9–11.
[13] For a cross-section of views on the concept of culture and its many meanings and contexts, see John W. Mohr eds, et al., *Measuring Culture* (New York: Columbia University Press, 2020); Tony Bennett, *Making Culture, Changing Society* (New York: Routledge, 2013); David Swartz, *Culture & Power: The Sociology of Pierre Bourdieu* (Chicago: The University of Chicago Press, 1997); James Clifford, *The Predicament of Culture: Twentieth Century Ethnography, Literature, and Art* (Cambridge, Mass: Harvard University Press, 1988); Clifford Geertz, *Works and Lives: The Anthropologist as Author* (Stanford: Stanford University Press, 1988); James Clifford, *Routes: Travel and Translation in the Late Twentieth Century* (Cambridge, Mass: Harvard University Press, 1997); Robert Edgerton, *Methods and Styles in the Study of Culture* (San Francisco: Chandler & Sharp, 1974); Michel Foucault, *The Hermeneutics of the Subject: Lectures at the Collège de France, 1981–82*, trans. Graham Burchell (New York: Picador, 2005); Seyla Benhabib, *The Claims of Culture: Equality and Diversity in the Global Era* (Princeton: Princeton University Press, 2002); Homi Bhabha, *The Location of Culture* (London: Routledge, 1994).
[14] Doris Bachmann-Medick, *Cultural Turns: New Orientations in the Study of Culture*, trans. Adam Blauhut (Berlin: De Gruyter, 2016), pp. 2–6.
[15] Ibid., p. 18.

extensive conceptual inflation'.[16] Despite this pluralism and 'unprecedented conceptual inflation', the scholarly turn toward broadly construed and protean notions of culture has prompted important methodological shifts in historical research in the last half century.[17]

Noteworthy in this theoretical reorientation is the use of a malleable cultural lens to advance a 'postmodernist critique of knowledge'.[18] As Victoria E. Bonnell and Lynn Hunt argue, Hayden White's *Metahistory: The Historical Imagination in Nineteenth Century Europe* and Clifford Geertz's *The Interpretation of Cultures: Selected Essays*, both published in 1973, 'profoundly influenced the orientation to the study of culture among American social scientists'.[19] Following the 'linguistic turn', semiotics and the arbitrary relationship between the signifier and the signified in Saussure's dyad, the cultural turn stresses the hermeneutic approaches of post-structuralism and deconstruction, and specifically the work of Michel Foucault, Jacques Derrida and Roland Barthes, which unsettles presuppositions about language and authorship; culture itself becomes a text to be read and interpreted. Moreover, the vast influence of Foucault's theorizations of power, language and the production of knowledge in *Discipline and Punish: The Birth of the Prison* (1977) and other germinal works moved beyond literary studies and shifted scholarly thought across disciplines.[20] Geertz refers to this mode of analysis, in the context of ethnographic writing, as 'sorting out structures of signification'.[21] He argues that 'culture is public because meaning is',[22] and elaborates on his notion of 'thick description':

> Our double task is to uncover the conceptual structures that inform our subjects' acts, the 'said' of social discourse, and to construct a system of analysis in whose terms what is generic to those structures, what belongs to them because they are what they are, will stand out against the other determinants of human behavior. In ethnography, the office of theory is to

---

[16]Gabriel Rockhill and Alfredo Gomez-Muller, *Politics of Culture and the Spirit of Critique: Dialogues* (New York: Columbia University Press, 2011), p. 1.
[17]Ibid., pp. 1–2.
[18]Bonnell and Hunt, eds, *Beyond the Cultural Turn*, p. 4.
[19]Ibid., p. 2. See Hayden White, *Metahistory: The Historical Imagination in 19th-Century Europe* (Baltimore: Johns Hopkins University Press, 2014); Clifford Geertz, *The Interpretation of Cultures: Selected Essays* (New York: Basic Books, 2017).
[20]Bachmann-Medick, *Cultural Turns*, pp. 107–9, p. 134; Bonnell and Hunt, eds, *Beyond the Cultural Turn*, p. 9. See also Michel Foucault, *Discipline and Punish: The Birth of the Prison*, trans. Alan Sheridan (New York: Vintage Books, 2012); Michel Foucault, *The Archaeology of Knowledge*, trans. A.M. Sheridan Smith (New York: Vintage Books, 2010).
[21]Geertz, *The Interpretation of Cultures*, p. 10.
[22]Ibid., p. 13.

provide a vocabulary in which what symbolic action has to say about itself – that is – about the role of culture inhuman life – can be expressed.[23]

The importance of uncovering and providing a vocabulary for analysis in the process of meaning making reiterates the textual nature of culture, always subject to interpretation. Ron Eyerman, following Hayden White, likewise emphasizes the process of uncovering as the task of the historian who engages with collective memory of the past to craft narrative which is instrumental in identity formation.[24] While these new directions in cultural analysis that emerged in the 1970s in the social sciences and crystallized in the 1980s and 1990s have been integrated and institutionalized in recent scholarship, the application of these critical approaches to the interdisciplinary studies of slavery has engendered a remarkable array of intersectional research methodologies.

Slavery studies and the 'Cultural Turn'

Drawing on discourses at the intersection of race, ethnicity, gender, sexuality, Black feminist and queer thought, performance, visual, post-colonial and disability studies, the 'cultural turn' in late twentieth- and twenty-first-century slavery studies advances theories and radical praxes that seek to make meaning of slavery's past in order to reckon with and respond to the crises of the present cultural and political moment.[25] Hartman's oft-cited clarion call in her sui generis *Lose Your Mother: A Journey along*

---

[23]Ibid., p. 30.
[24]Ron Eyerman, 'The Past in the Present: Culture and the Transmission of Memory', *Acta Sociologica* 47: 2 (2004), pp. 159–60. See also Ron Eyerman, *Cultural Trauma: Slavery and the Formation of African American Identity* (Cambridge: Cambridge University Press, 2001).
[25]For a sampling of key works that relate slavery's past to the condition of Black life in the contemporary, see Rinaldo Walcott, *On Property* (Windsor, Ontario: Biblioasis, 2021); Morrison, *The Origin of Others*; Christina Sharpe, *In the Wake: On Blackness and Being* (Durham: Duke University Press, 2016); Soyica Diggs Colbert, Robert J. Patterson, and Aida Levy-Hussen, eds, *The Psychic Hold of Slavery: Legacies in American Expressive Culture* (New Brunswick: Rutgers University Press, 2016); Claudia Rankine, 'Black Life is A Condition of Mourning', *New York Times*, 22 June 2015; Ta-Nehisi Coates, 'The Case for Reparations', *The Atlantic*, June 2014; Michelle Alexander, *The New Jim Crow: Mass Incarceration in the Age of Colorblindness* (New York: The New Press, 2012); Douglas A. Blackmon, *Slavery By Another Name: The Re-Enslavement of Black Americans from the Civil War to World War II* (New York: Random House, 2008); Achille Mbembe, *On the Postcolony* (Berkeley and Los Angeles, California: University of California Press, 2001).

the Atlantic Slave Route (2007) bridges past and present, declaring the persistent afterlife of slavery constitutes for African Americans 'skewed life chances, limited access to health and education, premature death, incarceration, and impoverishment'.[26] Relatedly, within Black Studies departments in particular, and Ethnic Studies departments in general, the study of 'culture', historical and contemporary, is foundational to the work and mission underpinning those disciplines. These fields therefore have not undergone a belated turn to culture; their founding premise necessarily takes into consideration race, gender and matrices of power in the formation of institutions and society.[27] As the astounding breadth of slavery scholarship indicates, the methods of cultural analysis have been as varied as the definitions of culture itself.

One vital facet of cultural analysis has focused on examining the cultural practices and identity of the subject. An extensive scholarly debate has centred on the question of 'retentions', 'survivals' and 'transformations', following VèVè Clark, of African cultural values, beliefs and customs among communities of African-descended people in the Americas. Scholars such as W. E. B. Du Bois, Melville Herskovits, Lawrence W. Levine and J. Lorand Matory, for example, have written extensively on the importance of specificity rather than generalization while clarifying the modes of transmission of various aspects of traditional African cultures, religions, languages and values.[28] As Levine writes, 'Culture is not a fixed condition but a process: the product of interaction between the past and the present. Its toughness and resiliency are determined not by a culture's ability to withstand change […] but by its ability to react creatively and responsively to the realities of a new situation'.[29] That culture spans past and present resonates with Eyerman's notion of collective, cultural memory shaping identity.

---

[26]Saidiya Hartman, *Lose Your Mother: A Journey along the Atlantic Slave Route* (New York: Farrar, Straus and Giroux, 2007), p. 6.

[27]Kehinde Andrews, 'Blackness, Empire and Migration: How Black Studies Transforms the Curriculum', *Area* 52:4 (February 2019), pp. 701–7; Maulana Karenga, 'Names and Notions of Black Studies', *Journal of Black Studies* 40: 1 (2009), pp. 41–64; Alexander Weheliye, 'Introduction: Black Studies and Black Life', *The Black Scholar* 44: 2 (2014), pp. 5–10.

[28]See, for example, W.E.B. Du Bois, *The World and Africa: Color and Democracy*, ed. Henry Louis Gates Jr (Oxford: Oxford University Press, 2007); Melville J. Herskovits, *Myth of the Negro Past* (Boston: Beacon Press, 2005); Lawrence W. Levine, *Black Culture and Black Consciousness: Afro-American Folk Thought from Slavery to Freedom* (Oxford: Oxford University Press, 2007); J. Lorand Matory, *Black Atlantic Religion: Tradition, Transnationalism, and Matriarchy in the Afro-Brazilian Candomblé* (Princeton: Princeton University Press, 2005).

[29]Levine, *Black Culture and Black Consciousness*, p. 5.

Three classic tomes – Orlando Patterson's *Slavery and Social Death* (1982), Paul Gilroy's *The Black Atlantic* (1993) and Saidiya Hartman's *Scenes of Subjection* (1997) – have profoundly enriched and radically transformed the critical landscape linking culture and slavery.[30] Each introduces new theoretical approaches to studying slavery during the cultural turn that have dramatically changed transdisciplinary thought and provided an indispensable critical vocabulary. Key concepts at the core of these extraordinarily influential books' arguments such as 'social death', the 'Black Atlantic', 'subjection', and the routinization of terror and racial violence permeate contemporary slavery scholarship to such a degree that these terms and ideas have been wholly absorbed into slavery's critical lexicon, even if challenged, often with only implicit reference to the original work. A keyword search in academic library databases reveals the sheer volume of scholarly monographs, dissertations, theses, articles, conference proceedings, special journal issues and journalistic writing that draws on the authors' transformative ideas, often incorporating their key terms into the titles of their work and at times, placing these ideas in unexpected contexts. Much like W. E. B. Du Bois's brilliant formulation of 'double consciousness' in *The Souls of Black Folk* (1903) or Mary Louise Pratt's enduring notion of 'contact zones' in *Imperial Eyes: Travel Writing and Transculturation* (1992), the salience of these critical terms transcends the academic fields of their authors and signals the importance of the cultural turn in thinking seriously about slavery across the disciplines.[31]

Each text configures culture as a dynamic process and contends, in different ways, with the questions of representation of the enslaved and the enslavers, identity formation, authenticity and freedom. A comparative study of historical sociology, Patterson's landmark *Slavery and Social Death*, rejecting the peculiarity claim, situates slavery as a global institution reflective of a universality, present in society from antiquity to the modern era, and in so doing, he insists on multiple scholarly conceptions of slavery.[32] Patterson

---

[30]Orlando Patterson, *Slavery and Social Death: A Comparative Study* (Cambridge, Mass: Harvard University Press, 1982); Paul Gilroy, *The Black Atlantic: Modernity and Double Consciousness* (Cambridge, Mass: Harvard University Press, 1993); Saidiya V. Hartman, *Scenes of Subjection: Terror, Slavery, and Self-Making in Nineteenth-Century America* (New York: Oxford University Press, 1997).
[31]W.E.B. Du Bois, *The Souls of Black Folk*, ed. Brent Hayes Edwards (Oxford: Oxford University Press, 2007); Mary Louise Pratt, *Imperial Eyes: Travel Writing and Transculturation* (New York: Routledge, 2007).
[32]Patterson, *Slavery and Social Death*, p. 44.

further theorizes that slavery is 'a highly symbolized domain of human experience' marked by 'the profound natal alienation of the slave'.[33] This line of enquiry and discussion of the enslaved as 'socially dead' and suffering from 'natal alienation' has shaped emerging theoretical traditions including Afro-pessimist thinkers like Frank B. Wilderson, III and Jared Sexton.[34] The expansive influence of Paul Gilroy's *The Black Atlantic*, which maps an oceanic geography of Atlantic slavery while attending to ideas connecting modernity, nation-state and identity likewise pervades current scholarship engaging questions of what Gilroy calls 'the overintegrated sense of cultural and ethnic particularity'.[35] Cautioning against the dangers of both ontological essentialism as a 'lazy, casual invocation of cultural insiderism', on the one hand, and strategic essentialism, or the 'pluralistic position which affirms blackness as open signifier' on the other hand, Gilroy offers the transnational perspective of the Black Atlantic diaspora and the 'vernacular' expressive cultures and countercultures it produces, opening up new scholarly terrain for thinking through Black geographies, the plantation, temporality and gender which Katherine McKittrick does so brilliantly in her work.[36] Just as Hartman's concept of the 'afterlife of slavery' compellingly sketched in *Lose Your Mother* is interwoven into the discourse of slavery studies and beyond, the powerful idea of emancipation as a 'nonevent' and 'yet unrealized freedom' presented in *Scenes of Subjection* demands a reassessment of the distinctions between juridical liberation and metaphysical freedom.[37]

Like the Barthesian notion of the 'tissue of quotations', the reverberating scholarly impact of the methodological approaches of Patterson, Gilroy and Hartman, and the interlacing of history, sociology, literary studies and cultural studies, has built ever-expanding, heterogeneous (counter)canons of research that exceed disciplinary boundaries in the cultural turn and problematize, extend, contradict, shift, dissent, revise and elaborate on the theories developed in these and other foundational texts, taking up strands

---

[33] Ibid., p. 38.
[34] See Wilderson for the argument that the category 'slave' cannot be dis-imbricated from 'Black person.' Frank B. Wilderson III, *Afropessimism* (New York: Liveright, 2020); Jared Sexton, 'The Social Life of Social Death: On Afro-Pessimism and Black Optimism', *InTensions* 5 (Fall/Winter 2011), pp. 1–47.
[35] Gilroy, *The Black Atlantic*, p. 31.
[36] Gilroy, *The Black Atlantic*, p. 38. Katherine McKittrick, *Demonic Grounds: Black Women and the Cartographies of Struggle* (Minneapolis: University of Minnesota Press, 2006).
[37] Hartman, *Scenes of Subjection*, p. 42, p. 139.

left unresolved or unaddressed in the early work.[38] Joining conceptualizations of the Black Atlantic, social death and the afterlife of slavery are instructive notions of fugitivity, flesh, redress, the wake, frottage, vestige, monstruous intimacy, landscapes, geographies, haunting and spectres, psychic hold, enclosure, to name only a few, that flow out of and overlap with this tradition. Among the exciting currents in scholarship that further developed and extended the parameters of the 'cultural turn' into new theoretical terrain is the work of scholars such as Christina Sharpe, Alexander Weheliye, Nadia Ellis, Tavia Nyong'o, Samantha Pinto, Stephen Best, Keguro Macharia, Aliyyah Abdur-Rahman, Katherine McKittrick and many others.[39] Their interventions have extended analytic modes to interpret high and low artforms, materiality, music, queer readings of culture, violence, sexuality and slavery, advancing thinking about notions of non-normativity, escape, liberation and identity outside the constraints of the colonial gaze.[40]

Slavery databases and critical vocabulary

Probing the limits of the archive and questioning what exists beyond the quantitative data and archival material, Stephanie E. Smallwood in *Saltwater*

---

[38]See, for instance, Barbara Christian, *Black Women Novelists: The Development of a Tradition, 1892–1976* (Westport, CT: Greenwood Press, 1980); Hazel V. Carby, *Reconstructing Womanhood: The Emergence of the Afro-American Woman Novelist* (New York and Oxford: Oxford University Press, 1987); Spillers, 'Mama's Baby, Papa's Maybe: An American Grammar Book'; Jennifer L. Morgan, *Laboring Women: Reproduction and Gender in New World Slavery* (Philadelphia: University of Pennsylvania Press, 2004).

[39]Sharpe, *In the Wake: On Blackness and Being*; Alexander Weheliye, *Habeas Viscus: Racializing Assemblages, Biopolitics, and Black Feminist Theories of the Human* (Durham: Duke University Press, 2014); Nadia Ellis, *Territories of the Soul: Queered Belonging in the Black Diaspora* (Durham: Duke University Press, 2015); Tavia Nyong'o, *The Amalgamation Waltz: Race, Performance, and the Ruses of Memory* (Minneapolis: University of Minnesota Press, 2009); Samantha Pinto, *Difficult Diasporas: The Transnational Feminist Aesthetic of the Black Atlantic* (New York: New York University Press, 2013); Stephen Best, *The Fugitive's Property: Law and the Poetics of Possession* (Chicago: The University of Chicago Press, 2004); Keguro Macharia, *Frottage: Frictions of Intimacy across the Black Diaspora* (New York: New York University Press, 2019); Aliyyah Abdur-Rahman, *Against the Closet: Black Political Longing and the Erotics of Race* (Durham: Duke University Press, 2012); McKittrick, *Demonic Grounds*.

[40]Recent innovative research provides analyses of Black feminist theory, sexuality, and slavery. See, for example, in response to the controversial so-called 'Harriet Tubman sex tape', Treva B. Lindsey and Jessica Marie Johnson, 'Searching for Climax: Black Erotic Lives in Slavery and Freedom', *Meridians* 12: 2 (September 2014), pp. 169–95, doi: https://doi.org/10.2979/meridians.12.2.169. See also Aliyyah Abdur-Rahman, '"The Strangest Freaks of Despotism": Queer Sexuality in Antebellum African American Slave Narratives', *African American Review* 40: 2 (2006), pp. 223–37.

Slavery (2007) discusses what is known and unknown not only to historians, but also to seventeenth- and early eighteenth-century West Africans living in 'the forest pocket that became known as the Gold Coast'.[41] As she queries the epistemologies of the Atlantic world, Smallwood observes that 'it was the quantitative content of the archives that entered most directly into the public domain, in the form of commercial vital statistics published for British consumption. Circulating alongside the formal accounting of economic exchange, the correspondence formed a more private transcript that was largely hidden from public view'.[42] Smallwood focuses on these correspondences between agents in London, Cape Coast Castle and the American colonies to 'gain a remarkably detailed picture, a window opening out onto the day-to-day conduct of the commerce in human beings'.[43] Although quantification of 'slave exports from the Gold Coast in the first half of the seventeenth century' is 'impossible to determine', the crafting of narrative from textual fragments of correspondence provides a 'picture' and 'window', even if not 'full narrative disclosure', into the lives of enslaved and enslavers.[44] Like the insoluble calculation implied in Morrison's dedication to *Beloved*, the methodologies of the cultural turn in slavery studies and critical fabulation enable scholars to sketch new pictures and windows of understanding.

A fascinating corollary to ongoing questions regarding slavery's archive, tabulation and cultural representation is the evolution of the digital *SlaveVoyages* database which originally launched in 1999 in CD-ROM format.[45] It represents an international collaborative effort – 'four decades of archival research on four continents' – to consolidate multisource datasets of slave voyages that individual historians and teams of historians had gathered starting with Herbert S. Klein in the late 1960s.[46] Since its initial launch, it has evolved into an open access website, supported by multiple funding sources, presenting over 36,000 slave voyages from Africa to the New World and over 11,000 newly added voyages between different sites in the Americas. Useful to scholars, economic historians of slavery, researchers and students, it attests to the technological advances in the last twenty years and standardizations in the slave voyages data. Perhaps the most interesting transformation of

---

[41]Smallwood, *Saltwater Slavery*, p. 12.
[42]Ibid., pp. 4–5.
[43]Ibid., p. 5.
[44]Ibid., p. 19, p. 207.
[45]*Slave Voyages* Database, 'History of the Project', https://www.slavevoyages.org/.
[46]*Slave Voyages* 2.0 Database, https://www.slavevoyages.org/.

the slave trade database is its ethos, organizing principles and treatment of qualitative information. Added to the searchable online archives is the African Names Database which contains the records of Africans captured during 'the last 60 years of the trans-Atlantic slave trade' who were captive on one of the 'two thousand vessels' that were 'condemned' by courts.[47] The inclusion of the African names and the attempt to identify African origins and languages signal the *SlaveVoyages* project's acknowledgement that catalogues of disembarkations do not tell the full story; it is not enough to extract data without the cultural narrative. I suggest that we might read these changes over time as a microcosm of some of the major trends in the cultural turn in modern slavery studies, closely related to questions of the archive, digital history and an injunction to craft narrative from those silences in the archive.

Scholars have been increasingly mindful of the terms used in slavery research, published monographs and articles, library finding aids, algorithms for key word searches in online databases and archives, academic conferences and pedagogical practice. As David Stefan Doddington observes in his chapter, 'A hallmark of the cultural turn was the concept that language shapes worlds', and recent scholarly imperatives to re-evaluate the metalanguage of slavery and the power dynamics it reinforces have supported this notion.[48] What is the language we use to talk about slavery? The once ubiquitous academic and popular use of terms such as 'slave masters', 'mistresses', 'slaves', 'slave owners', 'Black slaves' and euphemisms such as 'planters', 'servants' or even 'workers', employed uncritically in the influential work of some prominent historians, sociologists, social and cultural anthropologists, and literary scholars of the twentieth century, has been subjected to scrutiny and calls for re-evaluation of the academic discourse within the last few decades. Drawing attention to the cultural, political, social and psychic ramifications of this common usage and the ways in which it might signal a tacit endorsement of the white supremacist structures and mechanisms of power on which the institutions of slavery were built, a cadre of scholars have made persuasive arguments for, and indeed initiated, a lexical change. Their arguments have shown how unquestioningly equating 'slave' with 'African' or 'Black person' in scholarly writing functions to reinforce and normalize these racialized hierarchies of domination and subjugation. In response to this cultural turn, the *SlaveVoyages* website added the following 'Note on Terminology' in September 2020:

---

[47]Ibid., 'African Names Database', https://www.slavevoyages.org/.
[48]See David Stefan Doddington, 'Gender History and Slavery', in this volume.

The persistent and decontextualized use of the term 'slave,' in reference to an unfree person, is a needlessly dehumanizing word to describe someone who was captured, held in bondage, sold as a commodity and/or forced into servitude. The slavevoyages.org project is in the process of reviewing the website and its databases and considering how to best incorporate alternative language that will better recognize the dignity of the people who traveled on these vessels against their will. Unfortunately, some of the language used to label fields of information in our databases is embedded in the programming of our website. Changing the terms we use requires reprogramming the website, which takes technical skill.[49]

Although there is this tension between the coding methods within the *Slave Voyages* website, the increasing scholarly attention to cultural analysis, and funding sources, the critical move to recognize the humanity of the enslaved Africans requires that technology, and coding itself, conforms to these new developments in the cultural turn and slavery.

Calling for new grammars and vocabularies of slavery studies, Gabrielle P. Foreman has compiled and disseminated a dynamic, community-sourced slavery terminology guide with key contributions from other historians.[50] Refusing any proprietary claims and circulating primarily online and shared on social media, the guide, gently framed as mere 'suggestions', provides an excellent resource for professors, teachers, writers and students with recommended terms to replace those terms that have been used in scholarship uncritically for so long. A useful pedagogical tool and linguistic corrective to the conventional vocabularies which naturalize matrices of domination and power, the document serves to instruct scholars on terminology to consider adopting, even if it complicates syntax in scholarly writing. Reading the document as a cultural manifesto on the metalanguage of slavery, it is evident that here, too, scholars, artists, presses, students are working at the limits of language. As Laura Adderley poignantly states, all the terms we 'know to talk about enslaved people of African descent in these Americas prove insufficient, both for the brutality against them, and for their remarkable overcoming.'[51]

---

[49] *Slave Voyages* 2.0 Database, 'Note on Terminology', September 2020, https://www.slavevoyages.org/.
[50] P. Gabrielle Foreman, et al., 'Writing About Slavery/Teaching About Slavery: This Might Help.' Community-sourced document, 11 May 2020, docs.google.com/document/d/1A4TEdDgYslX-hlKezLodMIM71My3KTN0zxRv0IQTOQs/mobilebasic.
[51] Ibid., 'Writing About Slavery/Teaching About Slavery.'

'I Wish I Knew Your Name So I Could Remember You Right'

The imperative to reimagine the critical tools and language we use to tell the stories of slavery converges on the difficult issue of names and naming. As Morrison argues, the uncritical usage and circulation of 'slave' and its constellation of corresponding, dehumanizing, pejorative and stereotypical terms – Uncle Tom, Mammy, Sambo, pickaninny, etc. – structure racial hierarchies and propagate racial tropes and racial perception by naturalizing the condition of slavery with skin colour and the idea of 'race'.[52] The custom of ironic and denigrating naming practices for the enslaved with appellations such as Caesar and Venus to highlight their lowly status further contributed to their lexical subjugation.[53] In literature, according to Morrison, authors often use 'skin color to reveal character or drive narrative' as a type of 'narrative shortcut'.[54] The process of *Othering* in slavery scholarship similarly reinforces racial hierarchies, myths and hegemonies. Together, these linguistic logics of enslavement constitute the normalized discursive violence and racial order of slavery's archive and tradition of scholarship that Foreman and her colleagues seek to undo.

The cultural turn, then, urges scholars to learn the names of the enslaved, their family arrangements and kinship ties, and as much of their histories in their full complexity to supplant the erasures in the archive. An attention to naming counters the prevailing idea that people of African descent in the Americas, particularly the United States, had no culture or history, a notion underpinning so much of the scholarly orientation in early twentieth-century historiographies.[55] In the preface of Jennifer L. Morgan's *Reckoning with Slavery* (2021), she begins by closely analysing an Italian oil painting depicting a well-dressed African woman, *Portrait of an African Woman Holding a Clock* (ca. 1580s), which is the cover art for the book. Although

---

[52] Donald Bogle, *Toms, Coons, Mulattoes, Mammies, and Bucks: An Interpretive History of Blacks in American Films* (New York: Bloomsbury, 2015); Michelle Wallace, *Black Macho and the Myth of the Superwoman* (London: Verso, 2015); Raquel Kennon, 'Subtle Resistance: On Sugar and the Mammy Figure in Kara Walker's A Subtlety and Sherley Anne Williams's Dessa Rose', *African American Review* 52: 2 (Summer 2019), pp. 143–64.
[53] For a classic poetic example of ironic and demeaning naming of enslaved Africans and slave ships, see Robert Hayden, 'Middle Passage', *Phylon* 5: 3 (1945), pp. 247–53.
[54] Morrison, *The Origin of Others*, p. 41, pp. 44–5.
[55] John Henrik Clarke, *My Life in Search of Africa* (Chicago: Third World Press, 1999).

she knows the name of the famous painter, she announces to the reader, 'I won't give you his name because it's not important to the story that I am trying to tell. I can't tell you hers, although her anonymity is at the very heart of the story that I am trying to tell'. As Morgan uses the construction, 'she may or may not', to punctuate a series of speculations about the woman's condition as either enslaved or free, she finally concludes that art historians 'don't know who this woman is' and, in fact, 'can't'.[56] Morgan's refusal to provide the name of the artist registers as an attempt to level access to the archival material; we cannot know the African woman's name, and so we will not know the Italian painter's name either.[57]

Extending Hartman's invitation to embrace critical fabulation as methodology in slavery studies to carry out the crucial work of reclamation, we might then categorize fiction, specifically the genre of neo-slave narratives as delineated by Bernard Bell and popularized by Ashraf Rushdy, as its highest manifestation.[58] With the antebellum slave narrative as urtext, the genre of neo-slave narratives or contemporary narratives of slavery, flourishing from the 1970s to the present, has shaped our understandings and cultural engagements with slavery when the archive represented only unresolved questions and gaps. Recall the harrowing scene of escape in *Beloved*, the contemporary narrative of slavery par excellence, in which Sethe thanks Stamp Paid, in his first appearance in the novel, for helping her and her baby cross over the Ohio River. She poignantly remarks, 'I wish I knew your name so I could remember you right'.[59] It is this vital connection between knowing someone's name and remembering them 'right', that is, in their full, complicated humanity, that Sethe understands. If she could only know his name, she would be able to call forth the 'rememory' of this man: 'a picture floating around out there outside my head. I mean, even if I don't think it, even if I die, the picture of what I did, or knew, or saw is still out there. Right in the place where it happened'.[60]

---

[56]Jennifer L. Morgan, *Reckoning with Slavery: Gender, Kinship, and Capitalism in the Early Black Atlantic* (Durham: Duke University Press, 2021), p. ix.

[57]The failure to know one's name or paternal parentage with any degree of certainty is a trope of the antebellum slave narrative genre. Name changes are often linked to imposed or elected religious conversion. See, for example, the multiple names of the narrators in *The Interesting Life of Olaudah Equiano* (London: 1789); Harriet Jacobs, *Incidents in the Life of a Slave Girl* (Boston: 1861).

[58]Bernard W. Bell, *The Afro-American Novel and Its Tradition* (Amherst: University of Massachusetts Press, 1987); Ashraf H.A. Rushdy, *The Neo-Slave Narrative: Studies in the Social Logic of a Literary Form* (New York: Oxford University Press, 1999).

[59]Morrison, *Beloved*, p. 91.

[60]Ibid., p. 36.

Conclusion

Both a provocation and meditation, Morrison's dedication to *Beloved* reminds us that the suffering of the enslaved is multiplicative, the order of magnitude is at least in the tens of millions transtemporally and transgeographically, and the numerical accounting of this global atrocity is, at best, an imprecise estimation. Morrison deploys the tragic story of Margaret Garner, a single line in a newspaper notice, to design her novel and envision the life of one of those 'sixty million and more'. Employing *Beloved* as a literary touchstone in this chapter, I have attempted to trace several central moves of the 'cultural turn' in the field of slavery studies through the prism of quantification, incalculable tabulations and other silences of the archive, what it contains, what it withholds, what it cannot tell, to understand intriguing interdisciplinary directions in the field. New developments and shifts in cultural analyses, building on canonical scholarship of the 1980s and 1990s with its capacious theoretical framework, challenge positivist paradigms and the impulse to quantify. Moreover, these scholarly approaches counter notions of absolute 'scientific' objectivity in favour of representational possibility. The cultural turn enables novel articulations of what it means to dwell in the unknown of slavery's past, engaging the inexpressible through critical fabulation, that which extends across and beyond language and quantification. Urgent calls for a re-examination of critical terminology and naming in slave studies have prompted necessary theoretical reconceptualizations. As the refrain in the final paragraphs of *Beloved* reminds us, 'This is not a story to pass on'.[61] The irony, of course, is that in passing on this widely read and prize-winning novel, the reader comes to understand that which is left unresolved in the archive, and perhaps even remembers slavery right.

Bibliography

Gilroy, Paul, *The Black Atlantic: Modernity and Double Consciousness* (London: Verso, 1993).
Hartman, Saidiya, *Lose Your Mother: A Journey along the Atlantic Slave Route* (New York: Farrar, Straus and Giroux, 2007).

---

[61] Ibid., p. 275.

Hartman, Saidiya, *Scenes of Subjection: Terror, Slavery, and Self-Making in Nineteenth-Century America* (New York: Oxford University Press, 1997).

Hartman, Saidiya, *The Origin of Others* (Cambridge, MA: Harvard University Press, 2017).

McKittrick, Katherine, *Demonic Grounds: Black Women and the Cartographies of Struggle* (Minneapolis: University of Minnesota Press, 2006).

Morgan, Jennifer L., *Reckoning with Slavery: Gender, Kinship, and Capitalism in the Early Black Atlantic* (Durham: Duke University Press, 2021).

Morrison, Toni, *Beloved* (New York: Knopf, 1987).

Patterson, Orlando, *Slavery and Social Death: A Comparative Study* (Cambridge, MA: Harvard University Press, 1982).

Sharpe, Christina, *In the Wake: On Blackness and Being* (Durham: Duke University Press, 2016).

Sharpe, Christina, *Monstrous Intimacies: Making Post-Slavery Subjects* (Durham: Duke University Press, 2010).

Smallwood, Stephanie E., *Saltwater Slavery: A Middle Passage from Africa to American Diaspora* (Cambridge, MA: Harvard University Press, 2007).

Spillers, Hortense J., 'Mama's Baby, Papa's Maybe: An American Grammar Book.' *Black, White, and in Color: Essays on American Literature and Culture* (Chicago: The University of Chicago Press, 2003).

19

Re-tooling memory and memory tools: America's ongoing re-memory of slavery

Marcus Wood
University of Sussex

This whole city's a Freudian slip of the tongue, a concrete hard on for America's deeds and misdeeds. Slavery, manifest destiny, *Laverne & Shirley*? Standing idly by while Germany tried to kill every Jew in Europe. Why some of my best friends are the Museum of African Art, The Holocaust Museum, The Museum of the American Indian, The National Museum of Women in the Arts. And furthermore I'll have you know my sister's daughter is married to an orangutan.[1]

A short polemical introduction to slavery, memory, trauma and archives

The following writing thinks about the museological experiments now being conducted by John Cummings and Ibrahima Seck at the *Whitney Plantation*,

---

[1] Paul Beatty, *The Sellout* (London: Oneworld Publications, 2016), p. 5.

Louisiana, on the River Road, near New Orleans. There is also a discussion with some thoughts on the relatively new *Smithsonian National Museum of African American History & Culture* in Washington, DC. Both institutions are considered as vital test cases for where slavery and traumatic memory are now, and might go. The research materials on which the following writing is based have moved away from primary sources locked within the traditional printed and 'high art' archives. The work explores unstable, experimental, tangential, physical and perhaps challenging materials and institutions. In order to set an ideological frame for the following discussion, a brief introductory overview of the explosions of slavery studies and museological institutions during the last thirty years is necessary.

North American slavery, or rather its history and memory, is now, first and foremost, a massive academic industry. The book in which this piece of writing occurs is part of that industry and part of the printed archive of slavery. The industry is economically anchored within North American media and institutions. Yet the cultural and media juggernaut that now is 'Slavery Studies', or 'Atlantic Studies', generates a Global impact on writing, publishing, teaching, broadcasting, film and television, museology, university structures, the employment of academic staff and museum staff and, last but not least, social media. Over the last thirty years Brazil's academic interest in slavery is starting to catch up with that of the *gringos* and *gringas*. The perspectives of the literatures, bibliographies and historiographies generated by the archive of North American and Brazilian Atlantic slavery proliferate to such a degree that no individual is now in a position to master all of the materials in this vast and divergent set of archives. The published results of enormous research projects are frequently authoritative, often imaginative, sometimes apparently exhaustive, but do we even know how to ask the right questions when it comes to slavery and the memory of trauma? David Eltis and David Richardson have spent a large part of their lives forensically piecing together the information that allowed for the publication of the invaluable *Atlas of the Transatlantic Slave Trade*.[2] This for me is the most important book to explain the facts of how black bodies were moved, as slave merchandise, by the millions, over oceans and continents for a period of more than four centuries. The very clearness and coldness of the way

---

[2]David Eltis and David Richardson, *Atlas of the Transatlantic Slave Trade* (New Haven, CT: Yale University Press). See also *The Transatlantic Slave Trade Database*, https://www.slavevoyages.org/.

the information is set out gives it a tremendous traumatic force. These endless charts and maps have an abstract beauty and objectivity that reaches back to the greatest piece of antislavery propaganda ever made, *The Plan of the Slave Ship Brooks*. The *Atlas* stands as the *locus classicus* for a whole library of superbly detailed work in which socio-economic historians of the slave trade over the last half-century have increasingly provided remarkably precise maps indicating how slave importation, labour and mortality shifted and moved about. Through the sharing of electronic information we begin to see the patterns and populations of enforced African transmigration in terms of hard facts. Millions of abject bodies are moved around through space; dotted lines and swathes of coloured arrows show these unimaginably vast enforced migrations, from the interior of Africa, out to the holding factories on the Sub-Saharan African coast. Thousands of ships are plotted sailing to the Americas and the Caribbean and Europe, from the top of Africa's Atlantic slave coast to the bottom. Even the Portuguese East African trade around the Cape to Brazil is starting to get its due.

Slave-based economies and industries are subjected to ever more minute analysis and ever more sophisticated uncovering of their origins, development and influence. There are macro slave histories, chronicle histories, general surveys and global historiographies and bibliographies. There is micro slave history, impeccably researched projects and publications which now extend to minute case studies of individual economies within single plantations, or single slave states, or the specific studies of agrarian crop production, be it sugar, rum, rice, indigo or tobacco within specific territories, climates, cultures, diasporas and their sub divisions. The slavery archive takes it all in at different times and in different places across the Slave Diasporas of the Americas. The interpretation of the paper archive has increasingly stretched out, spreading its wings to include just about everything.

For decades I, like so many other historians, cultural historians, art historians, archaeologists and literary theorists, have written very long books all of which try and get into the 'proper historical' documents and art objects of the Slavery Archive. I tried to burrow into them and get under slavery's skin, and try to think about what these documents and images might uncover in terms of the suppressed life of the slave. There have been some rare and brilliant attempts to consider the operations of extreme revolutionary thought, on the exceptional occasions when slaves did manage to organize collective insurrectionary action against the slave power, and where their actions or thoughts or behaviour were recorded. The incomparable C.L.R. James's masterpiece *The Black Jacobins* remains the deepest, grandest and wittiest account of successful slave mass resistance.[3] Revolutionary slave violence still, however, remains a censored and often censured cultural space. Many other subjects connected to intimate violence remain taboo. These include slave mother infanticide, slave child abuse by both slaves and slave owners and sadomasochistic homosexuality and lesbianism within the confines of different slave settings.

What must never be forgotten is that this white paper archive is primarily the archive of the colonizers, of central European slave powers, of politically strategic abolitionists, or slave lobbyists, and of colonial power centres looking back at Europe. It is the archive of those with the power to record, of bookkeepers and bankers, of casual employees writing diaries and letters, of managers running the business of slavery, or negotiating the plantation household, or of abolitionists salving their consciences and investing in the (to use Chris Brown's ample phrase) 'moral capital' of the mythic, paradoxical and (to use one of my own book titles) 'horrible gift of freedom'.[4] It is an archive that is often arbitrarily formed, a colossal by-product of a global business enterprise. The more I work on this white paper archive the more I have a sense that it is a peculiarly homogeneous resource which always had, and in terms of the interpretative work it generates often has, terrifying and usually very blatant intellectual and creative constraints inscribed, or rather embedded, into its textual DNA.

Perhaps the most troubling aspect of the white paper archive of slavery, which stretches out across the Atlantic diaspora, is how little space it provides for the slave imaginary. Maybe we need to extend the still potent formulation of Orlando Patterson and to consider how slavery may have created not merely 'social death' as a space for the slave body, but also a slavery archive that has engendered a space of 'cultural death', or a nightmare of 'cultural life in death', for the slave imaginary.[5] Where is the authentic, let alone the creative, expression of the slaves? There were many, many, millions of slaves, we will never know exactly how many, and each individual slave had an inner life, an essence, an Africanity, a personally traumatized memory. These things, the heart of their mystery, do not lie in the white paper archive.

---

[3] C.L.R. James, *The Black Jacobins: Toussaint L'Ouverture and the San Domingo Revolution* (New York: Dial Press, 1938).
[4] Christopher Leslie Brown, *Moral Capital: Foundations of British Abolitionism* (Chapel Hill: University of North Carolina Press, 2006).
[5] Orlando Patterson, *Slavery and Social Death: A Comparative Study* (Cambridge, MA: Harvard University Press, 1982).

Even in exceptional circumstances when it is claimed that a space within the white paper archive has been cleared for, created by, satirically ironized by, the slave, the texts produced are frequently compromised in extreme ways. These ways are often sickly, anxious, and involve encoded and disguised methods for writing around a white imaginary.

Take one vastly influential example: the tradition of the putative *Slave Narratives* of nineteenth-century North America. These works, which have now been re-invented as a discreet genre, consist of a body of texts that are mired in agonistic struggles between the slave authors and the white abolitionist machine of production and of closure which policed the slave, or ex-slave, authors and what they put into the market. The ex-slave authors of the slave narratives nearly always had to negotiate white 'editors' (for which the word 'censors' is often a much more accurate substitute). Slave and ex-slave authors always had to work around the fact they were writing, or dictating, or being marketed, for white expectation, and under pressure from white prejudice. Most slave narratives do not let us into the slave consciousness in any unpolluted way, and if these texts are taken up and then re-injected into the mass entertainment industries the processes can be sinister, divisive and dishonest.

When it comes to black traumatic memory and slavery, this cultural up-scaling can be a most dangerous game. Consider for example the day when Steve McQueen's wife handed him a copy of Solomon Northup/David Wilson's 1853 *Twelve Years a Slave* to read, with the suggestion that it had a good film script in it. Wilson, the book's 'editor', states in his preface that he constructed the publication out of Northup's dictated life story, and that he vastly expanded it in his own words and style. Coming out less than a year after *Uncle Tom's Cabin,* Northup's narrative, heavily censored and pompously overwritten by Wilson, reads as if it were written by Harriet Beecher Stowe's less-talented brother. Messianic, evangelistic, it even starts with a long quotation from William Cowper. How much of this stuff ever came out of Northup's lips? We shall never know. Wilson's 1853 concoction was then avidly gobbled up by McQueen, his wife and their production team. Then television scriptwriter John Ridley transformed it into a predictable Hollywood screenplay. Ridley stripped down his Baroque and sentimental model and streamlined it into a shooting script. He spread thick layers of less-than-convincing 'Old South' plantation speak onto blacks, whites and white-trash alike. At the end of it all he garnered the Oscar, Best Adapted Screenplay, for his work, being only the second African-American to win that award.

It is pretty certain very few of Ridley's words ever came out of Northup's lips. The product was finally excreted in the form of a filmic blockbuster which is a violent and highly sentimental tale of male black survival against the odds. McQueen's film was and is the kind of plantation feel-good movie that could have been set just about anywhere, and anytime, in terms of the stereotypes of black servitude on the Old Plantation. Episodes of *Roots* come floating up at regular intervals. The product was the darling of the Motion Picture Academy, because it told the story of North American slavery precisely the way the Academy wanted it told. Finally after some wincing at the villains, and much coarse dialect dialogue, some crying with the victims, and with hero and heroine, and more dialect dialogue, and after just that necessary pinch or two of sadistic pornography, we come to the happy ending. Solomon is free, slavery is abolished, he and his family are reunited, and a good clean line is drawn in the sand making sure that slavery's memory is good and dead and isn't going to come back and bite, let alone haunt anyone's imagination, any time soon. Anyone. *Absolom Absalom* this is not. A new dawn awaits in the Home of the Free and the Land of the Brave, and all black lives matter. But with all those white α-male-A-listers creeping around and lining up for the pitifully clichéd minor roles, not to mention the superb camerawork of Sean Bobbitt laying on a glorious visual patina, the Pitt-Cumber-Bender *lusus naturae* was a great beast worthy of slouching towards the Academy Awards to be born. And once born it dived on in and dutifully ingested the many proffered Oscars. Why John Ridley, why not Toni Morrison? Why Solomon Northup, why not Nat Turner? Because no re-telling of the story of what actually happened during Nat Turner's Rebellion could have filled or fitted the bill in any way.[6] The fractured, haemorrhaged traumatic memories, the dark thoughts that won't go away, get buried. If they do surface as in Daniela Thomas's 2017 Brazilian masterpiece *Vazante*, a subtle and politically important study of the psychologies generated by slave systems far more ambitious than MacQueen's work, they get no exposure. When it comes to the memory of slavery some things are just too hard to look at.

---

[6]Nate Parker's 2016 film on Turner's rebellion, *Birth of a Nation*, suffered many of these problems. Criticism surrounded the depiction of Turner as an individual, the motives ascribed to the rebels, the presentation of violence in the rebellion, and on gender relations among slaves. *Birth of a Nation* (2016), [Film] Dir. Nate Parker, USA: Fox Searchlight. For examples of criticism, see, for example, Leslie M. Alexander, 'The Birth of a Nation Is an Epic Fail', *The Nation* (6 October 2016); Eileen Jones, 'Honoring the Real Nat Turner', *Jacobin* (15 October 2016).

The speculations below are evolved as a reaction to the pressures outlined above and have ended up in quite a simple space. The project is really just an attempt to answer a personal dilemma: where can the empathetic, baffled, defeated, impotent, but hopefully still open-minded scholar go in search of the inner life of the slave? Is this a pointless quest, is it unrecoverable in historical terms, and are we left only with the magnificent fictions of poets, novelists and painters? Will there ever be anything more important than the collective power of Toni Morrison's *Beloved*? This brave and frankly terrifying genius was many, many things as a traumatic testifier to slavery's horror. Among these things she was one of the world's great thinkers into the inter-bleeding of the traumatic and the beautiful. So the question remains, what part of the lost traumatic treasure of the inner life of the slave, as a human individual, can still be recovered from the cultural wreckage?

Attempts to uncover the history or memory of slavery through auras, residues, traces, cultural chimeras, hidden and mostly forgotten or ruined sites of slave culture and thought, are one way to go. Another is to look at what is out and about in post-slavery societies that strikes a chord with what we know of the lives and thoughts of slaves in former times. Find the living archive through the dead archive, and bring the dead archive back to life by investing in the living cultures of hybridity and creolization. Another way is to consider significant silence, African absence, what has been muzzled or zipped up. Above all my current work insists that most people who lived through and within slave systems didn't experience slavery through documents, and didn't record their responses as documents; they lived in slavery, and the vast majority of the Brazilian and North American slaves died as slaves. Slaves and slave owners responded to their world creatively on a day-to-day basis, eating, dancing, loving, co-existing, exploiting, surviving, calculating, suffering. We have only just started to think about the limitlessness of slavery's traces within what might be termed the spectre of memory. The Whitney plantation and the creative experiments it houses are saturated in slavery's spectres.

And so, if we turn our back on the printed archive, or even the 'high art' archive, which way should the bemused scholar of the memory of slavery turn? North America's institutions that tackle, or don't tackle, slavery fall into categories. There are the physical sites, houses, plantations, even whole towns (as in the case of Colonial Williamsburg) that formerly ran on slave labour. After a lot of scrubbing up, these sites are lovingly transformed into sanitized time capsules. Frequently these squeaky clean pieces of historical real estate are primarily there to remember the slave owners for their other accomplishments, as politicians, statesmen, authors, architects, collectors, men of letters or just fine examples of the white master race and Founding Fathers of the United States. Thomas Jefferson's *Monticello* is a prime example of such a model. The neo-Palladian folly embeds the memory of slavery within a larger aggrandizing, almost hagiographic (not to say pseudo-pornographic) white, male narrative.

Then at the other end of the scale exist very different museums which are prepared to keep slavery and its more terrifying aspects as their main focus. These institutions are often self-financing and culturally precarious. Precisely because they exist outside the grip of funding authorities, charity regulation and institutional consensus, they can attempt to remember the traumatic aspects of slavery – the Middle Passage, slave sale, slave torture and white sexual depravity as practised on slave bodies – in radical ways. *The Great Blacks in Wax Museum* is deliberately located in a challenged black area of Baltimore. It has constructed harrowing Middle Passage and Lynching exhibits and is a heroic example of how to kick against the pricks of museological officialdom. The *Great Blacks in Wax* is prepared to cross a line of 'good taste', and museological 'accuracy' which other museums will not dare even to approach. As a result, the place is despised and criticized by official museum culture as maverick, melodramatic, un-historical and sensationalist. Often the most severe and embarrassed resistance comes from affluent African-Americans who have appointed themselves guardians of 'their' version of history.[7]

Washington's SNMAAHC: Slavery, memory, and rounding up the usual suspects

Americans are still building big bespoke museums of African-American history. These places broadcast smooth teleological narratives which take in Atlantic slavery as part of a larger and determinedly, blindly, optimistic

---

[7]For relative cultural constructions of the *GBIW* within North American museology, see Marcus Wood, *Black Milk: Imagining Slavery in the Visual Cultures of Brazil and America* (New York: Oxford University Press, 2013), pp. 358–98.

National history focused upon the survival of slaves through and beyond the Civil War. America's slave population, given its freedom by Lincoln 'The Great Emancipator', march on into the heroism of the Civil Rights movement travelling via Rosa Park's inevitable bus seat to Martin Luther King's ubiquitous interracial 'Dream' vision. In this story slavery exists as a nasty stain now removed, as a small dark shadow that has been overcome, and triumphantly supplanted by African-American success stories from Booker T. Washington to Oprah. A typical example of an architecturally anodyne, massively financed and narrowly didactic venture into the gilding of American slavery's memory industries would be the *Reginald F. Lewis Museum of Maryland African American History and Culture* in Baltimore.[8] Hard on the heels of this experiment came an even bigger one, with a similarly grandiose, indeed obese, title *The Smithsonian National Museum of African American History & Culture* (hereafter SNMAAHC).

The museum is a little part of a much bigger whole in which Washington's mighty memory machinery dominates. The SNMAAHC official web site instructs: 'To the south and west are monuments and memorials to Thomas Jefferson, Martin Luther King Jr., Abraham Lincoln, and George Washington, whose contributions to African American history and culture are told in the museum.' This is an intriguing list, dominated by white patriarchs, not to say the ultimate white patriarchs, Founding Father Presidents. All these figures (including King) have, to put it mildly, less than spotless reputations when it comes to considering how their politics approached, or ignored, slavery, black agency, white racism and violent black activism. Jefferson indeed contributed much in tangible physical and generative terms to the African-American population. His contribution was very hands-on; DNA testing has now proved that he fathered multiple slave children with his hidden slave 'partner' Sally Hemings, who has recently been conjured back to life by some exceptional African-American historians.[9] Some insight into the perversions and erasures lying behind what Monticello does show and doesn't show lies in the fact that those in power over the estate/Jefferson tourist industry are finally converting Sally Hemings's bedroom back into a bedroom after mysteriously, some

---

[8]For a detailed comparative discussion of the Reginald Lewis, see Wood, *Black Milk*, pp. 378–99.
[9]See, for example, Annette Gordon-Reed, *Thomas Jefferson and Sally Hemings: An American Controversy* (Charlottesville: University of Virginia Press, 1997); Annette Gordon-Reed, *The Hemingses of Monticello: An American Family* (New York: W. W. Norton, 2009).

would say amazingly, turning it into a public female 'Rest Room' (Toilet in English) for several decades.[10] Yet the whole Hemings-Jefferson cultural battle ground remains largely taboo, a shadow of un-respectability hovers over it. The Hemings-Jefferson genealogy is certainly not to be placed as the jewel in the Smithsonian's Pure-African-Yoruban-American-post-abstract-post-futurist-three-tiered-museological-tiara.

The glitzy new museum is a shining ideological mess, a vast bauble, but a useful one in that it essentializes so much that is wrong with America's popular approach to the memory of slavery. The engineers, architects and cultural manipulators behind the venture basically built the first three stories of a bog-standard high-rise and encrusted a pseudo-Africanist concoction onto the exterior. The superstructure, or cultural cladding, we are told supposedly mimics some sort of African head gear, or as we are officially instructed, a form: 'inspired by the three-tiered crowns used in Yoruban art from West Africa'. In this context Sir David Adjaye O.B.E (the designer of the building's exterior encrustations and scabs) provides illuminating self-justification for his choices. In his pronouncements he combines vast generalization with an assertive aggressivity that idealizes, under slavery's shadow, one form of African sculpture, and indeed one Eurocentric myth of African Culture, at the expense of all others:

> **Sir David Adjaye O.B.E.**: Really I always wanted to premiate the arts as the central thing and anybody who knows anything about Central and West Africa knows that the Yoruba were really the high artisans of that period and of that time ['that time' being apparently the 15th to 19th centuries], there were many other sub-civilisations but they were really learning from the Yoruba.[11]

---

[10]https://www.washingtonpost.com/lifestyle/style/for-decades-they-hid-jeffersons-mistress-now-monticello-is-making-room-for-sally-hemings/2017/02/18/: 'The room where historians believe Sally Hemings slept was just steps away from Thomas Jefferson's bedroom. But in 1941, the caretakers of Monticello turned it into a restroom.' I have been fighting for this admission and this re-conversion for over a decade; see Marcus Wood, 'Strange Liberty Monuments: Lincoln, Jefferson, Freedom and Excretion' in Gordon Spark and Laura Findlay, eds, *Alienation and Resistance: Representation in Text and Image* (Newcastle upon Tyne: Cambridge Scholars Publishing, 2010), pp. 6–23; and Marcus Wood, 'Refurbishment, Responsibility and Historical Memory in Monticello's Slave "Dependencies,"' in Raphael Hormann and Gesa Mackenthun, eds, *Bonded Labor in the Cultural Contact Zone, Transdisciplinary Perspectives on Slavery and Its Discourses* (New York and Berlin: Waxman, 2010), pp. 187–207.

[11]BBC Radio 4, 'Only Artists Series 1: Yinka Shonibare Talks to David Adjaye' 28 mins. Wed. 26 April 2017, http://www.bbc.co.uk/programmes/b08n2y3b.

Here the mighty and noble Yoruba are lifted up on to the top of the podium at the expense of all other West, East, North and South African civilizations, or rather 'sub-civilizations'. This is an old colonial game, the same one Terre Blanche played when he praised the 'nobility' and cultural sophistication of the Zulu nation at the expense of all other black South Africans. For Adjaye, African cultures outside the Yoruba are simply written off: 'there were many other sub-civilisations'. This account completely ignores (or should one say complies with) the role of late Victorian Imperialism in 'premiating' Yoruban art and placing it on top of the pile. 'Anyone who knows anything about' the processing of African art by European so-called 'civilization' knows that British (not to mention German, Dutch and French) museums decided, in the late nineteenth century, to put Yoruban art at the top of their piles of African pillage and blood art. Once the art-historical tools of empire had assessed what to show and what to hide away from its vast mountains of stolen African art it ruthlessly promulgated its agendas of aesthetic racism. What Adjaye is doing is merely to parrot the arrogant but politically poisonous generalizing vision of African art laid out by British, and indeed Central European colonial powers.

The SNMAAHC sets itself out as the last word, as America's final Global testimony, accounting for the history and cultural memory of its slave and ex-slave populations. The institution now advertises itself with a blinking Hollywood neon sign of a slogan: 'A People's Journey, A Nation's Story'. This latest official, National, North American museological attempt to contain and simultaneously to abstain from slavery's memory is important. Sadly, the museum emerges as a lost opportunity, a stolidly backward-looking and sanctioned fiction claiming the Black American 'journey' as a closed-down narrative thrown into a box of clichés, or in Adjaye's words: 'A tragic story which is becoming a beautiful story'.

Once inside the great Yoruban crown the displays of the SNMAAHC all but squeeze out slave trauma as a subject of discussion; slave Rebellion is even more sternly shut down; slave mother infanticide remains a taboo. The museum does display the inevitable objects used by the torturers, which have always been deeply questionable as effective tools of traumatic memory. There are some rusty shackles here and some polished shackles there. These are typical of those forced onto the members of chain gangs and felons of many sorts across the world from the times of Roman slavery and Roman prisons. With no clear provenance there is no proof these shackles were ever put on an African slave.

When the museum finally opened, many African-Americans expressed outrage and horror on social media not only at the excision of slavery, but at the virtual exclusion of Malcolm X and the Black Panthers. Indeed, there seemed to be an overarching agenda which shut out all manifestations of extreme or violent black revolt, from the narrative. The only surprise here is that people would be surprised by this exclusion. I briefly mention the SNMAAHC because it is the culmination of a National tendency. The museum sets itself out as the last word, as America's final Global testimony, accounting for the history and cultural memory of its slave and ex-slave populations. In reality it emerges as yet another testament to a corporate fiction, a fiction encased in a museum of African-American History which skates over Diasporic Slave History. The price paid for committing to this transmogrifying African-American dream vision is any meaningful confrontation with the traumatic horror of slavery.

Extreme experimentation at Habitation Haydel

The remainder of this analysis is devoted to considering a radical – indeed ferociously non-establishment – museological experiment. This ongoing project flies in the face of the establishment Nationalist agendas and Colonial-Africanist Romanticisms which dominate, encase and pollute the SNMAAHC. What John Cummings and Ibrahima Seck are now doing on the River Road outside New Orleans with what was called Habitation Haydel, and what is currently known as the Whitney Plantation constitutes a uniquely ambitious, creative and daring museological, cultural and memorial experiment. The whole thing is a million miles away from Adjaye and Bunch's cultural folly on the Mall in Washington. The Whitney in the New Orleans area is a fascinating attempt to go where Washington and 'respectable' museums dare not go with the visual representation of slavery.

As it exists now John Cummings's memory experiment interfaces in intriguing ways with the institutional subdivisions set out at the start of my discussion. The Whitney also demonstrates a definite bias towards confronting slave suffering, slave abuse and the shadow of violence inherent in slave societies. The Plantation, originally named Habitation Haydel, was one of the plantations built on the banks of the Mississippi outside New

Orleans in the eighteenth century.[12] Where does this place locate itself around slavery's memorial boundaries, what sort of an institution is this? It's hard to tell looking at it and harder still to work out what's going on if you talk to the two men chiefly responsible for making what has happened there happen. I refer to the Irish American multi-millionaire Cummings who owns the Plantation, and who has poured as of now over fifteen million dollars into its development, and to the head of research programmes on the Plantation complex, the Senegambian Ibrahima Seck. Seck is also the author of the excellent microhistory of the plantation *Bouki Fait Gombo: A History of the Slave Community of Habitation Haydel (Whitney Plantation) Louisiana 1750–1860*.

Cummings bought the plantation purely as a piece of property to add to his vast real estate portfolio. Yet when he bought this plantation it had come with qualities which gave it unique potential as a place in which to develop a museum, or should one say creative and investigative site, devoted to the memory of slave life, experience, suffering and memory. Cummings's initial interest was sparked when he found that the Whitney Plantation came with a uniquely detailed history of its construction, planning and social organization. The Whitney is located near Wallace Town, 35 miles out of New Orleans along Louisiana's River Road. This fertile stretch of land hugs the banks of the Mississippi from New Orleans to Baton Rouge and used to comprise a solid swathe of Plantations producing indigo, some rice and then sugar. The plantations were physically long narrow strips of land, stretching more or less in parallel from both riverbanks inland. The river irrigated the sugar and rice fields and provided instant access to transport. Crops could be efficiently floated out through the ports in New Orleans, while goods and, of course, slaves could be transported inland along the Mississippi. From the mid-eighteenth century the plantations of River Road comprised a highly productive farmland known as the 'jardin de la Capitale' (garden of the capital) because it supplied the majority of rice, 'Indian' corn and vegetables consumed in New Orleans, the rapidly expanding state capital. During the twentieth century many of the old plantation sites were bought up by oil refineries and petrochemical plants. The remaining plantations are now either in ruins or have had squeaky-clean makeovers; the plantation Big Houses have been 'restored' into a state of pristine falsity. The Destrehan Plantation is a good and typical example of the historical fate of so many the

---

[12]For a fine microhistory of Habitation Haydel, see Ibrahima Seck, *A History of the Slave Community of Habitation Haydel (Whitney Plantation) Louisiana 1750–1850* (New Orleans, LA: University of New Orleans Press, 2014).

Big Houses of River Road. It is an over manicured historically anaesthetized place, which doesn't have a blade of grass out of place.

The Whitney almost became yet another victim of a petrochemical multinational takeover, and limited anodyne social makeover. The mighty Formosa company bought the property and planned to demolish most of the place to make way for a $700 million plant for manufacturing rayon. But the rayon market collapsed, and Formosa made the best of a bad job and sold off the Whitney Plantation to Cummings without having inflicted too much damage to its basic structure. Since he gained possession of the property, Cummings has launched a series of transformational initiatives which question how slavery might be memorialized or monumentalized within tangible heritage.

How is slave experience recovered, what is recoverable?

I am writing about the Whitney, in its present state, fully aware that Cummings and Seck have only been working on their concept full-on for five years and that things are changing there rapidly. It is exciting to think that the place and its sites of memory and creative response to slavery could go almost anywhere. The Whitney plantation, whatever else it is, is not complacently stable; it is moving and growing; it is something communal, porous, Protean, living, breathing, often generating vulgar failures as well as principled triumphs. Things get moved in and out, if they work they stay and get developed, if they fail they die and are moved off. There is then no point trying to provide a cut and dried cultural history of what is more of an ongoing creative experiment than a straightforward museum.

It is however useful to summarize some of the crucial, and currently permanent, sites at the Whitney at this stage of the experiment. The plantation breaks down into discreet categories; firstly the sites which did exist, and what Cummings has done to preserve and develop them, secondly the sites which Cummings has imported from outside which now function as part of the Whitney in despite of their original contexts, and lastly the works of memorial art which Cummings has so far commissioned and which are now set up as installations.

As far as the original main buildings are concerned, Cummings, when I interviewed him, summarized the site he purchased as follows. The plantation Big House 'was without porches and with a terrible termite problem', but is now fully restored, painted and pristine. The kitchen was, in Cummings's words, 'on the ground', and has been almost completely rebuilt. The blacksmith's forge consisted of 'some pieces of wood, which indicated something had been there but when we excavated we found anvils, horse shoes, enough to determine this was where the blacksmith's shop was, so we rebuilt it'.[13]

Yet Cummings's vision was not simply to recreate as authentically as possible a bygone era. He is not hampered by a frozen or indeed disciplined archaeological approach. He has no interest in 'doing' a Colonial Williamsburg, by which I mean re-establishing the Whitney as some form of, to use the ghastly phrase, 'authentic reproduction'.[14] This means that Cummings has no problem with commissioning large contemporary memorial art works or with moving in buildings wholesale from other locations if he considers they will enrich the environment and bounce off its history in some energized way. To the consternation of reconstructive purists Cummings has moved whole buildings plank by plank onto the Whitney site. He has also shipped in from other sites a number of primitive agricultural shacks which probably operated as slave cabins. In many ways he seems accountable only to his sense of creative possibility, more like a lawyer-artist than a dry-as-dust historical curator. What Seck and Cummings are doing is quite simply unique.

From 'Anti-Yoke' to 'Antioch' to Antique – Authenticity and transplantation at the Whitney

One dominant example of Cummings's creative latitude is the Antioch Baptist Chapel. The first church was built in Paulina in St James' Parish. It was

---

[13]Interview conducted by Marcus Wood with the owner of the Whitney Plantation John Cummings, Whitney Plantation, Louisiana, 27 February 2017, tape 1, 13 mins. 42–52 seconds. A copy of the full interview tapes is held at the Whitney Museum Library and Archive.
[14]For Colonial Williamsburg as the world's most formidable experiment in the 'authentic reproduction' of a year in the life of American Slavery, see Marcus Wood, 'Historic Williamsburg and the Memorial Limits of a Theatre of Colonial Slavery' in Julia Swindells, ed., *The Oxford Companion to the Georgian Theatre* (New York: Oxford University Press, 2014), Cap. 40, pp. 707–25.

Figure 1 The 'Anti-Yoke' Church, Whitney Plantation.

erected by free blacks after the Civil War in the 1870s and was the focal point for a burial society ensuring that African-Americans had decent funerals. The society and church first carried the startling name of 'Anti-Yoke' clearly foregrounding the function of the building as a symbol of freedom which stood against the Yoke of slavery, whether literal or metaphorical. But in 1890 the re-naming of the Church as 'The Antioch Baptist Church' disguised the original force of the name. When the society moved to a new church in 1999 the old Church was donated to the Whitney; the new Church has an even longer and more disguised title.

The Anti-Yoke church was, and remains, an astonishingly beautiful building, a little classic, with delicate proportions, carefully varied tile patterns, subtle internal space, astonishing acoustics, and this alone makes its preservation invaluable. Yet what this church now does and what it means on a site in an ex-slave plantation, and no longer standing on its own land as a functioning Free Black Church, defending the African American's right to a funeral plot, are more difficult to know. This church, in terms of slave religion, has little, maybe no connection, with religious buildings that were on the old plantation. Does it now reach out to a vision of African-American religion as a powerful force that exists through slavery and after slavery?

Viewed across the entire history of Louisiana's development New Orleans and Christianity are an immensely complicated phenomenon. Christianity as used by the slave masters, whether Catholic or Evangelical, was a pro-slavery policing mechanism, and Christianity was built into the system, as it was across the Atlantic slave Diaspora. The primary function of such a didactically organized dogma was to teach the slaves passivity, gratitude, meekness and doglike obedience. Does the transplanted Whiney chapel ask any serious questions about Christianity and slavery, does it try and interrogate the depraved uses to which Slavery put Christianity? Then again there are serious questions to be asked about how this Church relates to the places of worship which slaves on the plantation inhabited. As far as slave religion on Habitation Haydel is concerned there is little evidence of what went on. There can, however, be no doubt that a proportion of the slaves would have been involved in their own hybrid or syncretic forms of religion which would have had a tangential relationship to Catholicism and its Hagiographic inheritance. Indeed, in the first decades of the nineteenth century, Louisiana had unique syncretic forms of slave religion. The importation of Haitian slaves on most River Road plantations meant that Vodoun evolved into Louisiana Voodoo, but there may well have been many variants incorporating Catholic iconographic and mythic elements to a greater or lesser extent. Such slave religions were of their essence secret and disguised social phenomena, and as a result cannot be reconstructed through imagery or surviving objects, in any detail. The Whitney does not at the moment incorporate any reference to slave hybrid religion coming out of Voodoo, although Seck is keen to try and develop this angle. As it stands Christianity, and fairly orthodox sometimes anachronistic Christianity, predominates the Whitney's memorials. The Antioch chapel has arguably lost most of its Anti-Yoke punch and its function is hard to define.

Children of the Whitney

The resituated and restored Anti-Yoke Chapel has also had its interior altered with a permanent installation. A series of ceramic sculptures show black children male and female in dungarees and simple shifts. They stand about, sit in corners of the church or stand near the aisle. The conceptual justification for their creation and presence is complicated and again confused.

The sculptures were commissioned by Cummings from Woodrow Nash, a Wisconsin-based African-American artist. The figures are supposed to represent the former slaves who were interviewed by the FWP (Federal

Figure 2 Sculptures of Slave Children in 'Anti-Yoke' Church's Chapel.

Writer's Project) as part of the vast WPA depression-era employment project. As a result of the FWP initiative a core of ex-slaves were interviewed seventy-five years after the Emancipation declaration. Responding to a series of white-evolved questions the ex-slaves gave their policed versions of their life under and memory of slavery. The present sculptures of young African-Americans are intended to show the interviewees 'as they were at the time of emancipation: children'. The sculptures are intended to form a visual and creative link between the only recorded narratives by former slaves, and the existence of these people as children at the point when their status changed from slave to free. In this sense the figures form part of that vast body of commemorative art and propaganda dedicated to the celebration of the Emancipation moment. The idea seems to be that in a Church which was originally built by newly freed blacks these sculptures will embody the new sense of freedom within the frame of each child who would later testify as an adult to their experience under slavery.

Are they supposed to be a collective reference back to the generations of forgotten slave children who grew up on the plantation? Are they supposed to be completely free, or still living in the shadow of slavery? It is hard to know what to make of them, falling as they do between so many representational codes and historical periods. Placed in this church, and occupying its social spaces, they appear primarily as catalysts for charitable emotions rather than as potential revolutionaries or artists. They raise a question which at the moment runs through much of the art introduced to the Whitney: how committed to representing slave agency and violent slave resistance is this place?

The 'Field of Angels'

One key example of how orthodox Christianity has been incorporated into the installation art of the plantation is the 'Field of Angels' installation. This is a memorial in the form of a statue surrounded by inscribed granite slabs set into concrete. The installation is intended to be a memorial to the 2,200 slave children who are recorded as dying before their third birthday and who are registered in 'the Sacramental Records of the Archdiocese of New Orleans'. It consists of an outer wall of low granite slabs with the recorded names of the children engraved on them together with images of plantation life. In the centre of these slabs is a chained-off bronze sculpture on a plinth by Mississippi sculptor Rod Moorhead.

The piece is titled *Slave Angel with Wings* and is intended, according to the Whitney website, to show 'A black angel carrying a baby to Heaven'. The sculpture of black female angel and baby is semiotically conflicted, not to say confused. It might be an empowering image, but it might also be rather naïve in the way it draws upon themes of female slave fertility, motherhood and sexual exploitation. It might also be a disempowering image, in that

Figure 3 *Slave Angel with Wings* in the 'Field of Angels', Whitney Plantation.

it wraps the memory of slave motherhood and slave infant mortality in a cloak of sentimental and patronizing Christianity. After all there is no concrete evidence that any of the slave mothers or their children enslaved on the plantation were conventional Catholic Christians. Do we know, can we assume, these black slave children were Christian if brought up in the syncretic religion of African-Americans of the eighteenth and nineteenth centuries? The assumption cannot be made with any certainty.

The central figure begs many questions. Where do the enormous feathered wings accreted onto what is otherwise a naturalistic young female semi-nude form come from? The artist does not seem to have thought about the old religious conundrum – do angels have wings? Fritz Saxl showed that Rembrandt in a series of drawings destroying wings he initially put on an Angel fought through to a vital textual truth, the fact that Angels clearly did not have wings. People visited by angels in the scriptures often had trouble working out who they were. Many biblical figures took their visitors for humans when they appeared. Obviously these messengers from God did not have enormous feathered wings. Then again why is this a black angel, are angels racially specific, should they be black or white or beyond race?

The sculpture seeks to impose a certain optimistic narrative onto the life and death of the slave infants who died on the Whitney and surrounding plantations. They are turned from names and figures into a sentimentalized vision of redemption, each infant soul taken up to some imagined heaven (white or black?) by a huge nurturing black female 'Angel'. Yet the woman is also an attractive young black woman, who relates undeniably to a tradition of statuary which shows young women on the auction block with their bodies exposed to public view. In this context the partial undressing of the figure is significant. If the figure were completely nude she would mean one thing, and would relate to a tradition of classical statuary which places human nudity in a privileged and relatively, or at least ideally, un-sexualized symbolic space; she would clearly be a supernatural being. If she were fully clothed she would again be a very different figure, her modesty would be established, and the extent to which she is or is not sexually on display for a public viewership would not be an issue. But to have her clothing stripped from her upper body and bunched up at her waist suggests countless images of slave women either stripped on the auction block to be examined or stripped to the waist in order to be whipped. What emerges is a semiotic chaos in which neither the religious nor the gender agenda is clearly thought through, and in which the artist appears to have been absorbed into an iconographic inheritance of women and exploitation which is contaminated by pornography.

The 'Field of Angels' unsatisfactorily interprets what remains one of the most traumatic and taboo areas of slavery's memory. Slave fertility, slave pregnancy and birth, the relation of slave women to children they could not legally lay claim to, are all highly traumatized memorial sites. Slave women were often impregnated through rape for the ends of property production. The death of slave children takes us into some very dark places. Slave mother infanticide was an option for resistance which still remains largely taboo as a subject of discussion let alone the production of public art. Dead slave babies are not just unproblematic little angels wafted up to some divine La La land. Slave babies could also be the victims of murder by their own mothers. How many slave mothers deliberately aborted children who were the unwanted product of slave rape will not be known. Whether this is a subject which art can or should engage with remains an open question. Then again in the eyes of a slave mother the death of a slave child might be a cause for agonized celebration not because the 'little angel' is going to heaven but because the mother has taken property from out of the system and thus struck a blow at the base of the slave economy. The death of a child might be celebrated because it meant that another child had escaped the appalling and potentially limitless abuse of life within slavery. As Toni Morrison's *Beloved* suggests slave mother infanticide in all its horror might be a final gesture of empowerment for the black female. As Toni Morrison's *Beloved* also suggests it might be an insurrectionary act that is too hard and too emotionally extreme for males, white and black, to confront let alone comprehend.

Memorial walls and historical roll calls of honour

There are two wall-like installations at the Whitney, the '*Allées* Gwendolyn Midlo Hall' and the 'Wall of Honour'.

The latter is not in fact a wall, but a free-standing concrete plinth with a series of disconnected highly polished granite slabs with the names of all the slaves who can be identified as working on the Whitney plantation. The '*Allées* Gwendolyn Midlo Hall' is a series of concrete plinths, which have an overhang to protect the granite plaques from the weather. The granite slabs are inscribed with the names of the 107,000 people enslaved in Louisiana and documented in the 'Louisiana Slave Database', a project inaugurated and built up by the white female historian of the American

Figure 4 The 'Wall of Honour', Whitney Plantation.

Figure 5 The '*Allées* Gwendolyn Midlo Hall', Whitney Plantation.

South, Gwendolyn Midlo Hall. The naming of this monument after a great white historian has drawn some criticism from black visitors. The granite slabs also have imagery inscribed into them; the images take the form of woodcuts and early photographs of slave life and experience, many of them reproductions of popular propaganda from North American but also European abolition engravings, woodcuts and photographs. Many of these images are reproduced more than once on different panels and so have a series of different and often irrelevant contexts; their original sources are not cited and so they float before the viewer as a sort of cut-and-paste image bank in which context and semiotic message seem transferable from one panel to the next.

Clearly, as several commentators have pointed out, this installation has a relation to Maya Lyn's Vietnam monument, but what sort of relation? Although at an immediate visual level the two works might seem to have certain things in common, they are in fact very different memorial creatures. The significant thing about Maya Lyn's memorial is its monumental one sidedness; its perfection is based in its completely unilateral inclusiveness, and simultaneous unilateral exclusiveness. Lyn's sculpture has been thought through as a three-dimensional work from every angle. It takes the form of an arrowhead, cut into a gently rising hillside, with the walls rising towards the apex to a height of five meters. The polished surface of this rising and falling wall face is made up of conjoined highly polished black granite slabs, and they carry a continuous line of engraved names, alphabetically arranged. These are the names of all the known and recorded dead American soldiers from the entirety of the Vietnam conflict. The wall is first and foremost a monument to warriors, almost exclusively male it records fallen soldiers, all equal in death, and all dying for the same cause. At one level the work is a tribute to American military efficiency; the dog-tagging of each solider meant that just about everyone lost in action, regardless of rank, could be named, a bureaucratic and a democratic triumph for the Grim Reaper. Only total obliteration of the body, or the permanent loss of a corpse in swamp or jungle, would prevent each soldier's death being recorded. Of course, the memorial also alludes through denial, closure, deliberate self-blinding, to a far greater space outside itself, that of the Vietnamese mass fatalities. Unlike the American names these include not only dead male soldiers but thousands of dead female soldiers, and millions of dead civilians, strafed, burned up with Napalm, embalmed in Agent Orange, a ghostly army of casualties the majority of which consisted of women and children. How many millions will of course never be known; it is an open-ended and debated figure, as is the figure for how many slaves died during the course of the Middle Passage. If these hordes of lost Vietnamese people have an American visual monument, it is in the chance snapshots of the My Lai massacre, a few colour slides of begging victims and casually strewn and heaped corpses which evaded the military censor quite by chance. In the main however the slaughtered Vietnamese population remained nameless, uncounted and unaccounted for. These anonymous dead can never have their equivalent of the Maya Lyn Wall; the American Military machine simply obliterated them without recording them.

The Midlo Hall Wall can then in one sense be seen as an attempt to do for the slaves what the Maya Lyn Wall could not do for the Vietnamese. It attempts to name, and to give a memorial space to, the dead slaves as victims, or at least a small portion of them in one geographical location. But what form of identity can be given back or do we have access to; even the process of reproducing the names of these enslaved Afro-Americans is not innocent, easy or necessarily empowering let alone true. How the citing of these names constitutes an act of 'honouring' the lives of slaves is not clear. One of the first symbolic acts of enslavement involved the stripping of slave identity through the act of un-naming and then re-naming, sometimes multiple times. The vast majority of the names recorded on the Whitney plaques are, after all, the names which the masters 'gave' or arbitrarily foisted upon slave property. The thoroughness of these processes of identity imposition is evident from the evidence of the journals of slave captains, from ship inventories, from plantation inventories and from the accounts of slave narratives. African names were erased; new names, the names of masters, or whimsical acts of nomenclature coming out of classical mythology or European history were imposed – all those Caesars, Clytemnestras, Cleopatras, Caiuses, Chloes, Pompeys, Brutuses, Marcuses and Brunhildas. These arbitrary processes of enforced false identity are described with excruciating power in the opening pages of one of the earliest American slave narratives, *The Interesting Narrative of the Life of Olaudah Equiano, or Gustavus Vassa, the African. Written by Himself.* Even the title makes ambiguous statements involving multiple naming, uncertain nationality and unstable identity as the boy with an African birth name 'Olaudah Equiano' becomes, at the ironic whim of an English naval officer, 'Gustavas Vassa', who was a Swedish king and now transforms into a slave child.

In reproducing the names imposed upon slave bodies by the slave owners, the Midlo Hall Wall and the Wall of Honour at the Whitney are again in danger of remembering the slaves in terms of the labels of disempowerment imposed by the slave power in order to strip away African identities. Consequently, the names on the Whitney's memorials have a very different historical weight from the authentic American identities recorded on the Vietnam Memorial, and record a ghastly set of dehumanized false identities super-scribed upon what were once real people with real identities.

Heads on poles, ritual decapitation and the space of terror from Islamic State to the German Coast Slave Rebellion of 1811

Operating in stark contrast to the 'Field of Angels' is the memorial to the 1811 Louisiana Slave Revolt. This is to date the most violent and controversial exhibit at the Whitney, and indeed one of the most confrontational pieces of memorial art generated by North American slavery. It is not a monument which could ever have passed a selection committee at the Smithsonian. Yet what this piece of art finally says is hard to work out, and I am not certain how to evaluate this work; it is definitely thought-provoking, but does it provoke thought that is useful?

In January 1811 under the leadership of Charles Deslandes several hundred slaves began a military style march along what was then termed the 'German Coast', now River Road, with the intent of invading and taking over not only the plantations but New Orleans. Many plantations were overrun and burned, although the rebels killed only three slave owners and did not molest or harm any women or children. Local militias were called out and they soon suppressed the revolt. A period of mass terror and persecution followed. Slaves were rapidly executed, either at the moment of capture or in hastily convened trials. After being shot or hanged, the bodies of slave rebels were decapitated and their heads displayed on sharpened poles along River Road. The display was organized, heads were exhibited outside violated plantations, and in a show space in what is now Jackson Square in the French Quarter.[15]

Cummings and Seck decided that they wanted to create a monument to the Insurrection. In looking for a powerful central symbol they decided to focus the work on the ceremonial display of severed heads by the slave power. Woodrow Nash, an African-American sculptor, was commissioned to make sixty ceramic severed heads. It was then decided to display these set atop stainless steel poles of different heights. The sixty poles with heads

---

[15]The standard account of the revolt is Albert Thrasher, *'On to New Orleans' Louisiana's Heroic 1811 Slave Revolt* (New Orleans, LA: Cyprus Press, 1995).

were arranged geometrically, in rows of descending height, in a tight rectangular space, like a well-tended herbaceous border, on the periphery of the plantation grounds near the exit. The ground of this rectangle had been strewn with a thick bed of deep-red wood-chippings.

These long slim shining poles, with the uneven dark brown and black spheres of the heads at their tips, give the eerie effect of an obscene and violent institutional flower bed. Walking round the display the heads float and shift in space. This satiric use of generative natural imagery to describe racial atrocity against ritually murdered black bodies is not a new idea. One thinks of the deeply ironic re-deployment of the imagery of fruit trees to describe the bodies of lynch victims in the lyrics of Abel Meeropol's elegiac masterpiece *Strange Fruit*: 'Southern trees bear strange fruit/Blood on the leaves and blood at the root/Black bodies swinging in the Southern breeze/Strange fruit are hanging from the Poplar trees./Pastoral scene of the gallant South.'

Woodrow Nash's sculpture provides another pastoral scene of the gallant South, but it has proved controversial for blacks and whites alike.

The installation raises many immediate questions. The bodies are not present; only the heads remain. What does this signify? Why remember the rebellion in terms of its failure and the reduction of the slave body to a deliberately gruesome and de-humanized trophy for the slave power? J.C. Young, in his thought-provoking examination of trauma and memory *Holocaust Memorials and Meaning*, states that there are dangers inherent in

Figure 6 The Memorial to the 1811 Louisiana Slave Revolt, Whitney Plantation.

remembering the victims in terms of the memory tools left by, or indeed created by, the murderers. He extends this warning even to the glass tanks in Madjanek full of the suitcases, eyeglasses, the prosthetic limbs and the shorn hair of the victims. It is these human remains, or the intimate objects connected to the lost lives, which often get the most emotional and visceral reactions from visitors. Clearly the heads on poles installation at the Whitney operates in a somewhat different symbolic and historical domain. The heads are an artist's impression, somewhat reduced from life-sized, of what the decapitated heads may have looked like. They are not human remains but float, like some sort of ceramic shrunken heads, somewhere between symbolism and representational realism. Yet despite this element of historical re-enactment does this exhibit succeed in getting beyond the deliberate terror tactics that were the original intention of the Slave Power? Is the heads on poles exhibit not in danger of merely rehearsing its origin, of setting out the slave in precisely the degraded terms the slave power had already chosen as its preferred option? How do the ceramic heads relate to the actual heads? Do they reclaim the slaves as art? Do they re-humanize or dehumanize the victims? None of these are easy questions to answer.

Historically the slaves were captured, summarily executed, their corpses were then mutilated, and the heads exhibited on stakes. It was a brutal and atavistic warning, and a mutilation of slave bodies, but this form of display had a long tradition within European cultures. The public display of the severed head upon a pole or pike had been historically reserved in Europe for traitors and heretics. Yet this mode of display had not been widely used in Europe for over a century at the time of its use in Louisiana in 1811, and takes the Slave Power into a space of primitive terror.

While the display of heads on poles is in one sense historically distant in Europe, in certain contexts it is very much alive and contemporary. In the current flood of atrocity imagery generated by events in Syria there has been a large amount of carefully choreographed and visually extremely violent propaganda. Much of this is deliberately aimed at the intimidation of the West and by ridiculing its rules for what is acceptable and what is unacceptable when it comes to the public display of state-sanctioned violence. Group decapitation and the symbolic display of heads on poles have emerged as one chosen indeed privileged element within the lexicon of extreme terror. Isis Jihadists have been mass exploiters of this symbolism. There were depraved ritualistic displays of the decapitated heads of children set on poles in Mosul as part of the Isis murder of Christians. Is it useful to set up any sort of interpretative comparison between this real space of abject horror and the mediating aesthetic space of Nash's sculpture? Are we now re-entering a semiotic space of utter barbarity where the propaganda of terror can usefully equate the Plantation owners of Louisiana in 1811 with the executioners of ISIS in Northern Syria in 2017?

The final status of the Whitney's slave insurrection monument revisits and to an extent re-activates the Terror tactics of slave owners in the early nineteenth century. Suddenly the slave masters of Louisiana are seen to have created a theatre of violence retroactively related to the obscene aesthetic choreography of ISIS. If this is a transcultural, trans-historical or trans-racial equation of human violence that does anything valuable, then the final lesson seems to boil down to a single brutal insight. There are, it seems, no decent limits to how extremists whose absolute authority is finally based in terror will advertise their capacity to terrify. Whether the Whitney plantation should contribute to an artwork which arguably perpetuates this language of terror remains a very difficult question to answer.

African-American artists have visited this terrain before. The front and back covers of the catalogue produced by MIT press around the Williams College 2003 major retrospective exhibition of Kara Walker's Work entitled *Narrative of a Negress* is a case in point. The front cover shows one of Walker's signature style silhouette works. This shows two armed white men, apparently Confederate soldiers. One of them squats in front of a flaming fire and holds a tree branch which has four subsidiary branches growing out of it. Impaled on the end of each branch is the decapitated head of a young black figure, shown in full profile silhouette. The central pair is definitely female, the gender of the other two, one of whom is a small child, is impossible to determine. On the back cover of the volume is another silhouette group. This shows a young naked black woman leaning against what may be a tree or a pillar of fire. The profile head of this young black woman is grotesquely caricatured according to negrophobe stereotypes. She holds a long-sharpened stake on top of which is impaled the head of a white adult male. Another eight heads of white figures, two of whom may be female, are also impaled on poles, one through the mouth. Some of the male heads have the hair in pigtails implying eighteenth-century dress. If these two group compositions exist as a diptych, and if they carry any intended meaning (Walker's semiotics are often confused and chaotic as a matter of policy), it would seem to be that black slaves and white slave owners are equally capable of barbarism. Her black and white figures appear locked in a state of self-cancelling attritional barbarity, a meaningless horror without end. If it is hard to take anything uplifting from the imagery, then at least blacks are allowed violent agency, an agency which drags them down to the nadir of moral degradation in which the slave owners exist.

The Whitney exhibit confronts a very different set of problems from those of Walker's work and allows a limited space for slave agency. Encircling the entire artistic venture is the fact that it is a specific, and historically proven, slave revolt that the decapitation monument supposedly commemorates. Yet this artwork remembers the slave insurgents in partially symbolic partially realistic terms which prioritize the failure of their venture. What we see is a re-invention of the brutal punishment of the slaves via a set of white-evolved rituals fixated on the public display of the mutilated body parts of black slave leaders. Why is this so when there are so many other more inspiring memorial options available?

Apparently, this mini revolt or abortive coup rapidly swelled into a small army, a revolutionary army of liberation. The accounts tell of them drilling in organized fashion, singing, drumming, marching, dancing, singing. Their activities during the course of the insurrection did not involve random violence and eschewed sexual violation. There is no evidence that any women were sexually abused, or that any children were harmed. The attitude towards violence and homicide was clearly notably more restrained than that of the Nat Turner Revolt in Virginia two decades later. The slaves also did not mimic, despite the extreme claims of some of the Slave Power publicity, and despite the presence of individuals who had been involved in the Haitian slave revolt, the extremes of ritual violence which occurred during the early stages of the great slave revolt on the North Plain of San Domingo in 1791. The slave insurrectionaries clearly had a policy of destroying crops, property and the machinery of sugar production. Should there then be a more balanced and more celebratory monument at the Whitney which remembers the slaves in triumphant terms and in terms of their revolutionary ideology. A monument emphasizing inspiration, organization focused on a disciplined maybe also vengeful group? This group could include women and even children; it would show strong armed politically informed revolutionaries. Such an embodiment of American Black Jacobinism, a display of individuals who have made the heroic decision to fight for their freedom, would be a most welcome addition to the public political statuary at the Whitney.

Bibliography

Alpers, Svetlana, 'The Museum as a Way of Seeing' in Ivan Karp and Steven Levine, eds, *Exhibiting Cultures the Poetics and Politics of Museum Display* (Washington, DC: Smithsonian Institution Press, 1991), pp. 25–32.

Glissant, Edouard, *Faulkner, Mississippi*, trans. Barbara Lewis and Thomas Spier (Chicago, IL: University of Chicago Press, 1996).

Gordon-Reed, Annette, *Thomas Jefferson and Sally Hemings: An American Controversy* (Charlottesville: University of Virginia Press, 1997).

Hall, Gwendolyn Midlo, *Africans in Colonial Louisiana: The Development of Afro-Creole Culture in the Eighteenth Century* (Baton Rouge: Louisiana State University Press, 1992).

Matory, J. Lorand, 'The "New World" Surrounds and Ocean: Theorising the Living Dialogue between African and African American Cultures' in Kevin A. Yelvington, ed., *Afro Atlantic Dialogues Anthropology in the Diaspora* (Santa Fe, NM: School of American Research Press, 2005), pp. 151–77.

Palmié, Stephen, ed., *Slave Cultures and the Cultures of Slavery* (Knoxville: University of Tennessee Press, 1995).

Pilgrim, David, 'The Garbage Man: Why I Collect Racist Objects', available at: http://www.ferris.edu/jimcrow/collect/

Tim Barringer, Gillian Forrester, and Barbaro Martinez-Ruiz, eds, *Art and Emancipation in Jamaica Isaac Mendes Belisario and His Worlds, Exhibition Catalogue* (New Haven, CT; London: Yale Centre for British Art and Yale University Press, 2007).

Wood, Marcus, 'Atlantic Slavery and Traumatic Representation in Museums: The National Great Blacks in Wax Museum as a Test Case' in Celeste Marie Bernier and Judie Newman, eds, *Slavery and Abolition*, Special Issue: *Public Art, Artefacts and Atlantic Slavery*, 29: 2 (2008), pp. 151–73.

Wood, Marcus, *Black Milk: Imagining Slavery in the Visual Cultures of Brazil and America* (New York: Oxford University Press, 2013).

Wood, Marcus, *The Horrible Gift of Freedom* (Athens: University of Georgia Press, 2010).

Index

abolitionism/abolition 42, 46, 49, 65, 73–4, 89, 114, 124, 154, 162–7, 242, 347, 420
   abolitionist movement 34, 36, 84, 113–14, 118, 158, 160, 167, 195, 220
   African American 119
   Afro-Asia 121, 123–4
   Anglo-American 118
   British 64–5, 71–2, 74, 114–15, 117, 121–3, 214, 217, 262, 292, 295
   Euro-American 125
   European 121–2, 438
   of slave trade 71, 84, 86–9, 91–2, 94, 130
   Western discourse of 47
Adelman, Jeremy 50
Adjaye O. B. E., Sir David 426
Africa 8, 14, 29, 43–4, 117, 123, 142, 198, 236, 378, 388, 419
   African-American 14, 118–19, 234, 245, 253, 374–5, 377, 388–92, 424–5, 428, 432, 434, 436
   African Atlantic approach 206–7, 221
   African descent 164, 190, 194, 204, 219, 221–2, 229–30, 234, 240, 242, 389, 391
   antislavery 116, 124, 216
   East Africa 54, 63, 385
   Europeans in 62, 99, 121, 260
   Indigenous/descent 124, 190, 228–9, 237
   religions 11, 52, 199–205, 209–12, 217–19, 221–3
   removal of identities 440
   slave trade 53, 121, 145–8, 208, 288, 296–7
   slaves/slavery in 28–30, 32, 45, 127, 143–4, 156, 163, 192, 197, 203–4, 206–7, 213, 234, 298, 300, 315, 394, 427
   South Africa 127, 142, 427
   West Africa 53, 156, 191, 202, 205, 384, 391, 393, 426
Age of Revolution 109, 115, 119
agricultural colonization 66
agricultural labour/slavery 303
Ahat-abiša 19
Allain, Jean 21, 37
Allen, Richard 212
Alpers, Edward
   Resisting Bondage in Indian Ocean Africa and Asia 148
   Slavery and Resistance in Africa and Asia 143
Altink, Henrice 262
American Black Jacobinism 445
American Civil Rights Movement 163
American Civil War 119–20, 158, 160, 162, 166
American Historical Association 368
American Psychiatric Association 374
American Revolution 91, 94
American slavery 42, 161, 222, 249, 341, 352–3, 371, 377, 425
Amitai, Reuven 55
ancient Rome 155, 310, 393
Anglo-American case law 42
antebellum psychology 361–3
anthropology 6, 32–3, 378, 387, 389
Antioch Baptist Church 432
antislavery 115–16
   Brazilian 120
   campaigns against 'Chinese slavery' in South Africa 127

Caribbean slaves 115
Eastern Hemisphere 121
in Haiti 117, 119
historical permutations and combinations 125–7
in historiography 127–31
history of 113
humanitarian intervention 126, 128
Indian Ocean World 122–5
legacy 127
movement 116, 123, 127, 164
Muslim world 121–2
Nat Turner's revolt in Virginia 119
propaganda 419
rejected and transformed 115
state and non-state actors 113
transnational antislavery exchanges 120 n.11, 120
Western Hemisphere 117–20
Anti-Yoke church 432–3
slave children in 434
Aponte rebellion in Cuba 217
Aptheker, Herbert 373
American Negro Slave Revolts 371
archaeology 14–15, 377–80
Archer, Leonie J. 137
archives 10, 52–3, 253, 288, 294, 352, 364, 417–24
Aristarchus 19
Armitage, David 64
Arrighi, Giovanni 106
Atlantic Creole 202, 205, 207–8
Atlantic slavery 54, 56, 84, 99, 142, 147, 155, 159, 165, 190, 192, 197, 201, 203, 296, 304, 418, 424
Atlantic slave trade 44, 52, 54, 61–2, 71, 111, 145–7, 167, 288
autobiography 167–9. *See also* biography; microhistory

Bailey, Rahn K. 374
Bales, Kevin 21, 36, 131

Baptist, Edward 341
The Half Has Never Been Told: Slavery and the Making of American Capitalism 14, 353–5, 373
Baptist War 215
Bashford, Alison 64–5
Cambridge History of Australia 65
Bay, Edna 200
Bayly, Christopher, *Birth of the Modern World* 66
Beckert, Sven 13, 76–7, 353
Empire of Cotton: A Global History 141
Beckles, Hilary 253
Belich, James, *Replenishing the Earth* 67
Benot, Yves 69
Bentinck, Lord William 296
Bergad, Laird, *The Comparative Histories of Slavery in Brazil, Cuba, and the United States* 140
Berlin, Ira 140, 205
Berry, Daina Ramey 341
The Price for Their Pound of Flesh: The Value of the Enslaved, from Womb to Grave, in the Building of the Nation 358
Bhabha, Homi 293
biography 167–9. *See also* autobiography; microhistory
black activism 425
Blackburn, Robin 115, 164–5
The American Crucible 115, 142, 165
The Making of New World Slavery 77, 142
The Overthrow of Colonial Slavery 164
Black Lives Matter movement 374
Black Panthers 428
black traumatic memory 421
black women 72, 251, 257, 260
Blight, David 369
Blumenthal, Debra 264
body-capitalism 56
Bolívar, Simón 50

Bonaparte, Napoleon 166
bonded labour 45, 64, 113, 129, 143–4, 190. *See also* child labour
Book-of-the-Month Club 369
bourgeois revolutions 51
Bowman, Shearer Davis, *Masters and Lords* 142
Bradley, Keith 13, 138, 155, 307
Braudel, Fernand 82
Brazil 21, 42, 44, 66, 68, 83, 88, 108–9, 111, 120–1, 139, 141, 159, 162–3, 166, 169, 192, 194, 202–3, 209, 211, 216–17, 223, 239, 419
    antislavery movement 116
    Atlantic slavery 418
    coffee frontier 9, 109
    Islamic faith in 216
    Rio Branco Law of 1871, 166
Breen, Patrick H. 14, 361
bride-wealth 31
Britain/British 47, 70, 84, 91, 114, 119, 196
    abolitionism 64–5, 71–2, 74, 114–15, 117, 121–3, 214, 217, 262, 292, 295
    antislavery movement 116, 128
    British-colonized India 12
    expansion in India 45
    expansion of industrial capital 85, 87, 98
    imperialism 67, 76
British Empire 64–5, 67, 70–1, 75, 88, 165
British West Indian sugar industry 91
Brodie, Fawn M., *Thomas Jefferson: An Intimate History* 368
Bronze Age 43
Brown, Chris 420
Brown, Gordon 71
Brown, Kathleen 260
Brussels Convention in 1890 126
Bryson 311, 326, 328
Buchanan, Francis 298
    A Journey from Madras through the Countries of Mysore, Canara and Malabar 292

burial certificates of slaves 193
Burnard, Trevor 8, 59, 138, 262, 355
    The Plantation Machine 141
    Planters, Merchants, and Slaves 140
Bush, Barbara 253, 258
Bush, Michael, *Servitude in Modern Times* 143
Butler, Judith 259

Cambridge World History of Slavery 4, 131, 138
Cameron, Catherine M. 55
Camp, Stephanie 383
Campbell, Gwyn 55, 63, 137, 143–4
capitalism 6, 8–9, 54, 56–7, 74, 76–7, 81–5, 87–91, 93, 95–6, 102–4, 106, 108, 111, 114–15, 139, 141, 228, 341, 353–4
    Anglo-American interpretation 353 n.46
    slavery and 13–14, 44, 82, 84–9
capitalization 53
Caribbean
    antislavery movement 116
    profits and culture of 74
    slave uprisings in 119
    slavery 42
Carretta, Vincent 220
Cartledge, Paul 138
Cartwright, Samuel 362
Catterall, Helen Tunnicliff, *Judicial Cases Concerning American Slavery and the Negro* 160
Chandler, Joel 365
chattel slavery 229, 287–8, 290, 297
Chatterjee, Indrani 288, 294, 297, 301–2, 304–5
Chesapeake 391
child abuse, slave 420
child labour 129. *See also* bonded labour
Childs, Matt 11, 189
Chirac, Jacques 69

Index

Christianity 11, 121, 190, 193, 201–3, 209, 211–12, 214–15, 220–1, 223, 235, 432–3, 435–6
  creolization 222
  rise of 61
  slave owners 308
Christopher, Emma 145
Chrysostom, John 331
Church 190–1, 197, 212, 215, 219, 244, 432, 434. *See also specific Church*
  Catholic 139, 193, 196, 210, 234
  ecclesiastical sources 190–7, 221
  in Iberian slave societies 196
  investigation of abuses of slaves 194
  in Paulina 431
  Protestant 196–7
citizenship, rights of 159, 221
Civil Rights movement 160, 339, 341–2, 425
Clarence-Smith, William G. 55
Clarkson, Thomas, *History of the Rise, Progress, and Accomplishment of the Abolition of the Slave Trade by British Parliament* 114
classical slavery 126, 129
  vs. contemporary slavery 130
  Hebrew slave (*eved*) 25
Clinton, Catherine 252
cliometrics/cliometricians 6, 339
Cobb, Thomas R. R., *An Inquiry into the Law of Negro Slavery in the United States of America* 160
Code of Hammurabi, Babylonian 154
Code Noir slave code 157
Colebrooke, Henry 301
collective slavery 43, 45, 47 n.25
colonial/colonialism
  colonial-Africanist romanticisms 428
  colonial mercantile regime 88
  colonial policies 46, 305
  impact of 73
colonoware 390–1, 393

comedies (and dialogues)
  enslaved women 256
  of Plautus 319–20
  Roman 320
commercial capitalism 41, 85
commodification 53, 228, 358
comparative approaches 9, 133, 149–50. *See also* transnational approaches
  histories of slavery 135–8
  second slavery 141
  in specific regions 138–44
concubines 156, 159, 305, 385
Conermann, Stephan 55
Constitutional Convention (1787) 161
contemporary slavery 37, 129–30, 130 n.32
Corn Laws, abolition of 88
Covey, Herbert 386
Cowper, William 421
creolization model 11, 205, 207–8
  vs. African-Atlantic approaches 221
  of Yoruba 209
Cropper, James 64
cross-fertilization 140
Cuba 8, 44, 48, 51–4, 66, 76, 83, 88, 108–9, 139–41, 166, 192, 209–11, 217, 234, 239, 381, 384
  National Archives 53
  sugar frontier 9, 109
cultural death 420
cultural turn 81, 248, 259–60, 265
Cummings, John 417, 428
Curtin, Philip 61, 66, 142, 145
  The Atlantic Slave Trade 145–7
  The Rise and Fall of the Plantation Complex 142
Cycladic Thera 312

Dal Lago, Enrico 9, 10, 137, 142, 143
  Agrarian Elites 142
  American Slavery, Atlantic Slavery, and Beyond 143
Darcy, Robert 338

Darwin, John 66
Da Silva, Daniel Domingues 147
da Vinci, Leonardo 367
Davis, Angela 251
Davis, David Brion 19–20, 38, 135–6, 153, 191, 290, 295
   Inhuman Bondage 115, 142
   The Problem of Slavery in the Age of Emancipation 135
   The Problem of Slavery in the Age of Revolutions 135
   The Problem of Slavery in Western Culture 135
   Slavery and Human Progress 135
Davis, Natalie Zemon 168
de Alencastro, Felipe Luiz, *The Trade in the Living: The Formation of Brazil in the South Atlantic, Sixteenth to Seventeenth Centuries* 147
debt bondage 29, 43, 288, 297, 301, 303
Degler, Carl 163
   Neither Black Nor White: Slavery and Race Relations in the U.S. and Brazil 139
DeGruy, Joy 374
Delbourgo, James 74
delegalization 124
Delle, James 381
Demerara Rebellion 215
de Miranda, Francisco 50
Deslandes, Charles 441
Deuteronomy (Old Testament) 190–1
Di-Capua, Yoav 375
diversity 2, 8, 10, 16, 60, 65, 338, 388, 393
divide-and-conquer strategy 312
Doddington, David Stefan 1, 11, 247
domestic slaves 302–3
domination-and-resistance models 390, 392
Douglass, Frederick 28, 119, 257, 369
   Narrative of the Life of Frederick Douglass 168, 363
doulos (slave) 25

Draper, Nicholas 73–4
'Drapetomania' 362
Drescher, Seymour 9, 90–2, 94–5, 113, 115, 138, 142, 165
   Abolition 115, 142, 165–6
   decline thesis 90–1, 94–5
   From Slavery to Freedom 142
Dresser, Madge 72
Dubois, Abbe 298
DuBois, Page, *Slaves and Other Objects* 261
Du Bois, W. E. B. 14, 363–6
   double-consciousness 221, 366, 366 n.10
   The Souls of Black Folks 365–6
Dunn, Richard, *A Tale of Two Plantations: Slave Life and Labor in Jamaica and Virginia* 140
Dunning, William Archibald 364
Dutch Republic 68
Dysæsthesia Æthiopica 362

Eastern Hemisphere, antislavery 121
East India Company 287, 291, 294–5, 297, 299
Eaton, Richard 290
economy 81, 87, 90, 93–4, 310, 341, 357, 419, 437
   economic dimensions of enslavement 9, 261
   economic theory 89–90, 92–5, 103–4 (*see also* neoclassical economic theory)
Eden, Jeff 63
   Slavery and Empire in Central Asia 148
Egerton, Douglas 217
ego 195, 367, 373
Eisnach, Dwight 386
Ekpe society 211
Elkins, Stanley 139, 365, 370–3
   Slavery 14
Eltis, David 138, 147, 206, 418

emancipation 44, 53, 63, 84, 86, 88–9, 92, 95, 114, 117–25, 127, 129, 158–9, 165–7, 214, 300, 302, 340, 434
Emancipation Act (1833) 158
Emmer, Pieter 68
Empire 8, 81, 91, 166, 202, 427. *See also* imperialism
  American 76
  Atlantic 47
  British 64–5, 67, 70–1, 73–5, 85–8, 165
  critiques of 63–77
  definition of 60
  empire-building age 221, 228, 231, 237, 316
  European 66, 76, 121–2, 126, 154, 165, 234
  French 69–70
  Indian 234
  modern 60, 66
  Oyo 216
  Roman 49, 59, 65, 190, 192, 199, 264, 309
  and slavery 60–3, 66, 78, 154, 193
  Spanish 210, 234
  traditional 60
  transatlantic 113
Engerman, Stanley, L. 9, 90, 138, 142, 146, 165, 357
  Time on the Cross: The Economics of American Slavery 13, 90, 337, 339–43, 346, 350, 353, 356–7
English Heritage 72
English-originated slave systems 141
English Royal Society 231
Epictetus 323–5, 334
Equiano, Olaudah 195
  The Interesting Narrative of the Life of Olaudah Equiano 167, 440
Erikson, Erik, *Young Man Luther: A Study in Psychoanalysis and History* 368

Escott, Paul 351
  Slavery Remembered: A Record of Twentieth Century Slave Narratives 349
ethnic identification 14, 391
Eurasia 128, 144
Euripides, *Trojan Women* 256
Europe 100–1
  European 'miracle' 77, 97
  industrialization 95, 98–100, 105
  market-driven development 97
  military and commercial superiority 61
  overseas slave systems 126
'exclusion' 38
Exodus (Old Testament) 155, 190–1
extra-economic factors, slavery 93–4, 96, 100, 102–4, 288
Eyerman, Ron 375

Fairbanks, Charles 377–8
Farge, Arlette 168
Federal Writer's Project (FWP) 338, 386, 433–4
female slaves 26, 159, 253, 258, 363, 435. *See also* gender history
femininity, relation with masculinity 12
feminist activism 248, 250
Ferrer, Ramón 53–4
  Bella Antonia 53
fetishism 358
feudalism 250
fertility, slave 340 n.8, 345, 347
Field of Angels 435–7, 441
Finch, Aisha 217
Finkelman, Paul 31, 161
Finley, Moses 42, 65
  Ancient Slavery and Modern Ideology 155
Finley's Law 22, 28–33
First World War 34, 128
Fogel, Robert 9, 90

Without Consent or Contract:
  Evidence and Methods 337, 357
Time on the Cross: The Economics
  of American Slavery 13, 90, 337,
  339–43, 346, 350, 353, 356–7
Foner, Laura 140
forced labour 21, 29, 34, 36, 38, 45, 128,
  233
forced marriage 35, 129
forced reproduction 343–7
Forret, Jeff 374
Foucault, Michel 381
Fox-Genovese, Elizabeth 353, 373
Franklin, Benjamin 75, 220
Frazier, E. Franklin 389
Fredrickson, George, *White Supremacy:*
  A Comparative Study of South
  Africa and The U.S. 142
Free Black Church 432
freedmen monuments 321
freedom of speech 318–26
freedom suit (1772) 158
Free Soil Principle 157–8, 162, 167
Free the Slaves organization 21, 36
free wage labourers 303
'Free Womb' laws 166
French revolution 50, 119, 166
French slavery 47, 51
Fuente, Alejandro de la 164
Fuentes, Marisa, J., *Dispossessed Lives*
  263
Füllberg-Stolberg, Katja, *The End of*
  Slavery in Africa and the Americas
  144
Fynn-Paul, Jeffrey 192

Gabriel's Conspiracy 214, 216
Gaca, Kathy 264
gang labour 391
Gardner, Jane 256
Gaspar, David Barry 258
  More than Chattel 140
Gellner, Ernest 293

gender history 247
  disciplinary shifts 248
  racial slavery 253, 259
  reproductive exploitation 247, 252
  sexual exploitation/violence 247, 254,
    258, 262, 264
  and slavery 252–8, 261–2
  women's history 249–52
General History of the Modern Era
  (1500–1917) 50
Genesis 26
Genovese, Eugene 14, 139–40, 161, 353,
  365, 370–3
  From Rebellion to Revolution 140
  Roll, Jordan, Roll: The World the Slaves
    Made 14, 139, 161, 372–3
  The World the Slaveholders Made 139
George, Alexander L. 368
George, Juliette L. 368
German Coast slave rebellion (1811) 15,
  373, 441–5
German re-unification 51
German Society for the Advancement of
  Scientific Research (DFG) 51
Gerrigus, John, *The Plantation Machine*
  141
Gibbon, Edward 75
Gilroy, Paul 73, 205
  The Black Atlantic 146
Ginzburg, Carlo 168
Gladstone, Sir John 64
Glancy, Jennifer 264
Glazebrook, Allison 264
Gobineau, Arthur 232
Golden Age 307–8
Gomez, Michael A. 222
Goody, Jack 23
Gordon-Reed, Annette 369
  The Hemingses of Monticello: An
    American Family 168
The Great Blacks in Wax Museum,
  Baltimore 424
Great Dismal Swamp 394

Great Divergence 93, 95–104
Greco-Roman civilization 136
Greene, Jack P. 75
Greene, Sandra 200
Gregory, Cappadocian 307
Gronenborn, Detlef 55
Guha, Sumit 304
Gutman, Herbert 343

Habitation Haydel 428–30
Haggerty, Sheryllynne 72
Hall, Gwendolyn Midlo 140, 437–8
    Slavery and African Ethnicities in the Americas 146
    Social Control in Slave Plantation Societies 140
Haitian Revolution 69, 88, 109, 118, 213, 216, 445
Haiti, antislavery movement 116–17
Hann, Andrew, *Slavery and the British Country House* 72
Harper, Kyle 264
Hartman, Saidiya 255 n.29, 264, 265 n.62, 276 n.15, 277, 277 n.17, 278 n.19, 278 n.20, 402, 402 n.10, 405, 406 n.26, 407–8, 408 n.37, 414
Hayden, C. B. 361
    Southern Literary Messenger 361–2
Hebrew Bible 26, 190–1
Hemings, Sally 168, 368–9, 425
Henning, Joachim 55
Henry, Madeline 263
Henson, Josiah 257
Heritage Lottery 71
Herskovits, Melville 204, 389
Heuman, Gad 138
Heywood, Linda 200
hidden Atlantic 44, 48, 53–4
Higginbotham, Evelyn Brooks 259
Hine, Darlene Clark 258
historiography 2–3, 5–7, 9–11, 15, 21–2, 38, 47, 51, 60, 65–6, 69, 76, 78, 114, 117, 121, 127–30, 137, 149, 157, 190, 197, 200, 206, 212, 217, 220, 222–3, 244, 253, 291, 301, 341, 369, 373
Hodgson, Geoffrey 92
Hollande, Francoise 71
Holocaust Museum 417
Homer
    Homeric epics 26
    Iliad 256
    Odyssey 256
Hopkins, Keith 65
Hopkins, Terence K. 106
household slavery 156, 303
Housman, A. E. 307
Huggins, Nathan 77
human bondage 137, 150, 229, 231
human capitalism 56
humanitarianism 22, 33–6, 70, 84, 92, 125, 128
Hume, David 231
Hume, Ivor Noël 391, 396
Hyde, C. 300

Iberian Catholic *vs.* Protestant British slavery 221
identity imposition 440
Igbo religious shrines 392
imperialism 8, 59–61, 64, 67, 70, 76–7, 121–3
    imperial expansion 8, 59, 61–3, 65, 309
    imperial models 190–7
India 290
    antislavery movement 116
    caste system 293, 300–1
    colonial archive on slavery in 291–5, 297
    colonial constructions slavery in 295–302
    loss of citizenship 301
    Parliamentary Papers 291–2, 294, 297
    slave voices in 304
Indian Ocean World 122–5
industrial capitalism 76, 84–5, 87, 89–90, 115
Industrial Revolution 76–7, 85, 89, 98, 102, 105–6, 165

industrialization 9, 51, 67, 77, 83, 88–9, 95–6, 99–100, 103, 105, 109–10
infanticide, slave mother 420, 427, 437
Inglis, Robert 291
Inikori, Joseph 146
intercultural space 391
interdisciplinary approach 253, 396
International Centre for the Comparative History of Revolutions 50
ISIS (Islamic State) 441–5
Islamic law (*shari'ah*) 32, 156, 191–2

Jackson, Andrew 368
Jacobs, Harriet 247, 257, 345
   Incidents in the Life of a Slave Girl 168, 255, 363
Jamaica
   Clydesdale Plantation 381
   Jamaican Baptist War 215
   slave rebels 215
James, C. L. R., *The Black Jacobins* 115, 420
James, William 366
Jim Crow 160
Jefferson, Thomas 168, 232, 357, 368, 424–5
   Notes on the State of Virginia 237, 307, 362
Jones, Jacqueline 11, 227
Jones-Rogers, Stephanie E. 358
Joshel, Sandra, *Women and Slaves in Greco-Roman Culture* 261

Karras, Ruth Mazo 254
Kaye, Anthony 374
King, Martin Luther, Jr. 425
Kingsley plantation 'slave cabins' 377
kinlessness 38, 290, 304
kinship' 24, 43, 154, 235–6, 238, 254, 288, 290, 303–4
Klein, Herbert 139, 146
   African Slavery in Latin America and the Caribbean 141
   Slavery in the Americas 139

Klein, Martin A.
   Slavery and Colonial Rule in Africa 144
   Women and Slavery in Africa 144
Klooster, Wim 68
Knot, Gordian 208
Kolchin, Peter 142, 149, 342, 346, 374
   Unfree Labor: American Slavery and Russian Serfdom 142
Kopytoff, Igor 29–32
   Slavery in Africa 31, 144
Kossok, Manfred 53
Kumar, Dharma 297

ladinização (ladinoization) process 223
Ladurie, Emmanuel Leroy 168
La Escalera Rebellion 217
Landers, Jane 193, 210
Langer, William L. 368
language of slavery 22, 26
Latins, Junian 322
Laviña, Javier 143
law and metaphor 21, 25–8, 30
Law, Robin 200
League of Nations Convention on Slavery (1926) 20, 34, 126, 128, 164, 289
Legacies of British Slave-ownership (LBS) project 73–4
legal slavery 26–7, 130
   dimensions 47 n.25
   features 55
   regulation 25
legislature, Pennsylvania 166
legitimate biological ancestry 305
Lenski, Noel 55
lesbianism 420
Leviticus (Old testament) 26, 190–1
Lewis, David 8, 19
Lewis, Mary Agnes 371
liberal capitalism 54
Lincoln, Abraham 368, 425
Livesey, Andrea 13, 337

lobbyists, slave 420
Locke, John 74–5
Louis XIV 157
Louisiana Slave Database project 437
Lovejoy, Paul E. 24, 33, 55, 191, 200, 206–7, 211
  Transformations of Slavery: A History of Slavery in Africa 144
Lowe, Lisa 293
Lucumí, Carlota 218
Lushington, C. M. 298
Lévi-Strauss, Claude 380

Macaulay, Thomas Babington 73
Macaulay, Zachary 73
Macintyre, Stuart, *Cambridge History of Australia* 65
Mackenzie, John 67
macro-histories of slavery 48
Major, Andrea 11, 64, 287
Malê Rebellion 216
Manning, Patrick 55, 200
  Slavery and African Life 148
Mansfield, Lord 124, 158
Māori society 65
marginality 42, 148
market exchange 102
Marquese, Rafael 140
Marryat, Joseph 292
Marshall, Lydia Wilson 14, 377
Martí's, José 221
Marx, Karl 75, 77
masculinity, relation with femininity 12
master-slave relationship 161, 334, 393
material culture 14, 71, 255, 377–82, 384–8, 390, 393, 395
  space and enslaved 387–93
  space and study of slavery 380–7
material division of labour 102
material identification 395
material record 14
Maya Lyn's memorial 439–40
McAleer, John 71–2
McClelland, Keith 73

McCormick, Michael 55
McCurry, Stephanie 262
Meillassoux, Claude 33
  Anthropologie de l'esclavage: le ventre de fer et d'argent 30
memorial walls 437–40
mental habits of slave 309, 333
mercantilism 86–7, 89, 102
merits of slavery 64
Merivale, Herman 75
Mesopotamia 32
microhistory 167–8. *See also* autobiography; biography
Middle Passage 145–6, 384, 389, 424, 439
Miers, Suzanne 29, 33, 49
  Slavery in the Twentieth Century 34, 49
milagreiro (miracle worker) 224
military dictatorship 154
mimes (theatrical entertainments) 323
Mintz, Sidney 204
mixed race 217, 219, 230, 233, 237
modernity/modern slavery 5–6, 9, 21, 28–9, 36–8, 44, 47, 56, 59, 77, 93, 223
Molloy, Marie 358
monarchy 61, 75, 154, 157
monotheistic faiths 190–7
Moravian missionaries 220
Moret Law (1870) 166
Morgan, Jennifer, *Laboring Women* 259
Morgan, Philip 354
Morris, Thomas D., *Southern Slavery and the Law* 157
Morrison, Toni 399–402, 399 n.1, 400 n.2, 401 n.8, 410, 413, 413 n.54, 414 n.59, 415, 422–3, 437
Morton, Samuel George 232
Motion Picture Academy 422
Moya, Jose 198 n.9
Moynihan Report 342 n.12
Munford, Clarence J. 51
Murad, Nadia 20
Murdock, George P. 28
murgu 191–2

Murnaghan, Sheila, *Women and Slaves in Greco-Roman Culture* 261
Museum of African Art 417
Museum of Slavery 71
Museum of the American Indian 417
Muslim societies
　antislavery 116, 121–2
　household slavery 156
Mustakeem, Sowande', *Slavery at Sea: Terror, Sex, and Sea in the Middle Passage* 147, 263 n.57

'national-imperial' slaveries 47
National Museum of Women in the Arts 417
Nat Turner Revolt 119, 217, 232, 372, 422, 445
neo-abolitionism 36
neoclassical economic theory 92–3, 103
'neo-Tannenbaum' approach 196
New Archaeology movement 379
new economic history 9, 89–95, 340–2
　new economic historians 81, 83, 89–95, 100, 103, 110, 339–40
New History of Capitalism movement 76
New Netherlands 68
new world slavery 83, 95, 98–100, 102, 105, 123, 142–3, 196, 212
　periphery 101, 105
　systemic relation of 109
　expansion of zones 100, 104
Nolte, Hans-Heinrich 55
Northup, Solomon, *Twelve Years a Slave* 421
Nuremberg tribunals 128

Oakes, James 162
Ogboni society 211
Old Assyrian period 25
Old Babylonian period 25
Old Testament 154, 190–1, 212, 214
Olmsted, Frederick Law 362

Opium Wars in China 45
Orisas (deities) 209
Orser, Charles E., Jr. 386
Orthodox, Christianity 20–1, 199, 365, 433, 435
Ortiz, Fernando 204
Otto, John 385
Ottoman empire 61–2
Owens, Deirdre Cooper, *Medical Bondage* 263
ownership 8, 21, 29, 31–3, 38

Pacific Ocean World 64
Paquette, Robert 4, 140
Paris Constituent Assembly Declaration 166
Paris International Antislavery Conference 121
Park, Mungo 20
paternalism 139, 339, 373
patriarchy 154, 253
Patterson, Orlando 22, 28, 31–2, 49, 136, 289, 304, 387, 420
　Slavery and Social Death: A Comparative Study 28, 31, 49, 136, 387
Peabody, Sue 10, 153
peasants 63, 168, 194
　Indian 296
　Malaysian 390
　Roman 65
Peggs, Rev James, *India's Cries to British Humanity* 291
Penningroth, Dylan C. 374
Perry, Matthew 264
Pétré-Grenouilleau, Olivier 69
　The Black Slave Trades (*Les Traites Negrieres*) 145
Petty, William 231
Phillips, Ulrich B. 249, 339, 364–6
　American Negro Slavery 339, 365
'pigmentocracy' 241. *See also* race
The Plan of the Slave Ship Brooks 419

plantation slavery 165, 381
  plantation complexes 92 n.21, 105, 429
political/politics
  campaigns to abolish slavery 153
  domination 26–7
  economic transformation 86
  rhetoric 22, 27, 33–6
  political state 154–60
Pomeranz, Kenneth 9, 83, 95–103, 105
  The Great Divergence 81, 83, 95
Pomeroy, Sarah B., *Goddesses, Whores, Wives, and Slaves* 251
Porter, Bernard 67
Portuguese inquisition 194, 202
post-abolition societies of slavery 21–2, 27, 36–7, 130
post colonialism 12, 287, 291, 293, 295, 299, 305
  postcolonial theory 288
'post imperial melancholia' 73
post modernism 379
post processualist theory 379
post traumatic slave syndrome 374
Prakash, Gyan 288–9, 303
pre-colonial African history 200–3
pregnancy and childbirth, slave 247, 254, 332, 437
Prestholdt, Jeremy 385
Price, Rev Thomas 292
Price, Richard 204, 208, 223
Prior, Katherine 72
prison camps 47
process-oriented approach 395
proletarianization 87
Prosser, Thomas 214
Protestant/Protestantism 220
  African-American Christianity 219
  orthodoxy 199
  slave societies 195–6, 211
proto-industry 99
pseudo-scientific theory 228, 231
psychoanalysis 6, 367–70

psychobiography 367, 369–70
psychohistory
  antebellum psychology 361–3
  Freudian ego psychology 373
  psychoanalysis and 366–70
  psychology of slavery 363–6
  soul-killing effects of slavery 363
  trauma theory 375
  in twenty-first century 373–5
psychology, slave 14, 324, 362, 375
'pushing system' of labour 354–5
Pybus, Cassandra 145

quantitative histories 338–40
  criticisms of 352
  descriptive statistics 337
  economic vitality studies 352–9
  historians and counting 339–41
  new economic history 341–2
  post-1980s quantitative studies 347–52
  sampling process 346, 348
  social science research methods 346
Quirk, Joel 34–6
  The Online Anti-Slavery Directory 129
  Unfinished Business: A Comparative Survey of Historical and Contemporary Slavery 136–7
Quran, references to slaves in 191

race 5, 10–12, 66, 72–3, 124, 154–5, 162, 164, 193, 217, 219, 221, 227–45, 250, 260, 290, 424, 436
  African race 229, 234, 236
  black race 229, 234, 238–9, 241
  casta classification 241
  codification of racial slavery 157
  consequences of idea of 244
  Jewish race 233, 233 n.18
  notion of 228, 235, 243
  opposition of 228
  pseudo-scientific theory 231

race relations 230
racial difference 229
racial hierarchy 235, 244
racist psychology 362
racial slavery 230, 238
racial solidarity 228, 244
socio-racial status 240
tri-partite 'racial' classification 233
tropical workforces 239
uses of 237
raid slaveries 43
Rankin, David 163
Rawick, George P. 338, 349
Rediker, Marcus, *The Slave Ship: A Human History* 147
Reginald F. Lewis Museum of Maryland African American History and Culture museum 425
regionalization 7
Reis, João 216, 223
religious beliefs 206–7, 217–20
  African 204–12
  African-American 205
  Catholic religious associations 210, 218
  creolization model 205, 207
  Evangelical Christianity 212, 214
  slave revolts and 212–17
  syncretic 209–12
religious history 189, 200, 207, 217–18, 222–3
Research Center for the Comparative History of Bourgeois Revolutions 50–1, 53
Rhine-Danube frontier 317
Rhodes, Cecil 70
Richardson, David 138, 211
  Atlas of the Transatlantic Slave Trade 147, 418
Ridley, John 421–2
ritual decapitation 441–5
Roberts, Justin 384
Roberts, Richard 144

Robertson, Claire C., *Women and Slavery in Africa* 144
Rodney, Walter 61–2
Rodrigues, Nina 204
Rohrs, Richard 338
Roman slavery 13, 21, 42–3, 47–8, 155, 307–11, 322, 327, 330, 427, 320, 326–33
  contingency 312–18
  freedom of speech 318–26
  heterogeneity of slave population 309, 314
  regulation 311–12
  resolution 333–5
  slaves/ex-slaves in family business 326–7
Roman Empire 49, 59, 61, 190, 192, 199
Roman Law 32, 42, 155, 159, 251, 256, 312–13
Rotman, Youval 55
The Routledge History of Slavery 138
Rufus, Musonius 323
runaway slave 330, 362, 394
rural slave management 312
Russworm, John Brown 243

Saco, José Antonio 48, 56
sacrificial slavery 43
sadomasochistic homosexuality 420
Said, Edward 292
  Orientalism 292–3
Saintsbury, George 292
Salman, Michael 143, 148
Samford, Patricia 392
Sarkar, Tanika 288, 290, 302
Sawyer, P. H. 249
Saxl, Fritz 436
Schiel, Juliane 55
Schwartz, Stuart 140
Scottish Enlightenment 353 n.46
Scott, James C. 389–90
  Weapons of the Weak: Everyday Forms of Peasant Resistance 389

Scott, Joan 259
Scott, Rebecca J. 51
Seck, Ibrahima 417, 428–9
    Bouki Fait Gombo: A History of the Slave Community of Habitation Haydel (Whitney Plantation) Louisiana 1750–1860 429
second slavery 9, 44, 46, 48, 51, 56, 83, 104–11, 141, 143
Second World War 34, 128, 249
Sensbach, Jon 219
serfdom 62–3, 130, 142–4
servile 118, 123, 309, 312–15, 317–23, 326–30, 332–3
servitude 13, 121, 123–5, 129, 288, 290, 297, 300, 303, 309, 320, 322, 422
sex slavery 34, 43
sexual/hereditary bondage 124
Seymour, Susannne 72
Shmieder, Ulrike, *The End of Slavery in Africa and the Americas* 144
Sibylline tradition 334
Singleton, Theresa A. 381
Sivasundaram, Sujit 64
skin 'colourism' 243. *See also* race
slave-based production 9
slave-breeding 347
slave-castes 299, 301
'slave factories' (*factorías*), African 53
slave labour 64, 66, 76, 105, 109–10, 304, 344, 423
slave owners
    domination 385, 390
    strategies of coercion 381, 388
    terror tactics of 444
    unpredictability of authority 333
slave production 87, 98, 100, 104–5, 107
slaveocracy 390
slaveries with no name 46
slavery, definitions of 22–4, 30, 37–8, 289, 312
    global definition 23 n.12, 30

League of Nations (1926) definition 20, 25, 34, 37
    legal definition 23, 128
    standard definition 24
    unorthodox approaches 21
Slavery Abolition Act (1833) 166
Slavery Archive 419
Slave Societies Digital Archive 193
slave societies 10, 14–15, 42 n.5, 49, 55, 66, 105, 120, 133–4, 136–41, 144, 146, 148, 159, 191, 194–6, 209, 212, 214, 219, 262, 355, 428
Slave Systems: Ancient and Modern 137
slave trade 4, 10, 41, 43–4, 48, 50–1, 53–4, 56, 66, 68–9, 71–2, 76–7, 84–6, 88–9, 91–2, 94, 98–9, 102, 105, 110–11, 113–14, 117, 121–2, 126, 130, 134–5, 145–9, 156, 158, 163, 203–4, 206–8, 216, 236, 263, 288, 320, 340, 345, 347–8, 356, 419
    abolition of 71, 84, 86–9, 91–2, 94, 130, 164
    African 62, 156
    Angolan 146
    Atlantic 44, 52, 54, 61–2, 71, 111, 145–7, 167, 288
    French involvement in 69
    inter-regional 348
    origins of 61
slave traders 41, 53, 68, 156, 208, 229, 236, 294, 346, 348
    transnational historical practice of 135
slave village 381–2
slaving zones 44, 98, 100, 192
Smallwood, Stephanie, *Saltwater Slavery* 146
Smith, Adam 75, 127
    An Inquiry into the Nature and Causes of the Wealth of Nations 96
Smith, James McCune 362
Smith, Mark 140
Smith, Samuel Stanhope 232

Index

Smithsonian National Museum of African American History & Culture (SNMAAHC) 71, 418, 424–8
Snyder, Christina 35
Soares, Mariza de Carvalho 210, 219
social death 1 n.1, 49, 136, 289–90, 299, 304, 387–8, 420
socio-cultural significance 223, 261, 332
Solow, Barbara 66
 The Economic Consequences of the Atlantic Slave Trade 147
Somerset's case (1772) 124, 158, 220
spatial-analytical framework 92
spatial-chronological phases 42
spatial-temporal framework 88–9, 104
spatial-temporal structure 107
Spivak, Gayatri 293
Sreenivasan, Ramya 304
Stampp, Kenneth 249
Stanziani, Alessandro 55, 137, 143, 148
 Bondage 144
Stephen, James 287
Stetson, Erlene 250
Stevenson, Brenda 258, 374
Stillwell, Sean, *Slavery and Slaving in African History* 144
Stoic/Stoicism 324–6, 331
Stono Revolt 217
Stuard, Susan Mosher 250, 253
subjectivity 11
sugar duties, abolition of 86
Supplementary Convention (1956) 34
Suzuki, Hideaki, *Slave Trade Profiteers in the Western Indian Ocean* 148
Sweet, James 198, 202
 Domingos Álvarez 169
Syrus, Publilius 323

Tadman, Michael 340, 348, 355
 Speculators and Slaves: Masters Traders and Slaves in the Old South 348

Tannenbaum, Frank
 Slave and Citizen 138, 162–3
 thesis 196–7, 221
taxonomic toolbox 36
Taylor, Timothy 395
Temperley, Howard 301
terminology of slavery 21, 25–7, 33, 35, 240, 296, 304, 362
Testart, Alain 32
Texas Writers' Project 345
'Third World' populations 356
Thirteenth Amendment of the Constitution 160, 162, 166
Thistlewood, Thomas 262
Thornton, John 55, 61–2, 200–2, 205
 Africa and Africans in the Making of the Atlantic World 146, 201
Thorpe, Earl E. 371
Tilly, Charles 97
Toledano, Ehud R. 55
Tomich, Dale 9, 81
 Through the Prism of Slavery: Labor, Capital and World Economy 141
Torah 154
Torres-Cuevas, Eduardo 48
torture 155, 314, 317, 328, 355, 357, 363, 424, 427
'Total Factor Productivity' 357
Trans-Atlantic Slave Trade Database 201
transnational approaches 9, 133, 145–50. *See also* comparative approaches
trauma 352, 374–5, 389, 417–24, 427, 442
Trouillot, Michel-Rolph 199

UN Working Group on Slavery 34
United States
 abolition/abolitionists 162
 antislavery movement 116
 Civil Rights Movement 163
 cotton frontier 109
 law and slavery 160–2
 master-slave relationship 161
 methodological development of slavery studies in 338

Universal Declaration of Human Rights (1948) 128, 164
untouchables 299
Ur-Namma code 25

Vansina, Jan 379
Vaughan, J. 299
Vermont Republic 165
Vienna Declaration (1815) 126
Vietnam Memorial 440
Vink, Marcus 68
Vinson, Ben 141
Virginia act of 1662 252
Vlach, John 382
Vlassopoulos, Kostas 23
von Ranke, Leopold 364
Vorenberg, Michael 162

Walker, Kara, *Narrative of a Negress* 444
Wallerstein, Immanuel 106
Walpole, Robert 75
Walvin, James
    Crossings 147
    Questioning Slavery 141
war capitalism 44, 46, 76
wardum (slave) 25
Washington, Booker T. 425
Washington, George 220, 425
Watson, Alan 155
Watson, James L. 143
Wayles, Martha 168
West, Emily 340, 374
    Chains of Love 351
Western civilization 45, 117, 136, 207
Western European monarchies 61
'Western' subspecies 30
What Is a Slave Society? The Practice of Slavery in Global Perspective 137
Wheatley, Phillis 220
Whipper, William 243

whipping machine 352, 355–7
White, Deborah Gray, *Ar'n't I a Woman* 253
Whitney Plantation 15, 417, 423, 428–30, 432, 435, 437, 442, 444
    authenticity and transplantation at 431–3
    Slave Angel with Wings 435
    'Wall of Honour' 437–8, 440
William, Gwyn, *The Vikings* 249
Williams, Craig 262
Williamsburg, Colonial 391, 423, 431
Williams, Eric 9, 74, 83–4, 114, 340
    Capitalism and Slavery 9, 74, 83–4, 89–90, 114
    thesis 85 n.7, 89
Wilson, Lulu 345
Witzenrath, Christoph 55
Woodrow Wilson and Colonel House: A Personality Study (George and George) 368
Works Progress Administration (WPA) 339, 386
Wright, Gavin 354
Wyatt, David 254, 261

Xenophon, *Oikonomikos* 256, 311

Yazidi 20
Yellin, Jean Fagan 255
yoke of slavery 334
Young, J. C., *Holocaust Memorials and Meaning* 442

Zabdî 19
Zeuske, Michael 8, 10, 33, 41, 135–7, 143–4, 149
    Handbuch der Geschichte der Sklaverei 8, 56–7
    Slavery: A Human History 56
small slaveries 33, 55